# International
# Business Strategy
# and Administration

# International Business Strategy and Administration

John Fayerweather
*Professor of Management and*
*International Business*
*New York University*

Ballinger Publishing Company • Cambridge, Massachusetts
*A Subsidiary of Harper & Row, Publishers, Inc.*

This book is printed on recycled paper.

International Standard Book Number: 0-88410-669-1

Library of Congress Catalog Card Number: 78-5675

Printed in the United States of America


Library of Congress Cataloging in Publication Data

Fayerweather, John.
 International business strategy and administration.

 Includes bibliographical references.
 1. International business enterprises—Management.  I. Title.
HD69.I7F37                     658.1'8                  78-5675
ISBN 0-88410-669-1

To Jim

# Contents

# List of Tables

# List of Figures

# Preface

This book was written for readers seeking an intensive analytical approach to the major aspects of strategy and administration for international business. It evolved out of my earlier book, *International Business Management, A Conceptual Framework* (McGraw, 1969). The fundamental analytical scheme derived from the basic disciplines of economics, cultural anthropology, sociology, and political science has been carried forward into this book, largely appearing in Part I.

Two major components have been added to that base: application to management issues and experience from international business operations. In Parts II and III the fundamentals have been applied to the key aspects of strategy and administration including the product delivery system, the financial flow system, control, overall strategy, organization, and the managerial process. The analysis has been given a solid experiential base by drawing on the large body of research and writing on international business in recent years. The findings of over one hundred research projects have been summarized along with a number of writings by businessmen providing a synthesis of the current knowledge of international management.

Thus the book presents for the thoughtful reader a combination of fundamental concepts drawn from basic disciplines, an analytical approach to the main issues of strategy and administration, and a wealth of experiential information.

For one who has spent over thirty years in a professional field it is impractical to express fully the obligations owed to others for the content of this book. Innumerable businessmen, government officials, fellow academicians, and students in many lands have contributed insights and experience. The writer of a general book draws most of his knowledge from the efforts of others, essentially pulling together a state-of-the-art compendium. The amount of intellectual output in the field of international business in the past decade has been truly impressive and my work has benefited greatly from this large effort by others.

As to specific contributions, the works of individuals are indicated by the notes. However, two collective efforts deserve special note. First, the Multinational Enterprise Project at Harvard University directed by Raymond Vernon has made a tremendous contribution to this field. More than a dozen of the studies incorporated in this book were part of that project. Second, the United Nations Centre on Transnational Corporations is providing an invaluable service as a central hub in the evolution of knowledge. This book has benefited greatly from the data compiled by the Centre which appear in the Appendix to Chapter 1.

I especially want to thank those who have had a part in the actual writing of the book. My assistant, Gloria Hupka, performed a variety of helpful functions in developing data and other material. Lillian Ramirez and Helen Townsend did admirable work in typing the manuscript. And my family were ever patient as I pressed along with my writing.

John Fayerweather

Hastings-on-Hudson, N.Y.
August, 1978

**International
Business Strategy
and Administration**

※ *Chapter 1*

# An Overview

From 1966 to 1975 U.S. exports of manufactured products and other non-agricultural goods expanded 266 percent from $23.4 billion to $85.6 billion. But in the same period sales by majority-owned foreign affiliates of U.S. companies rose 370 percent, from $97.8 billion to $458.3 billion.[1]

Of the 2,422 foreign affiliates of the 187 largest U.S. firms formed before 1946, 18 percent included foreign partners. Of 5,898 affiliates of the firms formed between 1958 and 1967, 30 percent had local equity participation.[2]

A study of 1,100 foreign joint ventures entered into by 170 major U.S. firms showed that in about one-third of the cases there were subsequent changes in effective control. Typically the U.S. firm assumed greater ownership.[3]

These broad statistics are indicators of the field of management to which the following pages are devoted. Back of the statistics lie innumerable corporate strategy decisions. The relatively greater growth of manufacturing abroad compared to exports reflects a host of management conclusions on the complex question of how best to supply foreign markets. The ownership data are evidence of a further range of decisions on the equally complex problems of control of foreign operations with their implications for income, operating effectiveness, asset risks, and other factors. In addition to these major decision areas, there are a host of other strategy issues concerning product lines, financing, advertising, and the like which are of continuing importance to the many firms involved in international business. And there is the broad field of administration in a multicultural,

*1*

multinational, globe-spanning system which is essential to the implementation of strategy.

The great variations among company and country situations and the complexity of the strategy and administrative problems present a challenge for the international management analyst. A comprehensive prescriptive treatment appropriate to all circumstances would be prohibitively voluminous. The alternative approach employed in this book is to cut through the mass of situational specifics to the basic forces and factors bearing on the key strategy and administrative problems and present a fundamental framework of analysis which is applicable to all situations.

In this introductory chapter the main components of the framework will be presented. Such an initial overview is essential so that the reader may have from the very outset some sense of all of the key pieces of the analytical framework because all of the parts are interrelated in an intricate pattern. The interests of national governments, for example, are not treated in full until Chapter 5, but they will appear quite early as a significant element in Chapter 2. This interdependence of factors precludes a simple sequential build-up of one topic upon another, so the only practical course is to provide a brief preliminary statement of all the main components at the outset.

## SOME DEFINITIONS

Before launching into the heart of the analytical framework a few definitions are necessary. First, the *central actor* must be identified. "Multinational Corporation (MNC)," "International Corporation (IC)," "Multinational Enterprise (MNE)," "Transnational Corporation (TNC)," "Multinationals" and assorted other terms are variously used in the literature of international business. Some authors have attempted to make distinctions among these terms but to a large degree they are used interchangeably and this book accepts that reality. For the most part multinational corporation will be employed as it appears to have the greatest common currency but other terms may appear, particularly in references to writings of authors who use them in preference to MNC.

The definition of the central actor is more significant. For some purposes authors have found it useful to define firms according to degree of international involvement, foreign ownership, size, attitude toward international activities, and other variables. On the whole such distinctions are not appropriate in this book as our concern is very broadly directed at all firms involved in international business.

One variable, however, is of fundamental importance, namely control. The whole concept of strategy for the MNC presumes that there is ability to exercise central control for this is a necessary condition for the implementation of strategic goals and policies. Management may decide to allow foreign units to function with a high degree of autonomy, but this is in itself a strategic decision affirming the existence of ultimate central authority. So the definition of the MNC employed here has but two components: first, that the firm be significantly involved in international business having permanent operations in two or more countries; and second, that the capacity for central control of foreign operations exists.

A conceptual definition of *international business* is also desirable because it will provide a broad framework for the analytical approach. Although one can construct elaborate definitions of international business, it would appear to have only one central distinguishing characteristic—it is business involving two or more nations. Thus concepts unique to international business must stem directly from business processes intersected in some way by national borders. Although the presence of national borders in the conventional political and geographic sense is the basis for this definition, we must use a more flexible concept of the term *national border* to relate it meaningfully to international business processes. The points at which significant *inter-nation contact* occur range geographically from purchase by an Italian importer from a U.S. manufacturer in his plant in the middle of the United States to a French engineer supervising a worker in a Moroccan mine. Likewise, the impact of the intervention of national borders may be felt at two or more points in a continuous business process. For example, the relationships between a managing director of a British firm and an Englishman running its subsidiary in Brazil and between the latter and a Brazilian subordinate are both substantially affected by the intervention of national borders. National border is therefore used here to mean the border or contact line between people, companies and activities that are distinguished from each other for reasons arising from national borders in the conventional sense.

Focusing on the national-border element, we may identify two types of operational processes which are central to the analytical framework as shown in Figure 1–1. First we have essentially economic transactions in which resources from one nation are transmitted in exchange for resources from another in the form of shipments of goods, transfers of funds, movement of people, and so forth. Second, there are the interactions of a multinational firm with the host society. These may in a sense be considered a continuation of

**Figure 1–1.**   Analytical Framework for MNC Strategy Issues

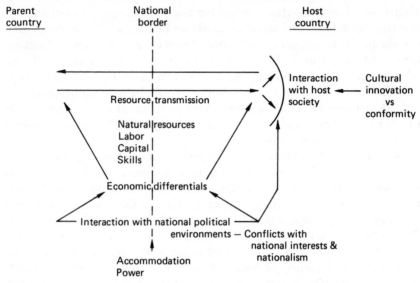

the first category as they involve the implementation of the processes of transmission of resources. However, it is conceptually useful to separate the cross-border transmission process from the subsequent processes of interaction with the host society.

From the two types of operational processes arises the third major process of international business shown at the bottom of Figure 1–1, the interaction of the MNC with national political environments.

The implications of these three processes will emerge as the book progresses so they will not be elaborated on here. However, it is useful to identify them in a broader context both to clarify their implications and to indicate the types of analytical approaches that are suitable to exploring them. The three processes are readily seen to relate to three major disciplines by which the phenomena of international relations are studied: transmission of resources is essentially the realm of international economics; interaction with host societies is fundamentally concerned with cultural anthropology; and relations with political systems is most readily associated with political science, though the social psychologists have also contributed to it substantially. Thus, the strategy analysis here will draw heavily upon thinking based on the basic behavioral disciplines that have studied the major dimensions of international relations.

*Strategy* is the primary focus of the book, administration being important but secondary as it exists essentially as a vehicle for implementing strategy. A precise definition of strategy is not essential for our purposes. It will suffice to understand that it refers to the main goals of the firm and the key policies and patterns of action by which those goals are pursued. There is an implication in the normative, prescriptive thrust of much of the literature on this subject that strategy is something that is planned. In fact, however, business strategies are to varying degrees unplanned, reactive, and intuitive. Thus in the pages that follow we will often be drawing conclusions from observation of past strategies in which planning was quite limited. The expectation, however, is that the extent and sophistication of preplanning of strategies will grow, an expectation reinforced by the steady expansion of long-range planning and analytical decision-making in managements.

Accompanying that development of corporate planning has been the emergence of a considerable body of thought on *strategy formulation*. It is not practical here to explore that field of management in depth. Readers who have no background in the subject are encouraged to delve into the considerable literature.[4] For present purposes a concise conceptualization of strategy formulation will be adequate. The key elements are identification of corporate capabilities and relevant environmental factors. The analyst must determine how best to capitalize on the strengths of the firm and minimize the effects of its shortcomings within the context of opportunities, competitive forces, and constraints in the environment.

## THE MAJOR COMPONENTS OF MNC
## STRATEGY ANALYSIS

Strategy analysis for a firm conducting business solely within one nation is essentially directed at sizing up the internal capabilities of the enterprise and determining how they may best be employed in the environmental context—the market, competition, governmental factors, and the like. These elements are also highly relevant for the multinational corporation. However, the basic approach to strategy analysis for the MNC must take a different direction. The underlying questions to be resolved stem from the rationale of the firm's role in international business. Not all companies belong in international business and the potentials for those that do differ. The strategist therefore must determine what corporate capabilities can be utilized in international business and how to use them most effectively considering the international economic, cultural, and political environment.

### Economic Differentials

The major elements to be incorporated in the MNC strategy analysis are shown in Figure 1-1. We start with the central process of transmission of resources—natural resources, labor, capital, and skills. As a point of departure the strategy analysis must determine in which resources the MNC has capabilities. The first level of this determination is made with the tools of the international economist looking at the basis for trade and other exchanges between nations. The essence of the approach is comparison of the relative advantages of each nation considering various supply and demand characteristics. The result is a determination of the *economic differentials* that create the commercial incentives necessary to justify business transactions.

Pure economic analysis, however, gives an inaccurate picture of world economic relations because of the heavy influence of governmental actions. In the pursuit of their national interests, governments substantially distort the basic relationships through imposition of a range of trade restrictions, controlled exchange rates, and the like. When these elements are taken into account, we have the true pattern of *effective economic differentials* that provide the range of real opportunities within which the MNC may find scope for its strategy.

### Resource Transmission Capabilities

The capabilities of the MNC must next be considered to determine which of those opportunities are appropriate for it. Two types of capabilities are particularly relevant. First, there are the general, non-international *characteristics of the firm* which establish its fundamental strengths and limitations. Two of these, the ability to integrate efforts of a large and diverse organization and the competence in application of skills in bringing products from inception to market, will be conspicuous in the analysis. Second, there are the capabilities arising from the *global span* of the MNC. Prominent among these are rationalization of activities with the benefits of specialization in particular locations, economies of large scale operations, and gains in effectiveness derived from interchange of capabilities based on communication of experience among units. From this stage of analysis the firm arrives at a determination of its *resource transmission capabilities*.

### Innovation versus Conformity

The interaction with the host society enters the analysis here as a determinant of the feasibility of resource transmission. Especially in transmitting skills the MNC is cast as a *cultural change agent* because the effect of the transmission process is to alter the existing patterns of the host society. A determination must therefore be made on the *innovation-conformity* issue which steers the analysis into the social structure of the society and the ways in which change takes place. The disposition of the MNC is in the direction of change to optimize its resource transmission capabilities but adequate weight to the conformity side is required by the costs of attempting change where it is questionable both in terms of MNC effort and in the adverse reactions often encountered in cultural change.

### Conflict with Nationalism
### and National Interests

The final major component is the interaction with the *nationalism and national interests* of home and host nation states. The analysis at this stage proceeds at two levels. First, there is a need to identify valid issues, eliminating misperceptions due to nationalistic and other attitudes, and attempting thereby to reach as much *accommodation of goals* as possible. The second level is the resolution of the valid differences in interests based on the *balance of power* between the MNC and the nation, essentially dependent upon their economic and political strengths. This is the tough level of strategy in which negotiation depends mainly on how the values of the MNC resource transmission capabilities to the host nation are weighted against the opportunities offered by the nation and its political strength.

### Bi-National and Multinational Dimensions

Strategy may also be usefully conceived in two dimensions. Much of it is *bi-national* in character having to do with the economic differentials between two nations, the interaction induced when resources based on the culture of one are brought into the other by MNC activities, and the convergence and conflicts of the nationalism and interests associated with individual nation–MNC interactions. The emphasis in this dimension is on optimizing the flow of resources.

The second dimension is the development of the *multinational* aspects of the strategy. Here the emphasis is on optimizing the benefits of *unification versus the fragmentation* fostered by the diversity of national environments. Figure 1–2 portrays the forces at work and the outcome which may emerge. Activities in some countries fall mainly into a globally unified pattern while others are largely fragmented because of the strength of local cultural, economic, and political forces.

**Figure 1–2.** A Conceptual Framework for Multinational Business Relationships

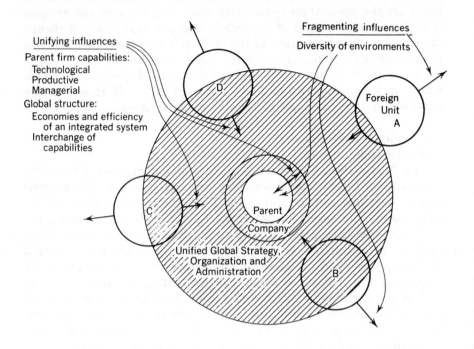

## THE PLAN OF THE BOOK

The book is divided into three parts with chapters that focus in the main on discrete aspects of MNC strategy analysis and its administrative implementation. However, the components of the analysis are so interrelated that pieces of the picture will be regularly intermingled. This may be somewhat confusing to the reader who favors clarity in distinctions and sequential progression of analysis. However, it is unavoidable and realistic. MNC strategy is a complex matter constantly requiring intermixture of assorted considerations. If anything, the presentation here errs on the side of over-simplification compared to real corporate planning. Thus, the best course for the reader is to acquire as quickly as possible a sense of all the major pieces of the picture and their broad totality so that their application in each issue in whatever mixture may appear is readily understood.

Part I analyzes the main sets of factors that enter into strategy formulation. Chapter 2 is directed at the determination of MNC resource transmission capabilities based on economic differentials among nations, government actions distorting the differentials, and MNC characteristics. Chapter 3 assesses the feasibility of resource transmission based on the cultural change process involved in the interaction with host societies. Chapters 4 and 5 examine the nature of the interaction between the MNC and nation states leading to the approach to conflicts with nationalism and national interests.

Part II applies the analytical thinking developed in Part I to strategy for specific aspects of MNC operations: product policy, research and development, logistics including production and supply systems, operating methods of foreign units including marketing, production and industrial relations, financial flow systems, and control and ownership, with a concluding chapter presenting composite strategy models.

In Part III organizational structures and their staffing will be analyzed, followed by consideration of decision-making and communication systems and the dynamics of the behavioral process.

As substantive background to faciliate understanding the nature of multinational corporations and their role in the world economy a variety of statistics have been provided in Appendix A to this chapter.

# Appendix A

# Some Statistical Dimensions of MNC Operations

To comprehend the strategy problems of multinational corporations, one must have a picture of the magnitude and character of their operations and their place in the global economy. For this purpose a variety of statistics will be presented here supplemented by others in later chapters.

## Concentration of Investment

The overall universe of MNCs is portrayed in Table A–1. According to these statistics, there were about 9,500 MNCs in 1973, of which half were very limited in scope, with affiliates in only one country. Only 10 percent of the MNCs had operations in more than ten countries. The concentration of major operations in a limited portion of firms is borne out in other data. U.S. statistics, for example, show that only 187 firms account for 80 percent of total U.S. foreign direct investment in manufacturing.[5] In brief there are a substantial number of multinationals but the field is dominated by a relatively small portion of them. As a consequence the actions of the big firms tend to be the prime focus of public attention.

Table A–1.   Firms with Affiliates in One or More Foreign Country

| Number of Host Countries in Which Firms Have Affiliates | Number of Firms Based in: | | | | |
| --- | --- | --- | --- | --- | --- |
| | European Economic Community | United States | Other Countries | Total | Percent of Total |
| 1 | 1,807 | 1,136 | 1,312 | 4,255 | 44.8 |
| 2 | 783 | 334 | 383 | 1,500 | 15.8 |
| 3 to 5 | 979 | 441 | 390 | 1,810 | 19.1 |
| 6 to 10 | 496 | 308 | 160 | 964 | 10.3 |
| 11 to 20 | 294 | 235 | 99 | 628 | 6.6 |
| more than 20 | 173 | 113 | 38 | 324 | 3.4 |
| | 4,532 | 2,567 | 2,382 | 9,481 | 100.0 |
| | 47.8% | 27.1% | 25.1% | 100.0% | |

Source: United Nations, Centre on Transnational Corporations, *Transnational Corporations in World Development Re-examined*, 1978.

A second striking feature of MNC activity seen in Table A−2 is the dominant role of just a few parent nations, notably the United States which accounts for almost half of the value of direct investments. The United Kingdom has an appreciable share, about 11 percent in 1976. West Germany, Japan, and Switzerland are clustered around 7 percent and the rest of the countries run progressively lower. The rapid rates of growth of direct investment of several countries observed in Table A−2 are producing some changes in this picture, but the absolute U.S. figures are so great that a significant alteration in its relative status is not likely. Thus the U.S. MNCs will continue to be the major factors in the field for the foreseeable future.

### Distribution by Geography and Industry

The broad pattern of geographic and industry distribution of MNC activities is shown in Tables A−3, A−4, and A−5. Overall about three-quarters of investments are in developed countries. In earlier periods investments in the LDCs were heavily concentrated in extractive industries. However, with the nationalization of many oil and mining operations and expansion of LDC manufacturing, the industrial distribution is now fairly similar among major areas.

**Table A−2.** Stock of Direct Investment of Developed Market Economies

|  | *Billions of Dollars* | | | *Percentages* | | |
|---|---|---|---|---|---|---|
|  | *1967* | *1971* | *1976* | *1967* | *1971* | *1976* |
| Unites States | $56.6 | $82.8 | $137.2 | 53.8% | 52.3% | 47.6% |
| United Kingdom | 17.5 | 23.7 | 32.1 | 16.6 | 15.0 | 11.2 |
| West Germany | 3.0 | 7.3 | 19.9 | 2.8 | 4.6 | 6.9 |
| Japan | 1.5 | 4.4 | 19.4 | 1.4 | 2.8 | 6.7 |
| Switzerland | 5.0 | 9.5 | 18.6 | 4.8 | 6.0 | 6.5 |
| France | 6.0 | 7.3 | 11.9 | 5.7 | 4.6 | 4.1 |
| Canada | 3.7 | 6.5 | 11.1 | 3.5 | 4.1 | 3.9 |
| Netherlands | 2.2 | 4.0 | 9.8 | 2.1 | 2.5 | 3.4 |
| Sweden | 1.7 | 2.4 | 5.0 | 1.6 | 1.5 | 1.7 |
| Belgium-Luxembourg | 2.0 | 2.4 | 3.6 | 1.9 | 1.5 | 1.2 |
| Italy | 2.1 | 3.0 | 2.9 | 2.0 | 1.9 | 1.0 |
| Total above | 101.1 | 153.1 | 270.4 | 96.1 | 96.7 | 94.2 |
| All other (estimate) | 4.0 | 5.1 | 16.8 | 3.8 | 3.2 | 5.8 |
| Grand total | 105.1 | 158.2 | 287.2 | 100.0 | 100.0 | 100.0 |

Source: United Nations, Centre on Transnational Corporations, *Transnational Corporations in World Development Re-examined*, 1978.

**Table A–5.   U.S. Stock of Direct International Investments by Major Industries (Billions of dollars)**

| Year | Manufacturing | Mining and Smelting | Petroleum | Transportation, Communication and Public Utilities | Finance and Insurance | Agriculture | Trade | Others | Total |
|---|---|---|---|---|---|---|---|---|---|
| 1897 | $0.1 | $0.1 | $0.1 | $0.2 | a | $ a | $ a | $0.1 | $0.6 |
| 1914 | 0.5 | 0.7 | 0.3 | 0.4 | a | 0.4 | a | 0.4 | 2.7 |
| 1919 | 0.8 | 0.9 | 0.6 | 0.4 | a | 0.6 | a | 0.6 | 3.9 |
| 1929 | 1.8 | 1.2 | 1.1 | 1.6 | a | 0.9 | 0.4 | 0.6 | 7.5 |
| 1936 | 1.7 | 1.0 | 1.1 | 1.6 | a | 0.5 | 0.4 | 0.4 | 6.7 |
| 1945 | 2.7 | 1.1 | 1.5 | 1.4 | a | 0.5 | 0.7 | 0.6 | 8.4 |
| 1950 | 3.8 | 1.1 | 3.4 | 1.4 | a | 0.6 | 0.8 | 0.7 | 11.8 |
| 1955 | 6.3 | 2.2 | 5.8 | 1.6 | a | a | 1.3 | 2.0 | 19.3 |
| 1960 | 11.2 | 3.0 | 10.9 | 2.5 | a | a | 2.4 | 2.7 | 32.7 |
| 1970 | 32.2 | 6.1 | 21.8 | 2.0 | 2.0 | a | 7.8 | 6.8 | 78.1 |
| 1975 | 55.8 | 6.5 | 26.2 | 3.2 | 3.2 | a | 12.5 | 5.3 | 124.2 |
| 1976 | 61.1 | 7.1 | 30.2 | 3.2 | 16.4 | a | 13.7 | 6.1 | 137.2 |

a Included in "Others."

Sources: E. R. Barlow and Ira T. Wender, *Foreign Investment & Taxation* and *Survey of Current Business*, 1955.

**Table A–6. Estimated Stock of Direct Investment of Major Parent Countries at End of 1967**

| Country of Origin | World (total book value,[a] millions of dollars) | Total Book Value (millions of dollars) | Developing Countries (percentage share) | | | | | |
|---|---|---|---|---|---|---|---|---|
| | | | Africa | Central America | South America | Middle East | Asia | Total Developing |
| United States | $59,486 | $16,703 | 2.3% | 7.4% | 12.4% | 3.0% | 3.0% | 28.1% |
| United Kingdom | 17,521 | 6,582 | 11.3 | 4.7 | 5.0 | 4.8 | 11.8 | 37.6 |
| France | 6,000 | 2,689 | 28.8 | 1.0 | 6.8 | 2.7 | 5.5 | 44.8 |
| Netherlands | 2,250 | 1,694 | 14.4 | 8.2 | 33.6 | 7.7 | 11.4 | 75.3 |
| Canada | 3,728 | 1,453 | 1.5 | 13.3 | 22.7 | 0.2 | 1.3 | 39.0 |
| Federal Republic of Germany | 3,015 | 1,018 | 4.6 | 3.4 | 22.8 | 0.8 | 2.2 | 33.8 |
| Japan | 1,458 | 700 | 0.9 | 6.9 | 20.9 | 5.8 | 13.5 | 48.0 |
| Italy | 2,110 | 696 | 11.7 | 1.0 | 17.6 | 1.2 | 1.4 | 33.0 |
| Belgium | 2,040 | 613 | 23.6 | — | 5.5 | 0.1 | 0.8 | 30.0 |
| Switzerland | 4,250 | 565 | 1.4 | 3.4 | 6.7 | 0.1 | 1.7 | 13.3 |
| Sweden | 1,514 | 180 | 5.3 | 0.8 | 4.6 | — | 1.2 | 11.9 |
| Australia | 380 | 100 | — | — | — | — | 26.3 | 26.3 |
| Portugal | 200 | 99 | — | — | 3.0 | — | — | 49.5 |
| Denmark | 190 | 29 | 8.7 | 1.5 | 1.2 | 1.0 | 2.7 | 15.3 |
| Norway | 60 | 9 | 5.0 | — | 10.0 | — | — | 15.0 |
| Austria | 30 | 5 | — | — | 16.7 | — | — | 16.7 |
| Total, DAC countries | 104,232 | 33,135 | 6.3 | 6.1 | 11.6 | 3.0 | 4.8 | 31.8 |

[a]Not including centrally planned economies.
Source: United Nations, Department of Economic and Social Affairs, *Multinational Corporations in World Development*, 1973.

Table A-7.   U.S. Direct Investment Position Abroad at Yearend—1976
*(Millions of dollars)*

| | *All Industries* | *Mining and Smelting* | *Petroleum* |
|---|---|---|---|
| All countries | $137,244 | $7,058 | $29,713 |
| Developed countries | 101,150 | 4,749 | 23,662 |
| Canada | 33,927 | 3,200 | 7,153 |
| Europe | 55,906 | 34 | 13,445 |
| European Communities (9) | 44,016 | 12 | 11,171 |
| Belgium and Luxembourg | 3,607 | 0 | 318 |
| France | 5,954 | −8 | 997 |
| West Germany | 10,410 | −1 | 2,294 |
| Italy | 2,944 | 8 | 635 |
| Netherlands | 3,771 | 1 | 1,298 |
| Denmark | 735 | 1 | 399 |
| Ireland | 897 | 1 | 114 |
| United Kingdom | 15,696 | 11 | 5,117 |
| Other Europe | 11,890 | 22 | 2,274 |
| Norway | 1,222 | (D) | 838 |
| Spain | 1,971 | (D) | 189 |
| Sweden | 1,152 | 0 | 406 |
| Switzerland | 5,733 | 0 | 106 |
| Other | 1,812 | 2 | 734 |
| Japan | 3,787 | 0 | 1,566 |
| Australia, New Zealand, and South Africa | 7,529 | 1,515 | 1,498 |
| Australia | 5,460 | 1,237 | 889 |
| New Zealand | 404 | (D) | (D) |
| South Africa | 1,665 | (D) | (D) |
| Developing countries | 29,050 | 2,309 | 2,882 |
| Latin America | 23,536 | 1,600 | 2,940 |
| Latin American Republics | 17,116 | 1,163 | 1,653 |
| Argentina | 1,364 | 53 | 174 |
| Brazil | 5,403 | 140 | 336 |
| Chile | 179 | 5 | (D) |
| Colombia | 653 | 11 | 56 |
| Mexico | 2,984 | 88 | 17 |
| Panama | 1,957 | 1 | 94 |
| Peru | 1,367 | (D) | (D) |
| Venezuela | 1,511 | −21 | 230 |
| Other Central America | 677 | 23 | 65 |
| Other | 1,020 | (D) | 367 |

*(Table A-7.  continued overleaf)*

Table A–7. continued

| Manufacturing | Transportation Communication and Public Utilities | Trade | Finance and Insurance | Other Industries |
|---|---|---|---|---|
| $61,062 | $3,247 | $13,691 | $16,392 | $6,082 |
| 49,699 | 957 | 9,910 | 8,946 | 3,227 |
| 15,984 | 771 | 2,153 | 3,796 | 871 |
| 28,702 | 155 | 6,766 | 4,767 | 2,037 |
| 25,121 | 84 | 3,485 | 2,960 | 1,182 |
| 2,221 | 5 | 591 | 419 | 54 |
| 3,968 | 5 | 715 | 186 | 90 |
| 6,638 | 17 | 537 | 811 | 114 |
| 1,870 | (*) | 281 | 82 | 67 |
| 1,770 | 1 | 364 | 204 | 133 |
| 140 | −2 | 104 | (D) | (D) |
| 738 | (*) | 33 | (D) | (D) |
| 7,776 | 56 | 860 | 1,233 | 643 |
| 3,581 | 71 | 3,281 | 1,806 | 855 |
| 298 | −1 | 27 | 2 | (D) |
| 1,221 | 17 | 218 | 81 | (D) |
| 607 | 9 | 106 | 15 | 8 |
| 948 | 1 | 2,756 | 1,541 | 381 |
| 507 | 44 | 173 | 167 | 185 |
| 1,689 | 30 | 361 | 103 | 38 |
| 3,324 | 1 | 630 | 281 | 280 |
| 2,505 | (*) | 372 | 291 | 166 |
| 114 | −1 | 55 | 2 | 48 |
| 705 | 1 | 204 | −12 | 66 |
| 11,362 | 567 | 3,229 | 5,986 | 2,715 |
| 9,242 | 285 | 2,404 | 5,478 | 1,587 |
| 8,642 | (D) | 2,126 | 1,927 | (D) |
| 895 | (D) | 105 | 72 | (D) |
| 3,667 | 26 | 496 | 422 | 31 |
| 49 | 6 | 34 | (*) | (D) |
| 387 | (D) | 64 | 100 | (D) |
| 2,223 | 47 | 453 | 51 | 105 |
| 139 | 45 | 512 | 785 | 381 |
| 168 | −1 | 64 | 8 | 43 |
| 747 | (D) | 289 | 150 | (D) |
| 226 | 65 | 60 | 53 | 185 |
| 139 | 28 | 49 | 285 | (D) |

*(Table A-7. continued overleaf)*

**Table A–7. continued**

|  | *All Industries* | *Mining and Smelting* | *Petroleum* |
|---|---|---|---|
| Developing Countries *(cont.)* |  |  |  |
| Other Western Hemisphere | 6,420 | 437 | 1,287 |
| Bahamas | 1,059 | (D) | 103 |
| Bermuda | 3,507 | 0 | 245 |
| Jamaica | 577 | 302 | 38 |
| Other | 1,277 | (D) | 901 |
| Africa | 2,802 | 534 | 1,599 |
| Liberia | 348 | (D) | 83 |
| Libya | 362 | 0 | 351 |
| Nigeria | 341 | (*) | 281 |
| Other | 1,750 | (D) | 884 |
| Middle East | −3,210 | 8 | −4,211 |
| Iran | −422 | (*) | −547 |
| Other | −2,788 | 8 | −3,665 |
| Other Asia and Pacific | 5,922 | 167 | 2,554 |
| India | 362 | (*) | 70 |
| Indonesia | 1,475 | (D) | 1,167 |
| Philippines | 831 | (D) | 192 |
| Other | 3,253 | 16 | 1,126 |
| International and unallocated | 7,044 | — | 3,169 |

*Less than $500,000 (±).
D Suppressed to avoid disclosure of data of individual companies.
Source: *Survey of Current Business*, August 1977.

Table A-7. continued

| Manufacturing | Transportation Communication and Public Utilities | Trade | Finance and Insurance | Other Industries |
|---|---|---|---|---|
| 601 | (D) | 278 | 3,551 | (D) |
| 94 | 12 | 89 | 616 | (D) |
| 225 | 29 | 149 | 2,810 | 49 |
| 226 | -26 | 8 | 4 | 26 |
| 56 | (D) | 32 | 121 | 30 |
| 257 | 98 | 102 | 63 | 149 |
| (D) | 88 | 8 | 32 | 67 |
| 1 | (*) | 3 | 1 | 6 |
| 35 | 2 | 23 | 9 | -9 |
| (D) | 8 | 68 | 22 | 85 |
| 185 | 13 | 73 | 122 | 600 |
| 76 | 6 | 11 | (D) | (D) |
| 110 | 8 | 62 | (D) | (D) |
| 1,678 | 170 | 650 | 322 | 381 |
| 259 | (D) | 8 | 8 | (D) |
| 100 | (D) | 3 | 7 | (D) |
| 352 | 21 | 111 | 84 | (D) |
| 967 | 137 | 527 | 223 | 258 |
| — | 1,723 | 552 | 1,460 | 140 |

Table A–8.   Direct Investment Flow and Investment Income Flow for Selected Developed Countries, Annual Average, 1968–1970 (Millions of dollars)

| Country | Direct Investment Flow | | | Income on Direct Investment | | |
|---|---|---|---|---|---|---|
| | Inward | Outward | Net | Inward | Outward | Net |
| United States | $727.0 | $ −3,621.0 | $ − 2,894.0 | $8,107.0 | $ − 866.3 | $7,240.7 |
| United Kingdom | 727.7 | −1,154.3 | −426.6 | 1,535.0 | −781.7 | 753.3 |
| Federal Republic of Germany | 338.7 | −542.7 | −204.0 | 49.3 | −547.7 | −498.4 |
| Netherlands | 404.7 | −450.7 | −46.0 | 496.0 | −192.7 | 303.3 |
| France | 371.0 | −303.0 | 68.0 | 268.0 | −33.2 | 234.8 |
| Canada | 651.3 | −273.7 | 377.6 | 171.0 | −579.3 | −408.3 |
| Japan | 80.7 | −260.3 | −179.6 | 56.0 | −89.3 | −33.3 |
| Italy | 452.0 | −217.7 | 234.3 | 344.7[a] | −325.0[a] | 19.7 |
| Sweden | 122.7 | −159.0 | −36.3 | 52.7 | −25.0 | 27.7 |
| Australia | 748.3 | −99.0 | 649.3 | 53.0 | −566.7 | −513.7 |
| Belgium-Luxembourg | 281.3 | −74.0 | 207.3 | 301.7[a] | −282.0[a] | 19.7 |
| Finland | 15.7 | −31.3 | −15.6 | — | −7.7 | −7.7 |
| South Africa | 319.7 | −26.3 | 293.4 | 109.3 | −365.0 | −255.7 |
| Spain | 191.3 | −21.7 | 169.6 | 2.3 | −16.7 | −14.4 |
| Norway | 28.7 | −19.3 | 9.4 | 23.0 | −17.7 | 5.3 |
| Denmark | 68.0 | −17.7 | 50.3 | 18.0 | −24.3 | −6.3 |
| Austria[b] | 48.0 | −7.3 | 40.7 | 4.7 | −29.3 | −24.6 |
| Portugal | 24.0 | −2.7 | 21.3 | — | — | — |
| New Zealand | 6.0 | −2.0 | 4.0 | — | −28.7 | −28.7 |
| Greece | 146.0 | — | 146.0 | 9.3 | −47.0 | −37.7 |

[a]Estimated.
[b]1969–1970.
Source: United Nations, Department of Economic and Social Affairs, *Multinational Corporations in World Development.* 1973.

**Table A—9. Direct Investment Inflow and Investment Income Payments for Sixty-One Developing Countries[a]**
(Millions of dollars)

|  | 1967 | 1971 | 1972 | 1973 | 1974 | 1975 |
|---|---|---|---|---|---|---|
| *Total, 61 countries:* | | | | | | |
| Direct investment | $1,200 | $1,942 | $1,359 | $3,094 | $ -2,100 | — |
| Income payments | -4,440 | -5,989 | -7,600 | -9,800 | -16,400* | — |
| *Oil producing countries[b]* | | | | | | |
| Direct investment | 370 | 618 | -375 | 134 | -5,268 | $3,104 |
| Income payments | -2,900 | -4,313 | -5,752 | -7,200 | -13,600* | -9,128* |
| *Non-oil producing countries:* | | | | | | |
| Direct investment | 836 | 1,324 | 1,734 | 2,960 | 3,169 | — |
| Income payments | -1,580 | -1,676 | -1,848 | -2,600 | -2,820* | — |
| of which: | | | | | | |
| *Africa* | | | | | | |
| Direct investment | 180 | 184 | 231 | 276 | 278 | — |
| Income payments | -240 | -196 | -212 | -340 | -350 | — |
| *Middle East* | | | | | | |
| Direct investment | — | -1 | — | — | — | 9 |
| Income payments | -31 | -9 | -16 | -14 | -12 | — |
| *Asia* | | | | | | |
| Direct investment | 136 | 310 | 452 | 755 | 1,277 | 1,317 |
| Income payments | -239 | -269 | -455 | -755 | -927 | — |
| *Western hemisphere* | | | | | | |
| Direct investment | 520 | 831 | 1,051 | 1,929 | 1,614 | 2,552 |
| Income payments | -1,068 | -1,202 | -1,165 | -1,456 | -1,550 | — |

Notes on next page

**Table A-9.** continued (*Notes*)

*Provisional figures.

*Note:*  In eighteen of the countries covered in this table, the direct investment inflow and investment income payments both exclude reinvested profits; in the remaining forty-three countries reinvested profits are in principle included in both entries; reinvested profits are included in the data for the following oil-producing countries: Nigeria, Ecuador, Venezuela, Iran, Saudi Arabia.

[a]Includes, in addition to the oil-producing countries listed in footnote *b*, nineteen African countries, twenty-two Latin American and Caribbean countries (excluding Bahamas and Bermuda), two Middle East countries and seven Asian countries (excluding India).

[b]Nine member countries of OPEC (Algeria, Libya, Nigeria, Ecuador, Venezuela, Iran, Iraq, Saudi Arabia, Indonesia); data for the other four OPEC members (Gabon, Kuwait, Qatar, and United Arab Emirates) are not available.

*Source:* United Nations, Centre on Transnational Corporations, *Transnational Corporations in World Development Re-examined.* 1978.

Table A–10. Direct Investment Flow from Selected Developed Market Economies to Developing Countries *(Millions of dollars)*

| | 1965–67 Average | 1970–72 Average | 1973 | 1974 | 1975 | 1976 |
|---|---|---|---|---|---|---|
| **Belgium** | | | | | | |
| Total | 47 | 44 | 48 | 49 | 69 | 236 |
| New Investment | 7 | 27 | 22 | 23 | 43 | 215 |
| Reinvested earnings | 40 | 17 | 26 | 26 | 26 | 20 |
| **Canada** | | | | | | |
| Total | 34 | 105 | 125 | 193 | 300 | 430 |
| New Investment | 25 | 39 | 50 | 109 | 150* | 205 |
| Reinvested earnings | 9 | 66 | 75 | 84 | 150* | 225 |
| **West Germany** | | | | | | |
| Total | 147 | 426 | 787 | 701 | 816 | 765 |
| New Investment | 84 | 265 | 543 | 431 | 532 | 487 |
| Reinvested earnings | 63 | 161 | 244 | 270 | 284 | 278 |
| **Italy** | | | | | | |
| Total | 59 | 206 | 246 | 100 | 150 | 213 |
| New Investment | 44 | 137 | 136 | −15 | 40 | 83 |
| Reinvested earnings | 15 | 69 | 110 | 115 | 110 | 130 |
| **Sweden** | | | | | | |
| Total | 27 | 39 | 22 | 49 | 82 | 125 |
| New Investment | 19 | 31 | 12 | 29 | 57 | 116 |
| Reinvested earnings | 8 | 8 | 10 | 20 | 26 | 9 |
| **United States** | | | | | | |
| Total | 1,147 | 1,909 | 2,881 | 3,788 | 7,241 | 3,119 |
| New Investment | 771 | 1,287 | 1,675 | 2,035 | 4,010 | 1,850 |
| Reinvested earnings | 376 | 622 | 1,212 | 1,753 | 3,231 | 1,269 |
| **Australia** | | | | | | |
| Total | 22 | 85 | 104 | 117 | 48 | 75 |
| New Investment | 22 | 67 | 26 | 28 | 43 | 44 |
| Reinvested earnings | — | 18 | 78 | 89 | 5 | 31 |
| **Total above countries** | | | | | | |
| Total | 1,483 | 2,814 | 4,221 | 4,997 | 8,705 | 4,963 |
| New Investment | 972 | 1,853 | 2,464 | 2,640 | 4,875 | 3,000 |
| Reinvested earnings | 511 | 961 | 1,757 | 2,357 | 3,830 | 1,963 |

Direct Investment Flows by Type for France, Netherlands, Switzerland, and United Kingdom.

| | France | Nether-lands | Switzer-land | United Kingdom |
|---|---|---|---|---|
| | | 1965–67 | | 1964–66 |
| Total flow (millions of dollars) | 339 | 90 | 46 | 206 |
| New direct investment | 161 | 52 | 37 | 96* |
| Reinvested earnings | 178 | 37 | 9 | 111* |

*Estimates.
Source: United Nations, Centre on Transnational Corporations, *Transnational Corporations in World Development Re-examined.* 1978.

majority-owned foreign affiliates (MOFAs) made by the U.S. Commerce Department. Comparisons were also made with statistics for all U.S. manufacturing corporations from the Internal Revenue Service. The after-tax rates of return on net worth for the MNC parents were 12.5 percent in 1966 and 8.8 percent in 1970 compared to 13.2 percent and 7.1 percent for all U.S. manufacturing firms in the same periods. The large decline for both types of firms reflected the cyclical downturn of the U.S. economy. As European business was still strong in 1970, the better performance of the MNCs relative to all U.S. firms presumably was due to the greater portion of foreign earnings in their results. In 1966 the highest rates of return among MNCs were in transportation equipment (15.7 percent) and chemicals (15 percent), whereas in 1970 mining was most profitable (13.3 percent) with food products next (12.3 percent).

For comparisons of MOFA performance, rates of return on total assets were preferred because the ready substitution of equity and debt by parents in financing made the meaning of net worth uncertain. In 1966, MOFAs showed a 6.4 percent return on assets compared to 7.4 percent for their parent MNCs, while in 1970 the MOFAs were up to 7.1 percent compared to 4.7 percent for the parents. A regional breakdown showed that profit rates for manufacturing MOFAs were relatively similar in both developed and developing countries. However, the petroleum firms had rates of return of about 50 percent in developing countries compared to 2 to 3 percent in developed countries. These differences reflected both intra-company pricing and heavy North Sea development costs. The data also were analyzed for the effects of size and age of investments. Of 1,077 European MOFAs, those of medium size had distinctly higher rates of return than either the large or small affiliates. Within size groups, 1970 rates of return were roughly 75 percent higher for MOFAs established before 1966 than for those formed after that.

A less refined analysis of profitability of MNCs is provided by the aggregate U.S. and U.K. data given in Table A–11. Here also the returns were about equal from investments in developed and developing countries. However, these aggregate figures disguise tremendous variations among countries, especially in LDCs.

**Table A-11.   U.S. and U.K. Average Returns on Book Value of Direct Investment[a]**   *(Percentage)*

| Area of Investment | United States Average (1965-1968) | | United Kingdom Average (1965-1968) |
| --- | --- | --- | --- |
| | All Sectors | Excluding Petroleum | Excluding Petroleum |
| *Developed market economies* | 7.9% | 9.6% | 9.3% |
| United States | — | — | 8.6 |
| Canada | 8.0 | 8.6 | 11.3 |
| Europe[b] | 7.1 | 10.0 | 7.9 |
| Japan | 14.2 | 20.2 | — |
| Southern hemisphere | 9.7 | 12.0 | 9.5 |
| *Developing countries* | 17.5 | 11.0 | 9.8 |
| Western hemisphere | 12.1 | 11.1 | 8.7 |
| Asia | 34.7 | 11.7 | 10.4 |
| Africa | 22.3 | 7.7 | |
| European developing countries[c] | — | — | — |
| Unallocated | 8.5 | 11.6 | — |
| Total | 10.7 | 10.0 | 9.5 |

[a] Adjusted earnings (branch earnings + dividends + interest + reinvested earnings) over book value at year end.
[b] United States data include investment in all European countries, other than Eastern Europe. United Kingdom data include investment in European developed countries as defined by the Organization for Economic Cooperation and Development.
[c] As defined by the Organization for Economic Cooperation and Development.
Source: United Nations, Department of Economic and Social Affairs, *Multinational Corporations in World Development.* 1973.

Table A–12.  International Production and Exports of Market Economies in 1971 (Millions of dollars)

| Country | Stock of Foreign Direct Investment (book value) | Estimated International Production[a] | Exports | International Production as Percentage of Exports |
|---|---|---|---|---|
| United States | $86,000 | $172,000 | $43,492 | $395.5% |
| United Kingdom | 24,020 | 48,000 | 22,367 | 214.6 |
| France | 9,540 | 19,100 | 20,420 | 93.5 |
| West Germany | 7,270 | 14,600 | 39,040 | 37.4 |
| Switzerland | 6,760 | 13,500 | 5,728 | 235.7 |
| Canada | 5,930 | 11,900 | 17,582 | 67.7 |
| Japan | 4,480 | 9,000 | 24,019 | 37.5 |
| Netherlands | 3,580 | 7,200 | 13,927 | 51.7 |
| Sweden | 3,450 | 6,900 | 7,465 | 92.4 |
| Italy | 3,350 | 6,700 | 15,111 | 44.3 |
| Belgium | 3,250 | 6,500 | 12,392[b] | 52.4 |
| Australia | 610 | 1,200 | 5,070 | 23.7 |
| Portugal | 320 | 600 | 1,052 | 57.0 |
| Denmark | 310 | 600 | 3,685 | 16.3 |
| Norway | 90 | 200 | 2,563 | 7.8 |
| Austria | 40 | 100 | 3,169 | 3.2 |
| Total, above | 159,000 | 318,000 | 237,082 | 133.7 |
| Other | 6,000 | 12,000 | 74,818 | 16.0 |
| Total, market economies | 165,000 | 330,000 | 311,900 | 105.8 |

**Table A-12. continued** *(Notes)*

a Estimated international production equals the book value of foreign direct investment multiplied by the factor 2.0. The estimate of this factor was derived as follows: the ratio of foreign sales to book value of foreign direct investment has been estimated from 1970 United States data on gross sales of majority-owned foreign affiliates and book value of United States foreign direct investment. "Gross sales of majority-owned foreign affiliates" (approximately $157 billion) includes transactions between foreign affiliates and parent corporations (approximately $20.3 billion) and interforeign affiliate sales (approximately $28.1 billion), which together account for about 30 percent of gross foreign affiliate sales. The book value of United States foreign direct investment in 1970 amounted to $78.1 billion. The resulting ratio of gross sales to book value is 2:1. This ratio has been used to estimate the international production of non-United States foreign affiliates.

b Includes Luxembourg.

Source: United Nations, Department of Economic and Social Affairs, *Multinational Corporations in World Development.* 1973.

Table A-12 gives the estimated volume of production by MNC operations in foreign countries and total national exports for developed countries. The overall totals are about equal but the prominence of MNC production is notable for the leading MNC nations, especially the United States. This point is reinforced by the data in Table A-13 for a sample of 298 U.S. MNCs and their 5,237 majority-owned foreign affiliates. The data show that of the total foreign sales of these firms in 1970 ($135 billion, sales to foreigners—$20 billion plus sales to affiliates—$115 billion) 84 percent was produced by the foreign affiliates. The balance included 6 percent—exports by the parent to the affiliates (about half for reprocessing, e.g., components and about half for resale without further manufacture) and 9 percent—exports to non-affiliated foreign buyers. Further data for all U.S. MNCs showing the aggregate of foreign affiliate sales broken down by industry and region is given in Table A-14.

Table A-13.  Worldwide Gross Sales by 298 U.S. Multinational Corporations for 1966 and 1970, by Industry of U.S. Reporter *(Millions of dollars)*

|  | Item | All Industries | |
|---|---|---|---|
|  |  | *1966* | *1970* |
|  | Gross Sales[1] | $307,993 | $423,960 |
| 1 | By U.S. reporter | 236,839 | 309,241 |
| 2 | To unaffiliated U.S. residents | 224,120 | 289,232 |
| 3 | To foreigners | 12,719 | 20,009 |
| 4 | To own majority-owned foreign affiliates | 5,038 | 8,623 |
| 5 | To others | 7,681 | 11,886 |
| 6 | By majority-owned foreign[2] affiliates | 71,154 | 114,719 |
| 7 | Sales to foreigners | 66,647 | 107,196 |
| 8 | Local sales | 52,400 | 80,827 |
| 9 | Exports to third countries | 14,247 | 26,369 |
| 10 | Exports to United States | 4,258 | 7,524 |
| 11 | By majority-owned foreign affiliates to affiliated customers | 16,028 | 26,696 |
| 12 | Sales to affiliated foreigners | 12,595 | 20,452 |
| 13 | Local | 4,006 | 5,799 |
| 14 | Exports to third countries | 8,589 | 14,653 |
| 15 | Exports to parent U.S. reporter | 3,433 | 6,244 |
| 16 | By majority-owned foreign affiliates to unaffiliated customers | 54,874 | 88,023 |
| 17 | Sales to unaffiliated foreigners | 54,052 | 86,744 |
| 18 | Local sales | 48,394 | 75,028 |
| 19 | Exports to third countries | 5,658 | 11,716 |
| 20 | Exports to unaffiliated U.S. residents | 822 | 1,279 |

1. Sales by U.S. reporter (lines 1 through 5) were reported on a partially consolidated basis, in that domestic intercompany sales were netted out; therefore line 1 contains sales to unaffiliated U.S. residents and all sales to foreigners by the consolidated U.S. reporter.

**Table A–13. continued**

| Manufacturing | | Petroleum | | Other Industries | |
|---|---|---|---|---|---|
| *1966* | *1970* | *1966* | *1970* | *1966* | *1970* |
| $202,955 | $270,921 | $ 61,250 | $ 91,439 | $ 43,789 | $ 61,601 |
| 164,004 | 207,993 | 34,814 | 47,690 | 38,022 | 53,559 |
| 154,029 | 191,954 | 34,015 | 46,542 | 36,077 | 50,837 |
| 9,975 | 16,139 | 799 | 1,148 | 1,945 | 2,722 |
| 4,208 | 7,079 | 378 | 553 | 451 | 991 |
| 5,767 | 9,060 | 421 | 595 | 1,495 | 1,730 |
| 38,951 | 62,928 | 26,436 | 43,749 | 5,767 | 8,042 |
| 36,213 | 58,139 | 25,007 | 41,379 | 5,427 | 7,677 |
| 29,940 | 46,817 | 18,473 | 28,266 | 3,987 | 5,744 |
| 6,273 | 11,322 | 6,534 | 13,113 | 1,440 | 1,933 |
| 2,588 | 4,788 | 1,370 | 2,369 | 299 | 366 |
| 6,307 | 11,462 | 9,164 | 14,742 | 557 | 492 |
| 4,146 | 7,309 | 8,090 | 12,766 | 359 | 377 |
| 884 | 1,140 | 3,100 | 4,556 | 22 | 103 |
| 3,262 | 6,169 | 4,990 | 8,210 | 337 | 274 |
| 2,161 | 4,153 | 1,074 | 1,976 | 198 | 115 |
| 32,492 | 51,465 | 17,213 | 29,006 | 5,169 | 7,552 |
| 32,067 | 50,830 | 16,917 | 28,613 | 5,068 | 7,300 |
| 29,056 | 45,677 | 15,373 | 23,710 | 3,965 | 5,641 |
| 3,011 | 5,153 | 1,544 | 4,903 | 1,103 | 1,659 |
| 425 | 635 | 296 | 393 | 101 | 252 |

2. Total sales by the foreign affiliates (line 6) include sales of finance and insurance affiliates but since such affiliates were not required to give any breakdown of sales by destination in 1966, lines 7 through 20 in 1966 exclude such sales. The amount involved was $249 million.

Table A–14.  Distribution of Sales by Majority-Owned Foreign Affiliates of U.S. Companies: Destination by Industry and Area of Affiliate *(Millions of dollars)*

|  | Total Sales | |
|---|---|---|
|  | *1974* | *1975* |
| Total | $437,685 | $458,310 |
| *By Industry* | | |
| Mining and smelting | 5,109 | 4,597 |
| Petroleum | 184,919 | 178,716 |
| Manufacturing | 175,703 | 192,253 |
| Food products | 17,001 | 18,277 |
| Paper and allied products | 9,259 | 9,246 |
| Chemicals and allied products | 36,206 | 37,552 |
| Rubber products | 4,952 | 5,444 |
| Primary and fabricated metals | 12,514 | 12,602 |
| Machinery, except electrical | 27,449 | 32,143 |
| Electrical machinery | 17,439 | 18,783 |
| Transportation equipment | 32,665 | 38,009 |
| Other | 18,216 | 20,196 |
| Trade | 46,062 | 52,152 |
| Other industries | 25,891 | 30,591 |
| *By Area* | | |
| Developed countries | 272,177 | 302,836 |
| Canada | 71,403 | 78,484 |
| Europe | 165,772 | 186,472 |
| European Communities (9)[b] | 138,536 | 155,774 |
| France | 22,061 | 26,100 |
| Germany | 34,557 | 38,102 |
| United Kingdom | 40,277 | 45,860 |
| Other | 41,640 | 45,710 |
| Other Europe | 27,236 | 30,699 |
| Japan | 16,849 | 17,778 |
| Australia, New Zealand, and South Africa | 18,152 | 20,101 |
| Developing countries | 148,303 | 141,786 |
| Latin America | 51,605 | 57,177 |
| Other Africa[c] | 10,139 | 9,185 |
| Middle East[c] | 64,078 | 53,689 |
| Other Asia and Pacific | 22,480 | 21,734 |
| International and unallocated | 17,204 | 13,688 |

[a]Sales by an affiliate in the country where it was located.

[b]Consists of Belgium, Luxembourg, France, Germany, Italy, the Netherlands, Denmark, Ireland, and the United Kingdom.

**Table A–14. continued**

| Local Sales[a] | | Exports to the United States | | Exports to Other Foreign Countries | |
|---|---|---|---|---|---|
| *1974* | *1975* | *1974* | *1975* | *1974* | *1975* |
| $276,533 | $301,546 | $ 31,801 | $ 31,571 | $129,351 | $125,193 |
| 1,025 | 1,142 | 1,788 | 1,138 | 2,295 | 2,317 |
| 89,569 | 93,835 | 16,053 | 15,145 | 79,297 | 69,736 |
| 134,705 | 148,007 | 11,228 | 11,371 | 29,770 | 32,875 |
| 15,488 | 16,727 | 334 | 227 | 1,179 | 1,324 |
| 6,574 | 6,631 | 1,023 | 1,067 | 1,663 | 1,548 |
| 27,876 | 29,819 | 451 | 445 | 7,879 | 7,288 |
| 4,197 | 4,615 | 33 | 59 | 723 | 770 |
| 10,316 | 10,411 | 394 | 383 | 1,804 | 1,808 |
| 18,093 | 20,761 | 1,431 | 1,506 | 7,925 | 9,876 |
| 14,486 | 15,674 | 946 | 742 | 2,007 | 2,367 |
| 22,954 | 26,968 | 5,637 | 5,885 | 4,074 | 5,156 |
| 14,723 | 16,401 | 977 | 1,058 | 2,516 | 2,738 |
| 29,152 | 31,954 | 1,418 | 2,595 | 15,493 | 17,604 |
| 22,081 | 26,607 | 1,314 | 1,322 | 2,497 | 2,661 |
| 209,788 | 231,571 | 14,831 | 16,061 | 47,558 | 55,204 |
| 55,528 | 61,015 | 11,411 | 12,694 | 4,464 | 4,775 |
| 121,938 | 135,752 | 3,077 | 3,065 | 40,757 | 47,656 |
| 105,710 | 117,084 | 2,515 | 2,511 | 30,311 | 36,178 |
| 18,328 | 21,249 | 298 | 301 | 3,435 | 4,550 |
| 28,521 | 31,651 | 822 | 637 | 5,215 | 5,814 |
| 32,093 | 34,821 | 576 | 649 | 7,608 | 10,390 |
| 26,769 | 29,363 | 819 | 925 | 14,053 | 15,424 |
| 16,227 | 18,667 | 563 | 554 | 10,446 | 11,478 |
| 15,940 | 16,848 | 127 | 124 | 782 | 806 |
| 16,381 | 17,956 | 215 | 179 | 1,555 | 1,966 |
| 55,364 | 59,713 | 14,763 | 14,618 | 78,176 | 67,455 |
| 33,187 | 37,668 | 6,415 | 6,669 | 12,003 | 12,841 |
| 3,958 | 4,339 | 1,541 | 1,804 | 4,641 | 3,042 |
| 6,648 | 5,227 | 4,725 | 3,591 | 52,705 | 44,871 |
| 11,571 | 12,480 | 2,082 | 2,554 | 8,827 | 6,700 |
| 11,381 | 10,262 | 2,207 | 892 | 3,617 | 2,534 |

[c] Egypt is included in "other Africa."
Source: *Survey of Current Business*, February 1977.

Tables A–15 and A–16 expand on the picture of international flows attributable to MNCs with data on payments of royalties and other fees for major parent and host nations. Table A–17 indicates that for U.S. firms the major portion of payments for skills are made by MNC affiliates, with licensing of independent foreign firms a lesser factor accounting for about a third of the total royalties and fees. However, the British data suggest that for firms of other nations licensing of independent firms may be a larger portion of MNC business.

## MNC Contribution to Economic Activity

Another indicator of the role of MNCs is the portion of economic activity they provide. A United Nations analysis of 422 of the world's

**Table A–15.** Payments of Royalties and Fees by Selected Developing Countries

|  |  | Payments of Royalties and Fees | |
| --- | --- | --- | --- |
|  | *Year* | *Millions of Dollars* | *Percentage of Exports* |
| Argentina | 1974 | $101 | 2.56% |
| Brazil | 1976 | 272 | 2.68 |
| Chile | 1972 | 17 | 1.98 |
| Colombia | 1975 | 17 | 1.16 |
| Mexico | 1971 | 167 | 11.11 |
| Trinidad and Tobago | 1975 | 18 | 1.02 |
| India | 1973 | 24 | 0.81 |

Source: United Nations, Centre on Transnational Corporations, *Transnational Corporations in World Development Reviewed,* 1978.

**Table A–16.  Receipts and Payments of Royalties and Fees for Selected Developed Countries** *(Millions of dollars)*

| | *1971* | | | *1973* | | |
|---|---|---|---|---|---|---|
| | *Receipts* | *Payments* | *Balance* | *Receipts* | *Payments* | *Balance* |
| United States | $2,545 | $ 241 | $+2,304 | $3,225 | $ 385 | $+2,840 |
| France | 397 | 466 | −69 | 845 | 743 | +102 |
| United Kingdom | 358 | 300 | +58 | 494 | 392 | +102 |
| Federal Republic of Germany | 156 | 425 | −269 | 223 | 619 | −396 |
| Belgium-Luxembourg | 129 | 169 | −40 | 206 | 248 | −42 |
| Netherlands | 105 | 117 | −12 | 142 | 191 | −49 |
| Sweden | 75[b] | 218[b] | −143 | 112 | 288 | −176 |
| Japan | 60 | 488 | −428 | 88 | 715 | −627 |
| Italy | 115 | 329 | −214 | 97 | 304 | −207 |
| Canada[a] | 60 | 327 | −267 | 94 | 500 | −406 |
| Spain | — | — | — | 29 | 261 | −232 |
| New Zealand | 13 | 9 | +4 | 16 | 17 | −1 |
| Austria | 8 | 33 | −25 | 8 | 48 | −40 |
| Australia | 7 | 73 | −66 | 6 | 107 | −101 |

*(Table A–16.  continued on next page)*

**Table A–16.  continued**

| | 1975 | | | 1976 | | |
|---|---|---|---|---|---|---|
| | *Receipts* | *Payments* | *Balance* | *Receipts* | *Payments* | *Balance* |
| United States | $4,302 | $ 480 | $+3,822 | $4,366 | $ 468 | $+3,898 |
| France | — | — | — | — | — | — |
| United Kingdom | 610 | 530 | +80 | — | — | — |
| Federal Republic of Germany | 324 | 834 | -510 | 304 | 806 | -502 |
| Belgium-Luxembourg | — | — | — | — | — | — |
| Netherlands | — | — | — | — | — | — |
| Sweden | 204 | 517 | -313 | 175 | 620 | -445 |
| Japan | 161 | 712 | -551 | — | — | — |
| Italy | — | — | — | — | — | — |
| Canada[a] | — | — | — | — | — | — |
| Spain | 50 | 301 | -251 | 61 | 467 | -406 |
| New Zealand | 25 | 20 | +5 | 20 | 23 | -3 |
| Austria | — | — | — | — | — | — |
| Australia | 12 | 98 | -86 | — | — | — |

[a]Figures for 1971 refer to 1969.
[b]For technical assistance including other items, separate figure not available.

Source: United Nations, Centre on Transnational Corporations, *Transnational Corporations in World Development Re-examined,* 1978.

**Table A-17.  Royalty and Fee Receipts and Payments for the United Kingdom and United States (Millions of dollars)**

| Country | Affiliate Firms (direct investment) | | | | Non-affiliate Firms | | | | Total | | | |
|---|---|---|---|---|---|---|---|---|---|---|---|---|
| | 1966 | 1968 | 1970 | 1971 | 1966 | 1968 | 1970 | 1971 | 1966 | 1968 | 1970 | 1971 |
| *United States* | | | | | | | | | | | | |
| Receipts | 1,030 | 1,246 | 1,620 | 1,874 | 353 | 461 | 600 | 695 | 1,383 | 1,707 | 2,220 | 2,569 |
| Payments | 64 | 80 | 111 | 91 | 76 | 107 | 119 | 125 | 140 | 187 | 230 | 216 |
| Balance | 966 | 1,166 | 1,509 | 1,783 | 277 | 354 | 481 | 570 | 1,243 | 1,520 | 1,990 | 2,353 |
| *United Kingdom* | | | | | | | | | | | | |
| Receipts | 54 (12)[a] | 63 (12) | 86 (20) | — | 101 (27) | 110 (36) | 133 (40) | — | 155 (38) | 172 (48) | 218 (60) | — |
| Payments | 73 (56)[a] | 99 (78) | 136 (111) | — | 51 (31) | 59 (30) | 68 (38) | — | 124 (87) | 156 (108) | 205 (145) | — |
| Balance | -19 | -36 | -50 | — | 50 | 51 | 65 | — | 31 | 16 | 13 | — |

[a]In parentheses, receipts and payments to the United States.

Source: United Nations, Department of Economic and Social Affairs, *Multinational Corporations in World Development*, 1973.

largest corporations (Table A—18) showed that 53 had more than half of the content of their operations abroad. For different parent nations the importance of MNCs varies greatly. In the total U.S. economy, MNC business has a fairly modest role. In the 1976 balance of payments data shown in Table A—19 the main exchange earning items to which MNCs contribute are:

| | |
|---|---:|
| Direct investment income | $12.4 billion |
| Royalties and fees | 4.4 |
| Exports | 115.0 |
| | $131.8 |

Much of the export volume, of course, is not by MNCs so the total is a high figure. Yet the total accounted for less than 8 percent of gross national product. The first two items, those directly attributable to foreign operations, compose a mere 1 percent of GNP.

For other parent countries the role of MNCs is substantially greater. Switzerland is probably the most prominent case. Some 5 percent of national income in 1974 was provided by earnings of MNCs and exports composed another 30 percent of the total.[7] For the 35 largest Swiss manufacturing firms, 68 percent of the employees in 1974 were in foreign operations. Here is a country strong in skills and entrepreneurship but with such a small domestic market that the only opportunities for major growth are in the world economy. Comparable data for most other countries are not readily available but presumably they would show a mix between the extremes of the Swiss and U.S. cases.

Table A—20 shows the share of industrial activity accounted for by MNC affiliates in several countries. The major MNC roles in countries like Nigeria, Malaysia, and Ghana reflect a colonial heritage in LDCs. Canada is an exceptional case of a developed nation with over 50 percent of industry foreign-controlled. This situation is the result of its closeness to the much larger U.S. economy and their relatively open border during the period of major industrial growth. In other countries aggregate MNC activity is of more modest proportions. However, in some industries in most countries MNCs tend to have large, often overwhelming prominence including electronics, chemicals, pharmaceuticals, and automobiles as shown in Table A—21.

The data presented thus far have documented a number of major facets of the role of MNCs in host nations. In an attempt to describe more fully the composite role, the U.S. Department of Commerce made a study of the operations of companies that accounted for 90

Table A–18.   Percentage of International Sales for 422 Largest Companies in 1976 (Number of companies)

| International Sales as a Percent of Total Company Sales | United States | United Kingdom | Japan | West Germany | Other Developed Countries | Less Developed Countries | Total |
|---|---|---|---|---|---|---|---|
| More than 75% | — | 6 | — | — | 14 | 1 | 21 |
| 51–75% | 13 | 9 | 1 | — | 9 | — | 32 |
| 26–50% | 68 | 14 | 3 | 4 | 9 | — | 98 |
| 6–25% | 99 | 10 | 22 | 14 | 14 | — | 159 |
| 1–5% | 20 | 1 | 16 | 1 | 6 | 2 | 46 |
| 0 | 14 | 1 | — | 3 | 4 | 4 | 26 |
| Unknown | 9 | — | 7 | 5 | 10 | 3 | 40 |
| Total | 223 | 41 | 49 | 27 | 66 | 10 | 422 |

Source: United Nations, Centre on Transnational Corporations, *Transnational Corporations in World Development Reviewed*, 1978.

**Table A–19.   U.S. Balance of Payments for 1976 (Millions of dollars)**

| Current Account | Exports of Goods and Services | Imports of Goods and Services |
|---|---|---|
| Merchandise, excluding military | $114,692 | $123,916 |
| Military goods and services | 5,604 | 5,213 |
| Travel | 5,755 | 6,831 |
| Passenger fares | 1,258 | 2,613 |
| Other transportation | 6,529 | 6,303 |
| Fees and royalties from and to affiliated foreigners | 3,616 | 271 |
| Fees and royalties from and to unaffiliated foreigners | 795 | 212 |
| Other private services | 3,227 | 1,500 |
| U.S. government miscellaneous services | 472 | 1,226 |
| Payments of income on capital assets: | | |
| Direct investment income | 12,416 | 2,167 |
| Other private receipts and payments | 8,893 | 5,426 |
| U.S. government receipts and payments | 1,285 | 4,523 |
| Unilateral transfers: | | |
| U.S. government grants | | 3,139 |
| U.S. government pensions and other transfers | | 923 |
| Private remittances and other transfers | | 943 |
| Subtotal, current account | 164,601 | 165,204 |

| Capital Account | Foreign Assets in U.S. (increase/capital inflow +) | U.S. Assets Abroad (increase/capital outflow +) |
|---|---|---|
| Foreign and U.S. official reserves | 18,107 | 2,530 |
| U.S. government loans and other assets (net) | | 4,925 |
| Direct investment | 561 | 5,000 |
| Private securities | 4,075 | 8,682 |
| Other U.S. liabilities and claims: | | |
| Long-term | -845 | 2,112 |
| Short-term | 11,232 | 20,402 |
| Subtotal, capital account | 33,129 | 43,021 |
| Statistical discrepancy | 10,495 | |

Source: *Survey of Current Business*, March 1977.

**Table A–20.   Estimated Shares of Manufacturing Held by Foreign Enterprises in Selected Countries**

| | Percentage Foreign Share of: | | | | Year | Criterion of Foreign Ownership |
|---|---|---|---|---|---|---|
| | Sales | Employment | Assets | Value Added | | |
| Nigeria | — | — | 70[a] | — | 1968 | — |
| Canada | 56 | 52 | — | — | 1973 | 50%+ |
| Malaysia | — | — | 50[b] | — | 1971 | — |
| Ghana | 50[c] | — | — | — | 1974 | — |
| Brazil | 49[d] | — | 29[e] | 37[e] | 1974 | — |
| Peru | 46 | — | — | — | 1969 | — |
| Australia | 36 | 29 | 42 | 34 | 1972/73 | 25+ |
| Turkey | — | — | 41 | — | 1974 | 10+ |
| South Africa | — | — | 40[c] | — | 1972 | — |
| Belgium | 33 | 18 | — | — | 1968 | — |
| Central American Common Market | 31 | — | — | — | 1971 | — |
| New Zealand | 33 | — | — | — | 1969/70 | — |
| Argentina | 31 | — | — | — | 1972 | — |
| Singapore | — | 30 | — | — | 1968 | — |
| Mexico | 27 | — | — | 23 | 1973 | 20+ |
| France | 27 | 19 | — | — | 1972 | — |
| West Germany | 25 | 22 | — | 23 | 1973 | 50+ |
| Austria | 23 | 23 | 20 | — | 1974 | — |
| Norway | 19 | 12 | 11 | 18 | 1971 | — |
| United Kingdom | 14 | 10 | 16 | 13 | 1973 | 50+ |
| India | 13 | — | — | — | 1971 | — |
| Denmark | 11[f] | — | — | — | 1974 | — |
| South Korea | 11 | — | — | — | 1971 | 50+ |
| Spain | 11 | — | — | — | 1971 | — |
| Hong Kong | — | 11 | 8 | — | 1974 | 20+ |
| Sweden | 10 | — | — | — | 1970 | — |
| Thailand | — | 9 | — | — | 1972 | 20+ |
| Finland | 5 | 4 | — | — | 1972 | 20+ |
| Japan | 4 | 2 | — | — | 1972 | 20+ |
| United States | 4 | 3 | — | — | 1974 | 10+ |

Notes on next page

**Table A–20.** continued *(Notes)*

[a] Based on the 625 largest manufacturing enterprises.
[b] Based on all commercial enterprises. Foreign share of assets based on all limited companies was 62 percent in 1971.
[c] Based on total industry.
[d] Based on the 1000 largest enterprises.
[e] Based on the 5,113 largest non-financial enterprises.
[f] Excluding car assembly and oil refining.

Source: United Nations, Centre on Transnational Corporations, *Transnational Corporations in World Development Re-examined*, 1978.

**Table A–21.  Indicators of Foreign Participation in Industries of Selected Host Countries**

| ISIC No. | Estimated Percentage of Foreign Share of: | | | | | | Year |
|---|---|---|---|---|---|---|---|
| | Chemicals (351–352) | Rubber (355) | Iron + Steel Basic Industry (371) | Non-electrical Machinery (382) | Electrical Machinery (383) | Motor Vehicles (3843) | |
| *Developed Countries* | | | | | | | |
| Australia | 84 (A) | — | 72 (A) | — | — | 83 (A) | 1972/73 |
| Austria | — | — | — | — | 40 (E) | — | 1973 |
| Belgium-Luxembourg | 21 (E)[a] | 56 (E)[a] | — | 32 (E)[a] | — | — | 1970 |
| Canada | 73 (O) | 70 (O) | — | — | 64 (A) | 84 (A) | 1973 |
| France | 33 (E) | 25 (E) | 11 (E) | 37 (A) | — | 21 (A) | 1973 |
| West Germany | 33 (A) | 48 (A) | — | — | 51 (A) | — | 1974 |
| New Zealand | — | — | 33 (R) | — | — | — | 1969/70 |
| Spain | — | — | — | — | 50 (O) | 84 (O) | 1973 |
| Sweden | — | — | 14 (O) | — | — | — | 1973 |
| Turkey | 54 (A) | 59 (A) | — | 43 (A) | — | 38 (A) | 1974 |
| *Developing Countries* | | | | | | | |
| Argentina | 37 (O) | 75 (O) | — | 82 (O) | 33 (O) | 84 (O) | 1969 |
| Brazil | 51 (O) | 44 (O) | 61 (O)[b] | 55 (A)[b] | 33 (A)[b] | 100 (A) | 1976 |
| India | 27 (O) | 52 (O) | 41 (O) | 25 (O) | — | 10 (O) | 1973 |
| Mexico | 67 (O) | 84 (O) | 37 (O) | 31 (O) | 63 (O) | — | 1973 |
| Peru | 67 (S) | 88 (S) | — | 25 (S) | 62 (S) | — | 1969 |
| Philippines | — | 73 (O) | — | — | — | 43 (A) | 1973 |
| Singapore | 46 (E) | 76 (E) | 21 (E) | — | — | — | 1968 |
| South Korea | 22 (E) | — | 37 (O) | 19 (O) | — | — | 1970 |

[a] Employment in U.S. majority-owned affiliates.

[b] Based on the 5,113 largest non-financial enterprises.

O = Output;  A = Assets;  S = Sales;  E = Employment;  R = Revenue.

Source: United Nations, Centre on Transnational Corporations, *Transnational Corporations in World Development Re-examined*, 1978.

percent of U.S. investment in Latin America using 1955 data.[8] Separate analyses were made of the two main categories of firms: primary material producers and manufacturing enterprises.

The chief function of the primary material producers is the generation of income from the resources of the country—metals, petroleum, food products, and so on. If these countries are to progress rapidly, they must import machinery and other products they cannot now manufacture. Food exports alone do not bring in enough income, and oil and minerals are their only other large marketable assets.

The figures in Figure A–1 show that the remissions of dollars by the American companies took $581 million or 29 percent of the $2,001 million earned from the exports of primary products. Only a part of the remissions were profits because a mine or an oil well is a wasting asset for the owner. The company makes an initial investment and then its "profits" are both a recovery of the value of its investment and true profits. The book value of the investments at the time of the study was $3,191 million. Hence, allowing a reasonable amount for return of capital, the rate of profit on investment was in the range of 10 to 15 percent. Considering the risks involved, this would not appear excessive. The importation of supplies and equipment for the operations required $372 million of foreign exchange, of which $43 million was supplied by new capital, leaving a net of $329 million to be met from the proceeds of the exports, about 16 percent of the total.

That left 53 percent of the export income as a net gain for the host countries, from which they benefited in two ways. First it was a major source of foreign exchange to finance imports. Exports by these American companies provided in all about 30 percent of the foreign exchange earnings of the Latin-American countries. Second, the income played an important role in the internal economies of Latin America, providing wages for workers, purchases from local suppliers, and so on as shown in Figure A–1.

The role of the manufacturing operations (Figure A–2) lies in saving foreign exchange and developing the internal economy. One cannot say precisely how much foreign exchange the operations saved. Undoubtedly some products were made internally by MNCs that would never have been imported—soap, for example. But observation of the nature of new manufacturing investments indicates that a large portion did replace imports. Most MNC factories produce refrigerators, automobiles, drugs, or other products which had previously been imported. So it is fair to say that a large portion of the $1,418 million of manufactured goods sold locally would have had to be imported or would not have been provided at all if the American

**Figure A–1.** Flow of Income and Expenditures of U.S.–Owned Primary Material Producers in Latin America in 1955 *(Millions of dollars)*

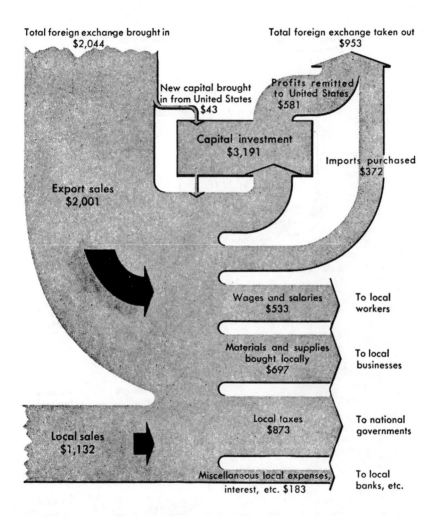

Total foreign exchange brought in
$2,044

Total foreign exchange taken out
$953

New capital brought in from United States
$43

Profits remitted to United States
$581

Capital investment
$3,191

Imports purchased
$372

Export sales
$2,001

Wages and salaries
$533

To local workers

Materials and supplies bought locally
$697

To local businesses

Local taxes
$873

To national governments

Local sales
$1,132

Miscellaneous local expenses, interest, etc. $183

To local banks, etc.

Source: U.S. Department of Commerce, *U.S. Investment in the Latin American Economy* 1957.

**Figure A–2.** Flow of Income and Expenditures of U.S.–Owned Manufacturing Operations in Latin America in 1955 *(millions of dollars)*

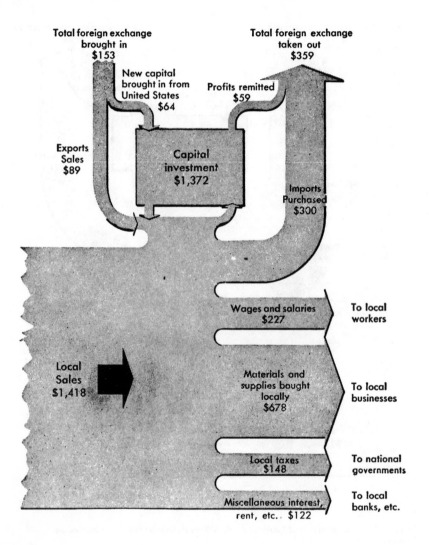

**Total foreign exchange brought in $153**

**Total foreign exchange taken out $359**

**New capital brought in from United States $64**

**Profits remitted $59**

**Exports Sales $89**

**Capital investment $1,372**

**Imports Purchased $300**

**Local Sales $1,418**

**Wages and salaries $227** — To local workers

**Materials and supplies bought locally $678** — To local businesses

**Local taxes $148** — To national governments

**Miscellaneous interest, rent, etc. $122** — To local banks, etc.

Source: U.S. Department of Commerce, *U.S. Investments in the Latin American Economy* 1957.

operations were not there. The $59 million required for dividends is therefore but a small portion of the amount saved in foreign exchange when related to the sales volume of $1,507 million.

The internal impact of these operations on the Latin-American countries is, of course, the very essence of the industrial revolution which has set them on the road from relatively primitive levels to a new way of life in the past half century. Without the tremendous infusion of foreign capital, manufacturing in Latin America would be far below its present level. The $227 million of direct wage payments indicated in Figure A–2, covering the employment of some 624,000 workers, is important. But even more important is the $678 million of purchases of local materials and supplies which fan out in the economies and multiply into many more jobs and purchases and the fostering of local manufacturing entrepreneurship. One more measure of the significance of these operations is the fact that new American investments accounted for about 10 percent of all new private investment in the Latin-American countries in 1955. The profits that the companies extracted from the economies amounted to only about 4 percent of the total income they generated.

## NOTES

1. William K. Chung, "Sales by Majority-Owned Foreign Affiliates of U.S. Companies, 1975," *Survey of Current Business*, Feb. 1977, p. 30, and "Foreign Trade of the United States," ibid., pp. S–23.

2. James W. Vaupel and Joan P. Curhan, *The Making of Multinational Enterprise* (Boston, Mass.: Graduate School of Business Administration, Harvard University, 1969), p. 384.

3. Lawrence G. Franko, "Joint Venture Divorce in the Multinational Company," *Columbia Journal of World Business*, May–June 1971, pp. 13–22.

4. For example: Kenneth R. Andrews, *The Concept of Corporate Strategy* (Homewood, Illinois: Dow Jones-Irwin, 1971); H. Ansoff, *Corporate Strategy* (New York: McGraw-Hill, 1965); and Alfred D. Chandler, Jr., *Strategy and Structure* (Cambridge, Mass.: M.I.T. Press, 1969).

5. James W. Vaupel and Joan P. Curhan, op. cit., p. v.

6. Robert B. Leftwich, "U.S. Multinational Companies: Profitability, Financial Leverage, and Effective Income Tax Rates," *Survey of Current Business*, May 1974, pp. 27–36.

7. Jurg Niehans, "Benefits of Multinational Firms for a Small Parent Economy: The Case of Switzerland," in Tamir Agmon and Charles P. Kindleberger, eds., *Multinationals from Small Countries* (Cambridge, Mass.: M.I.T. Press, 1977), pp. 1–39.

8. U.S. Department of Commerce, *U.S. Investments in the Latin American Economy* (Washington: Government Printing Office, 1957).

*Part I*

# The Environmental Context of MNC Strategy

The focus in Part I is on the opportunities, constraints, and problems for strategy which the MNC encounters in the economic, cultural, and political dimensions of the international environment. For each dimension groundwork will be laid by considering concepts drawn from basic disciplines and developing from them a fundamental analytical framework within which to consider the situation of the MNC. The nature of the strategy issues for the MNC will then be examined by both basic analysis and by reference to empirical evidence available from varied research studies and other sources. From this process emerge general concepts of strategy approaches in relation to the environment that will serve as the basis for development of specific patterns of strategy and administration in Parts II and III.

*Chapter 2*

# Determination of MNC Resource Transmission Capabilities

Marketing is the central nucleus around which business strategy must be built in a free economy. Success depends upon economical and effective delivery of products and services that satisfy buyer demands. For a firm operating within a single nation, a market strategy analysis directed at individual products and industry conditions is generally adequate. This approach is also relevant to international operations, but the analysis must extend to broader dimensions because of two distinctions between domestic and international markets.

First, doing business between countries adds to costs and complications of management; and

Second, there are greater differences in production factors and demand characteristics between countries than within countries.

It is the existence of the marketing opportunities presented by the latter which largely permits MNCs to overcome the impediments presented by the former. Thus, the MNC must assess the implications of the major patterns of economic relations among nations as a basis for its overall international strategy and then proceed to the domestic firm strategy approach within each country where it operates. It is the former aspect to which the analysis in this book is devoted, the reader being referred to standard books on strategy planning to pursue the latter.

The analytical approach adopted here starts with the determination of the resource transmission capabilities of the MNC, based on economic relationships among nations conditioned by political and cultural considerations and by the structural characteristics of MNCs.

The resource transmission capabilities then serve as fundamental factors in a variety of strategic questions spread through the rest of the book.

## DETERMINATION OF RESOURCE TRANSMISSION CAPABILITIES

The first stage of the strategy analysis process therefore is the determination of the resource capabilities of the MNC. In this discussion resources are considered to fall into six categories, adapted from the three factors of production identified in traditional economics: land, capital and labor. The six are natural resources, capital, labor and technological, managerial and entrepreneurial skills.

Natural resources include mineral, petroleum, forest and agricultural products. Extracting and converting these resources into usable raw materials requires application of labor and other resources. So the term natural resources as used here refers strictly to that portion of the value of raw materials that is derived without cost from natural sources.

Capital technically encompasses all forms of accumulated resources used for production of goods and services. The analysis in this book will be confined essentially to three forms of capital that are most prominent in international business: financial resources, industrial plant, and marketing systems. The latter include distribution facilities, trade names, and the like.

Labor is defined as the physical exertion of individuals. In classical economics the qualitative component of work is also included in the definition of labor. However, for the reasons given below, it seems more useful to separate them in this analytical framework. Thus, labor is treated here as essentially human energy, the physical input of individuals into economic processes.

Skills appear in the classical resource scheme only as a component of labor. That limitation is not satisfactory because skills are found in business in other forms than as personal capabilities. For example, technical skills as recorded in manuals and patents can be sold like a physical product. Skills have also been organized in such a way that they can function independently like an individual worker. The computer programs that direct machine tool operations are an example.

Thus skills in key respects fall as readily under the definition of capital as under labor. Just as various resources are diverted from immediate output to construct a factory for future production, so also are resources invested in developing technology for a new product. In both cases the values embodied in the initially diverted resources are subsequently disbursed through the useful life of the created resource, the factory and the product, which are consumed through depreciation and obsolescence respectively. If one considers only the personal side of skill, the investment of the time and resources in teaching individuals skills that are then applied over a finite working career is also similar generically to capital accumulation.

On the other hand, incorporating skills into the capital category is not entirely satisfactory either because they do differ from the strictly physical forms of capital included in the traditional definition. Their large human element, their less tangible character, and other attributes make them a quite different bird. All in all therefore it seems best to treat them as a separate type of resource.

Three subcategories of skills are employed in this analysis: technical, managerial, and entrepreneurial. The distinctions are not precise but insofar as they describe major skill areas the breakdown is useful. Technical skills are largely associated with the physical sciences and concerned for the most part with products, production and physical processes. Managerial skills deal mainly with the human aspects of business both within the organization and in relation to the environment and they draw most heavily on the behavioral sciences. There are clearly some hazy areas like the application of operations research in business planning which could be considered either technical or managerial. However, since it does not materially affect our analytical approach, no attempt will be made to refine the definition to eliminate that haziness.

Entrepreneurial skills are defined here in the quite broad sense of capacity to initiate and implement new uses and combinations of resources for business purposes. Again we have a hazy distinction, this time between the conscientious use of managerial skills and entrepreneurship. The distinction may be likened to that which the patent office must make between an unpatentable advancement in application of known science and a patentable "stroke of genius." For present purposes it will suffice to recognize in general terms that for a large portion of cases one can distinguish the application of known management methods from the imaginative, often risk-taking role of the entrepreneur.

Although the question of methods of resource transmission will be discussed fully in Chapter 7 it will clarify the present discussion to note that resources may be transmitted in various forms. The transmission can be in segregated form, for example, capital moving through the purchase of securities of foreign companies with no accompanying participation in management (i.e., portfolio investment). But most of the transmission process involves combinations of resources. Exports of goods typically represent varying portions of natural resources, capital (in the form of depreciation of the machinery used to make the goods), labor, and skills. Establishment of a factory abroad usually involves capital investment accompanied by commitments of technological, managerial and entrepreneurial skills. Thus the discussion of capacities to transmit individual resources appears here only as an analytical step, with no implication that they will necessarily be transmitted separately or in particular combinations. That question will be examined at a later stage of the strategy formulation process.

## BASIC ECONOMIC RELATIONSHIPS

Economic theory provides the foundation for analysis of resource transmission capabilities. For many years economists have been occupied with relations between nations. Although there are still gaps in their theories, they have laid out an approach that is adequate in its main character for our purposes. Essentially it focuses on concepts which account for the economic transactions between nations in terms of the differentials between them.

The main body of theory in this field deals with trade which until recently has been more prominent than investments, licensing, and other types of international business activity. The central concept for over two centuries has been the theory of comparative advantage which relates flows of trade to differences in productive capabilities.

Although substantial absolute differentials in resource distribution can be observed, these differentials are not controlling because of the necessity for balance in transactions among countries. The main proposition in the basic theory therefore is that nations export those products which they can produce most efficiently and import those in which they are least efficient as compared with other nations. In establishing the relationships, the dominant differentials are usually found in the availability of various resources used in production. Differentials in other cost factors such as transportation and size of production units also play a part as do differences in demand patterns. With appropriate adjustments of the foreign exchange rate between countries, the prices of the products a country makes most efficiently will be competitive in world markets, and those in which it is least efficient will be non-competitive.

The manufacture of machine tools and rugs in Germany and Turkey provides an illustration. The ratio of the supply of capital to labor in Germany is relatively much greater than in Turkey. Since machine-tool production requires greater portions of capital than making rugs, the Germans are comparatively more efficient in making machine tools than rugs. Thus the cost of a German-made machine tool may be twice that of the German-made rug, whereas for Turkish-made products the ratio is 10 to 1. That is, the cost of a particular German-made machine tool might be 20,000 marks and that of a fine rug made in Germany 10,000 marks. The same items if made in Turkey might cost 100,000 lira and 10,000 lira respectively. With the exchange rate of 3 lira per mark, Germany would sell the machine tools to Turkey and import rugs from Turkey.

Beyond the dominant resource differentials, the analysis would have to consider any other factors which might affect the costs. For example, German machine tool makers may benefit from larger scale output through access to the large European market, compared with the smaller local market a Turkish maker could serve. However, the Turkish maker would have a transportation cost advantage in his home market.

Theory incorporating all forms of resource transmission, not just the trade component, is notable by its absence from economic literature. Economists recognize the movement of resources (factors of production) and discuss some aspects of the process. For example, the international transfer of capital has been studied extensively. Differences in interest rates indicate effective differentials in capital resource supply-demand relations. These, along with marginal productivity in different countries, are cited as primary forces governing the flow of capital. But there is no comprehensive scheme which relates the flows of natural resources, capital, labor, and various skills.

Such a scheme will be slow in evolving because of the difficulty of sorting out and especially of quantifying the components. For example, licensing agreements result in transfer of technological skills in exchange for, let us say, raw materials (with intervening monetary transactions). But the supply of the skills in the licensing company is not reduced by the transfer, so it is difficult for the economist to develop an effective price theory for licensing which would be essential to a theory based on price relationships. Likewise, how is one to determine the relative availability of entrepreneurial resources in various countries? This is a fascinating question that has occupied many people concerned with economic development. As yet, however, differences have only been identified to a very crude degree by qualitative methods, typically by sociological approaches, rather than by quantifiable measures.

Despite this lack of economic theory, there would seem to be logic in extending to the whole resource transmission process the philosophy embodied in the trade theory. Both in it and in such theory as there is concerning direct resource movements, the influence of effective differentials in resource distribution is consistent with a comprehensive theory of resource transmission. Thus in this chapter it is assumed as a general proposition that basic economic forces work toward outflows from each country of the resources in relatively plentiful supply. "Relative" here is a function of the supply-demand structure for a specific resource and other resources both in the country and in other countries.

## GOVERNMENTAL INFLUENCES

Although the overall pattern of international transmission of resources is governed by the basic economic relationships in their distribution in and among nations, there are many distortions in the pattern induced by government actions. In the pursuit of various national objectives, governments may alter the effective relationships or directly intervene in the flow of resources.

Effective relationships are altered by any measure that changes the price of a resource relative to the price of another resource. In our modern, monetized societies all the economic relationships we have been discussing are stated in terms of price—wages, interest rates, prices of commodities, and so forth. The prices stated in terms of national currencies are related internationally by means of exchange rates. The prices of each resource and the exchange rates in the straightforward economic system assumed in the theory of comparative advantage will shift in response to supply-and-demand relationships to reach a level at which the appropriate flows will take place. If a government action alters a price, therefore, the amount or direction of flows will tend to change away from the pattern that had prevailed under the pure economic forces.

The government actions pertinent to this discussion affect two types of price relationships between nations: the overall differences and differences for individual resources. In the first category fall internal fiscal, monetary, and other policies affecting the general price level and regulation of exchange rates which affect the overall translation of internal prices into currencies of other nations. The result of a change in either the overall price level or the exchange rate of a nation is to cause a general shift in the apparent relative level of all of its resources. For example, if government policies cause a general inflation, the prices of each resource rise just as they would individually if their supply were actually limited. The international effect therefore is to attract greater flows of these resources from other nations, or if the prevailing flow has been outward for a particular resource, the effect is to reduce the outflow.

An alteration in the exchange rate has essentially the same effect: it changes the apparent across-the-board relationship of national prices and either attracts or discourages flow of resources. For the country whose overall price level is raised, the result is not only an increase in the tendency of individual resources to flow toward it but also a tendency toward a shift in the net balance of resource flows. If as a result total inflows and outflows are unequal, further change must come to restore the balance either in the internal price level or exchange rates or in one or more of the ways to be discussed.

International price relationships of individual resources may be altered by governments in a number of ways, chiefly by various forms of taxation and subsidies. The most common form of taxation employed is the tariff, whose effect is to raise the price of foreign goods relative to internal prices and thus to discourage them from flowing into the country. Though less common, taxes can be applied to affect international flows of other types of resources. For example, in 1964 the United States imposed an interest equalization tax on issues of foreign securities in the United States which in effect raised the interest rates (prices of capital) and thus discouraged the outflow of U. S. capital.

Subsidies typically are employed with the opposite effect. The government of a country makes some financial contribution to the supplier of a resource which permits the latter to sell at lower prices and encourages outflow of the resource from the country. The common form is the use of export subsidies which reduce the prices of certain products relative to those of other countries.

Direct intervention in the flow of resources can be accomplished by a government through the exercise of various controls over movements across its borders. Such regulations are commonly found restricting many types of flows: quotas restraining importing of products, exchange controls limiting the flow of capital, emigration and immigration restrictions regulating the movement of people, national security rules forbidding the transmission of certain technological skills, and so forth.

From the point of view of the policies of the multinational firm, we are concerned not only with the ways in which governments may influence the flows of resources but also with understanding the reasons for their actions as a basis for predicting government policies and relating company policies to them. Looking at the range of government actions since World War II, we can discern three main patterns:

efforts to foster economic development, moves to protect national groups, and measures to deal with balance of payments deficits.

### Fostering Economic Development

The concept of government initiative and control to further economic development is firmly established in the less developed countries and even to varying degrees in the advanced countries. To the extent that international flows of resources are important to economic development, it is common to find governments using their influence toward this end. Although there are assorted philosophies as to how to further economic development, a few guidelines are widely accepted and thus recur in patterns of government action often.

The main emphasis is upon development of national industrial production, so efforts are made to encourage the inflow of resources which contribute to this goal—especially capital, skills, and essential natural resources—and to discourage the inflow of finished products of which local production is being fostered. A second and related guideline is the desire to concentrate the utilization of receipts from the outflow of resources on uses which contribute to industrial development. This leads to controls which restrict the inflow of resources not regarded as essential, notably those incorporated in luxury goods. Third, efforts are made to decrease dependence upon foreign resources, an objective contributing to national security, economic strength, and nationalistic pride. This objective can lead to restriction of flows of any resource, ranging from limitations on employment of expatriate technicians which force the training of local nationals to "buy national" regulations requiring that locally made products be favored in government procurement. Fourth, increasing attention is being directed to increasing exports of manufactured goods which can capitalize on comparative advantage in labor resources and contribute to both employment creation and foreign exchange earnings, two major local needs.

### Protecting National Groups

Protection of national groups often runs counter to the best interests of a country in maximizing economic growth, but it is a common feature of society nonetheless. Individuals and groups with established economic activities seek to protect their positions. They may be able to obtain government support against internal threats, but they are likely to be most successful if the threat is from foreigners because of their superior political status as compared with outsiders, a subject to be discussed in Chapter 5. Thus it is quite common to find obstacles to the inflow of resources constructed to protect established economic interests. The commonest form of protection is the tariff that raises the prices of imported goods. Less commonly, the same end is achieved by import quotas or direct subsidies to local industries. Restrictions of this nature may be applied to other resource flows. For example, when small retailers in Mexico were threatened by the modern merchandising and entrepreneurial skills of Sears, Roebuck, they sought (though unsuccessfully) to have the government forbid foreign companies to enter the retailing field.[1]

## Balance of Payments Deficits

Measures taken to deal with balance of payments deficits vary greatly both in type and in the sophistication of government actions bearing on them. There have been cases where minor interference with economic relationships, soundly managed, was evidently effective in solving a transitory problem without serious distortion of resource transmission patterns. There have been others, of which the United States during the 1960s and early 1970s was a notable example, where measures of increasing magnitude affecting particularly capital flows substantially distorted natural economic relationships, though it is not at all clear what those relationships should be. Because of the overriding concern for maintaining the strength of the U.S. dollar as an international reserve currency, most responsible authorities felt that controls could not be relaxed and natural economic relationships were not, therefore, allowed to assert themselves.

Finally there have been a host of examples, chiefly among the less developed countries, of governments that have encountered balance of payments problems which have been caused by and perpetuated by various national shortcomings. In the typical case, the country is relatively immature politically, so that its government is unstable and its bureaucracy not very competent. These conditions result in the government pursuing unwise economic policies both from lack of competence and from fear of taking actions that may have adverse political impact. From these conditions emerge government deficits, wasteful use of government funds, and inflation. The inflation distorts the overall level of resource prices in relation to the rest of the world. The apparently sound economic corrective action should be a change of the country's exchange rate to reverse the distortion. At this point, however, inertia and national pride act to deter a devaluation, which is generally viewed as harmful to national prestige. So the country solves the imbalance in the economic pressures by other means, chiefly by restrictions permitting entry only of favored classifications of resources. The net effect is to limit the natural flow of some resources while others receive an unnatural push because of the price distortions.

## HOST SOCIETY CONSTRAINTS

The discussion thus far has focused essentially on the economic transaction phase of the resource transmission process considering economic and governmental influences. The other major environmental influence on resource transmission capabilities lies in the second phase of the process, the interaction with host societies.

The receptivity of the host societies is a critical determinant in governing the capabilities of the MNC in some aspects of resource transmission. In fields like the importing of standard commodities this factor has little significance. But where resource inputs impinge significantly on established cultural patterns in the receiving society the nature of the interactions is highly relevant.

In practical experience, the critical interactions are most commonly observed in the marketing of consumer products and in the adoption of various operational methods. In terms of our analytical framework, these activities are essentially associated with transmission of technological, managerial, and entrepreneurial skills initially derived from home or third country cultures. Casting the issue in yet broader terms, the character of the problems they involved in transmission of skills is quite readily identified. Skills compose one major part of culture as anthropologists define it. Any opportunity to transmit a skill from one country to another must be based on the fact that the skill is not presently established in the second country. The attempt to transfer therefore involves cross-cultural interaction and attempts at cultural change. Both points are critical to the analysis because, while cultural change may be possible at a given time, the interactions caused by an external agent like an MNC may not be the effective means for accomplishing it. The questions inherent in each skill transmission opportunity therefore are: "Can the skill be successfully introduced into the host society?" and "Is the MNC capable of accomplishing the introduction?"

The key questions having been set forth, the full discussion of this phase of the analysis will be set aside to be resumed in the next chapter as central to the major subject of relations with the host society with its central focus on cultural change. In a strictly logical sense this handling of the matter leaves a gap in the present analysis as full discussion of the cultural interaction problem would be required to complete the analytical framework for determination of which skill resources can be transmitted. However, in terms of strategy formulation for management, deferring the cultural issue makes more sense. The critical issues in the determination of operating methods are essentially concerned with selectivity and adaptation in application of skill transmission. It is therefore most effective in handling those questions to combine them with discussion of the cultural interaction process while it suffices here in our initial statement of the assessment of resource transmission capabilities simply to identify the basic issues presented by host society interaction as a constraint.

## MNC CHARACTERISTICS

The economic differentials, government actions and cultural patterns establish the range of opportunities and limitations for MNC resource transmission. The final determination of its resource transmission capabilities though depends upon factors within the corporation itself. The multinational corporation is not in its nature given to opportunistic, short-term profit maximization. It does not, therefore, exploit fully all economic differentials between nations, nor does it function with full flexibility in those which it does exploit. In the total international business community, there are individuals and groups that are both more opportunistic and more flexible—for example, consultants, individual investors, and traders. They tend to accomplish much of the flow of resources and as such serve a vital economic function. The multinational corporation is limited, therefore, to the role for which its characteristics are suitable.

The significant characteristics of the MNC may be viewed in two dimensions: basic and global. The key basic elements are that the corporation is an organization that has achieved a fair degree of effectiveness both in accomplishing group decision-making and in integrated productive activity among its members. The profitable roles for the organization in society lie in performance of those functions in which these characteristics are of particular utility. Furthermore, preservation of those characteristics gives prime importance to continuity in the nature and magnitude of activities in which it engages. Finally, the existence of the organization is rooted in the delivery of goods and services to society. Thus, two areas receive primary consideration in the corporation: the processes by which products and services are conceived and developed to marketable quality and the processes by which they are delivered profitably to the market, the two composing what will be called here the product-delivery system. Other activities within the firm must be considered secondary, of value as they serve the product-delivery system.

The key global characteristics were previewed in Chapter 1. First there are the economies and efficiency that can be achieved by an integrated system of global dimensions. Operating in a larger market area, the MNC is capable of achieving economies of scale superior to those of the typical national firm. With a global span of operations it has broader scope for specialization, selective location of activities, and other options. Second, the wider span of operations provides a greater range of interchange of capabilities among members of the organization.

How do the various opportunities for international resource transmission fit into this pattern of corporation characteristics?

### Natural Resources

In years past natural resources were one of the strongest areas of MNC endeavor. Oil, mining, and large segments of agricultural production were essentially controlled by international corporations. Much of that status still remains but the erosion of the MNCs dominance in this field is the critical clue to the lack of strong capabilities for this form of resource transmission. Natural resource transmission among countries per se is not a particularly complex process so the organizational capabilities of the MNC have no great advantage over trading between independent entities. The weakness of the oil companies in the Bechtel and Lube India cases in negotiating for raw material terms is indicative of the low value accorded to natural resource capabilities.[2]

The marketing process associated with the transmission is somewhat more complex, notably in fields like petroleum where distribution is carried down to the retail level. Likewise, there are technological requirements for production of some natural resources in which MNC capabilities are valuable. And, while capital for major extractive operations can be obtained from other sources than MNCs, the financial resources the firms control can be of significant value in many cases. Such marketing, technology, and capital inputs provide bases for the continuing role of MNCs in natural resource transmission. But, analytically, one must emphasize that this amounts to using other types of resource capabilities (to be discussed below) to maintain a role in natural resource transmission in the absence of real strength in the process itself which is essentially concerned with the buying and selling of quite staple and stable products. It is that fact which has permitted the steady takeover of the natural resource field by separate producing and marketing firms at the expense of the integrated MNC operations. The oil industry provides the conspicuous example in this respect but similar evolution may be found in aluminum, rubber, and other products.

Natural resource transmission as such is therefore no longer a prime area of MNC capability. For those firms already established in the natural resource industries, there remains wide scope for profitable operation based on strengths in technology, marketing, and financing. For manufacturing firms natural resource transmission offers relatively minor opportunity because most of the natural resources they use are quite staple commodities more efficiently and effectively traded in open-market competitive processes among independent firms.

## Capital

Overall MNCs are notable for their command of accumulated resources. Capital is therefore a key area of potential resource transmission. The potentials are quite different, however, among the major forms of capital: financial resources, industrial plant, and marketing system.

That MNCs engage in substantial transmission of *financial resources* across borders is self-evident from the magnitude of international direct investment. Clearly MNCs have financing capabilities and employ them extensively. Nonetheless, it appears that, for the most part, financial resources are not regarded by MNCs as a primary capability from which to benefit in international business. Rather, the prevailing attitude is to view funds as a supporting capability to be used to facilitate strategies primarily designed to make best use of other resources. This attitude is demonstrated in the common practice of financing a large portion of foreign investments from local sources, even in countries where interest rates and anticipated returns on investment are higher than in the parent country.

Underlying this practice are the dominant preoccupation of MNCs with production-marketing objectives and a tendency toward conservativism in financial matters. Thus the typical MNC does not make capital-return-optimizing decisions in the pure sense as, for example, a strictly financing institution might. That is, when a new facility is established abroad the MNC does not tend to put into it the full amount of its own money that it could justify strictly on the basis of anticipated return on investment computations. Rather, it weighs the risks and tends to limit its own investment to that necessary to assure a viable operation. In doing this it uses local financial resources to a considerable degree, thereby conceding to them some of the financial return it theoretically might have obtained. This is not to imply that financial optimization is not a primary criterion in MNC management decisions. The ultimate aim of market-oriented strategy is to achieve satisfactory financial returns and return-on-investment criteria are applied to new foreign investments by MNC managements.

A further element in this picture is the aggressive use of international financing sources by MNCs, especially since the development of the Euro-dollar market during the 1960s. Large MNCs have been one of the major participants in the Euro-dollar market and the proceeds of their Euro-dollar bond issues have been used throughout the world for development of new investments. This process composes a form of international capital resource transmission and the effectiveness of MNCs in using it demonstrates their capabilities based on skill in financial management and credit standing, along with their global scope characteristics.

The mention of credit standing adds the final element to the financial resource picture. Credit standing is a nebulous asset to include in the analytical framework employed here because one does not sell it in pieces like a product, nor even sell rights to it as with technical know-how. But it is a recognized resource, capitalized in the sale of a going company, typically as "good will," and it is of significant value in this area of international financing. Transmission of its real if nebulous value to a foreign unit provides a critical element of security on the basis of which local financial resources may be attracted on more favorable terms than would be possible without it.

Capital resources from *industrial plants* compose part of the value of every manufactured export (i.e., the depreciation cost of production), so they are in a sense a significant part of all MNC resource transmissions. However, in terms of our present process of identifying elements of distinctive resource capabilities, the role of the industrial plant is more limited. The key question is, "What advantages does the MNC plant system give as compared with national firms?" Leaving aside the elements of labor and skills, which will be considered below, we find the answer lies primarily in scale of operations. The benefits appear primarily in those product areas where the demand in some countries is smaller than the output of plants with optimal costs. Many industrial products and not a few consumer items fit this pattern, especially in smaller countries. In these circumstances the capital investment per unit of output of a large MNC plant, represented in the resource transmission process as the depreciation component of the cost of exported products, will be lower than that for products made by local firms. So where transportation or other costs do not wipe out the efficiency gains, larger scale MNC plants may have a potential economic advantage.

In practice, the major deterrent to this capability has been government action, especially in the LDCs, either in imposing tariffs which distort the cost relationships or directly preventing MNC imports to foster local production. As a consequence the capabilities for the MNC in this respect have been narrowed in product and geographic areas along lines that will be discussed in Chapter 7. But substantial opportunities are still available within the industrialized regions of the world for all types of products and for many products elsewhere.

Utilization of an established foreign *marketing system* is a major resource transmission capability for many MNCs. Building up a combination of strong brand names, good reputation in distribution channels, competent sales force, and other elements of a marketing system requires skilled effort and time. The development of a marketing system with its characteristics of interrelated parts, coordination among individuals and continuity of performance is just the type of thing for which the corporation characteristics we have noted at the start of this section are especially effective. Given the primary role accorded to marketing in modern management, the marketing system typically has a high priority and as a consequence is a hallmark of a strong MNC.

Once established, the marketing system is a vital capital resource and transmission of its values in the international system becomes a prime MNC capability. The initial utilization of the MNC marketing system is usually to accomplish the distribution of products made in the parent country and later in local plants as they are developed. The benefits of the resource utilization in these processes flow back to the parent company in the form of profitable sales of goods. This serves the MNC satisfactorily but is of no particular interest to host nations. Many LDCs in fact, giving a low priority to marketing as a social function, have a negative view of income gained through what amounts to the transmission of marketing system resources.

However, a new phase of MNC utilization of market system capabilities is emerging toward which the LDCs have a much higher regard. As noted earlier, the expansion of export of manufactured goods is receiving a high priority to create jobs and improve balance of payments. For this purpose, the MNC's capabilities for marketing goods in other countries have demonstrated strength and are accorded recognition in terms of preferred foreign exchange status, more lenient requirements for local ownership, and other benefits. In this respect the global character of an MNC marketing system is of especial value, since it provides LDCs with a network of distribution not available so readily when working with independent national importers. The same capability is also being used to a modest extent by MNCs like Massey-Ferguson as part of the basis for establishing plants in Eastern Europe with products delivered to Western markets as a basis for payments.[3]

### Labor

With a few exceptions, like the employment of foreign workers in European factories, labor resources are transmitted internationally as a component of processed goods. Every export includes some portion of labor value, so in a sense MNCs are all engaged in transmission of labor. But in the present consideration of MNC resource transmission capabilities, we are concerned with the potentials for companies to capitalize significantly on the major global labor differentials, notably those between the LDCs with their large, low-cost labor supplies as compared to the more fully utilized, higher-cost labor in industrialized countries.

The potentials here lie in manufactured goods that have a high labor content and a sufficiently high ratio of value to weight and volume so that the advantages of producing in low-wage areas are not lost through transportation costs. Products with these potentials may be divided roughly into two categories, one in which MNCs have little role and one which has proved quite profitable for them. The first is the manufacture of low-technology relative staple products like textiles, shoes, and garments. For the most part, MNC characteristics do not give them any particular advantage in cross-border shipment of such goods. Decision-making and interaction between market and production units seem to be as effective among independent firms as within integrated systems. As a consequence the major portion of trade in this field consists of exports by local producers in countries like Hong Kong and Taiwan, for example, to retailers in developed countries.

An exception might be noted in the case of Japanese basic commodity firms, many of which have established factories in Korea and Southeast Asia as Japanese wages have risen. For example, in 1975 about one-quarter of Japanese foreign investment was in textile plants (p. 266). However, it is questionable whether this phenomenon should be included in the MNC field. It appears more like the shift of U.S. textile production first from New England to the South and then to Puerto Rico. In the Japanese case the size and wage differentials within the national territory are much more limited so the same shift has required jumping borders. But the resultant pattern is of modest proportions in the spectrum of what are defined here as MNCs. Production is limited to a small number of sites from which sales are made very much in the manner of separate, local firms to independent firms (perhaps through trading offices) in varied foreign countries.

Because of the stability of technology the parent firm has a relatively modest continuing role in production management of foreign units. The strongest tie is the case where the parent provides a basic material like a synthetic fiber from a large, capital-intensive plant in the home country. One can identify MNC characteristics in such a pattern including benefits of structural integration and control but the ties are weak, and as in the case of raw materials, the mere fact that much business of a similar nature takes place among completely independent basic material, fabricating, and marketing units supports the view that this is a weak area for MNC resource transmission capability.

The second category, on the other hand, has emerged as a significant area for MNC resource transmission potential. It includes relatively high-technology products, portions of which involve labor-intensive manufacture, typically assembly. Electronic and electrical products are the notable examples but some automotive products and others may prove to have similar potentials. The significant distinction between these products and those in the first category is the degree of integration required between the parent and foreign country units in processing and marketing. In a typical case a U.S. television set manufacturer may have some components assembled in Taiwan. The efficient implementation of such a program requires that there be well-coordinated planning of production among the related factories in the United States and Taiwan, with further relating of plants to marketing developments in a changeable, competitive field. In addition, since the technology of the field changes steadily, there must be effective control over the foreign production management. These elements have given the integrated MNC organization capability for this sort of labor resource transmission, though local firms have been effective enough competitively to demonstrate that the MNC advantage is modest at best. Nonetheless capabilities in labor resource transmission are of great importance to MNCs because of their impact on the competitiveness which is central to their profitability. Significant opportunities to reduce production cost must be exploited, especially if they are readily available to competitors. Thus, MNCs may be expected to give close attention to labor resource transmission capabilities.

### Skills

Skills compose the strongest resource capabilities of most MNCs. This assessment is drawn from considerations in each of the four stages of analysis followed here. At the basic level of economic differentials among nations, the skill advantages of the industrialized nations compared to the less developed ones are great and, in a more selective pattern, there are significant differences in skill competence between industrialized nations which fundamentally account for the heavy flow of knowledge in commercial and non-commercial channels among them. Because governments have come to recognize that skills are a vital necessity for economic progress, their intent is universally to favor flows of skills into their countries. Their actions, influenced by other considerations, may not have implemented this intent as effectively as possible but the general thrust has been in a positive direction.

The effect at the host society interaction stage has been mixed but generally favorable. Because skill inflows clearly challenge established culture patterns, this aspect of the environment presents inherent obstacles to skill transmission not present in the economic differential and government policy aspects. However, there is also the inherently favorable consideration that improvement of human welfare desired by host societies requires modernization including cultural changes to which the inputs of MNC skills are on the whole contributory. Finally, skills are an especially strong capability in light of the MNC corporate characteristics. A large portion of the skills of conducting business are by their nature most competently understood by business managements and it is one of the ongoing functions of a corporation to transmit skills within its own system. Thus the MNC is both a natural source for international transmission of skills and an established vehicle for accomplishing the process. Within this broadly favorable picture, there are differences in the capabilities for the three types of skills.

**Technological Skills.** Technology is the MNC skill in greatest international demand, largely because of host government attitudes. Even the many LDC governments, which in certain important respects are relatively hostile to MNCs, have been quite explicit in their recognition of the value of MNC technical inputs for their development. The United Nations report preceding the study of the Group of Eminent Persons on Multinationals and the conclusions of the Group illustrate this viewpoint well.[4] They reflect the general feeling among LDCs that MNCs are overpowerful and that their operations benefit the firms far more than the host nations. However, the significance of their role in providing technology is clearly supported, the thrust of the reports being essentially the desire of LDCs to obtain the technology at lower cost and under greater national control, not to inhibit its flow.

The MNC has demonstrated its superiority as a system for developing and transmitting technology. A large portion of basic scientific innovation has been generated in non-business sources. But it is the industrial corporation which has accomplished the great bulk of application of scientific innovation into marketable products. The integrated organizational capabilities of the firm have been effectively employed, first in relating the efforts of R&D laboratories, production planners, market researchers, and others in developing effective technology, and then in providing the training, supervision, and control required to transmit technology to the production, marketing, and service arms of the enterprise. This transmission does not happen as easily internationally as it does domestically, for reasons which will emerge in later sections of this book. However, it is still a highly effective transmission system as compared to alternatives open to host nations like acquiring technology from consultants, or sending engineers to foreign schools. Finally, the MNC benefits from the advantages of amortizing the costs of centralized R&D work over a global market rather than the much smaller market a purely national firm serves. There are some offsetting factors, which will be discussed in Chapter 6, but by and large global scale is a major benefit in the technological skill picture.

Two quite different endorsements of the value of MNC technology even among advanced nations provide forceful evidence in this analysis. The first is the assessment of the basis upon which U.S. firms achieved their strong role in Europe in J.J. Servan-Schreiber's best-selling book, *The American Challenge.*[5] He discounted the importance of the size of U.S. firms, attributing their success precisely to their competence in commercial utilization of technology. Across the world, the Japanese provided a more convincing endorsement in the post-World War II era by engaging in a massive process of acquiring technology by licensing from MNCs while they held to a minimum all other forms of resource transmission from them.

**Managerial Skills.** The wide range of financial, marketing, personnel, labor and other managerial skills which are so important to the organizational effectiveness of the MNC are also significant for international resource transmission. However, their potentials are somewhat less than those of the technological skills for several reasons. With respect to LDCs much of the management approach of MNCs is too sophisticated, inappropriate for the smaller, less complex LDC operations. It follows that cultural resistance is greatest to managerial skills because of their high behavioral content and the resistance is greatest in the less industrialized, more traditional LDC societies. These two factors, combined perhaps with the greater difficulty of perceiving the values of management skills, have led LDC governments to give managerial skills a lower priority than technological skills. This is, however, strictly a relative appraisal for LDCs do recognize the need to improve managerial skills and have encouraged the MNC role to that end in various ways, for example, by pressures to upgrade the managerial abilities of local national employees.

In relations with developed nations, MNC managerial skills have a stronger role because the magnitude and operational requirements of the operations there are more similar to those in the parent nation. Indeed, because of the rapid diffusion of technology among developed countries, managerial skill differentials may in many cases be just as important as technological capabilities for MNC competitive status.

**Entrepreneurial Skills.** It is impossible to speak with any precision about the capacity of MNCs for international transmission of entrepreneurial skills. Sophisticated observers have concluded on the basis of economic performance, societal characteristics and other evidence that there are substantial differences in entrepreneurial qualities among countries and cultures. A number of LDCs are seen as deficient in this respect and some advanced countries like Britain and Canada are currently considered to have less entrepreneruship than others. Since MNCs largely come from countries which are considered strong in entrepreneurship, notably Germany, Japan and the United States, there is a reasonable presumption that a basic economic differential exists in their favor with respect to many other countries. Furthermore, the very strength and vitality of MNCs is apparent evidence of entrepreneurial capacity.

However, one must register at least two related reservations. First, entrepreneurship resting to a large degree on intuitive judgment and sensitivity is difficult for a management to exercise outside its native culture. Second, the scale and thrust toward unification in MNCs introduces inflexibility in management. This is a deterrent to the innovative, flexible decision-making associated with entrepreneurship.

## EMPIRICAL EVIDENCE

Results of several research studies provide tangible evidence of the resource transmission capabilities which multinational corporations have effectively employed.

1. Vernon classified the 3,784 product lines made by multinational corporations based in the United States, Europe and Japan into 376 categories grouped under three headings skill-intensive (122), advertising-intensive (89), and standardized (165).[6] Skill and advertising intensity were based on data showing high inputs of research and development and advertising expenditures. Analysis of the 3,784 product lines showed the following breakdown: skill-intensive 39 percent, advertising-intensive 17 percent, and standardized 44 percent.

2. Two studies have shown that high technology firms have a strong role in U.S. exports and foreign investment. Gruber, Mehta, and Vernon made an intensive analysis of the relation between research and development in U.S. industries and their export and direct investment performance.[7] Table 2—1 shows that the five industries with the highest research effort had a substantial excess of exports over imports while the fourteen industries with weak R&D programs had greater imports than exports. The authors further noted that the five high R&D industries accounted for 72 percent of U.S. exports of manufactured goods and 74.6 percent of company financed R&D expenditures. The analysis of direct investment and sales by foreign subsidiaries shown in Table 2—2 indicate that in foreign operations the high R&D firms were again more prominent than other companies.

3. The second study on the role of high technology firms in U.S. exports was done by Keesing.[8] He analyzed 1961—62 data for eighteen industries comparing U.S. exports, expressed as a percentage of the exports of the ten major exporting countries, with the percentage of total employment represented by scientists and engineers engaged in R&D. The general pattern of results closely parallelled that seen in Table 2—2. Keesing determined that the coefficient of rank correlation was 0.94. He went on to explore other explanatory variables for export performance. The capital intensity of industries was found not to be correlated with export strength, a finding confirmed in the Gruber, Mehta, and Vernon study. Likewise natural resource availability did not seem to affect exports of manufactures. The proportion of skilled workers in the industry labor force did not show a significant correlation with export performance. However, there was some systematic pattern of relation between level of R&D work and skilled labor.

The effect of economies of scale was also tested, using plant size as an indicator. A weak correlation was found but again there was some relation between R&D and scale. Keesing concluded that there was a powerful correlation between intensity of R&D activity and

Table 2–1.   Research Effort and World Trade Performance by U.S. Industries, 1962

| Industry Name* and SIC Number | Research Effort | | Export Performance | |
|---|---|---|---|---|
| | Total R&D Expenditures as Percentage of Sales ($R_1$) | Scientists and Engineers in R&D as a Percentage of Total Employment ($R_2$) | Exports as Percentage of Sales ($E_1$) | Excess of Exports Over Imports, as Percentage of Sales ($E_2$) |
| Transportation (37) | 10.0 | 3.4 | 5.5 | 4.1 |
| Aircraft (372) | 27.2 | 6.9 | 8.4 | 7.6 |
| Transportation (other than aircraft) (–) | 2.8 | 1.0 | 4.2 | 2.6 |
| Electrical machinery (36) | 7.3 | 3.6 | 4.1 | 2.9 |
| Instruments (38) | 7.1 | 3.4 | 6.7 | 3.2 |
| Chemicals (28) | 3.9 | 4.1 | 6.2 | 4.5 |
| Drugs (283) | 4.4 | 6.6 | 6.0 | 4.8 |
| Chemicals (other than drugs) (–) | 3.8 | 3.7 | 6.2 | 4.4 |
| Machines (non-electrical) (35) | 3.2 | 1.4 | 13.3 | 11.4 |
| Rubber and plastic (30) | 1.4 | 0.5 | 2.0 | 1.3 |
| Stone, clay, and glass (32) | 1.1 | † | 1.9 | −0.2 |
| Petroleum and coal (29) | 0.9 | 1.8 | 1.2 | −0.8 |
| Fabricated metal (34) | 0.8 | 0.4 | 2.1 | 0.7 |
| Primary metal (33) | 0.6 | 0.5 | 3.1 | −1.8 |
| Non-ferrous metal (333) | 0.8 | 0.5 | 4.2 | −4.7 |
| Ferrous metal (–) | 0.5 | 0.4 | 2.5 | −0.2 |
| Leather (31) | 0.6 | 0.1 | 1.7 | −3.4 |
| Printing and publishing (27) | 0.6 | 0.2 | 1.7 | 1.1 |
| Tobacco (21) | 0.3 | 0.2 | 2.2 | 2.1 |
| Food (20) | 0.2 | 0.3 | 0.9 | −1.2 |
| Textile (22) | 0.2 | 0.3 | 3.4 | −1.1 |

|  |  |  |  |  |
|---|---|---|---|---|
| Furniture and fixtures (25) | 0.1 | 0.2 | 0.7 | † |
| Lumber and wood (24) | 0.1 | † | 2.0 | −6.2 |
| Paper (26) | 0.1 | 0.3 | 2.1 | −3.5 |
| Apparel (23) | 0.1 | † | 0.7 | −2.1 |
| All 19 industries: | 2.0 | 1.1 | 3.2 | 0.6 |
| 5 industries with highest research effort | 6.3 | 3.2 | 7.2 | 5.2 |
| 14 other industries | 0.5 | 0.4 | 1.8 | −1.1 |

*Industries arranged in descending order of research effort, defined by R&D expenditures as a percentage of sales.

†Less than 0.05 percent.

Source: W. Gruber, D. Mehta, and R. Vernon, "The R&D Factor in Trade and International Investment of United States Industries," *Journal of Political Economy*, February 1967.

Table 2–2.   Plant and Equipment Expenditures, Investment Expenditures, and Sales in the United States and Foreign Countries by U.S. Industries*†

| | 4 Research-intensive Industries (billions of dollars) | 14 Other Industries (billions of dollars) | Ratio of 4 Research-intensive Industries to 14 Other Industries (percent) |
|---|---|---|---|
| Plant and equipment expenditures, 1958–64: | | | |
| In U.S. | $ 32.7 | $ 50.8 | 64.4% |
| In Europe, by U.S.-owned subsidiaries | 4.3 | 1.6 | 266.3 |
| In non-Europe, by U.S.-owned subsidiaries | 3.9 | 3.0 | 133.4 |
| Direct investment, 1964:‡ | | | |
| In U.S. | 71.7 | 94.9 | 75.6 |
| In U.S.-owned subsidiaries in Europe | 4.5 | 2.0 | 227.5 |
| In U.S.-owned subsidiaries in non-Europe | 5.2 | 4.9 | 106.0 |
| Sales, 1962: | | | |
| In U.S. | 143.4 | 205.7 | 69.7 |
| By U.S.-owned subsidiaries in Europe | 8.4 | 3.7 | 227.0 |
| By U.S.-owned subsidiaries in non-Europe | 8.7 | 7.3 | 119.3 |

*Data on the petroleum industry, SIC 29, are not included because not available for all parts of the table.

†Some of the data on the scientific instruments industry, SIC 38, are not available separately and have to be included in the "14 other industries" totals. This tends to blur slightly the otherwise sharp differences between the research-intensive industries and the other industries.

‡For United States, the figures presented represent total equity interest; for the non-U.S. data, the figures are equity and debt in foreign subsidiaries owned by U.S. parents.

Source: W. Gruber, D. Mehta, and R. Vernon, "The R&D Factor in Trade and International Investment of United States Industries," *Journal of Political Economy*, February 1967.

export performance, and the association was heightened by a tendency for industries with intensive R&D to exhibit economies of scale and high requirements of skills in production.

4. De la Torre made a study in Latin America which demonstrated the utilization of MNC marketing system and skill resource capabilities in exports of LDCs.[9] Manufacturing of U.S. multinational firms accounted for almost two-thirds of the increase in exports of manufactured goods from Latin America in the decade between 1957 and 1966. Their exports increased 704.8 percent during this period, while domestic firms increased their exports by only 51 percent. Since most foreign manufacturing subsidiaries as well as domestic firms in these countries were established primarily to substitute local production for imports, there was little reason to suspect that major differences existed between domestic and foreign firms regarding their principal commitment to domestic markets. Thus, the advantage of foreign firms in exporting manufactured goods could be attributed to a greater ability in international markets, rather than to differences in emphasis.

An intensive investigation of the situation in Colombia provided more specific identification of the bases for the MNC export role. De la Torre classified products into three groups, low, moderate, and great, according to the barriers to their entry into marketing. He considered such factors as product differentiation, promotional levels, service requirements, and captive distribution channels. He also determined a propensity-to-export index representing the ratio of exports to industrial output. In Colombia, industrial sectors with a low marketing barrier rating had an export propensity index of 2.75 while the moderate and great barrier groups had indices of 1.12 and 1.45 respectively. He also found that the higher the barrier, the more likely that exports would be initiated by an outside agent, and that they would be limited to neighboring markets and would be subject to less control by the local producer than his domestic business.

In examining the importance of marketing barriers, de la Torre used data for thirty-two industrial sectors in Colombia. They showed that foreign subsidiaries were responsible for 49.8 percent of exports in industries with low barriers compared to 80.6 percent and 90.2 percent for those with medium and high barriers.

5. Buckley and Dunning made an analysis of a number of variables to determine what factors influenced the relative importance of industrial groups in the composition of U.S. MNC operations in the United Kingdom.[10] The general hypothesis that was most strongly supported approached the question from the standpoint of the theory

of industrial organization and focused on the relative ease of U.S.-owned firms vis-à-vis domestic ones in overcoming barriers to entry in an industry. Several variables included in this analysis showed statistically significant correlations and one variation of the overall approach explained 82 percent of the variance. The analysis suggested that the most significant entry barriers in this case, i.e., the barriers in which U.S. affiliates had a comparative advantage, were skilled labor, entrepreneurial resources, R&D and control of know-how, and a concentrated market structure. Product differentiation did not seem to have an equivalent importance, but the evidence suggested it played a role in reinforcing other barriers. The proxy for economies-of-scale barriers proved less significant.

6. The potentials and limitations in the transmission of managerial and entrepreneurial resources are illustrated by the study made by Wright in Chile.[11] His research was designed to ascertain the impact of external environmental conditions on management in Chile and to compare the manner and success with which American and local firms responded to changes in the environment. His approach was to compare the performance and managerial characteristics of pairs of firms in seven industries in 1970. Each pair included one Chilean and one U.S.-owned firm, both of essentially similar nature in products, size, labor, and markets. As a similar study had been made with the same firms in 1965, a comparison of effectiveness in meeting changing environmental conditions over time was possible.

The performance of the firms was gauged by profits, sales, and market share. Virtually all firms were found to be less profitable than five years previously. However, the Chilean firms had fared substantially better than the American ones. Wright's analysis of the reasons for the difference related to four environmental factors, which interviews with executives indicated were most important: rapid cost inflation, price control, labor laws (notably restrictions on discharging employees), and small market size.

Wright concluded that the difference in performance was primarily due to managerial policies and practices of the firms that affected their reaction to environmental changes. The American firms operated essentially "by the book," that is, general policies and guidelines were applied with relatively little modification in both the United States and other countries of the world. In contrast, the management philosophy of the Chilean firms generally was based on highly individualized patterns. The Chilean approach apparently resulted in greater flexibility and better adaptation to the particular environmental situation in Chile.

Two main areas of difference were noted. First, the American firms tended to have a more complex and costly management structure. Their chief weakness apparently lay in employment of some managerial functions which were not essential and burdened the firms unduly in adjusting to the squeeze between cost inflation and controlled prices. Wright noted particularly the U.S. market research staffs which were of doubtful value in a market where nearly all of the firms could sell their productive capacity without difficulty. The Chileans operated more successfully with lean organizations supplemented in such functions as research by consultants when necessary.

Second, the U.S. firms were relatively inflexible in operating policies. For example, Chilean pharmaceutical firms adjusted to tight price controls by making minor modifications in products and bringing them out under new brand names at profitable prices. U.S. firms adhering, however, to established products and brand names found that prices could not be raised as fast as costs. Likewise, when cheap Japanese transistor radios hit the market, the largest Chilean firm quickly obtained a licensing agreement with the Japanese. Two years elapsed before the U.S. competitor, rigidly controlled by its parent, made an effective response by producing a lower quality unit. In the meantime its market share had dropped from 30 percent to 15 percent.

These studies support the previous general analysis of MNC resource transmission capabilities. Although there are a multitude of variations among individual MNCs, they indicate that there is a high frequency of patterns in MNC resource flows with industrialized and less developed nations along the lines shown in Figure 2-1.

Skills appear most consistently as the strongest MNC capability. The skill differentials between parent and LDC host countries are inherently greater than with developed host nations. However, the effective differentials are not so great because of the much lower absorptive capacity of the LDCs due to their economic levels and cultural characteristics.

Also of substantial importance are the capabilities derived from the established marketing systems of MNCs. The flow patterns here differ according to type of country, however. The typical relation with a developed country involves sale of U.S. exports and overseas production through the marketing system established in each host country. In the LDC case, on the other hand, the flow of resources may be in both directions. The traditional pattern is similar to that for developed countries. But there is rapidly emerging a pattern with a back flow of benefits to the LDC in the use of the MNC's home

**Figure 2-1.**   Major Resource Transmission Flow by Multinational Corporations

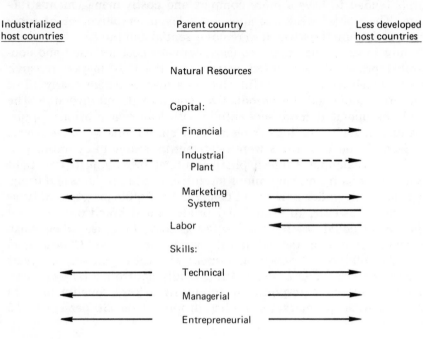

country marketing system to distribute the output of LDC plants. This latter capability is commonly married to the transmission of labor resources from LDCs, a capability which as yet does not appear prominently in the aggregate flow of resources managed by MNCs but is of critical importance in some industries.

Capital advantages either in financing or scale of industrial plants do not appear significant. Natural resources would, of course, be major factors if the studies included extractive industries but they are of no particular importance among the resource capabilities of manufacturing companies.

### NOTES

1. John Fayerweather, "Sears, Roebuck de Mexico," *Management of International Operations* (New York: McGraw-Hill, 1960), pp. 222-231.

2. John Fayerweather and Ashok Kapoor, *Strategy and Negotiation for the International Corporation* (Cambridge, Mass.: Ballinger Publishing Company, 1976), pp. 53-120.

3. Ibid., p. 121.

4. United Nations, Department of Economics and Social Affairs, *Multinational Corporations in World Development*, 1973, p. 49; and United Nations, Economic and Social Council, *The Impact of Multinational Corporations on the Development Process and on International Relations*, 1974, p. 51.

5. J.J. Servan-Schrieber, *The American Challenge* (New York: Atheneum, 1968), p. 28.

6. Raymond Vernon, *Storm over the Multinationals* (Cambridge, Mass: Harvard University Press, 1977), pp. 22–23.

7. W. Gruber, D. Mehta, and R. Vernon, "The R&D Factor in International Trade and International Investment of United States Industries," *Journal of Political Economy*, Feb. 1967, pp. 20–37.

8. Donald B. Keesing, "The Impact of Research and Development on United States Trade," *Journal of Political Economy*, Feb. 1967, pp. 38–48.

9. Jose de la Torre, "Foreign Investment and Export Dependency," *Economic Development and Cultural Change*, Oct. 1974, pp. 133–150.

10. Peter J. Buckley and John R. Dunning, "The Industrial Structure of U.S. Direct Investment in the U.K.," *Journal of International Business Studies*, Fall/Winter, 1976, pp. 5–13.

11. Richard W. Wright, "Organizational Ambiente: Management and Environment in Chile." *Academy of Management Journal*, March 1971, pp. 65–96.

*Chapter 3*

# MNC Interaction
# with Host Societies

Economic differentials between nations and MNC capabilities establish the potentials for resource transmission. The interaction of the transmission process with the receiving society is the other side of the coin. The receptivity of the society influenced by the actions of the MNC are prime determinants of the effectiveness of the process.

The host society interactions involved in resource transmission differ greatly in character. One way to classify them is according to impact on the two broad social institutional phases of society. A large portion of the interactions falls in the politico-economic area which is in the realm of the attributes of the national state and will be discussed in the next two chapters. Another large portion (with some overlap with the former) involves the sociocultural elements of society. They will be the focus of this chapter.

The extent of sociocultural impact induced by the transmission process varies according to the nature of resources. When standard physical commodities are imported or capital funds are provided for an ongoing enterprise, the sociocultural effects are usually negligible. When a quite new consumer product is introduced or parent company methods of handling worker complaints are adopted, the cultural impact may be substantial. Because of the emphasis on skills in the MNC resource capabilities, substantial impacts are prominent in MNC activities. Skills are by definition part of the culture of a society and introduction of new skills inherently therefore evokes attitudinal and behavioral reactions. Thus the question of cultural change is necessarily a major component of MNC strategy.

As a point of departure, we may usefully set the role of the MNC in this area in a very broad perspective, that of the cross-cultural change agent. Since the beginnings of civilization individuals and groups moving from one social group to another have contributed to the transmission of culture in its broadest sense of man-made ideas, attitudes, and practices. Early traders played a critical role in passing on not only material goods but assorted social traits from one society to another. Missionaries have actively spread religious ideas. In many ages migrants driven out of their parent societies by ethnic, religious, or other problems or seeking greater opportunities elsewhere have introduced into the societies they joined elements of their former way of life.

The MNC fits readily into this picture. The corporation and the parent country nationals who may be brought along to staff local units are generically similar to the other types of cross-cultural change agents observed over the course of time. Like them the MNC is a displaced or migrant social entity which carries with it assorted elements of its parent culture. In the process of adapting to its new home, it will to some degree conform to the local ways and to some degree it will attempt to perpetuate its former ways and to convert those around it to follow them as well.

With this sense of the broad social role of the MNC as a cultural change agent, this chapter will analyze the process of change in societies and consider the MNC's role in the process.

## BUSINESS AND SOCIETY

The essence of the concepts developed in this chapter is the interrelation of business with the structure of society and the nature of change in components of society. A few fundamental concepts drawn from the social sciences will set the stage for this discussion. Over the centuries human beings have organized themselves into groupings or societies of progressively broader character—families, tribes, small regional units, and now, most commonly, nations within which common patterns of life prevail. These patterns are typically described as institutions or systems and are classified according to their central purpose.

Individuals in all societies have just a few basic needs, and the systems they have evolved are directed toward serving these needs. Thus, as shown in Figure 3—1, spiritual needs are met by religious organizations, sexual and reproductive needs by the family system, intellectual needs by educational institutions, sustenance and physical needs by the economic system including business, and ego needs

**Figure 3-1.** The Needs of the Individual and the Systems Satisfying Them

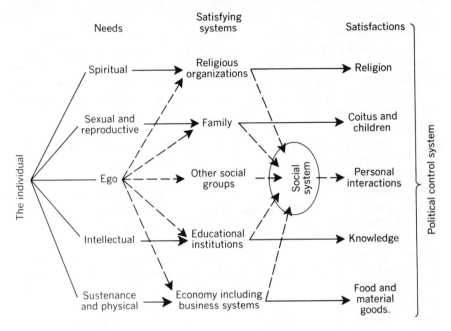

(chiefly love, status, and security) both by essentially social organizations (e.g., a fraternal association) and by the social interactions associated with the other institutions (e.g., the work group in a factory). There is also the political system which serves a control function in guiding the other systems for the benefit of the members of the society.

Within these systems people are able to function in a reasonably effective and orderly manner by virtue of two types of established and integrated networks of relationships, one economic and the other personal. The economic network involves the interrelation of the resources of society—natural resources, labor, skills, and capital. These resources are present in a society in varying quantities and qualities, and the demands for them form a particular pattern at a given time. The economic system provides the means for allocation of the resources and direction of economic effort. In completely free economies, most of this allocation and direction is accomplished by independent price and monetary mechanisms. In a highly controlled economy it may be determined by government decisions, though still with much use of monetary measures in planning and exchange. Thus the monetary measures in a society are typically indicators of the relative utilities and supplies of resources in that society, and the exchanges that take place on the basis of such measures keep the society functioning. For example, differences in wages attract people into particular jobs according to need and productivity; levels of interest encourage appropriate volumes of investment; and so on.

As any observer of the modern world knows, the monetary measure system often functions inadequately. For example, in many countries the inflationary spiral induced by fiscal problems has resulted in serious distortions in price relationships. But despite malfunctions, the system exists and does provide for the continuity of societies.

The personal network of relationships accommodates the needs of a society made up of human beings rather than robots. It is composed of integrated patterns of roles, expectations, values, and sanctions. Each individual as he or she operates within each system has a certain position or role, for example, as a priest or a customer or a student. Over the years the society will have evolved a set of expectations for the conduct of the individual in each role—how to lead, whom to respect, how much to know. The society will also have a system of values that will guide the conduct of people by telling them what is right and wrong, what is most desirable, and so on. And there will be some code of sanctions for meting out punishments and rewards according to how well people satisfy the established pattern of roles, expectations, and values. Sanctions range from jail terms for gross offenders, minor rebuffs like a curt response to an impolite question to praise or material benefits for those who perform correctly.

This combination of roles, expectations, values, and sanctions is essential to a society because it permits people to act for the most part according to tradition and habit, with confidence that they will be effective and that others will be proceeding in the same direction. By the same token it is vital for the perpetuation of the society as a whole. Because the individual aspects have over time evolved as an integrated, interdependent whole, the society is able to hold together and move in a purposeful manner.

Business is a basic component of this structure. It composes a major part of the economic system, providing the mechanism through which most goods and services reach the population wherever private enterprise is accepted. Furthermore, as shown in Figure 3–2, it is closely related to the other systems. The religious system propagates values and sanctions that affect the conduct of business. The family system is also a source of values, and its characteristics bear on business in other ways such as nepotism. The educational system affects business in both the extent and the type of intellectual development

Figure 3-2. Interaction of Systems of Society

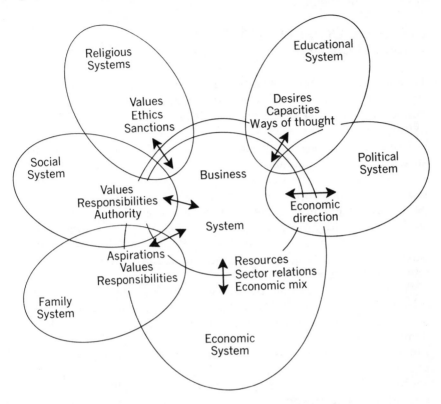

received by its customers, its employees, the government officials who control its operations, and so on. The social system is yet another source of values and sanctions, the interactions in business life being a major part of the social activities of people. Finally, one of the prime functions of the political system is direction of the economy, including the business system.

Insofar as the present analysis is concerned, the key point is clear —namely, that the individual aspects of each country are interdependent parts of a whole. Thus it is apparent in considering conformity-innovation problems, the MNC's decisions must be based on an understanding of the functioning of the surrounding society so that the business policies and practices adopted will effectively integrate with the assortment of environmental elements. This same observation can, of course, be made about purely domestic management, for every business must fit its methods to its environment. But in practical terms there is a major difference arising from the impetus for the multinational firm to seek changes from outside the established system of the society.

## DIFFERENCES IN RELATIONSHIPS AMONG SOCIETIES

To amplify the concepts outlined above, it will be helpful to illustrate them by describing some of the main dimensions of the economic and personal relationships within societies with which international business is concerned.

Notable on the *economic* side are income-structure, compensation-structure, and capital-labor relationships. The *income structures* of societies vary between the extremes shown in Figure 3—3. Type A represents undeveloped economies with the great majority of the people at the low end of the income scale, a small middle class, and a few quite wealthy people. Type B typifies the highly industrialized societies in which the bulk of the population falls in a relatively affluent middle class, with small numbers at both the bottom and top ends of the income scale.

A number of economic relationships are influenced heavily by the income structure. In the type A society the buying capacity of the masses is limited to a few staples and minor luxuries, so the effective demand for most consumer durables and many other products is found only among the small middle- and upper-class groups. A few typical consequences of this sort of structure are packaging of mass consumption items like chewing gum in very small units within the buying power of the poor; emphasis on luxury lines of durable goods with high margins to maximize profit from the upper class; and dis-

**Figure 3—3.**   Two Types of Income Structure of Societies

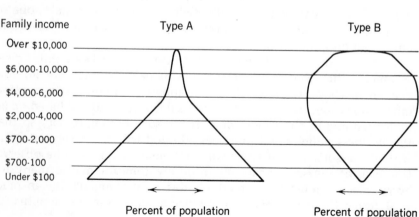

tribution and advertising methods designed to pinpoint coverage of one economic level, either the elite or the lower class, because their characteristics are so different. The closer one approaches the type B structure, the more emphasis there is on developing products suitable for the mass middle class, with less attention to the special demands of the upper and lower extremes. Likewise, advertising and distribution methods are directed more toward complete coverage of the market without distinction as to economic level.

The *compensation structure* is the other side of the coin related to manpower resources, skills, and productivity. In the type A society the great majority of the people are typically engaged in agriculture where they have low productivity due to small land units and unprogressive methods—lack of fertilizers, ineffective cultivation, and the like. The balance of the low-income groups are urban masses who are for the most part either unemployed or low-skill laborers. The relatively small portions of the population possessing the bulk of the technical, managerial, and entrepreneurial skills are found in the middle- and upper-income groups. Although this sort of compensation structure is disturbing by humanitarian standards, it reflects appropriately the economic contributions of the various groups and provides incentives in a constructive direction. That is, an individual with skills in such a society contributes relatively much more to economic output than a member of the low-skill masses, and the existence of high economic rewards encourages people at the lower end to develop skills that are badly needed. In the type B societies the disparity in economic contribution has been narrowed by mass education and by the broad dissemination and organization of skills in agriculture and industry, though a considerable span of compensation does of course remain.

The obvious relevance of the compensation relationships lies in the wage and salary structure established by a company, but it affects other aspects of business. For example, in type A societies the scarcity of skilled people and the low wages and unemployment among the unskilled encourage firms to avoid layoffs, thus reinforcing practices that have social support as will be indicated below.

The *capital-labor* relationship also relates to availability and productivity. In the less developed countries as compared with the advanced nations, capital is less available, and labor at lower-skill levels is more plentiful relative to needs. Indicative of these differences we find that interest rates are higher in the less developed countries, and wage rates are higher in the advanced countries. Putting the two together, we see that the ratio of cost of capital to cost of labor is higher in the less developed countries. This type of relationship bears most directly on the processes and technology employed in business. In the less developed countries it favors the use of low-investment, labor-intensive methods. The opposite tendency is favored as one moves up the scale of industrial development of nations. But to illustrate the complexity of the effects of various elements in a society, it is worth noting that the approach in less developed countries can be quite different because of other relationships. For example, companies have on occasion used quite automated processes requiring high investments because they found it easier to manage a few high-wage, high-skilled workers than to deal with larger numbers of people with low skills, sometimes because of irresponsible labor unions dominating the latter. This illustration simply emphasizes that the determination of policies that will fit best in a given society depends upon an understanding of all of the relationships in the society, not just a few obvious ones.

Turning to the *personal* relationship side, we find a much more variegated picture. There does seem to be some relation between level of economic development and cultural, social, and political characteristics. However, the human element has played such a strong part in the historical evolution of these characteristics that the nature of the personal relationships varies greatly even among countries at similar levels of economic achievement. Six are especially pertinent to the interaction of foreign business with the society: groupings of people, interpersonal obligations, authority systems, value systems, interbusiness relationships, and politico-economic controls.

The earliest *groupings of people* stemmed naturally from the reproduction process and elemental self-protection and subsistence needs. As human life became more sophisticated, it was natural that the family should remain the fundamental unit onto which people would attempt to graft new activities. Thus we find in many societies, especially those at early stages of development, that a large portion of the personal relationships have been built around familial ties. Frequently some version of the *extended family* (or clan or tribe) became an important unit with even quite distant relatives functioning on a fairly close and continuing basis. In such societies people do have other group affiliations, but they are not numerous and are not considered as important to their lives. A quite different structure is found in some of the more economically advanced countries. The family is still a significant unit but only in the limited nuclear form (husband, wife, and children). A large portion of the individual's activities takes place in a multiplicity of groupings, ranging from business firms to religious organizations, to political parties, to social clubs, any of which may be important enough to him to rival his family ties.

The nature of personal groupings affects business at many levels. The policies of a firm may be quite different if it is essentially an arm of a family unit rather than a widely owned independent economic unit. The economic objectives of the family, stemming from its other activities and even such non-economic considerations as family pride, may be determining factors, whereas the independent firm is better able to act on the basis of its separately determined objectives. In a number of aspects of operating, such as procurement and selling, managers imbued with strong extended-family orientation are likely to exert their efforts and develop relationships in the direction of family ties to a greater degree than persons from societies in which multiple affiliations prevail.

In employment practices the dominance of family ties leads naturally to nepotism. Hiring relatives is found in all societies. The difference in the family-oriented societies lies in the tendency to give much greater weight to family affiliation in selection as compared with technical proficiency or other qualifications. Because nepotism is often viewed critically in some advanced nations in which MNC managers are raised, it may be well to pause here for a moment to emphasize the point that each characteristic of a society has a logical place within that society. Nepotism is frequently found where general standards of business morality are not high and where the supply of competent managers is quite limited. These conditions provide a justification for emphasis on employing relatives because family codes can enforce morality and family loyalty can attract and hold managers. Thus under some circumstances nepotism is sound by both social and economic standards, even if it results in some sacrifice of managerial qualifications.

The system of *interpersonal obligations* in a society stems in part from the groupings of people and in part from the relations between groups. Variations are found among countries in both the patterns of obligations and their strength. Two illustrations will suggest the range of variations.

In the United States the multiple-group affiliations of the individual carry with them some obligations, so the general pattern is quite wide. On the other hand, few obligations seem to have great strength or durability: children leave home early and take little responsibility for their parents, compared to that in many countries; workers do the job for which they are paid, but they manifest little company loyalty and move on to other companies quite readily; consumers shift their buying from store to store and product to product with ease; and so on.

Japan presents a quite different picture. Traditional Japanese society was rigidly structured including a well-defined code of obligations for almost every relationship—parent–child, worker–employer, businessman–emperor, and so forth. Though some elements of these obligations have faded, many still remain. Thus, when a young man is hired for management in a Japanese firm, it is typically assumed that lifetime obligations have been assumed on both sides: the company assures the manager a job and steady increases in status and pay, and the man, in turn, remains in loyal employment in the firm. This type of paternalism is perhaps stronger in Japan than elsewhere, but to a degree it is common in many other countries. By the same token, in Japan and other societies one finds quite strong ties between housewives and small food merchants. Lower- and middle-class women tend to shop frequently, and they develop regular relationships with a small group of neighborhood merchants. It is hard to determine to what extent their actions are the result of simple habit, or of desire for regular social intercourse, or of sense of obligation to support the merchants who provide a convenient service. But a strong bond exists, which is a controlling factor in many distribution plans.

*Authority systems* are also largely a component of the groupings of individuals. The chief differences among societies are along the range between authoritarian-autocratic systems and democratic-participative systems. The former is the traditional pattern whose origins can be traced back to the way of life of primitive man. In simple societies it seems to have been natural for the strongest and wisest to achieve control and, with varying degrees of consultation with others, to make and enforce decisions within the group. In any case, in many countries we find today authoritarian patterns still well established in important sectors of life including the family, religion, education, government, and business. Democratic patterns are generally dominant in the United States, parts of Europe, Canada, and Australia. In a number of countries there is a mixed picture, with authoritarian systems dominant in some groups and democratic ones in others. In much of Latin America, for example, democratic concepts find a striking manifestation in student participation in important decisions, including faculty appointments in some public universities. On the other hand, authoritarian patterns persist for family life and for the student–teacher relationship within the classroom in most schools.

The obvious relevance of authority systems for business lies in the pattern of internal management. Where authoritarian relationships prevail, the multinational firm is likely, at least to some degree, to find it must relate itself to expectations of local employees along those lines, even though its expatriate managers may have come from societies where democratic approaches were common. But the authority system bears on other aspects of business. In marketing it is important in planning promotion and other activities to know whether it is the husband or the wife who makes purchasing decisions, and for industrial goods whether it is the president or the purchasing manager. In negotiating with governments on all sorts of problems, it is necessary to know whether lower level bureaucrats have true delegated authority or whether decisions can be made only by cabinet ministers or in some cases by the chief of state.

The question of *value systems* brings us into a different order of personal relationships. Values are pervasive mental attitudes that determine many of the standards of the individual as to what is right or wrong, good or bad, desirable or undesirable. Because they are the outgrowth of social, religious. educational, and other factors over many years, they form a very mixed picture around the world. Thus it is practical here to mention only a few interesting variations in values as they affect business.

One variation important to business is the respect accorded by societies to different occupations. In most traditional societies the highest prestige was given to scholars or warriors or government leaders, with business people typically falling fairly low on the scale. The low esteem of business arose from a lack of appreciation for its contributions, the image of the businessman as one who profited at the expense of the main body of the population, and the relatively weak power position of business vis-à-vis the governing elites. Even in most European countries, this low valuation of business careers persists, with only a few societies fitting the U.S. pattern in which business is at least reasonably close to other ways of life in prestige. All of this, of course, bears heavily on such matters as the type of personnel who can be recruited into management and the acceptability and conduct of the businessmen in other circles of national society.

Another set of values affecting business is the way in which people view different forms of achievement in life. People attach various relative weights to material goods, social standing, intellectual accomplishment, power, and so forth. The United States has often been characterized as a highly materialistic society. However, although the acquisition of material goods is thoroughly approved in the U.S. middle class, it appears that the attainment of social status is more important. Material goods are sometimes valued more as status symbols indicative of social standing than for their material benefits (the *nouveau riche* lady perspiring under a mink stole at a summer concert being a classic case). In some other countries, on the other hand, ostentatious demonstrations of material wealth or, in fact, the whole idea of self-generated achievement is frowned upon. The British are often cited as an example of a society in which a person is born to a place in the social hierarchy and expected to stay there. Thus achievement per se is not to be praised, and status symbols accordingly are not a dominant element in social relations. This type of value affects both marketing decisions and the way in which personnel are managed, for the whole incentive system of business must be geared to the objectives which people feel will have social approval.

Yet another set of values concerns the ways in which people interact, including codes of frankness, courtesy, cooperation, and competition. An extreme example of contrast in the combinations of these components is seen in differences in the ways of U.S. and Japanese businessmen. Both work in industrialized nations dominated by large firms requiring internal collaboration among managers and extensive external relationships. Yet there are notable difference in the patterns of conduct approved by their respective value systems. The American is supposed to be "all business," not wasting time on "non-essentials," and to be frank and precise. The Japanese, on the other hand, devotes a great deal of time in business relationships to pleasantries and other non-business conversation, and he is more concerned with being agreeable than with complete or accurate discussion of business matters. Thus, whereas the American is conditioned to spelling out the full nature of a problem, including both the good and the bad aspects, the Japanese may reveal only part of his knowledge on the matter. Likewise, when the American agrees to a course of action, he is usually doing just that; but the Japanese may have no precise intentions as to whether he can or will fulfill the apparent agreement.

A final element of value systems worth noting for its business relevance is the question of honesty. In virtually all societies honesty is approved, but what that means in the complex of attitudes composing the value system varies greatly. In the United States a shoplifter or a man who forges checks or takes bribes will not only be prosecuted by the law but will also be looked down upon by his neighbors. Yet thousands of people pad insurance claims or engage in petty income tax evasion by not reporting small sources of income (incidental baby-sitting, for example) with the full knowledge of neighbors, with no significant loss of social standing. In many countries, large-scale tax evasion or taking of bribes is commonplace among people who regard themselves as "honest" by the values of their countrymen.[1]

This type of variation again emphasizes the fact that all elements of personal relationships have to be recognized as part of a total societal structure. Whatever the honesty system of a society may be, it is presumably related to and consistent with the other aspects of that society. For example, the mere fact that there is massive tax evasion does not mean that the government has less revenue than it might have, for it presumably can adjust tax rates and other processes to obtain the revenue it needs and that the country can afford to pay. More likely, tax evasion means that the tax load is proportionately heavier on some groups than it might be if evasion were not so great. But even this may serve a purpose, for the conditions in the country may be such that the added monetary return for particular activities provided by the tax evasion is necessary to foster these activities—for example, to encourage the wealthy to invest in new industrial operations. By the same token, bribery of government officials is often associated with low salary levels, the bribes providing in effect a means for direct taxation for government services and supplemental compensation of underpaid officials. Whether or not tax evasion and bribery are still suitable for these societies is another question. The only point being stressed here is that absolutes in honesty are no more relevant than any other absolutes in the study of the relationships in a society. The prime consideration is essentially to determine what degrees and forms of honesty are required by the prevailing value system.

The subject of *interbusiness relationships* brings us close to the economic aspects of society, but the personal element in it is strong. The basic issue in these relationships is how a society balances the benefits of competition and collaboration in economic endeavor. Some degree of competition is always beneficial as indicated, for example, by the virtual universality of patent laws which provide a protected incentive for those who develop new products. And collaboration in such matters as joint efforts to develop favorable business legislation has equally common acceptance. But there are many differences among societies which have evolved in other respects. Notable among these is the control of marketing activities.

There seems to be a natural tendency for large industrial firms to seek considerable collaboration to minimize price and volume uncertainty and maximize profit in the marketplace. This tendency was very much in evidence in the United States around the end of the nineteenth century and can be seen in Europe and Japan in the extensive cartelization of business and in less systematic but tangible form in many developing nations. In time, U.S. society decided that the substantial limitations on collaboration embodied in the Sherman Antitrust Act and other legislation were desirable.

Other nations have adopted some limitations but for the most part considerably fewer than the United States. Differences in their circumstances bear on the balance they have chosen. For one thing their markets are smaller, so there is less room for competitors to function. In some cases the economies of scale preclude the efficient operation of enough companies to achieve effective competition. Perhaps more important are temperamental differences. U.S. society has placed high values on economic progress with strong pressures for low costs, low prices, and increased output but relatively lower value placed on the human cost, whether it be in the strain on senior executives or the layoffs of workers in companies which could not survive competition. In other societies these values seem to be reversed. The managerial-entrepreneurial class with support of labor seems more concerned with stabilizing its situation and avoiding competitive pressures and casualties and is less anxious to maximize economic progress. Given this outlook, it is quite natural to accept a much greater degree of collaboration than is approved in the United States.

Under *politico-economic controls* fall the assortment of ways in which the people through their political system attempt to guide their economic life. The regulation of interbusiness relationships is part of this as are price controls, investment incentives, ownership of factories, and a host of other government activities. Without delving into the details of any of these, we can discern among societies certain basic patterns or philosophies of politico-economic controls which are most pertinent to our discussion. Again thinking in terms of a spectrum, we find the range runs from virtually full government control to quite free private enterprise. The archetype of the former would be a communist state in which the economy is entirely owned and managed by the state. From this we move to countries with varying degrees of state ownership and controls to a relatively few Western nations in which most economic activity is by private companies subject to numerous government regulations. There are no wide-open economies lacking any form of government control which would fall at the other extreme of the spectrum.

A number of factors have contributed to these differences in control structures. On the basis of historical experience we may judge that there is a human predisposition toward private enterprise, manifest, for example, in the persistence of some degree of small scale private agriculture in the U.S.S.R. Thus the decision of a society through its political system to exercise collective controls may be presumed to be based on the conclusion that the private system was not in some ways suitable to its situation. This presumption seems to be borne out by the nature of conditions around the world where several elements in different portions have made full reliance on private enterprise questionable. In some countries there have not been enough of the right type of entrepreneurs to stimulate economic growth, or they have lacked the essential capital; in others, the risks and problems have been too great a deterrent to entrepreneurs; in still others, there was an apparent need to push the economy in directions which private enterprise was not appropriate to pursue; and in many cases there has been a sense that speed and socially equitable development were best achieved under public controls.

This sketchy survey of economic and personal relationships within societies does not presume to cover all the relationships pertinent to business nor to describe the few which have been mentioned sufficiently to guide the manager in dealing with them.[2] Its objective rather has been to provide enough illustrations to give substantive meaning to the concepts of the relation of business to the systems of society and the interrelationship of various societal characteristics. The illustrations, even though presented in sketchy form, clearly show that in many ways operations will be subject to adjustment on the basis of aspects of the local business system which, in turn, are to some degree controlled by elements of the host-society environment. Sometimes just one element of societal systems will be relevant, but as often as not several interrelated elements exercise influence on a business action.

## THE PROCESS OF CHANGE

In order to determine the feasibility of innovation, we must go beyond the analysis of the interrelation of the elements of societies to a concept of the process of change in the elements. As a starting point, a further dimension must be added to the picture just presented. The integrity and self-perpetuation of the elements of society may imply a simple uniformity, but there is in all societies some diversity in the character of each element. One finds, for example, some variety in the nature of relations within a family or the conduct of businessmen. This variety is induced by the range in personal characteristics of people and lack of uniformity in other circumstances. Within limits a society is able to tolerate variations in the character of each of its elements as long as the tendency in most instances is confined to a narrow range centered about what is called the *norm* of the society as shown in Figure 3–4.[a]

When one considers the question of change in societies, it is helpful to recognize the significance of the characteristics which fall on the outer extremities of Figure 3–4 and the logic of change at work in the process. The infrequent characteristics are of two general types. First, there are those shown at the left of the figure which are for one reason or another not useful to the society. Some are bad like sadistic conduct of a father or poor workmanship by artisans. Others are ineffective or inappropriate to the society as, for example, celibate religious sects like the Shakers who have great difficulty perpetuating themselves. And a substantial group represents passing aspects of the society which linger on, though with decreasing frequency.

Second, there are those characteristics shown at the right. Though not frequent, these are definitely useful, representing innovations, experiments, or similar deviations which will in time become estab-

**Figure 3–4.** Norms, Deviants, and Change in Social Systems

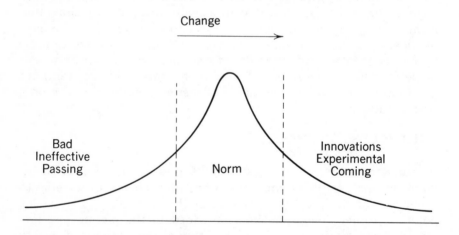

[a]The term *norm* is used here in the statistical sense of the average or mean. It is not to be confused with the use of the term by sociologists to describe a standard according to the value system of a society. In some cases, a characteristic of a society may be a norm by both definitions—for example, when honesty in business relations is both approved and commonly practiced. But for many characteristics there is a norm or prevailing mode which, as used here in the statistical sense, is either not guided by the value system or possibly runs counter to apparent values.

lished or at least will continue as constructive stimulants to the whole society. The idea of piece rates for factory workers fell into this category when it was first conceived; though initially unusual, it has now become a norm for industrial societies. The concept of the deviant as a useful stimulant is illustrated by the "stormy petrel" type, who emerges as a valuable member of some management groups. Such a type as a norm would result in chaos, but one provocative character in a group can be worth a great deal.

With the deviants from the norm categorized in this manner, the change process is readily incorporated in Figure 3–4 by adding the arrow at the top. Or a third dimension could be added showing the distribution of variations for a particular element of society at subsequent times. It would show some of the deviants on the right shifting in toward the center to become the norms. And it would show some of those on the left decreasing still more in frequency and being replaced by those close to the current norms. In food retailing in rural sections of the United States, for example, a chart a hundred years ago would have shown the norm as the general store run by an individual proprietor. Stores specializing in food would have been rather infrequent. Thirty years ago the general store would have shifted to the left, becoming a deviant. The store concentrating primarily on food—would have assumed the status of the norm but supermarkets would appear here and there. By the 1960s the true general store would have virtually disappeared, and the supermarket would have become the norm with various further modernization experiments to the right.

The magnitude of the dimensions both from right to left and in rate of transition through time will vary substantially according to the elements of society and the nature of the societies. In some aspects of life, like recreational interests for example, society tolerates a much wider range of variations than in others like religion. Thus the chart for recreational interests of boys in Mexico might show soccer as a norm but with baseball as a rapidly emerging variant and a number of other fairly common alternatives so that the chart would have a rather wide span and an irregular profile. In religious views, on the other hand, the vast majority of people would cluster around the norm of Catholicism, with a much smaller and narrower band of deviants. By the same token, there are differences in the general tolerance of deviations among societies. Typically the older societies have been the more rigid, with all elements within them held quite close to their norms, and newer societies have had greater tolerance.

The rate of transition typically is related to the range of tolerance in the society. That is, those societies that are fairly rigid in their tolerance of deviations from a norm at any given time are also likely to change slowly. Those tolerating substantial variations are likely to change more rapidly. However, the rate of change is also subject to other influences, notably from the outside. Especially relevant to this discussion is the influence of the more developed nations on the less developed ones, particularly in business methods. Thus a number of societies that of themselves were quite rigid have been changing fairly rapidly as a result of influence from the United States, the U.S.S.R., and other countries.

In analyzing and especially in predicting the process of change, one must have some guides as to why change takes place. The most practical concept for this purpose is that the evolution of norms and deviants depends upon their usefulness to the society, whether they are *functional* or *dysfunctional.* This concept postulates that a particular norm for one element of a society will persist as long as it is functionally the most effective available alternative. When it ceases to serve well and a preferable alternative emerges, it becomes dysfunctional, the alternative taking over as the norm. A large portion of the changes through history certainly fit this general concept. The automobile superseded the horse and buggy when its utility was established by technological improvements and by economic progress that made it a feasible purchase for the average person. The publicly owned corporation has largely taken the place of the family firm in the more advanced countries because of the greater effectiveness of the corporation in mobilizing large capital requirements for major industrial projects and in building the strong managerial organizations required for a dynamic, large enterprise, and so on.

The usefulness criterion is not adequate as a total explanation of the process of change because other causes must be considered, notably the need for sources of initiative to set change in motion which have been greater at some times and in some societies than in others. But usefulness is an essential criterion inasmuch as few dysfunctional variants make substantial progress, and the main thrust of development in societies has been toward useful change. We come, therefore, to the conclusion that the critical test in evaluating the feasibility of an innovation is whether it will be functional or dysfunctional within the evolving elements and systems of the host society.

## THE ROLE OF THE MULTINATIONAL CORPORATION

The foregoing discussion provides the basis for setting forth a conceptual scheme for determining the strategy of the multinational corporation in its relations with the internal structure of the host society (as distinguished from the nationalism and national interest aspects to be considered in the next two chapters). The special role of the firm as a foreign body within the host society lies in the introduction of innovations as part of the transmission of resources. Thus a primary disposition toward innovation in the strategy is conceptually sound. The critical decisions lie in determining the feasibility of the innovation. The useful criteria in this determination are (1) whether an innovation fits with the interrelated elements of the host society, and (2) whether it will be functionally effective for the society.

The proposition that the MNC should be ever anxious to introduce innovations drawn from experience in its home country is inevitably subject to charges of chauvinism and even imperialism. However, the proposition is supported by the logic of the situation. "When in Rome, do as the Romans do" is a nice adage, but it is useful primarily for tourists and diplomats whose main objective is to get along well with their hosts. It is of doubtful value as an overall guide for anyone who is going to participate actively in the give-and-take of the life of the society, for the obvious query is, "Can a non-Roman ever hope to do better at acting like a Roman than a true Roman?" The answer almost certainly is "no." This leads to the conclusion that a strong competitive status for an MNC requires departure from local norms either in product design, or in training methods, or in any number of other directions. Furthermore, since the main competence of the MNC to innovate must rest on its parent–country experience, it will presumably be most effective if the innovations it attempts are based on that experience. And to further counter the imperialistic implication, this form of innovation represents one of the clear values to the host society of the presence of the firm in its midst. To a substantial degree the firm must conform to the host society if it is to function effectively, but its special strengths both competitively and for the benefit of the host society lie in the innovations it is able to contribute.

Yet another aspect must also be brought in to put the role of the MNC in proper perspective. Although the inputs by foreign firms are important contributors to cultural change in host societies, their extent is often overstated, especially by nationalistic critics. Much of the change attributed to MNCs is in fact part of the natural evolution going on throughout the world toward more urbanized, higher income, industrialized life. While the patterns have a degree of difference related to cultures of each country, there is also a high degree of similarity in the way in which societies are evolving. The concept presented in this chapter of innovations being sound when they are functional for the host society carries with it the implication that even without the role of the MNC such changes would more than likely appear through natural evolution. Thus the MNC's innovative impact, while it may arouse some overt negative response, is in the main simply one of expediting and facilitating change that is part of the steady evolution of societies throughout the world toward rather similar models of culture appropriate to various stages of development.

While the case for a strategy disposition toward innovation is strong, the considerations favoring conformity must be given full attention. Basic support for conformity lies in the observation that an MNC will arouse less adverse reaction if it accommodates its ways to the local society. Given the strong general negative reaction toward the MNC which will be brought out in the next two chapters, this observation strongly encourages a disposition toward conformity. To this must be added a sense of the cost of innovation. Introducing new products, technological processes, and management methods requires substantial expenditure of time and effort. Thus the innovation-conformity issue is usually not a simple can-or-cannot matter but rather a can-at-this-cost proposition that must be weighed against the cost of other opportunities.

Overall then the MNC strategist is faced with a range of innovation possibilities. A sound strategy will call for undertaking some while conformity is accepted as a wiser course in others, because innovation efforts are too costly or to limit negative societal reactions, thus improving the prospects of success for the total strategy. To give this concept of a mixed innovation-conformity strategy fuller realism, we must observe that it will involve many compromises, adaptations of products, skills and the like, in which innovative characteristics will be combined with elements of the traditional culture. Thus, practical strategy will be a gray mixture of the two elements based on specific judgments regarding cost, practicality, and broader societal reaction.

## CASE HISTORIES OF INNOVATION

To give fuller meaning to the basic guidelines presented here, they will now be tested by application to some concrete situations. Four cases of varied character and complexity are outlined for this purpose: a product innovation, a change in personnel management, the introduction of a new marketing institution, and a complex case involving political-business relations and personal interactions.

## The Sewing Machine

One of the first of the multitude of new products introduced into countries by foreign firms was the sewing machine brought to Europe by Singer from the United States in the 1850s. The norm for domestic sewing at the time was, of course, the handwork of the housewife, and it remained that for many years. As long as most people were quite poor and their labor cheap, the investment in a sewing machine was not economically sound. But for a few more affluent housewives, along with many tailors and seamstresses, the investment was feasible and the higher productivity proved economically beneficial. Thus, in time, machine sewing shifted from being a promising deviant to become the norm for home sewing in European society and now for all but the poorest nations.

There is nothing very subtle about this story, but it is highly relevant because so much of the innovation done by MNCs is in the product area, and the economic aspects of product acceptance are so strong. One can find cultural and other factors at work in this and similar product changes. For example, in some societies skilled hand seamstresses have doubtless deplored the loss of their status to a machine. But by and large, companies introducing labor-saving products consistent with the evolution of economic relationships in host societies have succeeded. They have a natural advantage in doing so because their home-country economy has typically already passed through the stages of economic development found in host nations, and thus they are skilled in producing goods suitable for such markets. We find in the multiplicity of such cases, therefore, a clearly visible confirmation of the general concept of innovation being feasible and desirable if it fits with the functionally effective deviations from the norms of the host society.

## Paternalism and the Personnel Manager

A classic case of cultural innovation revolves around the role of the personnel manager. In major companies in the more advanced societies, the personnel manager is the focal point for many of the personal problems and grievances of workers. The supervisor of course has a role in this aspect of the lives of his subordinates. But consistent with the concepts of organizational specialization, the personnel manager is given the time and responsibility for doing a large part of the job. On the other hand, in the paternalistic systems characteristic of many host nations, the supervisor and quite commonly the senior manager of the plant assume this function. It is fundamental to the whole structure of paternalism that the organizational leader looks out for all the needs of his people.

One's first reaction to this situation is likely to be that conformity is in order, that an attempt to substitute the personnel manager in part of the role of the supervisor is unwise. By and large this reaction is sound. Paternalistic dependency among workers is usually reinforced by similar relationships throughout the host society—in family, in schools, in church, and in government. A norm of this sort based on pervasive, strong emotional attitudes is not readily altered. Thus a company that attempts to shift part of the prime paternalistic responsibilities to someone who is not the leader of the organization risks disruption of worker morale.

However, in terms of the concepts advanced in this chapter the situation requires a careful second look. Paternalism was once the norm in U.S. industry, but it has largely disappeared. Looking at other countries over time, one can clearly discern shifts in the same direction. Changes in the surrounding society provide a logical explanation. Paternalism is related to the economic and educational weakness of workers. As this weakness declines, the logic of dependency declines. By the same token, industrial efficiency is impaired if senior supervisors devote excessive time to personal problems of individual workers. The productivity of the organization as a whole increases as this function is channeled into the specialized hands of the personnel manager.

So it appears that given the commitment of virtually all societies to advancement of the status of workers and greater industrial output, the role of the personnel manager will at some point be a functionally effective deviation. The question then becomes not "yes" or "no" but "when" and "how." That is to say, the MNC must judge in each host society where paternalism is still the norm just how strong the bases for the norm are and how ready the workers may be for the deviant pattern. Then it must determine what pattern of deviant structure may be feasible, typically following a pattern substantially modified from its home-country norm. For example, a small start may be made by having the personnel manager sit with the senior manager in listening to the workers' problems and gradually take an increasing role in dealing with them until the workers begin to look to him rather than the senior manager as the natural person to go to with problems. Note that the innovation in this case is functionally effective but still reasonably consistent with the underlying attitudes fostering paternalism. No attempt has been made to alter the degree of dependence among the workers. This may change in time. But for the moment the objective of production efficiency is achieved by redirecting the dependency.

## Supermarkets in Less Developed Countries

In 1965 International Basic Economy Corporation opened a super-market in Venezuela, the first of its kind in Latin America. Since then supermarkets have appeared throughout Latin America and in many other less developed regions. To a degree these stores represent a transfer of retailing methods from the United States, but in consid-erable part they are new institutions that have evolved out of the changing characteristics of their host societies. For centuries food marketing in less developed countries was dominated by the charac-teristics of two groups: the impoverished masses who purchased the bulk of the food with primary emphasis on essentials and low prices and the affluent upper class which consumed many types of food with little concern for prices. The needs of these groups were served effectively by small merchants operating out of little stores or more commonly in large open markets with low overhead and minimal labor costs. The lower classes haggled directly with the merchants for their simple needs, and the upper classes sent their servants to shop around among the tradesmen. The small middle class fitted itself into this picture uncomfortably but adequately. The middle-class house-wife might be able to afford a servant to do her shopping but often as not she would go out herself to find the best bargains in the open market, accepting the noise and dirt as part of life.

The notable change in recent years to which the supermarket is geared has been the rapid growth of the middle class along with the availability of greater variety of foods. However, the story is not simply one of the transfer of a marketing institution developed in middle-class United States to fill comparable middle-class needs else-where. The logics of the institution are different.

A crucial element in the success of the supermarket in the United States was the rising cost of labor. The convenience of a large store with a broad product selection and a parking lot has been a factor in its success, but these features could have been provided by another type of store. The unique contribution of the supermarket, especially during its formative period in the Depression of the 1930s was the efficiency achieved by combining large volume and self-service with consequent low unit labor costs and prices appreciably lower than in smaller, clerk-served stores.

But the rising cost of labor is not a major factor in the less devel-oped countries. Labor there is still cheap, and because of their high investment and overhead costs, the prices in supermarkets are gener-ally higher than those of small merchants, especially for fresh foods. Although a simplistic analysis of the evolution of the host societies might have projected the feasibility of introducing a middle-class U.S. retailing institution from the emergence of the middle class, that analysis per se would have been incorrect.

The supermarket is succeeding as an effective deviant from the traditional norm for other reasons centering around convenience and sanitation. The middle-class housewife in the less developed countries is hard pressed for both time and money. In a status-conscious society she is trying hard to stretch the income her husband earns as an engineer or bureaucrat or teacher. So economy is important to her, but that does not mean buying at the place with the lowest price. She may have a servant who can do her shopping, but servants are becoming more expensive as industrialization raises wages; so it costs money to send a maid on a tour of small merchants, and the net cost of buying everything from the supermarket may be less. More commonly, however, the housewife will do much of the shopping herself because choices among the variety of foods available today cannot be delegated to the caliber of maid she can hire. For her the time factor, plus the nuisance of going from merchant to merchant, is a strong incentive favoring one-stop shopping at the supermarket.

Sanitation provides a decisive push. Modernity and Western standards have become prime cultural values among the new middle class. They want very much to live the life of the housewife of the advanced countries as they see it in magazines and the movies. A prominent aspect of that way of life is cleanliness. So the housewife is increasingly repelled by the dirt and shabbiness of the old stores and street markets and is attracted to the bright, clean supermarkets.

One more feature should be noted to underscore the fact that these supermarkets are not carbon copies of U.S. counterparts. In some less developed countries the stores provide boys to push carts around for shoppers and even to put things in the carts for them. This clearly is a product of status values in societies where manual labor is considered beneath the dignity of people of reasonable social standing. It inevitably adds to the cost of the food, so we can readily conclude that economy beyond a certain point is less important to these people than social status.

### The Canton Drug Company

The Canton Drug Company had set up a joint venture in Zardin, a Middle Eastern country, with a local businessman, Abdul Baba, and an associate of his, Ali Tabrizi.[3] This move was precipitated by a Zardinian government decree requiring that certain drug products be manufactured in the country. Canton had built a good business in

Zardin, relying on imports from the United States sold by a distribution company owned by Baba. The joint venture, Wadi Drug Company, was started with $280,000 capital of which Canton supplied $120,000, Baba $120,000 and Tabrizi $40,000. Baba was generally considered an able man both in business circles and in politics. He was a member of parliament in the majority party and was recognized as a potential prime minister. Tabrizi was also in parliament in the same party and was employed as an attorney by many local and foreign firms. The chief spokesman for Canton was Thomas Phillips, the Middle Eastern manager, who made his headquarters in Zardin.

The venture proceeded well at the outset. Although several companies sought manufacturing licenses, Wadi quickly received full approval for its plans. Two other firms obtained licenses a little later. One of these was entirely owned by a U.S. company and one was a joint effort of European and Zardinian capital. As only a few drugs were to be manufactured, all firms continued to import most of their requirements. An old warehouse was purchased by Wadi and fitted out with obsolete equipment from the U.S. parent, which was quite adequate for the simple mixing, tablet-making, and bottling to be undertaken.

Wadi earned a profit of $110,000 in the first year of operation and the board of directors voted a dividend of the full amount. Phillips expressed some doubts at this action, but as there was no immediate need for funds he did not feel he had a basis for arguing his point. During the next year the company continued to do well and an interim dividend of $140,000 was proposed in August. Phillips again objected, feeling some profits should be retained; but as there was still no clear need for funds, he felt unable to press his view, and the dividend was approved. At the end of the year the accounts showed $72,000 of undistributed profits, and Baba proposed that it be paid out in dividends.

Phillips felt at this point that there was good reason for retaining profits, and he found that the local auditor, Iktisat, agreed. Iktisat prepared a statement pointing out that the old equipment in the plant was rapidly wearing out. Even though 20 percent depreciation was being taken each year, the reserves would not be adequate because inflation in Zardin was running about 20 percent per year. Thus it would be wise to retain the balance of the profits as a reserve for renewing the equipment. Subsequently, Phillips advised Baba that Iktisat concurred in his views and that he was now unequivocally opposed to a further dividend.

The following day Baba proposed a limited dividend of $30,000. He produced a statement written, he said, by Iktisat, suggesting such a dividend. Baba was not aware of the statement Iktisat had already given Phillips. Phillips immediately went to Iktisat and asked what had happened. Iktisat said he had given Baba the same opinion he had given Phillips. But Baba had then asked what procedure would be followed if a limited dividend were voted, and the paper was Iktisat's response to that hypothetical question.

Iktisat and Phillips then went to Baba and asked him to explain his position. Baba asserted that Phillips had misunderstood him and that he had said, "If! If Wadi were to declare a dividend, Mr. Iktisat suggested one of $30,000." There was no further discussion of a dividend.

Early in the following year, plans for a new factory evolved. The government was pressing for production of more drugs. The other two firms were planning new factories whose modern, clean appearance would give them a competitive lift. A team of Canton technical experts advised that new equipment would cut costs. Plans were made for a new plant capable of producing 25 percent more output at 20 percent lower labor costs per unit of output. The plant would cost $1,000,000 of which $100,000 would be recovered from sale of the existing facilities.

There was some reluctance among the Zardinian members of the board over this major investment, but on the whole they accepted it as sound. There was substantial disagreement over the method of financing. Baba proposed that the bulk of the money be raised by issuing new stock which he felt could be sold at a premium of 400 percent; i.e., whereas the founders had paid $40 per share, the new issue would be sold at $200 per share. He felt he could sell the shares to the oil-rich emirs and sheiks of the Persian Gulf. To attract these buyers, he proposed that an interim dividend of 50 percent of the original capital be issued.

But Phillips believed Wadi should retain its full earnings, then estimated at about $200,000, for use in the new investment. He felt that investors would look more to the company's earnings than to its dividends and that a large dividend might actually discourage them. He also felt that a much smaller premium in the stock price was all that could be expected.

This case involves some interesting operational questions, but its relevance in the context of this chapter lies in the interaction of American ways with two aspects of the host society: the political-business system and interpersonal relations.

Analysis of the political-business system suggests that a significant change may be imminent in which the U.S. company may play a constructive role. Figure 3−5 shows the main elements of the estab-

**Figure 3–5.**  Zardinian Political-Business System *(Canton Drug Company Case)*

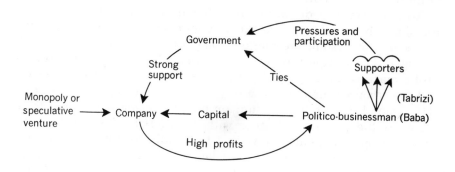

Established system

Emerging deviant system

lished system and of the new one that may be emerging. The norm shown at the top is dominated by politico-businessmen like Baba. They provide the initiative and capital for business ventures. The success of the ventures stems in large part from the influence of these men in government circles, which results in various forms of support for their enterprises. With this support the ventures are able to generate substantial profits which are fed through the political system to assure the continuation of support.

In its initial stages the Wadi Drug Company fitted this pattern. Baba demonstrated his influence in getting the production license promptly to the exclusion of most competitors. The company made a handsome profit of about 80 percent on initial capital in its first full year, suggesting that prices and other factors were adjusted very favorably. And virtually all earnings were being drained off into the supporting system immediately. This pattern has clearly been effective and must, therefore, be regarded as functional and a satisfactory norm for the moment.

Now, however, a deviation from this norm is taking shape along the lines shown at the bottom of Figure 3–5. The dominant elements of this system are market competition and the professional manager. The competition does two things. First, it greatly reduces profit margins, destroying the incentives for the politician–investor and the resources he could use to obtain support in government circles. Second, it puts a premium on efficient management and thus enhances the position of those with managerial skills. Analysis of projected operating data shows that the Wadi profit would be about 20 percent of capital in light of the large investment for the new factory required to meet the competition of the other firms. Baba being a pretty shrewd man, it is a fair guess that he has figured out these results. Thus his scheme to pay out a large dividend and obtain the capital from new investors looks like a move to withdraw the maximum possible money and extract himself as far as possible from a situation which is no longer suited to his *modus operandi*. On the other hand, Phillips is responding to the situation in a manner consistent with the logic of the emerging system, moving essentially in the direction of U.S. business norms.

One can expand in detail along these lines but our immediate purpose has been served by observing the basic contrasts of these two systems. The first has been the norm throughout most of the Middle East over the recent past. It is functional in a society at a low stage of industrial development dominated by the merchant's speculative psychology and unstable politics. With increasing industrialization and the development of more stable, responsible government, one can see functional utility in the second system, and the Wadi case clearly demonstrates that it is emerging.

Without a broad study of the Zardinian situation, it is, of course, impossible to determine the degree to which each of these systems prevails. It is a fair guess that the first is still the norm and that the second is as yet just a significant deviant. If this is so, then Canton has a difficult problem in deciding how to handle the conformity-innovation issue. Over the long term, innovation seems in order so as to participate fully in the achievements of those who work with the emerging system. That is, the company should be adjusting the operations of Wadi so that it has managerial effectiveness to meet the new competition aggressively. One may speculate, for example, that it would be harmful to this objective to bring into the structure people greedy for profit and unsophisticated in management. On the other hand, over the short run, if the politico-businessman system remains the norm, the support of men like Baba can be of great value. So the optimum strategy for the company would seem to be some plan that will provide Baba with a continuing flow of good profits but that will leave Canton relatively free to control the operations of Wadi.

The question of interpersonal relations is not so complex, but it does provide a striking case of cultural difference and the hazards an American faces when trying to deal with a foreigner by American ways. Baba is a product of merchant society, a system of relatively small enterprises each of which deals with others on an arm's-length basis; discontinuity is possible at any time with no great loss of effectiveness. In such a society the merchant is a lone wolf, keeping most of his thoughts to himself, bargaining and maneuvering in relations with others according to what seems best for his immediate purposes. Phillips, on the other hand, is a product of the U.S. big-company, industrial society in which the manager has wide-ranging contacts both within his company and outside it based on continuity and mutual trust. He has been conditioned to put a high value on teamwork, the exchange of information, and the generation of trust in others.

The contrast appears clearly in the exchange centering around Iktisat. Baba, it appears, was doing some tricky maneuvering to get his own way about the dividend. By his standards the obvious deceit was subject to criticism only to the extent that it failed. It seems that Phillips has adjusted his ways to conform to the norms of Baba's society. At least, the fact that he did not immediately disclose to Baba that he had the written statement from Iktisat suggests that. But one wonders if he is really doing an effective job of conforming or whether he is somehow trying to innovate by putting pressure on Baba. Because of Baba's importance in Canton's operations, it scarcely seemed useful to confront him with the statement at a point that would surely embarrass him.

This story illustrates the conformity-innovation problem at the personal level. As the overall norms change from the political-business system to the managerial system, the norms of personal attitudes and behavior in business will also change. The role of external businessmen like Phillips is likely overall to be positive: by example, by teaching, and so forth. But it will vary from case to case. Sometimes it will be quite effective, for example, when the foreigner works with a young, flexible management recruit. But it may be unproductive or even counterproductive if the local national is incapable of change. This is probably true in the relations between

Phillips and Baba; if Phillips is in fact trying to change Baba's ways of thinking and acting by his own combination of U.S. and Middle Eastern behavior patterns, he is probably wasting his time.

## SUMMARY

These four situations have only been sketched in broad outline. The reader may wish to fill out in greater detail the business activities involved and the environmental factors affecting them. The sketched outlines, however, are sufficient to validate the conceptual framework proposed in this chapter. In each situation we have seen that the norms of business were tied in with the prevailing structure of economic and personal relationships, but that deviants from these were feasible if they were functionally effective. Their effectiveness stemmed essentially from changes in the host society for which the old norms were no longer a fully satisfactory response.

All these confirm the basic conceptual guidelines developed in the chapter. The roles of the multinational corporation as a transmitter of resources and as a cross-cultural change agent inherently favor efforts toward innovation in the host society. The critical limiting factor in determination of strategy is the feasibility of accomplishing innovations. In this determination the main criterion is the usefulness of the innovation in the evolving pattern of the host society. A strategy of introduction of functionally effective innovations should be successful. For aspects of operations in which innovation appears dysfunctional, conformity is a sound strategy to maximize the acceptability of the firm in the host systems. These concepts are broadly sufficient with respect to the internal structure of the host society.

### NOTES

1. Illustrations of these variations in values with respect to honesty and their effect on MNCs are found in John Fayerweather and Ashok Kapoor, *Strategy and Negotiation for the International Corporation*, (Cambridge, Mass.: Ballinger Publishing Company, 1976). For the Gulf Oil Corporation case see pp. 369–398. This case involved political payments to the government of Korea. For the General Foods Corporation (A) case see pp. 241–270. Here the Italian subsidiary was posed with problems stemming from the traditional double-book, tax-avoidance system.

2. The reader who wishes to supplement this brief review of the elements of societies and their interrelation may consult several sources. The basic systems of economic and personal relationship are drawn from fundamental economics and sociology which are described in many books, e.g., Paul A. Samuelson, *Econom-*

*ics* (New York: McGraw-Hill, 1967) and Paul B. Horton and Chester L. Hunt, *Sociology* (New York: McGraw-Hill, 1964). The variations among these in different countries are best pursued in the small but growing literature of comparative business including J. Boddewyn, *Comparative Management and Marketing* (Chicago: Scott, Foresman, 1968) and R.N. Farmer and B.M. Richman, *Comparative Management and Economic Progress* (Homewood, Ill.: Richard D. Irwin, 1965).

3. This case is summarized from a fuller version in Fayerweather and Kapoor, op. cit., pp. 271–276.

✳  *Chapter 4*


# The Nation State and the
# Multinational Corporation[a]


Economic calculations must be the central determinants of
MNC strategy. However, nationalism, national interests,
national governments, and other elements associated with
the nation state are powerful influences. They interact directly with
MNC activities at almost every turn and affect in many ways the economic environment to which the MNC must relate. In broad terms,
there is an institutional conflict with a vying for power between nations and MNCs. The nations seek to manage geographic segments of
society as total units while the MNCs seek global control over industrial segments.

Thus the nation state is a central feature of practically every aspect of strategy formulation. This chapter will lay the groundwork
for considering its influence on specific elements of strategy by out-
lining the main attributes of the nation state with which MNCs interact and identifying the key dimensions of the interactions. The
greater part of this analysis is devoted to MNC interactions with host
nations because they pose the more significant strategy problems.
The same analytical framework, however, is pertinent to parent nation relations which will be considered at the end of the chapter. The
next chapter will carry the analysis on to the strategy stage discussing
how the more significant aspects of nation state–MNC relations may
be handled.

[a]The first part of this chapter is essentially quoted from John Fayerweather,
"A Conceptual Scheme of the Interaction of the Multinational Firm and Nationalism," *Journal of Business Administration* (University of British Columbia), Fall
1975, pp. 67–89. Reproduced by permission.

A few words need to be defined at the outset to avoid confusion in this discussion. A *nation state* is a self-governing, independent political unit. The term nation will generally be used interchangeably with nation state here though by exact definitions the two concepts differ. A *nation* is properly understood to be a people willing and capable of essentially governing their own affairs, those affairs being substantially self-contained. Some nation states do not fully meet those criteria; in a few cases their inability to govern their own affairs has been demonstrated by breakdowns as when Pakistan fell apart and Bangladesh split off as a separate nation state. Even in advanced nation states such splits may occur, as in Scotland and Quebec, both of which are classed as nations by many even though they are part of larger nation states. The term *national system* will be used frequently to describe the main components of the nation state which interact to make it a functional organization.

Among the attributes of the nation a distinction will be made between national interests and nationalism. *National interests* are considered to be the tangible goals of the nation including physical security, economic needs, and the like. *Nationalism* is limited to the emotional relationship of people to their nation. This usage must be distinguished from the broader applications often found in popular literature, for example, economic nationalism which is usually used to describe concrete manifestations of the attitudes of nationalism married to national interests in such actions as economic protectionism. In this book nationalism will be used only to describe the ways people feel about aspects of their nation though, of course, those feelings are substantially influenced by concrete experience and goals.

## THE NATION STATE

The main components of the nation essential to the MNC interaction analysis are shown schematically in Figure 4–1: goals, culture including national ideology, political system, and relation of individual nationals to the system.

### Goals

Fundamentally, the nation exists to fulfill the goals of its members. The goals are of three types: (1) *organic*, relating to the system unto itself; (2) *functional*, relating to specific achievements the group seeks for the benefit of its members; and (3) *implementing*, relating to the capacity of the group to achieve goals.

(1) The *organic* goal of a national group is self-rule, the ability of the people to make their own decisions and direct their own affairs,

**Figure 4—1.** Components of the Nation State System

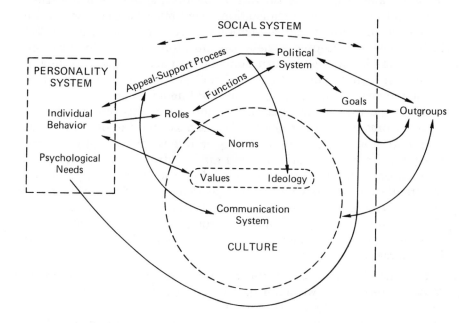

in effect to constitute themselves as a viable organization. In the words of Hans Kohn, the pioneer scholar of modern nationalism, "Every people awakened to nationalism sees political self-determination as its goal."[1] This organic goal is sufficiently straightforward that it need not be elaborated on at length. However, the brevity of treatment should not detract from its very great importance, for the attitudes it engenders are among the most powerful sources of the strength of nationalism. Thus, it is central to MNC interactions and in the subsequent analysis it will appear frequently in various ways.

(2) *Functional* goals compose the broad range of needs and desires which people seek to achieve through their national system. Common to all of them is the presumption that a major role for the nation in their achievement will be effective as compared to greater reliance upon subnational or supranational systems. The functional goals pertinent to MNC relations which people seek through their national organizational system are subsumed under four headings: general governance, welfare gains in external relations, internal development, and psychological well being.

(a) The *general governance* goal is the functional counterpart of the organic goal of self-determination. While people as a group may seek independence as a separate body, they also require the ordering of the affairs of their life through a governing system. For the effective functioning of any organization, there must be a system for the resolution of conflicts and allocation of resources. The nation, as the highest level of accepted societal organization, provides in our civilization the ultimate vehicle for human governance. Thus according to Silvert, the central concept of "nationalism is acceptance of the state as the impersonal and ultimate arbiter of human affairs."[2]

The logic that determines the assignment of this function to the national organization is rooted in Deutsch's definition of a society as "a group of individuals connected by an intense division of labor and separated from other societies by a marked drop in this intensity."[3] The nation in these terms may be seen as a social grouping in which differentiation of roles and interdependency (the division of labor) are so advanced yet self-contained that a substantial degree of effectiveness and efficiency is achieved through its functioning as a single unit, as compared to being divided into smaller units or incorporated into a larger entity.

(b) The goal of fostering the welfare of the national group in *external relations* has two main facets: physical security and maximizing economic benefits. A large portion of nations have at some time engaged in wars of liberation or defense against foreign powers. Thus the concept of the nation as a vehicle for achieving physical security is firmly implanted in the attitudes of the citizenry.

The role of the nation as an economic optimizing unit vis-à-vis the rest of the world also has a long tradition and is confirmed through continuing, day-to-day experience. The mercantilist concept of national benefit through trade imbalance and Adam Smith's *Wealth of Nations* are conspicuous examples to illustrate the focus on the nation as an economic optimizing unit even in earlier years. This tradition carries down clearly to the present in such matters as the preoccupation of less developed countries with their trade and investment relations with advanced nations and the employment-oriented protectionism of the United States and other industrialized countries.

The national approach to external relations issues is supported by practical logics of defense and economics. In addition it is reinforced by the tendency toward xenophobic feeling about external groups which will be discussed more fully later. The value of the national organization is magnified by the image of outsiders as aggressively threatening and economically predatory.

(c) While a multitude of organizations are concerned with the *internal development* goals of societies, the national system typically is viewed as a major vehicle. In some cases the goals are of such a nature that achieving them through the national organization is the only sound approach. Basic monetary controls are clearly its domain, for example. In many major industrial or infrastructure projects in less developed countries, the national government is the only institution capable of mobilizing and directing sufficient resources. Likewise the achievement of some forms of major scientific research or economic planning in developed countries clearly requires initiative at the national level. But beyond these essentially national roles, in many cases the assignment of internal development goals to national governments rests on the secondary logic of the dominant general capabilities at that level rather than the specific logics for the individual case. Thus, for example, in the United States responsibility for development of many aspects of education and social welfare which were and still could be administratively handled at lower levels, has shifted upward with the growing strength of the national government.

(d) At the *psychological* level the nation serves on a collective basis two important goals for the individual: a group structure and an outlet for certain emotional needs.

An individual as a social animal has a need to relate within some groups and with respect to other groups outside his circle: "in-groups" and "out-groups" or "we-groups" and "they-groups." The psychology of the individual in his or her relation to we- and they-groups is an extensive subject. Suffice it to say that belonging to the we-group provides the individual with a substantial sense of emotional support and security both in social relations within the group and vis-à-vis external theys. The initial we-group was the mating unit. Over time groups of progressively greater size have evolved. The essential determinant of the size of grouping appears to be the dimension of the socioeconomic space to which the individual finds he or she must relate.

Since there are socioeconomic relations between an individual and people throughout the world, a we-group is required that satisfies psychological needs at that level. The world having become structured in national groups, the nation then becomes the vehicle for satisfying the we-group need at the highest level of social structuring. Within it there is the potential for the individual to have the sense of common support with co-nationals in major concerns and the security of knowing that he or she is part of an entity that is at least structurally (if not in size and strength) on a par with the groupings of the "theys" composing the rest of the world. In the modern world, belonging to a national group is one of the most important elements in an individual's sense of social security.

A somewhat related value of the nation is its function as an outlet for certain emotions of the individual. Central to this function is the capacity of the individual to identify, at least to some extent, with the actions and character of the nation, projecting his personality into them. Identification with a major group of this nature provides a special form of emotional outlet for the individual which Lasswell has described as follows: "Nations, classes, tribes and churches have been treated as collective symbols in the name of which the individual may indulge his elementary urges for supreme power, for omniscience, for amorality, for security."[4] Of a somewhat similar nature is the possibility Tajfel has described "to attribute to an out-group the responsibility for unfavorable social changes."[5] The individual identifying with the nation can readily make the theys external to it the scapegoats for its failures and for the larger shortcomings and disappointments of his life.

3. The *implementing* goals of the nation are those that are sought as means of providing the national system with the capability to achieve the organic and functional goals. The element of overriding importance in this respect is the establishment of sufficient power to assure the preservation of self-rule and to advance the functional goals, particularly in relation with external groups. Thus the primary emphasis in the implementing goal is on the status of national units in the global system and the importance to each national group of the strength of its particular unit in this system. Of somewhat lesser importance, though still an essential goal, is the establishment of sufficient internal strength for the national government to permit it to achieve the governance and development goals within the nation.

### Culture

The cultural system of the nation state provides a large portion of its attitudinal content. The dominant cultural characteristics of the people are the main basis for differentiating themselves from other national groups. Propagation and protection of the culture takes on nationalistic importance as its characteristics are identified with the national ideology. The pride and defensiveness of people with respect to their national way of life are similar in nature, if not in full vigor, to their fundamental support of the nation as a self-governing entity.

The close relation of national culture and nationalism can be followed in historical evolution. Some nations have been built with disparate cultural groups, but in the great majority of cases they have evolved out of peoples with a large degree of commonality of cultural characteristics. There is a logical interrelation of a common culture with key characteristics of the nation: goals, group cohesion, and the political system. The probability of agreement on national goals is high among people with a common culture. The similarity of way of life, values, and expectations that contribute to functional goals is greater among people of a single culture; and, on a more basic level, the agreement on the organic goal of self-determination as a group is dependent upon a sense of mutual confidence and basic cohesion in which a common culture is a major factor.

By the same token a common culture greatly facilitates the cohesion of the national group. The role of the national culture for this purpose may be identified in three ways though each is essentially a different facet of social integration. First, as Tajfel has observed, people sharing a common culture benefit from cognitive simplification and economy which have benefits both in saving of time and energy and also in the minimizing of personal tensions and conflicts.[6] Second, communication is more efficient and effective within a cultural group. This element is the central theme of Deutsch's analysis, "Membership in a people essentially consists in wide complementarity of social communication."[7] Third, the similarity among the people who share a culture provides a cognitive logic to the sense of group cohesion and an inherent basis for personal identification with the group as differentiated from other groups. The cultural group is a highly satisfactory we-group with which the individual can readily identify and it provides a clear basis for differentiating external "theys."

The requirements of an effective political system are aided, as Gellner has observed, by the existence of a common culture because the populace will place greater confidence in the elite and follow them more readily if they are looked upon as people of a like nature.[8] The populace in these circumstances can more readily identify with the decision-makers and thus perceive their decisions as emanating truly from the "we" body rather than from the "they's."

These ways in which a common culture relate to national goals, cohesion, and the political system establish readily the logics for the coincidence of cultural and national groups. The requirements of the effective functioning of the national organizational system and the characteristics of the common culture are so useful to each other and so mutually self-supporting that they naturally blend. Thus, the national culture becomes an integral part of the nation and associated with nationalism in the minds of the people.

**National Ideology.** National ideology is technically part of culture, since it is an aspect of the value system. However, it requires separate treatment because of its prominence in nationalism. There are two key aspects: the central concept of the nation in general and the specific elements of the ideology of each nation. There is a parallel here between national and religious ideologies, both in character and in the role they tend to play in people's lives.

As in the case of religion, the general concept of the nation as a primary institution is strongly established among people. The convergence of philosophical, practical, and emotional considerations relating to goals, the political system, culture, and personal involvement results in a strong conviction in modern society that the nation is *the* way, the *essential* way, to organize people. While in the early stages of nation-building it is necessary to argue for the merits of the nation, once nations are well established, acceptance at the ideological level places the status of the system substantially outside the range of argumentation. For a large portion of the population in well established nations and among elites even in immature nations there is no question but that grouping as a nation is the way things should be, and those who argue for reliance on larger or smaller social groupings as the primary political institutions are heretics.

The special ideology of each nation, like particular religions, is the substantive form with which people of the nation fill out the general ideology. Typically the ideology will embody many elements of political system and culture. It often includes concepts of national character or mission like the American "manifest destiny," Nazi "super race" and Jewish "chosen people" images. In sum, the special ideology of each nation composes for the people a central core of attributes about which they have common convictions. As such they provide on-going guidance and a sense of certainty, resulting in an essential degree of momentum and stability for the group.

### The Political System

The political system is the vehicle through which national collective action is mobilized. While many facets of the system affect the MNC, of particular relevance are the attitudes and interactions.

In its role as the prime vehicle for the achievement of national goals, the political system must accomplish the basic functions of any organization, namely decision-making and the implementation of decisions. The decision-making of the elites is most visibly governed by their perception of national goals and the pressures of interest groups upon them. Their personal nationalism enters into the process to the extent that they have feelings about national independence and commitments to the national ideology. Their nationalistic attitudes also have an impact on decision-making resulting from the feedback accompanying the use of nationalism in implementation of authority. This process will be traced through its various stages to indicate its implications.

In his analysis Deutsch has placed the emphasis on the authority element because of his focus on nation-building. "In the age of nationalism, a nationality is a people pressing to acquire a measure of effective control over the behavior of its members. It is a people striving to equip itself with power, with some machinery for compulsion strong enough to make enforcement of its commands sufficiently probable to aid in the spread of habits of voluntary compliance with them."[9] But for the present analysis equal emphasis should be given to the feedback from this process on the way decisions are made by leaders who must relate themselves to the nationalistic attitudes they have propagated if those attitudes are to be effective in fostering continuance of support for their authority.

Amplifying Deutsch's concept one observes nationalism employed in two ways in the communications from the elite to the general populace. Both are necessary to the implementing-authority process. First, there is the long-term, continuing communication designed to preserve and augment the commitment to the national system. This aspect is particularly evident in the socialization process, notably in education where the ideology of the nation and its related components are impressed on young minds.

Second, there is the employment of nationalism in the appeal-support process required for the effective functioning of the political system in specific issues. Despite broad support of the nation by the general population, conformance to a multitude of specific government decisions is required.

In seeking support on these matters the elite rely substantially on appeal to the nationalistic attitudes because of the diversity of the population and its limited capacity to respond to other appeals. Many issues at the national level are too complex for the people as a whole to understand. Many decisions serve the immediate interests of one group at the expense of others. In these circumstances appeals for support based on rational argumentation are of limited value. To a substantial degree the elite must rely on the overall confidence and acceptance of the national political system for support in such matters, or at least for support of the formal laws and the process through which they are implemented, i.e., basic respect for law and order. But, especially in controversial matters of broad concern, the direct employment of nationalistic appeals for support has utility.

The employment of nationalism to build the general respect for national authority and in the appeal-support process on specific matters feeds back on the elite level in the form of constraints on decision-making. The actions of the decision-makers must, at least, to a reasonable degree, conform to the standards of nationalism which they have set forth to the populace. People are to some extent inured to the difference between what politicians say and what they do. But there are limits to their credulity, tolerance, and patience, and there is always an ample supply of opposing politicians ready to take advantage of these limits. Therefore the aspects of nationalism which the decision-makers have employed in appeals to the people become constraints to which they must relate their own actions if the support is to continue. Thus, while in early stages of nation-building one may conceive that nationalism is essentially generated at the elite level and propagated down to the general population, in more sophisticated structures there is a mutual interplay between the elite and the populace in which neither can be readily identified as the controlling factor.

### Individual Involvement

As in any organization, the relation of individuals to the nation is a function of their emotional response to it, the expectations which the system presses upon them, and the practical values for their lives which they perceive in it. Delamater, Katz, and Kelman have labeled these three forms of involvement symbolic, normative, and functional.[10] All three forms are major factors in the functioning of the nation.

The nature of the *symbolic* involvement of the individual in the nation has already been discussed in connection with functional goals earlier in this chapter. Essentially the individual finds psychological satisfaction from the nation both in its character as the highest level of we-group to which he or she is affiliated and because, through identification with it, he or she can find an outlet for certain basic emotions. Both of these elements lead the individual to internalize the national ideology and its associated cultural characteristics.

The *normative* form of involvement describes the conformance of the individual to what the nation requires in response to the pattern of roles and sanctions of the national social system. In its pure form it would presume an individual who does not accept nationalism but who responds to the signals of the surrounding social system. Since that social system is geared to support the operational needs of the national group, its influence on the individual would lead to satisfactory performance despite a lack of internalized conviction as to the merits of the actions.

*Functional* involvement describes the pragmatic relationship of the individual to the nation. For some people, government officials and military personnel for example, functional roles in society are substantially dependent upon the nation. For others, the functional benefits are smaller or more diffuse, for example, government services for small businessmen and tariff protection supporting the jobs of textile workers. Regardless of the specific form of functional benefit, the basic concept lies in the outlook of the individual toward the nation. Again considering the extreme form, the individual's involvement in this case rests entirely upon his or her judgment of the extent to which the nation is providing practical benefits for personal satisfaction.

While it is conceptually useful to separately define these three forms of involvement—symbolic, normative, and functional—in practice all three are generally found in varying proportions in each individual. However, the pilot study conducted by Delamater, Katz, and Kelman did indicate that in many individuals there was a tendency for one of the forms of involvement to be dominant. Of particular interest to the present analysis are two ways in which the groups differ: in their demographic makeup and in their attitudes toward external groups. The main differentiation was between the symbolic and functional groups with the normative tending to fall somewhat between them in these respects. The symbolic group tended to represent the lower end of the social scale, having much less income and education than the other groups, whereas the functional group represented the upper to middle class with substantially greater income and education. As to relations with external groups the symbolic group was more inclined to rely on military strength and disinclined to cooperate with supranational organizations like the United Nations. The functional group, on the other hand, expressed greater willingness to deal with problems with other nations by negotiation and to support a supranational government system.

The demographic differences fit the general pattern outlined in the previous discussion of the political system. The elite group intimately absorbed with the ongoing management of the nation's affairs is more strongly influenced by the functional type of involvement. Those at the lower end of the socioeconomic scale are least absorbed in the management of the nation's affairs and are least able to understand their character. So the symbolic emotional ties reach them most strongly.

## NATION STATE–MNC INTERACTION

The varied aspects of the nation state and multinational corporation result in a complex pattern of interactions which is outlined in Table 4–1. The elements of the nation state which have just been described

**Table 4–1.   Interactions of the Multinational Corporation with the Nation State**

| | As Business Entity | | Socio-Economic Impacts of Resource Transmission Role | | | As Agent of Home Nation |
|---|---|---|---|---|---|---|
| Components of National System | Central Control | Profit Extraction | Economic Inputs | Cultural Change | Global Rationalization | |
| *Goals* | | | | | | |
| Organic (self-determination) | F | | | | U | F |
| Functional | F | | | C | F–U | F |
| *Governance* | | | | | | |
| External relations | | R | R | | | R |
| Internal development | | | C–F | C | C–F | |
| Psychological benefits | R | | | U | U | R |
| Implementing (power) | F | | C–F | U | C–F | F |
| *Culture* | | | | | | |
| Ideology | R | | | U | U | R |
| *Political System* | R | | | | | R |
| *Individual Involvement* | | | | | | |
| Symbolic | R | | | U | | R |
| Normative | | | | F | | |
| Functional | F | | R | | U | F |

F = Frustrating   C = Contributory   R = Reinforcing   U = Undermining are listed at the left. The key attributes of the MNC are indicated in the column heads. The first set, central control and profit extraction, are inherent characteristics of the operations of the firm requiring little explanation. A capacity for the exercise of central control has been identified in Chapter 1 as part of the definition of the MNC. Extraction of profit from host nations is inherent in the MNC as a profit-making institution. The second set, economic inputs, cultural change, and global rationalization, are derived from the three elements of the resource transmission scheme presented in Chapter 1 (Figures 1–1, page 4 and 1–2, page 8). But they have been restated to emphasize their chief impact on the host nation. The economic transaction phase results in economic inputs and costs; the host society interactions initiate changes in the national culture; and the integrating capacities of the MNC work toward global rationalization of operations.

The final heading, home nation agent, is a new element in our analysis. Conceptually the assets which the multinational firm invests abroad are properly classed as owned by and a matter of interest to the home nation. In free enterprise countries such assets are essentially under the management of private firms, and it is assumed that the companies conducting business according to their own benefits will essentially serve the interests of the nation. Thus the MNC while largely autonomous in its business decision-making, is assumed to be utilizing the assets drawn from the home nation for its benefit, in effect serving as agent for the nation in this respect.

This concept of the MNC as an agent of the home nation coincides with the key aspects of the role of the business firm described previously. That is, by exercising control and by extracting profit on its own behalf, the company is doing the same thing in its social role of management of the home society assets placed abroad. The concept of the MNC as agent simply adds to the fact that the interests and weight of the home nation are present in the transactions.

Beyond that, however, the role of the MNC as agent, adds to our conceptualization the broad subject of extension of the control role of the home government into the sovereign realm of the host nation. So long as the MNC acts strictly in an independent private enterprise manner, the subject is only implicit. However, in the pursuit of their interests home nations are capable of, and in certain instances do, inject themselves directly into the relation between MNCs and host nations in two ways. First, home governments may try to support MNCs in conflicts with host nations. Most conspicuous in this respect are interventions on behalf of companies whose property has been expropriated. But, there are more numerous lesser affairs in which governmental officials give aid and to some degree exert pressure to help firms from their nations.

Second, there is a range of ways in which home nations assert controls to achieve their own objectives through the external activities of MNCs. In some cases the actions are confined physically to the home nation so spatially self-determination territory is not infringed. An example is the regulation of export of capital by many countries. Nonetheless in many such cases the domestically exerted controls of the home nation do have substantial impact on the host. Thus control of the flow of capital may have a critical impact on investment in a host society.

More conspicuous are those cases where a government seeks extraterritorial imposition of power. Notable examples are U.S. antitrust and trading-with-the-enemy laws under which actions of an MNC in a host country may be subject to legal action by its home government. While some purists argue for the strict limitation of government actions to their own territorial domain, this is not a sound proposition in light of the assorted extraterritorial interests of nations. In reality therefore conceptual thinking has to be directed at the manner in which extraterritorial application of sovereignty is related to the sovereignty of other nations. In this aspect of its agent role therefore the MNC stands in an uncertain, evolving area of overall intergovernmental relations.

### Analytical Scheme for Interaction Process

In analyzing the interaction process four main types of effects of the MNC on the nation will be considered. The distinction among these will be stated briefly here and will be clarified by the applications in the subsequent analysis.

C. *Contributory.* The MNC acts in such a way that it directly augments or contributes to the goals or achievements of the host nation without negative impact on it.

R. *Reinforcing.* The actions of the MNC stimulate the functioning and processes of the nation or enhance its usefulness so that its value and competence are reinforced.

F. *Frustrating.* Actions of the MNC are contrary to the goals of the nation or impede its immediate functioning in ways to which the nation cannot respond effectively so that it is frustrated.

U. *Undermining.* The effect of the MNC is to reduce the basic logics of the nation so that its functioning is weakened or undermined.

The symbols in Table 4—1 show the apparent effect of each inter-action of the MNC and nation according to this analytical scheme.

## Characteristics as a Business Entity

**Central Control.** The control exercised by the parent organiza-tion of the MNC affects many components of the national system. Most fundamental is its relation to the organic goal of self-determi-nation; other effects are largely corollaries of this aspect. The fact that decisions are made by an entity outside the boundaries of the nation deprives it of some degree of self-determination. Since the objective of self-determination is the central goal of a nation, the na-tion is frustrated in its goal, and the frustration is of critical signifi-cance. It appears explicitly in the weakening of the nation's ability to govern its affairs, notably in the allocation of resources. If signifi-cant investment and other industrial decisions are in the hands of business firms controlled from outside the country, resource alloca-tion is to some degree governed by goals other than those of mem-bers of the nation.

At the level of psychological goals, the effect is classified as rein-forcing because of the impingement upon the self-determination capability of the nation. The satisfactions of social-psychological se-curity within the "we-group" become more important as external threats to the national body increase. The extension of control by the MNC over operations within the nation triggers this sort of reac-tion, resulting in a strengthening of emotional national cohesion.

In the implementing goal of the nation, the effect of the external control exerted by the MNC is again frustrating. The assumption here is that the power of the nation is weakened by the fact that indus-trial decisions are not entirely within its control. There is a loss, for example, in economic bargaining power to the extent that some por-tion of the tactical or strategic options open to the nation are not subject to its own determination.

The effect of the MNC control function on the ideology of the nation is substantially reinforcing. The control function per se, that is, without regard to any benefits it may impart, is a challenge to the concept of the nation as the central societal institution. The interaction in this respect therefore takes on the character of a con-frontation in which the supporters of the nation are reinforced in their ideological stand by the threat of impairment to their institu-tion.

On the political system, the central control exerted by the multi-national firm has an effect similar to that at the psychological goal level. The chief impact is on the role of nationalistic attitudes in the appeal–support process directed by the governing elite toward the populace as a whole. The tangible evidence of impingement by the MNC on the self-determination capabilities of the nation provides the elites with solid evidence to back up their appeals for support along nationalistic lines. That is, it is easier to convince the people that foreign powers are a menace to the nation when one can point to actual decisions made by multinational firms. Thus the control function provides raw material for substantial reinforcement of the propagation and employment of nationalism through the appeal–support process in this aspect of the nation.

So far as individual involvement is concerned, the reinforcement provided for the symbolic form follows the same logics as were noted for the psychological goal aspects. The tendency of the individual to identify emotionally with the national system and the importance of that sort of involvement are enhanced to the extent that the external control function of the MNC is seen as an explicit threat. On the other hand, the functional form of involvement is to a degree frustrated by the external control. This is the operational counterpart of the effects already noted in the organic and functional goals. To the extent that individuals identify with the nation in functional roles, the control exerted by the foreign firms potentially or actually limits their accomplishment. This type of frustration is most explicit for the government bureaucrat whose objectives are impeded by the decisions made by the parent organizations of foreign-owned firms. But it may be perceived more generally by other members of the elite who identify broadly with the total governing system and sense therefore a personal loss of functional achievement and capability in the general loss to the system by virtue of the control in the hands of the parent MNC.

**Profit Extraction.**  The function of the MNC in extracting profit in transactions from its operations in a foreign country appears to affect chiefly the nation's efforts to optimize benefits in external relations. The effect here is classified as reinforcing the system because the interactions with the MNC are consistent with the nation's function and compose an important role requiring that the function be strengthened and performed effectively. In view of the magnitude of international investment and the various types of economic transactions involved (taxes, licensing fees, profit remission, etc.), the importance of this element in the picture is considerable.

The reinforcing impact noted by the functional form of involvement is the operational counterpart of the external relations effect.

A range of government officials and others are involved in negotiations with multinational firms and related activities, which give them a gratifying sense of functional role achievement as part of the national system.

## Socioeconomic Impacts

**Economic Inputs.** The economic transaction phase of the resource transmission role of the MNC has mixed effects on components of the nation because it does two quite distinct things to the host economy. On the one hand, the inputs of resources contribute to national wealth. Since the international economic interchanges are governed to a substantial degree by the efficiencies of comparative advantage, the productivity of the host economy is greater than if it were more self-contained. These effects lead to the contributing notations for the internal development goal and implementing goals, the latter being substantially dependent upon the economic power and strength of the nation.

The reinforcing classification appearing by the external relations goal is derived from the same process. While the economy is generally assumed to benefit from the input of resources, it is desirable for the nation that the cost paid for these benefits be minimized and the pursuit of this end reinforces that function of the nation. The same reinforcing impact appears in the functional individual involvement aspect.

The other side of the coin of the resource transmission process is that it creates a dependency in the national economic system which weakens its actual or perceived capabilities. For example, if research skills must be drawn from the foreign laboratories of MNCs rather than being available from local sources, the capabilities of the nation are different.

The dependency effect is classified as frustrating in three of the components of national goals. In the internal development goal, it is a potential frustrating factor to the extent that the access to the resources is less readily available to the nation. The qualification "potential" is noted because there is no reason to presuppose that access to the foreign resources of the MNC would necessarily be restricted. However, insofar as the point of view and attitudes within the nation are concerned, apprehension about potential limitations due to dependency on foreign sources may be just as important as real restrictions. For the implementing goal the dependency on foreign sources is a limitation inasmuch as it reduces the bargaining power of the host nation. These two elements in combination also cause some frustration of the functional form of involvement.

**Cultural Change.**  The role of the MNC as cross-cultural change agent has varied effects on the nation. In the governance and internal development aspects the impact may generally be considered contributory. The MNC induces changes in technological and management methods which, on balance, appear to make for better performance, primarily in business, but also to a degree affecting all of the host society.

On the other hand, by definition the impact of the MNC in this role is to reduce the cultural identity of the host national society by introducing some degree of commonality with the culture of its parent society. This effect appears in Table 4—1 as an undermining effect on the psychological goals, ideology, the culture, and the symbolic involvement of individuals. In all cases the undermining lies in the reduction of the degree of differentiation of the host culture from other cultures.

The frustrating effect noted beside the normative form of personal involvement is essentially a derived impact following on the assumed reduction in cultural distinctiveness. It follows conceptually from the latter that as the degree of cultural separation between societies is reduced the ability through the normative process of each to elicit conformity to distinctive, nation-directed behavior is lessened.

**Global Rationalization.**  The effect of the global rationalization impact of the MNC on the nation is both mixed and strong. Most prominent is the undermining of the self-determination goal, the ideology, and the general governance function which are the purposive, philosophical, and operational manifestations of the same impact. The heart of this effect lies in the distinction between the orientation of the nation toward optimization at the national level and the global optimization perspective of the MNC. At the functional level, the immediate effect of the global rationalization systems of the MNC is to frustrate the capacity of the nation to allocate resources according to its nation-oriented optimization views. But more fundamentally, if the basic logic of the global approach as leading to a more effective utilization of resources is accepted, then the whole concept of achieving this functional goal through the national governance mechanism is rendered questionable. The logics would argue rather that the members of the nation seeking economic benefit in matters where rationalization at the global level is beneficial are better served by a form of governance that has a global perspective, rather than one restricted to the national level.

The undermining effect on the ideology is simply the philosophical expression of this functional effect. That is, the emotional commitment to the concept of the nation as the supreme and ultimate form of societal organization is weakened by the indications that a supranational approach, at least in certain economic matters, is more beneficial. By the same token, the quest for self-determination through the nation is undermined by a growing awareness that self-determination goals must be increasingly achieved through supranational systems.

Back a step from these elements, but related to them, is the impact at the psychological level. The general undermining of the nation as an institution tends to cut away its value for the individual as a projective device through which to realize satisfactions of power, achievement, and the like. As the nation is perceived to slip in importance in the affairs of mankind vis-à-vis the MNC along with other international institutions, the member of the national group finds it progressively less important in his projective psychology.

The C—F notations in Table 4—1 for the internal development and implementing goals represent extensions of this analysis of the impact of global rationalization. Host countries stand to receive some of the benefits of the efficiency of globally rationalized systems. For example, lower cost is provided by a unified logistic scheme. These benefits will contribute to the internal development and power goals. On the other hand, the dependence on the global system is frustrating to the nation in this respect just as it was in the economic inputs from resource transmission. Briefly stated, the outlook for the nation is contradictory because the global rationalization makes available potential benefits for the national society, but realization of those benefits lies only partially within the domain of the nation.

The notation U by the functional form of personal involvement records the undermining of the elite in their organizational role in this respect. They may achieve material benefit from the global rationalization process. But the direct impact on their functional role, for example as government bureaucrats, is affected by the weakening of the ability to direct resource allocation by nation-oriented thinking.

### Interactions as Agent of the Home Nation

The role of the MNC as an agent of its home nation represents conceptually a direct confrontation with the host nation resulting in a mixture of frustration and reinforcement for the latter. To the extent that this role causes actions of the MNC within the host nation to be determined by the home nations interests, the organic goal of self-determination of the host is frustrated. This frustration appears in the weakened capability of the host nation to accomplish its general governance function. Its power in the implementing goal is also impaired. At the personal level the result is frustration of the functionally involved roles through limitations on their effectiveness in management of the system.

It might be argued that these effects should be classified as undermining rather than frustrating. The thesis would be that they are indicative of the growing interdependence of nations, which progressively weakens the degree to which the nation actually exercises self-determination in its affairs. However, this effect is somewhat different from the institutional undermining effect observed in the global rationalization role of the MNC. In that case, the logic supports the shift of decision-making from the host nation to the MNC because only the latter can take the requisite global perspective. In the home-nation agent case, there is no shift in responsibility for decisions vis-à-vis the home nation or the MNC as its agent. The logics remain nation-oriented and the effect is simply to impose constraints on the decision-making of the host nation. It must be emphasized that the analysis here concerns only the ways in which the home nation affects the control function of the MNC, not the control function itself. The latter has already been dealt with in the section on central control.

The other main effects of the interactions are found in reinforcement of some components of the host nation. At the ideological level, the MNC in the home nation agent role is reinforcing. It affirms the basic context which establishes the institutional role of the nation. It is pursuing the goals of its home national group, participating in and supporting the nation game. The host nationals are therefore reinforced in their perception of the nation as the central institution for social affairs.

From this conclusion it naturally follows that the functional roles of achievement of security and pursuit of national interests in external relations are enhanced because of the perceived utility of the nation as the vehicle for dealing with the agent role of the MNC. The nation-nation interaction is implemented through the activities of a great variety of specific agencies (ministries, embassies, etc.). The concept of the MNC as part of the range of agencies acting on behalf of the home nation fits readily into this picture. The MNC incursions in its home nation agent role in effect have opened up a whole new battlefield in the nation-nation interaction process and the host nationals must direct their attention to developing capabilities adequate to cope with it lest other nations gain the upper hand in this expanding field.

At the psychological level, the perception of the MNC as an agent of the home nation is conceptually a strongly reinforcing element. As compared to the MNC as a business entity, external nations appear as much larger and more menacing "theys" to host nationals. Perceiving the MNC therefore as an adjunct of its home nation inspires substantially greater apprehension in the minds of the hosts. Thus the value of the host nation as a "we-group" providing psychological security for its members is enhanced.

In the political system, this psychological element has a reinforcing effect, just as was true with the control function of the MNC. The government elite may effectively employ the image of the MNC as an agent of a foreign nation to increase the general worries about external threats to the host nation, enhancing thereby their national appeals for support. In the same manner, the symbolic form of involvement is strengthened by this increment to the worries about external problems and the importance of the nation as an institution to cope with them.

## NATIONALISM AND THE MNC

The patterns of interaction between the host nation and the MNC engender a variety of attitudes among host nationals. Because attitudes play a prominent part in MNC relations, it is useful to carry the analysis a step further by systematically defining the resulting attitudes. Two general types of effects on nationalistic attitudes may be discerned. First there are the immediate reactions of people to their perception of the MNC, its actions, policies, and basic character. Second, there are the longer term effects of the MNC on the nation which bear on the evolution of nationalistic attitudes. The former may be viewed as reactions within an existing pattern of attitudes, while the latter affect the basic nature of those attitudes.

The reactions are classified as either *favorable* or *unfavorable*. Favorable reactions are presumed to be present when the MNC is perceived to be contributing to the nation. The negative responses fall under two headings—*antagonistic* and *protective*. The distinction here is determined by whether the MNC acts in a manner consistent with the nature of the nation or contrary to it. The antagonistic reaction is the result of interactions in which the MNC is cast as an external "they" against which the nation acts as an advocate of its group's interests. In these circumstances the attitudinal reaction is to perceive the MNC as an antagonist or adversary in a game whose main moves and rules are established and not under question.

The protective reaction is that evoked when the MNC is perceived to be playing the game by a different set of rules and the effectiveness of the nation is impaired. In these circumstances, the attitudinal reaction is protective of the system itself, viewing the MNC, not just as an antagonist in a viable, continuing game, but as one who may impair or destroy the ability of the nation to continue in the game.

The longer term effects on the nationalistic attitudes are classified as *strengthening* or *weakening*. Strengthening results from interaction in which the underlying impact is to confirm the value of the nation and thus to augment the basis for attitudinal reliance on it and support for it. A weakening effect is assumed to occur when the MNC decreases the usefulness of the nation, or impairs its capabilities, in such a way that its members will regard it as less effective for their goals or less worthy of their respect.

The direct responses and long-term effects noted in Table 4–2 fall into a pattern in line with the classification of results of the interaction of the MNC on the nation in Table 4–1.

*Contributory* impacts of the MNC on the nation are perceived favorably because of their immediate benefits to members of the nation. The long-term effects could theoretically be either to weaken or strengthen the bases for nationalism. In fact, however, the significant results observed in this analysis all move in the direction of weakening reliance on the nation. The contributions of the economic inputs of resources and global rationalization to the economic strength of the nation diminish the significance of the nation as the primary economic optimizing unit, enhancing internationalization as an alternative. The dependence of the power gained by the nation through the internationalization process has the same effect. The contributions to internal governance provided by inputs of managerial methods in the cultural change agent role are achieved at the expense of diminishing cultural distinctiveness, weakening somewhat that component of nationalism.

The *reinforcing* effects of the MNC on the nation result in *antagonistic* reactions and a tendency to *strengthen* nationalistic attitudes over the long term. The MNC is perceived as an antagonist in such functions as profit extraction and as an agent of the home nation. The reaction may relate to the material conflict over national interest benefits as in the external relations function or the psychological foil provided by the MNC itself or in the identified image with its home government. This form of interaction has the greatest strengthening effect because it affirms the usefulness of the nation as the means by which its members relate to and deal with the external adversaries.

The *frustrating* effects arouse protective reactions and somewhat strengthen the underlying attitude patterns. Of the several interactions falling in this classification, that of the control function of the MNC with the organic goal of self-determination, is illustrative and perhaps most significant. The protective reactions of host nations are readily apparent in efforts to limit the control capabilities of the MNC by requiring local ownership and putting constraints on operating freedom.

It might appear that the long-term impact of the control exercised by the MNC should be classified as weakening because the actual degree of self-determination of the host nation is diminished. But the classification here concerns the attitudes toward the nation as a vehicle for self-determination, not the practical results. The attitudinal result is governed by the fact that the MNC, in depriving the host national of a degree of self-determination, enhances the importance of protecting himself from further loss and thus strengthens his convictions as to the value of the nation.

The *undermining* interactions also inspire a protective reaction but their long-term effect is to weaken the bases for nationalism. The protective reaction results from the instinct of the system to resist structural change, especially when induced by external sources. The immediate response is essentially the same as that when the nation is frustrated, the system being unable to function according to its established pattern and not discerning whether the disability is due to immediate difficulties or long-term changes in its effectiveness. But the undermining interactions are distinguished from the frustrating ones by their basic weakening effect. The key elements here are the increasing practical value of global rationalization for the economic benefit of members of the nation and the diminishing cultural distinctiveness induced by the change agent role. Both functions result in a movement toward a structuring of society in which the nation is a less useful or relevant institution so the ideology and related attitudes of nationalism are weakened.

To summarize the effects of the nation—MNC interaction on nationalistic attitudes are classified as follows:

| *Effect of MNC interaction on nation* | *Direct reaction by attitude patterns* | *Long-term effect on attitude patterns* |
|---|---|---|
| Contributing | Favorable | Weakening |
| Reinforcing | Antagonistic | Strengthening |
| Frustrating | Protective | Strengthening |
| Undermining | Protective | Weakening |

Table 4-2. Interactions of the Multinational Corporation with Nationalism

| Components of National System | As Business Entity | | Socio-Economic Impacts of Resource Transmission Role | | | As Agent of Home Nation |
|---|---|---|---|---|---|---|
| | Central Control | Profit Extraction | Economic Inputs | Cultural Change | Global Rationalization | |
| **Goals** | | | | | | |
| Organic (self-determination) | Prot S | | | | Prot W | Prot S |
| Functional Governance | Prot S | | | Fav W | Prot S & W | Prot S |
| External relations | | Antag S | Antag S | | | Antag S |
| Internal development | | | Fav & Prot W S | Fav W | Fav & Prot W S | |
| Psychological benefits | Antag S | | | Prot W | Prot W | Antag S |
| Implementing (power) | Prot S | | Fav & Prot W S | | Fav & Prot W S | Prot S |
| **Culture** | | | | Prot W | | |
| Ideology | Antag S | | | Prot W | Prot W | Antag S |
| **Political System** | Antag S | | | | | Antag S |

*Individual Involvement*

| | | | |
|---|---|---|---|
| Symbolic | Antag S | Prot W | Antag S |
| Normative | | Prot S | Prot S |
| Functional | Prot S | Antag S | Prot W | Prot S |

Fav = Favorable   Antag = Antagonistic   Prot = Protective
S = Strengthening   W = Weakening

These effects are shown in Table 4−2 for the various types of interaction outlined in Table 4−1. It must be noted that the chart substantially oversimplifies the interaction process. Only the most significant effects are shown, lesser and in some cases contradictory effects not being included.

## THE HOME NATION−MNC INTERACTION

The interaction of the MNC with its home nation differs notably from that with host nations because it largely lacks the external, "they," adversary characteristics. The MNC is generically rooted in the home nation so there is a high degree of coincidence of its interests with the home national interests, and attitudinally home nationalism is not fundamentally antagonistic to it even though on occasion it may arouse various adverse feelings. The matrix shown in Table 4−1 may be used for this analysis as the components involved in the interaction are similar. However, the implications and importance of the components differ from the host nation case.

The "central control" element lacks the fundamental force present in the host national interaction because the core of control lies within the home nation. Thus for the most part MNC decision-making is perceived as a part of the integral national system. Within that system, various participants (e.g., labor and consumers) may express concern about public control over private corporations but the basic issues are internal, not international.

However, there is some degree of *control* problem involved. As previously noted, the MNC resources are properly to be considered home national resources which the MNC manages for the benefit of the nation under the concepts of the private enterprise system. As long as the firm functions entirely within the nation, the public may assert its own interest directly through the established governance system, e.g., to regulate labor practices or to influence the investment process by tax measures. However, when the MNC's resources are substantially employed abroad, the ability of the home nation to exercise control is greatly reduced. The limits are amply demonstrated by the problems encountered in those cases where the home nation does try to reach out to influence MNC activities in what it perceives as vital areas of national interest like military security. The U.S. government has applied the trading-with-the-enemy legislation in a few cases against actions by MNC subsidiaries abroad but with very limited success and at a high cost of adverse foreign reaction.[11] Thus, while the central and major decisions of the MNC are essentially subject to home nation control, there are a multitude of lesser decisions made outside that control, which cumulatively may have important effects for home national interests. Thus, to a lesser but still important extent, the pattern of frustrating and reinforcing effects noted in Table 4−1 applies in the home nation interactions.

*Profit extraction* composes a similar mirror image situation. The fact that in the main the flow is into the home nation makes the process essentially a favorable rather than antagonistic element in the interaction. However, a source of tension is present in the disposition of the profit, which was notably evident in the period of great controversy over "tax havens" in the late 1950s and early 1960s. U.S. MNCs were accumulating large amounts of profit from foreign operations in holding companies in low-tax countries like Switzerland and Panama for reinvestment abroad. Under prevailing U.S. laws overseas earnings of subsidiaries were not taxed until they were actually received in the form of dividends by the parent firm. Thus the MNCs could recycle profits through tax haven companies for new investments indefinitely without payment of U.S. taxes.

The tax haven issue was widely debated in terms of legal principles, practical business requirements, and economies with a fair amount of political byplay.[12] Suffice for our purposes to observe that a critical element was the feeling in Washington that the United States was not getting an adequate return from the U.S. capital employed overseas, that the multinational firms as its agents were keeping too much to themselves, and that the public was entitled to a greater share of the benefits. This view eventually prevailed in Congress, and the 1962 Revenue Act extended U.S. taxation to cover certain types of overseas retained earnings including those of the tax-haven companies.

This story is sufficient to demonstrate that, in modified form, the "reinforcing" effect of the interaction pertains to the home nation case because the home government must assert the national interest in relations with the MNC to assure that its members share adequately in the profit generated by the national assets used abroad by the MNC.

The *resource transmission, economic input* interactions are quite similar to those in the host nation case. We are dealing here with commercial processes in which the MNC is an implementing agent. Its bias is toward home nation interests but still it is operationally required to balance interests to accomplish transactions. The home nation, like the host nation, is bound to be ceaselessly concerned and press for its own interests and will always be dissatisfied with the balanced outcomes achieved by MNCs. The most difficult issues of MNC−host nation relations fall in this general category. Prominent among them are the charges of "exporting jobs" and "giving away technology" that are strongly pressed by labor in the United States and other home nations. The essence of the charges is that home-nation capital and skill resources which should be used for domestic production and exports have been sent abroad to the benefit of foreign economies and to the disadvantage of home-nation labor resources. The merits of this issue will be discussed later; suffice at this point to identify in it the reinforcement for the role of the nation in protecting the interests of its members along with the mixture of contributing and frustrating effects of the resource transmission process on the economy and power status of the nation.

The *cultural change* effect is theoretically present in home nation interaction with the MNC but it would not appear significant. Its importance rests on the extent to which MNC contact with foreign societies results in feedback to the home culture. We can speculate on some interesting possibilities here. One which has received some research attention is the effect of growing foreign exposure on management methods of Japanese MNCs. In general the Japanese have been less successful than Americans in getting local nationals to adapt to their distinctive managerial system. In the later 1970s they were still largely meeting this problem by heavy use of their own nationals abroad. However, the possibility exists that as more local nationals are used their points of view may result in modifications of the Japanese style which could work up through the system to the parent organization. This influence might then reinforce the impact that non–Japanese MNCs have had directly within Japan. However, the degree of feedback impact in this and other cases is not likely to be great and cannot be considered therefore a significant interaction element.

*Global rationalization*, like economic inputs of resource transmission, is just as significant in the home nation interaction as in host nation relations. Despite the economic benefits of global integration, the increasing interdependence of economies undermines the concept of self-contained economy, power, and governance which are as fundamental for the home as for the host nation. Globally unified systems, whether they be oriented toward natural resources as in petroleum operations or skills, labor-cost and marketing as in electronics and sewing machines are vivid evidence of the shortcomings of the national system for organizing society. That is, the home government's structural weaknesses have often been shown to be greater than those of the host governments, e.g., the OPEC oil embargo and price increases.

The final heading in Table 4–1 needs to be changed so that the home nation interaction reads "Obligations to host nation." Although to a large degree the MNC is an agent of its home nation, the legal and public relationships of the firm in host nations require that it conform to a high degree to the host's national interests. From the perspective of the home nation wishing the MNC to employ its capabilities according to home nation interests, therefore, the MNC appears to be substantially under the power of host governments, not its own. With this reversal of perspective, the pattern of interactions is essentially the same as in the host nation relationship, even though the magnitude of the problems and feelings is less.

## MAJOR ISSUES OF MNC–NATION STATE INTERACTION

To give greater focus to the MNC–nation state interactions outlined in the preceding pages, this chapter will conclude by identifying those aspects of the interaction which are most critical for MNC strategy. The conspicuous character of MNC–nation state tensions has resulted in a flood of literature on the subject including many solid research studies. The results of a handful of these will be summarized here to provide a factual picture of the major issues present in MNC–nation state interactions. A number of other sources are listed in the notes.[13]

1. On the basis of extensive research, chiefly in the North Atlantic area, Behrman presented an analysis of the sources of tensions between MNCs and host governments of industrialized nations. He dealt with two major sources of tension: those derived from MNC actions and those attributable to the home government.[14] On the first he observed that the host government was caught in a 'love-hate' syndrome. It wanted the contributions to wealth and economic growth that the multinational enterprise could provide because they added to its power within the country, as well as internationally. At the same time it disliked and feared the resulting incursions on national sovereignty and technological dependence.

The key tensions stemming from MNC operations fell in three groups: industrial dominance, technological dependence, and disturbance of economic plans. The fear of industrial dominance by MNCs stemmed in part from the size of U.S. enterprises and their affiliates, in part from their concentration in a few key industry sectors, and in part from their aggressive behavior. According to Behrman, the concern was that vital sectors of the economy would be dominated by MNCs responsive to interests other than those of the host nation.

To inject for the moment another author's views, a vivid sense of the character of this concern is conveyed in the journalistic style of Servan-Schreiber's best-selling *The American Challenge.*

> Citizens would continue to vote, trade unions to strike, and parliaments to deliberate. But it would all take place in a vacuum. With our growth rate, our investment priorities and the distribution of our national income determined by the United States, it is not even necessary to imagine secret meetings between Wall Street bankers and European cabinet ministers to understand that the areas that really count would lie outside the democratic process.[15]

The second source of tension identified by Behrman, fear of technological dependence, is an extension of the fear of MNC dominance into an area of special national interest because of the great importance of technology for economic and security goals. Although host countries want the advanced technologies that come with direct investment by multinational enterprises, they did not always like the time and form of the transfers or the fact that the decision is up to the enterprise. They fear that their companies and economies will become dependent on the United States because of its control over the new technological advances.

The third element, disturbance to economic plans, describes concerns of host governments in a broader context. Governments are assuming more responsibilities for the achievement of economic growth and social goals; and many of them consider that without planning, these goals cannot be realized. Consequently, the role accorded to private enterprise is changing, and acceptance by business of expanded responsibility on the part of the government is altering the government–business relationship. The entrance of the multinational enterprise has made it more difficult for host governments to work out this new relationship. These same responsibilities have made governments more nationalistic, for the national economy is all that they are able to control.

In addition to these tensions in direct, issue-oriented relations with host nations, Behrman also made brief reference to the fundamental conflict between the global outlook of the MNC and the national perspective of the host government. "The multinational enterprise tends to integrate economics before governments are ready for this to happen. The further the enterprise proceeds in this direction and the more significant it becomes economically, the tighter the tensions with governments will become."[16]

Interspersed among the main body of his analysis of concrete national interest issues, Behrman made observations on three points concerned with the quality of the issues and thinking about them. First, he observed that each problem tended to have a set of interrelated facets involving costs, benefits, dependency, and control effects which were conflicting and hard to disentangle. For example, a requirement forcing a larger inflow of foreign funds, to help international payments or reduce the degree of 'leverage' or 'gearing' with domestic borrowing, lessened the government's control over the affiliate through local monetary and financial policies. Second, many problems arose more from uncertainty and fear than fact.

> Precisely when this loss of sovereign control occurs and how much is lost is not clear. It may be impossible to determine precisely, but the fear exists. Coupled with this fear is another over the potential loss of national identity. . . . When fear of a present or future threat exists, the important fact is not whether there is adequate justification for the fear but that it exists.[17]

Third, Behrman anticipated "Governments will, undoubtedly, continue to try to demonstrate to their citizens that national well-being is protected and enhanced by their policies. If effective alternatives cannot be found, restrictions of some kind will probably be adopted as the only feasible course of action."[18]

A second major source of tensions analyzed by Behrman was interference by the U.S. government, specifically through foreign investment controls related to the U.S. balance of payments program, export of technology controls arising from policies on trading with communist countries, and anti-trust extraterritoriality. He enumerated the concrete experiences which host governments have encountered in each of these areas. While the number and impact of the cases have been modest, their implications and image have cast a heavy shadow over the whole international business field.

2. Tables 4−3 and 4−4 summarize the results of surveys I made in Britain, Canada and France in 1970−71 of members of elite groups (national legislators, permanent government officials, heads of business firms and labor union leaders).[19] Although there was considerable diversity among the opinions, several patterns appeared strongly. With the exception of the labor leaders, it was the general consensus that foreign firms had a favorable effect on the host nation. Effects on control of national affairs were viewed most unfavorably and ranked highest in importance along with the economic effects. A divergence of views existed on the latter with the internal economic effect being generally considered favorable while the balance of pay-

Table 4–3.  Criteria for Evaluating Foreign Firms (Computed Rank Order Scores, 1 = Most Important)

| | Britain | | | | | France | | | | |
|---|---|---|---|---|---|---|---|---|---|---|
| | Leg | PG | Lab | Bus | Aver | Leg | PG | Lab | Bus | Aver |
| Effect on X national income | 1.0 (2.2) | 1.0 (2.3) | 1.0 (2.1) | 1.0 (2.8) | 1.0 | 1.0 (2.5) | 1.0 (2.5) | 1.1 (2.1) | 1.0 (2.4) | 1.0 |
| Effect on balance of payments | 1.0 | 1.0 | 1.1 | 1.1 | 1.1 | 1.3 | 1.3 | 1.1 | 1.4 | 1.3 |
| Control over national affairs | 1.4 | 1.7 | 1.6 | 1.3 | 1.5 | 1.2 | 1.0 | 1.1 | 1.5 | 1.2 |
| Benefits for X workers | 1.1 | 2.0 | 1.0 | 1.1 | 1.3 | 1.3 | 1.6 | 1.0 | 1.9 | 1.4 |
| Opportunities for X managers | 1.8 | 2.4 | 2.0 | 1.6 | 2.0 | 2.1 | 3.0 | 2.7 | 2.1 | 2.2 |
| Role of X in the world | 1.8 | 2.8 | 2.1 | 1.3 | 2.0 | 1.1 | 1.5 | 1.6 | 1.7 | 1.5 |
| Changes in X way of life | 2.4 | 3.0 | 2.6 | 2.4 | 2.6 | 1.8 | 2.0 | 2.0 | 2.1 | 2.0 |
| Opportunities for X investors | 3.1 | 3.4 | 2.9 | 2.0 | 2.8 | 2.7 | 3.6 | 3.2 | 1.8 | 2.8 |

X = British, French or Canadian

BASIS. Question "How important should the following considerations be in judging the value of foreign companies operating in X?" Major Importance = 1; Minor = 7.

Note: In the above table the consideration with the lowest average score for each group was given the rank of 1.0. The ranks of the other criteria are the sum of 1.0 plus the difference between their scores and those of the top ranked criteria for the group, e.g. for British MP's. Effects on National Income had an actual score of 2.2 and Opportunities for Investors, 4.3. The actual average scores of first item are given in parentheses.

Source: John Fayerweather, "Elite Attitudes toward Multinational Firms," International Studies Quarterly, Dec. 1972.

**Table 4-3.** continued

|  | Canada | | | | |
|---|---|---|---|---|---|
|  | Leg | PG | Lab | Bus | Aver |
| Effect on X national income | 1.5 (2.9) | 1.4 (2.4) | 1.0 (2.0) | 1.2 (2.6) | 1.3 |
| Effect on balance of payments | 1.1 | 1.6 | 1.8 | 1.1 | 1.4 |
| Control over national affairs | 1.0 | 1.0 | 1.1 | 1.2 | 1.1 |
| Benefits for X workers | 1.8 | 1.6 | 1.0 | 1.3 | 1.4 |
| Opportunities for X managers | 1.5 | 1.9 | 1.9 | 1.0 | 1.6 |
| Role of X in the world | 1.5 | 1.4 | 1.0 | 1.2 | 1.3 |
| Changes in X way of life | 2.1 | 2.3 | 2.2 | 2.4 | 2.2 |
| Opportunities for X investors | 2.1 | 2.1 | 1.9 | 1.2 | 1.8 |

## Table 4–4. Attitudes of Elites Toward Foreign Firms

For "X" in all questions read "Great Britain" (British); "France" (French) or "Canada" (Canadian).

Q. 1 — In your opinion what is the overall effect on X of the activities of foreign companies in X? Good = 1; Bad = 7.

Q. 2 — What will be the result for X if foreign companies have greater control over policy decisions in X industry? Good = 1; Bad = 7.

Q. 3 — How often do you think a typical foreign company operating in X acts in ways contrary to X national interests as compared to a typical X firm? No difference = 1; Frequently = 7.

Q. 4 — What do you believe is the net economic result of the operations of foreign companies in X? They give more than they take = 1; They take more than they give = 7.

Q. 5 — In relation to their economic contributions, the dividends, royalties, and other payments which foreign companies receive from their operations in X are: Too small = 1; Too large = 7.

Q. 6 — To what degree do you believe that the influence of foreign ways of life brought in by foreign companies in X changes the X way of life? Small change = 1; Large change = 7.

Q. 7 — Are the changes in way of life referred to in Question (6) good or bad? Good = 1; Bad = 7.

Leg = National legislators; PG = Permanent government officials; Lab = Labor union leaders; and Bus = Heads of business firms

|  |  | Leg | PG | Lab | Bus | Average |
|---|---|---|---|---|---|---|
| Q. 1 — | Br. | 3.2 | 2.8 | 4.0 | 2.9 | 3.2 |
|  | Fr. | 3.1 | 3.1 | 4.3 | 2.8 | 3.3 |
|  | Can. | 3.5 | 3.2 | 4.2 | 2.6 | 3.4 |
| Q. 2 — | Br. | 5.3 | 4.6 | 6.0 | 5.0 | 5.2 |
|  | Fr. | 4.8 | 5.0 | 5.8 | 5.1 | 5.2 |
|  | Can. | 6.0 | 5.8 | 6.3 | 5.3 | 5.8 |
| Q. 3 — | Br. | 3.5 | 3.0 | 4.1 | 3.1 | 3.4 |
|  | Fr. | 3.7 | 4.0 | 4.3 | 3.0 | 3.8 |
|  | Can. | 3.5 | 3.8 | 4.0 | 3.3 | 3.6 |
| Q. 4 — | Br. | 3.8 | 3.2 | 4.8 | 3.4 | 3.8 |
|  | Fr. | 4.1 | 3.8 | 5.2 | 3.3 | 4.1 |
|  | Can. | 4.6 | 4.2 | 5.2 | 3.8 | 4.4 |
| Q. 5 — | Br. | 4.5 | 4.4 | 4.9 | 4.3 | 4.5 |
|  | Fr. | 4.5 | 4.5 | 5.3 | 4.2 | 4.6 |
|  | Can. | 4.7 | 4.8 | 5.6 | 4.5 | 4.9 |
| Q. 6 — | Br. | 3.5 | 3.2 | 3.3 | 3.2 | 3.3 |
|  | Fr. | 3.6 | 4.5 | 3.6 | 3.7 | 3.8 |
|  | Can. | 4.3 | 4.0 | 4.5 | 3.7 | 4.1 |
| Q. 7 — | Br. | 3.3 | 3.8 | 3.9 | 3.7 | 3.7 |
|  | Fr. | 3.2 | 3.4 | 4.3 | 3.1 | 3.5 |
|  | Can. | 3.7 | 3.9 | 3.9 | 3.2 | 3.7 |

Source: John Fayerweather, "Elite Attitudes toward Multinational Firms," *International Studies Quarterly*, Dec. 1972.

ments effects were considered less beneficial. Effects on the national way of life, the cultural impact, were seen generally in a favorable light but were also not considered particularly important.

3. The third study shifts our attention to MNC interactions with less developed countries. With the assistance of several foreign collaborators, Robinson made a study of investment entry control processes in fifteen countries.[20] Ranked according to degree of restrictiveness, the countries covered were Burma, Mexico, Indonesia, Philippines, ANCOM (Peru, Venezuela, Colombia, Ecuador, Bolivia and Chile), Thailand, Malaysia, Brazil, Sweden, and Japan. He presented an overall assessment of the status, trends, and problems of government control of the investment entry process.

The inquiry demonstrated that national sovereignty was not "at bay." And its impact on corporations with global reach was such as to restrict significantly their options. Furthermore it appeared that national controls were becoming increasingly sophisticated, pragmatic, honest, and effective. A variety of policy options and control system measures were available and their goals, implementation, and interrelation characteristics composed a complex area of action. Robinson identified a substantial problem in the fact that no government had worked out how the various measures should be weighted. He felt that it became critically important for a society, via its political processes, to derive some degree of consensus as to the balance of its priorities among such objectives as maximum growth in production, maximum growth in consumption, and maximum growth in international reserves. To these he added considerations of domestic income distribution and economic or technical independence. Without such a set of national priorities, any entry control system, he concluded, was doomed to failure.

The host country emphasis was on technology, skills, and ownership. While most often ownership goals were sought by requiring local equity participation, Robinson observed that if a government could induce a foreign firm to transfer the greater part of its skills and technology, it might then weaken external control, thereby facilitating equity spinoff and a more favorable division of equity. He concluded that several countries were pushing fairly rapidly toward effective control of the direct foreign investor, notably the Philippines, Malaysia, and Brazil, precisely because they seemed to be giving priority to skill and technology transfer and were willing to waive local ownership requirements if the technology transfer was sufficiently great.

Another major question was identified in the capital requirements for local participation which might substantially exceed available local private resources. Robinson suspected that some government agency would in fact become the national purchaser of most of the spun-off equity, but he questioned whether governments would be willing to utilize their funds for this purpose when the flows got very large. A second problem lay in the effect on management of forced spin-offs which were likely to produce massive conflict of interest in the longer run. As foreign firms were forced to spin off equity to a level that threatened their control, they were very likely to start transferring profits via routes other than dividends such as transfer pricing. The author found some perception of these problems among governments but no effective solutions were apparent.

A further element was the enforcement of entry agreements. For the most part, they were not viewed as enforceable contracts. Only two countries, Indonesia and Malaysia, were willing to submit them to arbitration by the World Bank's Center for the International Settlement of Investment Disputes. Government efforts to monitor agreements were as yet largely limited to requirement of performance reports. Monitoring must rest ultimately on plant inspection and the audit of books, both of which require a cadre of trained and honest personnel. No country examined had mounted a serious effort on this level. One of the weakest parts of any entry control system was the demonstrable inability of a government to police transfer prices.

4. Table 4—5 gives key findings for surveys of elite attitudes toward MNCs in Chile and Venezuela by Truitt and Blake in collaboration with local associates.[21] Studies in other LDCs have not provided the depth of information available in this survey but suggest that the broad pattern of attitudes is similar. The overall social and economic impact in both countries was overwhelmingly rated as either very beneficial or beneficial, but national and mixed firms were rated significantly higher than multinationals. Chilean leaders stressed capital contributions as the main advantages of multinationals while Venezuelans were more impressed with technology inputs and general economic contribution. Perceptions of disadvantages were fairly similar in both countries with the stress on dependency and a feeling that the companies benefited more than the country.

The fifth and sixth studies deal with MNC—home country issues.

5. Stobaugh with a research team explored the employment and balance of payments effects of foreign investments by U.S. firms.[22] The approach was to make a group of case studies which would indicate in tangible terms the actual outcome of investments and the probable effects if the investments had not been made. One major investment case was studied in each of nine industry categories which

Table 4–5.  Attitudes Toward MNCs of Elites in Chile and Venezuela[a]

Views of Social and Economic Impact

| | Chile | | | | Venezuela | | | |
| | Type of firm | | | | Type of firm | | | |
| | National | U.S. | Other Foreign | Mixed Ownership | National | U.S. | Other Foreign | Mixed Ownership |
|---|---|---|---|---|---|---|---|---|
| Very beneficial | 43.2% | 24.1% | 24.2% | 38.8% | 59.3% | 16.1% | 15.9% | 30.0% |
| Beneficial | 41.7 | 50.4 | 50.0 | 44.2 | 30.7 | 53.1 | 50.0 | 54.6 |
| Neutral | 14.4 | 18.8 | 20.5 | 16.3 | 8.7 | 16.8 | 19.7 | 12.3 |
| Harmful | .8 | 6.8 | 5.3 | 0.8 | 1.3 | 9.1 | 9.8 | 1.5 |
| Very harmful | 0 | 0 | 0 | 0 | 0 | 4.9 | 4.5 | 1.5 |
| *Principal Advantage of Foreign Investment for Country* | | | | | | | | |
| Brings in capital | | | 48% | | | 20% | | |
| Brings and develops technology | | | 19 | | | 31 | | |
| Economic support and development | | | 18 | | | 25 | | |
| Creates employment | | | 7 | | | 7 | | |
| Other | | | 8 | | | 17 | | |

(Table 4–5.  continued overleaf)

**Table 4–5.  continued**

| Principal Disadvantage | Chile | Venezuela |
|---|---|---|
| Political and economic dependency | 24% | 27% |
| Company benefits more than host country | 23 | 26 |
| Harmful to economy | 20 | 15 |
| Negative effect on balance of payments | 10 | 17 |
| Other | 23 | 15 |

[a]Survey of businessmen, government officials, and students.
Source: Truitt and Blake, *Opinion Leaders and Private Investment.*

in total represented 90 percent of U.S. direct investment in foreign manufacturing.

The basic theme which ran through all the cases was that foreign investments were essentially defensive requirements to protect a firm's international market position; that if they were not made, business would have been lost to foreign competitors. Thus, despite immediate loss of employment and adverse balance of payments effects, the long term consequence of not making the investments would have been even greater loss of employment and foregoing future income and other benefits which ultimately helped the balance of payments.

In light of the national debate within the United States the most important case was that in the electrical products category. The case concerned a plant in Taiwan. Radio components manufactured in the United States were assembled into sub-units in Taiwan and returned to the United States for final assembly and sale. There was an immediate loss of 243 U.S. man-years of work. But the authors concluded that if the U.S. company tried to continue complete manufacture in the United States, it would within five years have lost the full U.S. market to foreign firms which did take advantage of the lower wages in the Far East. On the other hand, by making the investment the company strengthened its market position. By ultimately increasing its total sales, the employment in manufacturing within the United States rose, whereas it would have substantially decreased if competitors had taken over the market. Thus the authors estimated that U.S. employment from this phase of operations actually increased by some 734 employees within five years because the investment was made.

The other cases differed in details. In most the motivation for investment was to avoid foreign tariffs or other obstacles threatening loss of foreign markets. But in all cases, the basic strategic benefits to the United States were similar. The foreign investment permitted the firm to prevent foreign producers from eroding the U.S. market position. This enabled the firms to retain export sales of components and associated goods, i.e., products whose effective marketing required that the company carry a full line of products, some of which it was competitively forced to manufacture abroad. In addition, the U.S. investor typically purchased much of his manufacturing equipment for new plants from the United States, whereas a foreign competitor might not do so.

The authors presented some overall estimates of effects. They emphasized that these were crude, both because of the limits of their cases and because they did not deal with a variety of secondary effects of investments. Considering just the type of direct impact covered by their cases, they estimated that 250,000 jobs would have been lost if there were no U.S. foreign manufacturing investment. Adding in the employment in home offices of multinational firms, they arrived at a figure of 600,000 jobs in the United States dependent upon foreign manufacturing investment.

   6. Root and Mennis made another study of MNC–home country effects. They reported the results of interviews made during 1972–74 with 188 top executives of 46 U.S. multinational corporations, 17 officials in 15 government agencies closely associated with trade and investment matters, and an official in each of 10 U.S. labor unions that had issued statements on international trade and investment policy plus some people in AFL–CIO headquarters.[23] The authors observed that for 30 years from the mid–thirties to the mid–sixties American businessmen, unions, and government agreed on the fundamental proposition that liberal international trade and investment policies were good for the United States. In the 1970s this consensus had been replaced by a bitter confrontation between American multinational corporations and organized labor spearheaded by the AFL–CIO. During the dispute the U.S. government tried to sustain traditional policies amid growing uncertainty as to their desirability and effectiveness. The research was undertaken to identify the nature of the present gaps in perception. The principal findings were listed as:

> Both Administration and Union officials perceive U.S. MNCs as more dynamic, larger, and more technologically advanced, becoming more important in the U.S. economy and more powerful politically than U.S. domestic corporations. Unions, however, perceive wider differences between MNCs and domestic corporations. Administration and Union officials disagree significantly on the sensitivity of MNCs to U.S. interests and on the support MNCs obtain from the U.S. government. For Unions the single most important reason why U.S. manufacturers go abroad to set up production plants is to exploit cheap labor. For Administration officials the single most important reason is to penetrate foreign markets. . . . Unions generally perceive MNCs as a threat to the well-being of the United States and to Union power. . . . In contrast to Unions, Administration officials do not perceive U.S. MNCs as a threat to the well-being of the United States and the power of the U.S. Government. They do not view MNCs as 'independent actors' in the international system or to have escaped U.S. jurisdiction to the detriment of U.S. national interests. Union spokesmen perceive the U.S. Government as responsive to the interests of the MNCs to the disadvantage of labor.

Multinational executives are ambivalent in their attitudes toward the Government. On the one hand, they would like to be 'left alone' by the Government; on the other hand, they would like to have more supportive government policies. Multinational executives reveal little appreciation of the factors that motivate Union opposition to MNCs. They view such opposition to be based on out-dated conceptions of the world economy, and believe that the true interests of labor are helped rather than harmed by MNCs. Unions perceive U.S. international trade and investment policies to be supportive of U.S. MNCs. In contrast, Administration officials view U.S. policies as substantially 'neutral' although individual policies may be modestly restrictive or supportive. MNC executives lean slightly toward a restrictive view of U.S. policies. . . . A wide perceptual gap separates Unions from MNCs and the Administration on U.S. policies. Unions perceive the absence of restrictions to be supportive whereas MNCs and the Administration perceive an absence of restrictions to be 'neutral' toward MNCs.[24]

The Unions . . . condemn . . . the continuing give-away of American capital and technology. . . . An implicit working assumption of the Unions . . . is that extensive international transfers of capital and technology have made wage-cost differentials among countries the critical factors of success or failure in world competition. As a relatively high wage-cost area, therefore, the United States must preserve whatever advantages it possesses in capital and technology. . . . MNCs and Administration appose a very different perspective that echoes the free trade arguments of Adam Smith. . . . The Unions see MNCs as independent actors, politically powerful, unresponsive to national interests, detrimental to the U.S. economy, and (most important perhaps) a threat to Union bargaining power. But Administration officials see MNCs as economic institutions bringing benefits to the U.S. economy, weaker than the nation-state with only limited decision-making autonomy, and meriting the same policy treatment as domestic companies.[25]

These six studies are diverse in character but in total they provide a comprehensive picture of the concrete issues and attitudes dominant in MNC interactions with the nation state. From them we may extract certain basic points that will serve as the core to the approach to strategy analysis.

1. It is clear that on balance the MNC role is beneficial for both host and home nations and is perceived as such except for substantial dissent in labor circles.

2. Concern about MNC control in general and in varied major areas of application is central to MNC interactions with the host nation.

3. The economic effects are equally important among host nations and are the major concern in home nations.

4. The key issues in MNC–nation state interaction tend to be quite complex with conflicting evidence and interrelationships, so that clear-cut conclusions and solutions are generally difficult.

5. Divided viewpoints among sectors of national populations are common, so that governments have difficulty in arriving at positions on national interest in any given situation and their positions may shift over time.

6. Nationalistic feelings are present and may exert substantial influence in the complex and uncertain situations attributable to points 4 and 5.

## NOTES

1. Hans Kohn, "Nationalism," in David Sills, ed., *International Encyclopedia of the Social Sciences* (New York: Crowell, Collier, and Macmillan, 1968), Vol. 11, p. 63.

2. Kalman H. Silvert, *Expectant Peoples* (New York: Vintage Press, 1963), p. 19.

3. Karl W. Deutsch, *Nationalism and Social Communication* (Cambridge, Mass.: M.I.T. Press, 1962), p. 89.

4. H.D. Lasswell, *World Politics and Personal Insecurity* (New York: McGraw-Hill, 1935).

5. H. Tajfel, "Aspects of National and Ethnic Loyalty," *Social Science Information*, 9(3), p. 140.

6. Ibid., p. 51.

7. Deutsch, op. cit., p. 97.

8. Ernest Geller, *Thought and Change* (London: Weidenfield & Nicolson, 1964), p. 155.

9. Deutsch, op. cit., p. 104.

10. John DeLamater, Daniel Katz, and Herbert C. Kelman, "On the Nature of National Involvement: A Preliminary Study," *The Journal of Conflict Resolution*, Sept. 1969, pp. 322–323.

11. Jack N. Behrman, *National Interests and the Multinational Enterprise* (Englewood Cliffs, N.J.: Prentice Hall, 1970); pp. 102–111.

12. For a fuller discussion, see John Fayerweather, *Facts and Fallacies of International Business* (New York: Holt, Rinehart, and Winston, 1962), pp. 50–64.

13. Richard J. Barnet and Ronald E. Muller, *Global Reach* (New York: Simon and Schuster, 1974); Donald T. Brash, *American Investment in Australian Industry* (Cambridge, Mass.: Harvard University Press, 1966); John H. Dunning, *The Role of American Investment in the British Economy* (London: Political and Economic Planning, 1969); John Fayerweather, *Foreign Investment in Canada* (White Plains, N.Y.: International Arts and Sciences Press, 1973); Rainer Hellmann, *The Challenge to U.S. Dominance of the International Corporation*

(Cambridge, Mass.: Dunellen, 1970); Michael Kidron, *Foreign Investments in India* (London: Oxford University Press, 1965); Kari Levitt, *Silent Surrender* (New York: St. Martin's Press, 1970); James McMillan and Bernard Harris, *The American Take-over of Britain* (New York: Hart, 1968); A.E. Safarian, *Foreign Ownership of Canadian Industry* (Toronto: McGraw-Hill, 1966); Hugh Stephenson, *The Coming Clash* (New York: Saturday Review Press, 1972); Christopher Tugendhat, *The Multinationals* (New York: Random House, 1972); and Raymond Vernon, *Sovereignty at Bay* (New York: Basic Books, 1971).

14. Behrman, op. cit.

15. J.J. Servan-Schrieber, *The American Challenge* (New York: Atheneum, 1968), p. 191.

16. Behrman, op. cit., p. 11.

17. Ibid., p. 30.

18. Ibid., p. 150.

19. John Fayerweather, "Elite Attitudes Towards Multinational Firms," *International Studies Quarterly*, Dec. 1972, pp. 472–490.

20. Richard D. Robinson, *National Control of Foreign Business Entry* (New York: Praeger, 1976).

21. Nancy S. Truitt, and David H. Blake, *Opinion Leaders and Private Investment* (New York: Fund for Multinational Management Education, 1976).

22. Robert B. Stobaugh, *U.S. Multinational Enterprises and the U.S. Economy* (Boston, Mass.: Harvard University, Graduate School of Business Administration, 1972).

23. Franklin R. Root and Bernard Mennis, "How U.S. Multinational Corporations, Unions, and Government View Each Other and the Direction of U.S. Policies," *Journal of International Business Studies*, Spring, 1976, pp. 17–30.

24. Ibid., pp. 18–19, reproduced by permission.

25. Ibid., pp. 29–30, reproduced by permission.

*Chapter 5*

# Strategy for MNC–Nation State Relations

The preceding chapter has described the pattern of interactions between multinational corporations and home and host nations. The present chapter will build on that base to develop strategy guidelines for the conduct of MNC relations with nations, and especially with their governments. This is no simple task. We have already seen that the interaction process is multifaceted and complex. One can readily observe that MNC–nation state relations are immensely varied, constantly changing, and of uneven quality and success. Realistically, therefore, the objective of this chapter can only be to provide broad guidelines and insights which will be useful to the practitioner in dealing with assorted case situations, each of which will be unique because of the many variables involved. With this intent in mind the chapter will start with a wide scanning of the environment and the forces and trends apparent in it and then narrow down progressively to discussion of strategy for the main forms of MNC–nation state interaction.

## TRENDS IN THE NATIONALISM CONTEXT

Although most MNC–nation state interactions center around tangible issues, typically involving questions of corporate and national interests, this analysis will start with the more nebulous area of nationalism because it has two fundamental effects on the more tangible issues. First, it is the strength of nationalism as a fundamental political philosophy that underlies the entire structure of nation-oriented institutions and interests so its strength and future course is basic to the whole subject area.

Second, the emotional character of nationalism creates an ever-present milieu for the tangible issues which should be emphasized at the outset because it is all too easy to overlook it in the factual analysis of strategy issues which will occupy most of this chapter. The inherent conflict between nationalism and the multinational corporation was brought out in full in Chapter 4. Briefly the MNC activities inevitably cast it as an aggressive outsider seeking to enter and control a portion of life within the national group and to extract economic benefits from the nation. It therefore arouses instinctive nationalistic distrust and protective resistance.

This inherent conflict manifests itself in a wide range of specific situations. It injects into business affairs a non-rational, adverse state of mind which typically magnifies conflicts arising from rational disagreements over the divergence of company activities and national interests. For example, the question of allocation of foreign exchange for profit repatriation for a multinational firm is frequently magnified by politicians and the press and ultimately in the minds of the populace by nationalistic reactions. Thus it becomes more of an emotional issue dominated by images of the outsider preying on the property of the we-group than a question to be thought out logically in terms of economic benefits and obligations. By the same token, within a local subsidiary the employment of an expatriate to fill a management position will be viewed unfavorably in practical terms by one or more local nationals who had aspired to the position just as would be expected even if no national differences were involved. But the action will frequently arouse far stronger sentiments both in the individuals immediately affected and in their countrymen in the organization because it appears as an affront to nationalistic sentiments. It is difficult, and probably fruitless, to try to determine just how much of the conflict in a given situation arises from rational differences and how much from nationalistic reactions. The only essential point for the MNC to recognize is that nationalism is there and that it is dealing with some deep-seated and intangible feelings, not to be dispelled by logical arguments.

### The Roots of Nationalism

With this sense of the underlying importance of nationalism in mind, we must consider its future role and to get at that some perspective on its history is needed. Although nationalism is relatively new, its psychological roots are not. As we noted in Chapter 4, it is a manifestation of the fundamental quest of man for security and other social satisfactions from participation in a group.

For centuries these feelings found their main expression in "we-groups" that lived in relatively close physical proximity—the family, the clan, the tribe, the village, and even the city-state. These were units in which the individual could share in a common life through direct interaction with other members and have a sense of participation in the group. There were large government units, to be sure, but they could not serve the functions of a we-group. The great empires of Ghengis Khan and the Romans were administrative systems run by a central dictator. Early "nations" like England were affiliations of feudal rulers. Patriotism toward one's country and its monarch existed. A citizen might admire, respect, and love his king and feel emotional ties to his country. But nationalism goes a good deal beyond patriotism. The mass of the people were too poorly educated to have much knowledge of or sense of unity with "countrymen" beyond their immediate community, and they had too little participation in the government to feel full identification with it.

But there was nothing in the psychological forces involved that inherently limited we-group attitudes to small units. Two important changes, reinforced by other developments, brought forth true nationalism around the end of the eighteenth century: mass education and popular government. As literacy became quite common, facilitated by the accomplishments of the printing press, people became better acquainted with the world around them and found in this knowledge an identification with the language, traditions, literature, and culture of their national group as distinguished from the foreignness of other peoples. Concurrently the rise of the middle class was being fostered by economic growth and by the new social structure associated with the industrial revolution and large-scale manufacturing. The middle class now had a strong interest in the functioning of the national government and capacity to participate in it which superseded that of the feudal landowning aristocracy.

In broad outline, these observations explain how and why the we-group psychology was elevated to the national level. From its middle-class base in Europe and North America, nationalism has now spread in the company of popular government, mass communications, and independence movements to every part of the globe and down deep into the ranks of the lower classes, leaving only the most primitive tribal groups outside its range. It is found in varying stages of development, ranging from the mature forms common in Europe to the early, unstable forms in many new African nations. But it is present everywhere. Most people are now able to comprehend their affiliation with their countrymen and are emotionally caught up in the sentimental affiliation to their nation state.

### Current Trends

Though the present strength of nationalism is unquestionable, it is appropriate to ask whether this may not be a passing phase, whether nationalism has seen its peak and will be of progressively less significance to international business. The historical review just presented has two implications along this line. First, there is no reason to expect that nationalism will disappear because it is the product of social immaturity. The underlying we-group psychology is basic and will not disappear. Second, the past changes in the manifestations of this psychology and the reasons for the changes suggest that under the influence of new factors in the environment new manifestations may appear.

Following the lines of historical evolution, one's instinct is to look for signs that we are moving toward a still broader span of we-group structure—the family, the tribe, the city, the nation, next perhaps an international cohesion. And indeed there are numerous things we can point to that seem to fit the requirements for such a transition. Mass communications media are making people all around the world aware of each other and familiar with each other's ways of life. There has been a steady growth of what might be called international subcultures. Teenagers, for example, in virtually all countries share tastes in hair styles, music, and the like. To at least a limited degree they show a mutual identification rising above national affiliation. The numbers involved are smaller, but we have similar trends among, for example, international businessmen, chess players, and radio hams.

The increasing integration of the world economy is also an encouraging sign. Just as the emergence of nationalism coincided with and apparently was related to the economic suitability of the nation state as the industrial revolution got under way, our modern economy seems to require a cohesion and cooperation among nations. The International Monetary Fund, multilateral trade agreements now centering around the GATT (General Agreement on Trade and Tariffs), and similar mechanisms rising above national sovereignties are critical to world trade and thus to the welfare of people in all nations.

Nevertheless, there is reason to doubt that we are on the threshold of a true international "we-groupism." First, if we look at the past, we find that no we-group has ever existed without a "they." That is, there has always been something external from which the we-group could distinguish itself. The need for security is generally accepted as a critical motivation in the individual's commitment to the we-group. While a person may need security in relation to the unknown or in isolation, his concern about tangible external threats is strong, and its absence removes a significant support of any we-group. For international subcultures there are "theys." Teenagers everywhere, for example, are unified by their separation from adults. The communist threat has created a degree of cohesion in the free world. But its potentials are sharply limited by the affiliation of appreciable portions of the populations of many countries to communism.

However, a "they" distinguishable from the peoples of the world as a whole is hard to identify. We do have a threat of sorts in the universal dread of nuclear war. Such cohesion as exists about the United Nations is due in considerable part to this fear. Yet it is hard to visualize such a nebulous threat providing bonds of the depth and variety required for a strong international we-group structure. Thus drawing the peoples of the world together tightly would seem possible only if some concrete "they" appears like a threat from outer space.

Likewise, for all the development of international subcultures, the differences among nations are still very great and in important respects show little sign of diminishing appreciably. In such vital respects as language, religion, and cultural values the Indian, the Japanese, the German, and the American are still a long way apart. One cannot, therefore, readily conceive of their developing a strong sense of mutual identification such as characterizes a we-group.

In Europe, it is just possible that we are seeing a true breakthrough from a national to a regional we-group structure. Although there are a multitude of differences among the countries, it is hard to identify any major deviations of political and social ideology that would prevent cohesion. A strong base for a community of interest has been laid economically, and there is a considerable common tradition, especially in the hardship of two major wars. The fact that much of the fighting has been internal is not a block, for most of our nations are composed of people who have at one time or another engaged in bitter internal fights. And, finally, between the United States and Russia, the Europeans have an ample supply of "theys" as foils for strong we-groupism.

Several studies have confirmed a growing sense of union among Europeans. For example, Mennis and Sauvant asked a sample of German businessmen to indicate the location of decision-making they preferred for eleven governmental areas with four alternatives: entire national, predominant national, predominant European Community (EC) and entire EC.[1] Overall the data indicated strong support for Western European integration on the part of the managers, regardless of the function considered. Only a very low percentage selected the "entire national" option. The support was strongest for military security, 57 percent preferring entire EC control of it.

Economic decision areas fell in the middle range with the "entire EC" preferences for monetary policy and tax policy at 42 percent and 25 percent respectively. At the lower end of the scale were social welfare and education, for which 22 percent and 19 percent respectively favored "entire EC."

But despite such favorable indications. European governments with popular support continue to vigorously pursue separate national interests and there is little evidence they are prepared to sacrifice much national sovereignty to unified European institutions.

This analysis suggests some reason to hope that the we-group instincts of people may be shifting from nationalism toward a broader base, especially toward regional affiliations. However, it also indicates that the prospects for major or rapid change are not encouraging. In the determination of management policies this conclusion is significant because some people have suggested that the hope for the future of international business lies in the creation of a supranational corporation. Ideally it would be chartered by the United Nations, have its headquarters in some center with minimal national character (like Luxembourg), be owned by stockholders of a broad range of nationalities, and be managed as a true world enterprise without partiality to any country.

Although this is an appealing idea, it will not be an effective response to nationalism unless the peoples of the world start to transfer their we-group emotions to the United Nations in substantial measure. It would reduce the impact of the association of the home country with the multinational corporation, but it would not alter the basic relationship with other countries. The supranational corporation would still be an outsider, still a "they" whether it be of U.S. origin or United Nations origin. Furthermore, the change would amount in large part to a fiction if, as seems likely, the capital and management of the corporation still came from a small number of major industrial countries. It might even have a negative effect because, despite all their adverse comments about capital from particular countries, especially the United States, many foreign nations would have considerably more confidence in the beneficence and responsibility of business based in a major industrial nation than in a floating corporation chartered by a weak world-government institution and presumably virtually free of overall government control.

There is another way to look at the role of nationalism which we should consider as a source of possible relief from current tensions. We can look at the degree to which nationalism is an effective force in different phases of life. For example, in pure scientific research nationalism is of much less importance than in political affairs. Regrettably business has been an area in which nationalism has played a prominent role because of the heavy influence external business has exerted on the internal social and political affairs of many nations, especially the less developed ones. Animosity toward foreign investment is therefore part of the nationalistic tradition that binds these people together. Thus we start at a tremendous handicap in proposing that multinational business affairs become disassociated from nationalism.

On the other hand, it is hard to escape the historical indications that government institutions and their underlying philosophies have always tended to support the basic economic and business system that was desirable for the effective use of the technology of the day. It follows that if the multinational corporation is in fact beneficial economically, the national sentiments behind government policies will in some way adjust to accommodate it.

In speculating about ways in which this might happen, another feature of past history is worth observing. Throughout the prenationalism eras, various forms of internationalism existed. There were administrative unifications like the Roman and Ottoman empires in which locally recruited bureaucracies served international systems, despite the gulf between their masters and the local we-groups to whom they had an initial loyalty. Likewise, in the Renaissance period in Europe, the elite intelligentsia of the whole area were in a sense a distinctive we-group unto themselves apart from the masses. They spurned localism in favor of a common mission in a unified Catholic society. Most spoke French rather than the tongue of their country, and they disdained association with petty local interests.

The evolution of international subcultures mentioned previously fits this concept. At least with respect to matters central to their bond of affiliation, the members of these groups do seem for the most part to rise above nationalism. A geographically more limited but still essentially similar grouping is found in the *third-culture* concept constructed by Useem, Donaghue, and Useem.[2] The third culture is composed of that group of local nationals and foreigners in a country who provide the bridge between the host society and activities originating in foreign cultures including foreign business, government (notably foreign aid programs), and educational and religious operations. The distinctive characteristic of these people is their capacity to work effectively with people from a different culture; as a corollary their emotional ties to their own culture are weakened.

Although the anthropologists who have developed this concept have emphasized the cultural aspect, the operational logics and personal associations involved provide a comparable basis for weakening of nationalistic ties. A more limited, yet more direct indication of potentials in this direction is found in a study in Canada by Smetanka and in a phase of the Mennis-Sauvant German research both of which demonstrated that executives with greater responsibilities for international business manifested a lower intensity of nationalism.[3] Their work suggests that direct involvement in multinational operations fosters both intellectual and behavioral acceptance of internationalism and weakens therefore the force of nationalism.

There would seem, therefore, to be at least some hope that localized third-culture groups or an international subculture composed of international businessmen and the government officials who work with them around the globe may achieve such a sense of unity and at least partial disassociation from internal nationalism. The prospects along this line are intriguing, and we shall return to them later in the chapter when management policies are examined.

### Scenario for the Future

Pulling these various threads together, it is possible to visualize a scenario of global sociopolitical transition in which the MNC is a central actor. Comprehension of this scenario will help in formulating feasible and productive MNC strategy.

The central theme of the scenario is the growing interdependence of the world. That is a clear reality. The horror of a major war forces political collaboration even among nations with profound differences. Economic interdependence likewise has an overwhelming reality, manifest in many ways—raw material dependencies, volume of trade among nations, and the like. So the need and the reality of interdependence are obvious to all peoples.

The areas of uncertainty lie in determining the processes by which interdependence is to be implemented and in achieving acceptance of those processes. Here is a vast territory of flux, confusion and pragmatic evolution. In it nation states and nationalism are vigorously present and the MNC is a prominent feature. MNC–nation state interaction is clearly one of the main components of the unfolding scenario.

To guide its strategy wisely, the MNC must have a sense of where the present confused situation is heading. Some seers have projected rather extreme outcomes. The "sovereignty at bay" concept on the one hand has been expanded by some to a picure of a few giant MNCs dominating global economic decisions with national powers greatly weakened. On the other hand, those who perceive the persisting strength of nations and new signs of mercantilism and protectionism suggest that the role of the MNC may have already reached its zenith and its part in national economics will be progressively re-stricted.

A reflective view both of history and economic realities suggests that the outcome will look rather different from either of these extremes; that we are at the moment experiencing a historic restructuring process, the outcome of which will include coexistence of both vigorous nationalism and effective MNC operations.

The central issue in the restructuring process must be control which we have identified as the crux of the MNC–nationalism conflict. To perceive the probable outcome of this conflict one must step back and look at patterns linking control and independence both in their macro form in full societies and in their micro form in the lives of individuals. In social groups, regardless of their size, people always seek independence. Yet interdependence is a necessity, so they adjust to it and to the controls by others on their lives that it entails.

The incursions on national self-determination created by international interdependence are generically no different. The broad concept of MNCs as global entities exercising decision-making controls within nations is an integral part of the overall process. Accepting this concept does not mean any greater submersion of nationalism than any social controls imply the full submersion of individualism. Rather the prospect is for a restructuring of control and decision-making in which MNCs and nations have roles which effectively permit the former to perform their useful social roles while the latter retain a sense of identity and self-determination.

In this perspective the problems today are those of transition and adjustment, not of extreme changes in status of institutions. Major elements of evolution are at work. In the first place, there is a complex process of determining just what decision-making and control scope MNCs need to perform their social role effectively and what controls are important to national interests. Then there is the yet more complex behavioral process of achieving social acceptance of the new distribution of decision-making and control roles. The complexity of this is very largely a function of the character of diverse, free, democratic societies and their slow acceptance of institutional change. In historical dimensions, the penetration of MNCs in host societies has been very rapid, much too rapid for people to accept regardless of the rational logics which support its role. The pace has been too great to permit orderly and receptive determination of roles, limits, procedures, and other aspects of the way in which MNCs will be integrated in the decision-making processes of nation states.

In brief, then, the essential characteristics of the environment of MNC–nation state interaction for the next decade or more will be one of adjustment and acceptance, with the emphasis on experimentation, testing, learning, and accommodation. All of these require time, patience, and imagination.

## IMPLICATIONS FOR MNC STRATEGY

To fit this scenario for the future, MNC strategy must be geared to the complex pattern of interactions necessary to evolve an effective blend of decision-making and control roles for the MNC and the nation and its component parts. The ramifications of this process are very broad, ranging from global efforts like the activities under the United Nations Centre on Transnational Corporations to a multitude of interactions between individual MNCs and government officials. Some will result in conspicuous official agreements and plans. Others will have little separate significance, but large or small, conspicuous or inconspicuous, they will all collectively contribute to the evolution of a mode of MNC–nation state relationships that will permit the MNC to perform its economic role while still preserving as far as possible the attributes of the nation important to its people.

In considering these subjects it will be useful to bear in mind a fundamental constraint rooted in the emotional character of nationalism. The economic and institutional requisites of a beneficial blend of MNC and nation state roles are not easy to determine but it should be susceptible to rational, objective analysis and a logically supportable outcome. But the adjustments to nationalistic attitudes it will entail are a far more difficult matter to define, and most of all to convey to people. Thus MNC managements face a dual task of major proportions in determining sound strategy and facilitating its acceptance by national populations with the latter a particularly difficult task in light of the varied cultural and nationalistic sensitivities of people.

It will be impractical here to explore at length the many avenues in which this evolutionary process will proceed. But the more conspicuous aspects will be discussed. First we will consider two specific issues of MNC–nation state interaction—collective approaches and MNC structure. We will then examine the central problems of dealing with specific issues in which MNC and national interests must be worked out.

### Collective Approaches

Collective efforts to improve relations between MNCs and nation states go well back in time and have been pursued actively by many people. The Havana conference shortly after World War II attempted to formulate a global approach to investment issues paralleling the General Agreement on Trade and Tariffs (GATT) which was established to facilitate the flow of trade. That proposal failed and numerous subsequent efforts met with little success in the 1950s and 1960s. Only in the late 1970s has the possibility of real progress in this direction emerged from serious negotiations over codes to govern foreign investment.

This brief historical report overstates somewhat the limits of accomplishment. Some collective efforts have succeeded. For example, governments have negotiated bilateral treaties which provide some guarantees for the rights of investors. The U.S. government, in implementing its investment insurance program backed up by the leverage of its aid expenditures, has provided some support for U.S. MNCs. But these have essentially been marginal protective measures which did little to affect the operating role of MNCs.

More fundamental has been the work of the Organization for Economic Cooperation and Development (OECD). After much discussion the OECD formulated a code of Liberalization of Capital Movements in 1961. The OECD code was adopted only by the United States and the advanced European countries, the investment liberalization terms being unacceptable to less developed countries (LDCs). Even Canada felt the code would unduly limit its ability to restrain foreign investment in its economy.

But the OECD code has had an impact. Most notable was its important influence on the liberalization of Japanese investment policy. Around 1970 Japan was moving steadily toward greater outward investment by its own firms. It therefore came under increasing pressure to play the game by the same rules as other major capital exporting nations. The OECD code served as an effective vehicle for defining the rules, and its acceptance of them became the symbolic milestone in positioning Japan among the nations supporting relatively open investment policies. In actually implementing its policy, Japan has moved slowly and MNCs have much less freedom in making major investment decisions there than in the United States or even France. But the official adherence to the OECD code is nonetheless a solid factor supporting more liberal government behavior.

The formulation of codes received a major impetus in the mid-1970s as a result of several developments, notably the revelation of large-scale extra-legal payments by MNCs, the intervention in Chilean politics by International Telephone and Telegraph Corporation, and more fundamentally the gathering momentum of the New International Economic Order backed up by the success of the Organization of Petroleum Exporting Countries. A broad band of public and official opinion perceived that the time was ripe to formalize standards for MNC operations.

As a consequence much discussion and negotiation developed and modest actual progress has been achieved. The OECD countries have set forth a code which establishes certain behavioral standards. It is voluntary, there being no legal force behind it. But it does have considerable moral weight. In the meantime, the LDCs, working to a large extent in collaboration with the UN Centre on Transnational Corporations, are formulating their own ideas on codes with particular emphasis on technology agreements, for example, establishing the right to renegotiate terms at any time, reducing the constraints on exports by licensees, and increasing the responsibility of suppliers of technology.

The impact of all this activity is as yet uncertain. The prospects of formal agreement by MNC parent and host nations on major provisions seem dim. Concurrence on a few conspicuous points like the impropriety of bribery is possible but there are fundamental obstacles to agreement on more significant matters. One is that agreement requires concessions on both sides and, at this stage of evolution, neither side appears ready to make them. On the one hand, the parent nations want strong assurances to protect the property and operating rights of MNCs. The host nations are unwilling to go far in this direction both because such protection may limit actions they wish to take and because they are resistant to apparent invasions of their sovereign rights—the basic problem of protective nationalism. On the other hand, the parent nations resist the types of code provisions being advanced by the LDCs because they see them as unduly impairing the functional roles of the MNCs.

A second major problem is the difficulty of achieving agreement among the LDCs. The character of this problem is demonstrated vividly in the experience of the Andean Common Market (ANCOM). When ANCOM was formed by Bolivia, Chile, Colombia, Ecuador, and Peru in 1969 (with later adherence of Venezuela), there appeared to be a large measure of agreement among competent government officials. ANCOM policy on foreign investment embodied in "Decision 24" spelled out varied terms including profit remission and ownership. The latter emphasized the "fade-out" concept, essentially proposing that MNCs reduce their ownership of affiliates to a minority over a specified period. ANCOM retained its cohesion for a few years, but then it began to weaken partly due to changes in governments and partly because of economic problems. In 1976 it suffered major setbacks notably in the withdrawal of Chile and in significant modification of policies on MNCs such as relaxation of limits on profit remission.

The causes of the ANCOM problems are common to all LDCs. The countries share certain broad feelings and policy goals toward MNCs but when they get down to specifics and implementation, important factors lead to dissention among them—differences in political and economic philosophies, competition to attract foreign investors, personal political rivalries, and underlying nationalistic jealousies. So it is not easy for them to concur on positions and maintain a united front in the long and difficult negotiation process necessary to achieve effective agreements with MNCs and their parent countries.

A third problem lies in the principle of discrimination between MNCs and domestic firms that is commonly embodied in LDC proposals. The OECD countries are firm in their position that any requirements, for example, on public disclosure of corporate financial data, be equally applied to both MNC affiliates and local national concerns. But LDCs stoutly reject this concept because of resistance by their local business communities. Indeed it is generally perceived that LDCs intend that codes should be discriminatory, that they be a means to readjust what they perceive as a balance competitively favoring the MNCs to the disadvantage of their local business communities. So the issue of discrimination stands as a basic obstacle to agreement on codes between parent and host nations.

The slow progress in developing codes and the fundamental difficulties deterring them add up to a bleak picture if concrete agreements are assumed to be the prime objective. In terms of the contextual evolution we have outlined, however, the extensive conversations, publicity, and thinking about codes are immensely important. Collectively they are doing much of the job that has to be done of educating people as to the areas in which MNCs and nations are going to have to reach accommodation and the options and problems of accommodation. All of this is essential groundwork for ultimate accomplishment in global accommodation among extremely diverse peoples. While the simile has many shortcomings, we may liken the situation to the confused evolutionary period between the achievement of independence at the end of the American Revolution in 1781 and the achievement of a workable accommodation of state and national interests with the completion of the Constitution in 1886. Working out the MNC relation to the nation state is vastly more complicated and a single code to govern it is unlikely. But the general concept of a massive interactional process as an educational and adjustmental preparation for mutual accommodation is sound. The code discussion is serving that purpose very well.

For the individual MNC the strategy implications of the code discussion process take two directions. First, collectively and individually, MNCs are active participants in parent nation and international organizations which are carrying on the necessary studies and negotiations. Second, there are opportunities for individual firm initiatives which move the process ahead. The most conspicuous examples are codes of conduct which MNCs have set forth on their own. Caterpillar Tractor, for example, published the code that appears as Appendix A to this chapter. These codes in substance do little more than formally document good management practice. But, again emphasizing the broad contextual evolution, they are a real contribution to expanding public understanding and progress toward mutual accommodation.

### Structural Relations

The second broad area of MNC strategy for facilitating interaction with host societies is the pattern of structural relations the firm establishes. Such activities as public relations, lobbying, and community service have been a common part of general business practice for many years. Each has its special characteristics in the differing cultural, social, and political environments abroad but space will not permit us to explore them fully here.

It is important, however, to identify the major structural features that have become important to strategy in relation to nation states. A useful point of departure for this discussion is the picture of the extent of interactions of MNC executives with host government officials revealed in a study by Boddewyn and Kapoor.[4] They estimated that in developing countries, senior executives spent an average of 45 percent of their time on government relations and even in Europe the portion ran up to 20 percent.

Despite this prominence of government relations, Boddewyn and Kapoor found wide diversity in management attitudes toward international business and government relations (IBGR). About 10 percent of those surveyed took a "We don't want any" attitude, feeling the effort outweighed the benefits. Another 25 percent felt that there might be some benefit but were not completely convinced or had more pressing problems to deal with. About half the firms felt they needed effective government relations but were just beginning to organize for the task. Only about 15 percent could be said to have an adequately organized and staffed function.

The message apparent in this study and in general observation of MNC experience is that the task of managing relations with host nations is a large and vital one. Firms are just beginning to deal with it systematically. In their study Boddewyn and Kapoor emphasize that the task goes well beyond the limited goals of seeking legitimacy and reducing risks. The wide scope of government authority and discretion mean that favorable relations offer many opportunities to improve business performance. Government relations in this perspective can be viewed as on a par with marketing, production, and other basic activities designed to improve profits. By the same token, the authors observe that managements should not assume that: "(1) Government relations is only an unpleasant chore or an inevitable nuisance to be dealt with as expeditiously as possible by whoever is handy; and (2) it is mostly a matter of waiting to react to government initiatives. Instead, IBGR represents an active and imaginative top management function, one requiring planning and deliberation in the face of governments that can be as wavering in their policies and actions as any other institution."[5]

In another study Boddewyn has elaborated on the character of the task.

External affairs refers . . . to the function of enlisting support and/or negating the opposition of 'nonmarket' and 'macromanagerial' units in the multinational firm's environment. More specifically, external affairs . . . deals with: (1) government in its multiple roles as legitimizer, regulator, and promoter; (2) business and professional associations as well as other firms in their pressure-group role; (3) the intellectual, moral and scientific communities as legitimizers and opinion makers; and (4) public opinion at large."[6]

He then goes on to define the respective roles of members of management in the task,

At the national level, external affairs is a prime function of top line executives. Lower level specialists in external affairs perform a supporting function, but the top line men have the primary role including four major tasks: (1) identifying problems and assigning responsibility for them; (2) gathering environmental information through meeting with various "elites"; (3) obtaining approval and support for the firm's actions from decision makers . . . , opinion makers . . . , and other relevant "publics"; (4) negotiating with external decision makers. The external affairs staff aid in these tasks by environmental analysis, education of line executives, presentation of the corporate view to the public, bringing executives and outsiders together, coordination of external affairs activities and traditional external support activities like charitable contributions.

The regional level is frequently the first to receive attention because it constitutes a half-way point between the world level which is very heterogeneous and often underdeveloped, and the national level which may not warrant a full-time expert. . . . At a more advanced state, the regional level typically reflects the presence of several subsidiaries in a single region, which tends to create conflicts of national sovereignties, interests and feelings, requiring some multinational coordination and supranational representation. Here, the regional headquarters can often better explain and obtain approval for difficult decisions including choices among countries or of decisions to withdraw from a country. A national manager is usually less qualified to perform such sensitive "bad news" diplomacy because of the tendency of governments to berate him (especially if he is a native of the country) for being "unpatriotic" and for ignoring "national interests." . . . U.S. citizens usually serve very adequately in a regional capacity because of lingering prejudices and rivalries among nations.

The regional office is also useful because of the tendency of governments to copy the policies of other nations. The external affairs unit serves an effective collecting and disseminating function for information about government policies on a regional basis. As a part of this role, it is common to find that the Regional External Affairs Director organizes meetings of national EA directors to exchange information and experiences in such matters as regulation, pollution control, plant relocation or closing, discharge of personnel, and press relations. The regional level has five main functions: (1) to oversee the development of the external-affairs function in national subsidiaries; (2) to supervise the collection of information about national developments of interest to other subsidiaries; (3) to monitor and influence developments in supranational bodies; (4) to disseminate relevant information to and from national and world levels; and (5) to make strategy recommendations to the Regional General Manager.[7]

Boddewyn observes that the world level is the least developed of external affairs. This situation is due to various factors: the limited commitment to global affairs in corporate headquarters, the high degree to which matters pertaining to external affairs are localized, and the small number of people in headquarters with experience and disposition for worldwide external relations. He notes that as yet the global level does not have much to export outside of the field of public relations. He predicts, however, that the world headquarters role will increase because of the growth of instantaneous communications, the precedent-setting effects of actions of governments in all parts of the world, and the apparent trend toward more centralized decision-making in multinational enterprises.

## SPECIFIC ISSUES

Collective efforts to improve MNC–nation state relations and structural organization to deal with them play a major role in establishing the milieu for MNC operations. But the main body of the interaction is an endless stream of specific issues, some major, some minor. The job of management in dealing with this challenge may be separated into two levels, strategy and negotiation. We will focus only on strategy. However, the importance and difficulty of the latter should be recognized and the value of gaining skill in it appreciated. For this purpose readers are particularly directed to the studies of international business negotiations by Kapoor and some case studies which bring out vividly the problems and skills significant in negotiation.[8]

The analysis in the balance of this chapter does not elaborate on the specifics of the negotiation process. However, it is integrated closely with the subject because a *sine qua non* of successful negotiation is sound preparation including full understanding of the interests and attitudes of the negotiating parties, a realistic assessment of their strengths and weaknesses, and a practical and well directed set of goals and strategic plans. These are the subjects which we will now examine. Our analysis of strategy will proceed through three stages: first, an examination of the MNC and national interests which are at the heart of most issues, then an exploration of ways in which accommodation of MNC and national viewpoints may be accomplished and, finally, an exposition of the bases on which the hard kernel of conflicts is resolved by balancing of power positions.

### MNC and National Interests

National interests compose a broad subject encompassing not only overall national concerns but also those of individuals and groups within countries. Indeed it would appear that practically every action of the firm which touches its environment involves some aspects of national interests.

To develop this subject as a part of our analytical framework, we may start with the transmission of resources between countries discussed in Chapter 2. In line with the interaction analysis developed in Chapter 4, a pattern of benefits, conflicts, and controls arises in this process whose key components are depicted in Figure 5—1. Country A, within which the multinational firm is based, has certain resources which offer sufficient benefit for Country B to justify payments to Country A. Thus in broad terms there is a mutually beneficial basis for economic interchange between the two nations, and national interest calls for execution of the interchange so that A may make good use of its resources and B receive the benefits that are economically desirable for it. The multinational corporation is the agent through which the process of interchange is accomplished. Thus many of the problems it encounters are in essence those of the nation-to-nation interchange process.

**Figure 5–1.** Nation-to-Nation Resource Transfers

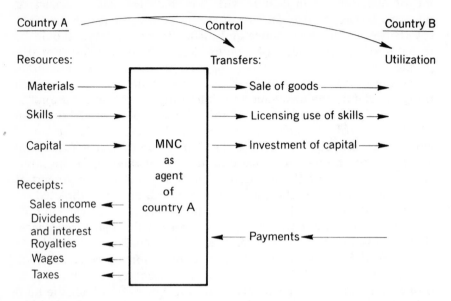

Although the interchange is assumed to be mutually beneficial, (otherwise it would not normally take place), its execution almost inevitably involves some degree of conflict both as to economic terms and control. The economic terms determine in effect the division of the benefits among the participants. Country A in our example naturally seeks the maximum return for the resources employed abroad, while Country B wishes to hold to a minimum the price it must pay. Likewise, Country A, wishing to assure that its resources are used in the manner most profitable to it and that they are adequately protected as long as it retains an interest in them, seeks to exercise certain controls over them. Country B, in receiving the resources, desires to exert its control to assure that they effectively serve its national interests. The MNC as the vehicle through which the exchange is taking place becomes the active agent on behalf of Country A in bargaining for the economic terms and establishing controls.

The problems for the MNC stem both from the inherent conflict between the two nations and from differences between the way the firm may see the situation and the viewpoint of the governments. These differences arise from divergences in opinions as to what is in the best national interest and from the difference in the terms of reference of the firm as compared with the nation as a whole. Without presuming to exhaust the many facets of this subject, we will find it useful to amplify the basic conceptual framework by citing a few of the key problems observed in international business.

First, to illustrate the *parent—nation* (Country A) side of the situation, we can look at the balance of payments and tax questions encountered by U.S. multinationals in relations with their government. Faced with persistent balance-of-payment deficits, the U.S. government arrived at the conclusion in the early 1960s that some limitation on the outflow of capital resources was in the best national interest as a means to protect the financial strength of the country. Many people, including much of the international business community, argued against this conclusion, believing that other measures would achieve the objective better. But ultimately the government view led to the voluntary restraint program instituted in 1965, followed by mandatory restrictions in 1968 which resulted in U.S. firms holding their export of capital below the level they would have set if their own judgment had been followed. In this case, the government view of the nation-to-nation exchange was that the overall interest of the United States was best served by a limitation of resource transfer, and the U.S. firms as the agents in the process acted accordingly despite opposing views among some of them.

The major tax issues have evolved in two stages. The first stage focused on the use of tax haven companies which permitted indefinite deferral of payment of U.S. taxes for profits reinvested abroad. As noted in Chapter 4 (p. 137) the U.S. government held that the national interest justified its assessing its tax share of these profits, even though they were held abroad. Thus, the 1962 tax law eliminated deferral of taxes for passive holding companies, leaving profits of actively operating subsidiaries still free of U.S. tax obligations.

While the U.S. national interest in MNC overseas profits was the basis for the 1962 tax changes, in the background was strong pressure by U.S. labor against foreign investment. MNCs were perceived as "exporting jobs" by setting up foreign factories to produce goods that had previously been made in U.S. plants with U.S. labor. Furthermore, MNCs were seen as dissipating U.S. technological strength by applying it in foreign manufacturing rather than retaining it for use only in U.S. factories where it would strengthen the competitive status of U.S. exports. Thus the labor unions had pushed for full elimination of tax deferral as a means to discourage foreign investment.

During the 1960s labor sentiment against foreign investment grew, especially as MNCs developed strategies to use plants in low-labor-cost countries as sources of products for the U.S. market to meet import competition by foreign firms based in those countries. The second stage of the tax issue emerged out of this pressure from labor in the Burke-Hartke bill proposed in 1972 which would have eliminated tax deferral from all foreign source income. It would also have repealed the foreign tax credit, substituting the tax deduction concept. The effect of the latter change would have been to raise the effective U.S. tax on earnings from foreign subsidiaries in major countries from the general range of 45−55 percent to 70−75 percent.

The Burke-Hartke bill was clearly based on the argument that foreign investments were counter to the U.S. national interest so taxes should be designed to discourage them. As compared to the previous tax haven issue, MNCs in this case were able to gain substantial support for their opposing view of national interest. Several studies including those by Stobaugh (p. 146) and Business International (p. 281) lent weight to their contention that the interests not only of the nation but labor itself would suffer if their capability to meet low-labor cost competition directly was impeded. The Burke-Hartke bill was therefore not passed. However, into the late 1970s it was still being pushed by labor and its allies in the U.S. government and the debate continued as to where the true national interest lay.

Turning now to relations with *the host nation* (Country B), we find a different range of problems. This is the point at which the terms of the nation-to-nation exchange of resources are worked out between the MNC as the agent for Country A and the government and/or businessmen representing Country B. The relatively wealthy industrialized countries are inclined to feel that their national interests will be best served by allowing these terms to be determined through the free functioning of economic relations in the private enterprise system. But among the less developed countries which are preoccupied with the problems of using limited resources to maximum advantage, it is common for the government to enter actively into the process of establishing both the economic and control terms.

The *economic* terms cover the full range of business arrangements affecting the profitability of the transfer of resources—prices, credit terms, and so on. In large part their negotiation is no different from similar processes in domestic business. The chief distinction is the critical role of governments, especially in the less developed countries, in such issues as price controls and taxes, which will influence profits, and in foreign-exchange controls and exchange rates which will determine the amount of income which can be transferred back to Country A. The multinational firm commonly finds itself either confronted with established policies (e.g., Country B will allow repatriation of profits up to only 8 percent of capital per year) or flexible situations in which it can negotiate with the government (e.g., Country B will exempt a new investment from taxation for five years if the company can argue effectively that it fills an essential national need). The firm, of course, pursues its negotiations and decision-making essentially on the basis of its private interests (though the effect of such measures as the U.S. government investment guarantees is to inject some extra weighting of the parent-government's view of national interest). In the process, however, it fulfills the role of agent for its country, establishing the terms of the nation-to-nation exchange. Whether the economic terms are determined in relations with private enterprise or the government of Country B, the difference in the national interests of the two countries, each seeking to maximize its net benefits from the exchange, makes a degree of conflict inevitable.

The questions concerning *control* were broadly defined in Chapter 4. They are not so readily defined in concrete terms as those relating to the division of economic benefits. They are of frequent concern, however, not only because of the national interests involved, but also because the extent of controls exercised by the MNC within a host country has much to do with the nationalistic antagonism it arouses. One can set forth two extreme viewpoints: (1) that Country A and the multinational corporation as its agent would like to have complete control over the use of its resources in Country B and (2) that Country B would like to see the resources turned over completely to its own nationals as soon as the resources enter the country. However, neither extreme is a close approximation to the positions found in reality. Typically, the Country A viewpoint accepts as beneficial to its own national interest substantial control by people in Country B, who are assumed to be competent to make more effective use of the resources in some respects than Country A nationals could achieve. The Country B position sees merit in some degree of active participation by the MNC in the control of the resources in its country. The problems therefore lie in a limited band of disagreement representative of (1) situations in which the national interests of the two countries diverge and (2) situations in which the MNC disagrees with Country B as to how the national interests of that country will be best served.

The clearest example of the first category, the difference in national interests, is the question of property protection. If capital resources of Country A are transferred to Country B but with ownership retained by one of its companies, Country A has an obvious national interest in protecting them. Although such extremes are rare today, in the not too distant past this interest was periodically manifested by active military intervention in foreign countries by nations which saw the property of their citizens threatened. Country B, on the other hand, has no great worry on this count. Typically, responsible host governments are concerned with the problem to some degree because they know they cannot attract investments unless they have a reputation for giving them reasonable protection. But this is a much less forceful concern than that of the actual owner of the capital resources. Thus capital-exporting nations and their businessmen are usually very anxious to negotiate controls to protect their property. The recipient countries are reluctant to agree as the terms involved usually restrict them in ways that may impair other efforts to further national interests such as their freedom to allocate foreign exchange to other uses than capital repatriation.

The situations in the second category are by definition of a hazier nature because they are matters in which there are differences of opinion regarding how to accomplish the same goal—the advancement of the interests of the host nation. There is a natural disposition along the lines discussed in Chapter 2 (which will be elaborated in several places in Part II) for the MNC to feel that its resources will be utilized most effectively if it exercises substantial control. The better utilization is seen as beneficial both to the firm and to the country.

To provide one illustration, this position is supported by the intensive study of foreign firms in Brazil by McMillan, Gonzales, and Erickson, which concluded that the general effect of national restrictions and sentiments was to prevent the foreign firms from making their full potential contribution to Brazilian economic development.[9] It is difficult to reach any sure determination on such matters, however, because much depends on how one defines "effective utilization of the resources." For example, on the employment of local national managers, these authors observed that "general criticism of the prevalent practice of staffing top management positions with U.S. citizens is difficult to justify. The most significant import for the developing nation is the economic decision-maker and initiator. The more and the better the quality of this class, the more rapid the pace of growth and the greater the opportunity for the development of national economic leadership."[10]

In the immediate sense of the effectiveness of specific company decisions, this conclusion seems well grounded. However, the host government may be more concerned with the development of managerial skills and the amenability of companies to acceptance of government guidance, feeling that both of these are more beneficial to the overall, long-term utilization of the resources brought in by foreign firms. Those criteria lead toward maximum use of local nationals even if there is a short-term lowering of the quality of decision-making in their firms. This type of difference in basic frame of reference can be found behind divergences in opinion about control of other aspects of the flow of resources such as marketing, technology, and finance.

Summarizing this section, we have observed that the activities of the multinational corporation inevitably affect the national interests of both the parent and host countries. Although a degree of mutual benefit for both countries must underlie these activities, some degree of conflict of interests is generally present. Further complications arise because of differences in perceptions of what the true national interests are and because of the special interests of the MNC. The interplay of the various interests appears most in the establishment of terms of exchange and the degree of control to be exercised by the firm and the host nation in the transmission of resources.

In the establishment of policies for the MNC, two features of the nationalism-national interest complex we have been examining are fundamental: first, that there is a substantial degree of uncertainty among the various parties as to what is in the best interests of each and, second, that some degree of conflict with nationalism and national interests is inevitable. These features, in turn, suggest two levels of policy formulation. At the first level the corporation should devote its efforts to the achievement of all feasible accommodations to nationalism and national interests, seeking to minimize conflicts and to maximize the achievement of mutual benefits. At the second level, policies must be designed that recognize valid conflicts and achieve a workable dynamic balance based on relative benefits and power relationships.

Our discussion will be confined to policies in relations between the multinational corporation and host nations. The other side of the question—relations with the parent country—is not considered unimportant; but relatively speaking, such relations are much less difficult. Insofar as this book is concerned, it is not essential to deal with them because conceptually the approaches to them are essentially the same as with host nations. That is, in broad concept (though not of course in specific detail), the accommodation and power-balance approaches are fully applicable to relations with the parent country.

### The Accommodation Approach
The achievement of feasible accommodation between the multinational firm and a host nation is directed at the range of decision

options in which differences in views are due to deficiencies of perception, inertia, or related causes rather than valid conflicts. Figure 5−2 illustrates this concept. On most questions there will be some span of difference X−Y, which represents a range of valid conflict in the interests of the host nation and the MNC. But each party will quite commonly conceive its interest as extending beyond these limits because of failure to understand the full situation, unwillingness to shift from an earlier position, nationalistic emotions, or some other reason. This misconceived extension of self-interest is represented by the added bands A−X and B−Y on either side of the span of valid conflict. Thus in many issues the parties find they are divided by an A−B span, which is much wider than the X−Y span over which conflict is really justified. The distinction between the scope of valid self-interest and the misconceived range of its extensions is, of course, impossible to determine accurately in practice. Because of the varied values and goals of people and the difficulty of obtaining full and objective facts and predictions of consequences of actions, one can never arrive at a clear determination as to the true interest of a group in any situation. However, the distinction is meaningful in broad terms.

The question of the use of local nationals in management jobs in subsidiaries can be used as an example. In a particular situation an MNC, we will assume, has sound logic in arguing that *corporate interests* are best served if the general manager and perhaps the senior financial officer are parent-country nationals, but the host government has equal logic in saying that *its national interests* call for using local nationals in these positions. This is the X−Y span of basic conflict, and its disposition will be considered later.

**Figure 5−2.**  Conflicts in Views of Self-Interest

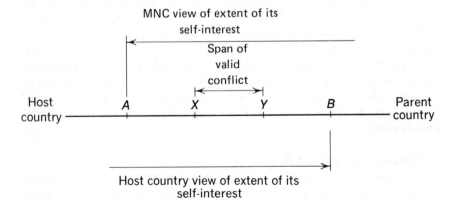

But on either side of this span there may well be other viewpoints. The A—X range indicates the views of those executives in the firm who advocate employment of expatriates in middle and perhaps even lower ranges of management, and the B—Y range covers host-nation views that expatriates should be excluded from even such activities within the subsidiary as staff advisors or a permanent stockholder's representative. These viewpoints are apparently not based on sound conceptions of self-interest.

The A—X range may be due to a biased underrating of the managerial capabilities of local nationals or the determination of expatriates presently holding jobs abroad to keep them when actually very able local nationals can be found who could do a good and perhaps better job with lower total compensation than expatriates. The B—Y range, on the other hand, can be traced to excessive nationalistic worry over foreign control of national industry or pressures from professional groups seeking to capture every possible job for local nationals without recognition of the real gain to the nation in some degree of facilitation of the inflow of resources by representatives of the parent company on the spot.

The problems of achieving feasible accommodation are readily apparent in this example. In the first place, it is no easy matter to determine the X—Y span. In practically every situation it will differ. Thus while the general manager–financial officer issue is very often the point at which valid interests collide, in other cases such as oil companies in highly undeveloped countries, employment of expatriates at much lower positions is clearly beneficial to the host nations because of the lack of competent local nationals. On the other hand, in a number of cases, especially in Europe, a company can find a local national who is both highly competent and sufficiently loyal to company interests so that his employment as general manager is in its best interests. But any conclusion is clearly based on subjective evaluation of many ill-defined variables and human characteristics. The same is true of other issues such as how much ownership should be shared with nationals, proper competitive relationships, and the like.

The underlying problem therefore is one of discernment—to determine what the A—X and B—Y spans are—and then of implementation. For the multinational firm these are essentially human problems involving intellectual effort, emotional discipline, and personal motivations. Their character is illustrated by one conclusion coming out of the intensive research among U.S. companies conducted by Robinson: "An inflexible policy against entering any joint ventures was nearly always a veneer covering basic distrust by United States businessmen, and possibly dislike, of non–Americans."[11] That such attitudes should be encountered among Americans is not at all surprising because they are fully consistent with the nature of nationalism. American executives are as prone to nationalistic attitudes as those of any other nation. But they, along with equally difficult deterrents in lack of intellectual perception and in personal interests, make it hard for managements to pull back from A to X, that is, to accommodate their own policies to host-nation viewpoints where there is a valid coincidence of interests.

Dealing with the B–Y span, the host-nation side, is yet harder because essentially the same human problems are involved, but the corporation can influence them only as an outsider. There is at the outset the nationalistic resistance problem. Any view advanced by the outsider, the multinational corporation, is instinctively resisted as coming from a suspect and distrusted source. Many people in a host country will instinctively support the full use of local nationals in management for this sort of emotional reason. One of the prime objectives of the corporation must be to tone down these attitudes.

In the design of a strategy to approach this problem, it is useful to think in terms of sectors of the host society as indicated schematically in Figure 5–3. The groups are plotted roughly along a curve according to the relative strength in their views of two factors: nationalism and "industrialism" (a term coined to show both interest in industrial development and awareness of the realities of accomplishing it).

At the outer extremes of Figure 5–3 we have the average citizen who is strongly influenced by nationalistic views. He is interested in industrial development but has little rational understanding of its requirements. Illustrative of the attitudes toward foreign investment found at the extremities are the results of an opinion survey in Brazil which showed that two-thirds of the people felt that foreign investors should take no profits out of the country.[12] Views of this nature are characteristic of the typical "man in the street," especially in less developed countries. As a general proposition he wishes industrial development and wants foreign companies to help. But when confronted by a specific issue in which the foreign company appears to be benefiting at the expense of his country or exercising control over internal affairs, he will instinctively give a negative response arising essentially from nationalistic emotions, with little or no realistic evaluation of the merits of the issue.

As we move toward the central axis, the nationalistic views come under greater restraint with rational understanding of economic factors coming to the fore. In the center the attitudes of people on both

**Figure 5–3.** Nationalism Versus Industrialism

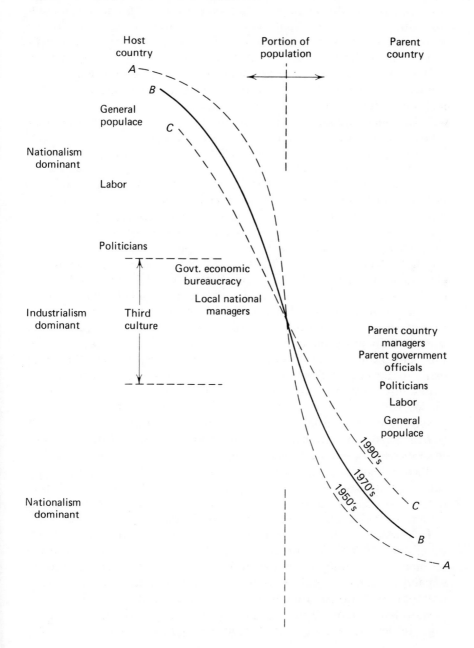

sides of the nationality break are fairly close because in many economic considerations they are thinking alike. These people are often members of the third culture described earlier in this chapter, including both national and expatriate executives and government officials who have a substantial community of interests themselves. The attitude surveys cited at the end of Chapter 4 (Table 4–5) demonstrate that the views among elites are much more diverse than Figure 5–3 implies. But the general proposition that national support for MNCs may be found among many elites is valid.

Although some public relations efforts directed at the general population are doubtless worthwhile, it is not realistic to expect a notable change to be accomplished by this means. Antiforeign investment attitudes are so deeply imbedded in the nationalistic traditions of the less developed countries and have become such prominent political footballs in even such advanced societies as France and Canada that the efforts of MNCs to change them can have little effect. With respect to this great sector of society, therefore, the most effective strategy is likely to be to minimize public exposure of specific conflicts. Though broad efforts to improve public image as noted elsewhere are beneficial, on specific issues the MNC faces not only a generally adverse public view but also a nationalistic bias in press and public reaction which greatly handicaps it in trying to convey its side of an issue to the public. Striking examples of the weak role of the MNC in press relations and its adverse effect in relations with host governments can be observed in the Bechtel and Mercantile cases in India and Canada.[13] For some large companies and major issues, low visibility may not be practical, but in many cases companies can in one way or another handle relations with the host government or local individuals or groups so that they do not attract public attention. Full attention can then be directed toward people in or close to the third-culture group.

Two elements of strategy appear to be productive in approaching the third-culture sector; first, efforts to expand the sector and, second, efforts to reduce the degree of misconceptions of national interest among its members, to reduce the B–Y span of Figure 5–2.

In pursuit of the first element, companies find they are accelerating and facilitating a process which has already gained substantial momentum. A number of developments in recent times have been expanding the third culture group quite rapidly, notably many international educational programs, large-scale international contacts of government personnel in aid, military, and other activities, and growing interdependence of nations. Thus we might schematically indicate the growth of the third culture group by shifting the curve in Figure 5–3 from A–A in 1950 to B–B in the mid–1970s and go on readily to visualize a C–C position as a natural evolution by 1990.

The typical MNC will have significant interactions with only a limited number of local nationals in business and government positions. The strategic proposition advanced here is simply that a concerted effort be made to attract these people away from strong attachment to their basic cultural and nationalistic attitudes toward more neutral viewpoints. The feasibility of this strategy has been proved by many overseas managers. Their success is due in no small part to the way in which they have broadened their own immediate third-culture social orbit.

A related dimension of the approach to the public is suggested in a study by Blake and Driscoll of pulp and paper operations of U.S. firms in Brazil.[14] Opinion surveys showed that familiarity with actual operations of the subsidiaries led to more favorable views. Positive attitudes were significantly correlated with employees and suppliers (vs. community and government leaders), those who followed the operations of the company closely, and those who lived closest to the operations. Sources of information showed a related pattern. The 132 respondents who said their information came from employees of the company were more positive in their assessments than the 23 who relied primarily on news media.

Although the reduction of emotional, nationalistic attitudes implicit in belonging to the third culture eases the task, the second element of the strategy, reducing misconceptions, poses real problems. There are just as many intellectual and personal blocks among host nationals as there are among managements of MNCs, resulting in the same inability or unwillingness to see where true national interest lies. Just to cite one striking illustration of the type of problem encountered, we may recall the expropriation of the Iranian oil properties in 1951. Quite well-educated Iranians sincerely believed that their nationals could step right in and run the great Abadan refinery. Only bitter failure showed them that the technological complexities were beyond their capacities so that in their own national interests they found it wise ultimately to bring in a new group of Westerners to run the industry.

In a less dramatic way this sort of education by experience is constantly under way, and the essence of the second element of company strategy is to make a deliberate effort to facilitate the process. It is essentially an educational job though it may proceed in many ways. Sometimes a large-scale effort may be helpful. For example, in 1964 the Business Council for International Understanding, a group of progressively minded U.S. firms, organized a program of meetings with Indian government officials which was aimed at giving the Indians a clearer understanding of the needs and capabilities of U.S. industry and how government policies related to them. More commonly the strategy calls for many and varied communications with businessmen, government bureaucrats, and other local nationals in which the facts and implications of each area of conflict are progressively discussed and understanding advanced. Again the details of the execution of such a strategy require more space than is feasible here. For one example of a well-executed effort, the reader is commended to Richard Robinson's case history of Merck's negotiations with the Indian government for establishment of a pharmaceutical plant.[15]

### The Power-Balance Approach

Although the accommodation approach may establish a broader range of coincidence of interests, there remain inevitably the valid conflicts, the X—Y span in Figure 5—2. These valid conflicts call for a different type of strategy built essentially around power relationships.

Two prefatory remarks are needed to set this discussion in perspective. First, it is commonplace to observe that conflicts in human affairs are settled by power, sometimes by raw force, but more typically by the exercise of economic, legal, and political strength: workers win higher wages according to their power to withhold their productive contributions from an enterprise by striking; the price of a house emerges as a balance between the strength available to the seller (the merits of his house and often his financial staying power) and that of the buyer (chiefly his opportunity to buy alternative houses); the politician beats out his rival if he has the ability to marshal power through popular support; and so on. Thus there is nothing unusual in the observation that conflicts confronting the MNC must be resolved through the use of power.

The second remark takes another tack. Given the nature of nationalism, the idea that a foreign company's status in a host country is the result of the exercise of power is disturbing. There is a great temptation to sweep the whole idea under a rug and talk about "nicer" things. We have no business doing that, however. Not only is it unrealistic but, more important, it encourages a fallacious line of thinking which is all too common. There are those who propose that companies operating abroad must go all the way to satisfy the valid interests of host governments, asserting in effect that the exercise of power by the multinational firm in this context is improper. Because this position is often related to humanitarian consideration of the lower-income levels of the less developed countries, and past and present shortcomings of the performance of foreign firms, it is appealing. But looking at the matter objectively, one can see no logical reason why power should not be just as normal and proper a basis for settling conflicts in the relationships of the multinational corporation as in any other type of conflict.

Working from this philosophical base, we may go on to consider the elements of power present. Our analysis can be limited to economic and political power, physical force being rarely employed except as an adjunct to the former. Legal power is also not covered per se because it is essentially a consequence of economic and political power, though of course in all its ramifications it composes a very large subject quite pertinent to the effective use of power. We will look first at the power available to the MNC and then at the host-nation side of the balance. In this discussion a broad distinction can often be made between the situations encountered in developed as compared to less developed countries, recognizing all the while that the problems in each country will be unique to some degree.

*The power of the multinational corporation* stems primarily from its own resources, the role of other MNCs, and the political and economic strength of the parent country. The forms the power takes are best described by reference to the types of situations in which they appear.

In the precommitment stage of any transfer of resources, the corporation has available the power to withhold the resources whether they be goods proposed for sale, capital funds for a new investment, or technical skills for a licensing arrangement. The strength of this form of power will, of course, vary greatly depending upon the value of the resources to the host nation. This value is essentially determined in the marketplace rather than by a determination of the intrinsic productive contribution of the resources. The marketplace value, in turn, is a function of the competitive strength of the corporation in relation to other companies and countries.

The weakest situation is that of the exporter of a staple commodity in ample world supply—sugar for example. A firm selling such a product can do little more than sell at the price and terms prevailing on the world market as it will gain nothing by threatening not to sell unless better terms are offered. At the other extreme we have a few companies with highly developed technological skills and great competence in applying them. The Merck case mentioned earlier is a good example.[16] While the company showed skill in accommodating

Indian interests, it was negotiating from very substantial strength in its technology both relative to other Western companies and in competition with the Russians who were not considered to be as competent by the Indians. The power of the MNC is underscored in those cases where the initiative has come from the host country—for example, when a host-country firm seeks a licensing agreement from a multinational firm because it lacks certain technical skills. In between these extremes lies a broad range in which companies have varying degrees of power, depending upon the combination of financial resources, technical skill, managerial competence, and productive capacity at their command.

Once the initial commitment to transfer resources has been made, the power to withhold them loses much of its force, though in most cases there is a degree of future flow of resources which gives some continuing power. A drug firm, for example, will be producing new technology, the future availability of which provides at all times some power for the corporation in relations with host nations.

Although the resources under its immediate control give the corporation considerable power, it benefits substantially from other forms of power. One of the major forms is the collective willingness of other corporations, both from its own country and from other nations, to transfer resources to a country arising from opinions about its *investment climate.* With many investment opportunities available to them, MNCs are relatively selective, and one of the prime criteria in judging new proposals is their view of the treatment they may expect from the government. Their conclusions on this count are very largely determined by their observation of the way in which foreign firms presently in the country have been treated, and therein lies the power available to the individual firm.

This form of power is most pertinent in the less developed countries, which are anxious to attract private investment. The situation in each country is different, but we can identify a fairly common evolution. A few years ago, the nation with an inexperienced government staffed by anticapitalist, highly nationalistic people treated foreign firms already established within its borders quite harshly. Expropriations may have occurred, but more commonly there were severe regulations; foreign exchange for dividends and even for essential material imports was erratically available, and so forth. At the same time the government was hard-pressed to find resources to support economic development, and there was a growing feeling that private foreign capital must play a bigger role. Unfortunately it appeared that MNCs were not much interested. Before long, government officials began to see that there was a connection between this fact and the way they were treating the established firms, and from this learning process arose a degree of power for the latter.

Another source of power in the less developed countries is the economic aid provided by the wealthier countries individually and collectively through international institutions. The donors of aid have been loath to use it in an overt manner to pressure less developed countries in their relations with MNCs, but in assorted ways the aid programs have been a source of power to the companies. The receiving countries have had some very clear signs of the potential relationship between treatment of foreign companies and contributions of aid. For example, in 1962 the U.S. Congress passed the Hickenlooper amendment which required that U.S. aid be cut off from any nation that expropriated property of U.S. companies without prompt and adequate compensation. Although the amendment itself has not been particularly effective, this and numerous other U.S. government actions have shown less developed countries that the way U.S. firms are treated in their countries will be one factor determining how they fare when aid decisions are made, and so the firms have acquired a degree of power from the aid program.

In relations in the highly industrialized countries, multinational corporations draw power from the presence of foreign investments in the parent country. For example, U.S. subsidiaries in France benefit from the fact that French companies have subsidiaries in the United States. Each government tends to refrain from actions in its own country which may lead to retaliation against the investments of its nationals abroad. This is a matter of mutual respect for which the power idea may seem inappropriate, but it is fundamentally part of the same concept. The chief difference between it and the forms of power discussed previously is that the situation is much more stabilized and institutionalized. That is, the extent of the power has already been largely recognized for some time; and it has been given effect in treaties and in routine patterns of government conduct.

Finally MNCs may draw some direct support for their interests by direct intervention of their parent governments on their behalf. There were cases in the past where this factor weighed heavily for the foreign firms. For example, in China a century ago by virtue of treaty obligations imposed by their parent countries, foreign firms had extensive extraterritorial rights including being subject to their own laws, not those of China. But today, parent governments exert far less influence on foreign governments on behalf of their nationals. The U.S. government typically does not take a strong position to aid U.S. firms in their relations with foreign governments except where a pressing U.S. national interest seems to be involved. Most of its efforts are of a generalized nature in seeking, for example, non-discriminatory treatment of investors or encouraging foreign countries to establish monetary reforms that will give greater assurance of ability to repatriate profits. Sometimes the magnitude of issues and arrangements with host nations require U.S. government intervention as in the negotiations with the Organization of Petroleum Exporting Countries and with Canada over the automotive products agreement. At other times it has played a modest but often crucial role where the national interest seemed significantly involved, for example, in helping Chrysler to enter the Japanese auto market, setting the pace for general investment liberalization. However, there are considerable risks in such intervention as could be seen in the Bechtel case in India and the Mercantile Bank affair in Canada.[17] U.S. government actions on behalf of these MNCs aroused nationalistic reactions which made its role of uncertain value. Other parent governments often take a stronger position supporting their MNCs. For example, when a European MNC was faced with a severe problem by a Latin American government in the early 1970s, its parent government made a sizable loan to the host nation with the explicit *quid pro quo* that the problem of the MNC be favorably resolved. The outcome of any parent government's efforts is, of course, highly dependent upon the overall relationships between the governments involved which inject into the conceptual relationship issues of broad international political affairs which are too big to discuss in this brief treatise, even though they are quite significant to it.

*The power held by the host country* comes more from political relationships, though economic power is also significant. The key element in this part of the power structure is the special political status of the MNC which arises from its interaction with various components of the host society and the related interactions with the host government. The nature of this status and its relation to the subject of national interests can be explained by comparison of domestic and multinational firms illustrated in Figure 5–4. In modern democratic nations the political system provides a means for satisfying and blending individual, group, and broad national interests.

On the left side of the figure we have a self-contained political system in which the main components interacting with the domestic business firm are shown. Each of the interactions contains some degree of mutual benefit and some degree of conflict. For example, competitors will often collaborate in the sharing of industry statistics through an association while they battle in the marketplace. Workers earn wages by virtue of the success of a business, but they are ever anxious for a greater share of the company's income.

**Figure 5–4.** Political Power Relationships

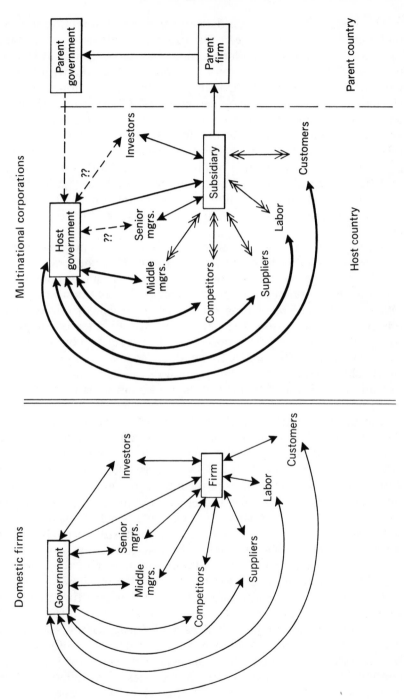

The resolution of the conflict aspect of the interaction is a complex matter; however, we can identify certain elements of it that are significant variables in understanding the status of the MNC to be considered below. First, there is the sense of identity with the company which is important particularly for the groups closest to it. The clearest illustration is the expectation of future top management careers which contributes to acceptance by middle management of salary, assignment, and other conditions which, if treated on an immediate reaction basis, might lead to greater conflict. Among workers there is at least a degree of moderation of conflict due to a sense that the corporation's profits contribute to local and national development; and in some firms like Sears, Roebuck, one finds that workers own directly or through pension funds significant portions of company stock.

Second, there is the assurance that comes from knowing that each component is subject to similar conditions. Competitors, for example, have access to similar financial institutions and suppliers. Thus they can more readily accept the character of the conflict as a fair match. This point must immediately be qualified, of course, by the observation that within a society there are all sorts of inequalities which favor one side of a conflict. With respect to competitors, for example, greater size tends to facilitate access to financial institutions. This is true, but it does not nullify the significance of the idea of similar conditions for this comparative analysis as we shall see in a moment.

The third element is equal status in voting rights and treatment by the government. A company does not, of course, have a direct vote, but through its top management and owners it is able to exercise an effective influence on the political process. The other components with which it interacts can seek recourse through the government for resolution of conflicts with the company. In some cases they may succeed. In the United States, for example, small firms have gained some relief from the disadvantages of their size through antitrust legislation, the Small Business Administration, and other means. Sometimes they may not succeed, but the mere fact that they have recourse to the government eases somewhat the tension of conflict.

Turning now to the situation of the multinational firm in a foreign society, on the right side of Figure 5–4 we find a different story. The immediate interactions will generally lead to the same mutual benefits and conflicts. Middle managers, workers, competitors and the like will have much the same degree of common interests and conflicts of interest in their regular activities with domestic firms as with a subsidiary of an MNC. The nature of the three elements affecting the resolution of the conflicts is, however, appreciably different with regard to the MNC because of its ties to the parent country and its political status in the host country.

The sense of identity with the company is to some degree weakened by the flow of income back to the parent country and the control exerted by non-nationals. The workers are, therefore, somewhat less easily satisfied in their wage demands because they feel that company profits when they leave the country do not benefit them even in the small way they might if they stayed in the host nation. Middle managers with virtually no prospect of reaching the top executive ranks in the parent firm and perhaps even cut off from senior subsidiary levels have less sense of identity with company goals.

By the same token, there is no longer the assurance of being subject to similar conditions. The MNC is seen by local national firms as operating under more advantageous conditions. It can, for example, draw on a broader range of financial resources both in its parent treasury and in access to the capital markets of other nations.

On the other hand, in the third element, political status, the multinational firm as shown in Figure 5—4 is clearly weaker. If it works through a fully owned subsidiary whose top executives are all nonnationals, it has very little political status in the normal electoral scheme. If it has a joint venture with some local stockholders and employs local nationals in senior positions, it will have some exponents with votes, but it is still weaker than a completely national firm in its direct relations with the government.

The limits on its political role are in themselves a difficult policy question. The crude manner in which ITT tried to buy political support to defeat Allende in Chile gave support to the view that MNCs should have no role in host nation political processes. But that extreme view is neither realistic nor sound. Its fallacy is best illustrated by the Canadian case where 60 percent of manufacturing is controlled by MNCs. To exclude the views of managements of 60 percent of a nation's industry from national decision-making would result in unbalanced analysis which would not be sound in any country. In other nations the role of MNCs is less but the general proposition still holds. It is fundamentally appropriate in democratic societies for all the views of all participants in the society to be vigorously represented in national decision-making.

While accepting this basic proposition, some people attempt to make a distinction between participation in national decision-making and political activity. Specifically they propose that MNCs energetically present their views to host governments but that they refrain from involvement in electoral processes. This is a useful distinction and in general terms, especially for public consumption, it is probably the best stance an MNC can adopt.

However, it is not in reality feasible to adhere to this stance fully. In the first place, there are inevitably a host of borderline situations involved in personal relations between MNC executives and political figures and in MNC public statements which have political impact. But more importantly, the electoral process is the ultimate heart of national decision-making and in one way or another the MNC, through its executives, its friends, and other means, will and probably should play a part in it. Nonetheless, even if we accept the proposition that the MNC will have some role in the host nation political process, it is inevitable that its power will be less than that of domestic participants.

To this picture we must also add the effect of bribery and related exceptional action by many MNCs revealed in the mid-1970s, such as have been described in the Gulf case.[18] These payments added a form of political power to the MNCs but the reaction against them has probably limited their widespread use in the future.

The combined effect of the differences in these three elements between the purely domestic situation and that of the multinational firm in a foreign nation is to set up a quite different flow of political forces and resultant actions as shown in Figure 5–4. The local groups interacting with the firm having less sense of identity and assurance of equal opportunity feel a greater sense of conflict in their relations with the firm. This, combined with an underlying nationalistic reaction, results in a greater flow of feelings up to the government.

The government, being a politically sensitive organ, tends to respond to these greater pressures and to the weaker ones coming from the MNC whose political power is limited. On the other hand, the politicians in the government often do or say things that encourage the anti-foreign investment component of nationalistic attitudes—a political stratagem which has proved effective for leaders in a great many countries. This creates a further component of pressure related to both nationalism and internal political byplay (e.g., the anti-foreign investment campaign oratory which must be implemented if the politician is not to be subject to opposition criticism).

The government might or might not meet fully the wishes of a particular national group or individual, depending upon other political considerations and its own view of national interest. But as often as not, there is a coincidence of national and special interests so that the political process fosters actions that in effect favor the special interests of the various groups in conflict with MNCs. For example, the desire of individual local nationals to obtain high management positions fits with government concern for greater national control, so assorted restrictions on the use of expatriates had been formulated. Although in public statements discriminatory treatment is usually adjured by all governments, workers can generally be sure that government labor officials will give them stronger support in negotiations with foreign firms than with local ones because of national interest in capturing as much income for the country as possible. Where special interests diverge from national interest, the outcome is unpredictable, but the weight of the political forces is likely to be significant, especially in matters such as were discussed earlier where the national interest is subject to some debate. For example, in a number of cases it would appear that joint ventures have been required by foreign governments more to satisfy the desire of local investors than to achieve optimum national economic advantage. As far as the power balance is concerned, therefore, the political status of the multinational corporation abroad is one of notable weakness.

The *economic power* of the host country comes from the value of the opportunity it offers to the MNC and the controls it commands. In a sale of goods this is simply a one-shot monetary payment, though there may be prospects of future sales to strengthen the buyer's hand. In investment and licensing situations the economic factor has a longer time dimension. As was noted in Chapter 2, market strategy is a prime factor in investment decisions. Multinational firms are extremely anxious to establish and maintain a strong position in foreign markets, especially the large and emerging ones. Thus host governments are well aware that they hold substantial economic power in their ability to give or withhold permission to operate in a market.

In addition, on a continuing basis the host government can control a number of factors affecting the economic performance of the firm —foreign exchange, imports, and prices. In those many countries where extensive economic planning and control are exercised, it is accurate in fact to characterize the private firm as being completely at the mercy of the government. Its profitability is dependent in large measure on the decisions of bureaucrats. Whether or not decisions are made which are economically adverse to the firm will, of course, depend upon many important considerations including such countering elements of power as have already been mentioned. But that is a further question. The point being made here is simply that the government does have the capacity and facilities to take these economic measures if it wishes, and therein lies a strong element of economic power.

## The Changing Balance of Power

Before leaving the subject of power relations, we must add one more dimension to the picture, namely, the element of *change*. Nationalism, national interests, and the elements of power are all subject to substantial change over time. The significance of these changes for business policies is perhaps best explained by an example—that of the oil companies in the Middle East.

In the 1920s, when exploration started in the Middle East, the host countries lacked the skills and capital needed to develop a petroleum industry, so their national interests were clearly served by the resources the oil companies could bring in. Their power position was very weak because, since the presence of vast reserves of oil was as yet unknown, they were offering an opportunity of uncertain value. The seven major oil companies still had modest natural resource requirements and functioning in a restrained, oligopolistic pattern, did not compete among themselves vigorously in the quest for oil reserves. Thus they did not contribute to the power of the host nations. All of these factors led to concession agreements which provided for modest 12.5 percent royalties for the host nations and a relatively free hand for the companies in management of oil operations.

By the 1960s this situation had changed notably. The host nations had now greatly increased their financial resources, and many of their nationals had acquired technical competence (though in most cases not enough to fully operate the oil industry). The existence of vast, proved reserves established the great value to oil companies of concession rights. The world demand for petroleum had mushroomed so that the companies were under constant pressure to acquire new reserves. Furthermore, instead of dealing with seven mildly competing major companies, the host countries were now receiving highly competitive offers from a variety of companies from many countries. They had still further strengthened their position by banding together with other oil-producing countries in the Organization of Petroleum Exporting Countries (OPEC) to negotiate key issues with the companies.

The net effect of these basic changes was that the interests and power relationships had shifted radically in favor of the host nations. Accordingly, there had been a notable change in the terms of their relationships. Concession agreements generally were giving the host nations about 60 percent of profits and sometimes more. There were also agreements limiting significantly the management control of the companies. OPEC, for example, was exerting considerable control over pricing.

Then in the early 1970s the power balance swung yet further. The OPEC nations dramatically demonstrated their strength in the 1974 oil embargo and subsequent quadrupling of oil prices. For the MNCs the process has led to virtually complete loss of pricing power and in some major cases liquidation of ownership status in petroleum production. Significantly, however, they do retain some power from two important resources: their control of much of the marketing structure and their technology.

Although this story of oil companies is a rather extreme example, the types of changes involved are quite common both over the long term and in relatively short periods. Richard Robinson's penetrating historical analysis of external investments in the less developed countries points up the major long-term trends and their significance.[19] In the nineteenth century, when the investments started, the host countries were weak in economic resources, and in many cases their governmental systems were so poorly organized that they did not even have strong political power. In these circumstances, the companies providing badly needed capital and skills were powerful enough to obtain very favorable terms. With the passage of time these countries have made appreciable economic progress, and their political competence has advanced. They still have great needs for capital and skills that multinational firms can provide, but the power differential has shifted substantially in their favor.

Robinson discusses at length the difficult policy problem this shift has caused for companies whose operations span a considerable time period. The favorable terms that were soundly established in an early period were typically formalized in legal documents, concession agreements, and licensing contracts, for example. The companies, adhering to the principles of private property rights and the enforceability of contracts, have felt justified in trying to hold the countries to these terms. The host countries, on the other hand, seeing that the balance of interests and power positions have changed, say that the terms are no longer justified. This readjustment of distribution of the benefits of international investment is a major component of the New International Economic Order which has emerged as the rallying point of joint LDC efforts in the late 1970s.

There is probably no "just" resolution to this problem. Both sides are "right" in a way. As a practical matter, however, such issues will be resolved on the basis of the new power positions. The shortcomings on both sides have been in the failure to properly assess these positions. The host countries have sometimes given too much weight to their growing economic and political strength, which has been supported in the public image by charges of excessive past use of power and exploitation by the Western nations and their companies. This view has led them to press harder on the multinational corporations than the true power relations justify, considering their continuing needs for capital and skills. As a result they have created images of poor investment climate and their national interests have suffered. On the other hand, many established companies have held too rigidly to the legal-right position and have been overconfident of their economic strength, not recognizing the degree to which the power of the host nations has grown. This view has led to unsatisfactory relations and, in some cases, even loss of property.

The shorter term shifts have been succinctly analyzed by Peter Gabriel:

> It is characteristic of direct-investment projects that their first-order benefits are greatest, certainly most spectacular, in the initial stages of the undertaking; capital flows in, plants are built, local workers are hired and trained, local supply contracts are let. Subsequently, the benefits from the investment change in nature and become diffused. The straightforward inflow of capital is followed by export production or domestic production of goods formerly imported (import substitution). Job creation shifts from the foreign enterprise to local contractors and suppliers. The importance of new technology changes from its direct use by the foreign firm to the more subtle demonstration effects on local entrepreneurship. These benefits seldom phase out completely. Yet over time they lose much of the impact associated with the inception and initial operation of the enterprise.
>
> The explicit costs of the foreign investment to the host economy generally behave in an exactly opposite fashion. They accrue almost imperceptibly at first, rise with the usual increase in the company's capital stock through plowback of earnings, and finally begin to abrade national sensitivities—in the form of dividend payouts—when the front-page benefits of the foreign investment have already sunk into oblivion, and discussion of second-, third-, and fourth-order benefits continues only in economic journals. True, remissions of earnings—though perhaps huge in comparison with the amount of capital originally brought into the country—are often modest compared with total profits realized or total capital employed. But these distinctions do not usually inform public controversy, acknowledged as they may have become in theoretical analysis.[20]

He concludes:

> Now, it is characteristic of a developing country that . . . conditions change radically with time. A "fifty-fifty" agreement with a fo .gn corporation that is seen as highly advantageous today, in comparison with previous arrangements in the same country or concurrent deals in other countries, will look intolerably onerous if other countries succe sfully

bargain for 75 percent tomorrow. Moreover, both the need for and the uniqueness of the contribution made possible by a given foreign investment are bound to be vitiated by the very process of industrial development it was typically called in to assist.

It is not surprising, therefore, that host governments should continually be tempted to try to renegotiate or unilaterally alter existing contracts and long-term arrangements with foreign investors, or to revoke or "reinterpret" laws and regulations affecting them. Governments in the less-developed countries are subject to severe pressures to extract the best possible deal from the foreign businessman, even if it means taking liberties with specific contracts made or general promises given. It may be a matter of sheer economic necessity. In times of desperate foreign-exchange shortages, guarantees of free profit remission are more easily suspended than imports of essential goods. It may be a matter of political pledges for newly elected governments. It is easier to marshal popular support by squeezing additional levies out of the foreigner on grounds of alleged "exploitation" than by acknowledging responsibility for domestic fiscal problems or failures. And there are the pressures from local business interests for protection from "unfair competition" unleashed by the allegedly more powerful foreign firm, or for license to participate in industries which the foreigner may have pioneered in the economy.[21]

The policy implications of these long- and short-term shifts in interests and power relations are clear, though by no means simple to achieve. A company must adopt a reasonably flexible attitude toward the terms of its relationships in a host country. This does not mean that legal contracts should be viewed as meaningless, for they are not. They are in themselves a part of the power structure, providing to the companies some degree of strength in any negotiation. The key point is that they are not to be regarded as absolutes which can be rigidly enforced even if the conditions under which they are negotiated change notably.

For Western managements this has proved an extremely difficult point of view to accept because of the obsession of the Western mind with the letter of the law, reinforced by nationalism and by real concern for the welfare of investments.[a] Thus the problem for management adds up to the need both to assess accurately the changes in circumstances and to achieve in its own thinking a degree of flexibility.

---

[a]A striking example of this attitude was provided by a review written by a businessman of Richard Robinson's book in which his advocacy of a flexible attitude toward contracts was sharply criticized. See John W. Scott, "A Critical Review of Intellectual Treason," *Business Abroad*, Aug. 10, 1964, pp. 30–31.

### Intermediaries in Conflict Resolution

Before leaving this subject, note must be taken of the role of agreements between governments and of supranational organizations in resolution of conflicts. For the most part this role is minor. If the earlier prediction that the shift of affiliation from the nation state to a supranational state will be slow, the role is likely to remain minor. In the analytical framework we have been developing the role lies largely in the institutionalizing of certain phases of conflict resolution. That is, the agreements among nations and the functions of supranational organizations provide a means for dealing in a collective or systematic way with conflict issues. The governments of pairs of countries have gotten together and threshed out problems of overlap in taxation. The World Bank in its Center for the International Settlement of Investment Disputes is evolving a system of mediation involving multinational corporations and host countries. In these matters the primary protagonists remain the nation states and the multinational firms. Where there is a conflict, the resolution is dependent upon the processes of accommodation we have been considering, with definition of interests and ultimately of power relations. The added element is the facilitating intervention of the government-to-government agreement or the establishment of an institution by multigovernment agreement, as the World Bank Center.

There is every reason to assume that the role of these intermediaries will expand because it is an efficient and a systematic way to deal with situations which recur and affect many companies. Thus it is important to the strategy of the MNC to know when and how to employ the devices which evolve. But this is essentially part of the execution stage of the strategy, not of the determination of its basic lines. There will remain the effort to clearly define the true interests of each party and to accommodate as far as possible to them, and to reach effective compromise on the residual conflict through sound application of relative power status.

### A Broader Perspective

The discussion in this chapter and the last has concentrated on the manner in which nationalism, national interests, and the multinational corporation interact in the types of situations normally encountered in international business. Recognizing the effects of change over time, we have evolved a strategy approach adapted to the environment that generally prevails in the free world today—a mixture of private- and public-enterprise economies functioning with a modicum of respect for property rights and continuity of responsible government. In this environment the resolution of conflicts by negotiation based on power relationships along the lines presented here is, in fact, functioning and may, therefore, be regarded as viable.

A thoughtful student of history must, however, ask whether the environmental characteristics upon which the resolution process rests are assured. We must recognize that the compromises resulting from the present power balance are far from satisfactory to either side. Many MNCs feel that their interests and those of their parent nations have suffered severely from the encroachments of foreign governments. But the dissatisfaction among the host nations is far greater, particularly in the tremendous body of accumulated resentment among the less developed countries against the industrial countries and their companies. The LDCs harbor a strong feeling that the industrialized countries have maltreated them in the past and are still trying to hold them back and milk their economies. For the most part, these feelings are held in check by national political leaders who, recognizing their dependence on Western capital and skills, have been willing to work within the environmental constraints assumed in this chapter. But from time to time, the feelings break out in convulsions like those in Cuba, Chile, and Indonesia, when foreign business is swept under for substantial periods by a fundamental change in the environmental conditions.

In principle, this type of development is still consistent with the balance-of-power concept. The difference is that the great reserve powers of the host nations in their ultimate sovereignty have been brought to play. Such eventualities suggest the possibility of even more radical changes in the environmental constraints. What, for example, would be the effect if all of the less developed countries agreed among themselves to demand that the industrial countries supply them with capital and skills on modest economic terms and with no control (i.e., no further establishment of subsidiaries in their countries)? What if they agreed to enforce this with the same type of collective political power (with military force in reserve) which countries like Cuba have exercised internally? We have already seen the beginnings of such collective action by the less developed countries in the United Nations Conference on Trade and Development (UNCTAD) and the early implementation of the New International Economic Order. So far, the demands of the LDCs have been modest and quite within the environmental constraints assumed in this chapter. But it is not impossible that, if conditions in their economies do not improve rapidly enough and political pressures grow, a more radical approach might appear. In a century that has seen such massive areas as Russia and China pass through radical changes in political-economic environment, one must recognize the possibility that other large areas may experience equally extreme changes.

The implications for corporate strategy are uncertain. The firm as a small social entity must, by and large, relate its strategy to the environment existent at any one time, making modest efforts to adjust its decisions to expected changes. If the environmental constraints are in themselves inconsistent with overall social needs, it can do little to change them. That sort of adjustment is essentially the job of major social institutions like national governments and the United Nations. The MNC may well participate as a citizen in the efforts of the governing bodies, but its individual influence is small. On an overall basis, therefore, the question that must remain unanswered is whether the processes of accommodating conflicts of interests among nations at the government level can evolve satisfactorily within the present general pattern. If not, then the ground rules upon which the conceptual framework for corporate strategy have been evolved may have to be radically altered.

## SUMMARY

A mutuality of interests between the MNC and host and home nations in processes of the transmission of resources and innovation in host societies is the sine qua non for international business. But some degree of conflict is inevitable in these processes. This chapter has added to the analytical framework an approach to understanding and dealing with the conflict component of the processes.

The conflicts have been considered as composed of two parts: first, an area of valid conflict in which soundly based positions on each side are mutually exclusive, and second, an extension of the area of conflict because of misconceptions as to what is the true interest of each. The misconceptions arise from ignorance, prejudice, and other causes, prominent among which are the nationalistic attitudes of the participants. There is an inherent conflict in the xenophobic reaction of the members of the national we-group toward the multinational firm which attempts at least to some degree to penetrate their society with objectives of profit and control. These reactions add a component of emotion to discussions of conflicts of interests which might otherwise be dealt with in a relatively objective manner.

The resolution of these problems in international business has been found to lie along two main lines. First, there is the effort to achieve maximum accommodation by reducing the misconceptions of interests on the part of the management of the multinational firm, parent-country government officials, and host-country nationals. An important component of this process is the effort to minimize nationalistic emotional reactions in the interests of rational discussion of issues. Measures to achieve this goal range from avoidance of heated public debate to broadening and effectively utilizing the third-culture groups which are most capable of objective action. Second, the resolution of the hard core of valid conflict must inevitably come through negotiation based on relative economic and political power relationships. The power available to the multinational firms and to host countries varies greatly from situation to situation and over the course of time. Thus a flexible approach to corporate policies affected by national interests and nationalism is required.

## Appendix A

## A CODE OF WORLDWIDE BUSINESS CONDUCT
## Issued by the Caterpillar Tractor Co., October 1974

### Ownership and investment

In the case of business investment in any country, the principle of mutual benefit to the investor and the country should prevail.

We affirm that Caterpillar investment must be compatible with social and economic priorities of host countries and with local customs, tradition and sovereignty. We intend to conduct our business in a way that will earn acceptance and respect for Caterpillar, and allay concerns—by host country governments—about "foreign" ownership.

In turn, we are entitled to ask that such countries give careful consideration to our need for stability, business success and growth; that they avoid discrimination against "foreign" ownership; and that they honor their agreements, including those relating to rights and properties of citizens of other nations.

We recognize the existence of arguments favoring joint ventures and other forms of local sharing in the ownership of a business enterprise.

Good arguments also exist for full ownership of operations by the parent company: the high degree of control necessary to maintain product uniformity and protect patents and trademarks, and the fact that a single facility's profitability may not be as important (or as attractive to local investors) as its long-term significance to the integrated, corporate whole.

Caterpillar's experience inclines toward the latter view—full ownership—but with the goal of worldwide ownership of the total enterprise being encouraged through listing of parent company stock on many of the world's major stock exchanges.

Since defensible arguments exist on both sides of the issue, we believe there should be freedom and flexibility—for negotiating whatever investment arrangements and corporate forms best suit the long-term interests of the host country and the investing business, in each case.

### Corporate facilities

Caterpillar plants, parts warehouses, proving grounds, product demonstration areas and offices are to be located wherever in the world it is most economically advantageous to do so, from a long-term standpoint.

Decisions as to location of facilities will, of course, consider such conventional factors as nearness to sources of supply and markets, possibilities for volume production and resulting economies of scale, and availability of a trained or trainable work force. Also considered will be political and fiscal stability, demonstrated governmental attitudes, and other factors normally included in defining the local investment or business "climate."

We do not seek special treatment in the sense of extraordinary investment incentives, assurances that competition from new manufacturers in the same market will be limited, or protection against import-competition. However, where incentives have been offered to make local investment viable, they should be applied as offered in a timely, equitable manner.

We desire to build functional, safe, attractive factories to the same high standard worldwide, but with whatever modifications are appropriate to make them harmonious with national modes. Facilities are to be located so as to complement public planning and be compatible with local environmental considerations.

Facility operations should be planned with the long-term view in mind, in order to minimize impact of sudden change on the local work force and economy. Other things being equal, facilities will give preference to local sources of supply, and to local candidates for employment and promotion.

### Relationships with employees

We aspire to a single, worldwide standard of fair treatment of employees. Specifically, we intend:

1. To select and place employees on the basis of their qualifications for the work to be performed—without discrimination in terms of race, religion, national origin, color or sex.
2. To protect the health and lives of employees by creating a clean, safe work environment.
3. To maintain uniform, reasonable work standards, worldwide, and strive to provide work that challenges the individual—so that he or she may feel a sense of satisfaction resulting from it.
4. To attempt to provide continuous employment and avoid capricous hiring practices. Employment stabilization is a major factor in corporate decisions.
5. To compensate people fairly, according to their contribution to the Company, within the framework of prevailing practices.
6. To promote self-development, and assist employees in improving and broadening job skills.
7. To encourage expression by individuals about their work, including ideas for improving the work result.
8. To inform employees about Company matters affecting them.
9. To accept without prejudice the decision of employees on matters pertaining to union membership and union representation; and where a group of employees is lawfully represented by a union, to build a Company-Union relationship based upon mutual respect and trust.
10. To refrain from employing persons closely related to members of the board of directors, administrative officers and department heads—in the belief that nepotism is neither fair to present employees, nor in the long-term interests of the business.

## Product quality

Wherever in the world Caterpillar products are manufactured, they will be of uniform design and quality. Wherever possible, parts and components are to be identical. When such isn't practicable, they will be manufactured to the same high quality standard, with maximum interchangeability.

We strive to assure worldwide users of after-sale parts and service availability at fair prices. Wherever possible, such product support is to be offered by locally based, financially strong, independently owned dealers. We back the availability of parts from dealers with a worldwide network of corporate parts facilities.

We acknowledge that the pursuit of product quality is not only a matter of providing the best value in terms of cost, but also of providing products responsive to the public's desire for lower equipment noise levels, compliance with reasonable emission standards, and safe operating characteristics. We shall continually monitor the impact of Caterpillar products on the environment—striving to minimize any potentially harmful aspects, and maximizing their substantial capability for beneficial contributions.

## Technology

We intend to take a worldwide view of technology. We locate engineering facilities in accordance with need, and without reference to countries or nationalities involved. We exchange design and specification data from facility to facility, on a worldwide basis, while recognizing local restrictions that may exist.

We desire to raise the technical capacity of employees and suppliers in all countries in which Company facilities are located. And we provide access, as appropriate, to technical competence which we have elsewhere in the organization.

## Finance

The principal purpose of money is to facilitate trade. Any company involved in international trade is, therefore, unavoidably involved in dealing in several of the world's currencies, and in exchanges of currencies on the basis of their relative values.

Our policy is to conduct such currency dealings only to the extent they may be necessary to operate the business and protect our interests.

We buy and sell currencies only in amounts large enough to cover requirements for the business, and to protect our financial positions in those currencies whose relative values may change in foreign exchange markets. We manage currencies the way we manage materials inventories—attempting to have on hand the right amounts of the various kinds and specifications used in the business. We don't buy unneeded materials or currencies for the purpose of holding them for speculative resale.

## Intercompany pricing

With respect to pricing of goods and services transferred within the Caterpillar organization, typically from one country to another: such pricing is to be based on ethical business principles consistently applied throughout the enterprise. It is to reflect cost and a reasonable assessment of the value of the good or service transferred. Prices are not to be influenced by superficial differences in taxation between countries.

### Differing business practices

While there are business differences from country to country that merit preservation, there are others which are sources of continuing dispute and which tend to distort and inhibit—rather than promote—competition. Such differences deserve more discussion and resolution. Among these are varying views regarding anti-competitive practices, international mergers, accounting procedures, tax systems, transfer pricing, product labeling, labor standards, repatriation of profit and securities transactions. We favor multilateral action aimed at harmonizing or resolving differences of this nature.

### Competitive conduct

Fair competition is fundamental to continuation of the free enterprise system. We support laws of all countries which prohibit restraints of trade, unfair practices, or abuse of economic power. And we avoid such practices in areas of the world where laws do not prohibit them.

We recognize that in large companies like Caterpillar, particular care must be exercised to avoid practices which seek to increase sales by any other basis than quality, price and product support.

In relationships with competitors, dealers, suppliers and users, Caterpillar employees are directed to avoid arrangements which restrict our ability to compete with others—or the ability of any other business organization to compete freely with us, and with others.

Relationships with dealers are established in the Caterpillar dealership agreements. These embody our commitment to fair competitive practices, and reflect the customs and laws of the various countries in which Caterpillar products are sold. The dealership agreements are to be scrupulously observed.

In relations with competitors, Caterpillar personnel shall avoid any arrangements or understandings which affect our pricing policies, terms upon which we sell our products, and the number and type of products manufactured or sold—or which might be construed as dividing customers or sales territories with a competitor.

Suppliers are not required to forego trade with our competitors in order to merit Caterpillar's purchases. Suppliers are free to sell products in competition with Caterpillar, except in a situation where the product involved is one in which we have a substantial proprietary interest—because of an important contribution to the concept, design, or manufacturing process.

No supplier shall be asked to buy Caterpillar products in order to continue as a supplier. The purchase of supplies shall not be influenced because the supplier is a user of Caterpillar products—unless evaluations of quality, price and service provide no substantial basis for choosing a different supplier.

### Observance of local laws

A basic requirement levied against any business enterprise is that it know and obey the law. This is demanded by those who govern; and it is widely acknowledged by business managers.

However, a corporation operating on a global scale will inevitably encounter laws from country to country that are incompatible, and which may even conflict with each other.

For example, laws in some countries may encourage or require business practices which—based on experience elsewhere in the world—we believe to be wasteful or unfair. Under such conditions it scarcely seems sufficient for a business manager to merely say: we obey the law, whatever it may be!

We are guided by the belief that the law is not an end but a means to an end—the end presumably being order, justice, and, not infrequently, strengthening of the governmental unit involved. If it is to achieve these ends in changing times and circumstances, law itself cannot be insusceptible to change or free of criticism. The law can benefit from both.

Therefore, in a world increasingly characterized by a multiplicity of divergent laws at national, state and local levels, Caterpillar's intentions fall in three parts: (1) to obey the law; (2) to neither obstruct nor defy the law; and (3) to offer, where appropriate, constructive ideas for change in the law—based on our worldwide experience with the advancement of the wisest, fairest usage of human and natural resources.

### Business ethics

The law is a floor. Ethical business conduct should normally exist at a level well above the minimum required by law.

One of a company's most valuable assets is a reputation for integrity. If that be tarnished, customers, investors and desirable employees will seek affiliation with other, more attractive companies. We intend to hold to a single standard of integrity everywhere. We will keep our word. We will not promise more than we can reasonably hope to deliver; nor will we make commitments we do not intend to keep.

In our advertising and other public communications, we will avoid not only untruths, but also exaggeration, over-statement and boastfulness.

Caterpillar employees shall not accept costly entertainment or gifts (excepting mementos and novelties of nominal value) from dealers, suppliers, and others with whom we do business. And we will not tolerate circumstances that produce, or reasonably appear to produce, conflict between the personal interests of an employee and the interests of the Company.

We seek long lasting relationships—based on integrity—with employees, dealers, suppliers and all whose activities touch upon our own.

### Public responsibility

We believe there are three basic categories of possible social impact by business:

1. First is the straightforward pursuit of daily business affairs. This involves the conventional, but often misunderstood, dynamics of private enterprise; developing desired goods and services, providing jobs and training, investing in manufacturing and technical facilities, dealing with suppliers, paying taxes, attracting and holding customers, earning a profit.

2.  The second category has to do with conducting business affairs in a *way* that is socially responsible. It isn't enough to design, manufacture and sell useful products. A business enterprise should, for example, employ people without discrimination, see to their job safety and the safety of its products, help protect the quality of the environment, and conserve energy and other valuable resources.

3.  The third category relates to initiatives beyond our operations, such as helping solve community problems. To the extent our resources permit—and if a host country or community wishes—we will participate selectively in such matters, especially where our facilities are located. Each corporate facility is an integral part of the community in which it operates. Like individuals, it benefits from character building, health, welfare, educational and cultural activities. And like individuals, it also has citizen responsibilities to support and develop such activities.

All Caterpillar employees are encouraged to participate in public matters of their individual choice. Further it is recognized that employee participation in political processes or in organizations that may be termed "controversial" can be public service of a high order.

But clearly, partisan political activity is a matter for individual effort, The Company will not attempt to influence such activity in any city, state or union. Caterpillar will not contribute money, goods or services to political parties and candidates, or support them in any way.

Where its worldwide experience can be helpful, the Company will offer recommendations to governments concerning legislation and regulation being considered. Further, it will selectively analyze and take public positions on *issues* that have a relationship to operations, when Caterpillar's experience can add to the understanding of such issues.

Finally, we affirm that the basic reason for the existence of any company is to serve the needs of people. The public is, therefore, entitled to a reasonable explanation of operations of a business, especially as those operations bear on the public interest. Larger economic size begets an increased responsibility for such public communication.

### International business

We believe the pursuit of business excellence and profit—in a climate of fair, free competition—is the best means yet found for efficient development and distribution of goods and services. And we believe the international exchange of goods and ideas promotes human understanding, and thus harmony and peace.

These are not unproven theories. The enormous rise in post-World War II gross national product and living standards in countries participating significantly in international commerce has demonstrated the benefits to such countries. And it has also shown their ability to mutually develop and live by common rules, among them the gradual dismantling of trade barriers.

As a company that manufactures and distributes on a global scale, Caterpillar recognizes the world is an admixture of differing races, religions, cultures, customs, languages, economic resources and geography. We respect these differences.

Human pluralism can be a strength, not a weakness; no nation has a monopoly on wisdom.

It is not our aim to attempt to remake the world in the image of any one country. Rather, we would hope to help improve the quality of life, wherever we do business, by serving as a means of transmission and application of knowledge that has been found useful elsewhere. We intend to learn and benefit from human diversity.

We ask all governments to permit us to compete on equal terms with our competitors. This applies not just to the government of a particular country; it also applies to the substantial way such a government can control or impact on the business of a company in *other* lands.

We aim to compete successfully in terms of design, manufacture and sale of our products, not in terms of artificial barriers and incentives.

## NOTES

1. Bernard Mennis and Karl P. Sauvant, "Describing and Explaining Support for Regional Integration," *International Organization*, Autumn, 1975, pp. 973–995.

2. John Useem, John D. Donoghue, and Ruth H. Useem, "Men in the Middle of the Third Culture," *Human Organization*, Fall, 1963, pp. 169–179.

3. Karl P. Sauvant and Bernard Mennis, "Puzzling over the Immaculate Conception of Indifference Curves," German Studies Notes, Indiana University, 1977, and John A. Smetanka, *International Business and the Dialects of Global Integration*, Unpublished doctoral dissertation, Harvard University, 1977.

4. J.J. Boddewyn and Ashok Kapoor, *International Business-Government Relations* (New York: American Management Association, 1973).

5. Ibid., p. 10.

6. J.J. Boddewyn, "External Affairs at Four Levels for U.S. Multinationals," *Industrial Relations*, May, 1973, p. 240. Reproduced by permission.

7. Ibid., pp. 240–243.

8. Ashok Kapoor, *Planning for International Business Negotiations* (Cambridge, Mass.: Ballinger Publishing Company, 1975).

9. Claude McMillan, Jr., Richard F. Gongalez, and Lee G. Erikson, *International Enterprise in a Developing Economy* (East Lansing, Mich.: The Michigan State University Press, 1964).

10. Ibid., p. 223.

11. Richard D. Robinson, *International Business Policy* (New York: Holt, Rinehart and Winston, 1964), p. 148.

12. McMillan et al., op. cit., p. 45.

13. John Fayerweather and Ashok Kapoor, *Strategy and Negotiation for the International Corporation* (Cambridge, Mass.: Ballinger Publishing Company, 1976), p. 98 and pp. 180–182.

14. David H. Blake and Robert E. Driscoll, *The Social and Economic Impacts of Transnational Corporations* (New York: Fund for Multinational Education, 1977).

15. Richard D. Robinson, *Cases in International Business* (New York: Holt, Rinehart and Winston, 1962), pp. 100–118.

16. Ibid.

17. Fayerweather and Kapoor, op. cit., pp. 89, 139, and 161.

18. Ibid., pp. 369–398.

19. Robinson, *International Business Policy*, op. cit.

20. Peter P. Gabriel, "The Investment in the LDC: Asset with a Fixed Maturity," *Columbia Journal of World Business*, Summer 1966, p. 114. Reproduced by permission.

21. Ibid., p. 117.

✳ *Part II*

# Strategy Formulation

The discussion in Part I of economic differentials, cultural changes, interaction with the nation state, and corporate capabilities has laid the analytical basis for determining MNC strategy. Part II will apply this basic thinking to specific aspects of strategy. Most attention will be devoted to the MNC's product delivery system, the set of interrelated activities by which a firm generates products and places them in the buyer's possession. This includes product line policy, research and development, the logistic system including production sites and the manner in which markets are supplied, and the operational character of foreign units which accomplish the production and marketing of products. Chapter 9 will deal with the financial flow system—the provision of funds to affiliates and return of income from them—which has the secondary role for the MNC of supporting the functioning of the product delivery system. Control will appear as a factor in all of these aspects of strategy and a separate chapter will pull the varied control considerations together. Finally, four composite strategy models will be presented in Chapter 11.

To facilitate the discussion in Part II and to lead it more directly toward the situation of a specific firm, a further analytical tool will be introduced, the International Strategy Analysis Grid (ISAGRID) shown in Table 6–1. Across the top of the ISAGRID are listed the major variables to consider in determining strategy. The importance in a particular aspect of strategy of each variable with respect to transmission of each type of resource is noted as High or Moderate. No entry indicates that the variable does not have sufficient impact

**Table 6–1. The ISAGRID**

| Company Resources | Strategy Context Variables | | | | National Interests | |
|---|---|---|---|---|---|---|
| | Economic Differentials | MNC Capabilities | Cultural Change | Global Unification | Home | Host |
| Natural resources | | | | | | |
| Labor | | | | | | |
| Capital: Finance | | | | | | |
| Production | | | | Hc | | |
| Marketing | | | | | | |
| Skills: Technological | M | M | | | | |
| Managerial | | | | | | |
| Entrepreneurial | | | | | | |

Importance in strategy: H = High; M = Moderate; c = Control by parent MNC significant.

to appreciably affect the analysis. Where the exercise of parent MNC control is important to a particular element of the strategy analysis, a subscript "c" is shown. Thus in the sample notations shown in Table 6—1, global unification of the MNC production system is of high importance and requires central control by the MNC while the economic differentials and MNC capabilities in technical skill transmission are of moderate importance.

The ISAGRID provides a convenient means for holding all the variables affecting strategy in mind in analyzing each specific situation. It also permits the presentation in concise form of specific examples of strategy options and factors bearing on them.

For the specific cases to be discussed in this chapter, frequent reference will be made to three companies which cover a span of types of MNCs. Descriptions of two of them, Singer and General Foods, appear in the casebook by Fayerweather and Kapoor.[1] The third, High Technology Industries, is a fictitious firm but its characteristics are quite similar to those of international Business Machines whose international operations have been described in a variety of published sources.[2] As a prelude to the discussion of the specific phases of strategy, the key considerations noted in abbreviated form on the top of the ISAGRID will be summarized here.

**Economic Differentials.** The differentials in supply–demand relations of resources among nations analyzed in Chapter 2 are the starting point for strategy analysis as they identify the range of opportunities open to the MNC. The objective is to exploit these differentials as far as possible by transmission of resources in the *directions of flow* which they support.

Because resources are commonly transmitted in combinations, notably as exports or through manufacturing abroad, a further strategy consideration is *efficiency* in flow patterns. The goal is to develop a plan in which combinations are largely composed of resources flowing in the direction favored by economic differentials with the content of resources flowing against the differentials held to a minimum. Another basic criterion is *effectiveness* in the transmission, optimum assurance that the process will accomplish the operational application of the resources in the host society.

**MNC Capabilities.** Within the range of opportunities offered by existing economic differentials among nations, strategy is directed at those in which *MNC characteristics* give it particular capabilities.

Most prominent is the area of skills for which the integrated managerial structure of the MNC gives it a special competence. A second area which is emerging steadily combines the capital resource strengths of the firm in marketing and industrial production systems with economic differentials in labor resources for an effective combination of resource flows. A third major capability lies in the large financial capital of MNCs but in the nature of the firm it is useful primarily as a supporting resource to facilitate implementation of strategies based on other resource capabilities.

**Cultural Change.** Resource transmission, especially for the skills that are a prime capability of the MNC, inherently results in cultural change in host societies. Cultural change is a complex process which must be critically viewed as to both feasibility and cost in terms of resource expenditures and adverse reactions. MNC strategy is predisposed toward cultural *innovation* as it is essential to resource transmission so the analysis is primarily directed toward identifying changes which will be *functional* within the host society. However, where innovation appears *dysfunctional* or is too costly, a strategy of *conformity* or compromises in *adaptation* of innovations is judicious to foster overall acceptance of the firm in the host society.

**Global Unification.** The global unification aspects of strategy have been noted in previous chapters and some effects of them appear in the resource capability analysis. However, the unification potentials are of sufficient value that capitalizing on them should be treated as a strategic objective unto itself which will be discussed briefly here and become more evident in the subsequent discussion of functional issues.

The main elements of this subject are summarized in Figure 6–1. Essentially the issues arise from the conflict between the influences on the left which favor a strategy of *fragmentation* in the pattern of operations and those on the right which work toward a strategy of *unification.*[a]

[a] The term unification is not perfect for the purposes intended in this chapter, but it seems to be the most appropriate word available in the English language. Integration would fit some aspects of the subject, but it does not go far enough to encompass the standardization and uniformity which are intended by the unification idea. That is, one can have substantial integration in the structuring of activities, even though they may be quite diverse in character. Centralization is also pertinent in some sections, but in common parlance it pertains only to certain types of structural features such as decision-making and production sources and not to others like the flow of product know-how from one subsidiary to another, so it is not adequate. Similar alternatives to fragmentation have been considered. On balance, it appears that unification and fragmentation pro-

**Figure 6-1.**  Fragmentation Versus Unification

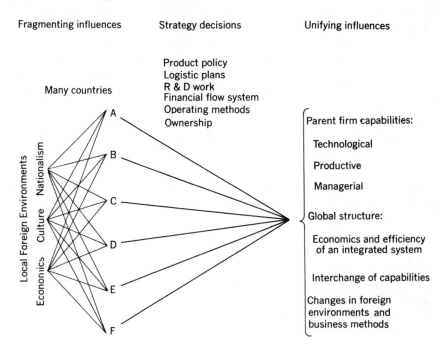

The fragmenting influences encourage managements to tailor operations in each country (A, B, C, etc.) to its unique combination of economics, culture and nationalism. Effective relations with the host society, as discussed in Chapter 3, frequently argue for policies and practices which conform to the particular system of economic and interpersonal relations of the local environment. The satisfaction of national interests and minimization of the emotional resistances of nationalism, considered in Chapters 4 and 5, favor approaches which are oriented toward localism rather than global unity. If these influences were given full play, the ultimate result would be a family of foreign units, with substantial diversity in a number of phases of operations.

The unifying influences, however, represent a substantial portion of the basic rationale for the existence of the MNC and the source of a considerable part of its competitive advantage. The predisposition in strategy planning should therefore always be towards the unifica-

---

vide the best available means of expressing the basic idea of this analysis. The reader is cautioned, however, to use them here according to the meaning which emerges from the discussion in this book rather than being limited by an initial dictionary definition.

tion approach. There is, in the first instance, the strength embodied in the various capabilities available within the parent company, notably its technological competence, its managerial know-how, and its productive facilities. This aspect is substantively linked to the resource transmission capabilities but adds a new dimension to them in emphasizing the value of structurally unifying those capabilities. In general, the capabilities are at their peak effectiveness when applied to the company's established pattern of activities. They can, therefore, be most effectively drawn upon to strengthen the operations of overseas units when the activities of the units fall in the same pattern.

Second, the multinational firm must capitalize as fully as possible on the potential advantages of size in its global span as compared to strictly local, smaller firms. The possibilities for economies and greater efficiency available to it lie largely in capabilities for specialization of activities in individual units with substantial interchange among them and are therefore dependent upon a high degree of uniformity in the activities of the units composing the structure. Likewise, the potential benefits from the large financial capabilities of a global organization are generally realized most effectively in a system with a high degree of unification of planning and operations.

Third, there is the apparently reasonable assumption indicated in Chapter 3 that all nations as they arrive at advanced stages of industrial development will have substantially similar characteristics. This assumption provides management with a sound conceptual basis for working toward greater uniformity of activities in many countries around the world as opposed to the assumption that existing diversities among nations have an expectation of permanence. Unlike the first two points, this one is not in itself an argument for unification. That is, it does not in its own logic provide any direct gain in effectiveness for a particular policy or action. Rather it is a counterargument to some of the fragmenting influences shown on the left of Figure 6-1. Thus in any given situation where there is a rough balance between the local environmental factors favoring a fragmentation approach and elements in the multinational corporation structure favoring unification, the assumption of change in foreign business systems weakens the force of the former to the benefit of the latter.

It should be emphasized that the discussion at this point concerns the operational processes in the firm, not its organizational processes. The unification-fragmentation issue is also pertinent to the latter and will be considered accordingly in Part III. However, the strategy employed in the operational processes is not necessarily the same as that of the administrative processes. That is, it is quite possible for a firm with a high degree of unification of decision-making in headquarters to deliberately choose various operational patterns of a fragmented nature which appear to be more effective than unified approaches. Likewise, a company in which decision-making is very fragmented, with much authority delegated to field units, might have a unified approach on some aspects of operations because the field managers found such an approach beneficial. As a practical matter, one does observe that in many companies the pattern in both respects is similar; and this is natural, for the administrative pattern reinforces the operational and vice versa. Indeed, from time to time in subsequent chapters, elements of fragmentation in organizations will be noted as variables favoring fragmentation of operations. But in an objective analysis such as we are pursuing here, the two must be recognized as separate characteristics.

**Interactions with the Nation State.**   A complex pattern of positive and negative interactions prevails in relations between the MNC and various attributes of *parent* and *host* nation states. They are roughly classified under two headings: *attitudes*, notably various manifestations of *nationalism*, and *national interest* issues. Strategy with respect to attitudes involves attempts to communicate with host national groups in ways which do not readily fit into the strategy pattern being analyzed here so it does not appear on the ISAGRID. The critical strategy issues lie in the disposition of conflicts among national and MNC interests. Two phases of strategy were proposed in Chapter 5 for dealing with these issues: the *accommodation* approach in which the MNC attempts as far as possible to meet the desires of the nation by not pressing for objectives that are not based on valid requirements of sound strategy, and the *power balance* approach in which resolution of valid differences in interests is reached on the basis of the economic and political power of the nation and the MNC.

**Control.**   In Chapter 1 the capability of the parent firm to control its foreign units was established as the one essential distinguishing characteristic in defining the multinational corporation. In Chapters 4 and 5 control emerged as a primary source of conflict between the MNC and the nation state. For each phase of strategy therefore it will be essential to determine how important control by the parent is and what significance the exercise of control has for the national interests involved. The assessments of the control implications of each component of strategy will then provide the basis for an overall strategy for control itself as manifest in ownership policy and other approaches to achieving its objectives.

Each chapter in this part except the last two will follow the same format. The first section, labelled "Strategy Issues," will outline an analytical framework for the subject, identifying the central issues and conceptualizing the types of considerations that should be included in the analysis of strategy options. The second section, "MNC Experience," will summarize reports of varied authors describing business practices and results. For the most part this material is derived from research studies of U.S. multinationals with a few on foreign MNCs, the balance being articles based on the observations of people closely associated with business operations. The final section, "Strategy Guidelines," will present such general recommendations for strategy planning as the analysis and experience justify.


Notes at end of Chapter 6

✳ *Chapter 6*

# Product Policy
# and R&D Strategy

Product policy and research and development are logical
starting points for strategic analysis because of their interdependence and importance for corporate success.
Products commanding satisfactory market demand are the vital requirement of an effective strategy taking precedence over all of the
components. R&D achievement is a critical underlying element because of its contribution to product competence and for the MNC
because it is the source of technical skills that are prime resource
transmission capabilities.

## PRODUCT POLICY

The domestic product line of an MNC is determined by a combination of corporate capabilities and market conditions. In its international operations the relevance of the capabilities is different and
market conditions vary substantially. The firm must therefore determine whether to modify the broad parameters of its product line
and whether to make lesser product adaptations within the parameters.

### Strategy Issues

Two subjects appear most commonly in discussion of MNC product strategy: (1) the feasibility of introducing new products into various markets and (2) the degree of world-wide standardization of
products. The fundamental issue in the former lies in the area of cultural change, the question of whether the host society is receptive to
the innovative attributes of a product. The latter falls in the global

strategy area. These two subjects are interrelated. The desire to achieve the benefits of unification creates a pressure to maximize cultural innovation so that globally standardized products will be accepted in many markets. On the other hand, limits on the feasibility of innovation encourage a fragmented product policy. The bias of the strategist is toward the unification-innovation potentials which tend to give greatest scope to the MNC resource transmission capabilities.

**Fragmentation-conformity Influences.**  In product policy the fragmentation influences have varying degrees of force, depending upon their nature and the types of products involved. The most compelling influences are those derived from those environmental conditions that critically affect the functional utility of products. For example, where 220-volt power systems are employed, electrical appliances must be adapted to them. The steering wheels of automobiles must be placed on the right or left side according to the traffic laws of each country if a company wishes to achieve good market acceptance. From these obvious cases we move off into a spectrum of situations with varying degrees of compulsion for local adaptation to environmental features. The ESFAC case is a conspicuous example. The company's efforts to convince Philippine farmers of the value of using more fertilizers present a classic case of the difficulties of achieving a cultural change in rural societies.[3]

A survey of the evolution of refrigerator sales in two major areas is more representative of the types of problems confronted by MNCs manufacturing consumer products. The 20-cubic-foot refrigerator is standard in the United States where housewives use it for storage of a large variety and amount of food and where families are affluent enough to be able to afford its luxury. In Europe kitchens are smaller, housewives shop more frequently, and the cost of a refrigerator is a greater burden because incomes in most countries are lower. These factors combined through most of the post–World War II era to establish the 6-cubic-foot refrigerator as standard in Europe. In the 1970s, however, the pattern was changing significantly as Europeans became more affluent and buying from large supermarkets aided by expanded car ownership led to less-frequent, larger-volume food purchases. Thus, while the 6-foot models were still prevalent among lower classes, larger models were increasingly found in middle-class homes.

In Latin America, although the same factors prevailing in Europe apparently argue for small refrigerators, companies found until a few years ago that the main demand was for larger, U.S.-style units. At the outset only the well-heeled upper classes could afford refrigerators, and they bought the U.S. models not only because they were the ones the U.S. companies could most readily supply to them, but also because among many Latin Americans U.S. standards of material life style were viewed with favor. Subsequently, the middle classes became able to buy refrigerators. From a practical viewpoint, they might have been better off buying smaller units. But refrigerators became a status symbol, and many middle-class families felt impelled to buy the bigger units. More recently, the smaller models have gained a larger share of the market, perhaps because in the lower economic levels the utilitarian-economic factors are more compelling and perhaps because cars and television sets have superseded the refrigerator as prime status symbols.

For each product the influences for fragmentation will differ. One can identify certain patterns in the ways in which they affect products, for example, according to their convenience and labor utilization features or their requirements for service. But extended analysis along these lines is not essential for our present purposes.[4] It is sufficient to observe that a company seeking maximum market penetration in each country will attempt to adjust to assorted local environmental conditions. Some of the conditions are so compelling that they must be accepted. For most, however, companies have a practical choice. They can adapt by using a fragmented-conformity policy or they can seek a more unified policy by counteracting the fragmenting influences with innovative efforts.

The innovative approach often finds support in the tendency of foreign countries to move toward some approximation of a uniform model of an advanced industrial society. In the refrigerator case, for example, it would appear that aside from some climatic differences, the basic utilitarian features of the device have a certain recurring relationship to the economics of human life which would support uniformity of product patterns among peoples at similar levels of economic development. If such tendencies are valid, then efforts to persuade peoples to move away from their present localized preferences have an underlying support.

**Unification Influences.** The influences favoring unification are the means through which an MNC with reasonable standardization in its worldwide product line can either produce products at lower costs or generate a stronger selling program than a company following a fragmented policy.

First, there are the advantages to the foreign units of being able to draw on the technological capabilities of the parent company. If the units wander off into product areas in which they have no technical support beyond their own limited resources, they are relatively weaker in a competitive world. Richard Robinson describes a somewhat extreme but certainly illustrative case in the experience of Minneapolis-Moline, which got into the manufacture of septic tanks in Argentina and textile machinery parts in Turkey because government restrictions cut off imports of components for manufacture of tractors.[5] The foreign units could not benefit from technological support from the parent in such product lines, so they were on the same competitive level in this regard as local national firms.

Second, for all but the simplest products, individual foreign units benefit by drawing upon the productive capacities of the parent concern or of other foreign units as part of an integrated world production system. This sort of structure has underlying logics which will be discussed in the next chapter. If such a system is to operate most efficiently, the product lines must be essentially the same.

Finally, the opportunities for benefiting by the interchange of knowledge among various units around the world are dependent upon their being engaged in essentially the same type of business. For example, if company X introduces a particular new food product in Mexico and learns how to promote it effectively, the company can then apply this same know-how in introducing the identical product in other Latin American countries. The approach in each country will, of course, have to be different to some degree, but the company will have a substantial initial advantage over the position it would be in if it started off with quite different products in each country each time. Singer had such an experience in Brazil several years ago. Hampered by import restrictions, the company took on several locally made products, including baby carriages, and even started selling life insurance policies to hold its sewing machine retail stores together. On a short-term basis these expedients had a certain operational logic, but the potentials for the transfer of know-how from other parts of its international organization to help the Brazilian unit were much lower in these product lines than in the normal company fields. The marketing experts in the home office would have been hard put to advise the Brazilians on how to increase sales of insurance policies.

These arguments are generally so persuasive that most companies do have essentially the same product lines throughout the world. They are considerably less convincing, however, when applied to minor product variations to fit needs of individual markets—for example, modest changes in styling or of size of units or perhaps even of quality standards. There is no significant loss of the gains from parent technological assistance or the exchange of knowledge among units with this type of product variation. However, even minor variations limit the amount of component and product exchange that is possible within the international structure. The significance of this will obviously depend upon the nature of the product line. In office machinery, for example, it is a real disadvantage; whereas for cosmetics it probably has little relevance.

## MNC Experience

Information on prevailing patterns of MNC product policy has appeared in several research studies. These studies have covered broader areas including R&D programs, operating methods, and logistic systems which will be discussed in later sections. However, they are described in full here both as a matter of convenience and to bring out the interrelation of product policy and other aspects of strategy.

1. On the basis of a study of the historical development of the operations of 187 major U.S. MNCs, Vernon formulated the concept of the product life cycle in international trade.[6] The model set forth as typical of historical MNC experience four stages in the evolution of a product as shown in Figure 6−2. In the first stage, the product was developed in the United States in response to characteristics of that market, notably relatively high-cost labor and lower-cost materials and a dominant middle class with a quite high standard of living. This mix particularly favored the emergence of labor-saving, convenience products. By contrast, the model would presume that European industry generated products with more concern for material savings in view of the greater limitations of its natural resources and that the lower general level of income and greater split between high- and low-income classes favored differentiated products geared to their needs. The nature of new products being tied to the home market. the firm tended to limit initial production to domestic plants where proximity permitted ready adjustment of production to market needs. This might be a deliberate decision or it might be the natural evolution especially when a company had not operated abroad before. Thus the first stage might be perceived simply as the normal process of a domestic business developing new products for its regular market without consideration of international sales at the outset.

In the second stage exports to other markets started. Presumably there was potential demand in these markets previously but the product had not been developed because the demand was too small or because business initiative had been inadequate. At first. with the demand modest, the MNC serviced the markets by exports and pre-

**Figure 6-2.** The Product Life Cycle in International Trade and Investment

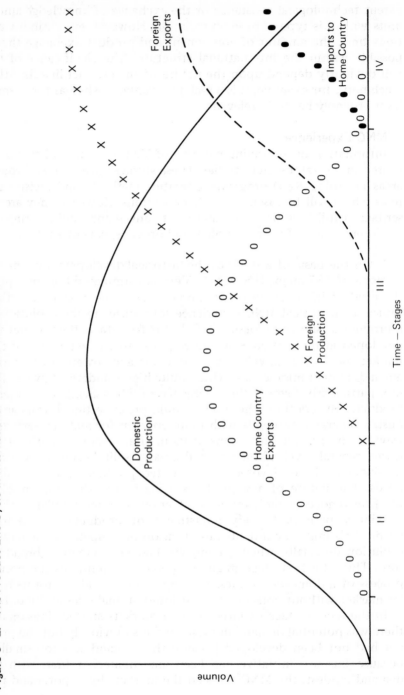

ferred to do so because that system used its domestic productive capacity effectively and limited its capital investment. Through this stage, the firm was perceived to still have control of the market, either a monopoly or at least a strong lead, through its initiation of the product.

In time, however, the market position of the firm was eroded as the product technology was acquired by other firms at home and abroad. As the volume of sales abroad grew, competition increased both from other U.S. exporters and from local producers. From these conditions, the third stage, foreign manufacturing by the MNC, evolved providing a competitively more effective means of servicing foreign markets. Local factories with lower costs, protection from imports and advantages of market proximity were able for a time to sustain the MNC's market position.

Eventually, when technology of the product was diffused and its initial market dominance lost, the competitive status of the MNC would be weakened further versus local producers. The fourth stage presumed that it might revitalize its position by shifting production to low-labor-cost plants from which it could import into the domestic and other high-cost markets. Vernon's research did not identify firms in which a full progression to this stage was observed, but he hypothesized it as a natural development to be expected in the future.

In subsequent writing Vernon observed that while the product life cycle was a useful way to explain the historical evolution of MNC operations, it was not so appropriate for later situations.

> By 1970, the product cycle model was beginning in some respects to be inadequate as a way of looking at the U.S.-controlled multinational enterprise. The assumption of the product cycle model—that innovations were generally transmitted from the U.S. market for production and marketing in overseas areas—was beginning to be challenged by illustrations that did not fit this pattern. The new pattern that these illustrations suggested was one in which stimulation to the system could come from the exposure of any element in the system to its local environment, and response could come from any part of the system that was appropriate for the purpose.[7]

2. Ginsburg analyzed the application of the international product life cycle concept to the pharmaceutical industry and concluded that a broadening of its conditions was appropriate.[8] He presented data showing that the rate of introduction of new drugs had decreased greatly with an associated increase in basic research. A greater portion of R&D funds had in turn been expended abroad. Industry data showed that the percentage allocated for R&D in foreign units had

risen from about 5 percent of the worldwide total in 1960 to almost 10 percent in 1970.

Ginsburg observed that in view of the spatial-temporal relationship and the comparative ease with which new drugs were introduced abroad, Vernon's product life cycle theory was confronted with a theoretical anomaly. Original discovery did not need take place in the high income or high technology (such as the U.S.) economy. Instead, it might take place in a lower income country first. It was not the discovery of a new drug that was the determining factor in market control, but its commercialization, i.e., development, that was the prerequisite of market control. In the early stages of the life cycle, the product was marketed abroad with only negligible exports to the home country (U.S.), usually for experimental and efficacy tests. This was the reversal of the flow stated by Vernon's life cycle theory. Only after an extended period of time, when required U.S. government product approval was obtained, based on a positive feedback of the new drug, did the firm begin to manufacture and promote the product in the United States.

3. Leroy made a study with the primary goal of development of a typology of product strategies of multinational firms.[9] His work was based on the history of close to 100 products in the operations of five firms: Gillette, Dymo Industries, Hewlett-Packard, Alcan, and Massey-Ferguson. Leroy particularly selected firms with significant experience in originating products in host nations. They provided effective illustrations of varied patterns of product innovation and diffusion in world markets and the influences affecting the patterns.

In the typology the product was defined as representing "a set of technologies, or different elements of know-how." Three elements were the main variables in the typology: country of origin of product know-how, country of marketing, and country of production. Where the know-how originated in the parent country, eleven different states of the firm existed at a given moment representing combinations of parent and host country sales and production with or without export from one to the other. From these alternatives were derived the alternative sequences of states which composed the multinational product strategies. Some eighteen possible strategies were identified for the case when the parent country originated the know-how and was the low-cost producer and another eighteen when the host country was low-cost producer. With an equal number of alternatives for the case of know-how originating in the host country (and eliminating a few duplications), the author had sixty possible strategy sequences.

Classification of the data for the products of the five companies studied showed that they included eleven of these strategies for the case of know-how originating in the parent country and eight where it originated in the host country. The great majority of products fell into three common strategies for parent country know-how: (1) domestic production followed by exports only; (2) domestic production followed by exports, then foreign production; and (3) domestic production followed directly by foreign production with no exports. Products fell mostly into two strategies for host country know-how (1) production and marketing simply in the host country and (2) production there with export to the parent country. However, the substantial number of cases in the fourteen other strategy patterns observed demonstrated the variety of options employed by companies.

Leroy analyzed the various concepts advanced by other scholars to explain the evolution of foreign investment and related them to his typology and the pattern observed in the five companies. He found that the bulk of his strategies fitted the other concepts but that clearly no one scheme was comprehensive, particularly in light of the many variations outside the dominant pattern. He devoted particular attention to Vernon's product life cycle theory, but found no example of its full sequence: the final stage of supply of the parent market from foreign sources did not appear. He advanced the possible explanation that firms other than the MNC might have taken over exports to the home country, the product by then being widely copied. However, Leroy leaned to the conclusion that firms used a variety of alternative paths to diffuse their products which conformed to Vernon's conclusion that the international product cycle was losing much of its relevance as a model.

A large part of Leroy's book was devoted to specific descriptions of the product histories in the five companies and to a summary of the rationales for the strategies based on systematic questioning of the company officials. Environmental factors were found to be significant but chief attention was given to firm and product characteristics. He noted that as the firms gained experience abroad they increasingly used product strategies originating in host countries. Eight characteristics of products were considered of which four did not show a clear relation to strategy. The four were: novelty of product, size of demand, economies of scale in production, and labor intensity. Type of product did have an impact on strategy, as industrial products were commonly made at home and exported while consumer products were made at home and then were made abroad.

Complexity of product strongly favored developmental production in the country of know-how origin. A high value-to-weight ratio favored exporting. The greater the competition, the more likely the firm was to produce its products close to the market.

4. Sorenson and Wiechmann explored the question of standardization in international marketing.[10] Their study was confined to twenty-seven consumer packaged goods companies in Western Europe and the United States. In each company they studied the marketing decisions covering one to three products, each of which had been marketed in three to five countries. To measure the degree of standardization they gathered a large number of paired country comparisons. They asked the executives to look at two countries at a time and to say how similar or different they thought the decisions were regarding, for example, product formulation, packaging, and advertising. A similar pairing approach was employed to gauge the degree of similarity of marketing conditions among countries.

The analysis covered the total marketing program for each product and twelve aspects of the program. For the total marketing program, 63 percent of the paired comparisons showed a high degree of standardization and only 27 percent low standardization. Three specific aspects fell roughly in the area of "product." Among them high standardization was found to be very strong in 93 percent of decisions on brand names, 81 percent for product characteristics, and 75 percent for packaging. Standardization was high for product decisions because of trademark considerations and because of the apparent dream of most managements to have recognizable worldwide brand franchises some day. Pricing decisions showed much less standardization; only 56 percent were in the high category.

Four aspects of advertising showed a varied pattern, with high standardization at 71 percent for basic advertising message, 62 percent for creative expression, 56 percent for sales promotion, and 43 percent for media allocation. The common pattern seemed to be that subsidiaries adapted both slogan and copy to local conditions but made sure the adaptations were in keeping with the prototype campaign that had been developed at headquarters. Distribution aspects showed a considerable uniformity with high standardization at 80 percent for role of middlemen, 74 percent for role of sales force, 72 percent for management of sales force, and 59 percent for type of retail outlet. However, the authors observed that the similarity of distribution decisions from country to country had been more accidental than intentional. As one executive put it "This is not because we make any special effort to have similarity, but simply because in all these countries there is only one sensible way in which our products can be distributed." [11]

Seeking explanations of degrees of standardization, the authors analyzed their relation to seven aspects of market conditions. Overall they found a high degree of cross-border similarity of market conditions seemed to concur with high standardization. However, the tendency to custom-tailor marketing when market conditions were dissimilar was not as marked. A number of companies seemed to be engaging in cross-border standardization despite strong differences in market conditions. This was most pronounced for certain food products. Cross-border similarity of market share position seemed to have a modest impact on the tendency to standardize marketing programs, while the nature of competition did not appear to lead to either more or less standardization.

Overall the authors concluded that the mistake of standardizing when market conditions were significantly dissimilar was generally more serious than not standardizing under highly similar market conditions. The authors observed that actual decisions to standardize might have been carried too far among the firms they studied in view of significant differences between countries. Standardization under such conditions could seriously endanger a multinational corporation's marketing success and market position.

The arguments for standardization were noted, including the transfer of strategies successful in one country to others, the value of a worldwide image when media cross borders, especially for European TV and publications, and economies in product design, ad copy development, etc. The latter point was considered of doubtful importance. In only one of the twenty-seven companies were executives able to offer documented evidence of specific savings that had resulted from standardization. Key factors in this respect were the low relative cost of product design and the limited economies of scale in consumer packaged goods companies.

From their findings the authors concluded that MNCs in consumer packaged goods generally could not gain significant competitive advantage by transferring marketing programs across borders. The key to their strength they found lay rather in that they had better systems for planning and implementing their local marketing efforts. The important thing was that the *process* through which programs were developed was standardized rather than the programs themselves. The major emphasis was placed on the annual planning format. The planning, budgeting, and control systems provided a disciplined framework for analyzing marketing situations and problems. These systems inspired a discipline within a company that resulted in marketing orientation, good management, and profit consciousness. Such a system was also of great educational value, an effective vehicle for the international transfer of marketing skills and thus an important source of international competitive strength.

5. Kacker interviewed managers of twenty-six U.S. companies operating in India to determine what adaptations they made from U.S. marketing patterns to fit Indian conditions.[12] The companies spanned a range of consumer and industrial products. A minimal amount of adaptation in product characteristics was found. The companies did no substantial research and development in India. Most firms made only such minor changes as were necessary to meet government requirements or climatic needs. Of the twenty-six firms only twelve reported appreciable modifications and in those usually only four or five products were involved. The types of changes noted included making dry rather than liquid fertilizer because farmers did not have equipment to use the latter, and changing the valves of shock absorbers to adapt to the poorly maintained and unpaved roads.

### Product Strategy Guidelines

Certain basic guidelines come through clearly from the analytical framework and MNC experience with a gray area of options beyond them. Global adherence to those broad product areas in which the MNC has acquired technical and marketing competence is sound strategy because the competences represent prime skill transmission capabilities and competitive strength. By the same reasoning, a basic thrust toward product innovation in international markets makes sense because new products are significant carriers of technological skill. Historically, as Vernon has described, (1 in the preceding section), the innovative process has usually proceeded from the home base of the MNC. The R&D strategy to be discussed in the next section suggests that this pattern will continue to be true for a large portion of MNCs. However, the studies of Ginsburg and Leroy (2 and 3 in the preceding section) confirm that product initiation can quite readily take place outside the parent country. The central points from a strategy point of view are that the capability for product innovation be fostered wherever it is viable in the MNC system and that a unified overall product strategy be maintained so the potentials for propagation of innovations elsewhere in the system are high and may be implemented readily.

In regard to specific products, however, the determination of strategy becomes more difficult and, in the final analysis, it is a company-by-company matter. The study by Sorenson and Wiechmann (4 in the preceding section) gives us some sense of the problems though their work is limited to a small segment industrially and geographically. One can mark out just a few strong determinants of strategy. Product diversity is inevitable where a different design is required by law or by firmly established practice, e.g., metric system or right-hand drive for cars. But standardization is in order for certain products of a non-cultural character, especially where a combination of limited global demand and economies of scale strongly favor centralized production; heart pacemakers and highly sophisticated computers come to mind as good examples.

But the great majority of products falls somewhere between these two poles. The choice lies between global standardization, which usually involves some degree of innovative thrust against host society culture, and a fragmented product strategy with conformity to host cultural characteristics. From their analysis Sorenson and Wiechmann concluded that MNCs were too inclined toward standardization and they felt the advantages of unification were overstated. This conclusion may have been valid for the limited range of firms they covered —consumer packaged goods in Western Europe. For all MNCs worldwide the pronouncement on the latter point is not valid; it would be hard to overstate the advantages of unification. The economies of standardization for product development and services are clearly significant for industrial products and larger consumer durables.

The potentials for rationalization of production and supply, at least on a regional basis, which will be discussed in the next chapter also argue strongly for standardized products. Singer provides an exceptional case in the degree to which it has integrated global logistics but its case is illustrative nonetheless of potentials that may exist for many companies in the future.[13] In earlier years when each factory was supplying its own limited market only, many small product variations evolved. When Singer began to rationalize production with major plants specializing in production of a limited range of products for sale to broad areas including markets previously served by other factories, the company found the large number of models, some only differing moderately from others, were a serious impediment. A program of product standardization, reducing the line was required. But because of the long life of the products and company commitment to high quality service, spare parts had to be maintained for all of the former models at significant cost.

Viewing this combination of factors, one must, as a strategic guideline, fall back on the prime consideration of market-competitive conditions. The general disposition toward standardization is sound

where there is any present or future prospect for significant economies by production rationalization. Its soundness rests primarily on
the market-competitive value of the price advantage which the economies can provide. Their value will, however, be dependent upon the
other market-competitive elements—taste, environmental traditions,
and the like. The varied nature of these elements is such that further
generalization is impractical here, though discussion of the ISAGRIDs
in Table 6—2 for our three sample companies will provide some illustrative guidance.

For High Technology Industries product strategy is primarily determined by the dominance of the parent firm's research in development of advanced computers and the limited demand and complex
production processes which confine output to a small number of
factories. Thus the ISAGRID notations emphasize the technical skill
transmission process through a highly controlled and integrated staff
and the centrally planned global production system. Within the limits set by these factors, moderate scope for product variations is feasible and competitively necessary to meet customer demand. Market
success for HTI requires an acute capacity for application to customer problems. Most of that success is achieved by the qualities
built into the basic products but moderate adaptations to customer
needs are normal and do not significantly detract from the basic
technical and production unification strategy.

The managerial skill considerations are moderately important but
essentially adjunct to the technological aspects. The interchange of
marketing competence developed among units of the firm is facilitated by standardization of products but it is not in itself an argument in deciding the degree of standardization. Technology and
production factors are far more important in this field.

In Singer's case, centrally controlled production rationalization is
the dominant factor in consideration of global standardization. There
are broad differences in market demand between advanced countries
where expensive, sophisticated machines may be sold and LDCs
where most buyers can only afford simple machines. But these differences can be handled by a modest number of models and there are
no significant culture-to-culture variations in sewing practices that
require refined product variations. Supplementing the production
rationalization factor is the importance of the Singer marketing organization and its reputation for life-long service for machines, which
also benefits from having a few, standardized models. Technological
innovation is slow in this field and not a prime competitive element
as, over most of the line, several firms have roughly equivalent tech-

**Table 6-2. ISAGRID for Product Strategy**

| Company | Resources | Strategy Context Variables | | | | National Interests | |
|---|---|---|---|---|---|---|---|
| | | Economic Differentials | MNC Capabilities | Cultural Change | Global Unification | Home | Host |
| High Technology Industries (HTI) | Natural resources | | | | | | |
| | Labor | | | | | | |
| | Capital: Finance | | | | | | |
| | Production | | | | Hc | | |
| | Marketing | | | | M | | |
| | Skills: Technological | Hc | H | M | H | | |
| | Managerial | M | | M | M | | |
| | Entrepreneurial | | | | | | |
| Singer | Natural resources | | | | | | |
| | Labor | | | | | | |
| | Capital: Finance | | | | | | |
| | Production | | | | Hc | | |
| | Marketing | | | | H | | |

**Table 6–2. continued**

| | | | | |
|---|---|---|---|---|
| **Singer** (*cont.*) | Skills: | | | |
| |   Technological | M | H | M |
| |   Managerial | | | M |
| |   Entrepreneurial | | | |
| | Natural resources | | | |
| | Labor | | | |
| | Capital: | | | |
| |   Finance | | | |
| | Production | | | M |
| | Marketing | | | M |
| **General Foods** | Skills: | | | |
| |   Technological | Mc | M | M |
| |   Managerial | Mc | H | M |
| |   Entrepreneurial | | | |

Importance in strategy: H = High; M = Moderate; c = Control by parent MNC significant.

nology. Thus the degree to which the product line is standardized only moderately affects the transmission of technological skill.

General Foods presents a different story because food tastes are so distinctive. The company's strength lies in its competence in convenience foods, both in their technology and in the marketing approaches they require. This characteristic defines the broad area of competition for its product strategy over which parent control is important. The value of holding to this area is clearly demonstrated by GF's ineffectiveness when it acquired a company making a staple food, pasta, in Italy.[14] Neither GF's technology nor the main body of its marketing competence could be transmitted effectively and the venture was a doubtful investment for the firm.

Beyond this definition of broad area of activity, the specific products a firm may introduce in each country are primarily determined by the receptivity of the host country culture to the product and to the marketing methods necessary to promote it. The failure of the effort to introduce Gravy Train dog food in Britain despite the success of other GF products developed in the United States illustrates the cultural sensitivity of problems in product strategy.[15] On the other hand, unification considerations are only a moderate influence. As will be seen in the next chapter rationalization does not figure significantly in the logistics of General Foods. There are some advantages in interchange and control through unification of technology and marketing methods among foreign affiliates but they are of moderate importance compared to the cultural considerations.

## R&D STRATEGY

Strategy for research and development in an MNC involves consideration of national interests at home and abroad, global unification–fragmentation factors, innovation in foreign societies, control, and organizational capabilities. The unification–fragmentation aspects require the most conspicuous decisions so the other factors will be considered as they bear on them.

### Strategy Issues

The unification–fragmentation issues lie in two dimensions as shown in Table 6–3. The horizontal dimension concerns the content of the R&D program. The program may be unified in that there is a centrally-determined overall plan and the activities of all R&D units are directed as part of this plan. Or the program may be fragmented in its content; in the extreme case each foreign unit would have its own self-planned R&D effort.

Table 6-3.  Unification-Fragmentation Patterns for R&D in the MNC

| Geographic Dispersion | Program Content | |
|---|---|---|
| | Unified | Fragmented |
| Unified | Centrally determined program conducted in home country | Foreign units initiate programs with work done in home country facilities by their direction |
| Fragmented | Centrally determined program conducted in two or more countries | Foreign units determine program and conduct work in own facilities |

The vertical dimension is the geographic dispersion, the location of the facilities in which the R&D work is actually performed. The first dimension is the important one from the point of view of achievement of unified global strategy, but the second has a significant effect on the degree to which that unification is achieved. Table 6-3 shows an option of a fragmented program initiated from foreign units but with the R&D work done entirely in home country facilities. To a limited degree such systems do exist. However, the physical presence of all R&D in the home country provides a powerful support for central control. By the same token, when R&D facilities are located in foreign countries, central control is both possible and common, but the proximity of the R&D operations to local management control and national influences provides a strong fragmenting potential. So a strategy of geographic dispersion of R&D work carries with it a potential impetus toward fragmentation of the actual R&D program. Thus both dimensions will be considered as significant elements in looking at the factors favoring fragmentation and unification.

The arguments for a primary emphasis on unification of the R&D system are overwhelming. It is inconceivable that a company should duplicate its basic research and product-development activities in all or even several foreign countries. The economies of concentrating research in limited locations where facilities are well developed are fundamental to the competitive advantage of the multinational firm. These logics are reinforced by the basic character of effective R&D management. It is recognized that a fairly high concentration of technological talent is most productive in this field, there being something comparable to the critical mass concept in technological productivity. The interaction and ready communication of a number of R&D people in a single location facilitates experimental processes and the advancement of knowledge. Thus we find that major firms tend not only to have large R&D facilities but that many of them are clustered together in the vicinity of major universities, e.g., Boston's "Route 128" complex of high technology firms near to Harvard and MIT.

Yet another important factor favoring unification is the existence or threat of limited ownership of foreign units. R&D capability is so valuable to a company that it does not wish to lose control over it. The complexities of communication and planning in a mixed owner-ship relationship deter assignment of technical work to partially con-trolled foreign affiliates.

Finally, at least as far as U.S. MNCs are concerned, there is some home nation pressure favoring unification. As we noted in Chapter 5, U.S. labor argues vigorously against what it perceives as the giving away of U.S. technological strength in the establishment of foreign factories and their stance would be even stronger if firms were seen to be also moving the source of technology creation out of the United States.

On the fragmentation side there are four main influences. First the strong pressure comes from host national governments. Because of their great preoccupation with the technological dependence associ-ated with MNC operations, they give a high priority to the develop-ment of R&D capability within their own borders and hopefully directed at special needs of their own nations.

As we have seen, the transmission of superior skills is the main contribution of international firms. Given the overwhelming scien-tific lead of a few countries, the flow of skills and resultant depen-dency seems inevitable for the foreseeable future. But no matter how useful the relationship may be, it is still a cause of practical concern and emotional resentment in the skill-importing countries; so they express a strong desire to have multinational firms do more research in their countries. For example, in a study conducted by the National Planning Association, the magnitude of local research ranked as one of six major causes of resentment toward U.S. firms in Canada on a par with such other sore issues as ownership and use of local manage-ment personnel.[16]

How the greater efficiency and effectiveness of a unified scheme may balance against national interest and nationalism depends very much on the types of analysis pursued in Chapter 5. The greatest power of most multinational firms appears to reside in its R&D pro-gram, so it could not readily be forced to accede to local pressures on this count. On the other hand, the sensitivity of this subject is so great that good relations with national groups may be substantially advanced by modest concessions in an otherwise unsound shift toward fragmentation. Or, to be specific, opening a small R&D facility may generate enough beneficial goodwill among local scientists, the government, and the public as a whole to be worth doing. It would compensate for some loss in direct research productivity as compared with an equal outlay in some other country as part of a unified R&D scheme.

Second, local market conditions argue for on-the-spot study to develop products for maximum local acceptance. To the extent that fragmentation of products has been justified on its own merits, there is a sound argument for developing these product variations locally as part of a unified R&D plan. The debatable area therefore lies in the extent to which local efforts go beyond such specific allocation of effort to study product innovations that are already the subject of study in other company units. The importance of this consideration is necessarily associated with the extent to which innovation in the host culture is part of the MNC strategy and particularly its adaptive character. A local R&D capability is logically a good vehicle for bringing in some parent technical skills and applying them to innovations particularly geared to the local culture.

Third, the presence in many countries of individuals capable of R&D contributions offers an opportunity which a multinational firm will often be wise to grasp. For example, able research chemists are scattered throughout the world. A chemical firm seeking to build a strong R&D organization might be inclined to hire and utilize these people wherever it could find them. At a minimum, such a policy may be supported as a defensive counter to the prospect that the same people will appear in the laboratories of competitors who have adopted a fragmentation strategy.

This sort of local employment of scientists in several countries might be made an effective part of a unified scheme by allocating different areas of investigation to each country. But this is often not the most efficient way to incorporate them into a unified system because of the communications difficulties and other shortcomings of a decentralized program. The shortcomings are especially significant when only one or two scientists in a relatively undeveloped country are involved. Such people are likely to be far less productive working in a local subsidiary than in a centralized research group with superior equipment and ready access to an advanced scientific community in one of the highly industrialized countries.

This leads us into the sensitive subject of the "brain drain," the flow of professional people from the less developed to the advanced countries and from Europe to the United States. Better salaries are a factor in this process, but studies have shown that the higher level of scientific work in the advanced countries coupled with superior research facilities offering greater professional opportunities are powerful attractions.[17] The loss to many countries of their intellectual resources is generally deplored, but the net effect of the process is subject to debate. There are those who believe that the scientist will be more productive in the advanced country, and that all countries will benefit from the dissemination of this greater productivity. Applied to the R&D program of the multinational firm, all of this argues for recruiting scientists wherever they may be found and bringing them together in laboratories in the more advanced countries rather than following a fragmentation strategy simply because of the initial dispersed locations of the scientists.

Finally, the managerial dynamics of the R&D system must be included. A prime objective of the parent MNC is to have its foreign affiliate managements wholeheartedly engaged in building their operations. Certainly nothing is more important to success in any operation than ability to respond to the product needs of a market. So the motivation of overseas managements is enhanced by policies which permit them to initiate and even conduct R&D designed to fit the needs they perceive in their own areas. And by the same token a policy of highly centralized R&D tends to stultify the initiative and interest of management abroad.

This problem may be partially overcome by establishing systems for communication of field proposals to the central R&D management. But the assorted communication problems from field to home organization which will be discussed in Part III are such that this sort of system will have only limited success compared with the ability of a field group to run their own R&D show.

## MNC Experience

The effect of these various factors on R&D strategy has been brought out in several studies. Three of the five studies cited in the section on MNC experience in strategy issues relate directly to this subject.[a] All three convey the picture of centrally determined R&D activities. This is inherent in the home-country product initiation process of Vernon's product life cycle and both Ginsburg and Leroy describe industry or company situations in which product diffusion suggests that the managements have centrally directed R&D in each area so that the output will be useful to the whole MNC system. However, the Ginsburg and Leroy cases are notable because they both involve significant geographic fragmentation. Ginsburg focuses

---

[a] Listed in Notes to Chapter 6 as 7, 8, and 9.

on the pharmaceutical industry in which stricter U.S. drug regulations have fostered a shift to product development abroad. Leroy deliberately picked companies which had stressed foreign R&D work and to some degree represent special cases. Gillette, for example, acquired the German firm, Braun, which had its own strong R&D and naturally continued it. Massey-Ferguson is a Canadian firm whose biggest market is in the United States and it has found it sound to shift much of its R&D to locations closer to the U.S. agricultural areas.

1. An overall picture of R&D in U.S. multinationals was provided in a report published by a U.S. Senate Committee.[18] In 1966 the firms spent $526 million or about 6 percent of their total R&D expenditures outside the United States. Manufacturing firms accounted for 90 percent of the total, geographically distributed as follows:

| | |
|---|---|
| Canada | 27% |
| United Kingdom | 25 |
| West Germany | 20 |
| France | 8 |
| Others (chiefly Australia, Belgium, Italy, and the Netherlands) | 20 |

Four specific industries were noted in which foreign R&D accounted for 10 percent or more of R&D outlays:

| | |
|---|---|
| Industrial machinery and equipment | 19% |
| Soaps and cosmetics | 16 |
| Food products (excl. grain mill products) | 14 |
| Farm machinery and equipment | 10 |

All of these were observed to be fields with a high level of product differentiation based on special factors that differed widely among countries. Industrial machinery had to fit differences in production systems while agricultural crops and farming methods varied greatly. Cosmetics and food were especially affected by cultural tastes.

2. The most comprehensive study of R&D by U.S. MNCs was a survey of 162 firms by Duerr for the Conference Board.[19] He observed that the function of R&D was not one that could be easily decentralized. In spite of the MNCs' desire to make maximum use of the capabilities of their foreign units, most companies cooperating in the survey made limited use of them for R&D. In spite of pres-

sures to decentralize research activity, most companies carried out the bulk of it in the United States. The greater portion of the R&D work that was done abroad was limited to product modification. However, the survey did reveal a few companies with substantial overseas R&D programs and indications that other companies might move in this direction.

Duerr found that some respondents felt that market and other forces were slowly pushing for greater foreign R&D. The main points in favor were the development of products for local markets and the use of skills found abroad. Two practical factors sometimes provided a critical push: the sharing of developmental costs with foreign companies and the use of non-convertible accumulations of funds. Much of the overseas R&D was on a country basis but one company had regional R&D centers in Canada, Japan and Switzerland with another planned for Latin America.

With the bulk of R&D concentrated in the United States, the organizational emphasis in most companies was on assuring that the overseas units derived maximum benefit from it. The report found that some bigger firms had established an international R&D coordinating unit to facilitate the communication process. The oil companies had the most comprehensive formal research coordination system. One firm held international meetings twice a year to facilitate direct communication. The objective of direct communication appeared in other forms among many firms. There was considerable stress on cutting through channels for direct exchanges between sources of know-how and users abroad. Travel was considered vital, many companies having technical specialists who regularly visited each foreign unit once or twice a year.

A chapter was devoted to financing of international R&D. The most common practice among the companies surveyed was to make no specific allocation for international R&D either because it was too small or in a minority of cases because it was fully decentralized and self-supporting from foreign income sources.

3. The character of foreign activities was studied by Ronstadt in seven multinational organizations which conducted a substantial percentage of their total corporate research and development abroad: Corning Glass Works, 9 percent; Union Carbide (chemicals and plastics only), 12 percent; Exxon Chemical, 23 percent; Exxon (energy only), 25 percent; IBM, 31 percent; CPC International, 39 percent; and Otis Elevator, 45 percent.[20] The firms created or acquired fifty-five R&D units abroad of which all but five were in Canada or Europe, the others being in India (two), Japan (two) and Australia.

Some thirteen of the units had been part of firms acquired by the multinationals. As the R&D capability was not a reason for the acquisition, these units were not considered in most of the analysis.

The forty-two units set up by the multinationals were classified into four categories as follows. Transfer Technology Units (TTUs). These thirty-one units were created to assist foreign manufacturing subsidiaries in the application of technology transmitted from the parent. TTUs were typically small, 32 percent started with only two professionals and 87 percent with six or less. Their work was limited to minor changes in existing technology so they involved little risk. TTUs were set up in only nine of the forty nations in which the seven parent companies had factories. It appeared that most had been established early in the foreign investment process before technology was standardized. Several managers noted that manufacturing subsidiaries in Latin America, Africa and the Far East did not require permanent R&D units to perform technology transfer services. Product process technologies had been standardized by the time manufacturing investments were made in these countries. When technical problems arose, they were handled by temporary R&D teams from the United States and Europe.

Indigenous Technology Units (ITUs). Two R&D units were created to develop new and improved products expressly for foreign markets, one by Otis and one by Corning. Continued growth in Europe became more difficult for both organizations to maintain as European market needs increasingly differed from the U.S. experience. As the European business expanded, European managers identified new investment opportunities that could not be exploited by using the technology developed by parent companies. U.S. product development in Otis, for example, was concentrated in high-rise building equipment. In the early 1960s the company found it was missing out on a major market in Europe in low-rise buildings for which the parent firm had no product line. So the decision was made to let Europe develop its own technology for small elevators. ITUs required much larger staffs and investments than TTUs.

Global Product Units (GPUs). Five foreign R&D units were created by IBM to develop new products for production in the United States and other foreign markets. These undertakings were part of the very large corporate program to develop the System/360 and subsequent System/370. The size of existing U.S. R&D facilities had passed the limit which the company felt was sound in terms of degree of community dependence (10 percent of an area's work force was set as the limit). IBM did not think it made economic sense to start new manufacturing centers in the United States solely for product development, especially since manufacturing and marketing resources already existed abroad that could be used for this work.

Corporate Technology Units (CTUs). Union Carbide created two R&D units to generate new technology expressly for the parent corporation in the United States; CPC created one, and IBM, one. These units were administratively and geographically separate from other foreign operations, having direct ties only with U.S. parent management. They typically came into being because of scientific advances made by non–U.S. scientists that were relevant to the parent business. It appeared most effective to set up units abroad to benefit from these advances, especially as foreign scientists could not always be persuaded to come to the United States. Two of the units were quite large (over twenty professionals) and two quite small.

Ronstadt discerned certain evolutionary patterns. All of the thirty-one TTUs grew and fourteen evolved into ITUs. The change to ITU activity was often based on the need to provide more challenging work than technical service to retain the best staff people. All of those transfer technology units that moved into indigenous technology work also assumed R&D responsibility at their regional level. Managers indicated that the company needed a large market base to underwrite new and improved product-process work. Three of IBM's TTUs evolved into ITUs and then GPUs. All eight of the firm's GPUs were successful. On the other hand, the four CPUs studied were of mixed success, two eventually being dissolved. The failures were variously due to small size, lack of clear direction of purpose and other causes.

Ronstadt noted that the research showed little evidence of non–R&D factors like government pressures and the "brain drain" playing a role in decisions on R&D units. In all cases the decision to place R&D abroad was based essentially on proximity to manufacturing facilities, market conditions, and/or foreign scientific competence. While units were usually established for limited service to the local manufacturing operations, they frequently expanded to a creative function generating technology which could flow to other foreign subsidiaries.

4. A comprehensive picture of the approach of European MNCs to R&D in the United States was provided in a study conducted by Franko for Business International.[21] Roughly 70 percent of the firms in the sample reported that they did R&D in the United States. The primary reason given was the rapid pace of product change and obsolescence in the North American market. Most managers stressed the speed with which U.S. competitors imitated even their most "revolutionary" European-originated products and the need to do their own

product development close to the U.S. market. There appeared to be no relationship between the existence of U.S.-based R&D and the rate of growth in U.S. sales although it did appear that companies doing R&D in the United States had considerably higher rates of U.S. profit growth and return on investment. Market-oriented "applications research" was apparently much more important in U.S. operations than was fundamental scientific research. Still, it was generally agreed that just "development" was rarely enough.

There were at least three reasons why European companies might wish to do R&D in the United States in addition to that of adapting and modifying products for the U.S. market: (1) To use a U.S. research base as a source of new products in order to enhance sales growth in the U.S. market. The managers of three European companies, whose U.S. operations had done classified research for the U.S. Defense Department at one time or another, appeared to have had this objective in mind occasionally. No other firms mentioned it; (2) To get product and process feedback. Although managers often expressed a desire to get "feedback" from R&D, there was no statistical relationship between the importance of it and the existence of U.S.-based R&D. Franko concluded that most companies would probably agree with the manager of a pharmaceutical firm who said: "We get a lot of insight into how research is done in the United States. We also get a lot of information on competitors' new products. But our own U.S.-based research has not really given the group as a whole too much, at least not yet."[23] (3) To minimize costs. Since U.S. R&D was tax-deductible in the United States, profits made on the application of results of U.S. R&D in low-tax countries could conceivably be greater than profits made in those countries were R&D to be done there. In other words, it would appear cheaper to get patents and licenses out of the United States than to take profits out.

Franko noted one of the reasons that European companies had not experienced much feedback might be the power implications of having an important subsidiary in the largest market in the world doing "its own thing" in R&D. Many European firms appeared to be fearful that an overly successful R&D effort by their U.S. subsidiaries would result in the parent losing control over the subsidiary or the parent company might become Americanized. He observed that one firm, in a high-technology field, had perhaps served as an object lesson to European headquarters managers concerned with keeping their relative power position over their U.S. subsidiary. The president of this company's subsidiary had at one time obtained approval for a major expansion of R&D activity in the United States. This activity was so successful that it was freely acknowledged that the U.S. subsidiary moved far ahead of the European parent in product technology and applications.

5. The tendency of European MNCs to move their R&D toward major markets is illustrated by data acquired as part of a broader study of trends in Swedish international business evolution by Hedlund and Otterback.[23] They found among forty major Swedish MNCs that 10 percent of R&D was being done abroad in 1971 but the managements predicted the portion would rise to 28 percent by 1982.

6. Crookell made a study in Canada most of which will be more pertinent to the ownership-control discussion in Chapter 10.[24] However, it is described in full here because it makes some key points about R&D which are best understood in the full context of his findings. He made a comparative analysis of the transmission of technology by MNCs to subsidiaries vs. licensing of independent firms. His central research base was limited to interviews with General Electric, Westinghouse and a major Canadian competitor. However, he also drew on broader research on transmission of technology done for Organization for Economic Cooperation and Development and the Canadian government. Overall the author's findings indicated that the licensing process was less satisfactory for the host country and that development of independent technology capability by licensees proceeded more slowly than in subsidiaries.

Subsidiaries were part of a more dynamic chain of technological communication than were their Canadian-owned competitors who secured their technology in the open market through arm's length licensing agreements. Effective technological development required specific measures to ensure a degree of direct relevance between the activities of the research center and the commercial needs of the firm. This process was achieved quite well in multinational firms whose subsidiaries had direct ties with parent research organizations and product divisions providing a regular outflow of new technology and feedback from the market. The process was facilitated by strong personal friendships between Canadian engineers and their American counterparts in the product divisions, which made the transfer of product technology virtually problem-free. The technological transfer process was facilitated by the parallel transmission process for other parent skills including market research, advertising, and cost and quality control techniques.

Special problems arose when the parent and the subsidiary chose different plans for the company products. Westinghouse decided to drop home appliances and color TV in the United States. Westinghouse Canada was successful in carrying on with small appliances that were not so research intensive. It established licenses with other firms and ultimately planned to have its own in-house technological capability. Continuation of color TV was also attempted by licensing, but it was difficult and costly to find personnel to absorb the licensed technology effectively. Ultimately the program failed because high costs precluded exports upon which its viability was dependent. GE maintained some product independence in Canada with two small research centers but their effectiveness was highly dependent upon basic technology from the United States. On the whole, product innovation from the in-house skills of subsidiaries was practical only in low technology work. High-technology innovation was left to the richer parent units with their larger sales volume.

Appraising the other side of the picture, Crookell found the Canadian-owned firms tended to operate through the distortion of transitory, arm's length relationships with foreign licensors and to overlook the development of in-house adaptive skills. It appeared that the firms remained dependent on the licensor for even minor changes in technology. Often the licensor would send skilled technicians into the Canadian firms to iron out problems. Canadian firms receiving this help developed what one executive described as a "foreman mentality in management." Operations tended to be run on a day-to-day basis. Managers had so little control over the speed and direction of the licensor's research that they were generally unable to formulate integrated long-range plans. Furthermore, the cost of technology to these firms seemed to be higher than the cost through a single administrative unit, such as an MNC. The speed of transmission was a good deal slower, and the range narrower. All of this put the Canadian-owned firm at a cost disadvantage for which it tried to compensate by operating with thin management and low overheads. Exports were minimal in these conditions since the Canadian licensee had neither a cost advantage nor a product advantage.

The development of in-house technological capability was slow in these circumstances. There was a real fear of severing the cord. Sizable commitments of funds would be required. Two strategies were possible: specific product projects and permanent investment in R&D capability. The first approach was the one most encouraged by the piecemeal research incentives offered on a project basis by the Canadian government. However, it was not so promising because subsidiaries with greater experience and facilities were competitively stronger on any single project. The second approach was preferred as it developed continuing strength. It was difficult, however, because of lack of funds and competent people. An executive pursuing this approach observed, "We were trying to do something so unusual, so uncharacteristic of Canadian industry, that the resources we needed were simply not available in the country. This is nothing short of a national disaster."[25]

7. John Bennet, a former manager of European Engineering Administration for International Telephone and Telegraph Corp. provided valuable insights into the actual planning of international R&D operations.[26] Bennet observed that the high engineering content of certain products and industrial operations made the cost of technical work a major factor in the competitiveness of a business. It was important therefore to obtain an effective assessment of the cost of technical work in foreign countries.

Communications in a foreign country between the people making this analysis and those actually carrying out the technical work were difficult. The European interpretation of English terminology often differed from U.S. understanding and although a foreign-trained technical executive might understand the words Americans were saying and writing, he might not fully comprehend the information they were trying to convey. In one German company, for example, English definitions of basic terms were prepared in cooperation with a German executive. Several weeks later this man translated the English definitions into German, rearranged the German to express his ideas more accurately and completely, and re-translated the revised German into English. The resulting definitions were much clearer expressions of the terms as they were actually used in the foreign company.

It was also necessary to spell out clearly the titles and especially the classification of technical personnel. Americans had to make sure that when they spoke of an engineer they meant the same thing their foreign colleague meant. Finally, total engineering effort had to be divided into major functional areas, a subject that had often been a subject of controversy.

Once a common understanding was established regarding the terms to use and the cost data related to those terms had been obtained, one could ask any number of questions about the actual costs of technical work. If, for example, the foreign companies were asked to report for each year the amount of money they spent in each technical area for every product group, comparisons could be made between different foreign and American operations. It was possible to find out in what country engineering expenses for a certain product were lowest and, from this, determine where the product could be engineered and produced most competitively. In one case, the technical operations of fifteen European companies located in many different product groups were analyzed by ITT. Such an analysis made it possible to determine where the greatest relative strength could be found for each product line and each functional type of technical effort.

### Strategy Guidelines

The weight of analysis and MNC experience is on the side of unification for MNC R&D strategy. However, it is equally clear that the circumstances of each company will lead to variations in the conclusions.

Two general strategy guidelines may be set forth as fundamental: the strategy should assure maintenance of the MNC's technological strength and it should provide effective responsiveness to market needs. These guidelines will apply to all MNCs, the differences in strategy being the result of differences in their implications for each firm's characteristics. The importance of these guidelines should be self-evident. The technological status is the heart of the MNC's strength in resource transmission, in competition, in power relations with nation states, and ultimately in its contributions to society. To compromise that strength significantly would be suicidal. The market sensitivity is tied to the importance of product demand emphasized in the previous section. It simply adds the obvious point that R&D output must be market-oriented.

The strong thrust toward unification is based on the combination of efficiency, effectiveness, and control which commonly result in centrally-directed R&D programs producing optimum technological output and in concentration of R&D in limited physical sites. Variations on this pattern are effective chiefly where key variables differ from the general pattern. In the largest MNCs R&D work may be divided among several physical sites with no loss in effectiveness. Placing one or more of these facilities overseas may induce some loss of operational effectiveness but that may be counterbalanced by advantages with respect to external factors including favorable host nation response, closeness to local markets, use of foreign personnel, and managerial motivation. The marketing situation of the firm will be the major variable. If adequate responsiveness to market conditions requires proximity to them, then the strategy will favor greater fragmentation.

The ISAGRID of HTI in Table 6−4 illustrates the typical case of a high technology firm whose international strength lies in its ability to maintain a steady flow of new product developments. In terms both of market responsiveness and basic scientific competence its effectiveness is supported by being located in the environment in which innovations in its type of product are in greatest demand, notably the United States and Western Europe. As a large firm in a field of critical interest it attracts strong host government pressures to locate R&D work abroad and its size permits it to allocate major pieces of the program to foreign facilities. Small to medium size firms in similar fields will generally find that analysis favors keeping all R&D within the parent country except for product modification and developmental work. The chief exception to this pattern, suggested by Franko's research is among non–U.S. MNCs. For them the size and product leadership of the U.S. market creates an argument for locating substantial R&D work in the United States. Regardless of the geographic location, however, in all of these high technology cases the wisdom of central control of R&D program planning is supported by the need for efficient and effective worldwide achievement, not only in the work itself but in gearing it into utilization of global plant and marketing capabilities.

General Foods represents a different mix, a more moderate sophistication of technology and a more sensitive interaction of product innovation with host society cultural characteristics. There are still substantial advantages in unification for the efficient development of basic technologies, useful for the whole global organization, interchange of know-how among units, and use of international marketing capabilities. But market needs of individual countries must be integrated with the R&D planning. This may be accomplished by a fragmented R&D system where foreign units undertake product development, or by close integration of local managements with home office R&D decisions or by some combination of the two.

For Singer's consumer sewing machine business R&D presents a simpler picture than for HTI and GF, primarily because new product development is so much less important in its total strategy than marketing skills and production organization. Except for top-of-the-line machines, the rate of product change has been fairly slow and product differentiation is not a major competitive factor. The company did suffer in the immediate post–World War II era because European firms got the jump on it with introduction of zig-zag models. But it is notable that Singer was able to recover quickly by adaptation of similar models it had sold for commercial use. It subsequently introduced the rotating hook system and then for higher priced machines the patented touch-and-sew system. The most significant consideration in its R&D strategy is the maintenance of central control, gearing the developments to serve the unified production system.

**Table 6–4. ISAGRID for Research and Development**

| Company | Resources | Strategy Context Variables | | | | National Interests | |
|---|---|---|---|---|---|---|---|
| | | Economic Differentials | MNC Capabilities | Cultural Change | Global Unification | Home | Host |
| High Technology Industries (HTI) | Natural resources | | | | | | |
| | Labor | | | | | | |
| | Capital: Finance | | | | | | |
| | Production | | | | M | | |
| | Marketing | | | | M | | |
| | Skills: Technological | Hc | H | | Hc | H | H |
| | Managerial | H | | | H | | |
| | Entrepreneurial | | M | | | | |
| Singer | Natural resources | | | | | | |
| | Labor | | | | | | |
| | Capital: Finance | | | | | | |
| | Production | | | | Hc | | |
| | Marketing | | | | | | |

| | Mc | M | | Hc |
|---|---|---|---|---|
| **Singer** *(cont.)* | | | | |
| Skills: | | | | |
| Technological | | | | |
| Managerial | | | | |
| Entrepreneurial | | | | |
| Natural resources | | | | |
| Labor | | | | |
| **General Foods** | | | | |
| Capital: Finance | | | | |
| Production | | | | |
| Marketing | | | H | M |
| Skills: | | | | |
| Technological | M | M | H | M |
| Managerial | H | H | H | |
| Entrepreneurial | H | | | |

Importance in strategy: H = High; M = Moderate; c = Control of parent MNC significant.

**NOTES**

1. John Fayerweather and Ashok Kapoor, *Strategy and Negotiation for the International Corporation* (Cambridge, Mass.: Ballinger Publishing Company, 1975), pp. 127–132, 241–270, 307–338, and 437–465.

2. Nancy Foy, *The Sun Never Sets on IBM* (New York: William Morrow, 1975); "IBM's International Integration," in Christopher Tugendhat, *The Multinationals* (New York: Random House, 1972), pp. 122–127; and R. Sheehan, "What Grows Faster than I.B.M.? I.B.M. Abroad," *Fortune*, Nov. 1960, pp. 166–170.

3. John Fayerweather and Ashok Kapoor, op. cit., pp. 205–232.

4. For further discussion of this subject see John Fayerweather, *International Marketing* (Englewood Cliffs, N.J.: Prentice-Hall, 1970).

5. Richard D. Robinson, *Cases in International Business* (New York: Holt, Rinehart and Winston, 1962), pp. 79–91.

6. Raymond Vernon, "International Investment and International Trade in the Product Cycle," *The Quarterly Journal of Economics*, May 1966, pp. 190–207.

7. F. Raymond Vernon, *Sovereignty at Bay* (New York: Basic Books, 1971), p. 108.

8. Chaim Ginsburg, "The Multinationalization Process," *The Journal of Business* (Seton Hall Univ.), Dec. 1973, pp. 17–26.

9. Georges Leroy, *Multinational Product Strategy: A Typology for Analysis of Worldwide Product Innovation and Diffusion* (New York, Praeger, 1976).

10. Ralph Z. Sorenson and Ulrich E. Wiechmann, "How Multinationals View Marketing Standardization," *Harvard Business Review*, May–June, 1975, pp. 38–55.

11. Ibid., p. 42.

12. M.P. Kacker, "Patterns of Marketing Adaptation in International Business," *Management International Review*, #4–5, 1972, pp. 111–118.

13. Fayerweather and Kapoor, op cit., pp. 307–338.

14. Ibid., pp. 241–270.

15. Ibid., p. 453.

16. John Lindeman and Donald Armstrong, *Policies and Practices of United States Subsidiaries in Canada* (Washington, D.C.: National Planning Association, 1960), pp. 57–64.

17. Thomas J. Mills, "Scientific Personnel and the Professions," *The Annals*, Sept. 1966, pp. 34–35.

18. U.S. Congress, Senate, Committee on Finance, *Implications of Multinational Firms for World Trade and Investment and U.S. Trade and Labor*, Washington, D.C., 1973, pp. 581–593.

19. Michael G. Duerr, *R&D in the Multinational Company* (New York: The Conference Board, 1970).

20. Robert Ronstadt, *Research and Development Abroad by U.S. Multinationals* (New York: Praeger, 1977).

21. Lawrence G. Franko, *European Business Strategies in the United States* (Geneva: Business International, 1971), pp. 23–24.

22. Ibid., pp. 23–24.

23. Gunnar Hedlund and Lars Otterbeck, *The Multinational Corporation, The Nation State and The Trade Unions* (Kent, Ohio: Kent State University Press, 1977), p. 74.

24. Harold Crookell, "The Transmission of Technology Across National Borders," *The Business Quarterly* (Autumn 1973), pp. 52–60.

25. Ibid., p. 59.

26. John B. Bennett, "Sizing Up the Costs of Research and Engineering Abroad," *Management Review* (June 1961), pp. 49–58.

# Chapter 7

# Logistic Strategy—The MNC Production and Supply System

The logistic strategy of the MNC encompasses the location and character of its production facilities and the way in which it services its markets from them, the broad operational framework of the product delivery system. Included in the strategy are a number of major decision areas:

- The choice between importing and local manufacture to serve each market
- Determination of the extent to which plants should specialize
- Decisions on alternative countries as sites for manufacture

## STRATEGY ISSUES

Logistic strategy analysis necessarily starts with economic factors because fundamentally the production-marketing system exists to implement resource transmission capabilities rooted in those factors. The major factors are the economic differentials and the efficiencies available in a unified global system. However, analysis based on economic factors must be modified by other influences including governmental actions and corporate characteristics.

### Economic Factors

The analysis in Chapter 2 indicated that the main MNC capabilities were in technological and managerial skills with somewhat less but still significant strengths in global productive and marketing systems and labor resource transmission, especially through combinations of these capabilities. What sort of logistic system is most appropriate for transmitting these resources? We should look first at binational transmission and then consider the multinational dimensions.

The MNC has two main options for resource transmission in its logistic system, to ship goods that embody combinations of resources or to convey resources to be manufactured in host countries. There are various suboptions under the latter heading providing different degrees of MNC control, including fully-owned operations, joint ventures, licensing independent firms, and management contracts. The key criterion in analyzing these alternatives is efficiency.

The *efficiency* criterion, as indicated in Chapter 2, directs strategy toward methods of transmission that avoid moving resources "upstream" and concentrates the process on those in which the firm has the greatest capabilities. The implications of these considerations may take many directions depending upon the circumstances of a particular firm but two main patterns are central to a wide range of MNCs. The first pattern is the substantial inefficiency of transmitting labor from more industrially advanced to less advanced countries. Because of their primary capabilities in skills, that is the chief direction in which MNCs tend to transmit resources. Yet it is inherently an upstream direction in which to transmit labor because wages are almost always lower in less advanced countries. This efficiency consideration is therefore a prime factor favoring foreign production over exports. The former approach permits transmitting useful skills to be incorporated with labor at the going rate in the host country rather than burdening the skills with the high cost of home country labor.

But the efficiency calculus is a good deal more complex than the simple elimination of upstream labor transmission. All of the resource components must be considered and in many cases the net result will favor export from the home country. The chief factor which can often offset high labor costs is efficient use of capital in large scale home country production units. Because of the small size of many foreign markets it is more economical to produce many manufactured goods in big parent country plants despite much lower foreign wages. For example, the cost of making an automobile in the United States is substantially less than in Mexico despite wages 50 percent below U.S. levels, simply because Mexican plants run at a fraction of the volume of U.S. counterparts.

The efficiency of transmission in this respect has been notably influenced by the expansion of the size of markets for many products accompanying rising standards of living. Such expansion has made it possible to utilize capital and skills more efficiently in overseas factories. Japan serves as a good illustration. Basic production skills have long been established there as was evident in the manufacture of high-technology arms for World War II. But despite low wages, local production of many products was not economical for many years because of limited demand. Production of sewing machines, for example, commenced in 1923, but up to World War II foreign firms like Singer continued to import into Japan on a large scale. In the postwar era, however, with the tremendous increase in per capita income (about 400 percent from 1960 to 1970) the market for many products grew so much that mass-production economies have become feasible and local manufacture is far more economical than importation. Thus Japan has not only ceased to import sewing machines, but it has become a powerful exporter in that field.

The efficiency criterion is effectively met in the emerging pattern of MNC exports from less developed countries in which a two-way flow of resources is combined. The first flow is of capital and skills to the LDCs consistent with the prevailing economic differentials. The skills and capital are combined with low-cost labor and the marketing capabilities of the MNC, the latter now also flowing in the proper economic direction. The second stage does involve upstream return transmission of the skills and capital, and this is inefficient. Thus the pattern is appropriate only where skills and capital represent only a modest protion of the value, i.e., in labor-intensive products, not capital-intensive ones.

In all efficiency analysis, the cost of transportation favors local production over transportation of manufactured goods. In this evolution of two-way resource transmission based on low labor costs it becomes a quite critical factor as high freight costs could offset labor cost advantages. Thus the weight–volume to value relationship is a critical variable. For products of high value per shipping unit the process is more likely to be profitable than for low value, bulky, or heavy items.

The second main pattern related to the efficiency criterion is structuring the system so that transmission is precisely limited to resources of particular MNC capability. There must be a presumption that for different resource differentials, different transmission structures will be efficient. For example, in one case the only superior resource outside a country may be technology, there being adequate natural resources, labor, capital, and other skills. In such a situation, a simple licensing arrangement between a multinational firm and a local manufacturer has an apparent logic. In another situation, a country may be deficient only in technological and managerial skills so that licensing and a management contract apparently fits.

The economic analysis of logistics takes on a substantially greater complexity when it is expanded to the global context. The ideal in a worldwide logistic system is to achieve the most profitable combination of flows among all of the countries. Since there are within the six major categories of resources (natural resources, labor, capital and technological, managerial, and entrepreneurial skills) a multitude of subcategories, each with its own pattern of international differentials, a planner equipped with a computer could work out a very complex logistic scheme to achieve optimum economic results of unification. Figure 7–1 indicates in a simplified form the type of scheme that might be forthcoming from this kind of analysis. The company in this case is assumed to be operating in five countries. A comparison of wages, productivity, and other production cost factors matched against the volume of demand for different types of products in individual markets and consideration of transportation costs and transfer

**Figure 7–1.**  Model of Logistic Planning Based on Economic Factors

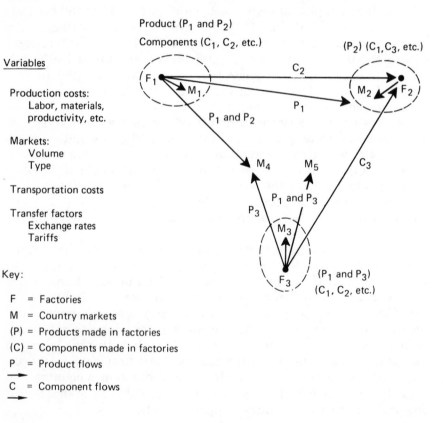

factors (tariffs and exchange rates) leads to locating factories, $F_1$, $F_2$, and $F_3$ in three countries. $F_1$ and $F_3$ are self-contained plants; and $F_2$ is partially an assembly operation dependent upon $F_1$ and $F_3$ for some components. The source for the components is dependent upon costs, $C_2$ being available at lowest cost from $F_1$ and $C_3$ from $F_3$. The source for end products is dependent upon costs and demand in each market. $F_1$, for example, appears to be generally the lowest cost supply point, so $M_4$ obtains $P_1$ from there rather than from $F_3$. On the other hand, it does buy $P_3$ from $F_3$ because $F_1$ does not make it.

## Government Influences

The potentials of the pure economic model developed thus far are substantially limited by the distortions introduced by government actions. These have commonly been directed toward national self-sufficiency rather than toward maximizing international trade flow. Most common are the government efforts noted in Chapter 2 designed to foster local manufacture, which force firms to adopt that strategy to protect markets even when import would be more economical. Somewhat less common but still very frequent are measures to limit MNC control, which may limit the range of resources transmitted. For example, Japan's policy through most of the post-World War II era has been to limit MNCs to minority ownership and strongly encourage licensing in preference to direct participation.

Another major thrust of host national policies is the fostering of exports of manufactured goods by LDCs which has become increasingly common. Export subsidies and other incentives can alter the economic differentials so that the MNC's capabilities to transmit low-cost labor incorporated into their manufactured products are enhanced.

The general thrust of the government actions has been toward fostering production within their borders and deterring the development of economically optimizing unified logistic systems. There have been sufficient obstacles and uncertainties to push multinational companies toward a fragmented approach, thinking of each overseas plant as a supply point for only the market in its own country. The major exceptions have been plants in England or Canada established to serve other countries in the British Commonwealth when the advantages of the Commonwealth tariff preference system were significant.

Environmental factors are now more favorable to intercountry flows. In a number of regional groupings barriers between countries are being lowered, notably in the European Common Market and the European Free Trade Area. Less well developed are the Central American Common Market and Latin American Free Trade Area. Progress in other regions is very limited but may become important. With the pressing need to earn foreign exchange in many countries, MNC subsidiaries are being encouraged to undertake export operations. There is a growing feeling among those concerned with economic growth of the less developed countries that the expansion of exports of labor intensive manufactured goods can be a major factor in further progress. As suggested in Chapter 2, the increasing participation of multinational firms in the reverse flow of resources from these countries is a quite likely development for the future. The concept of preferential tariff reduction favoring exports by LDCs to developed nations has received support from the latter and moves in this direction.

To these structural considerations must be added others that affect global logistic systems. One is that MNCs must be conservative in their approach, recognizing that the risks of extensive dependence on intercountry flows are significant and perhaps not worth the fairly modest economic gains available. Barriers to trade may be set up as long as we have independent nation states. Sometimes this action will be forced because of poorly developed methods of achieving international economic adjustments, even among nations that are committed to reducing trade barriers. For example, in 1963 Italy imposed restrictions against imports including those from other EEC countries. In 1964 Britain placed a surtax of 15 percent on manufactured imports including those from her EFTA partners, and in 1968 France took special measures restricting trade because of the crisis created by a national strike. In each case, severe balance of payment problems forced the hand of governments whose basic policies were to favor freer trade. In other cases, we may anticipate restrictions arising from protectionist sentiment not only among the newly industrializing nations but even among advanced countries. For example, the threat of assorted restrictions against low cost imports of steel, shoes, and textiles, are regularly proposed in the U.S. Congress.

The managements of multinational firms have therefore a legitimate cause for concern, and it may be sound practice to have plants in a somewhat greater number of countries than would be justified to achieve the optimum benefits of rationalization at a given moment.

Another consideration favoring diversification of sources is the diversity of foreign conditions. The politico-economic contexts to which MNCs must relate vary tremendously from country to country along key dimensions: authoritarian vs. democratic, socialism vs. private enterprise, receptivity to foreign business, economic vitality and others. Furthermore, the range of viewpoints among key groups in nations varies so that political change may produce a quite different context. And this in turn adds the degree of stability in the country to the analytical mix because it affects the prospects of a firm finding that the operating milieu will change substantially.

Classifying the countries of the world according to these varied characteristics presents a quite complex analytical matrix. Just to indicate its diversity we may note a few examples in the late 1970's: Germany—highly stable, strong economy, private enterprise secure, open to foreign investment; Japan—equally strong and stable but much less open to MNCs; Taiwan—quite strong and open but highly authoritarian and long-term stability uncertain; Brazil—fairly strong and open, also authoritarian but less rigid so prospects of near term political change greater; Peru—economically depressed, socialist philosophy, strong vein of opinion adverse to MNCs, quite unstable; Italy—economically weak, government ineffective, recent history of coexistence of private enterprise mixed with public enterprise, possibility of communists winning control but effect on private business uncertain. These varied conditions require many difficult decisions on logistic plans and reinforce the conservative policy of multiple sourcing points.

### Corporate Characteristics

The analysis of the effect of corporate characteristics on the logistic system must start with a few fundamental points. The chief objective of the typical corporation is to make its business grow and make profits over the long term by expanding its market position. In the accomplishment of this goal, it has been conditioned to acceptance of considerable risk in technological and marketing innovation. On the whole, however, managements demonstrate conservatism and particularly so with respect to finance. Their approach to the employment of capital resources is generally one of minimizing risk rather than of seeking maximum potential return.

In pursuit of their objectives, most corporations have also found that they perform most effectively in certain patterns with respect to the structure of operations and grouping of people. A typical company, for example, engages in some applied research but relies on other institutions for basic research; it does a substantial amount of manufacturing but also purchases many components from other firms; it conducts much of its own marketing operations but delegates a large portion of its advertising design to an agency, and so on through the range of business activities. The pattern for each company is partly the result of the logics of the situation in which it operates—its product and market, for example—and partly a matter of individual style, there being firms in the same industry which operate in different patterns. But regardless of the origins of the pattern, the corporation has become accustomed to its mode of operation, and a substantial part of its effectiveness is attributable to its ongoing competence in functioning in this pattern.

The corporation has a finite combination of resources under ready control. The critical resources are managerial and technical manpower and capital. Management of overseas operations requires individuals who are technically competent, familiar with a company's methods, and able to command the trust of senior executives. The number of parent country and local nationals meeting these criteria available to a given company at a particular time is always limited.

Availability of financial resources is a limiting factor chiefly for medium- and small-sized companies. Large companies typically have sufficient capital either within their own resources or through ready access to capital markets so that they can finance any undertaking they feel is sound. In a few cases the accumulation of financial resources may even be a factor encouraging overseas activities. For the most part, however, it appears that in the larger companies the supply of financial resources is a neutral factor in determining strategic plans. Among smaller companies it often restrains their capabilities.

Summing up these characteristics, the prime concern of the MNC is in maintaining its market position while using most effectively its skilled manpower and capital and limiting its asset risks, all within a pattern of operations it has learned to manage profitably. These characteristics have several significant effects in the analysis of logistic strategy. There must be a disposition to have a viable position in as many markets as possible and to strengthen the quality of service provided to markets. Broadly that reasoning leads to conforming to the pattern of economic differentials and government actions affecting them as they dictate the main pattern of market opportunities. However, there are ramifications of the logistic strategy analysis in this respect, particularly as the other corporate characteristics are brought into the picture.

First, there is a basic conflict between the market position, risk, and resource utilization goals of the MNC which is confronted in many investment decisions. The dominant objective of building the long-term strength of the firm creates strong pressure on management to protect any market that has been established through exports. The essentially conservative philosophy toward finance and property leads to quite guarded reactions to conditions abroad, especially in those countries where political and economic risks are high. The resources available within the firm at any one time must be directed at the most productive utilization.

The net effect of these factors is some pattern of selectivity among investment opportunities. Figure 7−2 illustrates the type of selective pattern the conflicting goals produce. Favorable investment decisions tend to fall in the shaded area. They include some countries with relatively small markets but also low risks, Belgium, for example, and at the other end some high-risk countries like Brazil which nonetheless have such large-market potentials that companies are willing to invest in them to assure their long-run market position.

A second combination of considerations argues against the economic advantages of a high degree of unification of the logistic system where that would require a limited number of specialized factories serving world markets. While such a system may produce certain cost advantages which strengthen the MNC's market position, the market orientation also argues for reliability of deliveries and some advantages in proximity of factories to customers to facilitate communication. To these general limitations must be added other factors including product characteristics and ownership factors in specific cases which work toward a further fragmentation of the logistic plan. If products must be varied substantially among coun-

**Figure 7−2.** Risk, Demand, and Investment Decisions

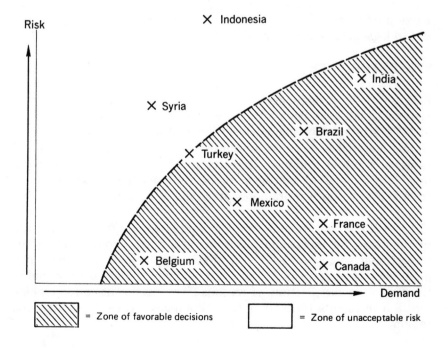

tries for cultural or other reasons, the feasibility of intercountry flows is naturally reduced. There is a wide range of products, including staples like gasoline and machinery products like trucks, for which this factor should not be of great importance as long as a company sticks to the same product line in all countries. Its chief influence is on more variable consumer lines like foods and on companies whose foreign units have been allowed to move into diverse product fields.

The ownership question is relevant because it limits the flexibility of management in making advantageous shifts in logistic plans and also because of antitrust considerations. If a company owns fully all of its foreign units, it can shift production of particular components or end products from one to another largely on the basis of overall corporate objectives. But if there are local investors as partners in one or more of the units, then their interests have to be considered. A partner in a joint venture will not be pleased if the company proposes that the production in his country be cut back and output shifted to another country. The antitrust problem stems from the prevailing view that under U.S. law joint ventures should be treated as independent companies, whereas wholly-owned subsidiaries are an integrated part of a company. Thus for an integrated company there is no legal deterrent to logistic plans under which the pattern of supply for the world is carefully laid out and controlled by the parent organization. But such a scheme worked out by a U.S. company with a group of foreign firms in which it has a partial interest may be subject to legal action as a form of restraint of trade.

## MNC EXPERIENCE

Because of the prominence of investment decisions as part of logistic systems, there have been a number of research studies of this phase of MNC strategy. By summarizing the findings of several studies and adding material from other writings a reasonably full picture of MNC experience can be obtained. Research in this field started with broad, pragmatic reports of management decision-making and has evolved from that into both more conceptual and more detailed approaches.

1. In 1955 Barlow and Wender completed the first broad study of the bases for investment decisions, using data from a Commerce Department survey of 247 U.S. MNCs supplemented by their own interviews in forty firms.[1] The heart of their findings is conveyed in the following distribution of reasons given by the firms for making direct investments (note that some companies gave more than one reason):[2]

| | |
|---|---|
| Favorable market or source of supply | 63% |
| Forced to invest to maintain market | 36 |
| Possibility of profit | 27 |
| Convertibility, favorable exchange | 4 |
| Government encouragement to company | 3 |
| Other | 15 |

The authors' interviews confirmed this picture. The usual reason for beginning assembly or manufacturing operations in a foreign country as indicated by the first two responses was to serve a market within the country that had already been established through export from the United States. Among the factors that necessitated the decision to invest were: government activity, local competition, inadequacy of local distributors, and marketing of related products. In the majority of cases the decision on whether to maintain a market or not was precipitated by government activity. In essence the U.S. MNC managements were motivated by marketing and defensive considerations when competitive and especially governmental actions created a risk of market loss. This picture of market-defensive strategy has been reinforced by subsequent studies, such as the intensive analysis of 100 investment decisions by Polk of the National Industrial Conference Board.[3]

2. The motivations of European firms were explored in an intensive study by Franko.[4] The study showed that Continental European foreign investments were almost always responses to trade barriers. The greater portion of operations was within the European area. The pattern of subsidiary plants set up to jump tariff barriers was not appreciably altered by the establishment of the Common Market. Intra-EEC trade was observed to have grown slowly in industries with many European MNCs. Probably proliferation of foreign manufacturing subsidiaries by European firms in Europe was a consequence of government or private efforts to limit integration by various nontariff barriers and subsidies. The notable exceptions to this pattern were in automobiles and appliances, in which a high degree of European industrial integration was achieved. Although some European MNCs had been in the United States for many years, a large portion of the Continental ventures there were recent. The most common motivation was essentially the same as in Europe and the LDCs: companies had jumped trade barriers to exploit innovative advantages born in Continental markets.

3. From an earlier study of thirty-eight major European firms, Franko provided a more refined examination of motivations for investment in the United States.[5] While exports from Europe had

grown, he noted that sales by firms with U.S. plants had grown much faster. An underlying motivation was that manufacturing in the United States brought far quicker and far closer access to the innovative stimuli of the U.S. business environment. He quoted a European manager to convey the overall philosophy. "Operating in the American market is no longer the natural consequence of success in other markets, but a precondition of success in the world market." On the negative side, antitrust and other legal complications were often noted as complications, but the research indicated that the main problems of the Europeans lay in the U.S. competitive environment with its rapid innovations and risk taking compared with the slower European response to competition.

4. On the basis of extensive research among Japanese international business firms, Yoshino reported a quite different pattern of motivations for its foreign investments.[6] He observed that whereas U.S. MNCs had been heavily concentrated in high technology industries and motor vehicles, much of Japanese investment had been in basic commodities, for example, nearly a quarter in textiles. The main impetus for the investment came from import substitution policies in LDCs, notably in Southeast Asia which threatened Japan's large export trade based on large-scale production and low costs. This pattern was dominant among the major Japanese trading companies which accounted for a considerable portion of foreign investment. Their strategy was to defend particular export markets and to become the major suppliers of intermediate materials or components, machinery, and equipment for the new plants overseas. Since the primary objective was simply to establish captive export customers, the trading companies had little interest in control and held less than 25 percent equity in two-thirds of their affiliates.

Yoshino concluded that the prospect of the trading companies becoming multinational enterprises with strong central systemwide coordination was limited. Their primary role was likely to be confined to facilitating multinational moves by others. They tended to be heavily oriented to short-term trading advantage. Although they had made some organizational adjustments to provide better management of foreign investments, they had not been able to guide adequately the multitude of joint ventures in which they had minority interests, many of which had floundered for lack of competent management. In one trading firm, for example, more than a hundred subsidiaries were monitored by a home office staff of four people. In the early 1970s the trading companies were trying to strengthen their positions by shifting from small- to large-scale ventures in basic commodities like petrochemicals, strengthening their multinational commercial networks and vertical integration. However, Yoshino doubted if their role in foreign manufacture would ever be great.

Investments by manufacturing firms had followed a similar export-related pattern. Subsidiaries were created to complement the firm's exports and the major competitive strength abroad initially was closely tied to the tremendous economies of scale in production enjoyed by the parent companies in Japan. In the average firm exports composed 25 percent of total sales so the international staff had to achieve its legitimacy and identity in the shadow of an extremely powerful export division. This status had been important as commitment of new resources was needed by managers of foreign subsidiaries in their desperate efforts to shore up their competitive strength after the initial cost advantages of home-based export supplies was lost.

As with the trading companies, the manufacturing firms found that the pattern of many weakly controlled joint ventures serving as captive outlets for exported intermediate products was not effective. Among the firms with the longest international experience, therefore Yoshino found a trend toward strategies stressing coordination and control and a preference for majority ownership. For certain strategies, control was especially important. For example, in a sample of fifty large firms, Yoshino found seventy-five wholly-owned subsidiaries of which fifty-two were off-shore production facilities designed to export their output to other markets. The Japanese were giving increasing emphasis to such plants in Korea, Taiwan, and so forth to maintain cost competitiveness lost in Japan due to wage rises. In such operations they found close control necessary to assure high quality, coordinate production and gain flexibility in transfer pricing. The few Japanese firms in which technology was a significant competitive advantage also stressed control of foreign units. Sony, for example, had a strong preference for wholly-owned units. And a variety of policy issues with partners were experienced in more mature joint-ventures which Japanese executives cited as arguments for shifting toward greater control. Thus, in making major investments, an increasing number of internationally active enterprises considered control so critical that in those cases where they could not obtain at least majority ownership, they insisted on an explicit agreement with the partner over certain key management decisions.

5. Wells described MNCs based in less developed countries on the basis of his research in Southeast Asia.[7] Data on direct investment by LDC firms were limited but some items were cited. Of 360 firms

granted promotion status in Thailand between 1966 and 1973, 93 were from Taiwan; 10-Malaysia, 5-Hong Kong, 15-India, and 16-Singapore. Wells observed that the foreign investors based in the developing countries appeared to thrive in industries or segments of the market where cost competition was severe and the advantages of economies of scale did not overwhelm small-scale manufacturers. The data available suggested that most LDC investors operated in industries that had mature technologies. Many of the developing-country investors appeared to have gained their initial advantage when they adapted large-scale technologies of the industrialized countries for manufacture at small scale in their home countries. Once mastered, the ability to manufacture efficiently for small markets gave the firms a skill that was exportable to other countries with small markets.

The advantage of the LDC investor was found chiefly in market segments where price competition was a viable strategy as distinguished from fields in which rapidly advancing technology and/or market intensity was critical. The LDC firm benefited both in economies of scaled-down and adapted technology and in lower costs of management and technical personnel. Wells identified refrigerators as a prime example of a field in which LDC MNCs had done well because the technology was stable, the opportunities for adaptation for cost economies in production were good, and the market was highly price-competitive. Detergents had been largely dominated by major MNCs with strong advertising and brand status. But there was a segment of this market also which was price-conscious so LDC firms with cost economies had a niche in it.

The vast majority of LDC investors entered foreign markets through joint ventures with partners of the host country. Quite commonly their only investment was provision of machinery. Home LDC governments often discouraged export of capital and the firms might also be more attuned to the political sensitivities of home countries on the ownership issue. More fundamentally, however, the LDC investor had little fear of having his strategy disrupted over marketing policies of the local partner, since sophisticated marketing strategies did not usually play a role in the firm's success. Likewise, subsidiaries did not play a role in a global strategy or require close relations for the continuing input of new technology as was true of the typical major MNC. For the most part it appeared that a subsidiary of an LDC investor was often "on its own" after a brief period of assistance from the parent at the outset. In fact, the links between the subsidiary and the parent might wither away with time. After a few years, the subsidiary of the LDC investor might be hardly distinguishable from a local enterprise.

The differences in U.S., European, Japanese, and LDC MNC experience suggest the difficulty of generalizing too fully from the nature of the former. However, as a practical matter U.S. firms do compose the greater portion of MNCs and the balance of the research on logistic strategy is largely focused on them.

6. The broadest conceptual analysis of MNC investment behavior is Vernon's product life cycle (PLC) which was described in Chapter 6 (p. 233). The concept is primarily an explanation of the evolution of logistic strategy of an MNC. It is consistent with the earlier market-defensive findings but carries the evolution further and in a more sophisticated form. Vernon found the historical evolution of MNC logistic strategies ran through a typical sequence starting with a product developed for the home market, followed by exports until diffusion of the product know-how weakened the firm's competitive status abroad. At that point production in other countries was undertaken displacing exports from the home country. Vernon hypothesized a fourth stage in which production would shift to low labor cost LDCs and the flow of products would be reversed. In his study of the history of firms, however, he did not find cases that carried through the full sequence.

Also noted in Chapter 6 was Vernon's subsequent assessment that the PLC was no longer adequate as an explanation for MNC behavior as firms were found to be responding to initiatives from varied points in their organizations. The key point is that the PLC assumed a process based upon market and management dynamics occurring in a set sequence with essentially a defensive orientation. When managements were new to the international field and their limited skill and facilities gave them few options, this sequence was common. However, Vernon's subsequent assessment is sound as sophisticated MNC managements now have a global outlook, many established facilities, and a skillful capacity to consider any logistic options that are economically feasible.

7. A prime example of the changed situation is the fact that what Vernon predicted as the final stage of the PLC sequence has appeared as a second move by many U.S. MNCs after establishment of home country production, namely sourcing from factories in low labor cost countries. Moxon undertook an intensive analysis of this process using the electronics industry as a case study.[8] He developed a con-

ceptual model for offshore production decisions and tested it with statistical evidence and interview survey results. The heart of the analysis concerned the circumstances under which offshore production was undertaken and the types of products involved.

For his statistical study Moxon determined an Offshore Production Propensity Index (imports divided by U.S. factory shipments) for three product categories: consumer and industrial electronic products and components. Correlation analysis was then employed using measures of import and price competition. The two concepts provided a rough indication of where the pressure to reduce costs was the greatest. The import competition index was more related to foreign competition, and the price trend more to domestic competition. His data indicated that the import competition index was a very important determinant of the offshore production propensity. The interviews confirmed this in company experience and supported the conclusion that many foreign investments were defensive in nature, and that executives needed a strong stimulus before they seriously considered a given foreign investment.

Several product characteristics were examined. The statistical analysis showed that labor intensity was probably important in determining which products were made offshore, while very highly capital-intensive products were not likely candidates. Skill requirements as measured by wage levels did not appear to be a significant factor. About three-quarters of the executives interviewed said that unit shipping costs were an important factor but the statistical measure used—value-to-weight ratio—did not show a significant correlation. Tariff considerations were mentioned by only a few executives and showed weak statistical relationship. Sales trends also showed no statistical relation to offshore production but executives did observe a connection. Generally foreign production increased with sales growth while in periods of sales decline the indications were that domestic output would be maintained to protect labor. Fluctuations and long-term contractions were absorbed abroad.

Several factors not susceptible to statistical analysis were examined only by interview evidence. Executives indicated that offshore production was more common for proven production processes than for recently developed ones, and for standardized simple products rather than for those with rapidly changing specifications and uncertain sales volume.

Executives were conscious of the risks of disruption of supply from foreign plants. It was quite common practice among the companies surveyed to have plants in more than one country to provide alternative sources to reduce the risk. Among semiconductor producers the average was two countries per firm while firms making tubes and other components averaged 1.5 countries per firm.

Moxon explored the alternatives to offshore production considered when companies encountered strong import competition. Automation of domestic facilities was favored by firms, the indications being that the products made offshore were those for which further automation was impossible or uneconomic. Subcontracting to independent foreign producers was considered desirable chiefly where the subcontractor already had the required knowledge, and where there was no great difficulty in coordinating the foreign and U.S. facilities. Two kinds of situations were mentioned in which subcontracting was a superior alternative to an offshore plant. The first was when a firm's production of a given product was too limited to take advantage of possible economies of scale. The second case was that of fluctuating production volumes. The products or manufacturing operations were invariably the most simple and standardized ones.

For semiconductors and computer parts the combination of offshore plants and a technological lead seemed to allow American manufacturers to compete effectively with foreign companies. But for older products, where the U.S. technological lead was smaller, even the use of offshore plants was not enough to stop imports from foreign producers from displacing the products of U.S. firms.

A substantial learning process was observed in offshore production. In the early stages, offshore production involved high perceived risks with unknown returns. But as companies gained experience the returns and risks become more predictable. Virtually all of the executives expressed satisfaction with the performance of their offshore plants. Moxon noted briefly the strength of offshore plants in relation to host governments because of their contribution to the economies and their mobility. In general he anticipated a continued expansion of offshore production, largely as a defensive mechanism against import pressure, and one therefore which was preferable for the U.S. economy to complete loss of domestic market position by U.S. firms.

8. Another perspective on the MNCs' role in export of manufactured goods from LDCs was provided by de la Torre's research described in Chapter 2 (p. 73). It emphasized their strength in global marketing capability.

9. A comparative analysis of three types of foreign operations with different logistic roles was made by Crookell in a study of eighty investment projects in LDCs undertaken by multinational firms from Europe, Japan, and North America.[9] He noted that the sample was probably biased in favor of successful ventures and large firms with

relatively large projects. The bias, however, would not materially change the types of conclusions he drew from the cases.

The investments studied were divided into three categories which provide the framework for the analysis. The first, export-oriented investment intended primarily to serve external markets, was typically motivated by cheap labor. In these ventures, much of the profit might accrue outside the host country as a result of transfer prices. In these circumstances, joint ventures with local partners were resisted by foreign investores, who found themselves in a strong bargaining position vis-à-vis host governments because of their total control over the market.

The second category, market-development investment intended primarily to produce for sale in the host country, was motivated by investor perceptions of that market potential. Incentives like tax holidays had little influence on these investments because profit expectations were often limited. Many firms mentioned that losses in the first three years of operation were regarded as a kind of "entry fee" into the market. Investors looked instead for evidence of long-term stability and attractive growth rates. Joint ventures were likely to be tolerated or even welcome in these projects.

The third category, government-initiated investment, was typically intended to displace imports. The foreign firm was expected to take a minority position in these operations and the firm most often viewed them as essentially portfolio investments where the main, and sometimes only, reason for going ahead was financial return. Hence the firm charged a fee or royalty for every function it performed.

Financial data from the research indicated that export-oriented projects tended to be very profitable and to use less LDC capital than other projects. Market development projects were the least profitable category, and involved more LDC capital and a higher rate of reinvestment for growth. Government-initiated investments showed rather good rates of profitability and the highest rates of reinvestment. The repatriation periods for the ventures in the sample were: export-oriented, 3.8 years; market-development, 10.5 years; and government-initiated, 8.1 years. The author emphasized that these were successful projects so the profitability was higher than for all investments.

As to government incentives, market-development investments were influenced most by protective measures while export-oriented ventures responded to financial incentives. Firms, after they decided to invest in order to reduce costs, began to "shop around" between countries for the best package of incentives offered by the most aggressive and accommodating LDC.

Export-oriented projects were found to have a positive net effect on host country balance of payments. Locally oriented projects had substantial negative effects and government-initiated projects had the most adverse impact. The increase in imports associated with locally oriented projects was due to complementary products as well as components and materials. Apparently the increased commitment to the country led to a stronger marketing effort including additional products to round out a line and make full use of the marketing investment. Some companies making market-oriented investments reported pressures to export. Crookell felt this was a short-sighted policy move in that it attempted to force projects to assume a function they were never intended to perform. A more efficient policy would be to encourage a number of export-oriented projects to offset the ongoing balance of payments drain of the locally oriented projects. Export-oriented firms were also found to transmit their technology intact while locally oriented projects often involved some adaptation. This was cited as a further reason why efforts to make them export might be rather inefficient.

Export-oriented projects had significantly less local ownership. The degree of local ownership was not found to affect other characteristics appreciably. The only items noted were that higher foreign ownership was associated with higher bilateral imports and exports, usually of component parts; greater international competitiveness, and higher foreign capital inputs with lower charges for foreign technology.

Crookell predicted that investment agreements would become more imaginative, complex, and carefully tailored. A distinction was seen in parent–subsidiary relations. Market-development ventures were sufficiently autonomous to be profit centers, while one could not reasonably delegate profit responsibility to a subsidiary manager who was denied control over prices and markets as was true of export-oriented projects. The positioning of operations in the corporate structure was also affected. The export-oriented project was usually developed by engineers and production people with emphasis on cost so responsibility for them logically lay with product or manufacturing divisions. The market development investments, on the other hand, might well be properly placed under international divisions.

As to host country policy, the author emphasized the need to relate policies to investor characteristics. He cited the Turkish foreign investment regulations of 1971 which set forth four criteria: introduction of up-to-date technology, international competitiveness and commitment to export, large-scale and majority Turkish ownership. Foreign firms had not responded because the criteria were inconsistent with investor motivations and other characteristics.

10. Another approach to distinguishing types of investment was the study by Buckley and Dunning cited in Chapter 2 (p. 73). They determined that U. S. MNC investments in the United Kingdom were strongest in industries where they had advantages in skilled labor, entrepreneurial resources, R&D and control of know-how, and a concentrated market structure.

11. The general studies of investment motivation all emphasize the frequency of defensive, competitive motivations. Knickerbocker pursued a major aspect of this behavior with an intensive statistical analysis of the degree to which multinational enterprises act to counter each other's investments in new foreign operations.[10] He found that the extent of defensive investments differed according to several variables.

The analysis was based on data for the 187 large U. S. multinational enterprises accumulated by the Harvard MNE project. The author included in his study all new investments by these firms during 1948– 1967 in 23 countries which accounted for about 83 percent of the total for the companies. His basic analytical measure was the Entry Concentration Index (ECI), the number of new investments within a given time period as a percentage of those over the total 20-year period. ECIs were computed for 3- , 5- , and 7-year periods.

Overall the analysis showed that 46 percent of the new investments in each industry in each country were clustered in 3-year periods, and 75 percent within 7-year periods. Thus his data demonstrated the inclination of companies to match each other's investment moves to maintain their market position in each foreign country.

Knickerbocker explored the correlation of the clustering to several variables with the following outcome: (1) On the whole ECIs were positively correlated to industry concentration. The latter was measured by the percentage of each industry controlled by the largest firms, using ratios for both four- and eight-firm concentration. The correlations indicated that in general firms' pursued the strategy of defensive investment more actively in industries of high seller concentration. However, a negative correlation was found in industries with the very highest concentration (eight-firm ratios above 70 percent). The author believed this was because high firm interdependency was coupled with high structural stability. (2) The countering of rivals' foreign direct investments seemed to be most energetic in those industries in which capacities of marketing organizations were the dominant basis of competitive strength as compared to those relying heavily on product characteristics or production economies.

(3) Entry concentration was negatively related to product diversity. Narrow product-line firms, because they had few options, tended to respond in kind when a rival made a foreign investment. Wide product-line firms, on the other hand, because they had the capacity to exploit foreign markets in a variety of ways, were not as inclined to oligopolistic reaction. (4) The few firms which reacted quickly to the moves of others tended to ignore production scale considerations. The others, which reacted more slowly, were deterred by this factor. This conclusion was based on the finding that the five- and seven-year ECIs were negatively correlated with measures of scale but the three-year ECIs were not. It appeared that the most aggressive firms would move to counter the establishment of new factories abroad by competitors even when markets were too small to permit optimum scale of units but that other firms were inclined to wait until an economical scale of production was more practical.

(5) ECIs were negatively correlated with intensity both of R&D and of advertising as a percentage of sales. These factors, like diversification, seemed to provide market strengths which decreased the need to match the immediate investment moves of rivals. (6) There was a positive correlation between profitability and entry concentration for which the author could provide no clear reason.

(7) Entry concentration by industry was positively related to measures of market growth much more so than it was to measures of market size. Likewise, stable political environments were found to be related to high ECIs, indicating that firms were anxious to protect their market positions in politically safer countries and not so concerned in unstable ones.

12. The unification aspects of logistic strategy have received relatively little research attention. The subject was covered briefly in Stopford and Wells' broader study of the organization of the 187 major firms included in the Harvard MNE project.[11] They found most unification strategies were on an area rather than a global basis. Many firms with area divisions attempted to lower their manufacturing costs by rationalizing production. Where economies of scale were significant the enterprise might use parts produced in a number of different countries to assemble its final product in a number of national locations; or it might assign a complete final product to a particular country, filling in the product line as necessary with models manufactured in other countries. But this strategy appeared to increase profitability only when the technology was stable, the overall

foreign production level high, and the products standardized to some extent in world markets.

Inability to standardize products was a major obstacle. Consumer preferences for such standard items as the washing machine could vary so widely between different national markets that even regional standardization of the product was impossible. Hoover, for instance, had to invest considerable sums of money and management time during the 1960s before a washing machine for the European market could be developed. And even after the development effort, only some of the components could be standardized throughout this one region. Hoover was able to make substantial savings in development costs, tooling and unit production costs, but the savings would have been even larger had a greater degree of standardization been possible.

Beyond product standardization the key questions in rationalization related to administration and marketing management. The disputes among subsidiary managers over such issues as transfer pricing and the allocation of production and markets could occupy an undue amount of senior management time unless some organizational mechanism for controlling and resolving the disputes was developed. Where global rationalization of production had been achieved, firms faced the problems of coordinating product flows across divisional boundaries. Massey-Ferguson, for example, assembled in Detroit a machine for sale in Canada that included an engine from England, a transmission from France, and an axle from Mexico.

The task of coordinating manufacturing, marketing, engineering, and the intersubsidiary movement of finished products and component parts posed huge problems. In spite of these inherent problems, firms that had built area divisions and had rationalized production through these structures had been successful in capturing major shares of the world market for their products. The potential costs of poor coordination of the product flows across the divisional boundaries could be held in check by developing planning committees and other organizational mechanisms that cut across the formal lines of responsibility. Provided that the tasks of coordination were relatively routine, the divisional managers or their representatives on the committees could learn how to act cooperatively without unduly restricting the autonomy of any one division. The structure of area divisions could be tailored to meet the conflicting requirements for centralized production and decentralized marketing.

The authors observed that greater control and a more far-reaching rationalization of production might be achieved if, instead of regional divisions, the organization had a structure in which each functional department had worldwide responsibilities. But this structural option was seldom adopted, even by firms with only a single product line. The marginal gains of increased rationalization of production and lower costs were normally judged to be more than offset by losses in marketing effectiveness. The functional departments centralized decision-making in the corporate office and inhibited rapid responses to changes in the foreign markets; delays and distortions in information processing occurred. Only under certain rare conditions could the worldwide functional structure be efficient.

If the operations were relatively stable, standardized procedures and short cuts in the lines of communication could be developed to maintain control without loss of efficiency. The National Cash Register Company during the first half of this century had efficient and successful worldwide functional departments. Some European firms, such as SKF (Sweden), had also used this structure. Only a few worldwide product divisions manufactured on a rationalized basis. Singer's sewing machine operations were cited as one example. Some other firms with worldwide product divisions were reported to be building specalized plants. But, in general, these firms had not developed a network of highly interrelated product flows as extensively as had firms with area management centers.

13. Logistic unification was also a significant factor in a study Franko made of the history of about 1,100 joint ventures of 170 U.S. firms.[12] About one-third of them were dissolved or ended in a substantial change in ownership control. In 182 cases the U.S. partner assumed full ownership while in 84 the foreign partner took over. In 46 instances, the U.S. firm assumed over 50 percent control replacing a 50−50 or foreign-controlled relationship. In two cases the foreign partner established such a status.

The study showed that the traditional explanations for joint venture instability, such problems as personality or intercultural clashes between partners were insufficient. It appeared that ownership changes occurred in clusters within a firm in a given period rather than one at a time as would be expected under the traditional explanation. The main cause apparently lay in changes in corporate strategy. Corporations pursuing a multinational strategy of foreign product-market diversification tolerated joint ventures and the decentralized decision-making they implied. MNCs pursuing a strategy of product-market concentration, thus specializing in selling one particular function to similar customers worldwide, eventually rid themselves of joint venture partners.

Franko found that at early stages of foreign operations, strong subsidiary managers were common and joint ventures were stable. The parent role was typically limited to providing technical advice, production know-how, and some capital; the foreign partner did the rest. As operations expanded, many firms shifted to the worldwide product division organization but this change was not inconsistent with the survival of joint ventures.

Something very different occurred, however, when a company with a limited foreign product line assigned regional managers direct responsibility for operations. The shift in these cases to a regional form of organization seemed to be a response to corporate perception that rationalization of production and standardization of marketing policies was required for maximum efficiency. When this shift was made the rate of joint-venture instability went up markedly. Joint ventures with local partners were no longer tolerated, primarily because of potential divergence of interest over marketing decision-making. Firms with a strong market position were more tolerant of the diversity of market decisions associated with joint ventures. In the tight competitive conditions of a more saturated market, however, companies were more likely to seek centralized decision-making and avoid joint ventures.

14. As the main thrust of logistic unification is at the regional level, two reports on corporate experience in developing it are useful. The first is a description by Valtz of the problems of a disguised company, Universal Manufacturing and Control Co. (UMCC), in achieving rationalization of its European operations after EEC for formed.[13] The company made heavy machinery for manufacturing and construction and control equipment for industrial processes. Since World War II it had built plants in nine European countries. Most products were made in three to six countries, but three products were made in all nine countries.

The main cause of this fragmentation was the level of tariffs which ran from 10 to 20 percent. Even though unit labor costs were only 40 percent of those in the United States, manufacturing costs were 105 to 115 percent of U.S. levels. According to one estimate, the latter would be cut to 75 percent or 85 percent if production of each item were centralized. These figures suggest the company was already tolerating somewhat greater cost disadvantages from fragmentation than the tariff levels necessitated. With the rapid reduction in tariffs within EEC the economic considerations favored rationalization.

Other factors, however, were strong deterrents to rationalization. Even though the products should have been uniform among countries, UMCC found that the management in each country had made small modifications to suit the desires of local customers. The company's public and government relations might suffer from breaking relations with various local suppliers or the loss of the "Made in ———" sales image. Managers in each country also resisted rationalization which would deprive them of much autonomy. And in the background of all this were the uncertainties of trade relations among the countries—the halting efforts at agreement between EEC and Britain and the other EFTA countries and the risk of obstacles such as the Italian and British import restriction cases cited earlier in this chapter. Thus even in a product field and a geographic area where movement toward an economically rational logistic scheme was apparently most logical, the practicalities of achievement were restricted.

15. The second source is an assessment by Behrman of the requirements and prospects of regional industrial integration in Latin America based upon detailed studies of two industries and a general examination of the situation.[14] The author's analysis identified several critical obstacles to integration and generally portrayed a pessimistic outlook. But he also conveyed an underlying conviction in the soundness and ultimate feasibility of the regional integration.

The basic idea of industrial integration is part of the Latin American Free Trade Association (LAFTA) pact. It provides for complementation agreements under which two or more countries allocate production among themselves to avoid duplication and achieve economies. Behrman recorded the slow progress in this direction with only nine agreements in effect, seven signed but not yet in operation and sixteen under negotiation, at the time of the study (1971). Even those which had been signed were of limited scope. Only three provided for allocation of plant location, the others merely reduced tariffs. They also covered only a few countries.

Behrman observed that the crux of the problem was to find an appropriate trade-off between efficiency (in an economic sense) and equity (in the sense of division of benefits) that still permitted world-wide competitiveness. He felt that the full LAFTA regional market offered major factors needed for efficiency: demand sufficient to support substantial levels of production, sufficient economies of scale at these levels, and additional nonscale reductions in cost. The major deterrents lay therefore in the conceptions of division of benefits such as employment and taxation and loss of control by each nation. Furthermore there were transitional deterrents in the commitments to existing plants by both primary producers and supporting industries. In this connection, Behrman noted with some concern the consequences of subregional integration such as the Andean nations proposed which would create costly deterrents to full integration later.

Four additional obstacles were identified: (1) Transportation was a problem because the main routes between Latin American countries and other parts of the world were developed while those between the Latin American were poorly developed. Some efforts were underway in this field and they would presumably be accelerated if substantial integration developed. (2) Exchange rate stability would be required to make certain that the shares in real terms were not altered by shifts in rates. Behrman predicted that unstable rates would result in continual conflicts as to equity. But in light of monetary history in the region he concluded that this dilemma seemed an almost impossible hurdle. (3) Intervention by foreign governments, notably the United States, could be disruptive in three areas—export control, antitrust, and balance of payments. Actions in any of these could prevent formation of integrated systems or interfere with the functioning of a system once set up. (4) There was the feeling among Latin American countries that government commitments were not necessarily credible. Too often government officials had violated their oral and written agreements or withdrawn a commitment. The large investments needed to implement complementation agreements would be difficult to induce in an atmosphere of government reversals.

16. While they were not as well focused on logistic decisions as the preceding reports, two other studies provide some interesting insights into the character and effects of organization of production on a global scale. Rowthorn made an econometric analysis of the patterns of growth of large corporations based in Europe, Japan, and North America.[15] The objective of the analysis was to determine whether the fear of the relatively greater growth of U.S. firms expressed in popular writings was based on reality, and particularly whether there was support for the thesis that U.S. firms had a growth advantage in their size and in their emphasis on certain industries.

The author analyzed the performance of groups of large firms listed annually by *Fortune* using three samples of varying composition. Data were analyzed for 1957–62 and 1962–67 as well as for the full period.

On the whole the analysis did not support the popular fears about the size impact of U.S. MNCs. It appeared that, if anything, the rate of growth decreased as the size of firms increased so the larger size of U.S. firms was no apparent advantage. As to nationality, over the ten years 1957–67, the leader was Japan followed by continental Europe. Well behind and closely bunched were Canada, the United States and the United Kingdom. While there were some differences according to industries, the Americans did not seem to have a consistent advantage in the high technology fields. They did relatively better in electrical and engineering but not as well in chemicals.

The author attempted to demonstrate that to a considerable degree the growth of multinational firms was due to interpenetration—a process of expanding into each other's market areas. Each firm might lose part of its home national market share to foreign firms in this manner. The data seemed to indicate, however, that the chief losers in this process are smaller domestic firms. The major firms held most of their home market share and gained sufficiently from acquiring shares of foreign markets so their overall growth pattern was better than that of their strictly home-based national competitors.

Another analysis was made to determine the sources of growth of U.S. firms. It appeared that about half was due to expansion of the U.S. economy, a sixth to increased share of the market and a third to increased overseas production. The latter figure varied from 21 percent for food to 51 percent for metals.

17. The second study was made by Business International as a response to the "exporting jobs" attack on the multinational corporation.[16] But it is useful here for its picture of the evolving logistics of U.S. MNCs. BI made a detailed statistical analysis of data from a sample of 125 companies over the period from 1960 to 1970. The main findings were (1) The international companies increased domestic employment two and one-half times faster than the average U.S. firm; (2) The firms with the highest rates of foreign investment increased their employment three times faster than those with the lowest rates; (3) The companies in the sample increased exports by 205 percent from 1960 to 1970 compared to a 128 percent increase for all U.S. non-agricultural exports; (4) Exports to their affiliates abroad rose even faster, 302 percent; (5) Companies with greater growth of foreign investment increased exports by 205 percent compared to 150 percent for those with lower growth rates; (6) Imports from affiliates as a percentage of total company sales rose from 0.6 percent in 1960 to 0.8 percent in 1970; (7) The balance of trade of the sample doubled from 1960 to 1970 while the overall U.S. balance of trade was cut in half; (8) Investment by the sample in the United States was 178 percent higher in 1970 than in 1960 compared to a rise of 121 percent for all U.S. manufacturers.

In part the BI study simply restated with new data points such as balance of payments effects which had already been well established. But it added important data on some points. The main thrust of these points was that expansion abroad contributed in a critical way to the overall vitality of a company, making possible greater investment and employment growth at home. In a nutshell the multinational firms had provided the greatest dynamic boost for the U.S. economy, not the firms which had abstained from foreign investment. The BI data showed this both in broad aggregate and on an industry basis. For example, it was noted that in the electrical machinery field, those companies with aggressive foreign investment programs increased U.S. employment while those which did not had declining U.S. employment.

The study advanced three mutually supporting concepts to explain this contribution of foreign investment to domestic strength. The first, the export continuation theory was that foreign operations permitted a firm to have a stronger overall market position. By making products abroad when that was necessary to serve markets, the company was able to field a full product line and meet competition effectively. This overall market strength provided opportunities to export both semi-finished products for use in affiliated plants and finished goods. This concept was illustrated by case examples of accelerated growth of exports by particular companies following investment in foreign plants.

The second concept, the continuity of expansion theory, argued that the greater and more stable rate of growth of sales of the multinational firm resulted in more consistent worldwide profits and greater financial capability for research and development. Firms in this position were better protected from U.S. cyclical problems and able to support a stronger product development effort. To a degree the foreign operations had the effect of subsidizing U.S. operations. In any case, the overall effect of being a stronger firm was greater capacity for domestic growth.

The third concept, the dollar overvaluation theory, was explained by comparing the firm to the individual who had got more for his money by buying abroad while the U.S. dollar had been overvalued. The thesis was that the multinational firm by economic gains of this nature had strengthened its overall resource position. Thus it was a stronger firm and better able to expand at home as well as abroad.

On the basis of interviews in thirty-five firms, BI confirmed that the typical motivation for foreign investments was maintenance or establishment of a strong market position. Sales to local markets absorbed 75 percent or more of the output of most foreign factories. Another point brought out was the importance of exports to affiliates. Some 50 percent of the exports of the sample firms were to affiliates abroad and the interviews indicated that there was an additional increment in exports by one multinational company to foreign units of another. BI was unable to indicate the magnitude of this increment because pertinent records were kept by foreign affiliates and they would be hard to isolate.

18. The importance of political risk in investment decisions has directed substantial research interest toward determining how MNCs handle and assess the risks. Root surveyed 124 companies which accounted for about one-sixth of U.S. industrial investment abroad

and interviewed executives in 18 companies to determine how they handled political risks.[17] He defined the main responses to these risks as avoidance, adaptation, and transfer. Noting that market opportunity and political risks were the dominant factors in most investment decisions, Root found that about a third of the executives interviewed gave market-defensive reasons for investments. Generally speaking, a defensive investment strategy went hand in hand with a policy of risk avoidance. On the other hand, about two-thirds of the executives emphasized market opportunity. This sort of aggressive investment strategy de-emphasized political risks, viewing them not as an obstacle to entry but as an environmental condition that called for skillful adaptation and possibly some sort of risk transfer.

The adaptation response presumed that a company might reduce risks by relating its activities to the national interests of the host society. Root found that few companies had formulated policies of this sort. Apparently, executives did not think in these broad terms. Joint ventures were cited as a prime medium for seeking political adaptation. But slightly less than half of the companies favored joint ventures, and of them less than two-thirds gave political advantages as a primary reason for their position. The author concluded that active adaptation to local national interests so as to minimize political risks did not appear to be a dominant policy. The chief means for risk transfer was the U.S. government AID Investment Guaranty Program. But Root found that only about 60 percent of the companies had used this program.

A further finding of the study was that no executive offered any evidence of a systematic evaluation of political risks. Root was critical of this evidence that American management was willing to render political judgments on the basis of vague impressions, newspaper accounts of recent events, and unexplored assumptions when, at the same time, it put time and money into a careful investigation of foreign markets and competition.

19. Thunell made an intensive statistical analysis to determine the relation between the investment decisions of multinational corporations and host country political conditions.[18] For the investment behavior he employed data from both the Harvard MNE project giving numbers of new subsidiaries established by leading European and U.S. firms, and IMF data for the flow of direct investment. Host country conditions were measured by statistics from the *World Handbook* under two headings: mass political events and government events. The former included riots, demonstrations, and political strikes; the latter, changes of government and coups. Only countries with thirty or more new investments recorded in the Harvard data in

the period 1948—67 were included except that Pakistan (twenty-nine) and Nigeria (twenty-three) were added to broaden the European-source sample. The other countries covered were Mexico, Colombia, Venezuela, Brazil, Argentina, France, Spain, Italy, South Africa, India, and the Philippines.

Data were analyzed to determine the relation of changes in the trend of investments to political events. It was found that the level of either or both government events and mass political events was higher the year of or before negative trend changes. For positive trend changes the results were more complicated. The reaction seemed to be asymmetrical. A high level of mass political violence made the companies decrease their investment relatively fast but a low level of political disturbances was not enough for them to increase their investment. Instead there often had to be an impulse in the form of government transfer. Whether such a transfer would cause a change in government policy was not known, but it could be guessed that it had to be perceived by the companies as resulting in revisions in the general economic policy in the country. Government events and especially transfers that seemed to be of vital importance both for positive and negative changes were, however, often preceded or accompanied by mass political disturbances. The years before positive trend changes were often violent.

Some differences were found among regions. The main difference between the European countries and the others seemed to be that in Europe the negative changes occurred together with mass political instability only, while in the other countries government events seemed to be relatively more important. Thunell concluded this meant that mass political instability as a phenomenon of its own was of more importance in Europe than elsewhere. This difference was probably because under normal conditions political variables were of little importance in Europe, but when the disturbance level increased above a certain threshold, it was perceived as a threat. In Latin America, on the other hand, political violence was a normal part of political life; managers were used to living with it and did not care much when it went up or down.

Tests made of hypotheses that reponses would vary according to whether companies were in industries which were capital intensive or labor intensive were not productive. However, positive results were obtained from the hypothesis that the higher the degree of oligopoly in the industry to which the company belonged, the weaker the relationship between political stability and foreign investment. This was true for the European countries, while in Latin America the opposite seemed to be true. Thunell speculated that this was caused by differences in market penetration by the international oligopolies. The alternative hypothesis valid for Latin America was: The higher the degree of oligopoly in an industry, the stronger the relationship between political stability and foreign investments, since the oligopolistic behavior would reinforce the normal reaction to changes in political stability.

20. Approaches to predicting political risk and the problems encountered were brought out in a book by Haendel, West, and Meadow.[19] They identified central problems of insuring investments in the lack of information and the difficulty of establishing an actuarial-based calculation of experience. Given these problems, political risk could not, in the ordinary sense, be considered insurable. A key distinction emphasized by the authors was that between the probability of occurrence of an undesired political event and the uncertainty generated by inadequate information concerning the occurrence of such an event. At least potentially, risk is measurable, insurable, and avoidable; uncertainty is not. Information, however, is useful on both counts, helping to calculate the risk and serving to reduce uncertainty. The investor therefore must always be in search of the most complete information available.

The authors describe two systems for the measurement of political risk: Business Environmental Risk Index (BERI) developed by Haner and the Business International Index of Environmental Risk. The BERI index is composed of fifteen variables grouped in three subindices: political, operations, and financial. The political component employs six variables: bureaucratic delays, balance of payments, monetary inflation, nationalization, attitudes toward the foreign investor and profits, and political stability. The authors see two main drawbacks to these systems: first, that they are strongly oriented toward short-term projections of less than a year and, second, that they are subjective, both employing the Delphi method of polling a panel of experts.

This analysis led to their own proposal of a Political System Stability Index (PSSI). Underlying PSSI is the assumption that the stability of the political system at any moment is directly related to its adaptability to the constant barrage of conflicting internal and external demands. The authors' objective was to employ hard data to measure indirect indicators of some of these characteristics of a political system's stability/adaptability. They chose fifteen data series which were grouped into three subindices: (1) Socioeconomic—ethnolinguistic fractionalization, GNP growth per capita and energy consumption per capita; (2) Societal Conflict further subdivided under three headings: (a) Political Unrest—riots, demonstrations and government crises, (b) Internal Violence—armed attacks, assassinations, coups d'etat and guerilla warfare, and (c) Coercion Potential—internal security forces per capita; and (3) Governmental Processes—political competition, legislative effectiveness, constitutional changes per year and irregular chief executive changes.

To test the data, the authors computed indices for sixty-five countries for the period 1961–65. They noted adverse scores for countries like Zaire and Dominican Republic which were clearly high political risks at the time. Their results did not, however, give any evidence as to whether the PSSI overcame the shortcomings noted for the other approaches of mainly identifying short-term risks.

## STRATEGY GUIDELINES

From the analysis and studies of MNC experience, we may isolate three main goals for MNC logistic strategy:

1. Efficiency in the transmission of resources, maximizing their flow in the natural direction determined by economic differentials and government actions.
2. Utilization of the potentials of unification in production facilities and other respects to make the maximum use of the special advantages of the MNC as a global organization.
3. Effectiveness in implementing resource transmission, especially with respect to skills for which communications are a critical factor.

While these goals must be applied in all aspects of logistic planning, three broad areas require particular attention. They will be discussed here in general terms and with reference to specific illustrations in the ISAGRIDs for HTI, GF and Singer (Table 7–1).

### Shifts in Economic Relationships

The basic function of the logistic system is to accomplish the transmission of resources. To that end it is inevitably geared into the pattern of economic differentials as modified by government-induced distortions. The efficiency of the gearing is a key to the success of the system. The general approach to efficiency was spelled out in the first part of this chapter. Adding inputs from the reports of MNC experience we can develop useful practical guidelines for strategy formulation. The emphasis in this process should be put on the element of change.

Stepping back to look at the broad perspective of world economic relationships and the nature of logistic systems, one can readily see why the element of change is so important. Over the past thirty years there have been tremendous shifts in the world economy affecting resource flows. Just to mention a few: the dynamic domestic and trade growth of Japan, the thrust to industrialization in LDCs emphasizing import substitution, the strength of a few LDCs like Brazil and Mexico, the formation of the European Economic Community and the emergence of OPEC, resulting in major changes in the world trade status of oil nations. On the other hand, at any one time the logistic systems of MNCs have a high degree of rigidity because of the nature of factories and organizations. The latter are technically more flexible than the former but considering the time required to train people and to develop effective working relations in global organizations, there is considerable cost in restructuring them. Thus there is an inherent inertia in a logistic system that substantially impedes it in adjusting to shifts in the economic relationships to which it should be geared efficiently.

The practical impact of this problem has been evident in many ways in MNC experience. Singer along with many other firms found its logistic system badly out of gear when the Japanese came into the export market with cheap products based on a combination of mass production and low-cost labor.[20] As indicated in the ISAGRID, Table 7—1, sewing machines being labor intensive are an effective vehicle for transmission of labor resources. Singer's global production system based on European and U.S. factories was not positioned to fit that pattern. A massive restructuring, in which export capacity was developed in Japan, Brazil, and Taiwan, eventually brought the system into a reasonably efficient relationship to the prevailing economic differentials but only after the company had lost a large portion of its share of the world market. Valtz's case history of the problems of UMCC in rationalizing its European production system to mesh with EEC is a lesser but still relevant facet of the inertia problem.

Because of the uncertainties of change and the rigidity of the logistic system, there can be no simple solution for this problem. However, the problem is manageable and dealing with it must be considered a regular part of logistic strategy formulation. The basic guideline involved is to determine the direction and prospects of change in economic differentials and related government policies and plan changes in the logistic structure to fit the expectations.

The forecasting requires work and attention but it is not as difficult as some types of forecasting because major shifts in economic relationships and patterns of government action usually evolve gradually. Typical examples are the evolution of EEC, the emergence of export manufacturing capabilities of low-cost-labor LDCs, and the

**Table 7-1.  ISAGRID for Logistic Strategy**

| Company | Resources | Strategy Context Variables | | | | National Interests | |
|---|---|---|---|---|---|---|---|
| | | Economic Differentials | MNC Capabilities | Cultural Change | Global Unification | Home | Host |
| High Technology Industries (HTI) | Natural resources | | | | | | |
| | Labor | | | | | | |
| | Capital: Finance | M | | | | | |
| | Production | | | Hc | Hc | | H |
| | Marketing | H | | Hc | Mc | | |
| | Skills: Technological | H | | | | | |
| | Managerial | Hc | | | H | M | H |
| | Entrepreneurial | | | | | | |
| Singer | Natural resources | | | | | | |
| | Labor | H | | | H | | H |
| | Capital: Finance | M | | | | | |
| | Production | M | | | Hc | | |
| | Marketing | M | | | Hc | | |

| | | | |
|---|---|---|---|
| **Singer** (*cont.*) | | | |
| Skills: | Technological | M | |
| | Managerial | H | M |
| | Entrepreneurial | M | |
| Natural resources | | | |
| Labor | | | |
| **General Foods** | Capital: Finance | | |
| | Production | | |
| | Marketing | M | |
| Skills: | Technological | M | H |
| | Managerial | H | M |
| | Entrepreneurial | H | Hc |

Importance in strategy: H = High; M = Moderate; c = Control of parent MNC significant.

shift from emphasis on import substitution to export promotion in them. The wave of Japanese exports that almost sank Singer in the 1950s had its roots in development of the Japanese industry that started several years earlier and could have been anticipated if the management had been alert.

The uncertainties involved must be recognized. For example, in the early 1970s Singer was apparently confronted with the need to unify production in the Andean Common Market because ANCOM announced a rationalization plan. To fit the plan Singer would have had to concentrate production which was then divided among three countries, and also pledge to sell 51 percent of its equity to local nationals in 15 years. In fact the company decided a wait-and-see policy was wise and, as Chile had dropped out of ANCOM and the whole thrust toward regional economic unity had lost much of its drive by the late 1970s, that decision seemed to have been sound.

Although each situation in this predictive planning process will have its unique characteristics, two general directions of guidance are in order. The first is that the company identify clearly its key resource transmission capabilities and the overall pattern of global evolution of economic and government conditions affecting those capabilities. From this process it may develop a long-term strategy concept. We have already noted that for Singer labor is a critical resource. In light of the past evolution it is relatively certain that there will be a steady progression toward more export manufacturing capability, at least for the less sophisticated machines, in countries at lower levels of development, while countries higher on the development scale lose export strength because of rising wages. Thus for Singer a long-term process of shift in production sites is predictable though the specific countries and timing involve much uncertainty and careful analysis. For HTI the critical element will be the technology capabilities of countries combined with labor costs, for example, in determining how quickly the more advanced LDCs can undertake manufacture of moderately sophisticated equipment. For General Foods, the key resource transmissions are in the combination of convenience food technology and marketing skills. GF therefore has to gauge the pace at which host country societies are evolving and the degree of cultural change to which they are susceptible.

The second direction concerns the unification aspect of the logistic system. Because of the special strength of the MNC in its capacity for integration of global production and marketing, strategy formulation in this area must have a predisposition always toward unification efforts. Servan-Schreiber in *The American Challenge* observed wryly that it was the U.S. MNCs which benefited most from the creation of the EEC because they had the structure and mentality to rationalize operations in Europe while the European firms were heavily oriented to their own nations.[21] The objective in logistic planning should be to apply this capability to the greatest extent feasible.

An example of a sound effort in this direction is the work of General Motors in Southeast Asia. GM has taken initiative in encouraging planners interested in the embryo ASEAN common market concept to adopt a program of rationalized local production of automotive parts integrated with its development of the Basic Transportation Vehicle for the area. We have already noted that Singer was confronted with such a situation in ANCOM. It appears that they were judicious in not pushing for rationalization there but under somewhat different circumstances it might have been wise because of their special capabilities and the prospects that it would have greatly entrenched their competitive status in the region as no other firm had that capability. HTI could expect to face similar opportunities in the more advanced LDCs in the near future. IBM, for example, has made a start in that direction in the Latin American Foreign Trade Area. It is a fairly simple matter involving rationalization of production of low sophistication products between Argentina and Chile. But the direction of movement is consistent with the utilization of the unification strength of the firm and a steady progression of the same nature is to be expected and desired. For General Foods, the degree of unification possible is greatly constrained by the cultural individuality of food tastes and the adverse economics of shipping foods. However, the company has demonstrated that many products like Kool-aid can be sold in several countries, so it also has a thrust in this direction with the planning orientation geared to market study.

## Political Risk and the Defensive Posture

A striking feature of the findings of many of the studies cited in this chapter is the extent to which logistic systems are based on defensive reactions to governmental and/or competitive actions. Barlow and Wender, Vernon and others emphasize that the shift from export to foreign production has often been motivated by government or competitive pressures which threatened the MNCs' tenure in the market unless local sources were developed. Knickerbocker's study is essentially focused on the psychology of oligopolistic managements which feel the necessity to imitate investments by others lest they lose industry market status; and Moxon found that MNCs did not generally initiate offshore procurement until forced to do so by competitors.

In many cases, the primacy of the defensive motivation is fully justified, for example, much of the manufacturing in LDCs is higher cost and less profitable than exports, at least at the start. However, other situations including a large part of the offshore procurement offer lower costs and could have been justified by higher profit potential before the firms were forced into them by competition. So the large influence of defensive motivation in logistic moves is notable, especially considering the aggressive, risk-taking character of the general run of big firms in such fields as product development and marketing.

The explanation for the prominence of defensive thinking lies substantially with the combination of the conservative thinking of corporate management about finances and property and the extent of political risk in international business. Thunell's study documents the readily observed sensitivity of MNCs to political events abroad. Managements are clearly guided in their investment decisions by positive and negative indications as to the conditions in host countries, and properly so in light of the history, not just of expropriations but also of lesser forms of adverse treatment by unsympathetic governments and the deterioration of local economies under many government conditions.

Caution in logistic strategy is therefore fully justified. The problem for planners is not to eliminate risk but rather to put it in perspective and to deal with it as rationally as possible. Specifically two things are needed which have apparently been deficient in many MNC managements: risk analysis and a concept of balance in handling risks.

For systematic study of political risk, the work of Haendel et al. indicates there is limited prospect at this point of scientific predictive methods or other refined analytical approaches such as may, for example, be possible in dealing with foreign exchange risk. However, it is possible to go considerably beyond the crude use of press reports and advice from local management commonly used by many MNCs in determining the course of political events and their implications for logistic decisions. A few major MNCs have already established political analysis units in which specialists engage in thorough study of these aspects of investment plans. Others may effectively use external advice such as the indices described by Haendel et al. And there are other approaches to applying expert analysis to the problems. The key point is the need to make systematic analysis of the political risks so that they are objectively assessed.

The second need is the determination of an effective balance between caution and an aggressive approach toward profit maximization in logistic decisions. It appears that the disposition of managements has been too much toward the defensive, cautious stance. The hesitant movement into strategies for transmission of low-cost labor is a useful example. Even a company like Singer which has made a substantial adaptation of logistic structure to meet competition in this regard has not gone as far as the profit computations would encourage. For example, in the late 1970s it continued to supply export markets from Italy with its simplest machines that could be made cheaper in Brazil and Taiwan.[22] It must be noted, however, that to return to the inertial forces affecting logistics, the company would face a major problem in trying to reduce output in Italy because of the strong labor and government resistance.

## Control and the Host Nation Pressures

The final point brings us back to the recurring issue of control and the conflicting goals of the MNC and host nations. The pressure on MNCs to take minority positions in joint ventures or to license local firms poses significant obstacles to achieving the full potentials of logistic systems. A unified logistic strategy is very difficult to manage with partially owned units, especially key export plants. The problems of equitable transfer pricing and allocation of export orders are sources of contention and time-consuming negotiation.

The basis for the host nation desires must be recognized. In addition to their general goals in seeking control which were discussed earlier, they have interests in the specific aspects of logistic systems. They presume that if local stockholders have a majority interest in an exporting plant, they will be in a stronger position to maintain the export volume if the MNC has inclinations to shift sourcing to some other plant and that transfer pricing will favor them more if local partners are involved. Both of these assumptions are subject to question because if the MNC anticipates problems in transfer pricing and sourcing, it may be deterred from placing export orders with the joint venture in the first place. So we may here be dealing with misperceptions of interest by host nationals. But their views are nonetheless a reality.

The question for guiding logistic strategy is therefore how the MNC should view the issue of control. While as always each case must be dealt with on its merits, the cumulative assessment to this point would suggest that pressing for control should have a high priority when skill transmission or logistic unification will be key determinants of overall success.

## NOTES

1. E.R. Barlow and Ira T. Wender, *Foreign Investment and Taxation* (Englwood Cliffs, N.J.: Prentice-Hall, 1955).

2. Ibid., p. 431.

3. Judd Polk et al., *U.S. Production Abroad and the Balance of Payments* (New York: National Industrial Conference Board, 1966), pp. 59–61.

4. Lawrence G. Franko, *The European Multinationals* (Stamford, Conn.: Greylock Publishers, 1976).

5. Lawrence G. Franko, *European Business Strategies in the United States* (Geneva: Business International, 1971).

6. M.Y. Yoshino, *Japan's Multinational Enterprises* (Cambridge, Mass.: Harvard University Press, 1971).

7. Louis T. Wells, Jr., "The Internationalization of Firms from Developing Countries," in Tamir Agmon and Charles P. Kindleberger, eds, *Multinationals from Small Countries* (Cambridge, Mass.: M.I.T. Press, 1977), pp. 133–156.

8. Richard W. Moxon, *Offshore Production in the Less Developed Countries* (New York: Graduate School of Business Administration, New York University, 1974).

9. Harold Crookell "Investing in Development—A Corporate View," *Columbia Journal of World Business*, Spring 1975, pp. 80–88.

10. Frederick T. Knickerbocker, *Oligopolistic Reaction and Multinational Enterprise* (Boston, Mass.: Harvard University, Graduate School of Business Administration, 1973).

11. John M. Stopford and Louis T. Wells, Jr., *Managing the Multinational Enterprise* (New York: Basic Books, 1972), pp. 58–62.

12. Lawrence G. Franko, "Joint Venture Divorce in the Multinational Company," *Columbia Journal of World Business*, May–June, 1971, pp. 13–22.

13. Robert C.V. Valtz, "The Case of the Multiplant Manufacturer," *Harvard Business Review*, March–April, 1964, pp. 12–30.

14. Jack N. Behrman, *The Role of International Companies in Latin American Integration* (Lexington, Mass.: D.C. Heath, 1972).

15. Robert Rowthorn, *International Big Business, 1957–67* (London: Cambridge University Press, 1971).

16. *The Effects of U.S. Corporate Foreign Investment, 1960–1970* (New York, Business International, 1972).

17. Franklin R. Root, "U.S. Business Abroad and Political Topics," *MSU Business Topics*, Winter 1968, pp. 73–79.

18. Lars S. Thunell, *Political Risks in International Business* (New York: Praeger, 1977).

19. Don Haendel, Gerald T. West, and Robert Meadow, *Overseas Investment and Political Risk* (Philadelphia: Foreign Policy Research Institute, 1975).

20. John Fayerweather and Ashok Kapoor, *Strategy and Negotiation for the International Corporation* (Cambridge, Mass.: Ballinger Publishing Company, 1976), pp. 310–311.

21. J.J. Servan-Schrieber, *The American Challenge* (New York: Atheneum, 1968), pp. 4–9.

22. Fayerweather and Kapoor, op cit., pp. 314–315.

*Chapter 8*

# Operating Methods of Foreign Affiliates—Production, Marketing, and Industrial Relations

In the MNC strategy the operating methods of foreign affiliates are the front line of interaction with host societies, with emphasis on skill resource transmission. It is in the range of operational activities of the affiliates that the application of technological, managerial and entrepreneurial skills becomes a reality.

The way in which these skills are applied is the essence of the interaction with the culture of the host society. Each bit of skill is put forward in some piece of the operations touching an element of the social system—workers, customers, the public. If it is accepted, the resource transmission has been accomplished. If not, there is no transmission. Thus, in considering the strategy for operating methods of affiliates, the main focus will be on skill transmission and the questions of innovation, conformity and adaptation central to interaction with host societies. Other aspects of resource transmission are significant to affiliate management but they will not be included in the analysis especially as the chief further item capital is examined in the next chapter. In addition to the host society interaction, other factors affecting strategy will be covered, notably unification–fragmentation factors as they affect the handling of skills in the operations of the foreign affiliates.

The analysis here will be limited to the three functions which, in addition to finance, compose the main body of operational activities: production, marketing, and industrial relations. The basic lines of analysis for them can be applied to other activities like purchasing and accounting and it would not be productive to devote space to each of them as well. The discussion here will also not focus explicitly on the skills embodied in products as that subject was part of the analysis in Chapter 6. However, product skills are so intimately associated with the production and marketing processes that they will inevitably appear in the present analysis.

To focus the discussion most effectively the production section will be confined to technology while the sections on marketing and industrial relations will deal only with managerial skills. This will avoid the redundancy in analysis which would otherwise appear because the basic considerations in transmission of production management skills are quite similar to those pertaining to marketing management. There is less similarity in the analysis of marketing and production technologies but the former are not critical strategically so little is lost in the basic purposes of this book by leaving them out.

## PRODUCTION TECHNOLOGY

A factory is much like a human organism. There must be a housing serving as the skeleton and skin to contain it. Energy and materials must be fed into it. But how much it accomplishes is largely dependent on the skills which like the brain and nervous system govern its functioning. Technological and managerial skills are the essence of the complex production processes of modern industry. Both types of skills are essential. Technological skills have received great public attention in international business because they have a certain visibility in physical form and in the materialistic achievement of industrial progress. Particularly among the less developed countries it is the technology held by the MNCs which is in great demand.

### Strategy Issues

Production technology composes the physical processes by which materials, labor, and capital are combined into a marketable product. That definition provides the two essential elements for analyzing the strategy of production technology. The inputs of resources identify the issue of balance among them. The production of a marketable product requires that the technology must result in both quality and cost levels which are acceptable to buyers. In turn these two elements indicate that production technology is by its nature a culture-oriented process. The character and availability of the inputs and the criteria for satisfactory outputs are affected by the society in which it takes place.

In line with the general discussion of interaction with host societies in Chapter 3, two main strategic issues follow from this characterization. First, there is the determination of what technology will be employed, and second, the means by which it will be transmitted.

The selection of technology in the context of host society interaction poses options of conformity to host nation practice, introduction of different methods by the MNC or adaptation of those methods. Because of the multiplicity of activities incorporated into a typical factory, all three options may well be exercised. For example, the handling of raw materials may be accomplished by traditional methods, production machinery of advanced MNC design may be used, or assembly lines may be adapted to fit some local characteristics while still achieving some innovative gains. Thus, while we will simplify the analysis here by speaking of distinct choices, in fact, in a given case, the outcome may be quite mixed in character.

Although the full range of host society characteristics bear on the choice of technology, primary emphasis is given to the economic elements because of the physical character of technology and its central role in determining the economic results of production. The other elements include worker skills, labor relations, and supervision capabilities. Technologies must be chosen that are within the abilities of the working organization and that minimize problems arising from the character of local labor and management. But within limits these elements may be regarded as subject to change to fit whatever technology is chosen. Workers may be taught skills, labor relations are subject to negotiation, and supervisors may be trained. The economic factors affecting technology, however, have a more fixed character. For the most part wage levels, capital costs, and other economic variables are givens to which the MNC must relate, subject only to modest influence by its decisions.

Thus the central issue in technology selection generally revolves around economic analysis. The options involve degrees of labor intensity and sophistication. In less developed countries two factors argue in favor of restraint in technological innovation: labor costs and scale of output. Where wages are relatively lower compared to capital costs, a strong case can be made for labor-intensive production methods. Likewise, where markets are smaller than in the parent country, the lower level of production argues for less sophisticated technology. It is presumed that there will in any case be a significant innovative thrust in the total production process, but the extent of innovation may be considerably limited by elements of conformity or adaptation which fit better with the calculus of costs and scale of the environment.

In addition to this central influence of interaction with the host society economic system, two other issues of the MNC strategy context are relevant to technology selection: the wishes of the host government and considerations of unification. The wishes of the host government are related to the economic analysis, though they are influenced by such considerations as increasing employment and improving balance of payments. The implications for MNC unification strategies lie both in skill transmission and product output. If the technologies employed in various affiliates differ significantly, the capacities for use of the central technical organization and of the interchange among affiliates is weakened. Also there are likely to be greater problems in the interchange of products among plants, reducing still further the possibility of unifying the logistics.

The second general strategic area, the methods by which technology is transmitted, involves to a large degree organizational and administrative questions that will be discussed in Part III. Here we will place particular emphasis on control. In the introduction to Part II the theoretical merits of *efficiency* in strategy formulation were noted. This approach has received great emphasis with respect to technology among many analysts. The general reasoning is that technology is the one resource that host nations strongly desire to obtain from MNCs so it is sound to transmit it separately by licensing agreements rather than by packaging it with capital and management. The latter way is seen as supported by weaker economic differentials and it arouses more adverse host nation reaction.

Two MNC considerations, however, oppose this approach, bearing on the greater *effectiveness* of transmission. First, there is the importance attached to ingegrated organizational control over the transmission process. Both the governments and businessmen of countries importing skills often tend to underestimate the complexity of skills and the problems of effectively acquiring them. This is a key factor in their advocacy of arrangements like joint ventures and licensing in which the role of the multinational corporation is limited to making information available with a modest instructional and advisory service. The skill-supplying firm, on the other hand, typically feels that the skills can be transferred more effectively if it has a close and intimate control over the operations in which they are employed, and furthermore, that there are certain aspects of skills which are so intimately tied to the corporation that they cannot be transferred separately.

In this respect the management contract has considerable merit because it does permit full integration of the multinational corporation with the skill transmission process even though there may be no financial commitment. However, it has short-comings which relate to the continuity of market position that is fundamental to the objectives of the corporation. This is the really vital distinction between the management contract and the controlled subsidiary, the former having a definite time limit after which the company is quite likely to lose its participation in the market. Although not so clear-cut, the same possibility is ever present in both licensing and minority positions in joint ventures. In both cases a firm may find that those controlling the enterprise in the host country will exclude them from the business at some time in the future.

## MNC Experience

1. The first extensive research on MNC factory operations was undertaken by Skinner in the early 1960s.[1] He started with an intensive study of plants in Turkey and then extended his work to cover thirty operations in seven less developed countries. Skinner found that in practice the choice of processes and equipment was seldom made for a particular set of circumstances in an overseas location. Instead the technology was more often exported unchanged from the domestic operation. This approach was not without its advantages. It required less engineering time, and it carried less risk, since it exported tested technological methods. But its disadvantages were that it was a crude fitting of technology to circumstances. It was safe but often expensive. The price was paid chiefly in cost and low productivity of the production system as a whole, including costs not only of direct labor and equipment but of inventories, overheads, and customer service. When operating margins were ample and competition was minor, it might be a good strategy. But as competition grew and margins narrowed, technological strategy needed to be more precisely tailored to maximize the fit of the production system to the critical environmental factors.

Despite the general practice of exporting parent technologies, Skinner cited several examples of modifications which demonstrated the feasibility of lower-capital, labor-intensive approaches. For example, a tractor firm modified an assembly line for Mexico cutting the cost from $175,000 to $29,000 by such means as substituting a tent and hand sprayer for its normal paint and drying rooms with elaborate equipment. Skinner noted that the unstudied application of parent production methods abroad was fundamentally incongruent with the high development of technological design in parent operations in which alternatives were carefully examined on the basis of such factors as scale of operations, labor and capital costs, and skill availability. Since these factors differ significantly abroad the technology should presumably be thoroughly reassessed.

The analysis examined the various factors which contributed to the prevailing pattern. Diverse influences from host government economists were observed. On the one hand, there were those who argued for labor-intensive, low-sophistication technologies to increase employment, decrease capital, widen distribution of purchasing power, lower skill requirements, and reduce setup and breakdown time. On the other hand, there were those who recommended capital-intensive policies for developing economies because they result in high efficiency and therefore larger production, higher national income, increased savings and investment, and hence a greater surplus for capital formation. India's decision to use the most modern technology in its steel mills was cited as an example.

Skinner observed that economists who conceptualized the choices as labor-intensive versus capital-intensive tended to overlook some less quantifiable factors, which could be very important. There was a wide gap between the theory of tailoring a production process to the environment and the actual, detailed plant design. Someone must tailor the process, and it was a problem to get the right people in the right place. Equally important was the fact that for some products and processes alternative choices were not readily available. For any new process the start-up and "debugging" problems were usually considerable, especially abroad. Special equipment might cause problems which were not readily solved by recourse to past experience. And judging from problems experienced abroad, maintenance of specially designed processes would often be a nightmare.

The MNC decision-making system and related decision criteria were found to play a major role. The research discovered that the primary reason for not innovating abroad appeared to be that these decisions were usually made by technical people employed to use their knowledge and experience to recommend processes that would consistently produce proper quality and volume. Companies were often under time pressures to meet tight schedules. They lacked the time and motivation to develop new processes tailored to the specific economics and practical realities in each different industrial location. Companies tended to explain their equipment decisions primarily on the basis of technological considerations, the need for achieving quality and keeping maintenance to a minimum, with relatively little consideration of the economics of a wide variety of alternatives and the industrial engineering aspects of different manufacturing approaches.

2. More recently Wells did research in Southeast Asia, primarily in basic consumer product plants—bottling, drugs, and cigarettes, for example.[21] His basic thesis was that multinational firms would often be better off to use "intermediate technology" for plants in less developed countries rather than the most advanced equipment. He accepted the proposition that automated plants were generally simpler

to manage with less quality-control difficulties, greater ease of adjusting volume when demand shifted, and more technical familiarity for the plant manager. However, intermediate technology with higher labor use was often cheaper and strongly desired by governments with large unemployment. Forfeiting the advantages of automation might in fact be offset by good relations from efforts to increase employment.

Wells observed that quality control was a critical factor and argued for a degree of automation in key functions. For example, hand soldering of zinc cans for dry cells may result in too many cracks and leaks. The intermediate technology approach assumes that such a job would be automated but that less critical tasks would be done by hand.

Several advantages of using less complex machines were noted. The author found that the only companies complaining about the quality of local labor were those that had introduced highly automated equipment; proper operation and maintenance were turning out to be serious problems. Absenteeism was more troublesome in automated plants because one missing worker on a critical machine could tie up a major operation. Most significant were the major economies often possible. The author cited investments of from $3,000 up to $20,000 per worker which were quite questionable in terms of economic return in low-wage countries.

An admitted problem with intermediate technology was the lack of established competence. For many companies it might actually mean developing new ways of manufacturing. The development of new technology was always risky; there were unforeseen expenses and what looked like a good design on paper might be a white elephant in metal. Only companies with many plants could afford the extra effort. The experience of Philips Lamp in developing special plant designs was noted in this respect.

Wells reported that overautomation was often encouraged by company practices which did not counteract the natural bias of multinational firm engineers toward greater automation. Companies should require that the economics of each proposed plant be compared with a less automated alternative. Engineers should be expected to look at local technologies in making designs. Surveys should be made of machinery which might be procured in developing countries like India, Mexico, and Brazil more attuned to low wage economies.

3. Morley and Smith made a detailed analysis of the question of adaptation of technology by multinational firms.[3] The authors employed four approaches: theory, aggregate investment data, case studies, and a questionnaire survey. All approaches led to the same

basic conclusion, that MNCs used different production techniques abroad but primarily because of differences in the scale of operations, not because of differences in factor costs, i.e., lower cost of labor and higher cost of capital.

The theoretical analysis was based on the interrelation of cost curves for production techniques with varying labor and capital content. Changes in labor and capital costs alter the curves, essentially rotating them so their slopes are different. This results in some change in the location of the intersection point at which one technique becomes less costly than another. However, the span of possible changes due to factor costs, called the price-sensitive range, is relatively narrow compared to the dominant influence of volume in determining the lowest cost technique.

The authors also noted a number of other factors which minimize the influence of low labor costs. In process industries, labor is generally a minor factor. Another form of economy of scale in capital involves the obvious but ignored fact that high-capacity machines generally save space. This element is also significant in expansion decisions. To produce an amount greater than the capacity of one manual machine, it is necessary to buy more manual machines and the space to put them in, and that is never profitable so long as the cost of the automatic machine rises at rates less than proportional with its increases in capacity.

The empirical research was concentrated on Brazil. Fixed capital per employee was determined for U.S. manufacturing industries and U.S. MNCs in Brazil. The ratios in fields like machinery and electrical products were two to three times greater in the United States indicating that firms did employ more labor-intensive production techniques in Brazil. The authors also found inventories of metal-cutting and metal-forming machinery employed by firms in the state of Sao Paulo and U.S. firms in roughly comparable years. The machines were classified as automatic and non-automatic. The firms were grouped in six industry categories (motor vehicles, household appliances, etc.). The data showed that Brazilian industry used two to three times as much non-automatic machinery as did its U.S. counterpart.

To obtain a concrete picture of the differences in production methods, the authors visited Brazilian and U.S. plants of eight firms in metal-working industries, the field in which price-sensitive factor substitution seemed most feasible. They made specific comparisons of the manner of performing seven types of functions. Some, notably assembly, were observed to be labor-intensive even in the United States, so little difference between the countries was found. For machining operations the picture was quite mixed. In some cases, especially machines in consumer durable factories with relatively high volume, the cost of the more highly mechanized or specialized models did not appear to make them uneconomic even at Brazilian output levels. Use of automatic controls (e.g., tapes or computer programs) in machining did vary, however. At U.S. establishments, all the capital goods producers visited were using such machines; in Brazil, none were. Painting and materials handling were noted as areas in which lower cost labor was a significant factor favoring labor-intensive methods. In the major portion of the processes, however, it appeared that the scale of output had determined the technique employed.

The questionnaire survey covered thirty-five MNCs of different nationalities in non-process industries, asking several questions relating to choice of technology. With remarkable regularity, scale emerged as the overwhelming determinant of machine choice and labor use. Multinationals used more, sometimes three or four times more, labor per unit of output in Brazil than in their home country, but they said this was primarily a result of their smaller scale operations in Brazil. In ranking factors by importance in choice of production methods, quality of product and size of market were clearly dominant. Labor costs were a distant third. In designing plants, firms tended to investigate methods employed in countries with similar output levels, not those with similar wages, thus indicating their minor attention to the latter. Asked how production might be planned if Brazilian output rose to the level in the home country, most firms said home plant techniques would be employed with certain very limited areas where differences would still persist because of cheaper labor.

From these findings the authors concluded that capital intensity of multinationals in Brazil was not a result of government policy incentives such as the importation of capital at subsidized exchange rates. Expansions underway would lead most firms to alter their production methods in the direction of even greater capital intensity. To increase employment, one must start one step back, in the choice of products. Here large improvements in labor absorption should be achievable by government inducements to produce labor-intensive products, rather than to produce any particular product in a labor-intensive manner.

Along this line, the authors noted that several of the firms interviewed in Brazil were planning to transfer many of their low volume products from the United States to Brazil. It appeared that further progress in this area could be achieved by removing artificial inducements to the importation of labor-intensive products like machinery. Or it could be furthered by not giving special incentives for establishment of mass production products, and by continuing the export incentive program, since the program tended to favor those labor-intensive products in which Brazil had a natural comparative advantage.

4. Teece, in his study of the resource costs of transferring technological know-how by MNCs,[4] confirmed the problems of instituting new processes that had been cited by Skinner. Teece analyzed the costs of twenty-six recent technology transfer projects by U.S. firms: fifteen to wholly owned subsidiaries, four to joint-venture partners, four to independent firms, and three to government enterprises. Some seventeen of the projects were in chemicals and petroleum refining and nine in machinery industries. The sample was also widely dispersed geographically.

The study did not include either royalty costs or the costs embodied in physical form such as tooling and equipment. The focus was on "unembodied" knowledge including the costs of transmitting and absorbing the information that must be acquired if the physical equipment is to be effectively used. This definition encompasses pre-engineering technology exchanges, engineering costs of project design, cost of R&D personnel engaged in the transfer, and pre-start-up expenses, and excess costs representing learning effort.

In the sample the transfer costs averaged 19 percent of total project costs with the range from 2 percent to 59 percent. Teece tested hypotheses concerning two groups of variables: characteristics of the technology/transferor and those of the transferee/host country. A critical factor in the transfer of technology was assumed to be the extent to which the transferor himself understood it. Teece hypothesized that the most difficult and thus costly technology to transfer would be characterized by very few previous applications, a short elapsed time since development, and limited diffusion.

The transferee/host country characteristics were essentially concerned with technical and managerial competence. Years of manufacturing experience was taken as one indicator. Size was another assuming that larger firms usually had a wider variety of technical and managerial talent. A third variable was R&D activity on the assumption that in-house R&D capability would facilitate transfer when technical problems were unexpectedly encountered. The final variable considered was the level of development of host country infrastructure for which GNP per capita was used as an indicator.

The data were divided into the two major industry categories in the analysis. For both groups the results strongly supported the hypotheses that transfer costs declined as the number of firms with identical or similar and competitive technology increased and as the experience of the transferee increased. For chemicals and petroleum refining, number of previous applications and for machinery, age of technology were also significantly correlated. However, the size and R&D activity of the transferee and the GNP per capita factors did not show significant correlations with cost.

In a second phase of the research the respondents were asked to estimate how the total transfer costs would vary for each project if one particular variable happened to take a different value, while all others remained constant. Analysis of data from this phase showed all of the coefficients were significantly greater than zero at the 0.20 level and the age of the technology, the number of manufacturing start-ups, transferee size, and experience achieved at least the 0.05 significance level in one or the other of the subsamples. Diffusion and manufacturing experience were especially important in the machinery category. The information also indicated that in chemicals and petroleum refining the second start-up could lower transfer costs by 34 percent over the first start-up, with a 19 percent further cut for the third start-up.

The respondents were also asked to estimate the differences between transfers domestically and internationally. The results varied greatly including five cases in which the international transfer was estimated to be less costly. An effort was made to relate the differences to variables but the sample was too small for good analysis. It was hypothesized that costs would be increased by cross-border communication problems, added documentation in dealing with governments, and lower diffusion internationally, while they would be decreased by lower labor costs.

The results did indicate that, in chemicals and petroleum refining, transfers to government enterprises and transfers before first commercialization involved substantial extra costs. But the level of host country development and degree of diffusion of an innovation had no bearing on the international–domestic transfer cost differential. Teece observed that the lack of correlation with level of economic development was consistent with speculation that international transfer was no more difficult than domestic transfer when the underlying technology was highly capital intensive. The perceived reluctance of multinational firms to adapt technology to suit the capital-labor endowments of less developed countries could therefore be due to their desire to avoid increasing transfer costs to unacceptable levels.

5. An intensive examination of the effectiveness of transfer of technological skills by MNCs was undertaken by Behrman and Wallender.[5] The heart of their study was a set of seven case studies: Ford in South Africa and Taiwan; ITT in South Africa and Mexico;

Pfizer in Nigeria and Brazil; and Motorola in Korea. The cases described in substantial detail the process by which technology was conveyed from the parent organization to foreign units though the authors observed that the process was one of continuous communication, and only an hourly replay could provide a detailed description. The cases were based on interviews with officials in the parent companies and foreign units and examination of the various forms of written communication employed in technology transfer and other documentation, for example, records of visits of technical personnel.

The authors identified seven phases of the transfer process and five general mechanisms that might be employed.

The transfer phases consist of:

- Initiation of the manufacturing proposal and initial planning
- Product design
- Design and construction of facilities
- Start-up activities involving industrial engineering and training
- Value engineering involving the establishment of controls and testing procedures
- Introduction of new products and product development
- Technical support to suppliers.

The five mechanisms that might be employed in transferring technology are:

- Documentation (manuals, specifications)
- Instruction programs
- Visits and exchanges of technical personnel
- Development and transfer of specialized equipment
- Trouble shooting

The strongest message, which came through repeatedly in the analysis, was the interrelation of the elements of the technology transfer process and the consequent efficiency and effectiveness of the integrated MNC with its varied specialists and established patterns of communication and collaboration. The research dealt only with fully owned subsidiaries. However, the authors made frequent reference to other modes of technology transfer that are less integrated. Overall they observed that a similarity among these cases was that full technology transfers would have been highly unlikely without at least majority ownership, and probably full ownership, simply because of the intricate relationships among affiliates, markets served, and nature of the technology. They concluded that the minority ownership and licensing favored by many host governments might occur at very high cost in terms of technical assistance from the international companies.

One of the major advantages of technical ties was the ability to tap the entire technical knowledge of the parent and the affiliates of an international company. In a non-integrated system this advantage would be undone by segmentation. This general theme was illustrated in the discussion of each of the elements of the process. A complementary conclusion was that the extent of technology transfer was limited in less integrated systems by their structural characteristics. For example, in the initial planning of a project, parent personnel will draw on experience both in the home office and in related facilities around the world. A variety of options was analyzed. A recipient country that purchased a turnkey operation would miss out almost completely on this phase of technical assistance, at least in terms of learning what was being done. Similarly, in straight sales of technology, the recipients had little information regarding how the supplier viewed the initial problems of use of manufacturing technology and why it recommended the techniques or machinery that were transferred. Likewise product design in a multinational enterprise involved use of varied elements of global experience. Few facilities in developing countries were capable of making such adaptations, and unless they were part of an international company, they would not obtain the technology necessary to do it. That is, they would be given an adapted product without even knowing why the adaptations were made or what problems they might lead to.

A further general observation in this same vein was the effect on administration and costing of the integrated multiple elements of the process. In each of the cases, technical transfers were continuous, that is, occurring over a wide range of activities and throughout the life of the association. There was no clear delimitation on what technology could or could not be transferred; rather, all the data and know-how necessary to do the job were transferred, not always without discussion, however. Since there was no precise delineation or even control over the technology transferred, there was no way in these cases to cost-out the assistance provided. Each company had a different method of charging for technology supplied, but none had developed precise cost-price methods that reflected the underlying value of the wide range of techniques, processes, specifications, and know-how provided the affiliates. Cost allocations were necessarily arbitrary; therefore, only 'out-of-pocket' charges were readily allocable. The value to the receiving country was also impossible to calculate without precise data bases. That is, any value set was either arbitrary or merely the result of negotiation among willing parties.

6. Complementing this research on technology transfer in integrated MNC organizations was an investigation of experience in licensing arrangements. Kapoor made an intensive study of the experience of fifty-three Indian companies and twenty-six U.S. and European firms with licensing collaborations.[6] His study covered all of the major aspects of collaborations—negotiations, use of foreign technicians, research and development, product modifications and compensation. Of broader significance was the overall picture of the effectiveness of the general system of collaborations found in India, most of which involved little or no financial participation by the licensor.

Kapoor concluded that although foreign collaborations had done much to help Indian industrial development, they had not contributed as much as they might have. Indian and foreign companies were dissatisfied with some areas of interbusiness relationships. And the government's policies and practices had hindered maximum contributions from foreign rights and services. A sharp distinction between large and medium-to-small firms emerged from the research. The large ones seem to have made effective use of collaborations, negotiating intelligently and having enough internal competence to utilize the technology provided from abroad. The large portion of situations in which an "average" Indian firm worked with a foreign firm with little overseas experience had been unsatisfactory in many respects. The notable shortcoming was the lack of sufficient competence in the Indian firms to effectively absorb and adapt the technology made available to them. They did not give sufficient authority to the foreign technicians and did not modify their businesses to make full use of the technology. While the author found that many firms criticized the technicians, he observed that those companies not technically qualified to evaluate were the ones who were criticizing. Those that were technically qualified to evaluate were satisfied.

Kapoor was quite critical of the Indian government's handling of collaborations. He found that more than half of the foreign companies felt the compensation permitted by the government was inadequate. The companies had gone ahead, typically because of a desire to establish a position in the potentially large Indian market. But this he observed was an unsatisfactory long-term basis for attracting foreign firms. Other shortcomings lay in the difficulties of negotiations and unrealistic insistence on export rights for Indian collaborators. Indications of the lack of interest of foreign firms in India were that over 80 percent of the collaborations were initiated by Indian firms and that some 30 percent of the foreign firms did not even visit the Indian partner during the negotiations. Emphasizing that large for-

eign firms had the most to offer India, the author concluded that the
government should have been aware of the fact that unless the
"atmosphere" of foreign collaborations was improved, the extension
of rights and services to Indian companies by these large companies
would continue to be limited—that is, they would be less than they
would like to extend and less than the country needed.

Interesting confirmation of the effect of control on effectiveness
in transmitting skills was provided in two case studies.

7. The first was a report by Broehl on the experience of the International Basic Economy Corporation (IBEC) established by the
Rockefeller family as a profit-making company, but primarily oriented toward upgrading the basic economies of less developed countries.[7] All its ventures were designed to provide critically needed
technological, managerial, or entrepreneurial inputs whose absence
was often attributable to strong cultural resistance. Thus its operations fit well into the model of the role of the MNC as a transmitter
of resources and innovator. At the same time, its social consciousness
(along with the Rockefeller association) had made it extremely sensitive to national attitudes. If any company would bend to nationalistic sentiment, it was IBEC. It had gone to great ends to serve other
countries' interests and convey a favorable image to the public. It
had no strong "market-position" objectives nor a great need to remit
profits home like the typical MNC. Given these characteristics, the
fact that IBEC held firmly to retention of control is most significant.
It had found that investment in less developed countries when not
accompanied by management control had a very poor record.

8. The second case was an analysis by Baranson of the experience
of the Cummins Engine Company in a joint venture with the Indian
firm Kirloskar for the manufacture of diesel engines.[8] The Cummins
case was a classic example of the trials and tribulations of multinational corporations pushed into overseas manufacture in less
developed countries by governments obsessed with the import-substi-
tution, save-foreign-exchange-at-any-cost philosophy with the added
complications of working with a foreign partner. Baranson's book
describes in detail the problems of inadequate suppliers, lack of technical skills, deficiencies of Indian management, the inefficiencies of
small scale operations, and the difficulties created by government
planning, especially a notable shift in industrial investment targets
which notably cut Cummins' market among end product manufacturers. A striking conclusion of the study was that costs of the Indian
plant were from three to four times those of U.S. plants. Furthermore, as of 1967 and for perhaps a few more years in the future it

was actually requiring more foreign exchange to manufacture in India than it would to import complete diesels. This ironic situation arose from the very slow development of local sources for the many high quality parts required, which had reached only 50 percent by 1966 as compared with the 90 percent by 1965 initially contemplated.

The joint venture aspects of the operation caused substantial trouble. The Indians proved relatively inept at planning, for example. No exhaustive listing of parts to be manufactured had been prepared and ordering equipment was equally haphazard. In addition, the transfer of technical skills was substantially harder than with Cummins's Japanese licensee whose plant was well staffed with experienced technicians. In India the dearth of experienced technicians severely inhibited technical interchange over manufacturing specifications and materials variations.

A general attitude of dissatisfaction on both sides prevailed. The Indians felt that American managers had arrogated Indian authority. They insisted that other Kirloskar plants were well run and that much of the chaos resulted from too many cooks for the broth. American managers tended to attribute failures to inadequate commitments on the part of plant management in such areas as production and quality control. Differences almost resulted in an impasse that would eventually have necessitated one party's selling his equity to the other. In the end, however, Cummins turned over the management completely to the Indians, accepting certain policies to which they did not agree. The key factor seemed to have been that, because of the powers of the Indian government, in any running encounter with the industrial control authorities, the American partner would probably lose out.

### Strategy Guidelines

The early production technology strategies of many MNCs, especially in LDCs as observed by Skinner, were notably loose. A general tendency to simply transfer parent methods with little consideration of the nature of the foreign environment led to lower productivity and higher costs than would have resulted from careful consideration of alternative approaches. The general low standards of local productivity and the high protection from external competition provided by governments anxious to develop local manufacture made it possible for firms to function profitably despite the inefficiency of inadequately planned technology strategy. As firms have gained more experience and, especially with growing competitive pressure from other MNCs, the rising standards of local national firms and increasing sophistication of government officials, this picture has changed notably and a well considered technology strategy has become essential to MNC success.

Despite the unsoundness of a strategy of indiscriminate transmission of parent firm technology, it appears that use of the MNC's established core of technology should be the heart of strategy for most firms. This conclusion is based both on the operating success of the great majority of MNCs following that course and the strong desires of host governments and businessmen to acquire MNC production technology. It is in the transmission of technology which it has mastered that the MNC can make its greatest contribution and exercise its greatest competitive strength. Furthermore, as the Behrman-Wallender and Teece studies demonstrate, the difficulties of technology transmission are large and they would be substantially increased if processes newly developed for overseas units were involved.

The real issues of technology selection therefore fall in a limited band of processes in which host environment conditions create strong logics for conformity to local methods or innovative adaptations of parent methods. For the most part these processes are those involving fairly low sophistication of technology, notably in materials handling and assembly and, to a lesser degree, machining operations. The primary emphasis of MNC parent technology in these processes has been in progressively adjusting the balance of capital and labor costs to fit the expanding scale of output and rising wage levels of their advanced societies. Depending upon the level of development of the host society, this aspect of MNC technological skill is more or less inappropriate. By contrast those aspects of production technology which are essentially related to product characteristics or quality generally do not raise questions of suitability for foreign applications, e.g., chemical processes and methods of producing electronic components.

Focusing attention on those processes most affected by labor-capital cost balance and scale of output provides an initial broad guidance for strategy analysis. Within that area the selection of technology inevitably must be based on case-by-case computations. The studies cited in the previous section, however, suggest some common tendencies which are useful leads for analysis. From the work of Morley and Smith it appears that scale effects are likely to have the greater influence, so adaptations where scale affects costs of output should be given prime attention especially in smaller markets. Wells' study emphasizes the host national government concerns which encourage firms to give visible attention to efforts to modify technological innovation to expand employment and reduce capital cost drains on the balance of payments. The degree to which it is economically sound to adapt technology to these considerations will depend upon the individual situation. However, in LDCs there is a high probability that some adjustments to the scale, labor-capital-cost context will be sound and that they will be well advised to gain government good will.

The studies of MNC experience do not give particular attention to problems that would fall under the heading of non-economic cultural receptivity of the host society to MNC technology inputs. Counterparts to the substantial resistance experienced by foreign aid programs in introducing agricultural and medical innovations in rural areas are not observed. On the whole, therefore, experience seems to confirm the assumption made earlier that workers' skills, supervisory competence and other environmental elements for which non-economic cultural considerations would apply are sufficiently receptive to production technology innovations so they are not major factors in selection of technology. On the other hand, there are ample indications, for example in Skinner's study that the "receptivity" requires considerable guidance and encouragement, that substantial training and other efforts must accompany technology if innovation is to be accomplished. The studies of Baranson and Kapoor reinforce this observation as the overall competence of local firms appears to be a major factor determining ability to absorb MNC technology.

This aspect of the analysis leads directly into the question of structural strategy as it affects technology transmission. Here the guidance from the MNC experience seems quite clear. The Behrman-Wallender and Kapoor studies both underscore the complexity of the transmission process and the value of strong communication links to accomplish it. The success of a multitude of licensing agreements including the massive technology acquisition program of Japan is ample demonstration that technology can be transmitted to independent firms, especially where their technological capabilities are already quite advanced. However, the general disposition of MNCs to feel that technology can be transmitted more effectively within their fully integrated organizations to controlled foreign affiliates seems soundly based. This, of course, is just one factor in the complex issue of ownership and control to be considered in Chapter 10. But as far as technology strategy by itself is concerned, the effort to maximize control is justified, especially in relations with LDC affiliates.

There is no significant mention in the various studies of unification considerations affecting technology transmission including effects on logistic systems and the interchange of skills among affiliates suggested at the start of this chapter. One may hypothesize that their non-appearance may be due to two reasons. First, most of the research has been directed at production units in LDCs which are not integrated into global or regional logistic rationalization systems. Second, the high degree of employment of parent technology based on the main logics identified above has assured sufficient unification of technological methods among affiliates so there is no cause for arguing its merits further for their own sake. If this reasoning is correct, then the absence of the unification considerations does not mean that they are irrelevant; just that they are redundant. This general pattern is affirmed by Ronstadt's research (p. 241) which showed that MNCs initially used technology transfer units to assist new production units to adapt parent methods, but that for latter ventures in LDCs these units were unnecessary because the process technologies had been so standardized that new operations could be aided adequately by teams of experts from existing operations in other countries. It would follow then that if in a given case the other logics for heavy use of parent technology were less pressing or the importance for logistic unification more critical, it might become a significant consideration. Thus logistic unification should be included in the general scheme of guidelines for technology strategy planning.

The ISAGRIDS in Table 8–1 reflect the difference in sophistication and importance to host countries of the production technologies of High Technology Industries, Singer and General Foods. HTI products require high quality, relatively complex and large-scale manufacture. Its capabilities in this regard are an important part of its resource capability, and one which is rated highly by host nations. The sophistication poses some need for cultural change, though it is rated as moderate because most HTI plants are in advanced industrial countries. Uniformity in methods among foreign factories is of some value in the effectiveness of the headquarters role of transmitting and monitoring production skills, i.e. the transmission is easier if each factory is using the same processes. But this is not a major concern. On the other hand, a high degree of control is vital because of the importance of quality control and effective transmission of the skills.

The key difference in the Singer situation is that the production technology is distinctly less sophisticated. However, Singer does require quality standards that are distinctly higher than those of all but the top competitors. The significance of its standards and their value to host nations was demonstrated by the fact that Taiwan went to considerable effort to entice Singer to set up a factory there so that its standards would upgrade the performance of the country's burgeoning but technologically weak sewing machine industry. Thus,

**Table 8–1.  ISAGRID for Affiliate Production Technology Strategy**

| Company | Resources | Strategy Context Variables | | | | National Interests | |
|---|---|---|---|---|---|---|---|
| | | Economic Differentials | MNC Capabilities | Cultural Change | Global Unification | Home | Host |
| High Technology Industries (HTI) | Natural resources | | | | | | |
| | Labor | | | | | | |
| | Capital: Finance | | | | | | |
| | Production | | | | | | |
| | Marketing | | | | | | |
| | Skills: Technological | Hc | H | M | M | | H |
| | Managerial | | | | | | |
| | Entrepreneurial | | | | | | |
| Singer | Natural resources | | | | | | |
| | Labor | | | | | | |
| | Capital: Finance | | | | | | |
| | Production | | | | H | | |
| | Marketing | | | | | | |

| | M | H | Hc | H |
|---|---|---|---|---|
| **Singer** (*cont.*) Skills: | | | | |
| Technological | | | | |
| Managerial | | | | |
| Entrepreneurial | | | | |
| Natural resources | | | | |
| Labor | | | | |
| Capital: Finance | | | | |
| Production | | | | |
| Marketing | | | | |
| **General Foods** Skills: | | | | |
| Technological | | M | | |
| Managerial | | | | |
| Entrepreneurial | | | | |

Importance in strategy: H = High; M = Moderate; c = Control of parent MNC significant.

though Singer's production technology is moderate, the firm's involvement in manufacture in many LDCs makes this a significant factor in both skill transmission and host culture interaction. The firm's extensive global logistic system further requires that there be uniformity in production processes, and with so many factories supervision is facilitated by standardization. Finally, control is an essential ingredient to accomplish these goals.

For General Foods production technology involves fairly low levels of sophistication. Because food industries are generally weak on technology worldwide, the introduction of even its modest skill involves moderate cultural change. This is evident from the problems General Foods encountered in the introduction of modest quality control and process improvement methods in Italy. Global unification is shown as a low importance factor because there is virtually no development of an interaffiliate logistic system. The value of standardization is limited therefore to helping with headquarters assistance to affiliates. However, the diversity of products limits carryover of experience from one affiliate to another. All of this adds up to moderate importance of control over production technology in the foreign units.

## MARKETING MANAGEMENT

Marketing is an area in which the counter influences affecting skill transmission are especially prominent. On the one hand, marketing is one phase of business in which companies in advanced countries, especially the United States, have developed a high degree of competence. On the other hand, marketing activities by their nature are associated very broadly and deeply with cultural characteristics, for example, people's tastes and motivations. And in the background are considerations of unification of global strategy. Fine judgment is therefore required to determine to what extent and how MNC marketing capabilities may be transmitted.

### Strategy Issues

Marketing encompasses a variety of technical, managerial, and entrepreneurial skills. The technical side composes the tools of the marketer ranging from sampling techniques for market research to balance of art and words in advertisements and approaches employed by salesmen. All of the elements of marketing technique have to be considered in the total international marketing work of an MNC. However, we will not look at them here because they are less significant to strategy then marketing management skills and because the approach to analysis of their transmission follows essentially the same pattern as that for the management skills.

Entrepreneurial skills will also not be considered *per se*. As they are inherently associated with many aspects of management skills, they will by implication be in the background of much of the discussion that follows. But systematic analysis of entrepreneurial skills transmission is not really practical. One can say that by its very nature, the aggressive, creative thrust of an MNC strategy embodies entrepreneurship and that its application must be limited and guided by the character of the host society. An elaboration of that statement can be generated in general terms and by citation of case situations. But any concrete strategy guidelines are likely to be tied to conclusions about the specific aspects of marketing management discussed below because they are to a large degree the outlets for entrepreneurial skills.

Our analysis will therefore focus on the transmission of marketing management skills, the approaches of the MNC to the main elements of the marketing process. The disposition in the analysis will be the search for opportunities for innovation which maximize the transmission of marketing managerial skills. A disposition toward unification by standardization of marketing methods in the global MNC system is also desirable considering its potential advantages. Economies may be possible if aspects of marketing are similar among units, e.g., development of a single advertising program for all countries. Also the skill transmission roles of headquarters personnel have certain efficiencies if all foreign affiliates are following similar managerial approaches and the opportunities for skill transmission between affiliates are enhanced under those circumstances. And administrative controls are facilitated by standardization of affiliate operations.

With the thrust toward innovation and unification taken as a fundamental goal, the strategy analysis focuses on the determination of its feasibility in the marketing context of host societies. Ultimately that determination boils down to case-by-case decisions but a broad view of the pattern of factors affecting feasibility will provide the basis for guiding the direction and aggressiveness of innovation efforts.

The matrix outlined in Table 8–2 provides an initial framework for this analysis. Three main determinants of the marketing characteristics of societies are listed on the left side. The economic factors include total market size, individual income levels and their distribution, and related characteristics. Structure encompasses the organizations and related physical features of the host environment through which marketing processes move or which impinge on them.

Table 8–2.　Influences on Market Characteristics of Societies

| Determinants | Fundamental Bases | Influences for Change | Sources of Resistance to Change |
|---|---|---|---|
| Economics | National wealth<br>Income distribution | Economic growth | Limits to growth |
| Structure | Economic system<br>Marketing institutions | Industrialization<br>Urbanization | Fixed assets<br>Vested interests |
| Values | Culture<br>Social norms | Modernization<br>Education<br>Professionalism | Tradition |

Values are used here to describe the attitudinal influences embodied in the host culture and social system. This breakdown of the influences is useful because it identifies three quite different patterns that affect potential marketing system changes.

The *economic* influences on marketing changes are directly tied to economic growth and its ramifications. Table 8—3 shows some measures of economic change in selected countries. Some, like Brazil, West Germany and Japan, have experienced rapid growth both overall and in per capita income. Other economies like India have expanded overall but show little improvement in per capita income because the growth is largely offset by population growth. The variations in income distribution patterns described in Chapter 3 (p. 84) are another significant factor in marketing operations. As per capita income rises the pattern tends to shift toward the more homogenous, middle-class pattern of the more advanced industrial nations.

A related element for which figures are not readily available is the distribution of growth among levels of society. It appears, for example, that the gains in Brazil have been heavily concentrated in the upper and middle classes with little progress for the lower classes, while in Japan the working people have shared more fully in national economic progress.

The *structural* features central to marketing are the system of organizations running from producers through channels of distribution to customers. Each has its human structure with associated physical properties: manufacturers with their factories, retailers with their stores, families with their homes, and so forth. Intimately involved with them are other structural features including banks, advertising agencies, government bureaucracies, and the like. These features have been subject to substantial change under the influence of broad structural evolution, e.g., industrialization and urbanization, and in response to fundamental economic and social change. However, by their nature they resist change. There is a strong inertial tendency built into established human organizational patterns with their internal ties, their pattern of vested interests in the ongoing system, and the rigidities of the physical assets they hold. A common example in the marketing field is the resistance of trade structure to change evident for example in the restrictive rules of European guilds whose pattern continues to this day in retail association control or in the fight against the chain stores by U.S. ma-and-pa stores in the 1930s.

The *values* of a society have much to do with the dynamics of marketing. Distinctions between what is right and wrong, what is good and bad, what is important and unimportant are at the heart of

**Table 8-3.  Market Data on Selected Countries**

| | Population | | Gross National Product | | | | |
| | | | Total | | Per Capita | | |
| | Total 1974 Millions | Annual Growth 1965-74 Percent | 1974 Billions of U.S. Dollars | Annual Growth 1971-74 Percent | 1974 U.S. Dollars | Annual Growth 1965-74 Percent | |
|---|---|---|---|---|---|---|
| United States | 211.9 | 1.0% | $1,413.5 | 10.8% | $6,670 | 2.4% |
| United Kingdom | 56.0 | 0.4 | 200.8 | 15.9 | 3,590 | 2.2 |
| West Germany | 62.0 | 0.6 | 388.7 | 32.5 | 6,260 | 3.9 |
| Italy | 55.4 | 0.7 | 156.5 | 18.6 | 2,820 | 4.0 |
| Brazil | 104.0 | 2.9 | 95.9 | 38.8 | 920 | 6.3 |
| Peru | 15.0 | 2.9 | 11.1 | 22.8 | 740 | 1.8 |
| Japan | 109.7 | 1.2 | 446.0 | 33.5 | 407 | 8.5 |
| India | 595.0 | 2.3 | 80.4 | 9.4 | 140 | 1.3 |

Sources: *World Bank Atlas*, 1973 and 1976.

the behavior of both marketing personnel and buyers. Changes in values are not readily documented but they are visibly observable over time, associated with educational progress, growing professionalism, shifts in family roles, and modernization of society in other respects. Economic growth and associated structural changes tend to be a major factor fostering these changes. But the inertial counterparts to the organizational structure and fixed assets resisting structural change are strong deterrents. The traditional patterns of socialization and value maintenance are firmly embedded and propagated by the family, educational system, religious organizations, and other elements of society. So values tend to change quite slowly.

The significance of economics, structure, and values to marketing innovation will be brought out by the examples in market research, distribution, and promotion. The illustrations could be expanded to other phases of marketing but, for present purposes of explaining the approach to strategy analysis, this coverage will suffice. Readers wishing to delve further into this subject may consult books in international marketing management.[9] In this discussion several references will be made to General Foods as it provides an excellent illustration of a company for which marketing skill transmission is a prime element of international strategy.

*Market research* has a conspicuous image in modern marketing management, because it combines analysis and consumer orientation, the key elements of the modern approach to the field. Market research developed first in the parent nations of MNCs, especially the United States, whereas it is at a very early stage in many LDC host nations. Thus there is a clear economic differential basis for transmission of its skills. The feasibility of the transmission is affected significantly, however, by host nation characteristics.

Market research is based upon a simple economic proposition. It is worthwhile to spend a certain amount of money to obtain information which will improve the chances of success in marketing programs. That proposition leads readily to an equation relating the cost of research to the money involved in the marketing programs. If millions of dollars are at stake in a highly risky venture, it may make sense to spend a considerable amount to buy information by research which will reduce the risk. If the program is small or the uncertainty minor, only a small expenditure on buying information is justified.

When market research is considered with this equation in mind, the relevance of the economics of the host society become significant. The total cost of determining a certain amount of information is generally as great or greater in a smaller or less advanced country than in a large, advanced one because the research program and the sample size must be roughly the same and the problems of research are greater. On the other hand, the amount at stake in terms of the marketing program is usually greater in the larger or more advanced country. Thus, the cost-benefit equation reduces the utility of market research steadily as one moves into smaller and less developed countries.

An interesting confirmation of this generalization is provided in the findings of Holton based on a survey of international executives.[10] His approach was to relate international management to game theory. He identified three main distinctive characteristics of international marketing in contrast to domestic operations: (1) greater uncertainty, stemming from differences in environment and less information among decision-makers; (2) more expense and more time required to provide market information to the international organization; (3) more effort required to determine what decisions should be decentralized.

In broad terms Holton found evidence in his research that firms made decisions in ways that were consistent with game theory thinking. In devising a strategy for entering a market, frequently the firm appeared to be looking for a means of minimizing risk and uncertainty, maximizing control, and yet maintaining flexibility. It was also common to find along with these objectives the strategy of entry by means of a series of moves which permitted the MNC to buy information over time. The process of first importing through a distributor, then forming some partnership with a local firm, and finally establishing a fully-owned subsidiary had these characteristics.

An apparent inconsistency was observed in the limited market research that many companies did before entering foreign markets. While the greater uncertainty apparently should lead to more research, Holton found a logic for the limited effort in two points: The value of the information generated by market research in many foreign markets is considerably lower than in the United States and there may be cheaper ways to acquire it. He presented some illustrative computations of costs, probabilities, and payoffs to show that the gain from research might often be insufficient to offset its cost, particularly for small markets. As a substitute for marketing research, the firm might employ what could be called the full-scale market-test approach. This is what many firms did when they started exporting into a market after only cursory research. The cost of supplying a market from a plant in another country might result in only limited profits at the outset but the process could provide a better test than research at reasonable cost.

The principal structural feature affecting market research in host societies is the availability of information both for direct use in research and for design of studies. There is a tremendous difference between the vast amount of well-based data that one can obtain from government and private sources in the United States and the small quantity and dubious quality of figures to be found in the least developed nations. The problems created by the less favorable structural conditions bring out the dependent character of market research by private firms. Even a market research organization which generates much of its own data cannot be effective if it does not have key information that can only be provided economically by an external organization. For example, the design of a field survey must be based on a breakdown of population units by key characteristics, e.g., income level range for city sections. Conclusions can be drawn only if the overall distribution of income in the national population is known. And more refined data like consumption of different products and expenditures on various media can greatly assist researchers.

Values affect both researchers and those upon whom research is being performed. The roots of market research go back to the scientific revolution which established the concept of systematic inquiry in Western society. That concept has now fanned out to the whole world but it has reached many societies quite recently and its impact has not gone deep. Depending upon the country, the values it embodies of independent inquiry, objectivity, and analysis often run counter to established values of acceptance of tradition, subjectivity, rote learning, etc. The educational system in particular is generally slow to adjust to new values required to prepare people for market research careers.

At the same time, the interview process, which is central to a large portion of market research, requires certain values of respondents, including honesty, frankness, and trust. The feasibility of market research is deterred by the lower level of these values in some societies. For example, in Latin societies honesty and frankness have traditionally been valued less than being agreeable with others, so it is harder for a researcher to get a candid reaction from a respondent to the qualities of a product. Even more difficult is the high degree of distrust researchers often meet in some countries where they are suspected of being secret investigators for government tax authorities.

These economic, structural, and value characteristics set the broad limits on the innovations in market research which MNCs may contemplate. Changes in these three fields will have much to do with the prospects to guide future strategy. As economies expand the cost-benefit equation becomes more favorable, justifying greater investment in research. As the national structural systems become stronger in provision of information, the feasibility of studies is increased. And the evolution of values in societies should generally help among both employees and the public.

Major differences in feasibility of innovation will undoubtedly continue, however, in the pattern illustrated in the General Foods case. In Great Britain, with its quite large market, the moves to strengthen market research were readily justified particularly after the $223,000 lost in the failure of the Gravy Train experience.[11] The structural and value foundations for market research are quite adequate in that country. The latter characteristics, however, were relatively much less favorable in Italy. With major decisions to be made in its tortellini business which accounted for $700,000 of annual sales, the $1,400 devoted to a market study seemed economically justified. But, in fact, the quality of the study done by an independent research firm was so low that it was of little value. The difficulties in terms of cost and competence in the local environment probably precluded GF bringing in its own research personnel, so it was impractical for it to implement much innovation in survey research despite considerable know-how in the area.

In Mexico, the Kool-Aid example illustrates the feasibility of substantial input of parent know-how in the test-market approach to research as the home staff provided a variety of useful suggestions. The approach itself suggests a variation of the economic basis for information buying noted by Holton. With total Kool-Aid sales running around $100,000 a year and modest uncertainties attached to sales program changes, large expenditures for separate research studies might be hard to justify, especially with the structural and value impediments of the Mexican environment. However, measured results of controlled variations in sales programs in two different markets would provide considerable information while paying for themselves out of sales income.

Advanced nations have experienced a major revolution in *distribution* processes in recent decades. The most conspicuous developments have been in mass retail merchandising channels but significant changes have come in other aspects of retailing and in wholesaling. The new approaches which have evolved have already spread to varying degrees to other countries and continuation of that diffusion process is to be expected as many of the forces underlying the changes in advanced countries are replicated elsewhere. The MNCs have been directly involved in these changes or closely associated with them, so they are well positioned to transmit the skills incorporated in them.

The economic, structural and value influences on the distribution process have already been illustrated by the supermarket example used in Chapter 3 (p. 101). Particularly significant is the idiosyncratic character of the evolution, supermarkets evolving in the United States according to one pattern and in other areas through different influences and in a different style therefore. This diversity is found in many other parts of the global distribution scene. For example, mass merchandising has made a giant leap ahead of U.S. practice in some European countries. Enormous self-service food and general merchandise stores running to 250,000 square feet or more compared with smaller U.S. operations. The European stores have notably higher turnover as well, e.g., figures cited in 1970 of $360 per square foot for Carrefour in France vs. a high of $87 in newer U.S. discount stores.

On another front, the studies of wholesalers in fifteen countries compiled by Bartels brings out considerable variation in their roles such as the degree to which they are sources of credit and capital and the extent to which they integrate their efforts with producers and retailers.[12] In some countries they tend to be contributing parts of the channel of distribution while in others they are more commonly independent traders with little loyalty or attachment to either manufacturers or retailers.

This idiosyncratic character of structural features of distribution was confirmed by Douglas in an intensive investigation of possible relationships between characteristics of marketing systems and levels of environmental development.[13] Three sets of characteristics were examined: size and organization of firms, managerial attitudes, and channel relationships. Five countries were covered to give a range of levels of development: Japan, Italy, Chile, Greece, and Ceylon.

Overall Douglas concluded that there was little evidence to support the theory that the development of marketing structure closely parallels that of the social, economic, and cultural environment. Only a few marketing characteristics seemed to be related to environmental variables. In Japan, the most developed country in the survey, the portion of marketing firms classed as large was greatest, while the greater portion of firms in Ceylon, the least developed, were small. But among the other three countries, the pattern of size among firms was quite disparate showing no relation to level of development.

The study gave interesting data on other characteristics, e.g., the attitudes toward vigorous competition vs. agreements among competitors, utilization of wholesalers, vs. direct selling to retailers, and extent of national distribution. But in none of these did Douglas find significant correlations related to the environment. In most cases there were considerable variations both among countries and within countries which could not be related to variables. In a few cases, there was substantial similarity among the countries, for example, in the portions of firms with local vs. national distribution.

The author concluded that either there is no relation between the marketing system and the environment or that the relationship might be more complex and indirect than that tested. In addition, aspects not considered in this survey—such as the concentration of economic and financial power and the rapidity of economic growth—might be important influences on the development of marketing structure.

Surveying this picture of distribution around the world we may draw a few general conclusions. First, because of the dominant role of many independent firms in distribution, the inertial deterrents to change that are common to structural features will be frequently experienced. Second, change has and will continue to come with prime impetus from economic growth factors and associated changes in values. Third, the prevailing distribution systems and their patterns of change will continue to show some commonalities among nations but also a high degree of diversity despite considerable similarity in the forces apparently influencing their character.

*Promotion*, especially advertising, is the other aspect of marketing in which advanced nations have a wide lead in experience with consequent substantial basic logic supporting skill transmission. One critical economic element has played a major role in the progress of promotional efforts, namely the expansion of discretionary income levels. When people are living at a subsistence level, there is little place for promotion because they have few marketing choices to make. At progressively higher levels of income, the choices increase and the utility of promotion efforts rises accordingly. This economic pattern is readily observed in the association of per capita income and per capita advertising expenditure data in Figure 8–1. The data also suggest cultural variations in the pattern, however; some Latin American countries have relatively high advertising outlays per capita compared to the cluster of high income European countries.

Along with this broad economic influence come a variety of specific effects of economic change on promotion methods. For example, the pattern of media availability and effectiveness is closely associated with economic development, especially as it affects radio, TV ownership, and car ownership. The economic relationship of various types of promotion is also subject to change. An extreme but illustrative example is the fact that door-to-door salesmen are so inexpensive in the least developed countries that for some consumer products their efforts are self-sustaining even with a low volume of

**Figure 8-1.**   Intensity of Advertising Effort

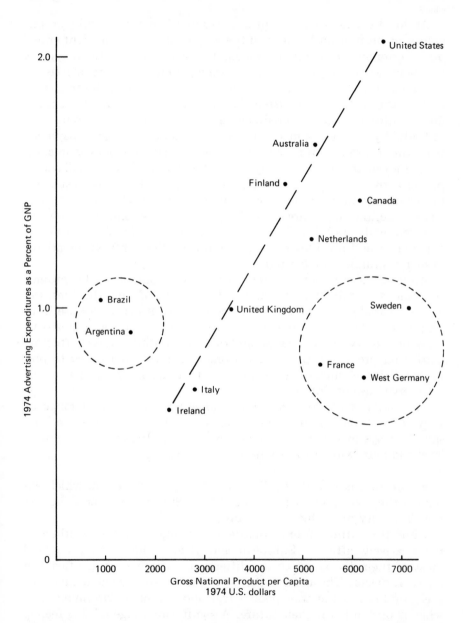

Sources: World Bank Atlas, 1976, and *World Advertising Expenditures,* 1976 edition, New York: International Advertising Association.

sales achievement and therefore they can be used as a medium of promotion that would be out of the question in high-income societies.

As in the case of distribution, structural features figure prominently in promotion because of the major role of independent enterprises, notably the advertising media. However, the intertial deterrent to change seems to be less, partly because some of the media like TV are quite new but especially because of the status of the media. A unit in the distribution system has an established status with trade links reinforced often by credit ties and control over an ongoing flow of trade. By contrast, a media unit is dependent upon direct payment from the advertiser and commands only partial control over an audience. Indeed the audience may be reached by alternative media competing actively for the advertiser's business. In these circumstances, the media are more responsive to the forces working for change. The chief structural departure from this pattern is government ownership of some media, notably TV in many countries. As the General Foods experience in Italy illustrates, the opportunities for MNC creativity in such a situation are limited.

While economic factors establish the basic foundation for promotion and structural features affect the pattern of opportunities, the greatest variations in host country conditions in this area arise from values. This fact is inherent in the role of promotion as a means to influence motivations, images, and other attitudinal aspects affecting marketing processes. Essentially promotion must be attuned to prevailing attitudes including the value system and influence aspects of it to serve business interests.

The findings of three research studies provide a useful range of views of the variety of value patterns affecting promotion and the specific ways in which the effects are felt, starting at a very general level and narrowing down to more specific aspects.

● The first is a study by Katona, Strumpel, and Zahn, which extended the consumer attitude work of the Survey Research Center at the University of Michigan into Europe.[14]

While the authors found considerable similarity in the members of the relatively affluent European and U.S. societies, they devoted most of their discussion to the differences. These were significant in many respects. The central theme to which they related many of their findings is the way people feel about their environment and what it portends for their future. A significant gauge of this feeling was the response of people to questions about how their financial situation had changed in the past four years and how they expected it to change in the next four years. The general pattern in the survey results was of a much more favorable, optimistic outlook in the United States than in Europe, although there were considerable differences between European countries.

The West Germans provided the greatest contrasts in most respects. For example, although per capita income had grown just as fast in West Germany as in the United States from 1964 to 1968, only 36 percent of the Germans said they felt better off in 1968 than four years before compared to 53 percent of Americans. Looking ahead four years, 43 percent of Americans expected to be better off and only 24 percent of the Germans. The authors felt that an important element contributing to the greater optimism of the Americans was their belief in their ability to progress through their own efforts. When asked to account for their progress in the past four years, 42 percent of Americans gave self-effort reasons such as "I worked hard," whereas only 10 percent of Germans credited their own efforts. The rest accepted progress as due to general economic progress, etc.

The other attitudes described in the book tended to fit into this central comparative theme but cultural attitudes also played a part. The German rate of saving was around 14 percent of disposable income compared to 7 percent in the United States. A large part of this difference was due to the steady increase of consumer debt in the United States which offset the other forms of saving there. In West Germany, a strong cultural influence persisted; two-thirds of respondents indicated unqualified opposition to buying on credit. Reflecting their lesser optimism, 70 percent of Germans listed economic security as their preference in selection of jobs, compared to 31–34 percent in the United States as well as in the Netherlands and Britain. The Germans also appeared at the bottom end of the scale in educational aspirations. Asked if they hoped their sons would receive a high level degree, only 41 percent of Germans responded positively while 66 percent of Americans hoped their sons would go to college. The British followed closely at 60 percent.

At the end of the book, the authors constructed profiles of the people in each of the four countries they studied intensively. Americans were characterized as adapted to the rapidly expanding economy around them with its emphasis on knowledge. They had high aspirations that were consistent with and thus supported the dynamic growth of the economy. In West Germany there was a gap between the reality of a rapidly developing mass-consumption economy and its perception by the people. Attitudes and behavior patterns taken over from agrarian and early industrial modes of living were still predominant. The Germans' lack of optimism, low consumption aspirations, emphasis on security, and low priority on education could be, the authors speculate, a significant drag on future economic progress in the country. The British were considerably closer to the Americans in optimism and economic aspirations. However, they were greatly worried about unemployment which led to tenaciously holding onto jobs and considerable feather-bedding and protective "spread the work" devices which made it impossible for the economy to advance fast enough to satisfy their aspirations. The Dutch were found to have only moderate material aspirations, the phrase "better happy than rich" being quoted to characterize their attitude. Symptomatic of their feeling was the fact that the share of married women in the labor force was lower than in any other Common Market country.

• Thorelli, Becker, and Engledow made a study of attitudes toward consumer information services which brings out variations in response to advertising and other information sources.[15] The main body of information was drawn from parallel research projects they conducted in West Germany and the United States. The basic components of the research were interviews in representative metropolitan areas in each country, Frankfurt and Indianapolis, covering 200 average consumers and 100 subscribers to testing services, *Consumer Reports* (CR) in the United States and *test* and *DM* in Germany. The study provided a penetrating look at two main subjects: consumer information (CI) and the relation of CI to advertising. The CI sections consisted largely of comparisons between the service subscribers and average consumers (ACs) within the two countries and between them. The subscribers in the two countries were found to be composed of substantially similar people whom the authors identified as the nucleus of the "information seekers" in the marketplace. As compared to ACs they were a relatively elite group economically and in educational background. This generalization persisted in studies in other countries except in Norway where a considerable portion of subscribers to a testing service were from the lower income groups. Subscribers of both nationalities were also found to be more disposed to plan new purchases and more inclined to seek information from other published sources. They watched less TV and thus saw less advertising on it. They were generally opinion leaders in the sense that their views on products were sought by others but they did not see themselves as early adopters of new products.

On the other hand, there were many points on which differences were found between the two groups, often related to the cultural or economic characteristics of their countries. Both groups were relatively favorable to business or at least did not have the strong antagonism that might be associated with those generally on the side of consumers. But whereas West German subscribers were convinced that welfare did not damage overall work output, American subscribers were even more certain that it did.

The same split existed on the question of more government control of business, where American subscribers were decidedly opposed and Germans quite in favor. Consistent with deep cultural differences was the tendency of the Germans to be distinctly less trusting of product information and business honesty than the Americans. A somewhat surprising finding was that U.S. subscribers rated brand reputation more important than did the average consumer, while German subscribers and ACs gave roughly equal ratings on this point. Likewise the Americans regarded advertising as a more useful source of information.

Broadly both Americans and Germans were found to be favorable to advertising but there were considerable differences in their views. Americans showed a greater overall support, 75 percent expressing positive opinions vs. 60 percent of Germans. Americans supported advertising from an economic view but criticized its social image. Germans, while not denying the necessity for advertising per se, did not greatly support it on either economic or social grounds.

The greater trustworthiness of information from product testing services stood out as the most important criterion in both countries. Otherwise a number of differences appeared in the ranking of criteria. For example, the American subscribers were less concerned with the lack of timeliness of product test information while they were more put off by the difficulty of understanding the content of product tests provided by the services.

Despite the wide readership of product testing services, the authors noted that the majority of the educated middle income people were still not information seekers in the sense defined in their study. They noted a French survey which showed that 53 percent of people felt sufficiently informed about products they bought. Their attitude would indicate that CI programs were really faced with the challenge of converting people to the notion that they needed more information, that is, they needed to create a market for their programs rather than merely satisfying already existing demand.

• A study by Green and Langeard provides a more concrete illustration of cultural differences in motivation of innovative consumers.[16] The purpose of the study was to compare the manner in which consumers came to try new products or new retailing services and the characteristics of consumer innovators in France and the United

States. A sample of 193 women was surveyed in Texas in 1973 and 226 women in Aix-en-Provence in 1974, the former by mail and the latter by questionnaires delivered and picked up personally because of poor response to mail surveys in France.

The survey covered fifteen grocery or grocery-related products and eight retail services at various stages of the adoption process. Because of differences between the countries, the lists for each were different. Innovators in each category were identified on the basis of the number of items they had purchased or used from the lists. The questionnaire also asked for information on age, income, education, employment, number of children, magazine subscriptions, sources of information, TV viewing, organization membership, willingness to try new products, and opinion leadership.

The respondents were asked whether their opinions had recently been solicited about innovations. It was found that the U.S. respondents tended to discuss grocery products significantly more than the French respondents (65 percent vs. 55 percent). Conversely, the French sample indicated significantly more discussion of retail services than the U.S. sample (66 percent vs. 33 percent). The authors hypothesized that the differences were due to national characteristics. American women were highly conscious of time and budget factors in cooking and alert to new products. French women were more traditional in their food habits. On the other hand, retailing in France had recently been in a substantial state of change as compared to the United States where the rate of change had stabilized since the rapid evolution after World War II. The U.S. sample expressed a greater willingness to try innovations in both categories: 84 percent vs. 71 percent for new products and 79 percent vs. 69 percent for new retail services.

The respondents were asked to identify the medium through which they usually learned about innovations. The U.S. respondents relied considerably more on friends and relatives and on television and print advertising than did the French respondents. Conversely, the French respondents indicated a greater propensity to notice new products for the first time in the store. These differences appeared to relate to various characteristics. TV viewing was much higher in the United States; only 9 percent of the French reported that they watched less than an hour per day compared to 36 percent in the United States. The U.S. sample subscribed to an average of 3.7 magazines compared to 2.4 for the French. On the other hand, shopping was more a part of the social life of the French and, with less storage space, they shopped more frequently. Thus there was more chance for them to notice innovations while shopping.

The authors suggested that these differences had implications for marketing management such as the need to give greater emphasis to packaging and point-of-sale promotion for innovation in France. The data showed that 32 percent of the U.S. sample were members of more than three formal organizations compared to 3 percent of the French. This suggested that the U.S. women might be subject to more social influences than the French.

The U.S. grocery product innovators could not be distinguished from the general population on any variables except that they watched more TV. Retail service innovators differed on several variables: higher on opinion leadership, more children, watch more TV, rely more on print media, and clustered more in the 35−49 age group. French grocery product innovators were distinguished from non-innovators in high opinion leadership rating, membership in more organizations, and clustering in the 35−49 age and middle income groups. The retail service innovators were distinguished only in subscribing to more magazines. The data also showed considerable overlap among innovators, i.e., people who were both product and service innovators, though the overlap was less strong in France than in the United States.

It is difficult to summarize the content of these and a number of other studies that have identified elements of value systems affecting marketing promotion. That difficulty may be the most useful concluding theme. Every study notes the substantial range of commonalities among peoples. But all observe many differences as well and the chief difficulty lies in the lack of any systematic pattern to the differences. Thus to a large degree the MNC strategist is faced with much the same idiosyncratic pattern as was observed in the structural features affecting distribution systems. In the same vein attitudes have an inertial character based in their cultural roots. Changes appear over time but only slowly. From the major influence of economic growth it is clear that promotion efforts in host societies will expand, providing ample opportunity for MNCs to participate in innovation in this phase of marketing. But substantial diversity among countries in innovational patterns is assured by the fact that promotional methods must be largely geared to the prevailing value system with both its similarities and differences in relation to other societies.

## MNC Experience
The modest number of research studies of international marketing management have largely been directed at the unification strategy

question and standardization of methods. However, by implication
they also provide insights into experience with the innovation-conformity issues of the skill transmission process.

1. A broad picture of MNC views, though rather limited in depth,
was provided in a survey by Kapoor and McKay of headquarters marketing executives in 116 MNCs spanning the range in size and other
characteristics of the *Fortune* list of the 500 largest U.S. firms.[17]
The main focus of their study was training of management personnel
but as background they asked questions about the needs for marketing management. The survey provided the ranking of major marketing problems shown in Table 8–4. Here and in another question
asking about future needs the integration of worldwide marketing
efforts was stressed. The survey did not ask questions elaborating on
this point, but in their analysis the authors observed that growing
competition and increasingly similar markets were key considerations. Senior corporate management was promoting integration at all
levels, including that of the international marketing function. The
process of integration was resulting in increasing centralization of
strategic decisions (such as product policy and pricing) at corporate
headquarters. Thus, new products should be developed with a view
to a worldwide market. The evolution of increasingly uniform markets at the regional level envisioned for the near future would be
largely restricted to North America, Western Europe and, gradually,

Table 8–4. Major International Marketing Problems

|  | MNCs Reporting | |
|---|---|---|
|  | *Number* | *Percent* |
| Integration of international marketing into worldwide corporate effort | 28 | 24% |
| Lack of marketing data | 18 | 16 |
| Unsuitable distribution channels | 14 | 12 |
| Trade barriers | 12 | 10 |
| Unfair competition | 10 | 9 |
| Local legal and political complications | 9 | 8 |
| Scarcity of personnel | 9 | 8 |
| Increasing nationalism | 6 | 4 |
| Product adaptation to local use | 5 | 4 |
| Other | 3 | 3 |
| No response | 2 | 2 |
| Total | 116 | 100 |

Source: Ashok Kapoor and Robert McKay, *Managing International Markets.*
Princeton, N.J.: Darwin, 1971.

Japan. Per capita income, discretionary spending power, level of industrialization and other major economic features would become more similar in the future. However, sociocultural factors in these countries would probably remain distinct.

2. The study by Sorenson and Wiechmann cited in Chapter 6 provided a penetrating examination of the experience of consumer packaged goods firms in Europe (p. 228). The main thrust of their conclusions was that the potential advantages of standardization of marketing programs for such goods were limited and that the firms seemed to have carried standardization further than was desirable in many cases. They did, however, stress the value of standardizing the processes by which marketing programs were developed as a prime means for transmitting marketing skills to affiliates and achieving a competitive edge over local firms.

3. The study by Kacker also cited in Chapter 6 covered experience of a range of U.S. MNCs in India with both consumer and industrial product marketing (p. 230). In their general promotion mix, four consumer goods companies reported that India differed from the United States in its major reliance on personal selling. The typical U.S. "pull" strategy was not effective because of low disposable income, high illiteracy, and media deficiencies. On the other hand, plentiful college educated young men and established promotion practices made a strong "push" strategy economical and effective. Drug companies, on the other hand, used essentially the same system of direct mail promotion and sales representatives as in the United States.

Of the seven consumer goods companies, five used only their established international brand names while two had also added some Indian brands. Kacker found that the advertising copy used by most of these companies was not as competitive in India as in the States. It did not emphasize value or the reasonableness of price with the exception of one manufacturer. The messages were stated in a simple, straightforward way.

As to distribution methods, the American firms had to rely on market channels very similar to those used by their local competitors. The adaptation here was thus substantial with relatively less control on market middle men and heavy reliance on wholesalers. There was little opportunity for direct contact with retailing in the absence of large scale retailers, mail order houses, and door-to-door selling organizations. However, fourteen of the twenty companies that used indirect distribution were satisfied with the support they received in the introduction of new products. The author noted that the very fact that a dealer was selected from among many prospective candidates gave him a feeling of distinctiveness and motivated him to extend full cooperation to his principal.

In the absence of strong independent retailers, only two companies sold under private brands. For the same reason and also because of the seller's market for most goods, there was little cooperative advertising. The market power of wholesalers and retailers was too weak to permit them to bargain for such support. The chief adaptation in pricing was in response to government regulation in many fields including drugs, tires, oil, and fertilizers.

4. An analysis of experience in a third area of the world is given in Wright's comparison of operations of pairs of Chilean and U.S. firms summarized in Chapter 2 (see p. 74). Overall Wright found that the Chilean firms had been more successful over the five-year period, 1965–70. Experience in several areas of management were examined with the general conclusion that U.S. firms were governed too much by general policies and guidelines applied with relatively little modification in all countries. The individualized methods of the Chilean firms permitted greater flexibility and better adaptation to local business conditions. Specifically, in the marketing area Wright cited the employment of market research staffs by U.S. firms. These were an unnecessary expense in the Chilean sellers' market of that period; local firms got along with limited staff, employing research consultants as needed. Also U.S. firms were more hampered by price controls as they stuck to their established product lines, while Chilean firms brought out products with minor changes or new brand names, permitting them to keep pace with cost increases.

5. Terpstra, Yoshino, and Sherbini came at the subject from a different direction, by exploring it from the headquarters point of view.[18] The objective in their study was to examine in depth the ways in which countries might be grouped according to similar characteristics and the usefulness of such grouping for marketing management.

One part set forth three main approaches to grouping countries for marketing analysis. The first, called the "Development Approach through Cluster Analysis," classified countries on three dimensions: level of development, environmental conditions (population, urbanization, etc.) and social factors (chiefly measures of homogeneity in ethnic and religious respects). Several measures of each dimension were used and a composite index was derived by which the countries were ranked and then classified in clusters of substantial similarity. The second method, called the "Regional Typology Approach," classified countries within each major continental area according to a composite analysis of twenty-five factors closely related to marketing: economic indicators, life expectancy, literacy, newspaper circulation, and motor vehicle ownership, among others. In the third method, called the "Two-Dimensional Direct-Score Approach," composite indices were determined for two major dimensions, one reflecting the degree of economic and demographic mobilization within each country, the other providing a rough measure of domestic stability and cohesion. Again a number of factors were used to derive the indices.

The other part of the book reported the results of a study of twelve leading companies and one advertising agency, together with the authors' conclusions as to the value of grouping countries for comparative analysis of marketing operations. The survey revealed that companies were not using such comparative methods to a significant degree. The authors found that, because of travel and other geographical factors, regional groupings had strong support for line management so their investigations were confined to staff problems. They identified three main functions in which groupings of countries by other than georgraphic criteria might be useful: goal setting, clearinghouse activities, and coordination and control.

In the performance of each function, the authors found that grouping countries by non-geographic means was rare but that it did appear in just enough cases to suggest its potentials. For example, one company had found that, in considering sales forecasts relative to potential, Japan, Mexico, and the United Kingdom were in the same growth category. Another corporate staff member, analyzing wide divergences in efficiency of manpower deployment, found it effective to group countries according to level of economic development and size of company sales.

Much of the book's content was devoted to development of the rationale for use of country groupings in staff functions. The logics were quite persuasive in many respects. For example, a recurring theme in the interviews was the emphasis on the importance of experienced personnel, as opposed to techniques or formulas. If experience had any value, it must be that there was a carryover from a previous situation to the present; i.e., that the experienced person was using his own comparative approach. The question being raised here was whether such comparisons could be made more general, formal, and explicit.

A significant obstacle to comparative analysis lay in the widespread management feeling that each operation and country was unique. The authors proposed, however, that more effective use of the many similarities among countries be made, with the hope of injecting some orderliness in the apparent confusion. Their recommendations generally run toward identifying a limited number of criteria for grouping countries, closely tied to the specific aspects of marketing under analysis. This approach would be preferable to the more comprehensive ones developed in the preliminary study, though the latter might be useful for some purposes.

6. The question of standardization in international advertising programs has been the subject of much literature by practitioners. One example, by Cranch, is summarized here and is followed by the findings of the only two research studies that have focused directly on this phase of marketing.[19] Cranch's point of departure was the active discussion in the mid-1960s of the prospects of increasing the use of common advertising campaigns. These would be run everywhere with the minimum of adaptations to local environments except for translation. He observed that there was very little identical advertising across national borders. Instead there was a great increase in advertising tailored to each country but within a common marketing plan. The identical look had given way to a strong sense of familiarity.

Behind this evolution the author saw a growing sophistication in marketing planning. The circumstances in each country were studied thoroughly including share of market, sources of competition, and consumer characteristics. With this information, those involved in planning international advertising analyzed the suitability of a campaign, element by element, to see what could be standardized and what had to be tailored to local requirements. Cranch noted that some arguments for standardization had little weight. A relatively small portion of the population travel and few people are impressed by the "international" character of a product. Thus the stress was on basic local competitiveness.

Cranch described the sophisticated modern approach as the two-tier system of inernational planning. The first tier was strategic, similar-looking campaigns crossing borders in international magazines, supported by advertising in the top-class local press and outdoor sites in urban centers. The second level of attack was the tougher, nearer-the-ground tactical advertising in local mass media, aiming at a larger audience. This advertising looked familiar to the visitor from abroad, but it looked local and spoke the local language to the native customer. The primary emphasis in the international familiarity approach was on the visual elements—package design and logotypes, point of sale material, and billboards with minimum copy.

Among industrial customers there was greater homogeneity of interests and requirements permitting greater centralization. Dow, for example, managed advertising for fourteen European countries from one office. Their campaigns were prepared in London to a single selling platform and layout, but with copy (and illustration if necessary) creatively adapted in the individual countries to the local language and idiom.

Cranch thought it was true that as time went on, people's buying habits tended to become more similar and their tastes more uniform. He therefore anticipated that the degree of commonality of advertising among countries would grow. However, it was likely that for some time the technical difficulties would require compromise between international theme and local presentation, particularly in the use of the TV medium.

A related global approach in another aspect of marketing was also foreseen. In an age of instant communication, one could anticipate that brands might soon be launched internationally in the same way that they were now introduced nationally. Just as heightened competition nationally had curtailed severely the classical procedure of the leisured and measured test market, increasing competition among internationally marketed products greatly increased the risk that a competing product would suddenly appear in countries D, F and M while an advertiser was still experimenting in country A. In fact, a few firms, notably Unilever, were already working this way. He expected that the managements of multinational companies would plan more and more brands globally, launching them wherever the markets dictated, without regard to home market location.

7. Dunn undertook a series of case studies designed to find under what conditions major U.S. advertisers transferred their campaigns successfully to other countries.[20] The thirty companies studied represented a variety of products and marketing problems. However, they did have certain characteristics in common: (1) all had been users of foreign advertising for at least thirty years, (2) all depended on advertising as an important part of their communications program, (3) all were at the time of study (1964) active in at least four markets outside the United States.

The focus was on specific brands and markets. An attempt was made to find out the extent to which the firm had used U.S. advertising for Product X in a single well-developed market in western Europe, usually France, and a single underdeveloped market in the Middle East. The companies tended on the whole to spend a little less in the foreign markets as a percentage of sales than they did in the United States. They seemed to be wary of heavy promotional commitments until they analyzed the market, media, and distribution. Some thought heavy spending in a particular market might upset the applecart and bring retaliatory advertising (perhaps more effective than theirs) from local competitors. Although most firms tended to increase their expenditures both absolutely and as a percentage of sales as they came to know a market, one large food company had moved in the opposite direction. The company had in 1960 advertised extensively in France, but it had experimented with other promotional means as it decreased its advertising budget. In 1964 it was making a satisfactory profit for the first time, depending entirely on sales promotion and good relations with dealers.

The degree of the specific changes that companies made in advertisements seemed to vary somewhat with the type of product advertised. On the one hand were the cosmetics and drug companies, transferring almost intact the U.S. approach. On the other, were the makers of packaged foods, who tended to look at each market almost as a market unto itself. Among cosmetics companies was one which ran a test in England to check the relative effectiveness of having an American woman as the star of the commercial versus an Englishwoman. Somewhat to their surprise, the test indicated that the American woman was definitely superior in communication effectiveness. A major soap company used the U.S. illustrations and copy in the United Kingdom because the campaign had been outstandingly successful in the United States, and limited copy testing in England indicated a favorable reception for the campaign. This step was taken even though the illustration (man or woman in a shower) was not particularly appropriate in a country where shower baths were the exception rather than the rule.

Most food companies made no special effort to use the U.S. advertisements. It should be pointed out, however, that products studied were all packaged or canned, in some cases varying from the U.S. formula. The decision-makers felt generally that food-buying habits and eating were so closely tied with customs and culture that changes in promotion were necessary when a product was transferred from one market to another.

What the competitors were doing affected transferability in a variety of ways. If the competition was very active, several executives thought that heavy advertising and a transfer of U.S. advertising techniques were logical.

Dunn observed that to a social scientist, a country's culture represents the logical starting place for a study of how to communicate effectively in that country. However, "cultural or psychological criteria" were mentioned by only twenty-three executives compared with thirty who mentioned one or more "market criteria." Many executives tended to find cultural concepts too fuzzy for day-to-day use, although they readily admitted that they were probably important. The acceptance of advertising by the people was mentioned by three executives. It was believed that in some countries (e.g., France) the average consumer was at least mildly anti-advertising, and that anything smacking of the American "hard sell" would not work. One respondent believed the subjectivity of a concept was one good measure of its transferability in that the more subjective the concept, the more difficult it was to transfer it effectively to another culture.

The more media available in a country paralleled those in the United States, the more likely the company was to use U.S. advertising. In cases where satisfactory magazine color was not available in a particular market, some companies modified their print advertisement so that they were less dependent on visual impact, more dependent on the copy and headlines.

8. Donnelly made a study to determine the extent to which management believed that advertising programs could be presented without basic modification around the world.[21] Some seventy firms composing a large portion of major U.S. manufacturers of non-durable products with extensive international business were surveyed. The questions concerned the amount of standardized advertising actually being done and the attitudes of the international advertising executives on the subject.

The survey revealed that 90 percent of the firms made at least some use of standardized advertising campaigns or individual advertisements. However, the general pattern was non-standardization. Only 17 percent of the respondents actually used standardized advertising for more than half of their advertising, and some 80 percent of the respondents said that they at least partially rewrote the copy when standardized advertising was used.

The managers were asked to indicate on a ten-point scale the degree of their agreement or disagreement with six quotations from the writings of advocates of the standardized approach. One example was, "Standardized ads can now be readily applied throughout the world because the cultural lag between most nations is minimal." The responses to each question varied somewhat. However, on four of the six questions there was a quite consistent pattern of 60 to 70 percent disagreement. Apparently the majority of international executives were hesitant to accept the basic philosophy underlying standardization.

### Strategy Guidelines
The assortment of environmental information and MNC experience available leads to a few clear guidelines for strategy on marketing management for foreign affiliates. It should be emphasized that

a large portion of this material has been concerned with consumer products associated with intensive marketing efforts. The nature of industrial products and consumer items subject to less intensive marketing efforts will suggest some differences in conclusions.

There is persuasive evidence that a unified strategy based on international standardization of marketing programs is of limited utility. The study by Kapoor and McKay brings out the strong desire of MNC parents to integrate worldwide marketing but the distinctiveness of foreign markets is recognized and the stress in integration is focused on product policy. The diversity of marketing characteristics of host societies discourages application of common methods. Available evidence, for example, in the study of Sorenson and Wiechmann, suggests that the potential efficiencies for MNCs from standardization are modest. Furthermore, there are indications, emphasized in Wright's research in Chile, that standardization may have an adverse effect by decreasing the flexibility and responsiveness of marketing management in relating to local conditions. In general therefore it appears that a fragmented pattern of specific marketing programs of affiliates is sound, though the basis for this conclusion makes it more convincing for consumer goods than for industrial items.

On the other hand, the information at hand suggests that standardization at another level is both feasible and useful. This concept is most explicitly expressed in Sorenson and Wiechmann's support of standardization of the development of marketing programs, but it can be supported by the weight of other evidence. The fundamental points are the obvious facts that (1) marketing is changing substantially in all countries under the influence particularly of economic growth but with substantial influence from structural and value system changes and (2) the MNCs based in the more advanced countries, which have experienced earlier and more advanced evolution of marketing management, have skills that are useful to countries at earlier stages of change.

Since the conclusions on the standardization issue rule out a strategy of broadly exporting parent marketing programs, the approach to capitalizing on the opportunities for skill transmission must shift to the level at which parent know-how is generally functional for affiliate operations. The focus on the generation of marketing programs meets this criterion.

The general guideline for strategy therefore is the objective of developing within the foreign affiliates the fundamental skills of marketing management. They include such basics as the focus on the consumer, analytical decision-making, forward planning, and aggressive pursuit of goals. At a more applied level certain broadly useful approaches may also be widely transmitted: the buying of information to reduce marketing risks, the identification of consumer motivation patterns as the basis for promotion programs, efficiency measurement in consideration of alternative channels of distribution, and others.

Beyond this level the form that marketing skill transmission takes will become progressively more selective and the outcome will become a case-by-case matter. The adverse conclusions on standardization of programs by no means preclude a large amount of direct application in a given affiliate of marketing programs originated at home or in other affiliates. But the functionality of each program must be thoroughly examined on its own merits with reference to the environment of the affiliate. It may also be that global standardization is practical in some respects at an even more specific level than is suggested as general strategy. For example, as Cranch's article indicates, many firms have found it effective to employ basic advertising themes on a worldwide basis with adaptation to local environments only at refined stages of content and translation. For industrial products and consumer items needing less marketing effort, the extent to which standardized programs may be utilized will be greater.

The merits of these strategy guidelines are well illustrated in the General Foods cases. GF had rather mixed success in the direct transfer of parent-generated marketing programs.[22] The main contributions of the parent organization to the success of foreign units lay in the managerial competence promoted by the rigorous planning and the effectiveness of certain basic elements of marketing management (the introduction of product managers and promotional methods in the form of premiums, packaging novelties, etc.). Many specific methods from the home parent were also utilized but only in a permissive system which provided reasonable selectivity to improve the chances of their being appropriate. Information on them was fed to the foreign affiliates by a newsletter and through the continuing communications from home office advisors who regularly reviewed affiliate plans. But the determination of what to use or not use was essentially up to the affiliates.

In the analysis to this point two major strategy considerations have been notable by their absence: national interests and control. The former is ignored because it is unimportant. In notable contrast to the intense interest of host nations in production technology, marketing skills are generally viewed by governments as of modest value for economic progress and of negligible strategic significance to national interests. Home nations have manifested no concern about their transmission abroad.

On the other hand, control does not appear in the literature because it is more or less taken for granted as of major value for transmission of marketing methods. It has not been a focal point in the general control issue with host nations as it has been in production technology. All the arguments put forward in the previous section supporting integrated communication as a means for more effective transmission of production skills are even more pertinent here because marketing skills are deeply imbued with behavioral qualities. As a practical matter it is difficult to contemplate a major program of transmitting marketing skills in a non-integrated relationship, e.g., to licensees.

As it happens, host nations giving low priority to marketing methods have not made a major issue of this subject. The more sophisticated marketing methods are also commonly associated with lower-technology firms in less essential consumer products. This fact has further diverted the control debate away from effect on marketing skill transmission strategy. Despite these favorable factors, there are many cases in which control is an issue for firms to whom marketing skill transmission is important. Because of the low priority given to the marketing skills by host nations, the MNC's interests bear virtually no power on this count. Thus, control rests as a highly desirable component of strategy for marketing management skills but one over which a firm has little strategy choice in this particular respect. That is the degree of control will usually be determined by other considerations, marketing being a minor influence.

The ISAGRIDS in Table 8–5 illustrate variations in strategy for foreign affiliate marketing methods following these guidelines. The main elements of the General Foods strategy have already been outlined and it is a good starting point because marketing is the major element in its overall strategy. Convenience food products requiring intensive marketing efforts are an extreme case of the general proposition that the transmission of marketing skill by MNCs is based on the advanced products and methods of highly industrialized societies. Notable economic differentials in marketing techniques, management methods, and entrepreneurship exist. The critical determinant of strategy is the element of cultural change. The nature of the products and the marketing methods involved are heavily affected by the values and other personal characteristics of the host environment. The other major factors affecting the strategy are both related to the importance of effective communication and action. One is the integrated character of the MNC, which is essential given the complementary character of the various components of marketing (product development, market research, distribution, and promotion). The other is control as a prime requirement for the intimate pattern of communication involved in transmission of the skills. The importance of control can be grasped only from a sense of the detailed processes seen in the GF cases. Finally global unification has some moderate significance in the managerial and technical skill transmission, chiefly through the transfer of know-how acquired in one affiliate to others facilitated by some degree of commonality of approaches.

Marketing is just as important for Singer as for GF but the skill transmission involved is of a quite different nature. The product has been well known all over the world for years, innovations are infrequent compared with GF, and the frequency of purchase is low. Essentially Singer's need is to continually upgrade its marketing programs but at a moderate pace to capitalize on the modest economic differential afforded by its leadership in the field. The essentially utilitarian, rather universal home-economics character of the product minimizes the cultural change effects of the marketing methods and facilitates global unification of methods. The utilization of the basic sewing center system combining distribution and promotion is a notable example of successful global marketing standardization. As with GF, the MNC character and control facilitate the marketing skill transmission but, given its well established basic character and slow rate of change, they are only of moderate importance in this case. The successful use of independent retail organizations is indicative of this fact.

The HTI ISAGRID illustrates the quite different situation of an industrial product in a rapidly developing field. The process of broadening the market and educating customers for a product essentially new to each market calls for strong transmission of skills. Their importance is underscored by the fact that IBM, the prototype of this sort of firm, is recognized to have achieved its leading position as much by marketing competence as by technological success. The position of HTI products in the more modern phases of the industrial sector limits the cultural change effect, though the marketing of any product involving highly innovative management methods will have to deal with resistances to change in the host society. The industrial character of the product and the high degree of commonality of characteristics among business customers should permit a substantial amount of global unification in marketing programs. In this instance, then, the values of control are supported both by the major flow of marketing skills to affiliates and by the feasibility of standardization in methods.

**Table 8–5.  ISAGRID for Affiliate Marketing Management**

| Company | Resources | Strategy Context Variables | | | | National Interests | |
|---|---|---|---|---|---|---|---|
| | | Economic Differentials | MNC Capabilities | Cultural Change | Global Unification | Home | Host |
| High Technology Industries (HTI) | Natural resources | | | | | | |
| | Labor | | | | | | |
| | Capital: Finance | | | | | | |
| | Production | | | | | | |
| | Marketing | | | | | | |
| | Skills: Technological | H | | | H | | |
| | Managerial | Hc | H | M | H | | |
| | Entrepreneurial | H | | | | | |
| Singer | Natural resources | | | | | | |
| | Labor | | | | | | |
| | Capital: Finance | | | | | | |
| | Production | | | | | | |
| | Marketing | | | | | | |

**Singer** *(cont.)*

| | | | | |
|---|---|---|---|---|
| Skills: | | | | |
| Technological | M | | | |
| Managerial | Mc | M | M | H |
| Entrepreneurial | M | | | |
| Natural resources | | | | |
| Labor | | | | |
| Capital: Finance | | | | |
| Production | | | | |
| Marketing | | | | |

**General Foods**

| | | | | |
|---|---|---|---|---|
| Skills: | | | | |
| Technological | H | | H | M |
| Managerial | Hc | H | H | M |
| Entrepreneurial | H | H | H | |

Importance in strategy: H = High; M = Moderate; c = Control of parent MNC significant.

## INDUSTRIAL RELATIONS

The heavy emphasis on transmission of parent skills to foreign affiliates found in production technology and marketing management does not appear in MNC industrial relations strategy. On the other hand, industrial relations issues are substantially influenced by national interest and global unification considerations. As a consequence MNC industrial relations strategy differs markedly from the strategies for other phases of affiliate operating methods.

### Strategy Issues

To analyze MNC industrial relations strategy it is necessary to place in proper perspective the special characteristics in this field of each of the major strategy factors: skill transmission and interaction with the host society, national interests, global unification, and control.

**Skill Transmission and Host Society Interaction.** There is no question but that there are great differences in industrial relations practices among the nations of the world. It will suffice to note such major distinctive features as the lifetime employment system in Japan, the highly developed codetermination in West Germany, and the non-legal force of labor agreements in Britain. Substantively more important than these conspicuous differences is the mass of differences among countries in the main body of industrial relations practices.

But skill transmission analysis starts with the identification of economic differentials between nations. These differences do not signify a comparable magnitude of economic differentials providing opportunities for skill transmission. The true opportunities are limited for reasons of both utility and feasibility. On the utility side, it is by no means certain in many cases whether one nation's industrial practices are better than those of another. Furthermore, in some cases, the ultimate movement may be toward the MNC's parent nation, not from it. For example, the industrial democracy approaches evolving in Europe may eventually be adopted in the United States, but then again they may not as they may not prove functional in the U.S. culture. A more modest but more likely import is the worker control over job design initiated by Volvo in Sweden. In any case, the central point is that by comparison with the widely accepted value of MNC production and marketing methods for foreign use, parent industrial relations practices are useful to only a limited degree abroad.

On the feasibility side, the obstacles to introduction of industrial relations innovations by MNCs are notably greater than for production and marketing changes. At the fundamental level of human resistance to change, industrial relations has a more significant impact than the largely physical character of production processes or even the managerial behavior involved in marketing management. Wage bargaining practices, job security provisions, ways of handling work grievances, and other key aspects of industrial relations strike to the heart of the motivations, satisfactions, and needs of employees. Significant changes in them therefore have a strong impact on feelings and are likely to result in great resistance; though beneficial changes may also be met with highly favorable reaction, of course. The depth of feelings involved come through vividly in the Textile Machinery Company case in which major worker discontent was aroused by a combination of pressures for modernized work methods, a deterioration of the traditional Mexican patron-supervision structure, and an increase in U.S. supervisory personnel all complicated by poor internal management and communications relations.[23]

This fundamental behavioral concern with industrial relations is reinforced, and to a large degree is the basis for structured rigidities supported variously by host society labor union, business, law, and government action. Over time the major components of industrial relations systems have to a large degree become formally established to serve the interests of the various parties involved. The wage negotiation process, the role of unions in handling worker issues in the company, limits on freedom to discharge workers, and other matters therefore are commonly subject to either formal constraints or at least to well established practice supported by powerful bodies of local opinion. An unusual but forceful example of these problems is provided by Ford's 1969 efforts in England to reduce wildcat strikes and subsequently to obtain legal force to support an agreement with union leaders to achieve that goal.[24] Grass roots shop steward resistance, reinforced by court support of the traditional non-legal force of contracts defeated the company effort. It is notable that broad national support for both innovations was demonstrated by the 1971 passage of an Industrial Relations Act giving labor contracts legal force. But even with government backing the innovation failed because of the fundamental resistances and the act was repealed in 1974.

Given these sources of resistance to industrial relations change, the range of real opportunities for innovations by MNCs is limited and the costs and uncertainties may be high. A further deterrent comes from the MNCs' own motivations. Transmission of production and marketing skills has a high priority in MNC strategy because of their major role in product costs and because they are effective in building market position. Innovations in industrial relations may contribute to costs and quality in production but the impact is generally less substantial and immediate. This generalization is confirmed by the relatively slight attention of top management to industrial relations. With the notable exception of major wage negotiations which govern overall costs, most industrial relations matters have a low priority compared to product development, plant investment, and marketing decisions. As far as changes in affiliate operations are concerned, therefore, relatively modest benefit is usually expected from industrial relations innovations which further discourages efforts in the face of the assorted resistances frequently faced.

These varied elements should not be read as a totally negative picture but rather one which poses exacting standards in determination of what innovations are functional and worth the efforts and risks of application. Examination of innovations is further complicated by the MNC industrial relations context, which is commonly clouded by issues of national interest and global strategy.

**National Interests.** The national interest aspects are more relevant to logistic strategy than to industrial relations. However, they are part of the union-government-MNC interaction that is fundamental to industrial relations. Unions may be conceived as agents or spokesmen for national interests with respect to labor just as business firms were identified in Chapter 5 in a similar role on behalf of the nation's business interests. This conceptualization embodies problems because there are clearly points on which the interests of labor may not be those of the nation as a whole. In the present context this is especially true in the issue of protecting domestic jobs against lower-cost imports. But certainly there is political reality in the power and effectiveness of unions in pressing their views. The national interest issues affecting labor inevitably become part of the industrial relations mix of affiliates. Again Ford in Britain provides a notable example: the company's threat to shift operations out of England was a conspicuous element in its 1971 negotiations.[25]

**Global Unification.** These national interest factors interact with the unification aspects of MNC strategy both in the logistic system and in specific aspects of industrial relations. Recently a multinational union effort has emerged which as yet is a minor factor in MNC affairs but contains the potentials for major influence and has therefore to be given serious attention. The multinational union movement centers around eighteen International Trade Secretariats which bring together unions of several nations in major industries.[26] The strongest groups are the metalworkers with eighty unions in 49 countries, and the chemical workers with eighty-six unions in 33 countries as of 1977. The U.S. unions with more members and money are leaders but have tried to avoid dominating the movement. Within the metalworkers, the automotive group established in 1966 has four divisions to deal on a worldwide basis with General Motors, Ford, Chrysler-Fiat-Simca-Rootes, and Volkswagen and Daimler-Benz. The chief accomplishment so far has been to systematically compile and disseminate contract information to members so bargainers in each country will know what agreements the company has elsewhere. The near-term goal of the automotive group is regional harmonization of wages and working conditions. A similar pattern of cooperation was in formation among electrical workers of General Electric and Philips in 1977.

There have been only a few cases of ITS involvement in actual negotiations. In 1969 workers in four countries confronted St. Gobain with coordinated bargaining supported by the chemical ITS. The U.S. union was successful in a strategy based on the global status of the firm. Even though the U.S. subsidiary was unprofitable, it won most of its demands in light of the overall corporate profits.

Another ITS objective is unified contract termination dates. Some unions have suffered from the ability of companies to bring imports in from other countries when plants in one country were struck. The unions would like to be able to shut down a company's entire global operations at one time.

Despite the progress to date, the movement faces major obstacles. Fundamentally, U.S. unions have been most concerned by growth of imports from low-wage countries. They would like to stop companies from setting up foreign facilities to serve U.S. markets at the expense of U.S. production. But this objective is directly in conflict with the interests of foreign workers who benefit from growth of production and exports in their countries. While they are sympathetic to a degree with U.S. labor efforts to see foreign wages pushed up to U.S. levels, they realistically see that this could hurt their objectives. Thus, for example, Mexican unions have made no real effort to support the position of the U.S. unions in trying to force up the wages in the U.S.–owned plants in Mexico's northern border zone. A further deterrent to cooperation lies in the political orientation of many foreign unions, notably those run by communists.

Because of these deterrents, progress will be slow. It will be seen chiefly in exchange of information, but potentials exist for more global financial support for strikes, some regional harmonization of wages, more use of the global financial position of the firm in bargaining demands, and possibly some global coordination of strikes.

**Control.** While control was important in production and marketing strategies because of its importance for effective skill transmission, with industrial relations the emphasis shifts to factors of national interests and global strategy. Labor circles in host societies are concerned over the capacity of the parent MNC to make decisions both over working conditions in affiliates and over the allocation of production, which determines the amount of employment in their countries. They are highly sensitive to the weakening of labor's status as compared with its status vis-à-vis purely domestic firms upon which it can exert power directly and through government channels. As a consequence labor has a general bias in favor of limiting the power and control of MNCs whether by opposing them directly by advocating limits on their ownership or indirectly through governmental constraints or the evolution of the multinational union system. For the MNCs the issue is seen in reverse so they benefit from retention of control. However, except with respect to logistic decisions which have already been discussed in Chapter 7, control does not appear to be a major issue in industrial relations strategy. With the introduction of innovations a low priority goal and the probability of common interest with local partners on wages and other issues, joint ventures or even licensing in this respect do not pose serious problems. On the other hand, the skill of a local associate in handling the distinctive and often complex character of labor relations in the host society may be of great value.

To summarize, global MNC industrial strategy revolves around the intermixed issues of the extent to which managerial innovations should be pursued and standardized among countries, the quest for a balance among home and host nation corporate interests, and the cost and service capabilities of the logistic system. The multinational union movement remains in the background, an as yet nebulous but potentially important factor.

### MNC Experience

Studies of MNC experience with overseas industrial relations are not plentiful but they do cover the main elements of strategy. It is significant that despite much literature on the general subject of labor relations in various countries, there is very little research bearing on experience with innovations by U.S. firms. The broadest assessment with reasonable authority on this subject is provided by a report of a 1974 conference at Michigan State University which included a highly qualified group of international academic, business, and labor experts.[27] The report observed that the general picture was one of conformity to local ways. Observations about adoption of U.S. union methods abroad led to the conclusion that they were the result of communication among unions, not MNC influence. The general view of most conference participants was that the overall impact of MNCs on industrial relations practices in industrialized nations had been small, that adaptation to local and national norms was more characteristic than aggressive innovation and change, and that the more experience an MNC gained in overseas operations, the less inclined it was to try to force home office policies and practices upon host country management.

1. Kujawa's study of labor management in the international operations of Chrysler, Ford, and General Motors presented a somewhat different view along with information on other aspects of industrial relations experience.[28] His observations were largely concerned with the relative roles of the parent and foreign managers with aspects of labor relations as illustrations of management processes.

The author's point of departure was that labor problems could be bigger for the multinational firm than for its domestic counterpart and they were even more probable. The size of the problems stemmed largely from the logistic integration of foreign units. The production cutbacks in other Ford European plants caused by the 1969 strike in England were cited as an example. There were two causes for the frequency: (1) the presence of expatriate management in decision-making areas affecting workers and working patterns, and (2) the ability and practice of the MNC to continually upgrade production and process technology. The research revealed considerable resentment over foreign control of work methods and other matters affecting the workers. This was given impetus by the emphasis on steadily improving productivity by introducing labor-saving methods.

The author firmly rejected the often-stated implication of these feelings that labor affairs should be the exclusive domain of subsidiary management. He concurred that subsidiary management would normally have superior local know-how and that local national executives should be the primary labor managers for psychological reasons. But he rejected the "exclusive domain" concept because it assumed that local nationals possessed adequate technical and managerial expertise to be successful in their endeavors. This he felt was not always the case.

He argued for a combination of local know-how and general labor management competence contributed by parent executives. In support of his proposal he cited errors made by the autonomous UK Ford labor management which contributed to the 1969 trouble and a successful joint effort of GM's West German and parent managers in the 1966–67 recession to support his philosophy. Some specific suggestions for bringing parent management skill to foreign units were made. These included modernization of foreign unit labor relations systems such as Chrysler and GM had undertaken and regional conferences of subsidiary executives. Kujawa also proposed more effective reporting of foreign labor conditions to the parent so its advice could be improved. Specifically he was critical of limited reporting of trade association labor negotiations and work council activities found among the auto companies.

2. The intermixture of national interests, global strategy and managerial innovations has been brought out in two country-oriented studies. In the first, Gennard described the attitudes of organized British labor toward the effects on them of multinational firms.[29]

The key attitudes of the labor people fell under six main headings:

- Job security. The union argument ran as follows: Operating on a global scale means company operations can be transferred from one country to another, from high wage to low wage areas and from countries with "unsatisfactory" labor relations to those with more "satisfactory" ones. The author noted that in fact British unions had experienced little runaway industry. But the job security worry persisted nonetheless.

- Superior bargaining power. The global scale of operations was also seen as giving a bargaining advantage in that firms might draw on sources in other countries to offset output losses when British plants were struck. The use of this tactic by Goodyear was cited. In its long 1971 strike, however, Ford apparently did not use it.

- Conflicts with national interest. In like vein it was feared that the power of the MNCs applied in bargaining with the British government would result in arrangements adverse to unions. A threat by Ford in 1965 to move its R&D to West Germany if it was not given freedom of choice in locating the facility was mentioned as an example.

- Source of decisions. The unions found it more difficult to bargain with MNCs because some key decisions were made in the parent organization by people with whom they could not communicate readily.

- Union recognition. Probably the most strongly expressed union feeling was that MNCs were less willing then domestic firms to recognize unions. On the basis of available data the author observed that non-recognition problems with foreign firms were perhaps exaggerated. The visibility of the issue seemed to stem from the fact that the foreign firms that did not recognize unions were often large and affluent (e.g., IBM and Kodak) while among British firms the practice was typical of small, weak firms.
- Management practices. Under this heading fell the interrelated matters of handling labor and production management. In both respects foreign firms had often departed from British practice. Many of them preferred to bargain on a company basis rather than through industry associations. The major reason appeared to be the desire for autonomy in industrial relations, so that managements could take initiatives in the introduction of innovation into labor-management relations. Some of these innovations had been beneficial to labor (e.g., the 1962 introduction of a wage rise tied to increased productivity by Esso) while others had been resisted (notably, the efforts by Ford and others to make labor agreements legally binding).

The author also looked at wage and strike experience. While popular opinion held that foreign firms paid better than British firms, he found that the facts did not justify generalization, the situation varying from industry to industry. Some highly publicized strikes had led people to believe that foreign firms were more strike-prone. The data here showed that for each dimension of strikes, viz. frequency, workers involved, and man-days lost, the foreign firm was less strike-prone than the domestic company. Gennard observed that one reason for the better experience was that company procedures in the U.S. subsidiaries tended to be speedier and thus lessened frustration and the need for workers to take unconstitutional action.

On balance it appeared from the study that in actual benefits to workers the foreign firms had been a positive factor in Britain but that unions had not benefited and might even have lost ground. The response of labor reflected this assessment. The major concern of the unions seemed to be with achieving stronger power in relation to the firms. Toward this end they had exerted pressure on the British government to take legislative or administrative action. The major thrust had been on getting the government to require that foreign firms recognize unions. The author noted that not much could be expected in this regard, because if the government were to impose too many restrictions on foreign companies, the MNCs might prefer to invest elsewhere, and the country would lose the benefits such companies brought.

A second concern of the unions was to improve the quality of labor negotiations by getting more information and better planning. Progress had been made in this direction but the author doubted that these were major power gains. Thus, much interest centered on the third approach, the development of the multinational trade union. The capacity to bargain with the same global control as the firm had was seen as the logical way to meet the power of the latter. Gennard noted some achievements along this line but he also observed assorted problems ranging from ideological differences among union movements of various countries to wage differentials which would be major deterrents.

3. In the second country-oriented study, Bomers reported the results of a survey in West Germany and the Netherlands of business and labor views of the impact of MNCs on industrial relations.[30] He made ninety-one in-depth interviews including twenty-five labor leaders, fifteen government officials, four outsiders and forty-seven industrial relations executives. The business sample encompassed MNCs based in Germany and the Netherlands and local subsidiaries of foreign (mainly U.S.) MNCs and was limited to three industries (metalworking, chemicals, and food processing) in which multinational union efforts were active.

Both union and employer responses rated the unilateral, transnational decision-making system of MNCs as the major concern of labor, followed closely by their "lack of transparency" or "elusiveness," particularly in their decision-making processes and financial policies. The production allocation capabilities of MNCs and the issue of exporting jobs came through as significant sources of adverse union feelings. However, Bomers noted that there were major deterrents to substantial shifts of production out of Europe because of views of the public, labor, and governments, and the survey turned up no significant actual shifts. The real "job export" problem lay with uninational firms in labor-intensive industries (textiles and leather) which had simply closed up shop in Europe and started anew in cheap labor countries. The survey revealed, however, that the unions were not basically adverse to this process, since it contributed to a more rationalized international division of labor with an upgrading of the quality of work at home. They desired only that it take place in an orderly, planned fashion. The author did emphasize, however, the low unemployment in Europe and the possibility that the union views might change as unemployment rose. The union leaders did not consider that the greater financial strength of MNCs gave them any special advantage in collective bargaining, a view related to the fact that bargaining in these countries was typically on an industry basis, not company one.

The union people generally thought of MNC industrial relations policy-making as more centralized than did the employers, especially in U.S. firms. The reactions to centralization were mixed. For example, union respondents in the Netherlands frequently indicated their intentions of getting home-based MNCs to centralize industrial relations policy-making, so that "superior" industrial relations standards might spread to less-advantaged countries. The implication was that union respondents wanted it both ways: centralized industrial relations policy-making in home-based MNCs and decentralized industrial relations policy-making for foreign-based MNCs. Centralization was a contributing factor in "non-transparency" of decision-making processes, a major source of suspicion and distrust. The way industrial relations policies were determined, the basis for financial results, and the use of manipulative transfer pricing were cited particularly. Union leaders believed that the latter was common, though employers claimed the opposite and cited major constraints to support their position.

Both union and employer respondents came out clearly against greater national control of MNCs. In part this related to the union support of the general economic role of MNCs as international integrating institutions but it also had practical logic. It was noted that regulation at the national level was apt to worsen the non-transparency problem, whose fundamental cause lay in the incongruence of national legal, accounting, and tax systems. National regulation would tend to increase that incongruence. Furthermore, greater national control would decrease the chance for regional (EEC) control which unions strongly favor along with the prospect of European-wide codetermination rules.

The codetermination objective was strongly and universally advocated by the West German unions which were fully committed to "social partnership" with private enterprise. The Dutch unions had mixed views; some were committed to a fundamental change, seeking a socialist society based on workers' democracy. Employers also tended to favor EEC-wide approaches. They felt EEC codetermination would inhibit further differentiating developments in industrial democracy within the Community and that in general such regulation would give MNCs a degree of legal protection from national regulatory action. International regulation was favorably viewed by unions but regarded as an unrealistic prospect.

Building an international union counterforce against MNCs was supported by unions and opposed by employers. The international information and consultation work of the International Trade Secretariats was recognized as currently strong and maturing rapidly. However, the majority of both unions and employers anticipated that international bargaining or full collective bargaining would not come for at least twelve years and perhaps never. Major deterrents to collective bargaining as well as to union influence on MNC production allocation decisions were cited both in the diversity of national union goals and practices and the views of national governments. The governments would often see overriding general national interests conflicting with the goals of multinational union efforts.

4. Another perspective on host nation attitudes toward labor management of MNCs is provided by the responses to three questions in my survey of elites in Britain, Canada, and France cited in Chapter 4 (p. 141). The data in Table 8−6 indicate some distinct differences in the image of various aspects of the labor relations of foreign firms. The responses to Question A affirmed the generally observed

### Table 8−6. Attitudes of Elites toward Labor Relations

How do you believe the treatment of workers by foreign companies in X compares with that by X firms in respect to wages and other working conditions (job security, handling of grievances, etc.)?

Q. A.  Wages: Foreign firms  Better = 1; Worse = 7

Q. B.  Other Conditions: Better = 1; Worse = 7

Q. C.  Do you believe that foreign companies in X are more *or* less willing to recognize trade unions than X firms are? More willing = 1; Less willing = 7.

Leg = National legislators;  PG = Permanent government officials;  Lab = Labor union leaders;  and Bus = Heads of business firms

|        |      | *Leg* | *PG* | *Lab* | *Bus* | *Aver* |
|--------|------|-------|------|-------|-------|--------|
| Q. A.  | Br.  | 2.6   | 3.3  | 3.5   | 2.8   | 3.1    |
|        | Fr.  | 2.9   | 2.7  | 3.2   | 3.1   | 3.0    |
|        | Can. | 3.3   | 3.4  | 3.3   | 3.3   | 3.3    |
| Q. B.  | Br.  | 3.5   | 3.8  | 4.5   | 3.6   | 3.8    |
|        | Fr.  | 3.8   | 3.5  | 4.8   | 3.8   | 4.0    |
|        | Can. | 3.7   | 3.8  | 3.6   | 3.5   | 3.6    |
| Q. C.  | Br.  | 4.9   | 4.3  | 5.6   | 4.3   | 4.7    |
|        | Fr.  | 3.8   | 3.6  | 5.0   | 4.0   | 4.1    |
|        | Can. | 3.3   | 3.4  | 3.4   | 3.1   | 3.3    |

Source: John Fayerweather, "Elite Attitudes toward Multinational Firms," *International Studies Quarterly*, Dec. 1972.

view that foreign firms pay higher wages than local firms. When it came to other working conditions like job security and handling of grievances (Question B), however, the weight of opinion shifted toward a less favorable image overall and a distinctly negative one with the British and French union leaders.

On the third point, union relations (Question C), the results presented a mixed picture. While the questions were not quite comparable, the data confirm a general impression that in France there was not the same intensity of struggle between unions and foreign firms as in Britain. In Canada, the situation was clearly quite different. It was notable that not only were the scores generally lower (less struggle), but the union leaders themselves rated the foreign firms as more tractable than domestic companies.

5. A report by Roberts and May dealt with the multinational union question by presenting the results of a survey of thirty-two British multinational corporations with comparisons of their responses to a survey by Blake of U.S. MNCs.[31] The majority of the companies indicated that labor relations were essentially delegated to their foreign units, eight firms declining to complete the questionnaire for that reason. The parent headquarters was involved to the extent of frequently giving policy advice in 23 percent of the cases and approving changes in pensions or other terms in 46 percent. On direct negotiation matters, however, only one firm had frequent involvement. The degree of involvement was less among those British firms with many foreign units, a finding in contrast to Blake's survey which showed that involvement increased with greater international spread. The authors suggested the difference might be related to the greater emphasis among U.S. vs British firms on tight financial control from headquarters and less sense among the British of company industrial relations policy as they negotiated more through employer associations.

The overall assessment from questions on the prospects of international unionism was one of scepticism as to the capability of unions to organize at this level, and of hostility to the idea of transnational negotiations and agreements. In the opinion of management every country was so very different as to make nonsense of transnational industrial relations policies. The companies were asked about the time periods within which trade union cooperative efforts might develop. In 10 percent of the cases labor councils were already established on an international basis but none of the firms had given them any recognition. The majority of the firms did not anticipate such councils sooner than five years. Stronger transnational action including coordinated collective bargaining was not expected to develop by the majority until the mid-1980s. These time expectations of the British firms were longer than those of U.S. firms in Blake's survey. In both surveys the chemical companies expected pressure in a relatively short time. The U.S. engineering firms (autos, etc.), however, expected international action much sooner than their British counterparts. In both countries it was the more international enterprises that anticipated multinational union pressure soonest.

The responses showed that the managements were more concerned with demonstrations of solidarity than with other international union efforts. A substantial majority felt that transnational solidarity actions such as strikes, overtime bans, and blacklisting of companies by unions could be very harmful. Apart from the disruptive effects of widening the scale of conflict, the upward pressure this could exert on wage levels and employment conditions could considerably alter the rationale of the MNC's distribution and scale of operations. The result of this type of pressure might be especially adverse to the industrially less advanced and less efficient countries.

A substantial portion of the managements indicated that they would resist cooperative union efforts. However, the number of firms that would resist such union efforts was significantly lower than the number suggesting that such actions would prove harmful. It was also noted that the engineering and chemical concerns were those most inclined to resist and that U.S. firms showed overall a greater inclination in that direction. The authors attributed the British attitudes to their genuine belief that the unions were not likely to be able to pose any serious threat to their commercial interests through international action in the near future. The doubts about serious problems were also manifest in the fact that over two-thirds of the companies had made no systematic studies of the impact of international unions and some firms had not even informed themselves on international union developments.

Looking to the future, the authors concluded that everything would depend on the ability of the unions to organize effectively. The barriers were not insuperable, but the task was considerable. The value of government support was noted. In this connection the 1971 British Industrial Relations Act limited the right of British unions to strike to support unions in other countries while the subsequent Labor government's Trade Unions and Labour Relations Act permitted such action. Nonetheless, the authors felt that it was difficult to see how differences could be effectively reconciled between countries that had extremely wide differences in labor costs and levels of economic development. Effective transnational mutuality of support was likely to be achieved only when the common interest was obvious and immediate.

## Strategy Guidelines

Thinking about industrial relations strategy for foreign affiliates must start from the understanding that action in this area has to be subordinate to other major considerations:

- Transmission of production technology skills. The effectiveness of innovative technological efforts is facilitated by industrial relations that assure a competent and receptive work force.
- Logistic strategy. The ability of an MNC to shift production globally is a significant source of dissatisfaction in relations with labor but, to the extent that important economic advantage is available through logistic shifts, they take priority over industrial relations goals because of their critical effect on competitive status.
- Control. Centralized decision-making is another prime source of labor concern with MNCs. But strategy here also must be determined by more critical criteria such as effect on skill transmission, logistic system, and financial flows. Industrial relations consequences are a lesser concern.

Three other underlying elements are additional key factors in strategy formulation.

The first is the inevitability of conflict with labor, especially labor unions. There is an inherent conflict in the interests of labor and management in the division of economic benefits of production which provides the basic raison d'être for the union movement. Unions represent a powerful force to propagate the conflict because it is the prime source of their existence and support. The direction and intensity of labor conflict with MNCs may vary greatly depending upon a number of variables including their industrial relations policies. But the existence of some degree of conflict is inevitable and even substantial conflict may be tolerable if it is a necessary consequence of higher priority goals.

The second key factor is the prominence of images that are often inaccurate in labor attitudes. This is a striking feature of all the attitude studies summarized in the preceding section. In such important matters as export of jobs, wage levels, and parent MNC control, host nationals seem very commonly to have perceptions of MNC actions affecting labor which are quite different from reality, usually on the unfavorable side.

The third key factor in strategy formulation is the major political power of labor. On many economic issues business and labor are the main protagonists and consumers a weakly represented third party. In every country maintaining a private enterprise system some sort of balance evolves among those forces which permits business to function. For the most part MNCs simply adhere to the system, allowing the main pattern of the balance to emerge from interaction of host national business and labor groups. But when it comes to the special problems of MNC operation—control of logistic systems, financial flows, and the like—the host national business community has limited and often opposing interests. Thus, where labor groups have positions vs MNCs their vastly greater local political power is a major factor with which the firms must contend.

In light of all the observations and experience accumulated to this point, it appears that the primary tool of industrial relations strategy for foreign affiliates should be the maintenance of satisfactory continuity and quality of production with a reasonably satisfied workforce. By implication this goal runs counter to two other options. First, a highly innovative industrial relations approach is discouraged because of the risks it entails of worker dissatisfaction and disruptive resistance to change. Second, it is opposed to a highly competitive posture in which management presses hard for economic advantage vis-à-vis labor, because of the political risks and delays in production that such an approach may cause. The innovative and competitive goal sets are not to be completely discarded but, given the total mix of MNC goals and environmental context, it seems wise to place them in a secondary status.

Specific strategy guidelines flow readily from these conclusions about goals. First, conformity should be the dominant mode in determining industrial relations approaches, as appears to be the reality of most MNC experience. This guideline does not preclude innovation and transmission of industrial relations skills. In fact, the diversity of industrial relations practice in most countries necessitates decisions that have an innovative thrust. Typically, there is a range among host national businesses running from traditional to quite progressive management of industrial relations. The progressive relations commonly contain new practices that to some degree are related to practices in other countries. Thus an MNC following a general "conformity" strategy may position itself to good effect as a member of the progressive wing of host national business. In that position it can engage in a degree of skill transmission bringing in new practices to upgrade its operations but in a context supported by progressive businessmen of the host nation and, hopefully, in many instances by labor.

Second, acceptance of a high degree of fragmentation is an inevitable consequence of the general thrust toward conformity along with the great diversity of industrial systems of the host nation. A modest effort in the direction of unification is, however, encouraged by the gradual development of the multinational union movement. At a minimum it is apparent that MNCs can expect an expansion of the exchange of information among unions already experienced in a few industries. Thus, the MNC within its own worldwide industrial relations system must have a full exchange of information. Some commonality of positions among foreign affiliates will often be desirable as well, especially in close-knit areas like EEC.

Third, the first two guidelines suggest only a modest need for parent control in industrial relations strategy. The objective of minimizing adverse labor attitudes further supports limitations of control. As a practical matter this objective is difficult to achieve because of the necessity for exercising control in critical decision areas like location of production. However, within the industrial relations area itself a deliberate effort to *visibly* vest control in the affiliate management can be productive. For example, much can be done to avoid the prime source of host nation criticism, the situation in which the local management in the midst of a negotiation says it must refer the issue to headquarters because a policy question is involved. A strategy of consistent prior provision of policy guidelines, quick phone consultations which need not be advertised to the unions, and other devices to provide necessary parent input without aggravating the external control issue are worthwhile alternatives.

ISAGRIDS for industrial relations strategy for our three sample companies are given in Table 8—7. For all three, moderate opportunities to transmit industrial relations managerial skills exist subject to questions of cultural suitability. The operations of the companies in this respect are not likely to present distinctly different opportunities.

Beyond this general pattern General Foods presents the simplest situation. Having no significant concern with either transmission of labor resources or a globally unified logistic system, GF has no need to consider other factors in its industrial relations, so strategy in this respect is not a particular concern. The minor problems experienced in GF's Italian factory compared to the serious problems in other phases of its operations are indicative of this fact. In these circumstances GF is relatively free to attempt skill transmission innovations without concern for their effects on other aspects of strategy. But in the interests of harmonious production operations, it is moderate in its efforts.

HTI has a somewhat more complex situation because of three factors: (1) its operations require the introduction of high technology production skills so maintenance of a high quality, cooperative work force is essential; (2) it utilizes plants in low-wage countries

**Table 8–7. ISAGRID for Affiliate Industrial Relations**

| Company | Resources | Strategy Context Variables | | | | National Interests | |
|---|---|---|---|---|---|---|---|
| | | Economic Differentials | MNC Capabilities | Cultural Change | Global Unification | Home | Host |
| High Technology Industries (HTI) | Natural resources | | | | | | |
| | Labor | M | | | M | | M |
| | Capital: Finance | | | | | | |
| | Production | M | | | M | | M |
| | Marketing | | | | | | |
| | Skills: Technological | M | | M | | | |
| | Managerial | M | | M | | | |
| | Entrepreneurial | | | | | | |
| Singer | Natural resources | | | | | | |
| | Labor | H | | | H | | H |
| | Capital: Finance | | | | | | |
| | Production | H | | | Hc | | |
| | Marketing | | | | | | |

General Foods

| | | M |
|---|---|---|
| Skills: | | |
| Technological | | |
| Managerial | M | |
| Entrepreneurial | | |
| Natural resources | | |
| Labor | | |
| Capital: | | |
| Finance | | |
| Production | | |
| Marketing | | |
| Skills: | | |
| Technological | | M |
| Managerial | M | |
| Entrepreneurial | | |

Importance in strategy: H = High; M = Moderate; c = Control of parent MNC significant.

for some labor-intensive work; and (3) it has a moderately rationalized logistic system with production allocated within major regions to large specialized plants. The latter two factors, combined with the general high visibility of the company, have led to substantial host nation attention to HTI labor policies. In these circumstances the firm's industrial relations policy should combine an attempt to be progressive to attract good workers while still maintaining a low profile to avoid aggravating adverse feelings.

Singer's situation parallels that of HTI to a large degree, but the importance of labor resource transmission and a few major exporting plants in the global logistic system magnify the effect of labor and unification considerations and consequent concern of the host nation. The critical importance of labor conditions in the Italian and Scottish plants is indicative of this weighting. On this basis a distinction has also been noted between HTI and Singer in the moderate importance of control for industrial relations strategy of the latter. A sharp distinction here is probably misleading but thinking in terms of the evolution of multinational unions, Singer with its few major exporting plants and emphasis on wage-cost differentials, is a likely prospect for cross-border union collaboration. For this reason, as well as the general importance of cross-fertilization of industrial relations management among affiliates, considerable parent control is justified. Much the same would be true of HTI but to a somewhat lesser degree and HTI, because of its high general visibility, might be more willing to forego pressing control in this area if that facilitated relations with labor and governments in host nations.

## NOTES

1. Wickham Skinner, *American Industry in Developing Economies* (New York: John Wiley & Sons, 1968).

2. Louis T. Wells, Jr., "Don't Overautomate Your Foreign Plant," *Harvard Business Review*, Jan.–Feb. 1974, pp. 111–118.

3. Samuel A. Morley and Gordon W. Smith, "The Choice of Technology," *Economic Development and Cultural Change*, Jan. 1977, pp. 239–264.

4. D.J. Teece, "Technology Transfer by Multinational Firms," *The Economic Journal*, June 1977, pp. 242–261.

5. Jack N. Behrman and Harvey W. Wallender, *Transfers of Manufacturing Technology within Multinational Enterprises* (Cambridge, Mass.: Ballinger Publishing Company, 1976).

6. Ashok Kapoor, "Foreign Collaborations in India," *The Patent, Trademark and Copyright Journal of Research and Education*, Summer 1966, pp. 213–258 and Fall 1966, pp. 349–389.

7. Wayne G. Broehl, Jr., *The International Basic Economy Corporation* (Washington: National Planning Association, 1968).

8. Jack Baranson, *Manufacturing Problems in India* (Syracuse, N.Y.: Syracuse University Press, 1967).

9. John Fayerweather, *International Marketing* (Englewood Cliffs, N.J.: Prentice-Hall, 1970) and Warren Keegan, *Multinational Marketing Management* (Englewood Cliffs, N.J.: Prentice-Hall, 1974).

10. Richard H. Holton, "Marketing Policies in Multinational Companies," *California Management Review*, Summer 1971, pp. 57–67.

11. John Fayerweather and Ashok Kapoor, *Strategy and Negotiations for the International Corporation* (Cambridge, Mass.: Ballinger Publishing Company, 1975), pp. 241–270 and 437–465.

12. Robert Bartels, ed., *Comparative Marketing* (Homewood, Ill.: Richard D. Irwin, 1963).

13. Susan P. Douglas, "Patterns and Parallels of Marketing Structures," *MSU Business Topics*, Spring 1971, pp. 38–46.

14. George Katona, Burkhard Strumpel, and Ernest Zahn, *Aspirations and Affluence* (New York: McGraw-Hill, 1976).

15. Hans B. Thorelli, Helmut Becker, and Jack Engledow, *The Information Seekers* (Cambridge, Mass.: Ballinger Publishing Company, 1975).

16. Robert T. Green and Eric Langeard, "The Cross-National Comparison of Consumer Habits and Innovator Characteristics," *Journal of Marketing*, July 1975, pp. 34–41.

17. Ashok Kapoor and Robert McKay, *Managing International Markets* (Princeton, N.J.: Darwin, 1971).

18. Vern Terpstra, Michael Y. Yoshino, and A.F. Sherbini, *Comparative Analysis for International Marketing* (Boston, Mass.: Allyn and Bacon, 1967).

19. A. Greame Cranch, "The Changing Faces of International Advertising," *The International Advertiser*, Spring 1972, pp. 4–6.

20. S. Watson Dunn, "The Case Study Approach in Cross Cultural Research," *Journal of Marketing Research*, Feb. 1966, pp. 26–31.

21. James H. Donnelly, Jr., "Standardized Global Marketing," *Journal of Marketing*, April 1967, pp. 57–60.

22. Fayerweather and Kapoor, op. cit., pp. 437–465.

23. Ibid., 363–368.

24. Ibid., pp. 339–362.

25. Ibid., p. 345.

26. Richard L. Barovick, "Labor Reacts to Multinationalism," *Columbia Journal of World Business*, July–Aug., 1970, pp. 40–46.

27. Robert F. Banks and Jack Stieber, eds., *Multinationals, Unions, and Labor Relations in Industrialized Countries* (Ithaca, N.Y.: N.Y. State School of Industrial & Labor Relations, Cornell University, 1977).

28. Duane Kujawa, "Planning a Global Labor Strategy," *Worldwide P & I Planning*, Mar.–Apr. 1971, pp. 38–49.

29. John Gennard, *Multinational Corporations and British Labour* (Washington, D.C.: British–North American Committee, 1972).

30. Gerard B.J. Bomers, *Multinational Corporations and Industrial Relations* (Assen, the Netherlands: Van Gorom & Co., 1976).

31. B.C. Roberts and Jonathan May, "The Response of Multinational Enterprises to International Trade Union Pressures," *British Journal of Industrial Relations*, Nov. 1974, pp. 403–416.

✳ *Chapter 9*

# Financial Flow System

The pattern of monetary flows within a multinational corporation may be viewed as a secondary system within a primary system. The basic character of the MNC activities is determined by the product delivery system governed by market requirements. The interrelated strategies of that system—research and development, product policy, logistics, and affiliate production and marketing—establish the main determinants of the financial system—the capital needs and the income sources. The pattern of monetary flow then evolves as a variety of options appear for optimizing financial results within the limits set by the product delivery system.

This subordinate, yet independent character of the financial flow system is notably confirmed in the comprehensive study of MNC finance by Robbins and Stobaugh which will be cited frequently in this chapter.[1] At the start of the book, the authors briefly note that market factors are the primary determinants of foreign investments. Throughout the book, however, these factors are scarcely mentioned again and the authors' explanation of the varied monetary flow options employed is based almost entirely on financial reasoning in response to capital market, foreign exchange, tax, and other monetary conditions. Thus, the area of strategy discussed in this chapter is something of a separate entity subordinate to the primary aspects of strategy. But it is an important one nonetheless because the options open to management offer substantial opportunities for increasing the profitability of international operations.

## STRATEGY ISSUES

The strategy analysis for MNC financial flow systems will be most heavily oriented toward unification–fragmentation issues. The greatest potentials for profit optimization lie in an assortment of options requiring unified planning, but there are significant managerial and environmental factors working in the direction of a fragmented system of financial management. National interests and government relations constitute a large portion of them. Capital resource transmission capabilities based on economic differentials figure prominently in the analysis but are often blended closely with the unification–fragmentation issues.

Interactions with host societies do not significantly affect financial flows, since MNC money flows per se have very little cultural impact. Financial management practices do have considerable cultural implications as was evident in the Canton case described in Chapter 3 (p. 102). However, the managerial aspects are not analyzed in this chapter as they raise essentially the same issues as the affiliate marketing management practices discussed in Chapter 8. The one notable difference lies in the effect of divided control. Innovations in marketing management methods are often impeded by the presence of joint venture partners but, more because of established practices and inertia than personal interest. In financial matters, however, the partners frequently have a significant personal stake, as was true with Mr. Baba in the Canton case. Therefore, while the analysis in Chapter 8 is in general approach equally applicable to financial management, the element of control must be noted as of much greater importance.

The essence of the financial flow strategy is a combination of capital and income mechanisms by which the MNC seeks to optimize profit for the parent-affiliate system as a whole. The main options available for the strategy are outlined in Table 9–1. The capital and income sets are analyzed as separate groups later in this section considering the advantages of each over the others. However, in the ultimate determination of strategy, the separate analyses must be blended because most of the capital and income options are related as shown by the lines. Equity capital leads to dividend income, various forms of loans call for interest income, and transfer prices are a factor in accounts receivable. Only royalty payments and management fees are independent of the capital structure.

The analysis of financial flow strategy is most readily understood through comparing directly the various options open to MNCs. However, as a basis for that approach, it is helpful first to outline the

Table 9—1. Financial Flow System Options

| *Financing for Affiliates* | *Income Flows from Affiliates* |
|---|---|
| Equity: Parent——————————— | Dividends |
| Local | |
| Loans by parent | |
| by other affiliates ——————— | Interest |
| from local sources | |
| Accounts receivable ——————— | Transfer prices |
| | Royalties |
| | Management fees |

main factors influencing the choice among the options: the elements that provide the opportunities for gain in the choice of options and various limiting considerations.

### Motivating Variables

The determination of the optimum combination of options revolves largely around three main variables: interest rates, foreign exchange, and taxation. Table 9—2 lists data from several countries for these variables, along with cost of living data which are a key factor in considering interest and foreign exchange rates. The *interest rates* shown are just one indicator of the array of differences among various forms of debt. The differences among countries are the result of a number of capital market influences, notably the supply of money, general risk conditions, inflation, and government monetary policies. In general, interest rates are lowest in the advanced countries where capital is relatively plentiful, in the more stable environments, in economies with low rates of inflation, and in countries where the governments are pursuing expansive monetary policies. The MNC may benefit from obtaining funds in such countries at low rates and transmitting them for use in countries where rates are higher because capital is less plentiful or because they are driven up by political instability, rapid inflation or tight monetary policies. In undertaking this sort of financial flow, the MNC is, of course, performing a sound resource transmission. The interest rate differentials are basically an indicator of economic differentials in the supply—demand relationship of capital. A number of other institutions including banks, private investors, and governmental aid organizations are major factors in financial capital resource transmission. Thus the MNC does not have the same sort of exceptional capability in this area as it does in skill transmission. But it does have a special opportunity-determined

**Table 9–2.  Selected Data on Motivational Variables for Financial Flow Strategy**

| | Prime Bank Interest Rate 1976 | Increase in Cost of Living 1967-1976 | Change in Exchange Rate 1967 to 1976 National Currency in U.S. Dollars | Basic Corporate Income Tax (top bracket) 1976 |
|---|---|---|---|---|
| United States | 6.8% | 78.3% | | 48% |
| United Kingdom | 11.1 | 101.8 | −34% | 52% |
| Italy | 15 | 87.1 | −25 | 25 |
| Brazil | 30 | 250.4 | −77 | 30 |
| Peru | 19.5 | 104.4 (1967–1975) | −33 | 55 |
| Japan | 8.3 | 90 | +26 | 40 |
| India | 14 | 69.7 | −15 | 63 |

Sources: Organization For Economic Cooperation and Development, *Main Economic Indicators*, 1976; Price, Waterhouse, *Doing Business in United Kingdom, . . . Italy*, etc. various 1972-76; and U.S. Department of Commerce, *Foreign Economic Trends* [for each country], 1977.

capability in its control over its own investment processes. Thus, to the extent that it is useful for these processes, it may effectively exploit the existing capital resource differentials.

The significance of the *foreign exchange rate* changes as a variable lies in its effect on completion of transactions and conversion of accounts. International business transactions for the sale of goods or other purposes necessarily involve two currencies, those of the party paying and of the party receiving payment. Intermediaries may be brought in to handle the cross-currency aspect of the transaction, but for the main body of commercial transactions one or the other of the principals agrees to accept or make payment in the currency of the other principal. (Even when intermediaries are involved the principals will have to carry in some way much of the cost of the currency risk.)

In the ongoing flow of business, export, import, and other transactions are constantly being undertaken by an MNC, basing terms on regular commercial considerations such as production costs and market prices. The transactions typically involve a time span including both a period for completion of the performance and for payment, e.g., an export shipment to be made in two months with payment in the importer's currency 60 days after delivery. Throughout the period until the transaction is completed there is a risk that the currency of the importer may devaluate and the seller will receive less in his own currency than was assumed when the sale was initially made. Thus for an MNC all of the obligations and incomplete transactions denominated in the currency of other countries represent transaction risks.

The effect of exchange rate changes in the conversion of accounts concerns the determination of profit and financial status for the MNC. If the currency of a host is devaluated in relation to that of the parent nation, the financial value to the MNC of an affiliate in that nation will be decreased. The amount of the decrease is a matter to which intensive discussion is devoted in accounting circles but its main dimensions are fairly well established. For current items including the income statement, cash, accounts receivable, inventories, and the like, the decrease is directly proportional to the change in the exchange rate because that rate reflects what the MNC can expect to realize under the new conditions from continuing operation of the business. For fixed obligations such as long-term debt, the change, of course, is determined by the currency in which the obligation is stated. The value of other fixed assets like plant and machinery generally continues to be converted at the exchange rate that existed when the items were initially recorded, the historical rate.

It will be readily seen that there is some overlap in the coverage of transaction and conversion risks. Accounts receivable, for example, fall in both. However, since our concern here is with the strategy implications and not with accounting niceties, the overlaps in fact are useful in reinforcing the understanding of the risk of foreign exchange rate changes. The essential point is that the MNC has at risk at any given time the value of all of the obligations it has assumed that are stated in foreign currencies and the assets that it holds abroad whose present or future profitable liquidation or use would be affected by changes in rates for conversion into parent currency. The extent to which these risks exist in each currency and ways to protect against them are therefore an important variable in determining the financial strategy of the firm.

There are two main approaches to dealing with exchange rate risks. One is to hedge the risks by entering into futures contracts to buy or sell foreign currencies in amounts that offset outstanding currency risks. Essentially, this approach results in transferring the risk of future changes to the seller of the futures contract, paying him a fee to carry the risk. In effect it is an insurance in which the risk of intermittent, large, and unpredictable losses is exchanged for a continuing cost.

The other approach is to structure the firm's finances in such a way that risks are offset within the system, so that exchange rate changes do not result in losses or that the losses are kept in a moderate range. The main thrust of this approach lies partly in balancing host country assets and liabilities to minimize net exposure to exchange rate changes and partly in offsetting various obligations and spreading them among currencies so that the risk position is reduced.

The significance of the *tax* variable lies in the advantages for an MNC in realizing profits in countries with low tax rates or in making the best use of the way governments in one country treat taxes paid in another. To take advantage of the first approach, U.S. MNCs established sales and holding companies in "tax haven" countries like Switzerland and Panama which had very low income taxes in the 1950s. By realizing most of their export and investment profits in these countries and making new investments out of them, the firms avoided giving up the roughly half of the profits that would have gone to the U.S. government in taxes had the income been routed through the U.S. parent. The U.S. tax changes in the early 1960s eliminated the greater portion of tax haven potentials (p. 173). However, there still remain opportunities in various ways to save taxes by maximizing the share of earnings realized in lower tax countries.

The other approach is to make the best use of the provisions governments establish to minimize the effects of double taxation for MNCs. The U.S. government permits a company either to deduct foreign income taxes paid by a subsidiary as a cost from dividend income received from that subsidiary or to take the foreign tax as a credit against the U.S. tax due on the dividend income. The second way is usually the most beneficial calculation. Thus, if the foreign tax is less than the U.S. tax rate, the parent is never obligated to pay more total tax (foreign and U.S.) than the U.S. rate. If the foreign rate is higher than that in the United States, there are possibilities for applying the excess credit against taxes on earnings from subsidiaries in other countries where the rates are lower. Given these tax provisions, the MNC finds it fruitful to consider various alternatives which distribute costs and income among the affiliates and the parent firm.

## Constraining Variables

These three factors—interest rates, foreign exchange risks, and taxes—establish the potentials that are the prime motivation for financial flow strategy. Other factors, however, enter into the choice of strategy and affect the feasibility and wisdom of employing various options. Notable among them are government actions beyond those directly affecting interest rates, foreign exchange rates, and taxes. Also significant are commercial and political risks, managerial process effects, corporate image, and ownership questions.

Acting primarily through various *regulatory* channels, governments exercise considerable influence on the types and magnitudes of financial flow options employed by MNCs because national interests are substantially involved in their strategies. The monetary flows they entail affect the balance of payments, tax revenue, and economic development processes such as capital allocation and costs. In all nations, therefore, governments take some measures which restrict the options open to management and, in those where government economic direction is strong, the controls narrow the choices of MNCs greatly.

*Commercial and political risk* considerations are an important restraining influence in financial planning because of the basic conservative stance of the MNC in this area of management. The primary concern of the MNC is with success in its product delivery strategy and it must necessarily take risks in that area. Among the options opened up by the global interest rate-foreign exchange-taxation environment are many which offer good profit opportunities but at considerable risk. As the basic role of the financial system is to support the product delivery strategy, risk taking in it must be subordinated to protect that role. It would be unwise to adopt some financial plan that might offer high profit potential if it also entailed risking capital which, if lost, would put a crimp into new investment plans with good market potential.

The *managerial process effects* of financial flow strategy are largely concerned with complexity and control. The multiple options open to an MNC, especially a large one, present a complicated picture both for decision-making and for subsequent implementation and control. Some firms have over one hundred subsidiaries in many countries. The permutations of options for financial flows among these units are enormous. Even with the help of the best computer techniques, they are immensely complex to analyze and monitor. At some point, therefore, complexity becomes a limiting factor not only in the difficulty of management but also in the doubtful wisdom of devoting scarce managerial resources to it as compared to more important efforts in the primary strategy concerns of the product delivery system.

On top of this general complexity problem, there is the specific effect of financial flow options on the control system. The main function of the financial system in the firm is to accomplish the flow of monetary resources supporting and derived from the product delivery system toward the ultimate end of providing income for the stockholders. But the system also serves a major secondary purpose in providing value measurements that are used for exchange and judgment of performance. Thus the costs and prices assigned as goods move through the system are used as measures of resources added and of the efficiency of the functioning of operating units. They are also used as the basis for decisions on allocation of future resources. To serve these functions best, the monetary designations appearing throughout the MNC corporate system should, as far as possible, accurately reflect the true value of resources, the efficiency of performance, and other economic realities.

The goals of financial flow strategy which dominate in this chapter take a different direction and one that can readily conflict with the control and measurement function. Many of the options require use of monetary designations which will distort the accuracy of the financial system for purposes of managerial economics. For example, if transfer prices are adjusted to allocate profits to low tax countries, they will not accurately record the performance of affiliates. An apparent ready solution for this problem is to run two sets of accounts, one for the financial flow system and one for performance measurement purposes. But that course presents its own complexities and time costs. Furthermore, it can be self-defeating as hiding the existence of separate accounts is impractical in big firms and may be powerful evidence against an MNC if the legitimacy of financial flow options is questioned. This is a prime concern especially in transfer pricing decisions. Therefore this consideration is a constraint limiting use of some options.

*Corporate image* enters into this analysis because of the impact of financial flows on national attitudes. The productive activities of MNCs are generally appreciated but their financial affairs much less so. In particular, the withdrawal of earnings from host nations is viewed adversely. The basic nationalistic instinct to protect national wealth and to view outsiders as predators establishes a strong foundation for this sort of attitude. Payments for dividends, royalties, and the like are readily perceived as excessive. Since the fundamental goal of financial flow strategy is to optimize the gain for the MNC, conflict with national interest in choice of options is inevitable. Accepting it as inevitable, the MNC must deal with the conflict as it does in other matters, by conformance with regulations, by taking opportunities where they are found, and by negotiations where flexibility exists.

In these processes the MNC helps its cause by minimizing as far as possible adverse attitudinal pressures. Toward this end, the image projected by its financial flow strategy can be a help or a hindrance. There have been a few notable cases which illustrate the potentials. In 1926 General Motors started operations in Australia with an investment of £1.75 million. For years thereafter it reinvested virtually all of its profits. By 1954 GM found it no longer needed a large accumulation of funds. Therefore it declared a dividend to the parent of £4.6 million. This sum was huge by normal Australian standards and amounted to 6 percent of total net investment income in the national balance of payments. These statistics were the meat for a large amount of adverse publicity for GM, charging the firm with draining the country excessively from high profits on a low capital input.

In 1968 when the British pound was very weak, one major U.S. MNC sensed the imminence of devaluation and shifted large funds out of the pound into other currencies. Their financial acumen was good and they realized a profit of some $4 million in the subsequent fall of the pound. When word of the profit leaked out, however, the British press made the company appear in a most adverse light as profiteering from the difficulties of the British nation.

These are extreme cases but they make the point. A company which appears to offensively disregard national interests can expect to suffer the consequences in adverse image. The potential gains may be worth the consequences, but considering the many ways in which an MNC must treat with national governments, the risk to image may be a cause for restraint.

Last, but far from least, is the question of *ownership* with its control implications which is as significant here as it has been in other aspects of strategy discussed in prior chapters. The question takes on special importance here because sharing control with local stockholders not only affects the power to make financial strategy decisions but also brings the interests of those stockholders forcefully into the decisions. Thus the whole approach of a unified financial flow strategy directed toward optimizing the overall profit of the MNC is greatly weakened, for the local stockholders inevitably are concerned only with optimizing at the affiliate level. The MNC may continue to seek options that serve the global optimization goal, but compromises to meet the suboptimization, affiliate-oriented viewpoints must be expected. The balance between the two depends upon the relative bargaining power of the parties.

To this pragmatic view of the implications of divided ownership may be added a more theoretical view which relates the problem of price linkages to MNC structure. This view was advanced by Brown[2] based upon the earlier work of Coase. Basically, Coase's idea was that the market is inefficient and costly in providing prices for many kinds of transactions. Firms therefore "coagulate" in areas where administrative allocation is cheaper and more accurate than market allocation. The costs of using the market, which Coase called transaction costs, are four: (1) the cost of finding a relevant price (the brokerage cost), (2) the cost of defining the obligations of both parties to a contract (the definition cost), (3) the risk associated with accepting such contracts, and (4) the taxes paid on market transactions. Where these costs are high, the firm sells to itself or to a fully owned affiliate.

These fundamental logics are seen to apply to the reluctance of MNCs to license. First, there is great difficulty in legally specifying the conditions involved in the complex tasks of promoting, manufacturing, and delivering some new product variant. Second, a reasonable estimate of the value of the licensor's contribution is difficult to make, even if it can be defined. Third, since the "result" of any license is very uncertain, both licensee and licensor tend to be wary of paying an inappropriate price. Brown suggests that by their very nature technological inventions and innovative products are easier to define and separate from the firm than are marketing or product-coordination advantages. Thus licensing is more practical in firms whose key strength is technology as compared to those that have developed a unique marketing competence.

The relation of oligopoly to international investment is found in the risk factor. The fewer the firms in an industry, the harder it is to establish market price. The more market processes become internalized, the thinner and less reliable becomes the free market, and the higher the risk costs of using it.

Five corollaries of the application of Coase's theory are proposed.

1. Firms that set up their own operations abroad because they cannot establish the value of their contribution to independent foreign enterprises, cannot establish meaningful transfer pricing.
2. The inability to set prices causes tightly organized multinationals, to eschew joint ventures.
3. Where transaction costs are high relative to cost differentials among tradeable goods and services, there can be no presumption that administrative allocation will be the same as market allocation.
4. Since some intrafirm costs are lower than transaction costs, some trade will take place between affiliates which would not take place at all between independent firms.
5. The fewer the industries in which an MNC operates and the more established its product types, the more administrative allocation replaces market allocation. Implications are also seen for the administrative structure of the firm. The availability of market prices facilitates decentralization and use of profit centers. Where transaction prices are hard to determine, centralization is fostered.

Brown observes that there are shortcomings for resource allocation in the functioning of the system based on Coase's concepts.

> The kind of allocation that goes on within islands or globs of butter need not be the same in direction or result as that which goes on in the ocean of unconscious forces. Moreover, the oligopolistic position and high degree of product differentiation among product concentration firms means that the firms themselves can make a considerable number of errors of judgment before market forces would put an end to them.[3]

### Comparison of Options

A financial flow strategy evolves through comparison of the merits of each option against those of others. In view of the varied options and the several considerations affecting choices among them, this process is in full form quite extensive and complex. Our analysis here must therefore be confined to the main dimensions of the process, identifying the conspicuous comparisons and major factors bearing on them.

**Financing Options.** Figure 9–1 shows schematically the main factors supporting each option for supplying funds to affiliates as compared with each of the other options. The starting point is the provision of capital in the form of stockholders equity by the parent firm. To a certain degree it is inevitable that the MNC will invest equity capital in an affiliate. But beyond a certain modest level, the support for greater portions of equity tends to come from government pressures requiring that some minimum debt-equity ratio be maintained. If tax authorities regard the amount of debt as excessive, they may rule that part of it is to be treated as equity. Another pressure comes in countries where dividend remissions are limited to a percentage of equity capital. To the extent that capacity to make

**Figure 9–1.** Comparison of Options for Financing Affiliates *(Advantages of each option in column heads over those listed at left)*

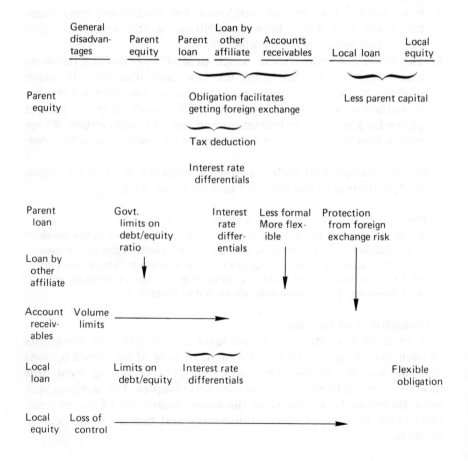

dividend payments is a useful option in the income flow strategy to be discussed next, it is desirable therefore to establish a reasonably large equity base.

The next three options—parent loan, loan by other affiliate, accounts receivable—are forms of debt to the rest of the MNC system. They are all preferable to parent equity in that they represent a firm obligation both as to principal and interest, which establishes a stronger case in seeking foreign exchange for remission of funds. There are differences among them, though, in other respects. The main distinction between the two types of loans and in comparison with local debt lies in their potentials for taking advantage of interest rate differentials. Loans from other affiliates provide the greater opportunities in this respect. Repayment of debt to the parent may be advantageous in income remission because it will not be treated as income for tax purposes for the parent. The process may simply defer the tax payment but, depending upon profit reinvestment and other circumstances, part or all of the benefit may be permanently realized.

Accounts receivable offer distinctive potentials. Their role lies in the possibilities for allowing longer terms for payment as a means for providing capital to an affiliate and shortening terms to withdraw capital, a practice known as "leads and lags." The advantage of this option is that it can be employed with less formality in relations with foreign exchange authorities than loans. However, its potentials are limited as to magnitude and timing by the volume of exports to the affiliate from the parent or from other affiliates, which govern the size of the accounts receivable. Thus for some firms like those in the food and toiletries industries, whose affiliates are largely self-sufficient, this option has little value. For others which may import a large volume of components or even finished goods, the use of leads and lags may be useful.

The two sources of local capital—local loan and local equity—both have the effect compared with other options of reducing the amount of capital the MNC must put into the host country. The value of this effect will depend upon the availability of capital within the MNC system and the degree of risk the firm perceives in the investment. For a well-heeled firm establishing an affiliate in a country with a good investment climate, this factor will be of negligible value for the financial strategy. For a financially weak firm entering a politically and economically unstable country, the employment of local capital may be quite valuable.

The other major advantage of use of local capital lies in protection against the risk of devaluation of the host nation currency. The lower the proportion of external capital in the affiliate the lower the amount that can be lost if the currency value declines. As between the two sources of local capital, the difference of overriding importance is the loss of control resulting from taking in equity partners. This carries with it all the serious disadvantages that have just been described, in that it greatly weakens efforts to benefit by a unified financial flow strategy. The only offsetting factor is that local loans carry a fixed obligation, but that is a minor concern compared with loss of control.

**Income Flow Options.**   The chief factors to be considered in comparing income flow options are shown in Figure 9–2. Dividends are potentially more flexible than other means for transmitting income to the parent. The extent to which that potential is realizable, however, depends upon the regulations of the host government. Some countries exercise no restraints on dividend payments to parent firms while others, typically those with balance of payments problems, restrict them or in a few cases allow no foreign exchange for dividends. Where controls are applied on various forms of payments, greater flexibility may lie with other options rather than with dividends depending upon the prevailing government policies.

The three options in the middle of Figure 9–2—interest, royalties, and management fees—share two advantages: tax deductibility and formality of obligation. These payments, being operating costs, are deductible from income and reduce the tax liability in the host nation. The payments are, of course, income fully taxable in the parent nation and there is no foreign tax credit to offset against them. Thus there is an ultimate advantage only where the host nation taxes are higher than those in the parent country. The results are also beneficial, however, as long as affiliate profits are being retained in the host nation, regardless of the tax rates.

The formal obligation characteristic is an advantage over dividends in any situation where there are restrictions on dividend payments or risks that such restrictions will be imposed. Each of these options can be justified to host government authorities as payment for a specific form of service, so the chances are greater that governments will give them a priority in allocation of foreign exchange.

Each of the three options has certain characteristics. Interest payments probably have the strongest formal status and they have a fixed magnitude regardless of the business situation. Royalties are sometimes on a fixed basis but most commonly they are tied to sales volume and thus provide a flow of payments that will vary with the course of the affiliate's business. The magnitude of royalties may

**Figure 9-2.** Comparison of Options for Income Flows from Affiliates
*(Advantages of each option in column heads over those listed on left)*

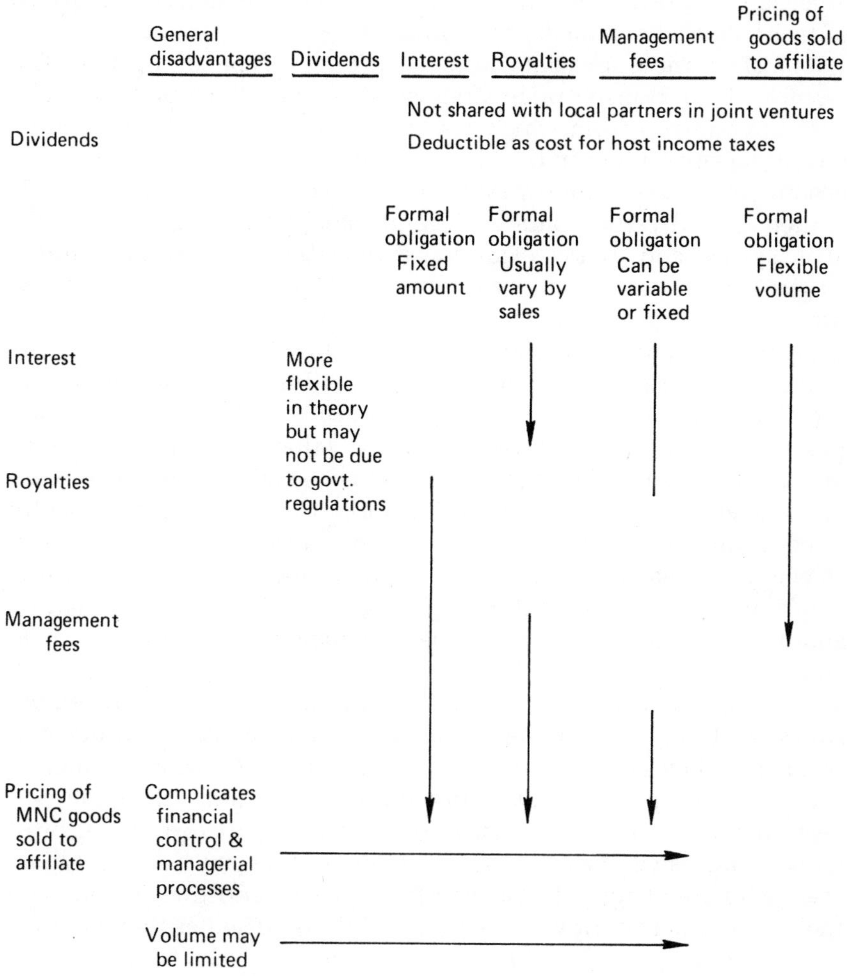

| | General disadvantages | Dividends | Interest | Royalties | Management fees | Pricing of goods sold to affiliate |
|---|---|---|---|---|---|---|
| Dividends | | | Not shared with local partners in joint ventures<br>Deductible as cost for host income taxes | | | |
| | | | Formal obligation Fixed amount | Formal obligation Usually vary by sales | Formal obligation Can be variable or fixed | Formal obligation Flexible volume |
| Interest | | More flexible in theory but may not be due to govt. regulations | | | | |
| Royalties | | | | | | |
| Management fees | | | | | | |
| Pricing of MNC goods sold to affiliate | Complicates financial control & managerial processes<br>Volume may be limited | | | | | |

also be quite flexible in many countries though in recent years some, chiefly less developed, countries have started to exercise strict control over royalty rates. Management fees are much the same as royalties though there is more flexibility in their bases and particularly so in those cases where LDC governments are sharply limiting royalty payments. Depending upon the nature of the firm, notably its technology, it may be easier to justify to government authorities, larger payments by one of these options than by the others.

A further factor favoring these options exists where there are local equity partners. They are means by which the MNC can receive income without sharing it with the local owners. This consideration is especially important where the MNC is making major contributions of technological and managerial skills.

Transfer prices present quite a different type of option. The essence of the transfer-price strategy is to charge high prices to affiliates in countries from which maximum payments are desired, maximizing receipts either in the parent country or in other countries, for example, in those with low taxes. The employment of this strategy is limited both by the volume of goods shipped among units of the MNC system and by tax regulations which generally require "arm's-length" prices or their equivalent in intracorporate sales. As there are often no identical open market sales to which tax authorities can compare intracorporate transactions, the tax regulations leave some room for management discretion. Within this range and the magnitude of trade with the affiliate, the transfer price option is a more flexible system of accomplishing payments than interest, royalties, or management fees. The transfer prices can be adjusted slightly without attracting government attention while the latter three are set by fixed formulas. The transfer prices may also be a more practical vehicle for transfers to other affiliates than the other options because it is more common to find shipments of goods from one affiliate to another than for interest, royalties, or management fees to be paid among them.

The major disadvantage of the use of transfer prices on any extensive scale lies in the complications to financial control and management that they entail. This option distorts the internal measurement process, making it difficult to determine results, judge the quality of performance, and make plans. Furthermore, the distortions of profits it produces can have an adverse effect on the psychology of managers who are attuned to gauging their success and their status with their superiors in terms of the profitability of affiliates they manage.

**Time-risk Considerations.** The discussion thus far has been cast in essentially timeless terms. To complete the analytical scheme, time must be introduced as a variable, which in some cases may bear substantially on handling of financial flows. Of course, time must be assumed as a general part of international financial decision-making just as it is in domestic planning, e.g., determination of pay-back for investment. But time takes on special dimensions in international financial management because of the eventualities that must be anticipated. In domestic business and to a large degree in the advanced industrial areas—Western Europe, Canada, and Australia—time considerations in planning for the return of capital and flow of earnings may be limited to the commercial outlook, notably the market life cycle of products, the rate of obsolescence of production processes and the deterioration of manufacturing facilities.

The major factor that must be added in international planning is the possibility of politically determined full or partial termination of operations which was outlined in Chapter 7 (p. 292). In some cases, the termination may be anticipated from the outset as in those nations which require a "fade-out" ownership plan for new investments. In others, it may be unexpected and severe—the experience of firms in Cuba when Castro took over, for example. In yet others, it may be unexpected but evolve in a tolerable manner, typically in laws requiring sale of full or majority of equity to nationals within a given period. Except where the termination is preplanned, this factor must be incorporated into the financial plans as an element of risk and the time aspects of the financial flows must be geared to it.

The approach to handling the time-risk considerations may take two directions. One is the general assessment of political risk which was covered in Chapter 7. Essentially, the MNC's strategy must be to seek more rapid return of capital and earlier profitability where political risks are higher. The second approach is to relate the risk to the economic quality of the operations in relation to the host nation context. The basic hypothesis in this approach is that the ability of the MNC to maintain financial flows out of a host nation that is inclined to terminate its operations will be determined by the MNC's economic power. This power in turn will depend mainly on the value of the resources it is providing. Thus, an MNC supplying a continuing stream of resources, say in improving technology or in provision of export marketing for host nation products, is in a good position to obtain a continuing flow of earnings and return of capital at its discretion. On the other hand, a firm that provides a one-shot input of technology, for example, setting up a fertilizer plant for which the host society does not need subsequent improvements, will be in a weak position if the host government wishes its ownership terminated. It follows that the choice among financial flow options should provide for adequate return within a safe period. A safe period then is defined as that in which the MNCs' inputs to the host country will be sufficiently valued to assure necessary income and provision of foreign exchange.

**Strategy Patterns of Financial Flow.** This outline of the relative merits of various forms of capital and income flow gives a broad picture of the factors management must consider in choosing among the options. Clearly no one option is superior on all counts to others. Thus the challenge for the strategist is to determine the mix of flows which will offer the optimum benefits. To put this task into perspective before examining information on MNC experience, we may define three quite distinctive patterns of financial flow strategy.

In the first pattern, each affiliate is run essentially as a separate company, financial relations with the parent being conducted on an arm's-length basis. Sales of products to the affiliate, licensing of know-how, and other contractual arrangements are handled just as though the affiliate were an independent firm. The parent, as controlling stockholder, has official authority over dividend payments, but even in this it defers to the affiliate managers, so that payments are determined in practice by them, just as is true of stockholders generally in relation to corporations. This pattern composes the extreme of a *fully fragmented* strategy. It would be expected either where a firm was not attuned to the benefits of many of the options discussed here or where it was prevented from seeking them by the viewpoint of a strong local joint-venture partner.

In the second pattern the affiliate finances are controlled closely by the parent corporation. A certain degree of independence in financial management is delegated to the affiliate, but in all transactions with the parent firm the headquarters determines the outcome according to a centrally established strategy. Thus export prices, royalty payments, dividends, and the like are all part of the parent plans to optimize financial flows for the affiliate's operations. This pattern may be designated as a *bilateral unified strategy*. It seems likely that this sort of strategy would appear as the first stage in evolution of a sophisticated approach to international financial management but one which is still limited to the relatively simple pattern of direct relations with each affiliate.

The third pattern carries the integration further to the point that all affiliates are treated in essentially the same manner as domestic divisions. Thus the income of each is absorbed into the common corporate pool, and its needs are met out of that pool according to determinations in which the parent management has the final word. Transactions among all parts of the corporation including those between affiliates are subject to central strategy planning. Goods are sold by one affiliate to another at prices giving the best overall corporate profit considering tax differences; funds are shifted among affiliates as needs develop; and other arrangements are made in which optimization of profits for each affiliate is subordinated to optimal return for the MNC system as a whole. This pattern should be classed as a *multi-lateral unified* strategy. It will involve the full range of options between parent and affiliates and among affiliates developed by an MNC management which has achieved advanced sophistication in the field.

## MNC EXPERIENCE

The financial flow systems of U.S. MNCs have been explored by one comprehensive research project. A few other studies have examined limited parts of the subject. Thus we have a fairly full picture of American experience in this area though relatively little information on it from the viewpoint of other types of MNCs.

1. The comprehensive study was made by Robbins and Stobaugh as part of the Harvard Multinational Enterprise Project.[4] They employed data from the 187 largest U.S. MNCs combined with intensive interviews with 39 selected with some care as representative in size and industry characteristics of the range among the top 500 U.S. companies. Broadly the research revealed that the financial flow strategies of MNCs fell into three general patterns which tended to be characteristic of firms in size groups: small, defined as having foreign sales below $50 million; medium, sales up to $200 million; and large, sales running around $1 billion.[5]

The small operation typically had a limited headquarters staff, sometimes with only one financial man. These companies gave wide latitude in financial decisions to subsidiaries. Since its central staff typically was not knowledgeable about foreign business, the small MNC employed few decision rules. In fact, it tended to view each subsidiary as an independent operation and made little attempt to take the overall system into account in its financing decisions. This attitude was reflected in various financial practices. Only 20 percent of the small MNCs invested additional funds in a foreign subsidiary after it was started compared to 71 percent of the medium and large MNCs. Only 50 percent of the small firms lent money to subsidiaries to save interest costs against 89 percent of the larger firms. The small firms also used relatively few sources of funds, for example, 11 percent utilized Euro-capital markets as compared to 67 percent of the larger firms.

The medium-sized MNC generally had a central staff and "system optimization" viewpoint. This approach was reflected in a continuous stream of instructions to the subsidiaries on both short-term and long-term problems. With a larger and more sophisticated central staff, these firms exercised a large degree of control over foreign units. They looked carefully for ways to optimize financial benefits. For example, 100 percent took advantage of interest differentials compared to 60 percent of small and large MNCs. During a monetary squeeze in the host country, the medium MNC was more likely (83 percent vs. 47 percent) than the small and large MNCs to furnish the subsidiary funds from outside the country.

The large firm leaned toward the system optimization but it was too large and complex to implement it. Thus the central staff devoted itself largely to issuing guidelines, leaving the decisions to the subsidiaries, which were generally quite large firms with strong financial staffs. Another distinction at this level was that because of their large size, these firms were much more concerned about public image than smaller companies. Thus many of them had guidelines like "let equity equal fixed assets" to minimize criticism of borrowing an overly large percentage of needs or paying too high dividends relative to equity. The larger firms were distinguished by the use of a wider range of financial sources. For example, 75 percent obtained funds from local non-banking sources compared to 44 percent of small and medium firms.

The research revealed some patterns of transition from one size category to the next. The move from the small to medium level generally came around the $100 million foreign sales mark. It was often the result of a shock in which some major loss in a foreign unit was experienced. At this point, if sales were great enough, the headquarters would react by setting up a central staff to exercise greater control over foreign units. The transition to the large category was usually more gradual with a progressive shift from the control to the guideline function by the central staff.

Two other variables were less prominent as determinants of financial management but they did have an influence. Companies with more joint ventures tended to exercise less central direction and overall system optimization than those with more fully owned subsidiaries. Likewise companies with high R&D expenditures were found to be less concerned with financial cost minimization for foreign units. This factor was considered to be due to a difference in basic corporate strategy, the high-technology firms generally devoting major attention to new product development while low-technology firms concentrated on cost minimization.

The findings of the study as to the options employed by MNCs were organized around three topics: financing of foreign affiliates, withdrawing funds from abroad, and protecting against exchange risks. The information from the firms was supplemented in this analysis by use of a computer model which showed how a company with a full-system-optimizing approach would handle options under various tax, foreign exchange, and other conditions.

The sets of figures shown in Table 9-3 and Table 9-4 provided an overall picture of *affiliate financing.* Both sets indicated the strong preference for debt over equity. Foreign sources were clearly preferred over parent sources for debt. The preference for U.S. entities

**Table 9-3. U.S. MNC Affiliate Financing**

Estimated Balance Sheet of Foreign Direct Investment
of U.S. Enterprises, December 31, 1970
(In Billions of Dollars)

| *Assets* | | *Liabilities and Equity* | | |
|---|---|---|---|---|
| Current | 62 | U.S. entities' share (Book value of U.S. foreign direct investment) | | 78 |
| Fixed | 60 | | | |
| | | Liabilities to U.S. entities | 21 | |
| | | Equity owned by U.S. entities | 57 | |
| Other | 12 | | | |
| | | Foreigners' share | | 56 |
| | | Short-term liabilities | 34 | |
| | | Long-term liabilities | 16 | |
| | | Equity | 6 | |
| Total Assets | 134 | Total liabilities and equity | | 134 |

**Table 9-4. U.S. MNC Affiliate Financing**

Sources of Funds, Majority-Owned Foreign Affiliates
of 313 U.S. Foreign Direct Investors Primarily
Engaged in Manufacturing, 1969

| | | | *Percentage* |
|---|---|---|---|
| *From within multinational enterprise* | | | 60 |
| Internally generated by affiliate | | 46 | |
| Depreciation | 29 | | |
| Retained earnings | 17 | | |
| From parent | | 14 | |
| Equity | 9 | | |
| Loans | 5 | | |
| *From outside multinational enterprise* | | | 40 |
| Loans | | 39 | |
| Equity | | 2 | |
| Total | | | 100 |

Source: Sidney Robbins and Robert Stobough, *Money in The Multinational Enterprise.* New York: Basic Books, 1973.

was equally clear for equity (Table 9−3). Managements explained their preference for debt in providing parent funds by the greater facility of bringing them back to the United States. Because of their apprehension about government controls on dividend and equity payments, they made particular efforts to limit equity in countries with weak currencies. Tax savings were also noted as a reason for use of debt, especially by smaller firms which tended to concentrate on limited subgoals in their initial overseas financing practices. The savings were realized both in the deductibility of interest payments and in the fact that debt repayments would not be considered income to the parent thus facilitating the first stages of remission of income. Businessmen generally considered that the U.S. tax authorities regarded a four-to-one debt-equity ratio as satisfactory. Most firms tended to keep their ratios below this level though one small firm was observed with $10,000 parent equity and $1,550,000 debt owed to the parent. The research found that most firms made use of intercompany accounts, e.g., accounts receivable, for financing affiliates with their flexibility a significant advantage. The major limitation observed was the quantity of goods and services sold to the affiliate.

Robbins and Stobaugh found that financing among affiliates was used much less than they would have imagined. The complexity of the task for headquarters in keeping track of intricate interaffiliate relationships was given as a common cause. In some cases it was also found that local institutions, e.g., banks, took an adverse view of providing funds for affiliates which then used some of their resources to finance affiliates in other countries. The local institutions felt disinclined to help the development of companies outside their own country. On the whole, therefore, interaffiliate financing was undertaken only among a minority of firms, mostly of middle size. The smaller and larger firms were both discouraged by the complexity of the process, the former being inexperienced and the latter confronted with too large a system to control effectively. A few cases were cited in which a high degree of this type of financing appeared, for example, a French subsidiary for which $10.6 million was provided, 34 percent by equity, 46 percent by loan and 20 percent by accounts receivable, with about half of the total from sister subsidiaries. The evidence from such firms reinforced the calculations of the study's computer model demonstrating large potentials that most firms were not exploiting.

Dividends were reported in the research to be the most common means of *withdrawing funds from abroad*, a finding confirmed by the data in Table 9−5 which show that a little more than half of the funds received from U.S. affiliates were dividends. Most of the bal-

Table 9–5.   Income of U.S. MNCs

Funds Received from Foreign Operations by U.S. Foreign
Direct Investors Engaged Primarily in Manufacturing,
1966, Excluding Capital Movements and Payments
for Merchandise (In Millions of Dollars)

|  | *Dollar Value* | *Percentage* |
|---|---|---|
| Dividends | 895 | 51 |
| Royalties | 304 | 17 |
| Management fees | 299 | 17 |
| Income from sales affiliates | 162 | 9 |
| Interest | 99 | 6 |
| Rentals | 5 | — |
| Total | 1,763 | 100 |

Source: Sidney Robbins and Robert Stobough, *Money in the Multinational Enterprise.* New York: Basic Books, 1973.

ance for manufacturing affiliates was composed of royalties, management fees, and interest in roughly equal proportions. No data are available to indicate the magnitude of earnings achieved by adjustments in transfer prices which would reflect earnings withdrawn from the affiliates in excess of normal profits on the sale of goods.[a] The research revealed that where overall withdrawal policies existed, they were likely to be geared to a limited subgoal like minimizing taxes or maximizing parent liquidity. The development of a policy for the whole MNC system which would optimize benefits with reference to all key objectives appeared to be too complicated for managements in most cases.

Dividend policies varied greatly among companies. Some firms used them substantially to take full advantage of tax credits, while other firms gave greater preference to fixed obligation payments with dividends composing a smaller portion as a residual channel for income. Likewise, dividends as a percentage of each affiliate's earnings tended to vary greatly; data for one firm showed a range from 117 percent to 0. In some firms, however, an effort was made to maintain some consistency in dividend payments to establish to government officials that they were a regular part of the company's financial program.

[a]Some indication of the potential may be derived from the U.S. government study of a sample of U.S. MNCs composing about 75 percent of total U.S. international manufacturing operations cited in Appendix A, Chapter 1 (p. 28). The exports of these firms to their foreign affiliates in 1970 totaled $8.6 billion. For comparative purposes, the profit remissions in that year of all U.S. manufacturing MNCs were $1.8 billion.

Royalties and management fees were commonly used by MNCs for the reasons given in the earlier analytical notes, namely that they provided income which did not have to be shared with local partners and provided tax benefits where host nation tax rates were higher than those of the parent firm. Varied experience was reported in negotiations with governments to ascertain the maximum royalty rates and management fees which could be charged.

The subject of transfer prices being quite sensitive, the researchers found it difficult to establish firm findings. In general it appeared that the larger firms tended to avoid possible problems with governments on this subject by establishing uniform policies setting standard mark-ups. Medium-size firms did tend to make use of the potentials in flexible pricing to take account of varied affiliate circumstances. For smaller firms, the niceties of transfer pricing were premature as they were typically absorbed with straightforward problems of getting new ventures to a satisfactorily profitable stage.

For *protection against foreign exchange risks*, the research indicated that companies relied mainly on attempts to minimize their net asset risk position. Many MNCs were reported to make little use of forward exchange markets, chiefly because of the costs. The researchers' computer model confirmed the economic hypothesis that hedging costs would roughly equal devaluation losses over time. Because of this cost deterrent, many firms tended to borrow funds in foreign currencies as the easiest and most satisfactory means of achieving some protection against devaluations. Exchange rate protection was found to be of greatest concern in medium sized firms. Smaller ones were often too unsophisticated to handle it and, since their affiliate accounts were often not consolidated with those of the parent, they were not confronted with translation problems. In large firms risks were reduced simply by the wide spread of operations.

Robbins and Stobaugh made an overall assessment of the effectiveness of MNC financial management by comparing the patterns they observed in practice with those followed in their computer model. On this basis they determined that U.S. firms on the average could increase their earnings by about 25 percent if they made full use of the potentials available from optimal choices among financial flow options. Applied to 1972 earnings this would have added some $3 billion to the income of U.S. MNCs.

2. From this broad view, we now turn to studies of specific aspects of MNC finance. Zenoff made an investigation of the practices of 30 U.S. MNCs, using 1960–65 data.[6] All firms agreed that the decision on the amount of earnings to be sent home belonged to the

parent rather than the subsidiary. But in all other respects variety in policies was the prevailing theme.

On the question of the interrelation of the types of flows of funds: dividends, management fess, royalties, repayment of parent loans, licensing fees, and sales commissions, Zenoff found that over half the companies determined the size of various remittances independent of dividends while the balance determined dividend size as part of a mix of the various flows to minimize tax payments.

As to providing funds for foreign units, three patterns emerged. One group of companies allowed subsidiaries to retain earnings for planned requirements though they were often nervous about the dangers of the foreign environment and greatly preferred the affiliate to operate on foreign borrowings. A second group was less malleable and decidedly more nervous. They called for regular remittance of 90 percent or more of earnings. The third group was characterized as permissive, allowing subsidiaries to build up funds to establish firm independent financial status. About one-quarter of the respondents, cutting across all three groups, made it mandatory that each of their subsidiaries develop a pattern of continuity and consistency in its dividend payout. They reasoned that if foreign exchange restrictions were imposed, their subsidiaries would have a much better chance for approval to remit their dividends than would subsidiaries with irregular payment records.

There were also substantial variations in the degree to which a total corporate viewpoint was taken. Only some firms, for example, attempted to work out a minimum overall tax load for the corporation based on adjustment of the many potential variables in the total financial flow system. Again, in a few firms, a sense of foreign government attitudes was more important than optimum tax schemes. For the many companies that had difficulties in getting dividend payouts from a portion of their subsidiaries in less developed countries, establishment of a uniform dividend payout rate throughout the corporate system—justified by their obligation to the stockholders—would, it was hoped, persuade officials of the justice of the claim.

Zenoff concluded that companies were making insufficient use of the leverage their borrowing strength could offer. He suggested that companies could consider borrowing money for dividend distribution in order to meet stockholder requirements, rather than foregoing profitable opportunities overseas by remitting their own funds. He also felt that few firms think in terms of a worldwide pool of company-controlled funds. A contributing factor here was that overseas managers were often men who had not had an overall view of the corporation. International operations had generally been segregated, marginal activities.

3. Focusing more specifically on dividends of European subsidiaries, Zenoff in a second study identified three main considerations: taxes, foreign exchange risks and sources of capital.[7] He found that there was a broad range in the degree to which taxes were influential. One-quarter of the firms surveyed made what could be regarded as "every attempt" to minimize the overall tax burden on the worldwide company. Another third gave about equal weight to taxes and exchange risks. The balance of the firms accepted taxes as "part of the cost of doing business," determining the amount of remittances primarily on other bases, for example, as a regular portion of subsidiary earnings or as remission of all excess funds.

Because of the West German tax differential between retained and disbursed earnings, the performance of German subsidiaries provided a good indication of these differences. Whereas the "non-tax-conscious" group showed little difference in dividend payout ratios for 1960–65 between German and other European subsidiaries (0.70 vs. 0.81), the "tax-conscious" group showed a notable difference, 0.73 for Germany vs. 0.47 for the rest of Europe.

The reaction of firms to exchange rate risks showed a somewhat similar pattern. About 25 percent of them varied the rate of remissions according to changes in risks while the balance seemed to be relatively unaffected by this factor. A comparison of remissions from England was used in this respect between data for 1965, a year of major devaluation rumors, and 1962, a year of less uncertainty. Companies with little concern for the risks showed little variation either between the years for England (0.81 in 1965 and 0.78 in 1962) or as compared with the rest of Europe (0.74 and 0.65). For the other 25 percent, however, the two years looked quite different: 0.93 in 1965 vs. 0.44 in 1962 and the ratios for the rest of Europe also varied more, 0.59 vs. 0.71.

As to sources of finance, Zenoff noted the major reliance on retained subsidiary funds ranging from 53 percent to 60 percent from 1962 to 1965 with from 24 percent to 39 percent coming from local sources and only 8 percent to 18 percent from the United States. He observed certain problems growing out of this pattern: the heavy drain on local capital sources, the impracticality of U.S. companies operating contrary to the objectives of local monetary policy, and the long-term burden on host countries' balance of payments.

4. No separate study is available which has systematically examined policies and experience of firms on royalties and management

fees of MNCs. However, the work of Mason and Masson provided some useful insights on this subject in the context of host nation attitudes which are the critical variable in determining the amount of income which may be transmitted in this manner.[8] Their research was undertaken in response to suggestions that the developing countries, and particularly those in Latin America, were incurring too heavy a burden for the technology they received from outside sources. The study had two phases: balance of payments analysis and field interviews. It was confined to Argentina, Brazil, Colombia, Mexico and Peru.

The goal of the balance of payments work was to determine the cost of technology payments. The data available proved inadequate for a full assessment. Current account items were generally recorded but consultants' fees, engineering services, and other items financed as part of loans were not. Neither could the technical assistance components of loans and grants be isolated. The data available showed that about a quarter of technology inflows were financed by loans and three-quarters on current account. The total cost for the five countries in 1969 was about $345 million, roughly 3 percent of total imports of goods and services, with the range from 1.3 percent for Peru to 4.2 percent for Brazil. Somewhat over 50 percent of the payments were to the United States.

In addition to observing that the balance of payments impact was minor, the authors noted that even if they had sound balance of payments accounting systems, they would have been unable to evaluate the financial effects of technology transfer—primarily because the impact is more indirect than direct. That is to say, technology transfer brings about structural changes and expenditure switching which indirectly affect the balance of payments.

The field interviews covered twenty large U.S. firms and fifty-three companies in Latin America. The former included companies having subsidiaries with and without licensing arrangements and some dealing with independent licensees. In all they had fifty-one manufacturing operations abroad, eighteen involving licenses. The firms covered thirteen manufacturing sectors, the object being to discuss typical industry practices with knowledgeable individuals among a fairly broad cross-section of industries. Licensing agreements tended to run for five to ten years or to be indefinite in length. Royalties ranged from 2 percent to 8 percent of sales, clustering about 5 percent. There were also variations including a sliding scale. Technical aid agreements were found to be more common than licensing. The authors found that access to the licensor's know-how was substantial and often without charge. Five of the companies restricted licensees or subsidiaries to marketing in their own countries, but the large majority of firms set no such restrictions. Many of the foreign affiliates were in fact restricted by their high costs which precluded exports but about one-third did some exporting.

Among the fifty-three firms visited in Latin America there were fifty-four licensing agreements. Roughly half of these provided for compensation on a percentage of sales basis, the rates ranging from 1 percent to over 5 percent with the average, 4.2 percent. Nine licenses had no fee while seven involved a lump sum payment and there were ten with other bases. About three-fourths of the contracts had fixed terms ranging from five to ten years, the balance being indefinite. The firms reported generally open access to licensor technical assistance and little or no restrictions on export markets or pricing.

The authors report their conclusion that practices across industries and countries did not vary greatly. Either firms followed some customary "rules of thumb" in setting standards of compensation for know-how or there was a reasonably competitive market which influenced firms to behave similarly to one another. Respecting the basic situation which motivated the research, the authors observed that their main conclusion was that many of the criticisms attacking the practices associated with technology transfer and the cost of that technology were largely ill-founded. Indeed, some of the suggested stringent controls on transfers might lead to a hurtful dampening of technological infusions. Additional research was needed on the real costs of controls on know-how payments. Some curious practices and aberrations associated with them were noted, including greater technological dependence, overbilling of imports, perhaps even limitations on exports.

5. Another relevant study was Lovell's research on the attitudes and practices in licensing agreements of 191 U.S. companies in 1969.[9] Underlying all of her findings was the theme of diversity. Motivations for licensing, types of arrangements, methods of management, and financial accounting varied greatly among firms. The diversity precluded even an approximation of standard practice or normative guidelines. For example, some companies were wholeheartedly committed to licensing as a primary means for overseas operations while others viewed it as a means for gaining some plus income with nominal effort or as a way to protect patent or trademark rights with little emphasis on income generation. These differences in motivations along with other variables led to a host of variations in other characteristics.

Overall Lovell reported that licensing continued to grow but apparently at a slower rate and in a different manner than in previous years. Both statistical data and comments from her survey suggested that straight licensing arrangements with non-related firms were less popular; instead the emphasis shifted more to licensing of subsidiaries and joint ventures. About half the firms reported they were moving in this direction. Presumably related to this trend was the finding that about one-third of the companies reported dissatisfaction with performance of individual licensing arrangements. The blending of investments and licensing as well as exports doubtless was also a major factor in the organizational handling of licensing. In the conpanies surveyed, only 19 percent had a full-time licensing coordinator or manager. The most common practice reported was for the top international executive to be responsible but with supervision of licensing operations to be disseminated among regional or other officers under him.

Lovell devoted a large portion of her report to accounting practices. The overall impression conveyed by these sections was that the accounting effort and thus the knowledge of full financial performance was quite limited. While in some respects this was undesirable, by and large it seemed to be consistent with the role of licensing and the options open to the firms. For example, where licensing was viewed as a defensive device for short-term market protection, full analysis of the costs involved might not be worthwhile. Or, if licensing was employed as but one of the structural ties with subsidiaries, it might not be either useful or practical to try to unravel its costs from all of those involved in the relationships. Lovell did note, however, that the limitations in accounting might prove troublesome in future tax questions though she had not explored this aspect in detail.

The report enumerated all of the types of financial gains and costs pertinent to licensing arrangements and indicated the incidence of each in the reporting companies and whether they were recorded in their accounts. Only a few obvious items such as royalties and costs of machinery provided were commonly recorded. A number of important ones were not. For example, of the 130 companies which incurred travel costs of supervisory and technical personnel to help licensees, only 56 percent kept separate records of these costs. On the income side, Lovell identified eighteen types of return but again only a few were generally recorded. For example, 122 firms indicated that they gained through sales of components or raw materials to licensees but only 46 percent of these kept separate records of the sales income.

6. Transfer pricing has received considerable research attention with five studies available to provide a range of analyses of MNC experience. Business International surveyed the methods and experi-

ence of a range of companies presenting a comprehensive analysis of practices which were adaptations to the pressures of competition, taxes, tariffs and costs, and the need to provide sales motivation at the factory, international division, and distribution levels.[10]

The main subjects covered were intracorporate pricing, intercorporate pricing, establishing market prices, and control mechanisms. Problems of pricing between domestic factories and export divisions were a major preoccupation in most firms. Consistent with prevailing managerial concepts, many companies had established profit centers at each level to improve motivation and control. But this resulted in numerous difficulties because the performance of each center was heavily influenced by the transfer prices whose level was determined by various competitive, cost, and tax considerations. Business International recommended as the best apparent solution the "carry-back" system under which some profit was earned for control purposes at the export level but was then carried back to the producing level. At the producing level a consolidated profit statement became the major management performance and pricing guide.

The study demonstrated the persistence in a great many companies of looking upon exports as "plus" business. That is, these managements had set their prices on an incremental cost basis. In a typical case the factory prices on goods for the export division were lower than those for domestic buyers. While part of this doctoring was justified by clear savings like lower selling costs, much of it was based on the fact that the out-of-pocket cost for producing an extra X per cent to fill export orders was all that had to be covered for these sales. The practices in many companies were more sophisticated than this but the incremental-cost attitude were still clearly evident.

The result of these practices was that export sales did not contribute as much to profits as domestic business. This colored the motivations and actions of key managers in servicing the export demand to the detriment of market development. Thus, while observing that prices should recognize that additional export volume for the production line spreads fixed costs, Business International generally felt that marginal costing tended to subsidize export sales. But sales to all markets should be evaluated in terms of contribution to corporate earnings on the same basis. In the same vein BI noted that few U.S. firms followed the practice of spreading out the R&D cost.

7. Greene and Duerr surveyed senior executives from 130 companies concerning various aspects of transactions between parent companies and overseas controlled subsidiaries.[11] The survey showed that in every aspect there was great diversity in corporate practices and viewpoints. Nonetheless there were a few dominant themes.

The study started with the observation that, theoretically, internal exchanges within the company network constituted a simple realignment in ways that would maximize financial return to the corporation. But, while this might be practical domestically, the survey showed it to be largely inapplicable in the international marketplace. External forces, including foreign and U.S. tax provisions, customs regulations, and balance of payments controls, greatly restricted the range of flexibility open to companies in adjusting intracorporate prices and other exchanges so as to maximize return.

Faced with these constraints, most respondents reported they had adopted the basic principle of "equity" in commercial relations with their subsidiary companies abroad. The equity concept was elaborated in quotations from one executive to include "a reasonable, rational distribution of profits, one that can be easily justified in terms of the interests of the host country." Within this general philosophy, however, the survey did indicate a tendency to seek overall corporate profit maximization by judicious shifting of profits when that was feasible. It also showed a desire to maximize return in dollars.

A major factor in company practices was the fact that nearly two-thirds of the companies managed their foreign subsidiaries as profit centers. These companies tried to treat the foreign units on roughly the same basis as an unrelated firm. Stress was also laid on the attitudes of overseas managers achieved in this approach, as compared to shifting profits around so that the foreign units could not control their own financial results.

A large part of the report was devoted to describing different approaches to allocations of profit and price setting. Some firms linked profit to the functions performed by the U.S. supply units and the foreign subsidiary. Others split gross margins on the basis of assets, costs, or some subjective concept of "equitable" treatment. Some felt so hemmed in by tax regulations that they were guided entirely by them. A few had foreign subsidiaries which were fully autonomous, food companies, for example, that had no significant transactions with the parent. And a minority of firms gave primacy to maximizing overall corporate profits. Methods of determining prices included the arm's-length concept required by U.S. tax law, negotiated pricing, and the cost-plus approach.

Taking a broader view, the survey found that a substantial number of senior international executives acknowledged the desirability of applying a uniform corporate policy to relations with all of their controlled foreign units. Because of differences in the operating environments of these units, however, very few stated that they were able to do this in practice. Most firms did try to hold to uniform broad underlying "concepts." But flexibility and regular review were necessary at the level of policies and operating practices.

8. Arpan made a survey of intracorporate pricing of foreign firms operating in the United States, comparing their practices with those of U.S. firms.[12] A questionnaire was sent to 145 firms with U.S. subsidiaries. The response of 40 percent was generally satisfactory; only the Japanese, Swiss, and oil companies made no replies. The author was able to round out his information by interviews with eight major accounting firms, which were familiar with the practices of companies of all countries. He also had follow-up visits with sixteen firms that responded to the questionnaire.

While Arpan found that foreign-owned subsidiaries in the United States had a relatively high degree of autonomy, the setting of transfer prices remained the absolute prerogative of the parent company executives, regardless of firm nationality. Degrees of subsidiary participation in transfer price determination varied, but the bargaining power and final say belonged to the parents. The person responsible for the prices was never lower in rank than treasurer and usually he was vice president or comptroller.

Transfer pricing systems of non–U.S. MNCs were generally less complex and more market-oriented. Sophistication was closely associated with orientation: market systems were less sophisticated because they did not rely on complex cost determination formulas. There was also less of a scientific approach to transfer price determination in non–U.S. firms. Sophisticated cost-oriented systems were characteristic of most large multinational companies, although they typically maintained additional records using market-price equivalents for subsequent management-performance evaluation. They also did the most maneuvering of liquid assets. Smaller firms tended to use market-oriented systems and did less maneuvering. Firms operating with a degree of monopoly power tended to use cost-oriented systems.

Finally, there are national preferences. U.S., French, British, and Japanese managements preferred cost-oriented systems, while the Canadians, Italians, and Scandinavians preferred market orientation. The West Germans, Belgians, Swiss, and Dutch did not exhibit a particularly distinctive orientation preference.

The research showed that the degree of competition and differences in income tax rates were the most important variables affecting pricing. Inflation, foreign exchange conditions, export subsidies, and customs duties were significant for a limited number of firms.

Non–U.S. multinational firms considered only roughly half as many internal parameters as their U.S. counterparts. The parameters that were not considered had to do with transfer pricing's relation to management performance evaluation. The use of profit centers and return on investment analysis was not widespread among non-U.S. firms; therefore problems caused by transfer pricing in these areas did not enter in as considerations. The most important internal criteria were acceptability of methods to governments, competition, and control. The latter was typically the key element, pricing being vital to parent control of financial performance.

Some national patterns were discerned. For the French and Italians income tax minimization was the dominant goal. This was due to the benign neglect of the French government and tax determination and collection procedures in Italy, which were considered to be so confused and subject to interpretation that maximum opportunities for tax avoidance and deferral existed. The Japanese preferred cost-oriented systems. Their intensive competitiveness could be attributed considerably to low transfer pricing. Among English firms pricing was manipulated to assure steady return on investment, which was demanded by British bankers. Canadian firms were distinctly market-oriented, but largely because Canadian-U.S. trade was subject to both Canadian and U.S. tax regulations specifying arm's-length prices. The West Germans gave least attention to pricing, their emphasis being on fixed asset position. The Scandinavians gave primary emphasis to host government acceptability.

Overall Arpan observed that two opposing trends appeared on a definite collision course. As a multinational firm's size and percentage of international operations increased, there was an increasing preference for, and use of, cost-oriented systems. As government awareness and concern over transfer pricing increased, there was an increasing preference for market-oriented systems.

9. Shulman reported his observations of intercorporate pricing practices among a small sample of U.S. companies.[13] He found that, in order to cope with the international environment, the companies typically engaged in continual adjustment of other than arm's-length prices. He noted the main incentives for price adjustments as differences in tax levels among countries, high tariffs whose effects were reduced by lower component prices, unstable foreign currency conditions encouraging maximum return to the parent, and regulations of foreign countries that encouraged high prices as a means to recoup parent company costs properly chargeable to the subsidiaries.

He also found some more subtle situations such as the use of low transfer prices on imports which gave the foreign enterprise the appearance of a sounder balance sheet. In some cases foreign lenders might be presented with profitable operating statements almost from the start, rendering them more willing to advance needed capital to the subsidiary. On the other hand, the effect upon foreign divisional managers might be to foster a false sense of accomplishment in getting a new venture off to a profitable start.

And yet more problems might arise when two subsidiaries were involved. In one company the United Kingdom division was directed to lower its price to a new French subsidiary so as to improve start-up operating results; but a good deal of ill feeling was generated when headquarters seemed to forget that the resulting poor performance in the United Kingdom was not a reflection of local management failure.

Shulman gave considerable attention to such effects on the management control system not only because they complicated the process of making intelligent management decisions but also because of their psychological effects. For example, in the case of a company whose highly directive transfer-pricing system caused a disproportionate share of income to arise overseas, its international managers were sometimes tempted to boast about their "contributions" to corporate profits. The fact that their profits were in effect allocated rather than earned did not deter their proprietary self-glorification, much to the frustration of domestic managers.

To minimize this problem, Shulman found that two companies made compensating adjustments in control data so that profit allocation was better balanced internally. In effect, dual sets of books were maintained. One was for public consumption and tax purposes, while the other was kept for internal measurement and evaluation. The sharp eye of the tax authorities was, of course, a critical factor. It was understood that company manipulation of transfer prices was within the range of tolerance of tax regulations.

10. Duerr made a survey of company experience with U.S. allocation of income and expenses under Section 482 of the Internal Revenue Code.[14] While a number of general points were made in the study, its chief value lay in the descriptions of 172 allocation cases. One of the main general points that emerged from the survey was the great variation in allocation methods. It appeared from the survey that both companies and tax agents had preferred to settle their differences privately.

Section 482 dates back to 1928 but until after World War II it was not used extensively. As the volume of international business has grown, it has become a major tool of the U.S. government in trying to capture what it regards as a fair share of the income generated in intracorporate transactions with foreign subsidiaries. Its use in the 1960s was further encouraged by the failure of the Treasury efforts to get Congress to tax all foreign income of U.S. firms. Many companies felt the allocation process had been used as an alternative device to tax as much of this income as possible.

The crux of Section 482 cases is the implementing regulation which says that allocations should be comparable to those in transactions made at "arm's length with another uncontrolled taxpayer." Since "arm's length" transactions under identical circumstances rarely exist, there is considerable uncertainty as to what allocation is proper in any given case. The regulations provide some further clarifying options such as cost-plus computations but there is still wide latitude for discretion.

The other major factor indicated in Duerr's survey was that companies tended to look first at the "big picture" and then arrange the details to conform, rather than the other way around. Thus intercorporate transactions were determined by competitive strategy, financial needs, and other corporate goals. The U.S. tax regulations were secondary or perhaps not even considered. When the tax agents questioned the allocations, therefore, the companies as often as not had to work out the logics as best they could according to the regulations rather than having already in hand a tax-based rationale. Given the primary importance of business strategy, this problem seemed inevitable. But it did mean that a tax agent working from the logics of the law would arrive at an allocation that was often unrelated to the way the company did business overseas.

The main concern of the study was with the shortcomings in administration of the regulations. Of the 512 companies surveyed, 271 had experienced allocations in the past ten years. Of these, 28 percent felt that the agent did not adhere to the tax regulations in making the allocations. Most of the complaints were directed not at the Treasury's policies but at the way they were carried out in the field. The complaints included questions about the competence or good faith of agents and the administrative system which explicitly or implicitly created pressures for agents to maximize allocations unfavorable to companies. These pressures, combined with the latitude offered by the regulations, resulted in what the companies often felt were unjustified allocations. The most common experiences concerned intracorporate pricing, but charges for services were almost as common. Loans, royalties, and transfer of intangibles were less important.

The report concluded with observations on the overall situation. While the allocations were a minor problem for most companies, forty-six firms said they had caused major changes in their operations. Some thirty-four reported that their competitive situation had been adversely affected, eight of these firms being in pharmaceuticals. It was noted, however, that in a number of the cases the problems were due more to the foreign-source income sections of the Revenue Act of 1962 than to Section 482 itself. A number of firms did report, though, that upward price adjustments due to allocations hurt their competitive export status. A more troublesome fundamental problem noted by several companies was that foreign governments were becoming more militant in their own enforcement of similar statutes. One executive felt that an important conflict between U.S. and foreign tax authorities was brewing, and that the U.S. government ought to be negotiating a settlement or modus vivendi with foreign governments.

## STRATEGY GUIDELINES

The primary motivational variables—interest rates, foreign exchange risks, and taxes—provide the basis for strong arguments favoring a sophisticated financial flow strategy. The estimate by Robbins and Stobaugh that U.S. MNCs could increase their profits by 25 percent if they exploited the full potentials of such a strategy is a persuasive push in that direction. The practical considerations lying behind the failure of MNCs to take advantage of the potentials, however, add up to a convincing case for something less than full exploitation. Prominent among the constraining influences are government relations and managerial effects.

The long-term trend of government actions is toward constraints on MNC financial flows, for example, increasing restrictions of royalty payments and forcing closer examination of intracorporate pricing. In vigorous pursuit of some options, therefore, MNCs run a substantial risk of conflict with governments. Conflict per se is not an absolute argument against a strategy, for the essence of the analysis in Chapters 4 and 5 was the inevitability of MNC–nation conflict. The question is rather whether conflict on any specific issue is productive. The answer will depend upon the issue. Undoubtedly on many financial matters an MNC must press its case, for example, if a host government seeks to cut royalties excessively. But for much of the more sophisticated thinking about financial strategy in such options as debt-equity ratios, intracorporate pricing, and taxation proposals, an MNC, even though technically within the law, may press against the intent and interests of nations in a manner which risks aggravating relations. Pressing conflict in these areas adds fuel to the general adverse image of MNCs.

The importance of incremental gains in these options must be given a lower priority than more critical aspects of MNC affairs, which may be impaired by adverse reactions. The emphasis here must again be placed on the primary status of the product delivery system and on issues determining its effectiveness. Government actions affecting market access, operational control, logistic flexibility, and other elements of the product delivery system are fundamental. Major financial system features affecting basic profitability are, of course, essential. But it is questionable whether incremental gains by sophisticated use of financial flow options are desirable, especially if they affect overall government relations to the ultimate disadvantage of more fundamental strategy needs.

The managerial process constraints follow much the same line of reasoning. If the financial flow strategy could be delegated to financial specialists and if it could be implemented independently of other corporate activities, there would be no significant concern on this count. But that is not practical. Finance is a central responsibility of top management. Decisions on capital allocations are a prime role of senior executives. Many financial strategy options involve considerable risks: capital deployment in countries of varying stability and handling of foreign exchange risks, for example. Others intimately affect important aspects of government relations as has been noted previously in this chapter. Independent implementation is not practical because of the intertwining of the control system and the dependence of decision-making on financial measurements of performance. To some degree it is possible to run independent accounting systems or supplementary measurement processes to overcome problems in this respect. However, they may be both overcomplicated and counterproductive in relations among management and with governments.

Again, the fundamental emphasis being on the product delivery system, these considerations temper the force with which one can argue for maximum exploitation of financial flow system options. Substantial diversion of top management time or loss in effectiveness of the measurement-control processes to the detriment of the product delivery system cannot be justified as a cost of achieving limited incremental gains for the financial flow system. The fundamental profitability of the MNC must, of course, be assured by careful attention to the main dimensions of the financial strategy. The managerial process considerations are, however, a realistic constraint on efforts to achieve the full potentials which purely economic calculations make seem so promising.

All things considered, therefore, the MNC should seek the optimum combination of financial flow system options which will be consistent with the primary goals of the product delivery system, especially in government relations and managerial processes. Basically, this stance calls for assurance of income from operations and protection of corporate assets. The specific applications will, of course, take many directions in considering the numerous options. Among them, guidelines for three main areas should be given particular attention: adequate flow of income from affiliates, reasonable attention to capital costs, and conservative handling of foreign exchange risks. Figure 9−3 schematically incorporates these guidelines.

The flow of income from affiliates is the "bottom line" of MNC operations in a financial sense. In terms of our strategy analysis it is the reciprocal component of the central MNC role of resource transmission. The latter point leads toward the fundamental guidelines for strategy. The financial flow system should be structured so that income flows from affiliates are soundly related to resource flows. This guideline requires considerable sophistication in costing and design of income flow options.

As the Business International and Lovell reports show, many firms especially in the early years of their international work view foreign income as "plus" business with little effort to refine the costs or to structure the income flows systematically in relation to the resource flows. In the practical circumstances of specific cases this approach may be sound; much depends upon the product delivery strategies involved. However, as a general guideline for the evolution of financial flow strategy, these characteristics are undesirable both by internal managerial economic standards and in the prevailing environmental context, especially in government relations. Managerial standards call for a systematic effort to determine costs and benefits as a basis for measuring the profitability of resource transmission. Effective government relations require a solidly based rationale for income flows to meet critical government reviews and to justify foreign exchange allocations in the many host countries that restrict international payments. This line of thinking supports the full use of each of the main options—dividends, interest, royalties, management fees, and intracorporate pricing—by designing the magnitude of each to return to the MNC the full value of resources transmitted to the affiliate.

Reasonable attention to capital costs is a major guideline because of the real but secondary role of financial resource transmission in MNC strategy. By "reasonable" it is implied that the firm will in broad terms be conscious of global interest rate differentials and will make use of low-cost capital when that does not conflict with other significant considerations. Frequently, however, it may be expected that interest costs will turn out to be a lesser concern. In particular, it is to be expected that frequently protection against foreign exchange rate risks will support borrowing local funds. A less common but in some cases strong consideration will be avoidance of direct

**Figure 9–3.** Financial Flow System for Bilateral Unified Strategy

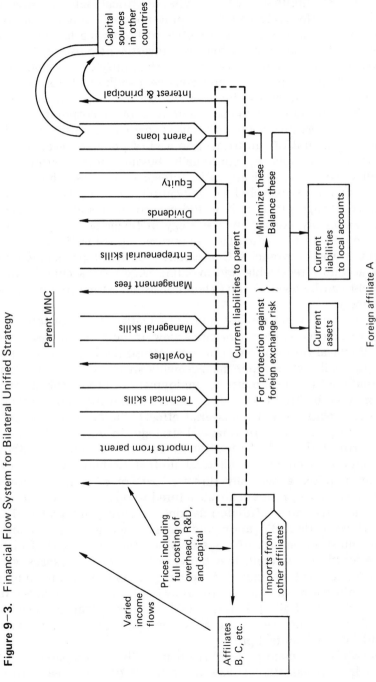

blockage of funds for payment of external interest and principal on debt. Within the limits set by these types of critical factors, however, the MNC may effectively benefit by movement of capital from low- to high-cost areas. The general practice of borrowing large sums in the Eurobond market for international investment purposes by major MNCs is a practical demonstration of the utility of this guideline.

The third main guideline, conservative handling of foreign exchange risks, is dictated by the international monetary environment and the responsibility of management to protect corporate assets. The term "conservative handling" is used advisedly to distinguish the approach from that of full protection against possible devaluations, which is possible only by continually buying future contracts to cover all outstanding obligations in foreign currencies. The cost of full protection is excessively high. Indications from the work of Robbins and Stobaugh are that it would exceed the losses experienced using a reasonably conservative strategy of financing. The latter essentially consists of avoiding large exposure to possible devaluations, especially in weak currencies. Conservative current steps include minimizing accounts receivable and avoiding large cash accumulations. Local debt can be used to the extent consistent with a sound capital flow strategy.

These guidelines are modest and conservative. It is not intended thereby to take a completely negative view of the more sophisticated uses of financial flow options. For some companies in particular situations, especially where their managements are especially competent in international financial matters, employment of more sophisticated means may be highly beneficial. However, within the constraints of government relations and managerial effects, these guidelines seem sound broad parameters for financial strategy. In terms of the models set forth at the end of the strategy patterns section (page 386), they compose essentially a bilateral unified strategy. Each of the guidelines requires a centrally directed pattern of financial flows. That is, the actions proposed are structured to optimize return to the parent when the parent-affiliate relations are closely integrated. The income flows, capital allocation, and foreign exchange risk avoidance measures must all be part of plans in which the parent and affiliate roles are jointly considered. Inevitably, in this process linkages with other affiliates will be included because of trade relations among them. Furthermore, a number of aspects of collective analysis of financial matters of all affiliates, notably financial strategy development, inherently involve capital allocation, foreign exchange exposure, and financial control processes.

Thus, while the main pattern of financial flow anticipated under the guidelines is essentially bilateral, from the parent to each affiliate, it inevitably is based on a substantial degree of unified planning for the MNC system as a whole. It does not, however, assume the character of the multilateral unified strategy in which the finances of all of the affiliates are in principle pooled. In practice such a system would result in a much greater flow of funds among units and much less discrete distinctiveness for the financial system of each unit and the flows of funds in and out of it. Substantial movement in this direction is discouraged by the complexities of management it would require given the nature of the international monetary environment.

In concluding previous chapters ISAGRIDS have been used to illustrate the application of strategy analysis to the situations of High Technology Industries, Singer, and General Foods. The ISAGRID is not particularly appropriate, however, to bring out the key distinctions in financial flow strategy. Table 9—6 showing the relative emphasis among the main income flow options will be used instead. The options for financing affiliates are not shown because there would not appear to be significant differences among them based on firms' characteristics. There are, however, distinct differences in income flow patterns related to the nature of the companies.

The relative emphasis on royalties reflects the importance of technology among the firms. HTI with its superior and important technology can expect to justify large royalty payments to tax and foreign exchange authorities so they compose a major source of income from HTI affiliates. Singer's technology is neither so distinctive nor so important, but it is still significant and of respected value to national authorities who have typically encouraged manufacture either for import substitution or export. Thus Singer can expect governments to be reasonably accepting of royalties from its affiliates. General Foods, on the other hand, is in a relatively weak position in justifying royalties to any government exercising appreciable controls on technology payments. Few host nations will see significant national interest benefits in convenience food technology.

The status of management fees has been noted as moderate for all firms, essentially to make the comparison with technology payments

**Table 9—6. Relative Emphasis of Income Flow Options for Sample Firms**

|  | *Royalties* | *Management Fees* | *Intracorporate Pricing* | *Dividends* |
|---|---|---|---|---|
| High Technology Industries (HTI) | High | Moderate | High | Low |
| Singer | Moderate | Moderate | Moderate | High |
| General Foods | Low | Moderate | Low | Moderate |

that is typical of most governments. The value of management skills is recognized but at a moderate level comparable to the intermediate technology inputs of Singer. The outcome is that management fees should be less significant for HTI than royalties but more important for General Foods.

The differences in importance of intracorporate pricing reflect the varied logistic characteristics of the firms. HTI makes a number of its more sophisticated products in just a few factories, shipping them to affiliates in many countries. With its strong competitive status, it is in a good position to price the products to bring a good return to the parent, including if appropriate, some portion of income from other aspects of the affiliate operations. Singer also has considerable trade from its major export plants. However, some substantial markets are self-sufficient in production so no income is earned by exports to them. And the sewing machine market is sufficiently price-competitive so that Singer is not in a position to push prices up appreciably in most markets to achieve any extranormal transfer price outflows from affiliates. For General Foods this option is largely precluded because food products are not exported to most affiliates.

The dividend flows are assumed in this presentation to be residual payments subject to both affiliate financing needs and government controls. HTI being in a rapid growth industry has a continuing need to expand facilities abroad so it will reinvest a considerable portion of affiliate earnings and remit limited dividends. Singer, an essentially mature industry with limited expansion needs, will have little need for reinvestment. While the company's retail-store, consumer-financing activities require large volumes of working capital, it will be well advised to obtain it by local borrowing and remit its cash as dividends to protect against foreign exchange risks. General Foods is a growth industry but from the problems apparent in the Brazilian, British, and Mexican situations, it appears that the difficulties of achieving acceptance for new convenience foods in foreign cultures results in relatively slow growth. Thus the rate of reinvestment would be smaller than with HTI, providing more opportunity for dividend remittances.

# NOTES

1. Sidney M. Robbins and Robert G. Stobaugh, *Money in the Multinational Enterprise* (New York: Basic Books, 1973).

2. Wilson B. Brown, "Islands of Conscious Power," *MSU Business Topics*, Summer 1976, pp. 37–45.

3. Ibid., p. 44.

4. Robbins and Stobaugh, op. cit.

5. Robeit G. Stobaugh, "Financing Foreign Subsidiaries," *Journal of International Business Studies*, Summer 1970, pp. 43–64.

6. David Zenoff, "Profitable, Fast Growing, but Still the Stepchild," *Columbia Journal of World Business*, July-Aug. 1967, pp. 51–56.

7. David Zenoff, "Remittance Policies of U.S. Subsidiaries in Europe," *The Banker*, May 1967, pp. 415–427.

8. R. Hal Mason and Francis G. Masson, "Balance of Payments Costs and Conditions of Technology Transfers to Latin America," *Journal of International Business Studies*, Spring 1974, pp. 73–89.

9. Enid Baird Lovell, *Appraising Foreign Licensing Performance* (New York: National Industrial Conference Board, 1969).

10. *Solving International Pricing Problems* (New York: Business International, 1965).

11. James Greene and Michael G. Duerr, *Intercompany Transaction in the Multinational Firm* (New York: National Industrial Conference Board, 1970).

12. Jeffrey S. Arpan, "International Intracorporate Pricing: Non American Systems and Views," *Journal of International Business Studies*, Spring 1972, pp. 1–18.

13. James Shulman, "When the Pricing Is Wrong by Design," *Columbia Journal of World Business*, May-June 1967, pp. 69–76.

14. Michael G. Duerr, *Tax Allocation and International Business* (New York: The Conference Board, 1972).

*Chapter 10*

# Strategy of Control
# and Ownership

The control and ownership of foreign affiliates is typically
the thorniest issue in relations between host nations and
multinational corporations. For both sides the issue has
important implications of a fundamental character and in particular
aspects of operating results. Many of these implications have appeared
in the preceding chapters. In the present chapter they will be pulled
together and other considerations added to develop a composite analysis of the subject.

A prime objective in this analysis is to clarify the real interests
of the parties involved. The need of both MNCs and host and home
countries to distinguish misperceived extensions of self-interest from
valid differences in interests is appropriate here. (See p. 178.) Because of the nationalism and other attitudes involved, perceptions
about the value of control and ownership are often distorted by both
host nationals and MNC executives.

Pursuing this objective of clarity, we should start with an understanding of the distinction between ownership and control, avoiding
the tendency to assume they are synonymous which is all too common. In a technical sense, ownership of 100 percent of the capital
stock of an affiliate gives an MNC the power to elect the board of
directors, who vote on major affiliate actions and choose the management that directs lesser actions. But these formal powers by no
means result in full parent control over the affiliate because the status of the host government gives it a wide range of direct power over
the operations. Such matters as provision of foreign exchange to
cover dividends to the parent and approval of construction of new

factories involving import of machinery and site acquisition are routinely subject to government approval in many nations. And governmental objectives may be pressed in many other ways, sometimes by direct action like price controls and in others by a range of indirect influences in areas such as relations with labor unions and tax administration. Thus the appearance of control conveyed by ownership is always limited and greatly so where the host government exerts its potential power aggressively.

On the other hand, neither is it correct to presume that giving up 51 percent or more of ownership to local stockholders means the loss of effective control of an affiliate. It may be true but not always so. Usually it is a matter of degree. The reality will depend upon the power that the MNC commands beyond technical ownership, a factor that is often critical even when it has 100 percent of the equity. The elements of its power were discussed in Chapter 5 and in this general discussion of control we are simply reformulating the MNC-nation state relationship examined there. We may say, for example, that an MNC offering high technology needed by the host nation or providing a good export market for its goods can exert a high degree of control over decisions of an affiliate even if it has less than 50 percent equity. Another MNC offering resources of minor value to the nation may find itself pushed around by the government even if it holds 100 percent of an affiliate's stock.

A second and related point requiring comment is the concept of corporate ownership embodying a bundle of ownership rights which may be used in different control modes. Within a single nation one is accustomed to dealing with a business corporation as a complete ownership entity which has a single operating mode, typically outright sale of finished goods. Therefore "unbundling" the elements does not come naturally to management thinking. But in principle it is quite practical, being commonplace in other phases of life. The individual enters into a time-limited contract for his work services, provides his financial capital to others in various arrangements like savings bank accounts and stocks, and may rent his house on occasion.

By disaggregating the resource capabilities of the MNC, we have already laid the groundwork for the concept of unbundling the assets. This is gaining increasing acceptance in international strategy thinking. In practical terms the firm applying the idea of unbundling, structures its activities so that the components of the ownership bundle are handled differently according to what is suitable for a given situation. For example, the technical know-how owned by a chemical firm may be sold outright in the construction of a plant; the managerial skills may be either rented in a continuing management contract or more commonly may be sold on a graduated payment basis in a term management contract, and the financial assets of the firm may not be utilized at all.

The value of the unbundling approach lies in the flexibility it permits in thinking out strategy where conflicting factors deter employment of the full corporate ownership package. We have already pursued that type of thinking in previous discussions, for example, the analysis of logistic system options using the efficiency and effectiveness criteria. However, it is well to identify the concept explicitly here as a prelude to the composite discussion of the ownership-control issue which will proceed by considering the host and parent nation viewpoints and conclude with the MNC strategic considerations.

## HOST NATION VIEWPOINTS

Consideration of host nation attitudes toward ownership and control must start with the fundamentals of nationalism and proceed outward toward more concrete problems.

### Nationalism

The basic role of self-determination in nationalism was emphasized in Chapter 4. The desire of host nationals to control their own affairs is the essence of the nationalistic spirit. We have also observed the thrust toward some degree of control exercised within the host society by the MNC. This inevitably means conflict with nationalism. Attention is given throughout this book to many ways in which the conflict may be ameliorated or resolved, but it can never be really eliminated. The self-determination goal of nationalism is always in opposition to the control requirements of management.

The disposition of this inherent conflict has already been dealt with at one level in the discussion of the power balance process for resolving issues in Chapter 5. However, it is well to go here to another level because, when applied to the deep human feelings associated with nationalism, the power balance concept leaves an image of a "cold war" relationship. Unfortunately this has a ring of truth in much public thinking but is undesirable and ultimately not necessary. The central issue is not really power but interdependence. How can the desire for self-determination be fitted into a world in which interdependence is firmly established as necessary for economic progress and physical security? The resolution of issues by power relationships is simply the means by which the interactions implementing interdependence are worked out. The fundamental adjustments have to come in a different pattern, which permits nationalistic people to accommodate to living confortably with interdependence.

This sort of adjustment has a parallel in the way individuals learn to live in the interdependent structures of society. All people have desires for independent action generically similar to those embodied in nationalism. As children they strive for freedom from parental control, only to find as adults that they must adjust to all manner of external controls at work, by government, and even in assorted voluntary relationships. Some maladjusted individuals never really accept these constraints and live in an endless state of rebellion and antagonism toward the controls exerted by society. But most adults adjust quite well. They often complain about restrictions on their life but the complaining is for the most part just a healthy release of emotions. On the whole, they accept the constraints as part of normal life and are content to find satisfactions within the considerable range of personal freedom allowed them by the system.

The problem at the international level is that the structural relationships are too new and are still changing so rapidly that a satisfactory pattern of accommodation has not yet evolved. It is clearly beyond the scope of this book to deal fully with such a complex subject. Its main dimensions must be understood, however, for the MNC–nationalism interaction is just one symptom of the fundamental process by which national peoples learn to live with the interdependent world.

The ultimate key to the necessary accommodation is acceptance of whatever degree of external control is required to make interdependence effective. But that acceptance can only come after a prolonged period of experimenting, testing and proving. Who should exercise the control? Probably many groups just as in domestic society—governments, businesses, and religious groups, for example. What will be the limits of control? We do not now know. For commodity prices? For military actions? For distribution of income? Today the basic adjustment in which the self-determination thrust of nationalism becomes tempered with the acceptance of international constraints is at a very early stage. Indeed, as the interaction analysis in Chapter 4 suggested, in many ways the current process is strengthening the basic nationalism.

To return to the central issue of control, it must be expected that the fundamental conflict will be with us for the foreseeable future. The MNC must accept as inevitable much of the "cold war," "I accept your invasion of national control because I am forced to" attitude. Only over the very long term will its control function be given basic acceptance as part of the overall adjustment to global interdependence.

### National Interests

There are two main areas of national interest which host nations see at stake in the control-ownership issue: direction of national economic decisions and economic benefits. They must be analyzed in terms of the ownership-control options available and the criteria for their effectiveness. Effectiveness criteria are best stated in the form of three questions:

Are the specific national interests sought being achieved?
Does the control-ownership pattern have other specific effects?
Are there secondary effects which are adverse to national interests?

The control-ownership options available cover a considerable range but for analytical purposes they may be grouped under four headings: general governmental control, direct control, unbundling, and joint ventures.

**General Governmental Control.**  Technically any affiliate of an MNC operating in a foreign country will fall under the sovereign powers of that country and be subject to the control of its government just like a domestic enterprise. Thus in principle the government should be able to influence its actions as it does those of other businesses in the country. Host nations observe, however, that in practice they have less ability to affect MNC affiliate decisions for at least three reasons.

First, the host is less able to affect affiliate decisions because an MNC subsidiary is less susceptible to some of the means by which governments attempt to direct economic processes. The example commonly cited is finance. Governments use various components of the financial system to achieve economic goals. France's indicative planning is an illustration. The government priorities are fostered by steering bank credit and other forms of financing into favored fields and discouraging it in low priority situations. This approach works well for domestic firms essentially dependent upon financing out of the national economy. But MNCs with ready access to parent and other international financing feel little pressure from the governmental financial measures and thus are under less influence to make decisions according to the government intent.

The second reason for inability to affect affiliate discussions is that the management decision-makers in the MNC affiliate are less oriented to host national interests. Some are likely to be non-nationals and even the local nationals are likely to have some sense of loyalty to the MNC interests as compared to executives in purely national firms. Thus as decisions are made the affiliate managers are presumed to give less weight to national interests and they will not be personally as susceptible to influence of government officials who attempt to guide their decisions.

The third reason is that many decisions, particularly major ones on investments, export policy, etc. will be made in the MNC headquarters away from the influence of the host government but subject to pressures from the home government and other countries.

These observations are ample basis for the conclusion that something more than the control system applied to domestic business is required if host governments are to substantially influence MNC decisions. One can make a case after considering all of the complications to be discussed that it may be unwise to attempt to exert substantial influence at all. But few host countries will entertain that concept so it is largely an academic proposition.

**Direct Control of MNCs.** The second approach is to go directly to the heart of matters of national interest by exercising specific influence on the MNC decisions. It is employed very widely when MNCs make new investments. In most LDCs and in not a few developed countries like Canada and Japan, new MNC investments must go through some sort of government screening. During the screening officials may press for arrangements that fit national objectives. The government views may be handled informally but quite commonly the process involves a formal agreement. Robinson's intensive survey of entry contracts in fifteen countries, summarized in Chapter 4 (p. 145) gives a thorough picture of this approach. It is clearly effective for acting on certain important goals, notably direction of investment into priority fields, establishment of major structural components (financing, employment of nationals, exports) and ownership. The limitations within the system seem to lie largely in its postinvestment capabilities. Robinson notes the very weak policing processes in LDCs that do not have the personnel to follow up on the performance of MNC entry contracts. But despite this shortcoming the entry contract and similar direct approaches to MNC decisionmaking appear in principle to provide an effective vehicle.

The main problem with them is their potential for adversely affecting national interests outside the specific issues to which they are directed. The big hazard is that a direct control system may discourage foreign investment in general. The evidence here is mixed but appears to indicate that the system per se is not adverse but that it is susceptible to use in ways that can be very adverse. Robinson's study indicated that firms were not necessarily less willing to invest in countries that were more restrictive. In fact, experience suggests that MNC managements are more concerned with stability and predictability, a point of view consistent with our prior discussion of reaction to political risk. Thus a strong investment control program is not in itself likely to discourage them. The key question is how it functions. If it involves endless delays, red tape, and difficult official relationships at the administrative level, that will discourage investment. More broadly if it embodies criteria and requirements that are unacceptable to managements it will have the same results. Crookell cites a set of Turkish requirements (p. 273) that were so inconsistent in this respect that they could not be accepted by MNC managements.

**Unbundling.** Unbundling is another direct means to deal with the control problem, in this case by excluding a large portion of the MNC control capability from the host society. The main options are licensing, management contracts, and turnkey operations. In each case the scope of the MNC operations is limited and the main decisions in the operation, since they are under the authority of national ownership, are subject to normal government controls. There is no question but that this approach is highly effective for specific goals and in assuring general host nation control. There are major limitations, however, in the extent to which it can be applied and to its utility for many national objectives. For some important industries like automobiles, the complications of skill transmission and unified logistic strategies are so great and the power of the firms so considerable that host nations cannot expect to apply the approach to them. For goals such as expansion of exports and development of national R&D capability, unbundling is not likely to attract MNC collaboration. There is the possibility that the national firms receiving the limited MNC inputs may develop their own R&D and export capabilities but that will depend upon their own competence. On the whole, therefore, it appears that the unbundling approach is effective but appropriate for only certain situations, notably operations requiring stable, relatively easily learned technologies (e.g., fertilizer plants) and transmission of technology among firms with relatively equal skill competence (e.g., cross-licensing among chemical firms of advanced nations).

**Joint Ventures.** There is wide support among host nations for the achievement of national control of MNC activities by requiring local ownership of 51 percent or more of equity. Much of this thinking is distorted by the confusion over ownership and control discussed at the beginning of this chapter. The actual control over decisions in a joint venture is likely to be determined more by the relative power of the partners than by their equity shares. But, other things being equal, there is no doubt that the party holding the greater equity has greater control. That still leaves other questions to be answered, though.

One major question is whether the joint-venture partner will be an effective vehicle for incorporating host national interests in joint-venture decision-making. If the partner is the government, then presumably the answer is positive. But there are good reasons for limiting the extent of government joint-venture participations. The process stretches government resources unduly, government management in industry is often ineffective, and private business capabilities are not developed. In most countries, there is a general disposition to favor private local businessmen as joint-venture partners. There is in fact a separate motivation in this direction which is an important part of the story in itself. Local businessmen have a strong personal motivation to participate in joint ventures with MNCs. For a modest financial investment and limited management role, many of them have profited greatly from the skills of MNCs. Indeed Kidron reports from his intensive study of foreign investment in India that the government was subject to charges of bias from some segments of the private sector in its decisions to approve joint ventures by specific Indian firms which thereby achieved lucrative profits.[1]

This consideration of local partners presents some questions of national welfare in itself but it also bears on the utility of joint ventures as a vehicle for exercise of host nation control. The key query is how effective the local business partner will be in serving the national interest. The presumption is that as a local national he will be more susceptible to the host government's influence than the MNC management. He may be. But he may also not be. It depends on the individual. If he sees greater profit in taking a direction proposed by the MNC, he may support it. Furthermore, with the external financial capabilities of the MNC behind him, combined with his skill in handling the local environment, he may be more effective in evading the government intent than the MNC by itself would have been.

As a practical matter, host governments find on occasion that MNC managements, because of their high visibility and more tenuous status, are more susceptible to direction than local businessmen. These comments are suggestive, not definitive. The reality in each case will depend on the nature of all the actors and on balance undoubtedly local businessmen will be more amenable to government influence than foreigners. However, the basic point made is that the injection of the local business partner as an intermediary adds a considerable element of uncertainty to the objective of exercising host nation control.

A second major question conerns the acceptability of the joint venture to the MNC and its response in critical management issues. In this respect the joint venture can be treated as a partial unbundling, subject to much the same problems of adverse MNC views in key areas, and it will be most effective to discuss it specifically in reference to them. Before getting to that, however, a significant variation of the joint-venture concept should be brought into the picture. That is the "fade-out" idea, the process by which an MNC makes an initial 100 percent equity investment in a new operation and then divests itself of a majority of the equity over a period of, say, fifteen to twenty years. This idea acquired a degree of interest during the 1960s and then was adopted as the official policy goal of the Andean Common Market nations in 1969. With the weakening of ANCOM, it is likely to lose its strength there and it has not developed a strong status elsewhere. However, it is still an option that may appear on the agenda in specific cases.

Intellectually the fade-out idea has a certain appeal. The proposition is that the full contributions of the MNC are needed at the outset and the MNC should gain the full profits from these initial efforts. Then as the need for its inputs decline with the acquisition of skills by the local unit, it should progressively fade out of the picture. The trouble with the idea is that it does not fit with the basic characteristics of the MNC identified early in this book, notably its primary focus on long-term strength and market position. The fade-out process would leave a firm with some residual role as a 49 percent partner but for a dynamic firm with new products, marketing skills, and production technology coming along steadily, the preferred status is 100 percent participation which both facilitates application of inputs and profit on them on a continuing basis. Thus, viewing opportunities around the world, the MNC is bound to rate the fade-out situation as having lower potential and in a variety of ways will give it less management attention. Overall therefore foreign investment is discouraged by the prospect of fade-out requirements.

It appears that the fade-out approach is even less favorable than an immediate requirement to divest majority ownership. In the fade-out there is a distinct possibility of an extended period in which the MNC management will be treating the affiliate as a step-child, withdrawing earnings from it and not putting new effort into it. The local management may be in a liquidation frame of mind before local part-ners step in with controlling interest and such drive and capabilities as they may have to build the business. A requirement of divestiture in a fairly short period, say a year, eliminates that period of potential deterioration.

**Control Issues.** These general comments are necessary to put the options into perspective but a determination of the utility of each for achievement of control of MNC activities by host nations is best seen by looking at specific aspects of national interest: nature of in-vestments, development of national industrial competence, export expansion, and fostering research and development capability.

Host governments have a major interest in maximizing new *invest-ment* and guiding it in directions conceived to be most useful for it. Back of this interest are the national desires for economic progress, employment and status. For this purpose the option of direct control by government appears both in principle and in practice to have the greatest utility. Unbundling and joint venture approaches are too clumsy as indirect vehicles, though it is possible that one of them may be adjunct to the negotiations or an outcome of them.

The exercise of the influence of the government on the MNC decisions to provide whatever inputs are involved calls for direct interaction with a combination of incentives, pressures, persuasion, and other elements of negotiation. The shortcoming of the approach lies, of course, in the discouragement to investment created by the negotiation process itself and the terms imposed. But these elements have become so commonplace today that most MNCs accept them as part of doing international business. Certainly they should be iden-tified as a deterrent to the whole international business system. Given the high priority host nations attach to direction of investment deci-sions, however, the general loss is an acceptable cost. The key then becomes the development of competence in handling the direct con-trol process so that individual firms find it tolerable. There seems to be a steady progression in this direction, Robinson noting in his study the growing sophistication and competence of the investment proces-sing systems he studied (see p. 145).

Development of national *industrial competence* encompasses a vari-ety of things but most importantly in this case the acquisition of technological and managerial skills. The direct government control is appropriate for this purpose as evident from training and related requirements commonly incorporated in entry contracts. But host nations generally see great value in the joint venture and some forms of unbundling as a more dynamic means to achieve the end. The key point argued by host governments is that local nationals will be given higher level positions more quickly in a joint venture and the overall development of skills will therefore be greater than with fully-foreign-owned operations. The other side of the coin is in part the lower effectiveness of the skill transmission process discussed earlier and in part the lower inclination of MNCs to transmit technology fully to partially owned operations.

There would not seem to be any clear evidence one way or the other as to which is the best means through which to exercise government influence in this respect. A significant point to guide thinking about it, however, is to stress the difficulty of directing the MNC actions in this area as compared to investment decisions. The latter have specific dimensions subject to explicit decisions and implementation. Skill transmission on the other hand is a continuing process involving a multitude of actions and requiring a high degree of voluntary behavior. If a host nation by direct influence can assure itself that host nationals will be placed in most management positions, then it is likely that the maximum skill transmission will occur in whatever structural option results in maximum MNC desire to achieve the transmission. The extent of skills conveyed will be greater than in options dependent on governmental compulsion or on theorized local dynamics. Thus, it is quite possible that the joint venture will not be as useful as the wholly owned subsidiary unless the former is perceived as ultimately becoming an independent entity. Reinforcement for this view is found in Robinson's observation that some countries were moving fairly rapidly toward effective control of MNCs by giving priority to technology transfer rather than ownership.

Where the government wishes to exert influence to *foster exports*, there seems no question but that the direct control process is preferable. The critical point which has been made previously is the strong aversion of MNCs to using partially owned units as sources for global logistic systems, essentially ruling out the joint venture and unbundling options. These observations are clearly confirmed in the outcome of entry negotiations in LDCs. Where significant export obligations are undertaken, the governments generally permit 100 percent ownership even though that is contrary to prevailing foreign investment policy.

Governments desiring to foster MNC *research and development* in their nations are also more likely to succeed by direct influence though the reasons are somewhat different than with export development. We have noted the very strong logics for unified R&D strategy. The prospective lack of control of R&D work and even the risk of loss of benefits of results virtually preclude assignment of significant R&D to units over which the parent does not have clear control. On the other hand, host governments, at least in the developed countries, have had modest success with direct efforts to persuade MNCs to place R&D in their areas. The MNCs are quite conscious of the importance of the subject to the host nations and they are susceptible to incentives to move in that direction. Thus, for example, Canada has been able to encourage a number of U.S. firms to place R&D work in subsidiaries there. A conspicuous but not untypical example was the placement in Canada of full R&D work for a complete new line of products by National Cash Register Company supported by a package of tax and financial benefits provided by the government.[2]

### Economic Benefits

All of the control issues just reviewed have important economic effects so that discussion carries over into this section. To it must be added certain effects on economic results related to the ownership of MNC affiliates, notably in balance of payments and capital formation.

There is a strong feeling among host nationals that MNC ownership makes them a hostage of the MNC for the payment of dividends in perpetuity. They feel this is contrary to national interest and unjust, since they think the MNC's contributions do not deserve these continuing rewards. Limited ownership arrangements are strongly preferred for this reason, the unbundling and fade-out approaches being particularly favored.

Rational analysis of this subject is difficult partly because it is complex and partly because the outflow of money is a point that especially arouses nationalistic feelings, the draining of national wealth syndrome. The complexity arises from the uncertainties which MNC financial practices and national borders inject into the idea of the role of profit in society. The basic concept supports the payment of dividends as part of the financial flows in the economy, as they are through various intermediation processes eventually routed back into new investments. The system may function with varying effectiveness, sometimes rather badly as in depressions. But within private enterprise societies, the basic concept is accepted.

When MNCs remit dividends, however, the recycling to new investment in the same country is less direct and under not uncommon circumstances it may not take place. Ideally the recycling comes in the form of new investment by other MNCs. Obviously one cannot identify a route by which dividends remitted to MNC A appear in new capital provided by MNC B, but the process conceptually is no different from that in the domestic recycling process. To this stage the difficulty lies in the near impossibility of explaining such a process convincingly to the great majority of host nationals who can see no structural connection between outgoing dividends and incoming capital of different companies. But the more serious problem arises from the frequency of real breakdowns in the recycling, especially in the very LDCs in which nationalism and anti–MNC attitudes are strongest. As we observed in Chapter 7, new investment often falls off when political or other deterrents are encountered. Thus it is absolutely true that in many cases the recycling concept is not valid, at least over periods which may extend for several years.

Given these real and perceptual problems, there is strong basis for the host national feelings that they will assure themselves of a fairer return if the dividend process is so structured that external payments are minimized. To a point this end may be accomplished by the restrictions on dividend payments, say to 8 percent of capital, which many countries impose. But the more certain means appears to many host nations the joint venture or unbundling route which structually and permanently limits the claims of the MNC on a share of the profits. This aspect of the joint venture–unbundling options has to be considered along with the other implications already discussed and particularly with the closely related aspect of domestic capital formation.

The effects of MNCs on host nation *capital formation* have been studied by a number of economists with inconclusive results. The key question is whether MNCs by their investments displace local capital, i.e., by putting money into opportunities that local capital might have undertaken, or whether they undertake ventures that would not have been developed otherwise and thereby stimulate the economy so that local people invest more than they would have. Analytically it is hard to isolate the effect of the variables affecting capital formation so answers to this question are elusive. It also seems quite likely that the answers will be different from one country to another.

The benefits to the host nation of the extent of MNC ownership are clearly affected by this question. In simplistic terms it would seem that the nation would be adversely affected by limiting ownership because it would reduce the capital inflow into the country. By the same token a requirement for divestiture resulting in repatriation of capital would be injurious to national interest. But that is not necessarily so if the inputs of skills by the MNC had stimulated new capital formation provided by the local national businessmen participating in the venture.

Finally, there is an overall economic benefit anticipated for the host nation by positioning a local business partner as an "agent" for it in relations with an MNC. In pursuit of his personal benefit the local partner should in effect also be pursuing the benefits of the host nation. He will bargain for lower prices in imported components, for limited licensing fees, for export rights, and other terms. There are points on which the host government itself may negotiate with the MNC except for the time required. The time factor is significant though because the typical LDC government has quite limited competent staff members. There is great practical utility therefore in positioning a body of local businessmen as joint-venture partners to serve as a corps of negotiating agents promoting the economic interests of the nation in MNC relations.

### A Selective Strategy

The net effect of the varied economic effects is hard to determine. This inconclusiveness has been affirmed by Vernon on the basis of his broad study of MNC performance. "In cold and narrow economic terms, there is no *a priori* basis for assuming that a greater measure of local control is associated with policies that yield a higher level of benefit for the host country; the opposite could well be the case. But the introduction of control as an end in itself changes the calculus of benefit and cost to a degree that depends on the perceived value of the control."[3] The value of control per se takes us back to the discussion of nationalism, which probably affects the thinking of host nationals who are often unable to grasp the involved relation of control and economic effects.

Despite this overall inconclusive picture of the effect of control and ownership, it does appear that there are certain patterns of relations between options and specific national interests and that their diversity favors a selective policy by host nations. Specifically, we have seen that partial ownership is probably self-defeating where export expansion and encouragement of local R&D are desired. On the other hand, where the inputs desired from the MNC are limited and not expected to continue over time, the economic benefits and the benefits in greater control may favor the unbundling options or joint ventures. Thus the general conclusion from the host nation point of view is that a selective policy is sound in contrast to the general policy advocating joint ventures that is common in many countries. This conclusion is reinforced by the selectivity evident in the entry contract practices of the more successful LDCs like Brazil and the Philippines, observed by Robinson which have avoided dogmatic overemphasis on host national control and ownership (p. 145).

## HOME NATION VIEWPOINTS

By and large home nations of MNCs have not taken significant positions in the control-ownership issue, nor would there seem to be important national interests at stake for them, except insofar as their interests coincide with the MNCs' interests. In theory one can make a case that greater MNC control is in the interests of the home nation because it more effectively permits achievement of policy goals. However, home nation goals concerning MNCs are largely not such that the extent of control over the foreign units is a significant issue. For example, the use of low-cost labor countries for manufacture by MNCs with its "exporting jobs" implications in home countries is affected by the willingness of the host countries to permit fully owned operations. But the home nations coping with the question are unlikely to find that influencing ownership is a useful move. Import quotas, tariffs, or other restraints are much more effective.

The instances of home influence have been varied therefore, and relate to specific national situations rather than to broad aspects of MNC–home nation relations. In the United States, the only significant government influence was during the early years of the aid program. The government then was giving strong support to the desire of host nations for joint ventures. This viewpoint could be attributed to the academic governmental economic background of aid officials, who had little appreciation for the management viewpoint. While that sort of viewpoint still provides considerable support for joint ventures in the U.S. government, it is strongly tempered now by greater influence of MNC managements in policy-making. Indeed the extended discussions of State Department officials with other countries on codes of investment behavior in which MNC managements have closely collaborated have brought the official and business thinking close together.

Japan provides a quite different case, the only one in which a parent nation has made broad statements officially encouraging joint ventures. As we will note presently, Yoshino's study shows that there have been distinctive circumstances which made joint ventures generally more desirable for Japanese firms than for U.S. counterparts (p. 267). In addition, the Japanese government has been especially concerned by the strong anti–Japanese sentiment aroused by operations of its MNCs in Southeast Asia and by the corrupt and callous practices of a significant portion of the firms. The policy position is part of a deliberate effort on the part of the government to act in a cooperative and sympathetic manner in line with the goals of these host nations. However, as Yoshino indicates, there is now a trend among the major Japanese MNCs to favor greater control, for much the same reasons as among U.S. firms, so the Japanese government is likely to take a less vocal position on the subject in the future.

But the main point is that both of these examples illustrate that the direct interests of the home nations in the issue are marginal so they should not be viewed as factors in its outcome.

## MNC VIEWPOINTS

MNC viewpoints on control and ownership as they affect components of strategy have been included in previous chapters. To put the total subject in perspective as the MNCs tend to see it, the findings of several studies analyzing the experience of Continental European, British, Japanese, and U.S. firms will be summarized. The main overall themes will then be pulled together to provide general guidelines for strategy in this area.

### Studies of MNC Experience

1. Franko's study of European MNCs provides the following picture of joint ventures in their operations.[4] Most European MNC operations were simply production units turning out parent-developed products for the local market. Joint ventures were widely accepted, composing over half the total. The ownership practices were influenced by limited capital of parent firms and their involvement in diverse, non-consumer product lines in which mixed ownership presented few management complications. Both at home and abroad, the European firms were generally accustomed to a cartel-type environment in which dynamic complications for management were minimized. The highly competitive U.S. environment was quite different. When U.S. competitors struck, European enterprises were often handicapped in their response both by reflexes conditioned to seek negotiated arrangements and by the frequent inapplicability of European production and distribution techniques to American relative-factor costs. Two responses were observed. The first was the nearly universal undertaking of research and development in the United States. The second was a tendency to seek full control, two-thirds of all U.S. affiliates being fully owned, to achieve quicker management decision-making in competitive responses.

2. Franko expanded on the latter subject in his study of European firms in the United States.[5] He found that over 70 percent of the U.S. subsidiaries of large European companies were fully owned. Of the fewer than 30 percent that were not wholly owned, only about

10 percent were joint ventures with corporate, family, or individual private shareholders. Thus European companies indicated a strong preference for wholly owned operations in the United States, and a general aversion to joint ventures with partners who might exercise some managerial responsibility. Not only was this the case but the divorce rate of joint ventures in the United States also seemed particularly high. At least ten of the sixty-seven wholly owned subsidiaries of the forty-nine companies examined started out as joint ventures with U.S. partners.

The primary reason for European companies' preference for wholly owned ventures in the United States seemed to be related to the nature of the U.S. market. In his findings cited in Chapter 6 (p. 243) Franko noted the desirability for a European company to do R&D in the United States. The management of technical innovation was seen as more than the maintenance of an R&D laboratory, rather it was a corporatewide task too important to be left to any specialized functional department. Therefore the subsidiary's response to the ever-changing U.S. market required a closer coordination between marketing and R&D than was possible with a joint-venture relationship.

3. Stopford and Haberick made an intensive study of the ownership of more than 2500 affiliates of eighty-three British firms which account for about three-quarters of Britain's overseas manufacturing output.[6] Most of the analysis excluded affiliates in the six countries where ownership had been closely controlled for some time—India, Japan, Mexico, Pakistan, Spain, and Sri Lanka. Data from the study of U.S. firms in which Stopford participated which is summarized below was cited in frequent comparisons.

Overall, British MNCs had a somewhat greater portion of joint ventures than U.S. firms, over half having partners in at least 40 percent of their affiliates. A strong trend toward shared ownership was observed with 90 percent of pre–World War I affiliates wholly owned compared to 64 percent of those established in the 1960s. There were indications that this trend was not only due to host nation influence on the firms but also because, lacking knowledge of local market conditions and wishing to catch up on their entrenched international competitors, they frequently turned to local partners to speed their entry. Some countervailing forces were observed, notably rationalization of production systems and adoption of area-based structures, both associated with buy-out policies.

U.S. data had shown that MNCs operating in four or more industries collaborated with partners nearly twice as frequently as those in one industry. British firms showed no such pattern. The reason for the difference was not clear. One factor was the number of British firms that merged during the 1960s with companies already established abroad. An analysis restricted to situations where diversification took place after acquisitions showed that few of the new affiliates were wholly owned. The authors also found that there were many MNCs which held very small share interests in some foreign companies which had been acquired in a variety of ways including sale of foreign affiliates to large firms for stock and technology exchanges.

Certain policies were found to favor absolute control, notably technological leadership and being in a marketing-intensive business. It was also observed that affiliates in the United States had the highest incidence of full control and that larger affiliates were more likely to be 100 percent-owned. The authors identified sixteen firms as "global investors," those with less than half their sales in Commonwealth countries and manufacturing in at least four continents. These companies typically were competitive leaders with strong research and advertising. The global investors' policies appeared insensitive to the location of the affiliates. By contrast, Commonwealth-based investors showed an increased preference for partners outside the Commonwealth where they were weakest. Data for the global investors related closely to that of U.S. firms. The strong implication was that, when equally strong competitively, British firms adopted ownership policies of the U.S. variety. It was the weaker British firm that had relied more frequently upon local partners abroad.

Data for the six countries that closely control ownership showed that they did have a higher portion of local participation than other nations. However, the number of affiliates was relatively low, suggesting that the countries paid some penalty for insistence on their policies in that firms had refused to consider investment. In like vein analysis showed that the proportion of all new affiliates had declined in recent years in LDCs. This was taken to suggest that British-based MNCs had been concentrating their efforts in the developed world and withholding both management and financial resources from the less developed world. While the proportion of new wholly owned affiliates had declined in the LDCs, it had risen in the U.S. and Commonwealth countries. In EEC and EFTA countries the proportion was static for new affiliates, but this region showed the greatest number of increases in management control indicative of rationalization of European units.

Overall the authors concluded that where the parent company possessed distinctive strengths in product lines critical to its continued survival, wholly owned positions have been preferred. Where the resources of the parent were less distinctive as compared to other international competitors, or where the business was peripheral to the main interests of the parent, partners were often preferred. Likewise where transfer of resources among units was required, control was preferred. Noting that this pattern resembled that of U.S. MNC policies, the authors observe that since many British-based MNCs are somewhat weaker in terms of technological resources, marketing skills, and even sheer size, they have exhibited a slightly higher propensity to work with partners abroad. Another observation was that many British managers increasingly felt impelled to develop stronger roots in developed economies to offset the problems of controlling a world business from a weakening home base. With this shift away from LDCs the risk to governments of losing British investments appeared to be increasing. Somewhat offsetting this shift was an apparent greater willingness of firms to contemplate management contracts and licensing.

4. Yoshino's analysis of the Japanese MNC outlook was reported fully in Chapter 7 because it was dominantly concerned with logistic strategy effects (see p. 267). For the trading companies, foreign ventures were largely undertaken to establish captive export customers and joint ventures were quite acceptable because control over operations was not important to this end. However, the system of many weakly controlled affiliates had not proved effective. The initial investments among manufacturing firms had followed a similar pattern. However, as the trend shifted toward operations established to take advantage of lower production costs abroad, the Japanese MNCs found close control important to assure quality standards, coordination of production, and flexible transfer pricing. For those having high technology advantages, control also became an important factor.

5. An interesting supplement to Yoshino's broad picture is the detailed study by Sim of decision-making in British, Japanese, and U.S. affiliates in Malaysia.[7] The main findings will be presented later (p. 549) but particularly relevant here is the conclusion that the Japanese parents exerted stronger control of management decisions than the Americans or British because they were more inclined to accept joint ventures. In other words, direct authority over decisions exercised through Japanese executives placed at the top of joint ventures was an effective substitute for ownership in asserting parent control.

6. Stopford and Wells made a study of basic organizational structure and ownership, drawing on the Harvard data bank on 187 U.S. MNCs and a substantial amount of interviewing.[8] The organization part of the report will be incorporated in Part III of this book.

The study of ownership patterns showed that a strong preference for wholly owned subsidiaries was generally associated with strategies that also required tight central controls, notably: (1) use of marketing techniques to differentiate products, (2) rationalization of production facilities to reduce manufacturing costs, (3) control of raw materials, and (4) development of new products ahead of competitors. Firms in the first category placed major emphasis on their own advertising and put a low value on marketing contributions of joint-venture partners. The degree of production rationalization and the related product standardization were clearly correlated with the utilization of joint ventures among the sample of firms.

Those who tended to use more joint ventures were generally other types of firms for whom resources available from local partners were useful. Companies with a high degree of product diversity more often took this approach as a means to acquire marketing skills. The data also showed that small firms had a greater propensity to enter joint ventures. The study indicated that changes in strategy and organization often led to changes in ownership policy. Specifically, when enterprises reorganized their structures primarily along geographical area lines—a clear sign of a desire to tighten central controls—they tended to change minority holdings to majority control, or to buy out the joint venture partners altogether.

The authors also discussed the range of host government policies and their effect on firms. They found evidence that the countries had not managed to persuade some foreign enterprises to deviate much from ownership patterns they were accustomed to apply elsewhere. The crux of this matter lay in the relative bargaining powers of the parties, which were examined briefly, along with the costs and benefits to the countries. The authors inclined to the view that no significant economic gain existed but that the political pressures along with growing power would lead to greater demands for shared ownership. At the same time, because of the evolving strategic requirements on organizations, the dominant pattern would probably be greater attempts by MNCs to exercise control over their scattered subsidiaries. Because of this trend it appeared that the majority of the existing multinational enterprises would try to move toward more complete ownership of their overseas facilities. They might become less capable of resisting growing host nation pressures for shared ownership, however, as access to technology and industrial capabilities in developing nations increased. Some counterbalancing strength for the firms was seen in their control of access to foreign markets. But on the whole the authors seemed to accept that the growing desire of firms for greater ownership control would be frustrated, especially in developing nations.

7. Franko made an analysis of historical experience with joint ventures which was summarized in Chapter 7 (p. 277). He confirmed Stopford and Wells's findings by showing that MNCs tended to eliminate joint ventures when they became complicating factors in centrally planned strategies. Franko concluded that there should be no universal policy on joint ventures because companies might choose either of two strategies. MNCs concentrating on serving one-product markets wherever they went eventually would find their joint-venture partners a hindrance to their desires to differentiate product, rationalize production, and recentralize organization. However, those following a strategy of constantly diversifying abroad by introducing new products into foreign markets would continue to use and have a high tolerance for joint ventures. It was important, he observed, however, for both the multinational corporation and the foreign partners to look ahead to understand the policy implications of different strategies. They should consciously prepare for the shock that could come when joint-venture partners wish to go in their own directions at the same time that corporate policy seeks to rationalize, centralize, and differentiate.

## BASIC THEMES IN MNC
## CONTROL-OWNERSHIP STRATEGY

While this global survey of MNC control-ownership experience shows considerable diversity, there is a notable consistency in certain basic themes. Adding the observations in previous chapters and some further information, we may identify five themes as the dominant determinants of strategy: role of local partners in operating effectiveness, effects on skill transmission, issues of foreign unit management, limiting risks, and compatibility with unification strategies.

### Operating Effectiveness

The role of local partners in operating effectiveness appears in the studies summarized in the preceding section as the primary benefit MNCs derive from joint ventures. It is especially important for smaller firms and those new to international business which lack overseas operating know-how. Characteristic is the observation of Stopford and Haberick that U.K. firms seeking to catch up with firms already established abroad sought local partners to speed their market entry. In part this strategy is often based simply on the value of buying an initial market position by joining an existing firm. But that portion of the strategy could be accomplished by full acquisition as General Foods did in most cases in starting up its overseas program.[9] The assumption in the joint venture entry method is that the competence of the partner will be substantially utilized in operating the firm and will be more effectively involved if he is a financial partner rather than just a general manager. Benefits are anticipated from his greater experience with the host national business system and especially in the sensitive area of relations with the government.

On the whole, this role has been demonstrated to be of real value. However, two reservations have to be noted which contribute to the downgrading of the values of the role by larger and more experienced firms. First some partners are not effective in integrating their local management know-how with the expectations and inputs of MNCs. The problem may be simply a matter of managerial abaptability. This would appear to be a factor, for example, with Mr. Gellini in the General Foods Italian case as he found it hard to adjust to the range of management innovations put forward by the parent. Or, at a more fundamental level, the partner sometimes proves to be quite inappropriate. The commonest example of this type of difficulty is the loss of effectiveness of the associate if he is a political figure and a change of government makes him an "out." One can visualize, for example, the radical change of Canton Drug Company's status in the volatile Middle Eastern political climate if Mr. Baba's party loses power (p. 102).

The second reservation is of a structural nature. The standard response of many experienced MNC managements to this pro–joint venture argument is that they can "buy" the same sort of local management competence by hiring appropriate local nationals. Experience has proved that they are to a large degree right, especially in the advanced Western nations and to a fair degree in Latin America. The executive employment market is quite open in those areas and an MNC can usually hire people of much the same quality as one would acquire in a joint venture.

To some extent in Latin America and to a high degree in other LDCs and non-Western nations, however, it is not so easy to buy the necessary competence. One deterrent is the adverse views of employment in MNCs due partly to nationalism and partly to perceptions of opportunities they offer for promotion. Truitt and Blake, for example, in their study of elite attitudes, found that opportunities for promotion were rated "good" or "very good" in national companies by 77 percent of respondents in Chile and 73 percent in Venezuela as compared with 32 percent "good" and 31 percent "very good" by respondents referring to U.S. firms.[10]

A second and more serious deterrent is a social structure which reduces managerial mobility. The prime example is Japan where the lifetime employment concept holds most able managers with the local firms they joined as young men. Even the large and experienced MNCs have found in Japan that it is very difficult to hire first class Japanese managers. This fact, combined with the complexities of the culture, language, and government relations, has led many companies that avoid joint ventures in most countries to conclude that in Japan they are desirable.

### Skill Transmission

The effects on skill transmission were discussed earlier (see p. 298) so they need not be elaborated on here. Analysis combined with the experience reported in research confirms the loss of effectiveness when skills are transmitted in a partially owned system.

### Foreign Unit Management

Issues of foreign unit management represent a convergence of the first two themes but they also present more general management problems. At the heart of the latter is the difference between unitary and joint management. The overwhelming dominance of unitary management in the corporate world is ample demonstration that by and large it is the more effective. In a unified management system a diversity of viewpoints can be resolved better than when two strong viewpoints are represented by substantial power at the top level of the organization. Where joint ventures are most common and successful, for example in mineral and petroleum operations, the partners share a large degree of common goals and management approaches and tend to pick operating teams which, being imbued with these characteristics, can be left alone to run the operations. A joint venture marrying an MNC with a strong foreign business organization is another matter. Differences in viewpoints are always encountered on many points, so a mixture of disagreements, delays, and frustrations are common deterrents to decision-making.

Viewed as a convergence of the role of the local partner in contributing host nation managerial competence and effect on skill transmission, however, this decision-making involving local partners process takes on another dimension. It establishes a dynamic managerial process for the resolution of questions which largely fall in the innovation-conformity area. When local managerial competence is "bought" by hiring local nationals, it has a weaker position in decision-making because the local managers rank below the parent headquarters staff and usually below one or more senior expatriate managers. Thus there is a built-in bias in the decision-making process in favor of the MNC viewpoint. This structural characteristic is another way of describing what we have noted as the greater effectiveness of a fully controlled organization in transmitting skills. Its value is quite clear on that count. However, in the determination of when innovation is appropriate, that is, which skills should be transmitted, the "effective" system may be less effective than the divided management of a joint venture.

The joint venture structure assures that the host society viewpoint will have a strong influence in decision-making. It may, of course, be too strong, in which case useful innovations may be blocked. One cannot generalize. It depends on the case. The Canton, Shave-All, and General Foods cases provide illustrations of the variations possible.[11] In the Canton case, it is by no means certain whether Mr. Phillips's approach to financial management is sounder than Mr. Baba's in the context of the local culture and, their power status being reasonably balanced, the outcome has been a compromise which may or may not be the best resolution. In the Shave-All case, Mr. Macy seems to have a strong case for his plan for more aggressive sales promotion and Mr. Rama's dominant status in the joint venture does appear therefore to be a real obstacle to a better approach to management. In General Foods, on the other hand, in several instances the power of the top management has resulted in adoption of product ideas in foreign units about which local management was doubtful and which proved unwise. But also in some cases top management showed greater perception than the local staff.

Although one cannot generalize about the merits of joint ventures in this respect, the components of decision-making are fairly clear. If in each case they are employed well, the chances for a sound strategy are improved. As the cases just cited indicate, the form in which innovation-conformity, skill-transmission issues appear is commonly fuzzy. In such conditions, the better the balance of strength in decision-making among different viewpoints, the greater the prospects that both sides will be thoroughly heard and that time will be taken to assure that whatever contributions thoughtful analysis can provide will be considered. Divided ownership is not necessarily the best way to achieve this end. For example, the balance seems better in the General Foods case than in Shave-All. However, the decision-making dynamics available in a fairly balanced structure like that of Canton do have real merit in this respect. The time and other costs involved in decision-making are an adverse consideration. But they may also be looked upon as a legitimate cost of accomplishing a difficult aspect of management if they result in better innovation-conformity decisions.

## Risk Limitations

The role of control and ownership in limiting risks does not appear substantially in the literature of MNC experience but it poses significant questions for strategy that must be considered here. These questions have been set forth persuasively by Robinson in an article whose name puts the issue concisely: "The Global Firm-To-Be: Who Needs Equity?"[12] The crux of Robinson's article is that international business in the future should be based primarily on the sale of skills rather than on investment in overseas production operations. He starts by commenting on the low level of participation of multinational firms in developing nations. He feels that clearly the global enterprise cannot push levels of return high enough to overcome the heightened risk factor in poor countries. The enterprise would run the very real risk of being charged with exploitation. He suggests that the alternative is some combination of return maximization and risk minimization.

The sale of services he proposes as such an alternative. Following conventional economic theory, he defends it as exporting the MNC's most capital-intensive output, high-level knowledge and skill, R&D, and modern technology. It is the sale of such services of skills in capital-poor countries that is likely to generate highest return on investment. A second major argument is that if one is to supply a rare and useful knowledge or skill, one is in a position of virtually no risk. Not only is one in a powerful bargaining position, but the major investment to exploit the foreign market in these terms is made in the United States in the development of exportable technology and skills. As further evidence Robinson points to the lively business in the marketing of skills among consultants, the number of firms willing to construct and start the operation of plants, and so forth.

Summing up his position, Robinson visualizes that the MNC of the future will probably sell its technology, its skills, and its distribution services on a contractual basis to largely locally owned firms. The international firm will justify itself because of economies of scale in (1) high-level staff work, including R&D, (2) the international recruitment of able people, and (3) the international organization of the market, whether on the supply or selling side.

This reasoning does not appear explicitly as a deliberate component of strategy in reports of MNC experience. There are probably two reasons for this. First, its general thrust is contrary to the primary objective of building market strength which underlies all MNC strategy. Second, the substance of the approach appears but in another form, namely the pressures from host governments for essentially the same outcome, e.g. unbundling. Combining these two factors, we find that the result Robinson advocates has been achieved increasingly but through a reluctant conformity to host government policies rather than by deliberate design on the part of MNC strategists.

The dynamics of the situation are such that this progression is both natural and likely to continue. Because a high degree of control is a priority objective for a large portion of MNCs, the deliberate adoption of a strategy of minimal equity in risky LDCs would be counterproductive. It would greatly weaken the hands of a firm's negotiators in any one country if it were known that the firm had taken such a concessional attitude in other negotiations. Adoption of the line of thinking proposed by Robinson would therefore have to result as he suggests in a full adoption of it as a general policy. But this would mean abandonment of the goal of maximum market strength which MNCs now generally perceive as still practical in wide areas of the world. Thus the prospect realistically is that the non-equity mode will continue to expand but under duress, not as a deliberate approach based on Robinson's reasoning.

### Unification

From the discussion in previous chapters and its prominence in the studies of MNC experience, compatibility with unification strategies is the major consideration favoring strong MNC control over foreign affiliates. Taken separately, a strong case was made for unification in four key areas: product lines, R&D, logistic system, and financial flow-system. Given the interrelation of these aspects of strategy, the case becomes yet more persuasive.

All of the five themes identified here have real significance for MNC strategy on control and ownership. As some lead in one direction and others in the opposite direction, a firm must reach some determination as to which are more significant and evolve some compromise in its control-ownership strategy which balances among them. The broad surveys summarized under "MNC Experience" give a sense of how firms have tended to act in recent years, and the analysis here suggests that by and large their strategies have been logical. In those MNCs for which unification has significant strategic value, the arguments for control become very great. The evidence in the studies of MNC experience supports both the strategic value and the trend in the direction of greater emphasis on control resulting from growing efforts to unify operations. This trend is reinforced by the value in high technology industries of control to achieve effective skill transmission. In the total MNC picture, therefore, the value of local partners in relating to host nations appears chiefly of significance to smaller or inexperienced firms. The risk reduction benefit of limiting equity seems to be a rationale to be accepted reluctantly as host nation attitudes require it. The chief compromises have appeared in situations where the issue lay between the merits of control for effective skill transmission versus the value of inputs of local partners or pressures of host governments to include them. Here joint ventures or even licensing with management contracts or contractual provisions giving the MNC a strong role in technological supervision and managerial decisions have been reasonably satisfactory. On the other hand, compromises are difficult where the MNC interest is in global unification, because the central control is important in precisely those issues where MNC goals can conflict seriously with the objectives of the host nations—sourcing shifts, transfer pricing, etc.

The variations in control-unification strategy which this analysis suggests are illustrated in the cases of the three companies for which ISAGRIDS are shown in Table 10—1. High Technology Industries' strength lies primarily in its superior technology and it is vital therefore that it retain that superiority through its R&D and that it assure that the product delivery system bring those skills effectively to the consumer in products and service. The prime control needs for this end are in direction and proprietary rights in the R&D system and in quality guidance and control in production and marketing systems.

HTI will also have some concern with unified logistics as the sophistication of its units and moderate size of national markets for them and the advantages of large-scale production dictate a degree of global rationalization of production. However, the sophistication precludes use of low-cost labor in LDCs for most products so it has only moderate concern with that factor in its logistic system. Moderate importance is also noted for the values of control in transmitting its managerial skills, especially marketing. These are a factor in the success of its business to which host national managers are relatively new. The cultural change entailed in local adoption of HTI products is also rated moderate because it is facilitated by control of the marketing process, but this sort of change among management of business customers is not difficult enough to be a major consideration. Global interchange within the marketing system is also of moderate importance. The host governments will have a keen interest in gaining as much benefit as possible by the transmission of the technology and especially in the possibility of reducing dependence by the shift of R&D to their countries. HTI cannot contemplate any concessions to this interest in the control of its R&D program as that could seri-

**Table 10-1.  ISAGRID for Control**

| Company | Resources | Economic Differentials | MNC Capabilities | Cultural Change | Global Unification | National Interests Home | National Interests Host |
|---|---|---|---|---|---|---|---|
| High Technology Industries (HTI) | Natural resources | | | | | | |
| | Labor | | | | M | | |
| | Capital: Finance | | | | | | |
| | Production | | | | H | | |
| | Marketing | | | | M | | |
| | Skills: Technological | H | | M | H | M | H |
| | Managerial | M | | | | | |
| | Entrepreneurial | | | | | | |
| Singer | Natural resources | | | | | | |
| | Labor | | | | H | | H |
| | Capital: Finance | | | | | | |
| | Production | | | | H | | H |
| | Marketing | | | | H | | |

|  |  | | |
|---|---|---|---|
| Skills: | | | |
| Technological | M | | |
| Managerial | H | | |
| Entrepreneurial | | | |
| Natural resources | | | |
| Labor | | | |
| Capital: | | | |
| Finance | | | |
| Production | | | |
| Marketing | | | |
| General Foods | Skills: | | |
| | Technological | M | M |
| | Managerial | H | M |
| | Entrepreneurial | | |

Importance in strategy: H = High; M = Moderate

ously impair its strength. However, if the host government of a major market puts strong pressure on it, some ground might be given on the production side. A plant might be set up as a joint venture for moderately sophisticated products as long as HTI was given strong technical control over the operation and as long as the output was entirely for the local market so no complications to the global unified logistic plan were involved. The chances are that the firm's technical strength would give it enough power to protect it from any demands more troublesome than that.

For General Foods the primary values of control lie in direction of management, especially the marketing processes which are its prime competitive strength. It finds it hard to transmit this sort of skill in a joint-venture relationship where it cannot pick key executives and provide strong direction for the methods they employ. Back of the importance of this process is the degree of cultural innovation involved and the value of pressing for change as much as possible. Transmission of the technical skills of making convenience foods is also furthered by control but it is neither so important nor so difficult to convey in less controlled relationships. Unification is significant for the firm only in the interchange among marketing and other management personnel. It is facilitated by control but it is not essential and the interchange is not in any case a vital component of success. GF does not face any particular host government pressures for local control beyond the general encouragement of local participation experienced by all MNCs. However, its own interests support some attention to the values of strong representation of local management viewpoints to guide innovation decision-making. So it is well advised to build into its control structure a strong status for top level local national managers.

In Singer's case unification of the logistic strategy, especially combining the large-scale production units with low-cost labor is crucial. The company could scarcely contemplate making the necessary investment, sourcing, and pricing decisions without essentially full control of the worldwide system. The complications arising from the one major exception the 50—50 joint venture in Japan, confirm this assessment. Control also facilitates the transmission of the marketing skills that have made the company's sewing centers such a success and of the technical skills required to make the machines, though the latter are sufficiently moderate in sophistication and rate of change so that this is not a crucial control concern. Host government pressures on the company's decision-making are strong, especially in the countries with major export plants. The company cannot concede sale of equity to permit the host nations to participate in decisions affecting the global logistic system. However, it is well advised to respond to the control desires of the host governments by close consultation on expansion and contraction of exports and it may expect the governments to apply direct influence in various ways, including both incentives and restrictions to press their objectives.

## A FUTURE PERSPECTIVE

Our analysis of control-ownership strategy ends inconclusively. The general guidelines for MNC effectiveness are reasonably clear. But their application will be greatly affected by individual company situations and especially by the direction and strength of host nation pressures. To put the outlook for this flexible situation in perspective, it is well to consider the whole control issue in the broader context of the basic structure of the multinational corporation with its emphasis on unification capabilities for which control is essential. Two extremes may be visualized: first, a close-knit, well-integrated structure in which all the basic decisions are made in the direction of unification and, second, a loosely related, highly variegated family of enterprises in which the decisions are made in the direction of fragmentation. The former is essentially an extension on an international scale of the typical domestic industrial concern. The latter appear as a group of independent national firms with quite diverse activities, tied together by licensing and similar arm's-length agreements and possibly by some exchange of capital, though with little ownership control exercised by one unit over another.

Looking at the nature of international enterprises today, one can readily see that there is a real question as to what type of structure we are moving toward. Elements of both extremes are present. Because they are accustomed to it at home, most firms have a natural bias toward the unified structure. But there is no reason to assume that it is clearly the best for international business. And indeed there are strong forces pulling in the other direction. It is extremely difficult to predict the outcome of a process of industrial evolution like this, but a few reflections on the forces at work will at least put the matter in perspective.

The fragmented structure appears to be favored by considerations of immediate operational effectiveness and organizational pressures. It seems clear the adaptation to local environmental conditions and giving way to host-country nationalism and national interests will, on a short-term basis, maximize the acceptability of a firm abroad and lead generally to the fullest realization of immediate operational potentials. The organizational problems due to distance and cultural and nationality differences will be discussed in Part III. They are also minimized over the short term by structures permitting autonomy and diversity among the field units. In addition, there are definite long-term strengths in the basic concept of fragmentation to the extent that it results in solidly integrating each foreign unit with the host society, counteracting the inherent conflict between the multinational firm and nationalism.

The unified structure, on the other hand, seems most suitable for performance of the role of cross-cultural agent of change, for the transmission of resources, and especially for global economic rationalization. For the most part it appears that the drive, coordination, continuity, economies, and other factors that contribute to the achievement of these missions are most effectively attained within a unified corporate organization.

Both of these sets of advantages are significant, but there would seem to be a fundamental logic in favor of the second. The main thrust of the fragmentation arguments is toward making the multinational corporation fit most comfortably into the host nation. This in a sense is a desirable objective, but it is essentially defensive, not positive or constructive. On the other hand, if the unified structure is most effective for introducing change and transmitting resources to the host nation and facilitating the economies for the world of integration, then it makes a greater contribution. It would appear, therefore, that this sort of structure is more consistent with the distinguishing functions and characteristics of the multinational corporation.

But such a general conclusion should not be interpreted to mean that international business will ultimately be conducted by large-scale carbon copies of integrated domestic industrial firms. Rather it is more likely that a different pattern will emerge in which the corporate structures will vary according to the situation of each industry and company. We have within domestic industry substantial variations in degrees of unification—auto companies that sell through dealers and a sewing machine company that has its own retail stores, aircraft makers that buy from many subcontractors and petrochemical firms that are largely self-sufficient for raw-material needs, and so forth.

It seems reasonable to expect that the international scene will be just as varied. The variations in this instance will be heavily influenced by the factors we have been discussing. For example, if transmission of a sophisticated combination of skills continues to be an essential element in the international computer enterprises, they will remain highly unified structures. On the other hand, if food tastes remain quite distinctive among countries and the skills of convenience food technology and marketing in which the United States has been dominant are mastered by many other countries, then a fragmented structure for food companies might be expected.

The form fragmented structures may take is yet another question. Because of the rapid spread of joint ventures, many people currently expect them to be a major feature of international business in the future. There is reason to doubt this, however. The operational weaknesses of joint ventures are clear. In decision-making and implementation they seem to have inherent shortcomings as compared to companies under unified control. Over the long term, therefore, it would seem more likely that where fragmentation is advantageous it will be accomplished by the emergence of a new structure of independent firms dealing at arm's length with each other. Thus we might expect that licensing agreements and even management contract arrangements would be more enduring than joint ventures. Joint ventures may be a useful but largely transitory phase in the evolution of multinational business. In fact, one can see signs of this evolution in the present scene. On the one hand, many firms, after entering into joint ventures that seemed of mutual advantage, have subsequently bought out the controlling interest from their partners to achieve the advantages of unified structures. On the other hand, there are situations in which local interests, often supported by their governments, have taken over progressively greater control from multinational firms, and it appears likely that they have the competence and strength to take full control ultimately. They may do it by expropriation but more likely, if the power relationships justify the host national position, the MNCs will withdraw on some mutually agreeable basis.

Finally, we may pitch this discussion at a yet higher level by pondering on the role of the multinational corporation as a socioeconomic institution. It seems safe to conclude at this point that the global company is useful as a part of world evolution. However, the ways in which it will be useful over the years and the characteristics that will best facilitate the performance of its role are by no means clear as yet.

By comparison, we have over the past fifty to seventy-five years developed a fairly clear concept of the role and values of the large, publicly owner private corporation within a reasonably integrated and homogeneous nation-state. This concept incorporates aspects of capital formation, distribution of the benefits of ownership and control among the public, relations to government and public objectives, accomplishment of innovation and economic growth, and provision of work opportunity and benefits from employment.

Though we may carry some of the thinking based upon these concepts into the international arena, the multinational corporation functions in quite a different manner, and it is likely that a somewhat different set of concepts must be evolved concerning its role and future evolution. The one sure characteristic of the firm is its unity as compared to the complete separation of fully independent national companies. Thus presumably its distinctive contributions as a socioeconomic institution should derive from the capabilities of unity.

Taking the broader social-value viewpoint permits us, however, to reexamine each of these issues to determine whether the multinational corporation in pursuit of its objectives evolves strategies that are beneficial to society as a whole. This analysis brings to light a notable deficiency in world society today—the lack of a medium to determine and foster world interests. In Chapter 5 we could effectively analyze the relations between the multinational corporation and the interests of the individual nation-state because the latter are fairly well defined and effectively organized. But turning to the multi-country analysis we are limited to discussing the diversities among nations because there is no effective concept of world interests. We have a start in institutions like the United Nations, the World Bank, and the International Monetary Fund, but just a bare beginning.

Thus discussion at this level is extremely vague, but it may nonetheless be useful for multinational corporate strategies because the long-term viability of their approaches presumably will depend upon it. Take, for example, the capital-formation question. A unified corporate strategy may at times call for movement of investment funds from one part of the world to another and at other times for maximum use of local capital drawn forth in part by guarantees offered by the strength of the parent firm. National interest is clearly an important factor bearing on each alternative; the first makes outside capital available to the country, the second fosters internal capital formation. But what is the world interest? Will the world as a whole benefit more from one of these functions than the other? Or more to the point, assuming both are needed, for which is the multinational corporation best suited?

At first glance we might say making outside capital available is the more important function, but this is not necessarily so. Perhaps the MNC's unique role lies in its capacity for global transmission of skills that provide foci for local capital formation and that anything facilitating maximum performance of this role is in the best world interest.

But this is a very cursory observation, which may be most convincing only in demonstrating how inadequately our views on such matters are thought out. Thus in opening up this further approach to the fragmentation-unification question, we can do little more than to emphasize the fact that the multinational corporation is already a world institution and that a conscious effort to think in terms of world social benefits is a movement in the right direction. Presumably this approach will lead to stress on those strategies in which the gains from unity are optimized.

The evolution of operations of U.S. firms within the European Common Market provides a useful illustration of this thesis. It is generally recognized that these companies have moved more quickly toward capitalizing on the economic unification of the area than the companies rooted in individual European countries. With their capacity for structuring operations on a global basis, the MNCs have more readily made changes in such areas as rationalization of production facilities to benefit from the lowering of trade barriers among countries.

The complexity of the move toward unification is brought out vividly in Terpstra's detailed study of operations of twenty-five U.S. companies within the European Economic Community made in the mid–1960s.[13] To varying degrees fragmenting influences have held back the process, especially in distribution and in many aspects of consumer goods operations. But the main thrust is undeniably in the direction of unification strategies. The more effective approach to unification by the multinational firms has regrettably stirred the resentment of local European firms and some of their governments. But if the basic objectives of the EEC are accepted as representative of *European interest*, as distinguished from *national interest* of the component countries, then the MNCs appear to be serving that interest best by pursuing the unification strategy vigorously. And it would seem quite reasonable to project this line of analysis to a world perspective by proposing that a global unification strategy tends to best serve *world interest*.

## NOTES

1. Michael Kidron, *Foreign Investments in India* (London: Oxford University Press, 1965), p. 262.

2. John Fayerweather, *Foreign Investment in Canada* (White Plains, N.Y.: International Arts & Sciences Press, 1973), p. 118.

3. Raymond Vernon, *Sovereignty at Bay* (New York: Basic Books, 1971), pp. 144–145.

4. Lawrence G. Franko, *The European Multinationals* (Stamford, Conn.: Greylock Publishers, 1976).

5. Lawrence G. Franko, *European Business Strategies in the United States* (Geneva: Business International, 1971).

6. John M. Stopford and Klaus O. Haberick, "Ownership and Control of Foreign Operations," *Journal of General Management*, Summer 1976, pp. 3–15.

7. A.B. Sim, "Decentralized Management of Subsidiaries and Their Performance," *Management International Review*, #22, 1977, pp. 45–52.

8. John M. Stopford and Louis T. Wells, *Managing the Multinational Enterprise* (New York: Basic Books 1972), pp. 90–170.

9. John Fayerweather and Ashok Kapoor, *Strategy and Negotiation for The International Corporation* (Cambridge, Mass.: Ballinger Publishing Company, 1976), pp. 241–270 and 437–465.

10. Nancy S. Truitt and David H. Blake, *Opinion Leaders and Private Investment* (New York: Fund for Multinational Management Education, 1976), p. 85 and p. 89.

11. Fayerweather and Kapoor, op. cit., pp. 235–276.

12. Richard D. Robinson, "The Global Firm-to-Be: Who Needs Equity?," *Columbia Journal of World Business*, Jan.–Feb. 1968, pp. 23–28.

13. Vern Terpstra, *American Marketing in the Common Market* (New York: Praeger, 1967).

✳ *Chapter 11*

# Composite Strategy Models[a]

The preceding chapters have analyzed strategy for the components of the MNC product delivery system, financial flow system, and control. These aspects of strategy may be treated to a large degree as freestanding entities to be determined according to the distinctive set of considerations bearing on them. However, throughout the analyses the substantial interrelation of the strategies has been apparent. We come readily therefore as the final stage to looking at MNC strategy from an overall viewpoint.

That approach could result in a complex matrix in which assorted mixtures of component elements of strategy were combined. But a more meaningful approach both conceptually and in terms of practical experience is found in putting together a limited number of composite models that capture the main threads of MNC effectiveness in the international environment. Four general models are presented in this chapter; their main characteristics are summarized in Table 11–1. These include the corporate capabilities underlying the models, the form of economic return anticipated, the requirements for effective operation including critical points subject to negotiation with host governments, and the power available to the MNC in the negotiation.

### Dynamic High-Technology Model
The dynamic, high-technology strategy assumes an MNC capability for generating a continuing flow of product and process innovations

[a]This chapter is essentially quoted from John Fayerweather and Ashok Kapoor, *Strategy and Negotiation for the International Corporation.* Cambridge, Mass.: Ballinger Publishing Company 1976.

**Table 11–1.   Strategy Patterns for Multinational Corporations**

| | MNC Capabilities | Economic Return System | Operating Structure Requirements | MNC Power Factors |
|---|---|---|---|---|
| Dynamic High-Technology Model | Continuing flow of technically significant new products | Steady flow of payments in royalties or from sales margins | Sustained high quality R&D program; Reasonable control of application of technology abroad | Strong, based on desire of host nations for future technological innovations |
| Low or Stable Technology Model | Useful technological skill but low sophistication or slow change | Full income realized in a short period | A short-term transmission arrangement; sale or turnkey installation; Sufficient control to assure income payment | Relatively weak, dependent on value of technology and competition |
| Advanced Management Skill Model | High competence in marketing or other management fields | Steady flow of dividends from ongoing operations | Continuing integrated operations in fields with management skill competitively effective | Weak, due to low priority for management skills |
| Unified Logistic, Labor-Transmission Model | High value to weight and/or volume ratio; High labor intensity in production; Strong global marketing system | Regular flow of dividends from either production units or marketing system | Low-cost production sites; Strong global marketing organization; Standardized products; High integrated control of operations; Full ownership preferred | Strong, based on high priority for exports in producing countries; Weak in importing countries |

for which there is demand in foreign countries. Of the three companies that have been used as illustrations in our strategy analyses, High Technology Industries fits this definition. For such a firm the profitability of the strategy rests upon arrangements rewarding the MNC for transmitting the skills. The chief alternatives are satisfactory profit margins for exports of completed products or components, royalties for the use of technology, and dividends from competitively profitable operation of overseas affiliates.

The most essential requirement for the satisfactory pursuit of this strategy is the maintenance of a strong R&D program that will generate the continuing flow of new technology. The importance of this requirement must be stressed because host nation pressure on MNCs to expand R&D within their countries may jeopardize it. The risk for the MNC is that distributing R&D among a number of host countries may reduce the efficiency and effectiveness of technological work so that the heart of the strategy is weakened. Thus concessions to host nation desires in this regard must be given grudgingly and carefully. The chief possibilities are that minor development work may be allocated to foreign affiliates or that large segments of work on certain parts of the product line may be allocated to major R&D facilities in particular countries. If the latter type of concession is made, however, it is essential that full control over the foreign unit be assured, including ownership, because of the possible loss of proprietary rights to products essential to the economic base of the strategy.

The second essential requirement is that sufficient income be generated by the operating arrangements so that the global R&D program can be adequately financed. In the current trend of host nation negotiations, particularly in less developed countries, this requirement is increasingly difficult to achieve. LDCs in the past few years have become much more aggressive in trying to reduce the balance of payments cost of paying for imported technology.

Some degree of control over foreign affiliates is required in this strategy but not as much as in some other strategies. A key assumption is that a substantial degree of effective managerial control can be achieved simply through the leverage of the continuing provision of technology. The minimum essential requirement is sufficient control over the application and quality of the technological work of the foreign affiliate so that the economic base of the transmission is not weakened over the long term. That is, the MNC must be able to assure that the technology is used in such a way that satisfactory products are produced. Otherwise the affiliate will not continue to generate income to flow back to the MNC.

This degree of control can be achieved by relatively limited means such as a quality control arrangement with an independent licensee if the latter is a competent manufacturing organization. Beyond this minimum essential, the MNC stands to gain by achieving greater degrees of control over the foreign affiliate. As a general matter, the effectiveness of the application of its technology will usually be greater if it has full control over the personnel employed in the foreign affiliates and key decisions in the operating processes. Furthermore, the greater the ownership the more readily and completely the MNC may obtain full financial benefits from the technological capabilities.

The strength of the MNC in negotiating these points depends essentially upon the quality of its technological capabilities. A company with a significant competitive lead in a field whose technology is considered very important to host nations commands strong power in such a strategy. Leaders in specialized fields like computers and pharmaceutical products are typical examples. Companies with somewhat less essential technologies or whose work is closely matched by competitors are in a less strong position. Firms producing nuclear reactors and various types of industrial machinery provide examples of this sort.

### Stable or Low-Technology Model

The second strategy model assumes the MNC has capability in a technological field that has a relatively slow rate of innovation (e.g. steel) or in which the technology is of a rather unsophisticated character (e.g. cement). For the main volume of its products, Singer's technology status should be considered in this category, though certainly more sophisticated than that associated with cement. The economic returns in such circumstances must usually be based on one-shot or short-term arrangements unless other factors provide supplementary strength. That is, the MNC's strategy calls for a system in which the technology in effect is sold in one immediate transaction or over some given period required to effectively transfer the skills involved. There can be no presumption of continuing income over an extended period, as in the first model.

The operating requirements for this strategy call for the same sort of short-term viewpoint. The key requirements are a sufficiently secure financial arrangement to assure adequate return coupled as may be appropriate to sufficient control over operations to support that financial return. The specific form these arrangements may take will vary considerably according to the country circumstances.

The simplest approach is an arrangement in which the technology is sold outright. In some cases this may merely amount to selling a piece of machinery with an instruction book or perhaps brief service of an engineer to assist in the installation and start-up. More complex arrangements grade up to the turnkey contract for large industrial installations, in which the MNC undertakes full responsibility for construction of a plant and for managing it until local personnel are competent to do so.

The other general approach to this strategy is the establishment of licensees, joint ventures or fully owner subsidiaries with a guarded time horizon. Host country attitudes are generally not favorable to the long-term income costs of arrangements like this based on relatively stable or low-sophistication technology. However, the general foreign investment policies or other conditions at a given moment in a country may permit a multinational corporation to establish a fully owned operation. In doing so, the MNC must realistically recognize that in the future, perhaps not far down the road, adverse attitudes of the host nation may assert themselves. Such has been the case in many situations in less developed countries and it has resulted in pressures on MNCs with weak technological positions to divest all or part of their ownership and terminate licensing agreements not seen as beneficial by the host government officials. Thus the strategy of a corporation in setting up operations should presume a relatively short-term payout against the risk of termination.

Although the power of the multinational corporations pursuing this strategy varies with the extent of competition and the degree of sophistication of their technology, the presumptions underlying the strategy assume that they do not have a particularly strong bargaining position.

### Advanced Managerial Skill Model

The third general strategy pattern is based on one or more areas of management expertise. The notable examples of this sort of strategy are found among MNCs in consumer non-durable fields whose competitive strength is based on advanced marketing skills often combined with management competence. General Foods is an example. The economic returns in this type of strategy call for a continuing operational system that generates a steady flow of business with a high operating margin.

While in theory it might be possible to implement the advanced management strategy through management contracts or minority joint venture arrangements, in practice majority ownership control seems to be a key requirement. Since advanced managerial skills incorporate a large degree of behavioral, non-scientific competence, it is extremely difficult to transmit them through anything but a well integrated organization system. Thus effective strategies of this sort are typically found in those firms that have a broad network of fully controlled foreign subsidiaries in which management and personnel work together over extended periods and acquire a thorough knowledge both of the management skills involved and of how to relate to other people in the organization.

MNCs find themselves in a relatively weak position in pursuing this strategy if resistance is encountered in host nations. The resistance is generally greatest among less developed countries, which regard advanced managerial skills with substantial scepticism, especially in areas like marketing of consumer goods. They give a low priority to this sort of skill as compared to technological skills and take a negative view therefore toward allocation of foreign exchange for repatriation of earnings derived from their application. Among more advanced countries there is greater acceptance of the value of managerial skills, particularly in the leading countries with MNCs of their own whose earnings are based on competence of this sort. Still, even in these countries, the MNC is in a relatively weak bargaining position in the pursuit of this strategy because little national benefit is perceived from the skills involved.

### Unified-Logistic, Labor-Transmission Model

Three elements of corporate capability are essential requirements for the fourth strategy model. First, the product involved must have a high enough ratio of value to weight and volume so that transportation over substantial distances is economically feasible. Second, the production processes must be sufficiently labor-intensive so that economic advantage greater than transportation costs is achieved by locating production in low-wage areas. Third, the MNC must have an effective global marketing organization. Electronic products, sewing machines, and to some extent automobiles are examples of products that fit these criteria. Singer is the prime example among our illustrative cases.

The economic return in the logistic strategy comes from achieving a satisfactory profit margin through the combination of the first two factors with a steady flow of business based on the third factor, the global marketing organization. The system is financially flexible so that the profit may be taken in whatever proportions are appropriate from the production locations or the marketing system.

The implementation of this strategy calls for a well integrated and efficient global system. Furthermore, the system must have a substantial capacity for flexibility and change over time because elements essential to it are subject to considerable change. Most important are changes in wage costs, which can radically alter the basis for the logistic structure. For example, in the early 1960s Japan was a sound production site for inclusion in such a strategy, but with the rapid rise of wage levels there it has become a poor competitive location compared to Southeast Asian countries. A different form of evolution is the transition of Brazil from a highly unstable political and economic status to a strong position in the mid–1970s with a booming economy providing a superior sourcing site for inclusion in a global logistic scheme.

The need for flexibility over time dictates essential elements to be included in the implementation of this strategy. It is important that there be a high degree of standardization of products so that production sites may be used interchangeably as sources for the marketing organization. Since maintenance of low costs is central to the logics of the strategy, continuing effort to improve efficiency of operations is required. Assuming the probability that rises in wage levels in some locations will reduce their competitive value while other locations emerge as more favorable sites, the strategy requires a continuing study of production locations and a sound concept as to how production mobility will be accomplished.

The control elements in implementation are also critical. To tie together widely separated production and marketing units there must be tight internal control. Market forecasts and production plans must be worked out carefully and changes in them must be transmitted rapidly. Clearly quality control must be maintained effectively. There must also be thorough coordination within the system as to changes in products and particularly in the evolution of production site mobility.

Given all of these requirements, it appears that a high degree of control by the multinational corporation is desirable, including full ownership of all units in the system. Without this degree of ownership some questions become difficult to deal with. In particular, the transfer of sourcing from one production site to another will raise very troublesome questions if there are equity partners in the foreign units. Likewise the extensive questions of pricing between production and marketing units are much more complicated when ownership partners are involved.

In both of these matters it may in fact be preferable as an alternative to full ownership to work with no ownership at all, handling the production phase of the strategy through manufacturing contract arrangements with independent national firms. Prices in these circumstances can be bargained over directly and cutbacks in sourcing can be accomplished within the terms of the contractual arrangements. However, independent manufacturers, particularly in less developed countries with low wage costs—the natural production sites in this strategy—may be less than fully satisfactory when it comes to reliability in meeting production schedules and quality standards. Thus the achievement of full ownership control is highly desirable for this strategy, though lesser degrees of control are feasible.

The negotiating power available to an MNC pursuing this strategy is great in the host countries serving as production sites and weak in those composing only marketing outlets. Among the former, with the desire to expand exports to improve their balance of payments and increase employment, the MNC following this strategy is looked on with great favor. In many cases, for example, the 100 percent ownership desired may be obtained on the basis of proposed export volume despite general nationalistic policy opposing foreign control of production facilities.

The weakness of the MNC in the marketing countries stems from the desire to reduce imports to help the balance of payments. This is often reinforced strongly by local manufacturers and unions protecting national production units. Where the latter are particularly strong the MNC may find that it cannot achieve entry for foreign production or that the entry is limited by quotas or tariffs. A number of European countries, for example, have been quite resistant to imports from Japan and other Asian countries. However, the MNC does have substantial support in the strategy of locating production in low-wage areas, from the international consensus favoring greater access to industrial areas for exports of less developed countries. This has been pressed by the United Nations Commission for Trade and Development (UNCTAD) and given substantive commitment through the agreements for preferential tariff treatment for imports of manufacturers from LDCs.

### Composite Strategies

The four strategy models have been set forth separately to facilitate analysis. Some firms can clearly be identified with just one model. However, the strategies of many firms combine the characteristics of two or more. The automobile companies, for example, blend a moderate level of technology and highly competent managerial skills with increasing use of unified-logistic, labor-transmission capabilities. In an operating sense the coexistence of strategies does not alter the analysis presented here appreciably. However, it can make a major difference in relations with host societies.

As we have noted, two of the models embody strength in relations with host nations, namely those based on high-technology transmission or on export logistics while two carry little power in this respect, those based on weak technology or on advanced management skills. In a combination strategy it may be possible to use the strength of one of the former to offset the weakness of the latter and thus make profitable use of the capabilities it embodies which otherwise might not be effectively employed internationally. IBM's strength in relations with host nations, for example, is strong primarily due to its technological superiority. In fact, however, it is widely recognized that IBM's marketing competence is what vaulted it to the lead in its field and it continues today to use that skill as a major basis for its profitability abroad. Singer represents a different combination, its greatest strength lying in the availability of its global marketing system to serve export plants like Brazil and Taiwan, while utilizing a technology for basic sewing machines little different from that of other leading firms in the field.

# ✳ *Part III*

# Administration

Strategy establishes the goals and direction for the efforts of the multinational corporation. Its implementation is essentially dependent upon administration, which will be the subject of Part III. A complete discourse on the requirements of administration for an MNC would require covering all elements of the full range of managerial functions—planning, organizing, staffing, directing and controlling (to use the classification of Koontz and O'Donnell).[1] As was true in our strategy analysis, however, the treatment in this area will be limited to the special aspects of administration derived from the international character of MNC operations. This limited treatment leads also to structuring the subject with a somewhat different classification of topics than in complete studies of administration. The discussion will be divided under two main headings: organization and managerial processes. Organization will cover staffing and organizational structures while managerial processes will deal with processes essential to strategy implementation, particularly decision-making, skill transmission, and managerial direction. As a foundation for this analysis, a diagnosis of the special characteristics of the international nature of the MNC administrative context will be presented first.

To start this diagnosis, it is well to go back to Parts I and II and relate administration to the strategy analysis for it is in one sense another facet of that subject. Administrative skills are among the key resources which the corporation may attempt to transmit; the question of conformity or change is ever present in determining administrative systems in host societies; nationalism and national interests are intimately associated with the people involved in overseas operations; and the use of unification versus fragmentation appears prominently in determining the structure of people and administrative systems of a worldwide enterprise. In this part, these elements must be considered, for they lie behind many of the distinguishing characteristics of the administration of the multinational corporation. So they will be very much in the background as we consider the elements of administration as the means for implementing strategic objectives and policies.

The framework for this analysis is a blend of the processes and strategic patterns already developed and of the effects of the intersection of administrative processes by national borders. The former establish the main lines of the firm's objectives in international operations. The latter inject into the administrative problems of any large-scale endeavour additional complications arising from the involvement of people of different nationalities located in many countries.

Figure 12–1 summarizes the key components of the analytical framework. Reference will be made to it throughout Part III. It describes schematically the organization of a typical MNC. The triangles at the top and bottom indicate the structures of the parent company and a subsidiary. As indicated by the $S_2$ and $S_3$ notations, there are a number of other subsidiaries. Supervision of the subsidiary in this illustration rests with an individual in the parent organization located at the bottom of the top triangle. Behind him spread out a variety of people whose work is in some way related to the activities of the subsidiary. These include line and staff personnel of the parent company, and a variety of people spread through the domestic organization who run factories making components for export to foreign assembly plants, establish worldwide quality standards, or in some other way affect the subsidiary. As one moves away from the point of the triangle, the intensity of the involvement of each individual with the subsidiary declines, but the number of people involved increases.

The structure of the subsidiary at the bottom is that of any operating unit, though usually on a relatively smaller scale than that of the domestic units of the parent firm. There is a senior manager in charge and a hierarchy of managers, supervisors, staff people, and workers spreading out below him. Connecting the parent structure and the subsidiary is one line, though as the notation "control lines" suggests, there may be multiple patterns of communication as will be seen in Chapter 13. There may also be some form of intervening regional supervisory unit.

**Figure 12–1.** Analytical Framework for the Administrative System of the Multinational Corporation

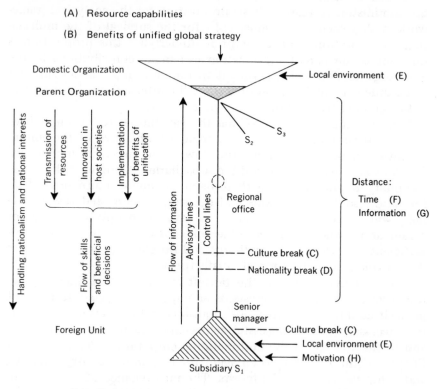

(A) Resource capabilities

(B) Benefits of unified global strategy

$$\Delta A + \Delta B \text{ must be} > \Delta C + \Delta D + \Delta E + \Delta F + \Delta G + \Delta H + \text{overhead}$$

The point of departure of this analysis is the set of objectives indicated on the left-hand side of Figure 12–1. Three of these objectives may be viewed as the constructive inputs from the center of the MNC into the foreign units, and they lead to a single general objective for the administrative processes. The three are the transmission of resources, innovation in host societies, and implementation of benefits of unification. The role of the parent organization in furthering these objectives is determined by (1) its access to the resource capabilities of the firm and (2) by its central position in achievement of the benefits of a unified global strategy including the experience with operation of subsidiaries in other parts of the world which are channeled through the headquarters and the specialization and centralized decision-making essential to unification of corporate operations, for example, in logistic planning.

If the parent organization is to play an effective role in achievement of these objectives, it must be through the "flow of skills and beneficial decisions," which is set forth as the general objective of the administrative plan. A basic proposition for the analytical framework is that such a flow must exist for the survival of the multinational corporation. The assumption underlying this proposition is that unless the parent organization can make contributions to the local organization which permit it to function in a manner superior to an independent local national unit, the international business will not be competitive and therefore will not survive.

If we assume that the MNC has the capabilities to be competitive in the international environment, then the objective of the administrative system is to facilitate the flow of the necessary implementing skills and decisions toward the subsidiaries. Along with this is the secondary requirement that there be an adequate return flow of information so that the skills and decisions transmitted toward the field will be appropriate. That is to say, the people in the parent organization who are responsible for overseas activities must have sufficient knowledge of conditions and problems in the subsidiaries if their role is to be performed satisfactorily.

The objective shown at the far left in Figure 12–1, handling nationalism and national interests, is an implementing goal. It does not in itself contain substantive contributions to the overseas units, but it is necessary to the successful achievement of the other objectives and to the welfare of the multinational corporation. As we noted in Chapter 4, the firm acts as an agent for its parent-country interests, and it has its own set of interests. The maintenance of a sound balance in the MNC's relations with home and host countries requires that these interests be pursued in their varied interactions with nationalism and national interests. The administrative plan must therefore provide an effective means for pursuit of interests by the combination of accommodation and power strategies discussed in Chapter 5.

These then are the objectives central to international administration. They establish at the outset a degree of mutual interdependence of the field and parent organizations requiring a flow of communications in both directions. The flow that may be appropriate obviously will depend upon the nature of the business. For example, it will be quite heavy in a high-technology globally unified industry in which the coordination among foreign units is great (e.g., the petroleum industry) and fairly small in low-technology industries with highly diversified foreign units.

The problems in achieving these objectives span a range from those which are found in any large, diversified activity to those which are distinctive to the multinational corporation stemming from the intersection of its administrative processes by national borders. The determination as to which problems are distinctive is hard to make because, as in many aspects of international business, the differences are often more of degree than kind. For example, some people might identify the need to adapt control systems to the greater risks of international business (devaluations, political change, etc.) as a special administrative problem for international operations. The risks themselves are certainly distinctive and have been considered in earlier chapters, for example, in the strategy on transmission of capital and in handling nationalism. However, the control systems related to them are, on the whole, similar to those employed in business in general where a range of degrees of risk is encountered. Thus the basic approach to frequency and detail of control measures employed for a subsidiary in an unstable foreign country will be similar to that for a risky, new product venture in the domestic market.

Accordingly the focus for our analytical framework must be on the effects of the intersection of national borders on the administrative processes themselves. Within this constraint the problems may be classified as arising from four communication gaps—culture, nationality, environment, and distance. Each of these is also found in domestic organizations, even the second if we note the parallel between nationalism and the we-group feelings of a factory manager toward his plant group and community. But the differences in the degree to which these problems exist in international as distinguished from domestic firms are great enough so that a substantially different analytical approach to them seems required.

The other distinctive element in international administrative systems is the presence of many currency systems which, for example, inject a distinctly different problem into comparative measurement methods in control systems. This problem is recognized but not dealt with systematically in the analysis which follows. A few words to explain its omission are in order. The presence of many currency systems would be no real problem if the relations between them (i.e., the price levels and the exchange rates) were fixed permanently. The problem stems therefore from the changes in relationships and the uncertainty as to the timing and extent of changes. Designing control systems and other administrative measures suitable to this situation is in large measure an economics-probability problem. As such, it is conceptually quite a different order of subject than the rest of the content of this book. Omission of this subject leaves out a trouble-some problem of administration for the MNC. However, as a practical matter in the design of administrative plans, the subject appears as a separate area worked out with reference to its special economics-probability considerations. Thus, its omission does not impair the analysis of the main administrative elements which follows.

The discussion in this chapter, therefore, focuses on the four types of communication gaps whose characteristics will be outlined in the paragraphs below.

### Cultural Gap

The cultural gap stems from the difficulty encountered in communication between people from groups that differ in values, social mores, and other aspects of interpersonal attitudes and relationships. There are of course many differences among people within a single cultural group. This point is brought out clearly in the intensive study of 3,641 managers in fourteen countries conducted by Mason Haire and his associates, which showed that "the differences among individuals are about 2½ times as great as the differences among countries."[2] But the people within each general cultural group are accustomed to this range of difference and have learned to communicate with each other despite it. Their communication patterns are guided by the norms and expectations of the group culture, not just by their individual characteristics. Thus two French managers may have quite different personalities, but from long conditioning by their cultures they will have acquired sufficient common patterns of communication so that they can communicate with reasonable effectiveness.

The problem for the multinational corporation lies in the need for communication between people from quite different cultural groups who do not have common norms and expectations. The dimensions of the differences between cultural groups have been described by several authors. They range from fairly easily observed features such as language and concepts of time[3] to attitudinal characteristics like job expectations and the degree of trust felt toward other people.[4] Managers whose cultural experiences differ in such dimensions find it quite hard to communicate even in a common language. An idea that has a particular meaning in one manager's cultural frame of reference may be received into the mind of a man from another culture with quite a different interpretation.

In addition to the problems of communication arising from differences in the content of cultures, further problems arise from attitudes about communication itself noted in Chapter 3. In the cultures found in Northern Europe and the Anglo-American countries, people are supposed to express their opinions relatively freely and the value systems stress honesty and precision. In many other parts of the world, however, the prevailing attitudes are quite different. People are supposed to speak much less openly, and under many circumstances they are permitted and even encouraged to say things which are misleading or not true. A subordinate in many authoritarian societies, for example, is not expected to say anything critical to his superior. In many situations Orientals and Latin Americans will give affirmative responses to requests simply to be agreeable without necessarily intending to fulfill the request. These patterns of miscommunication or lack of communication are frequently aggravated in relations with foreigners by emotions arising from insecurity, nationalism and pride, which are described in my research study of relations between U.S. and Mexican managers.[5] As a result, the international executive is often confronted with a facade which conveys an incomplete, often deceptive picture of the true thinking of the foreigner with whom he is attempting to communicate.

The cultural gap in the full organizational span of an international enterprise is very great indeed, for example, that between a U.S. parent corporation treasurer and a Japanese laborer. The full gap is rarely encountered between two individuals, however. Typically it is bridged by a series of individuals who have to a degree made an adjustment to those in organizational proximity to them so that there are a number of moderate gaps to be bridged rather than a single large one. The chief bridging process is usually accomplished by the third-culture group described in Chapter 5, composed of parent-country nationals who have become quite familiar with foreign cultures and local nationals who have become accustomed to foreigners. However, even among such individuals the basic cultural differences exist, so the cultural gap remains an important obstacle to communication in the MNC.

### Nationality Gap

The nationality gap tends to be more clear-cut than the cultural differences. There may be a few unusual individuals who are capable of a binational or non-national outlook. Most people in an organization, however, will identify themselves with a single nation which commands their nationalistic and patriotic loyalties. A substantial number of corporate activities affect national interest or may arouse nationalistic feelings. There are generally, therefore, opportunities for misunderstandings and disagreements because of the loyalties of managers which impede the functioning of the business. For example, local executives who are sympathetic with typical national attitudes are likely to disagree with their U.S. management associates in the degree to which they should press against their government for scarce foreign exchange for repatriation of profits or departure from prevailing policies on acceptance of host national capital in joint ventures. In individual cases, the attitudes of either the multinational parent management or the local nationals may be such that nationality differences are not a problem. The essence of the discussion of the characteristics of the third-culture group was that in many expatriates and local nationals the common interest in industrial objectives leads to subordination of nationalistic feelings. Yet we would be attributing non-human qualities to executives if we supposed that they could fully detach themselves from these feelings, and where valid differences in national interests are concerned, they must often, if only for practical political reasons, be loyal to the countries of which they are citizens.

Further complicating the communications process are attitudes arising from the psychology of nationalism discussed in Chapter 4. Howard Perlmutter has incorporated these attitudes into a general scheme for multinational organizations.[6] He identifies three types of attitudes: the ethnocentric, the xenophilic, and the geocentric. The ethnocentric is the aggressive, outward component of traditional nationalism. It describes the manager who is convinced that his ways are the best and should be accepted by others. The opposite side of the coin is the xenophobic reaction against the ways of others which is characteristic of many local nationals confronted by multinational firms. Perlmutter does not use this term, apparently incorporating the attitude into his concept of ethnocentricity in the attitudes of some local executives, i.e., the Frenchman whose resistance to American methods takes the form of vigorous assertion of the superiority of French ways. The xenophilic manager is one who says in effect, "We accept your superiority and our inferiority. We shall do as you say and shall comply with the methods and standards you apply to us." This is an unhealthy, negative nationalism existing among many people, particularly in the less developed regions, who extrapolate their country's inferiority in skills into a general sense of inferiority. Finally, Perlmutter identifies the geocentric manager as one who can take a balanced view of the local national ways, the parent-country viewpoint, and the world-enterprise objectives. The geocentric attitude assumes either a non-national or an internationalist viewpoint.

Individuals precisely fitting these stereotypes are rare; but the attitudes themselves in varying mixes are found in all managers, and they clearly complicate communication. A quite common pattern, for example, is a home-office group with a strong ethnocentric bias working with local nationals in subsidiaries who show a mixture of xenophilic and xenophobic reactions. The former are so sure of the merit of their own ways that they regularly issue orders, advice, etc., which are often inappropriate to the foreign situations. The latter alternate between passive acceptance of what they assume to be sound communications from the all-wise industrial masters and resistance, either explicit or of a submerged emotional nature, to the overwhelming, unsympathetic outsiders. As managements have acquired experience, they have learned how to function more effectively by careful attention, to these communications problems. However, this "careful attention" is in itself an added cost which the communications system must bear in terms of skills required of managers and of time and effort.

### Environmental Gap

The environmental gap emanates from both substantive differences and limitations in human psychology. It pertains especially to the problems of individuals in one location attempting to make decisions which are sound for other locations—most frequently the problem of the man in the home office with a responsibility for decisions affecting field operations. The substantive gap involves the acquisition of adequate information about a foreign environment. Even when substantial information has been gathered, however, there remains a psychological difficulty for the individual attempting to project his thinking into a foreign situation while immediately surrounded by his local culture which is typically his natural environment to which he is most fully adjusted. It is extremely difficult under such circumstances to switch in the proper variables so that the decision-making within the individual's mind incorporates all relevant aspects of the foreign environment.

Consider, for example, the problem of an international market-planning manager in Cleveland who is asked to evaluate a proposed plan for introduction of a consumer product in Japan. He may well have visited Japan and may even have lived abroad for a period, though the odds are it will have been in some other country. The program he is reviewing will be based on a variety of assumptions about buying power, reactions to advertising copy, and the like. There may be some evidence to back up these assumptions, but it will be incomplete; much depends on subjective impressions and interpretations. People on the spot will have gained part of their evidence from observations in store visits, reading newspapers, and assorted sources which they cannot readily convey in a report to the man in Cleveland. So he starts his review with an incomplete environmental picture. As he thinks, ideally he should be projecting himself into the Japanese home and the mind of the Japanese buyer, filling in gaps and making relevant interpretations. But all along the way he will, unless he is an exceptional person, unconsciously find bits of the Cleveland environment intruding in answering such questions as: How much benefit will we gain from brand association with our other products? How much influence will the children have on the parents' decision? He may be able to fight off the natural intrusion of the influence of the local environment, but the necessity for effort to fight it off is in itself an impediment to his effectiveness.

### Distance Gap

Distance taken in conjunction with the limitations of our current communications media causes both *time* impediments and obstructions to the *flow of information.* The time factor would appear to be a minor concern in an age of jet travel and communication satellites. In fact, however, the limitations on available personnel and the problems of communication by various media do result in a substantial addition to the time required to achieve communication in an international structure as compared to a domestic one. Likewise, although it should be possible to communicate information just as fully from Australia to New York as from Kansas to New York, in fact, the adequacy of information flow in the international organization generally appears to be less effective than domestically. Perhaps the problem lies in the greater diversity among units in the international structure. This requires a greater flow of information if people at each end are to be adequately informed.

The equation at the bottom of Figure 12—1 is a way of summarizing the significance of all the factors affecting international administration. The underlying assumption of the equation is that unless the multinational corporation provides inputs superior to those of local firms, it will not survive. The equation spells this out saying, in effect, that the incremental gains favoring the MNC from resource capabilities, and the benefits of unification with other components of the multinational structure must be greater than the incremental disadvantages arising from the obstacles to communication in the culture gap, the nationality gap, the environmental gap, and the time and information-flow problems arising from the distance gap, along with the possible lower motivation of hired managers in foreign units as compared with independent local entrepreneurs, and the cost of the overhead in the parent-organization structure.

The last two elements are not peculiar to an international business as they are found in any large enterprise in competition with smaller independent units. They are included here to complete the equation. Obviously it is impossible to insert figures in such an equation, but it is a helpful way of looking at the basic problem of the multinational organization. Essentially the problem lies in optimizing the input increments and minimizing the obstacles to communications and other disadvantages.

Notes at end of Chapter 12

*Chapter 12*

# Organization

If the managerial processes to be discussed in Chapter 13 are categorized as the dynamic aspects of administration, the organizational matters dealt with here might be called the static aspects. That characterization, however, is not really appropriate if it implies a sterile or passive quality. The structure of management and the personnel who staff it have a substantial impact on the capabilities of an organization. Thus it is best not to imply anything by initial categorizations. The distinctive nature of the content of this chapter is simply that we are dealing with the material form of the MNC organization—the nature of the people in it and the way in which they are positioned relative to each other while in the next chapter we will talk about how relations among them are conducted. The present subject matter falls under two main headings: organizational structure and staffing.

## ORGANIZATIONAL STRUCTURE

Organizational design is a never-ending subject of discussion among MNC managers. There is no ideal structure to deal with the complex management needs of large, globe-spanning, multiproduct MNCs nor even of firms of lesser magnitude given the variations in company characteristics. Furthermore, it appears that over the course of time as its situation changes, the organizational form most suitable for a company will change substantially. Thus, the discussion of organization must necessarily be cast in terms of varied options and criteria with the expectation that substantial diversity among companies will result from case-by-case conclusions.

The evolution of MNC organizational patterns can best be seen by a review of the literature describing the history of experience in the era of major MNC development from World War II to the present. The critical determinants of organization are operating requirements and the evolutionary process provides a sense of the needs felt by business and how it has adjusted to them.

For the vast majority of firms the initial organizational pattern for supervision of international activities has been a single unit, typically an international division, which very often evolved out of an earlier export department. With international activities composing a small part of the firm's business, a unit staffed with experts competent to deal with such special problems as export transactions, foreign currencies, and host government negotiations, was efficient.

1. Gilbert Clee who, as a consultant with McKinsey & Company, was in close contact with the largest corporations sensed the emergence of new patterns in the late 1950s. He wrote a landmark article at this point with a colleague, Alfred Discipio, proposing as a model for the future the "world corporation."[7] The essence of the world corporation was that the entire upper-management echelon would become skilled in international management problems and assume full responsibility for global strategic planning and decisions. The functions of the international division would be disseminated through the regular line and staff organization. By the late 1970s the world enterprise model as Clee envisioned it had been adopted by only a few companies. It appears that he underestimated the operational problems it involves. But he was entirely correct in his basic assessment that as international business became more significant to the MNC, organizational changes would be necessary to assure that it was given effective attention by top management and the key operating components of the parent firm.

2. In the mid–1960s, Clee and Sachtjen reported how the organization evolution was in fact proceeding.[8] They identified the three main structures shown in Figure 12–2. In structure A, responsibility for broad policy and strategic planning for overseas operations, previously in the hands of an international division, had shifted to executives at the corporate level without significant change in the traditional formal structure. Operational responsibilities were handled by the subsidiaries and affiliates, with corporate or international division assistance given as required. The international division in some cases also functioned as a coordinating "middle-man" between production facilities anywhere in the world and worldwide markets.

**Figure 12–2.**  Organizational Structures for Worldwide Business

A.  International Division Structure

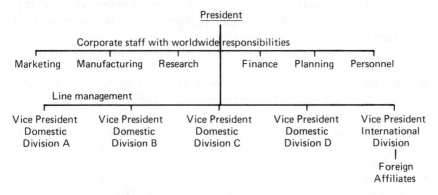

B.  Geographic Structure

C.  Product Structure

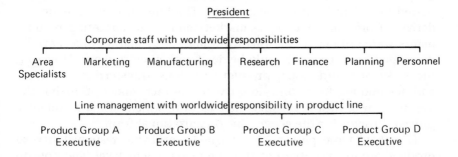

Source:  Clee and Sachtjen, "Organizing a Worldwide Business," *Harvard Business Review,*
Nov.–Dec., 1964.

One or more of five reasons were given for retaining the international division form:

- Formal organizational changes sometimes threatened to disrupt delicate working relationships, particularly in the case of long-established overseas subsidiaries.
- Foreign activities might get better direction with an international division.
- The company's key executives might be domestically oriented even though they participated in policy and strategy formulation for the overseas activities.
- The company might have worked out special ways of deriving the key benefits of another organizational pattern without relinquishing the international division form.
- The company might not have enough trained, capable executive personnel to staff a worldwide organization effectively.

Clee and Sachtjen noted the disadvantages of this structure. The international division form could become ineffective when overseas activities shifted significantly from "exporting" to self-contained overseas operations. For a company with a reasonably diverse product line, too strong an international division might impede management's efforts to mobilize the resources of the total company to accomplish a global objective. Even with superb coordination, planning would be carried out at best awkwardly by two "semi-autonomous" organizations—the domestic company and the international division.

The second basic organizational form, B, was the assignment of operational responsibility for geographic areas to line managers, with corporate headquarters retaining responsibility for worldwide strategic planning and control. Companies successfully using this structure shared two significant characteristics: The bulk of sales revenue was derived from similar end-use markets and local marketing requirements were critical. Variations from market to market in a centrally developed basic product could be dealt with at close range. However, the tasks of coordinating product variations, transferring new ideas and techniques from one country to another, and optimizing the logistic flow of product from source to worldwide markets frequently proved difficult for the geographic organizational form.

The third basic pattern, C, assigned worldwide responsibility to product group executives at the line management level, and coordinated activity in a given geographical area through area specialists at the corporate staff level. There were two situations where the product structure was likely to be advantageous: (1) when the product line was widely diversified and went into a variety of end-use markets; (2) when high shipping costs, tariffs, or other considerations dictated local manufacture, and a relatively high level of technological capability was required.

The product organization had brought the foreign operations into close contact with the latest technology in every product field. Perhaps the most important problem lay in turning worldwide responsibility over to executives whose working experience had been largely domestic and who might either lack sufficient understanding of international problems or be disinclined to devote enough attention to them.

The choice of organizational pattern, the authors observed, had historically been largely determined by a small number of key variables. The rapidity with which an emerging world enterprise moved toward a basic organizational structure was inevitably influenced by its past experience, by management traits and the capabilities of key individuals, and by the nature of the business itself. They posed three questions as pertinent variables: What kinds of management decisions are really critical to the success of the enterprise? How often must they be made, and at what organizational level? How much control can and should corporate headquarters exercise over planning decisions for individual businesses around the world?

Clee and Sachtjen also stressed the need for change. Many of the problems observed in working with world enterprises could be traced directly to a single mistake—that of allowing the corporation to remain locked in an organizational form originally chosen in the light of company history and current management limitations.

3. Another perception of the evolutionary process in the mid-1960s was provided in a study of 150 companies by Lovell.[9] While a discernible trend was found toward the "global" management structure in which international responsibility was dispersed among a number of top corporate executives, only 5 percent of the firms in Lovell's sample had such structures while 85 percent gave primary responsibility for international activities to one executive. The logics of this structure in terms of special skills, concentrated attention and drive, and other practical benefits were affirmed from the experience of many companies.

But the study brought out clearly that this centralization of responsibility was not to be equated with segregation and lack of coordination with other corporate personnel. To the contrary, Lovell noted a frequent pattern of collateral responsibility for international matters entrusted to operating and service units of the parent company that were predominantly concerned with domestic operations. There was also a substantial degree of communication among central corporate and international managements. Looking ahead, she found no clear indication that the "global" structure would ultimately be the dominant pattern. In response to a question asking in which direction they expected to move, 33 percent of the companies foresaw a gradual merging of their domestic and foreign operations but some 23 percent expected a shift in the opposite direction toward more centralization and autonomy for their foreign operations.

One significant point bearing on the pros and cons of alternative types of organization was the observation that in either system skilled experts in various aspects of international work (taxation, law, finance, etc.) were needed, and it didn't seem to matter much whether the qualified expert was on the staff of the international manager or the central corporate staff as long as his expertise could be brought to bear promptly and effectively. In like vein Lovell brought out the fact that to the two dimensions common to most organizations—function and product—a third must be added in international activities—geographic region. Effectively blending the expertise and directional effectiveness related to these three dimensions precluded any simple organizational system.

> Taken alone, the internal structure of the international units may give the impression of fairly discrete divisional assignments, with a fixed line of command within each division. But, viewed in perspective, as part of a 'going' company organization, one discovers a web of liaison, dotted-line, and committee relationships that cut across formal organization structure and provide the communicating and coordinating links that make it a flexible, three-dimensional management pattern.[10]

4. A few years later Stopford and Wells completed an intensive study of the organization of 187 of the largest U.S. MNCs.[11] Slightly more than half the firms in the study had international divisions but the evolution seemed to be away from that form. The analysis focused on the factors affecting the timing of change and choice of area, product, or mixed approaches to global organization. The authors found that greater product diversity was correlated with the global types. In them it appeared that the worldwide product division provided the shortest and most effective link for the transmission of technology-oriented communication. However, as products aged, the technology matured, marketing became the critical function, and potential benefits from area coordination increased. Size was also a key factor. Of the seventeen firms with area organizations, thirteen had foreign sales that were 39 percent or more of total company

sales. These thirteen in turn composed a large majority of the nineteen in the over–39 percent category of the full sample.

The authors set forth a schematic pattern demonstrating that the shift from an international to a global organization is a function of the combination of size and product diversity. They noted, however, that there may often be a lag between the point at which changes in these two factors logically support a new system and the actual reorganization. For example, of the nineteen firms which abandoned their international divisions in 1967 or 1968, thirteen were already beyond the size-diversity boundary favoring change by 1966. The authors found some, if slight, evidence that companies whose organization was not suitable by these criteria were financially less profitable.

With expanding size and diversification of operations, both area and product global organization become excessively complex. As a consequence new systems were emerging in a few companies of which the grid approach was most conspicuous. In it foreign unit managers had direct relations with product managers, regional offices, and sometimes other executives. While the grid approach reduced barriers to communication and overhead, the authors noted that the practical difficulties of making this structure work suggested that its adoption by a large number of firms would be slow in coming. Useful contributions toward this goal in some firms were extensive management development programs that appeared designed to create an elite cadre who all knew one another. Such people, conditioned, by common experience and goals, could more readily communicate with each other at a distance in varied reporting relations. Furthermore, greater delegation was possible where the manager was known to be conditioned to predictable patterns of behavior in line with the policies of the firm.

Three other studies broaden this picture by bringing in the experience of European firms and the special role of export departments.

5. Schollhammer set out to determine the difference between the organizations of European and U.S. multinational firms.[12] He concentrated on large firms in a single sector so as to minimize the number of variables affecting the organizations. His sample was composed of twelve chemical pharmaceutical companies, all falling among the 500 largest firms worldwide with at least 30 percent of total sales from international business. Their base countries were: France, two companies; Germany, three; Switzerland, two; U.K., two; and U.S., three.

In overall organizational structure, six of the nine European firms favored the global concept in which foreign units were related to the parent in the same manner as domestic units, whereas two of the three U.S. firms preferred the international division structure. Moreover, in two of the three European firms with an international division, the division had a limited role. Schollhammer could find no evidence in growth of sales or earnings that one organizational structure was superior to the other. He also noted that during the past decade none of the firms had changed its structure and none had expressed any intention to do so. He concluded that the experience of the twelve companies refuted the idea that with an increasing magnitude of international business activities a firm would shift its organizational structure from a domestic orientation to an international division approach and, finally, to a global approach.

The primary organizational pattern of six of the European firms was along functional lines and three along product lines, while one U.S. firm had a product organization and two regional structure. The author observed that European-based MNCs tended to adopt a structure that facilitated a potentially more centralized, but looser control over the totality of corporate operations by a few key executives. In contrast, the U.S. firms favored a structure that provided greater opportunities for decentralized decision-making but that also allowed for a more strict supervision, control, and coordination. Again, he noted that performance data provided no evidence that one approach was superior to the other.

In all U.S. companies there were direct line authority reporting relationships between heads of foreign units and parent headquarters, two with single executive ties and one with multiple executive authority in headquarters. There were three European firms with similar direct line authority ties. The other six European firms either assigned loose, coordinative authority to headquarters men (two cases) or had a poorly defined, nominal line authority. Schollhammer noted that the ill-structured European patterns related to the functional-type organization, the appointment of senior executives with long company experience to head foreign units and their balance between autonomy and centralization of authority.

6. In his study of U.S. operations of a sample of European MNCs,[13] Franko divided their organizational structures into four categories as listed:

- "Mother-daughter" reporting relationships, in which the president of the U.S. subsidiary reported directly to the head of the parent, had the greatest number of firms (thirteen). The pattern was a natural outgrowth of traditional European organization with the top man in direct control of all key aspects of the business. However, the operating results showed the lowest rates of growth and return on investment for these firms and their managers reported the greatest dissatisfaction with technical and marketing information communication. The communication and decision-making patterns were apparently too slow and encumbered for the task.

- Product division supervision was the next most common (eight cases). The results were generally better here though marketing communications were considered less satisfactory.
- There were five firms with international divisions. Two had fast-growing, new U.S. operations but the evidence as to effectiveness was slim.
- In the eight other firms there was an executive in Europe with full-time responsibility for U.S. operations. These firms seemed to be the most effective, the man in Europe providing the necessary facilitation for decision-making and communications.

7. Suzman studied the operations of nine U.S. companies of different sizes and in different industries over a ten-year period, observing in particular the effect of changing circumstances on the organizational structure of the units responsible for exports.[14] In all cases there was a trend toward greater importance of foreign sales and a transition of products from exporting to foreign production. As this transition took place, the export organization assumed two roles with rather different requirements of competence: finding new markets for already established products, basically an entrepreneurial selling function requiring extensive knowledge of international markets, and introducing new products in established markets, which required that managers either had acquired the new technical and marketing product know-how themselves or could provide coordination between the domestic product divisions and the foreign marketing units.

The location of the export function was considered. The initial decision whether to organize the company's early export activities into one independent department or to concentrate them within product divisions could be related to the feedback required between sales and the product design and production functions. In a machine tool firm there was frequent need for product modification to fit customer requests, and this called for close coordination and contact between export and domestic production groups, so export responsibility remained with the product divisions. In two chemical companies exporting standardized products, however, centralized export departments could effectively serve all domestic product divisions.

Five companies in Suzman's survey had moved from an export department to an international division organization when they had at least two foreign manufacturing affiliates and when exports to them reached 10 to 25 percent of total exports. At this stage coordination of exports and foreign manufacture required a common organizational unit and a senior executive responsible for both export and foreign affiliate operations. Likewise there was a need to coordinate sourcing to serve foreign markets.

In this structure, however, adequate contact and coordination with domestic product divisions began to emerge as significant problems. Some companies responded by appointing product managers within the export department or within the international division who could maintain closer relations with domestic counterparts, while in other companies product divisions retained responsibility for exports. In spite of these moves, the research clearly indicated that in the companies with an international division form of organization the relations between the domestic product divisions and the export department were a significant problem, especially with respect to obtaining technical and marketing assistance from the domestic product divisions.

The worldwide product division organization was adopted by three companies to meet these problems but it encountered other difficulties. New and smaller units often lacked international expertise, while in all companies there was competition for management personnel and attention between foreign and domestic units. To minimize these problems, Suzman suggested a gradual rather than complete shift in the organization. Worldwide product divisions were to be formed only where the domestic management was able to take on the added responsibilities. Another step could be formation of worldwide product planning groups made up of representatives from the domestic and the international headquarters and from overseas management. These were contemplated only for those product lines that would benefit most from worldwide coordination. The assignment of worldwide responsibility then could take place for each product group or division separately at the appropriate time. The international division eventually would be retained as a staff group with area subdivisions. In this way it could provide area coordination and long-range planning on a company-wide basis. It could also be responsible for the development of totally new product lines or areas of business activity.

A key problem was transfer pricing. Conflict appeared to arise largely as a result of a transfer pricing system that gave the local manager little or no profit from selling U.S. exports. The author advocated a system in which the domestic product division management, the export department, and the overseas regional and subsidiary management all would receive a memorandum report showing gross sales revenue less all incremental costs to arrive at a net export contribution.

In his concluding comments, Suzman emphasized that in large firms the export department changed from an operating unit to a staff coordinating unit but still retained some residual operating or line responsibilities. There was a need to avoid ambiguities in this role. Most significant, however, was the function of the export group which stands in the middle of some major conflict issues such as the allocation of effort between exports and foreign production. These issues require considerable work by intracompany teams and committees. The unit responsible for export operations is in a position to play a key role in such integrating activities.

8. To complete the picture of the organizational options open to MNCs, we need to bring in two types of bodies which are appropriate for certain situations, chiefly in bigger firms: regional offices and advisory boards. From the vantage point of an international consultant, Williams provided an analysis of the evolution and role of regional offices.[15] He observed that once a company's European operations reached an advanced level of complexity, geographic spread and size, individual national subsidiaries became less rational as independent operating units and profit centers. There were several reasons for this: production runs were too short, engineering and research expenditures were often redundant, and market and product planning were sometimes invalidated by developments occurring on the other side of a national border.

Noting the risk of oversimplifying, Williams classified companies into four broad categories, characterized by: (1) operations in initial stages of activity, (2) European operations dominated by one or two sizable national subsidiaries with large management staffs, (3) European operations comprised of several large, strong, historically independent national operating subsidiaries, with rationalization of production and marketing required for maximum efficiency, and (4) large Europewide operations that had been closely integrated according to a worldwide plan and were undergoing evolution of management structure as the size, complexity, and needs of the operation changed.

While it was difficult to determine the need for regional management on the basis of the stage of development alone, it appeared that companies in Category 3 had the most acute need for utilizing a regional management approach. Several companies in the Category 1 phase had used a small, high-powered regional group to plan, launch, and execute their entry into the European market. Companies in Category 4 were not required to make a radical change in their management organization, but could move naturally into the regional form when their operating subsidiaries reached a certain level of size and complexity. The companies which were probably least in need of regional management were those in Category 2.

An industrial products or technology-oriented company was more likely to utilize a regional-approach organization, while a consumer goods company was more involved with individual national marketing problems. When consumer product companies reached a size and geographic scope where marketing strategy had to be coordinated on a Europewide basis, however, it was probably necessary to utilize an on-the-spot, well-informed, senior regional management group.

Most regional managements with line authority for European profit performance had review authority over capital budgets and operating budgets, subject to the approval and guidelines of the worldwide top management. They also had direct line authority over the appraisal, promotion, and development of managers in the operating subsidiaries, coordinating authority over the marketing function, including product planning and other factors of Europewide importance, and line authority over production rationalization and specialization programs. In addition, regional offices could play an important role in developing recommendations for long-term corporate strategy, diversification, and financing.

There were some significant disadvantages to the regional management concept. Probably the most serious was the difficulty of reconciling product emphasis with a geographically oriented management approach. This could be particularly difficult if the company's product line was diverse and if it had to be marketed through different types of distribution channels. Moreover, such requirements frustrated the approach of worldwide product management combined with worldwide staff departments. Since a certain amount of product expertise had to be developed by the regional unit, a duplication of product development and technical knowledge was often required. At the same time, there was some overlap of functional staff responsibilities with the worldwide headquarters. All this added to overhead costs and created an additional tier of communications. Despite such problems, the majority of regional managers agreed that there was no better solution at the present time than an on-the-scene regional management unit, at least where there was a real need for coordinated, Europewide decision-making.

9. Heenan and Reynolds reported from a survey that thirty-six of sixty-four U.S. multinationals had regional units. Two-thirds had regional personnel offices (RPOs), upon which they focused their analysis. Several factors had contributed to regionalization. The rise of regional political and economic institutions had fostered clustering of corporate activities, including manpower decisions. There was also intense competition for managerial talent in which the possibility of a career with shifts of jobs to several countries was significant, an option multinationals could offer to offset some advantages strictly national firms provided. RPOs were useful in facilitating regional shifts of managers. An RPO was in addition an appropriate vehicle through which local managers could ascend the corporate hierarchy. Typically, 40 to 70 percent of the key executives in a regional headquarters were nationals of companies in the area, the remainder from the parent company. By encouraging the interaction of executives of different nationalities, the RPO might ease the transition to a truly multinational management team in corporate headquarters. A further element was the value of the RPO as a means of upgrading the quality of local personnel activities, in some cases facilitating a better balance in such matters as training programs by consolidating them on a regional basis.

Certain factors were identified as critical to the success of an RPO. There had to be a top level commitment to assure that the RPO had the resources needed to do its job. Operational planning had to be integrated on a regional basis. Premature attempts to establish full-fledged RPOs in an area not ripe for truly regional factor mobility—as, for example, the Andean Common Market—would be futile. For most firms, this meant that Europe might be the primary locus of regionalism in the seventies. Another concern was "regional chauvinism," overidentification with the area at the expense of global goals leading to suboptimization. The thrust toward regionalism should also be realistically restrained. MNCs should not create an atmosphere that forces local managers with neither regional ability nor mobility to work abroad. In some cases, regional approaches might best be limited to tasks that were dissolved upon completion.

A critical question was whether the regional personnel officer should report to the senior parent personnel executive or to the senior regional line manager. Where the regional unit was a profit center there was a strong case for the latter. If it was not a profit center, the authors favored the former relationship. In either case, top quality managers for the RPO were essential, and they were often lacking. For example, only about one-third of the Americans working abroad as regional personnel executives in U.S. multinationals had had any previous overseas experience. All too often the authors observed RPOs staffed by those who couldn't make the grade elsewhere.

The formation of regional task forces was noted as a useful adjunct to the RPO. General Foods was cited as an example. The RPO had a skeletal staff; the bulk of the regional efforts was performed by a task force composed of personnel managers of subsidiaries in countries within the region. Country men received periodic regional assignments based on their expertise, e.g., the British manager handled regional benefits studies because of his competence in compensation. Regional seminars, rotational assignments, and regional audits had a similar thrust. In the latter, personnel officers from various countries visited each other to review their programs along with parent and regional staff.

10. On the basis of interviews with a number of multinational corporations, Kenny reported the trend of experience and thinking about the use of top level advisory committees in Europe.[17] The advisory committee was conceived as a non-management body that supported the regional manager and acted as a sounding board, interpreted events, and contributed to strategies. The position of these corporations was essentially that their plans should be considered valid and beneficial for the host country before they could actually be sound from a strategic standpoint. To facilitate this end, the members were leaders who could speak for their own country, whose contact tentacles were alive, and whose views on current trends within their countries were sought after.

Kenny's survey revealed that companies were generally very pleased with their experience. The main value of boards had been in review of local country strategies and trends and policy implementation. The underlying and frequently non-stated purposes were to help with specific new business developments and to improve relationships and positioning with local governments. A few companies were especially candid about these purposes. Board members were also useful in identifying new business opportunities.

A major element in the picture was the emphasis on relations of the advisory committee with top corporate management rather than with the regional or local management. In fact, some advisory boards, such as General Motors, deliberately excluded area management from their formal structure. Moreover, their chairman ex-officio is chairman of the board. Since the highest level candidate in each country should be attracted, it was natural that nationals would expect contact with the corporate office of the multinational. Ideally, someone at least at the executive vice president or vice chairman level should be assigned the responsibility as advisory board chairman. Top level ties were also consistent with the goal of some companies to affect management at that level. For example, IBM was more concerned about its USA-influenced management policy. They believed from the beginning that the whole corporation, and not just IBM Europe, would be a large benefactor through greater dialogue with leading European nationals.

This approach implied limited local operational involvement. Where multinational companies had established international executive boards consisting of product managers and area managers, merely adding on leading foreign nationals as participative members of that board had not been successful. It was difficult for such internal international boards to operate effectively since they were more concerned with tactics and, therefore, required detailed product and market knowledge. This kind of operating board should not be confused with the area advisory committee. By the same token, the members of advisory boards were not intensively concerned with product knowledge; and one sure way of losing interest was to provide them with a heavy product orientation.

While the general pattern was to employ boards covering several countries, a few firms had taken a more limited approach. For example, ITT and Westinghouse did not believe a formalized system for Europe was appropriate and thought it might hinder local assistance. Westinghouse, in support of the management-by-committee concept for that complex area, didn't believe any one advisory system would suffice.

Substantial effort was required to make an advisory board effective. The normally expected gestation period was about two years. Orientation of members and development of satisfactory informal relationships called for considerable effort. Typically, the area general manager could not spend sufficient time to make the committee successful; and, therefore, he probably should not have an official status on the board. Thus, liaison with the board was best handled from the top corporate level. GM, for example, had a coordinator from the executive vice president's office as board chairman.

Kenny also observed that an advisory board represented a substantial commitment. It was expensive and should be maintained only on a first class basis. Annual budgets ran from approximately $200,000 to $1 million. Direct remuneration was usually nominal. In some cases board members served for a specified term while in others indefinite commitments were involved. The author favored the latter as it facilitated changes without hurting sensitivities while being still consistent with the goal of long-term participation.

The selection of members was critical. The major product and marketing issues had to be faced up to on a country-by-country basis before selection began. It was conceivable that the representatives from each country should have totally different backgrounds. Even though the board member was not going to be technically concerned with the product issues, that member should be acceptable to a number of major product representatives. He should be able to receive an audience with other industry spokemen and responsible public officials. Other qualifications were that he should be prominent in his native country, active socially, someone who had had a recent history of leading and acting as spokesman for his local environment, including government and business, but politically neutral.

11. An alternative to the advisory board, as a means for providing top level input into management, especially in medium-sized to small firms, is the use of outside directors.[18] Samuel C. Johnson, Chairman, S.C. Johnson & Son, Inc., and Richard M. Thomson, President, Toronto-Dominion Bank, drawing on practical experience from their own operations, discussed their role. They observed that the chief executive of the MNC should not delegate to others the invitation of outside directors to serve. His personal involvement indicates the significance he ascribes to the position. With the advice of other board members and nationals in the subsidiary operation, he should seek persons with local and national standing in both civic and business affairs. Although the chosen director might have specialized expertise of use to the subsidiary, such as in law, technology, or real estate, ideally he would be a businessman with a viewpoint gained from management experience. The outside director's compensation has to be large enough to make him feel he is an important member of the worldwide organization and to stimulate his desire to help out locally. And he has to be informed of what is expected of him.

The authors specified that the director become familiar with the subsidiary's operations and keep abreast of economic, legal political developments which might affect it. He should be certain that the subsidiary was following the goals and policies set by the parent. He should present an independent view on how the subsidiary's business should be conducted, with the goal of making the subsidiary both a business success and a good corporate citizen of its host country. Other functions, in the authors' view, include advising on relations with financial institutions and the government and counseling on local compensation standards.

The capacity of the director to view operations as an outsider was stressed. At times the subsidiary's interests would differ from those of the parent. If the directors who were also officers of the subsidiary were not in a position to take a strong stand, it was the outsider's duty to express an independent viewpoint, particularly when the matter involved the host country's interests. The outsider could also help challenge the branch-plant mentality of the home office, although he had to keep in mind the fact that the subsidiary was just part of a global enterprise.

The authors suggested as an area in which a local director could be helpful the question of undertaking research and development in a subsidiary. The director could mediate between the desire of the MNC to avoid diversion of R&D resources and complication of R&D management and the feelings of the host government that minimal R&D in the subsidiary was a form of exploitation. An independent director could help both subsidiary and parent company managements avoid the extremes of, on the one hand, refusing to help develop or adequately capitalize local technical resources or, on the other hand, undertaking programs that had little chance of eventual success in response to local pressures.

### Organization Guidelines

Sorting through the MNC experience just reported, three guidelines are suggested for the relationship of the components of MNC organization.

1. The organization should be so structured that planning and decision-making on each aspect of operations may be done by people with the functional, geographic, and/or product responsibility necessary to achieve the degree of unified strategy appropriate in that aspect.
2. The channels for the flow of important or recurring decisions and information should be as direct and short as possible and structured that motivation for communication is fostered.
3. Individuals with expert international knowledge and competence in overcoming the obstacles to communication and dealing with specialized problems should be readily available within the organization to be utilized wherever their capacities are needed.

The operational implications of these guidelines will depend upon the strategy needs in each company, of which a few common patterns may be observed.

First, there are situations in which a significant degree of unification of some aspects of the product delivery system are feasible—product, logistic, or marketing strategy. Here the first criterion is the primary consideration and the outcome leans toward assignment of primary responsibility on a global product division basis because the product-oriented activities are the core of the unification strategies. In the late 1970s it appeared that the pressure of competitive conditions encouraging firms to maximize the advantages of their global unification capabilities was the strongest factor moving MNCs toward greater product division control of international operations. The case history described by Prahalad, which will be cited in the next chapter (p. 557), is a good illustration of this evolution.

A second type of situation is that in which a high degree of coordination of activities of diverse product groups within a country or perhaps a region are required. This requirement is most important where host government relations are sensitive. However, it can be significant in other aspects of operations. The managers of three factories in France, for example, even though they make different products, will have much to gain by exchanging information and coordinating their approaches to labor relations. Undoubtedly there will be benefits from substantial cooperation in financial affairs—dealings with banks, balancing of surplus funds in one unit against needs in another, and so forth. Under these circumstances the limitations implied in the first criterion by "degree of unified strategy appropriate" and the utilization of special competences covered in the third criterion are primary considerations. An organizational structure emphasizing geographic allocation of responsibility is desirable.

Third, there are the situations in which skill transmission is central to success. Here the second criterion is typically the dominant consideration and a structure is favored which provides a direct line of communication from the prime source of the skills to the foreign affiliates. Most commonly in larger MNCs, this approach calls for assignment of responsibility for foreign operations to each product division. The international division structure is undesirable because of the deterrents to communication in passing through a non-contributing layer of management.

This structure also increases the motivations for the product divisions to put their best efforts and personnel into the overseas operations. If product X is manufactured abroad under a separate international division, the managers of product X operations in the United States will have less incentive to assign their better production experts to overseas factories than if they have direct profit responsibility for the factories.

Finally, there are the situations in which the evolution of the MNC's international business has not yet reached the stage where assumption throughout the management of international responsibility is feasible. A large portion of the small and medium size firms, especially those new to global business, fit this category. For such firms adoption of any variations of the global structure raises real questions as to whether the incremental disadvantages of communication are increased unduly, particularly with respect to the cultural and environment gaps.

Here the third criterion comes into play. The international division is a device for organizational specialization bringing together individuals with special aptitudes and skills in understanding foreign environments and communicating across cultural and nationality gaps. In the global organization many parent-company personnel with substantially less competence in these communication skills are expected to deal with overseas personnel, and it is quite possible that the lower level of communication achieved would substantially offset any gains from having their capabilities readily available to the overseas personnel.

In most MNCs the situation will provide sufficiently strong arguments for one type of organization pattern so that adopting it as the dominant structure is justified. Still it will generally be true that to some degree all of the considerations favoring alternatives will be present. Thus, the most effective outcome as indicated by the Lovell and Stopford-Wells studies is a system which assures that either formally or informally channels are open for the planning, decision-making, and implementation which in effect permit the personnel to function according to the scheme of alternative organizational patterns when they are more appropriate. As we will see when we get to discussing the dynamics of the managerial process, this is not an easy goal to achieve. But it is a necessary one given the impossibility of designing a single organization structure which will serve all strategy requirements.

## STAFFING

In broad outline the main considerations affecting the use of parent country nationals (PCNs), host country nationals (HCNs) and third country nationals (TCNs) in management of foreign affiliates are readily stated. There is a general disposition toward maximum use of HCNs because that policy is favorably viewed in host nations, because it involves less cost and complications than assignment of expatriates and because HCNs do not have problems in relating to the host culture. On the other hand, some degree of PCN and TCN utilization is fostered by significant operational advantages in three areas: skill transmission, implementation of parent firm strategy, and communication with the parent organization. But as the human and operational implications of these factors are explored, one finds that the issue is quite complex.

As a starting point for this analysis, we may look at evidence of the patterns of employment of different types of managers in MNCs and then proceed out from that into underlying characteristics of the patterns, focusing on HCNs first and then PCNs. Three studies provide a picture of managerial staffing patterns, identifying particularly their relation to strategic considerations and to a lesser degree environmental conditions.

1. Franko made a survey of twenty-five European and U.S. multinational enterprises which showed the historical evolution of the use of host and parent nationals in international operations.[19] He found a constantly repeating cycle that varied in its details for each individual company, but whose overall pattern was quite consistent.

During a firm's initial export stage, foreign sales management generally was left in the hands of local nationals. As production was undertaken, however, there was a sharp rise in the use of headquarters nationals to transfer technical skills abroad. The use of local nationals in top positions dropped to around 25 percent at this stage. For U.S. firms, however, the portion of expatriates historically had dropped quite quickly after production was established. A 1971 survey of 200 U.S. subsidiaries in Belgium, for example, showed that only 22 percent of the presidents of those formed between 1966 and 1968 were Belgian but of those subsidiaries formed prior to 1958, 59 percent had Belgian heads. The tendency apparently had been to rely on local managers heavily once basic skills were acquired. However, the Belgian survey showed that European multinational firms did not follow a similar course, the percent of parent country nationals in top positions holding at a consistently high level from the inception of production.

Yet another stage appeared in the U.S. subsidiary staffing of firms which adopted a strategy of a limited product line worldwide. These firms gathered in once relatively independent subsidiaries under common strategies. In the words of one European headquarters official: "We needed to put a stop to every country subsidiary going off in its own direction, and this dictated a realignment of power positions in the firm."[20] The realignment apparently often called for replacing local nationals in top subsidiary jobs with headquarters personnel. Franko's data showed that the portion of local nationals in top positions fell at this stage to essentially the level of the earlier stage of initial production.

Subsequent to this process, the author found a reemergence of local managers to head subsidiary operations. Some of these local managers moved into the previously inaccessible upper reaches of multinational corporate management. However, the global rationalization process had changed the role of the local managers. Unlike the first round, their role was less to adapt to local environments than to interpret the innovation of multinational coordination to their compatriots.

2. Galbraith and Edstrom made intensive studies of four large European firms.[21] Key data on managerial transfers within these firms showed striking differences which were the focus of the analysis (Table 12-1). The first two companies were in the same industry and the second two were in another industry.

The personnel managers of the firms gave three main reasons for transfers which the authors tested on the data. The first was filling a position for which a local national was not available. The data showed that 50 percent of the World Wide and 80 percent of the European transfers were technical people and that a major portion of the transfers of all companies could be explained by the need to transmit technical expertise to LDCs.

A second motivation was utilization of management—a job opportunity and a promotable individual did not always occur in the same subsidiary. The authors concluded that this motive was not generally valid because most transfers were of parent nationals (70 to 90 percent in the firms studied). Only in World Wide did people move commonly between subsidiaries as well as to and from the parent. Furthermore, only World Wide had a sufficiently staffed and detailed system to be aware of job-person matchings between subsidiaries.

The third motive was to provide international experience for managers. The only basis found to test this motive was the source of initiative for transfers and who paid for them. In two companies the initiative and payment lay with the subsidiaries, suggesting that train-

Table 12-1.  Managerial Transfers within Four Firms

| Disguised Firm Name | Employees Total | Transfers (1972) | Employees Europe | Transfers in Europe | |
|---|---|---|---|---|---|
| | | | | Central Offices | Subsidiaries |
| World Wide | 174,000 | 3,600 | 88,000 | 491 | 545 |
| National | 160,000 | 1,000 | 77,000 | 70 | 250 |
| European | 91,600 | 300 | 70,000 | – | 63 |
| Occidental | 67,700 | 245 | 50,000 | 45 | 38 |

ing was not a primary motive, while in two the opposite was often true.

The central thesis of the authors' analysis was that, although these three motivations explained much of the transfer process, a fourth factor was important, especially in the developed countries. Their analysis supported this thesis though the personnel managers denied it. They suggested that differences in transfers in the developed world were related to differences in the need for coordination, control, and communications among subsidiaries and between subsidiaries and central offices and that transfer was a facilitator of those processes. The great variations in transfer data among the companies suggested the need for such an explanation since major variations based on the first three motivations were not reasonable. Likewise, data within the companies were found to support their view. For example, European had a number of expatriates in Belgium, Britain, and the United States, but none in other European countries where the subsidiaries were larger. They found that in these countries there were large efforts to "crack the local market." Thus it appeared that when organizations changed strategies, implemented new systems, or had start-up activities, transfers tended to be used. It was also found that there was little interdependence among the subsidiaries of European and Occidental while there was substantial specialization and need for coordination among those of the other two firms. The latter had substantially more transfers. The authors concluded that the presence of expatriates facilitated coordination.

Further thinking was advanced to explain the greater number of transfers in World Wide compared to National. Two approaches were observed for achieving coordinated strategy. One, believed to be the case in National, used a central corps of executives who visited subsidiaries with great frequency. The other, presumed to be true of World Wide, was control by socialization. That is, functional behaviors and rules for determining them were learned and internalized by individuals, thereby obviating the need for procedures, hierarchical communication, and surveillance. An important adjunct to this element was the development of multiple contacts among executives through the transfer process. It was observed that much key information within large organizations is transmitted verbally. For those interested in decentralizing power in organizations, the transfer of top management between interdependent units may generate the contacts and communications to bring about the power shift. The large amount of transfer needed to maintain contacts and network knowledge was the reason why World Wide transferred more than National in the developed world.

3. Youssef made a comparative study of the integration of local nationals into management of the Argentine (AF) and Mexican (MF) operations of a U.S. firm.[22] The AF was opened in 1956 and consistently had about three times as many workers as the MF which started in 1958. In 1958 the ratio of U.S. to local national managers in both plants was 8:1. By 1966 the integration in the AF had moved far ahead—17:12 compared to 17:4 in Mexico. By 1970, both were about equal: AF at 21:20 and MF at 19:18.

The author identified a number of variables influencing the rate of integration. In both countries there was a shortage of qualified managers and the company was under competitive pressure to get going fast, so initially both units were heavily staffed with U.S. nationals but the U.S. personnel did differ. In the MF the top U.S. managers were not familiar with the foreign language and the culture, while in the AF they were. To make communication possible between the local employees and their U.S. superiors, knowledge of English was sometimes emphasized more than technical qualifications in the selection of Mexican personnel. The top U.S. personnel in Argentina also had more favorable attitudes toward the abilities of local nationals than those in the MF.

The plants both started with a relatively simple product. A more complex one was introduced in 1961 in the AF and 1965 in the MF. Thus the AF personnel had an earlier exposure to more sophisticated technology in addition to their larger size. Youssef observed that the smaller, simpler MF could be run more readily by a few top home country nationals than the AF. This factor in turn led to the earlier introduction of management training and a greater amount of training in the AF.

The main impetus for integration in the MF came after 1965 when the company was forced by the government to sell 51 percent of its stock to Mexicans. U.S. personnel were promptly withdrawn and Mexicans were given responsibilities even though their preparation was limited in some cases.

Youssef concluded that integration of local nationals in the AF was induced largely by internal forces in the multinational firm, while in the MF it was induced largely by an external force (host government pressure). This difference resulted in differences in the experience and training backgrounds of the two management groups. The turnover rate of management and clerical people in the AF was notably lower than that in the MF at most times. The author's interviews with U.S. managers from the AF indicated that this was largely because of the difference in advancement opportunities and employment prestige associated with the growth picture of the two units.

Shorter training periods for managers in the MF might have been due to the high turnover. Because of the weaker training program in the MF, the company was hard pressed to find able people when integration was forced. For example, it had two local nationals as factory manager within three years, neither really satisfactory, while the AF had no trouble filling this slot with a local national when it decided to do so.

4. It is well to add a picture of the staffing pattern at the parent level because it has some bearing on the evolution of the relative use of parent and host country nationals throughout the MNC organization. Franko's study (case 1) provided some basic data on this subject.[23] The fourteen firms responding to his questionnaire reported that they employed a total of thirteen headquarters managers of foreign nationalities in 1972 as opposed to one in 1960. But the thirteen in 1972 were out of a total number of approximately 400 headquarters managers. The author's research led him to suspect that a multinational management might be an unrealistic target for the headquarters. Moreover, the association of "geocentric" headquarters staffing with industries under threat led him to question company preoccupation with nationality mix. He thought it might in some cases constitute a distraction from the main problem: that of restructuring the corporate strengths that underpin viable long-term multinational operations.

5. Earlier Simmonds made a study of the national origins of all top corporate officers and directors of the 150 largest U.S. industrial corporations in terms of sales in 1965.[24] This covered 3,847 executives. About one-fifth of the total employment in these firms was foreign, yet only 1.6 percent of their top corporate management could be classified as representative of the corporation's foreign employment. For 71 corporations with heavy foreign activity, foreign employment jumped to 33 percent while foreign participation in top management remained at 1.6 percent. Simmonds recognized that data for 1965 on senior management would not reflect current movement upward but the slim host country national representation was still significant.

Simmonds added some explanatory notes on the reasons for the limited use of foreign nationals in headquarters. He found a tendency for a self-perpetuating management to fill vacancies with men of a similar cultural background. Altogether apart from any prejudice, such a tendency might be a simple necessity if management did not feel capable of evaluating the potential of someone from a different background. Another advantage of the home country national was that he had been closer to the head office for a longer time than his foreign counterpart. This lack of exposure to head office affairs was compounded in those worldwide corporations that centralized strategic planning and decision-making. Furthermore, although he generally had a quality university education, the lack of a business education hampered the foreigner in competing with a U.S. national.

The foreign manager himself might also be reluctant to move from his subsidiary status. Why leave the top position in a large subsidiary in one's own cultural environment where the headaches of operating at the top are lessened by the load assumed by parent leadership?

Finally, the foreigner who had not spent a considerable time in the United States might be at a considerable disadvantage in a top management post in a company that was responsible to U.S. shareholders, still had a large percentage of its sales in the United States, and therefore required that the incumbent possess an intimate knowledge of U.S. institutions. This would be particularly true on the government relations side.

6. Tugendhat's broad analysis of multinationals resulted in an assessment that reinforces Simmonds' comments.[25] He observed that the idea of including people of varied nationalities in the top management of multinational firms was generally favored. There was an assortment of problems to be overcome in accomplishing it, however. One had to deal with the resistance of those who had fundamental objections. A British board member, for example, observed, "We have to be able to speak freely together and trust each other implicitly. If we have a foreigner here his loyalties would be divided. He might sometimes be tempted to give undue weight to the interests of his own national subsidiary, or tell his home government of our deliberations."[26]

The practicality of accomplishment was demonstrated by a few cases like Nestle in which about one-third of the headquarters executives were non-Swiss. But the rarity of such cases demonstrated the impediments. There was also a time factor in accomplishment. In 1959 Massey-Ferguson reorganized to facilitate incorporation of all nationalities in top management but except for a few Britishers, the top ranks were all North American. It was estimated that real change would not appear till 1980.

A substantial impediment was the attitude of foreign executives. The international executive wanted equal opportunity with his company's home country nationals, while retaining the option to jump off the promotion ladder if he found that he did not want to take up permanent residence abroad. While men early in their careers might value a stint abroad, the senior men suitable for top management were less likely to accept a long-term or permanent shift to the home country of the firm. This deterrent applied especially to those of nationalities to whom family ties were of great value. Southern Europeans were an example. The firm faced the prospect that it might make major investments of time and money to develop promising young foreigners for top management only to have the investment lost through the personal feelings of the men. Companies could therefore be forgiven if they preferred to rely on men who were unlikely to drop out of the race, and these were more likely to come from their home countries than any other.

Language was not a major problem for English-speaking companies because all international businessmen tended to learn it. But for other European and especially for Japanese firms, it was hard to get foreigners who had sufficient home country language competence to be fully effective in the parent organization. Related to this was the problem of culture and management style. Even with substantial language competence, a foreigner might find many small and large differences in national characteristics which rendered him less effective than a native of the home country culture. There was also a cost factor comparable to the expense of sending home country nationals overseas. The foreign national brought to the parent headquarters would expect a salary comparable to his peers and extra compensation to cover the costs of moving, special educational expenses for his children, etc.

Despite these problems, Tugendhat felt there would be steady progress toward multinationalizing top management. The overriding reason would be the need to attract and retain the best available executive talent of all nationalities. Companies that refused to promote foreigners beyond a certain point would find that many of their best men left, and that they could not recruit their fair share of able and ambitious young men for their subsidiaries.

### Focus on the Host Country National

The staffing questions in which the host country national is of particular concern are internal relations in foreign affiliates, communications, and attitudes. While strategic objectives and external pressures seem to have been the major determinants of policy on use of host and foreign nationals, the interactions among parent country nationals (PCNs), host country nationals (HCNs), and third country nationals (TCNs) have significant implications for operational effectiveness. At the heart of the implications are problems of personal motivations and cultural interaction, so it is useful to observe their character in varied cross-national patterns.

1. First, there are reports on two parts of a research program directed by Zeira.[27] One part reported the results of an intensive study of management attitudes in the U.S. subsidiary of a foreign airline, supplemented by a less intensive study of subsidiaries in Japan, Western Europe, and the Middle East of three other airlines. The authors found that the U.S. host country nationals had substantially lower morale than the parent country nationals who held four of the five top positions, 80 percent of the upper middle jobs, and a few of the lower middle ones. The problems were attributed largely to the ethnocentric outlook of the firm and policies and attitudes stemming from its home culture which was quite authoritarian and inconsiderate of subordinates. The heavy use of PCNs was due to the desire of the corporation to assure international integration and to the interest of the parent personnel who viewed assignments in the United States and Western Europe as promotions and opportunities for self-development. For example, they valued the high standard of living, the broadening of technological and managerial horizons, and the opportunities for personal ties with other airline people.

It was found that the expressed desires of both groups were similar as to managerial patterns—decision participation, information flow, etc. However, the actual behavior patterns differed substantially along national lines and satisfaction was correlated with these differences. The only top HCN was head of the finance division, which was distinctive in its pattern of sharing information, coaching, and other administrative actions and enjoyed substantially greater satisfaction among HCNs.

The HCNs complained that decisions were made at levels above those where adequate information was available, and that their PCN superiors disregarded subordinates' organizational and personal problems when making decisions. This disregard reduced the motivation of HCN subordinates to pass unfiltered information. They were also, sceptical about the quality of managerial decisions. Likewise, the practice among PCN superiors of not sharing relevant information greatly hampered HCN performance, and had a deleterious effect on their job commitment. PCNs were relatively more satisfied with communication and decision-making. In the interviews they revealed that they were not aware that subordinates were reluctant to pass on unscreened information.

The PCNs also received a number of fringe benefits not open to HCNs and their promotion opportunities were superior because the top jobs were generally reserved for them. The latter inequality resulted in high dissatisfaction. Older managers stuck to their jobs but a number of younger ones seeking better opportunities had left the company for this reason.

The authors reflect on why the PCNs did not adapt their managerial style to be more congruent with the expectations of HCNs as well as with the requirements of the host environment. All of those studied had been in the host country for at least three years. Several reasons are proposed, all related to culture. Basically, the PCNs, having been raised in their home culture, felt the idea of participative leadership was contrary to their assessment of effective management. Reinforcing this feeling were three sources of psychological resistance to change: (1) They feared that changing their way of managing people would imply that they had not been as successful in the role of manager as they would have liked to believe or, at least as they would have liked others to believe. (2) They were apprehensive that they would fail to be able to learn new methods or would be ineffective in applying them. (3) They believed that a change in managerial behavior would result in considerable frustration for them upon their return to headquarters.

Another key factor was that PCNs were not aware that their managerial practices were a source of considerable dissatisfaction. Turnover among HCNs was relatively low. And in the absence of open communication channels it was difficult for PCNs to discover the extent of dissatisfaction in the organization. In addition, the "easy life" of the PCNs seems to have dulled their sensitivity to the needs of subordinates. Their relatively high standard of living compared with home country conditions, high status, autonomy and other factors led them to a sense of satisfaction which was not conducive to objective self-evaluation, an important prerequisite for change.

2. The second part of the Zeira-directed research was from a questionnaire and interview survey covering forty-nine personnel vice presidents of leading MNCs.[28] Broadly the survey revealed that the high officials responsible for personnel policies abroad were not familiar with several important personnel issues. This created serious morale and organizational problems in their subsidiaries. Their unfamiliarity was highly criticized by expatriates (PCNs and TCNs) and also by senior HCNs, who regarded this phenomenon as characteristic of their detachment and low professional standards.

The survey showed that headquarters officials were aware of the effect on morale of blocking promotion opportunities for senior HCNs (as had been shown by the first stage of the research). However, all the vice presidents interviewed tended to underrate its importance in organizational effectiveness. They believed that the most effective solution was to limit the number of PCNs in top positions abroad.

Utilization of third country nationals received considerable attention. Most of the directors were confident that the policy of rotating and promoting TCNs to key positions was an effective method of uniting different ethnic groups; they felt that it indicated a true multinational policy and was welcomed by HCNs abroad. The actual situation in subsidiaries was found, however, to be quite complex. In multinational corporations that rotated many TCNs at middle and lower levels, they were favorably perceived by HCNs because the latter saw their assignments as temporary, not blocking promotion. TCNs were eager for favorable evaluations by host-country superiors and HCNs felt obligated to help the newcomers. Some recognized that they also might be transferred and might be in the same position elsewhere. On the other hand, where only a limited number of senior TCNs were used, they were not welcomed by HCNs who viewed them essentially in the same terms as PCNs.

Since HCNs had little chance to move into higher positions in corporation headquarters, many of them were willing to assume TCN status and live permanently in foreign countries. Their status in this role became dependent upon headquarters officers with whom they developed close contacts. They adapted their behavior therefore to PCN expectations, and the need to adapt their managerial behavior to the expectations of their local deputies became less important to their personal success. Although HCNs tended to understand the policy of having PCNs occupy the subsidiary's top positions, they did not understand having third country nationals occupying these key positions. TCNs, aware of this problem, felt obligated to demonstrate their managerial superiority in their new positions, even more than PCNs. Many refrained from delegating authority and maintained as much power for themselves as possible.

The research indicated that most personnel directors were not sufficiently aware of the dilemma, and therefore had not yet developed proper personnel techniques for coping effectively with this complex situation. Furthermore, lacking adequate awareness, they did not provide orientation for parent country nationals going on foreign assignments to prepare them to deal with the situation. Senior PCNs abroad criticized the selection and training processes, which they felt were not tailored to help them with their adaptation problems in the subsidiaries.

Differences were also found in perceptions of responsibility. Personnel directors felt that the chief executive of each subsidiary was fully responsible for all morale problems in his subsidiary. He should, therefore, initiate the appropriate steps for solving these problems. However, the chief executives had a different view. First, they did not think of themselves as personnel executives. They claimed that all corrective steps in this area should be initiated by headquarters. Second, since the evaluation of their performance as chief executives was not based on their ability to deal with local morale problems, they did not tend to be highly involved with such personnel activities. Third, they believed that the organizational advantages of the existing staffing policy outweighed the shortcomings; that it was senseless to invest time and energy treating a problem which couldn't be eliminated as long as the personnel policy, which they themselves supported, would not be changed. Fourth, they preferred to be as independent as possible. They did not encourage their local personnel directors to seek advice from experts at headquarters; this would reveal human problems that they wanted to conceal. Four personnel directors of Western European corporations said they did not initiate any special evaluation methods because they expected loyal HCNs to change their own attitudes and to behave in accordance with headquarters managerial patterns. They insisted that expatriates should not change their own leadership style and that headquarters patterns should be maintained in all their subsidiaries abroad.

3. A different perspective is provided by three views of Japanese experience with management relations in affiliates. In a study by Johnson and Ouchi of Japanese MNC operations in the United States, the point of departure was the authors' observation that the operations in a number of cases had higher productivity or in some other ways seemed to be managed better than U.S. counterparts.[29] In-depth interviews with the managements of the Japanese operations provided a picture of the nature of their methods upon which the performance record was based.

To a substantial degree the Japanese had imported their national managerial styles, usually employing a half dozen to twenty or more expatriates in the top executive ranks and expecting Americans to adapt to their style. The Americans had considerable difficulty in the adaptation. An American in this position found himself in a topsy turvy world in which many of the conventions of western style management were reversed. However, those who persisted through the adaptation seemed favorably impressed with the Japanese style.

The report elaborated on the distinctive characteristics. Major attention was given to the heavy reliance upon flows of ideas and information up from the bottom. The role of the superior was perceived as eliciting initiative and asking questions to improve the quality of the proposals coming from below, rather than taking initiative and directing action as was common among Americans. Along with this practice went major emphasis on communication both vertically and horizontally. Decision-making, Japanese style, involved a process of "rolling consensus." The process required much time and many meetings which in turn called for skillful personal relations. This style was contrasted with the quicker decision-making and individualism of the Americans, whose meetings varied from adversary proceedings in which individuals either strove for supremacy or, alternatively, accepted meaningless generalization as their only common ground. The continuing close communication of the Japanese pattern and gradual evolution resulted in the ultimate decisions being fully understood and essentially concurred in by all, and this was presumed to strengthen the implementation phase.

Another major difference was in the area of employee relations. While the Japanese had not imported major features of their traditional methods like lifetime employment, they had applied the basic philosophy of the national approach. Japanese managers expressed great concern for the employee as a whole person. Managers were expected to know their employees well, including their personal lives. The researchers interviewed a number of workers and found that they sensed a difference in the Japanese methods to which they responded favorably.

The authors gave a brief case history describing the difficulties of integrating American managers with the Japanese style. The crux of the problem was that the Americans accustomed to strong top level leadership waited for guidance from above, while the Japanese senior men waited for initiatives in the bottom-up pattern. The problem was eventually solved by the role of junior Japanese coordinators who bridged the gap. But the authors stressed the risk of such a debilitating stand-off in other mixed management groups.

The authors cited several cultural obstacles to American adaptation to the Japanese style. The concept of authority had to be revised from the action-initiator role to that of improving upon the initiatives of others and creating an atmosphere in which subordinates were motivated to seek better solutions. The emphasis for the manager had to change from getting ahead individually to going along effectively with the continuing group process. The Americans eschewed ambiguity, seeking clarity in decisions, while the Japanese accepted ambiguity as well as vagueness in organizational matters.

The bottom-up process and rolling consensus resulted in a gradual evolution based upon the reactions of younger men to the environment with which they worked closely. Strategy in U.S. firms often dominated by initiatives of strong top men and major changes in strategy were not uncommon, frequently associated with changes of top personnel. The comparison caused the authors to ponder the advantages of the Japanese system which adapted continuously and which, while changing direction slowly, rarely turned in the wrong direction.

4. Yoshino found in his broad study of Japanese MNCs that, whereas the U.S. managerial methods on the whole were an asset for U.S. MNCs abroad, Japan's distinctive managerial system was an important factor inhibiting the growth of Japanese multinational enterprice.[30] The intimate communications and group decision-making patterns based on the distinctive Japanese culture had been taken abroad by the Japanese firms. The process had involved heavy staffing by Japanese fostered partly by the language barrier but mainly by the need for critical mass in the number of Japanese managers in each subsidiary if the system was to function. The Japanese manager would find it impossible to manage an organization without the support of subordinates who shared the same work style. Yet the heavy use of Japanese had offended host governments, discouraged local nationals who saw poor prospects of promotion and complicated relations with joint venture partners.

A further complication was the resistance of most Japanese managers to foreign assignments because of the importance to them of remaining at home where they could maintain the intimate personal relationships so important in their system. Thus, there had been a tendency to send less competent personnel abroad. Yoshino concluded that Japanese management faced a serious dilemma. In order to undertake major expansion internationally, the Japanese had to bring about basic changes in their management system—changes not easy to achieve. And in the process they might well sacrifice those elements that had made their system so effective internally.

5. Another perception of Japanese overseas management relations is provided by Sakamoto's description of problems with joint–venture associates arising from cultural differences.[31] He observed that at the board of directors level in both the United States and Europe non-management custodial members were named and were viewed as representatives of stockholders and the public. The U.S. version was the outside director while in Europe it was the custodial board which supervised the managing board. In both cases the board functioned as a body by voting on decisions. The Japanese boards were quite different. They had no non-management members and decisions were made by the chief executive with no vote. Sharply-defined dif-

ferences in status among directors gave the board the nature of a superior-subordinate arrangement.

Sakamoto observed that Japanese executives assigned to top positions in joint ventures in Europe or the United States and not understanding these role characteristics might act improperly. An executive having custodial status might perform as a managing executive and an executive having operational tasks might act as if he were chairman of the counsellor board. This activity invited distrust of the Japanese. Likewise, since the custodial function was not active in Japanese firms, the Japanese might make it powerless in the joint venture, also generating distrust.

Differences also arose because the Japanese assigned to the joint venture were non-owner technocrats whose viewpoints differed from the partners who might be owner-managers. Often it was the Japanese-type manager who acted rashly in regard to business planning. The classic behavior pattern of the technocrat might be seen in his concern for accomplishments during his term of assignment and in his feeling that since distribution of profits outside the company was of little personal benefit, profits should be reinvested in the company. At the top management level the same difference noted at the board level was seen. European top management made decisions in the collegiate style by voting. In the Japanese style, even though there might be full discussion, it was the president who made the decisions.

At the middle management level in Europe, the transmission of commands was extremely directive and was handled by line managers. Therefore, each middle manager, in executing his command attempted to make suitable decisions within the scope of authority allocated to him. In contrast to this, in Japanese organizations the content of commands was often indicative and informative. Therefore, although each middle manager made the necessary decisions within the range of his own authority, he sought to obtain the consent of others who were involved in the matter at hand by the *ringisho* method. (This term defines the traditional Japanese system of circulating proposals through all interested managers to solicit views and work toward ultimate consensus decisions.) Thus responsibility is shared. Sakamoto described a type of situation in which a Japanese department manager supervising three foreign section chiefs would confuse them by acting as if the Japanese style prevailed. If there were a failure in a matter under one section chief, he would speak to all three section chiefs considering that the other two were also responsible. The other two, not being Japanese, would wonder why on earth they were being held responsible. This might easily lead to feelings of dissatisfaction, distrust, and even animosity.

Also as a result of the collective responsibility concept, the share of responsibility borne by each person was diminished. Thus, situations might arise in which by foreign standards of individual responsibility employees who should certainly be released for failing to perform their duties were permitted to remain in the company because of application of the Japanese standards. Such acts by Japanese managers inevitably dulled the interest of serious employees.

Finally, it was noted that for individual Japanese managers, there was only one "company." The complete loyalty of the expatriate to his parent company impaired his ability to associate with the point of view of the joint venture. In extreme cases, even when the equity share of the Japanese partner was low, the other partner might be considered as being subordinate. At least for the term of his assignment, the manager must think of himself as being part of the management of the company to which he had been sent, but Japanese could not do this very well.

The differences in managerial behavior that appear as part of the problem in these commentaries have been the subject of a number of studies in recent years. Summaries of four comprehensive projects are helpful in giving a sense of both the similarities and differences in managerial characteristics around the world.

6. Haire, Ghiselli, and Porter surveyed 3,641 managers in fourteen countries, ascertaining attitudes under three main headings: leadership, the role of the manager, and motivations and satisfactions.[32] Overall they found substantial similarity among managers of every nation. The differences among individuals within countries were found to be about two and one-half times as great as the differences among countries. Working with national average data, however, it was possible to define a number of distinct differences both among countries and among groups of countries, which apparently arise from cultural differences.

Broadly the authors found that the attitudes in certain countries tended to cluster, resulting in natural groupings as follows: Nordic-European (Denmark, Germany, Norway, and Sweden), Latin-European (Belgium, France, Italy, and Spain), Anglo-American (England and United States), developing countries (Argentina, Chile, and India), and Japan. The results confirmed the unique pattern of managerial thinking in Japan that could not be tied in with that of the other groups. The study also confirmed that the developing nations were more similar to each other than to what might seem their natural cultural relatives in the more developed nations (e.g., India and England).

The leadership analysis was essentially concerned with the difference between democratic and authoritarian approaches. Overall, the study revealed a somewhat paradoxical situation: the tendency to disagree with the belief that the average individual has a capacity for initiative and leadership and, at the same time, a tendency to agree that the best methods of leadership are the democratic-participative methods. The authors pondered whether this paradox was due to a tendency of managers to give lip service to modern management concepts while retaining a traditional outlook. A number of differences among individual countries were noted. Some fitted what might be expected of them: e.g., the pattern in Germany was autocratic. Some differed from expectations: the Japanese, for example, showed greater similarity to Americans than was anticipated.

In the section on the role of the manager, considerable emphasis was given to the differences managers perceived between "directing" and "persuading." It was found that in the Nordic countries, and to a lesser degree in developing countries, these roles were considered quite different while in the other countries they were close—a pattern related, but only partially so, to basic leadership attitudes.

The third section explored feelings as to the extent of fulfillment, the degree of personal satisfaction, and the importance attached to five categories of needs: security, social, esteem, autonomy, and self-actualization. Again certain broad similarities among all nations emerged, notably that while most managers were relatively well satisfied on the first three counts, there was almost universal dissatisfaction with the extent to which desires for autonomy and self-actualization were realized at work.

Among the more specific findings, the most interesting was the high degree of dissatisfaction among two groups of nations for different reasons. Argentinian, Chilean, and Indian managers reported receiving fairly adequate need fulfillment, but they were dissatisfied with this degree of fulfillment because of exceptionally high expectations which in many instances exceeded the expectations of managers in much more economically-developed countries. In the Latin-European countries, on the other hand, the relatively low satisfaction expressed by the managers seemed to stem from relatively low fulfillment rather than from unreasonably high expectations. The authors took especial note of the situation in the less developed countries because people in them uniformly ranked the satisfaction of human needs as being of high importance and the degree of dissatisfaction expressed by managers could be troublesome for the future of private enterprise.

7. England made a ten-year study of the value systems of 2,556 managers in Australia, India, Japan, Korea, and the United States.[33] The study questionnaire included sixty-six value concepts in five categories: goals of business organizations, personal goals, views about groups of people and institutions, ideas associated with people, and ideas about general topics. The respondents rated each concept according to a three-point scale of low to high importance and according to a three-step ranking among "right," "successful," and "pleasant," the latter identified with moralist, pragmatic, and affective orientations. The author also employed responses to incidents to determine the relation between values and behavior. In addition, by the use of age, rank, and salary information, the success of the managers could be roughly determined.

England found a wide variation in values among managers in all countries. However, many patterns permitted conclusions as to general tendencies of characteristics and of differences between countries. Overall England found that successful managers favored pragmatic, dynamic, achievement-oriented values while less successful managers preferred more static and passive values. More successful managers were oriented to achievement and preferred an active role in interaction with other individuals useful in achieving the manager's organizational goals. They valued a dynamic environment and were willing to take risks to achieve organizationally valued goals. Relatively less successful managers had values associated with a static, protected environment in which they took relatively passive roles and often enjoyed extended seniority in their organizational positions. It was also found that among all countries there was a general trend for organizational goals to become a more important part of managers' value systems in larger firms.

Comparing overall patterns among countries, the author found that the United States and Australia were most similar, Japan and Korea next in similarity, and India and Australia fairly similar. The greatest differences were between Korea and Australia and between Japan and Australia. In aggregate about one-half of the managers were pragmatists, one-fourth moralists, one-twentieth affect-oriented and the balance mixed in value orientation. The Japanese were most pragmatic, followed closely by Koreans and Americans. The Indians and Australians were the most concerned with morality. The Japanese were also found to have the highest adherence to organizational goals such as high productivity and organizational stability. In other countries the relevance of these goals varied; the Indians placed high value on organizational stability but low value on profit maximization. Both ratings seemed consistent with a heavily planned Indian economy.

With respect to goals of individuals, the first major difference was the high relevance attached to personal goals by Indian managers, specifically to job satisfaction, security, individuality, dignity, prestige, and power. A high level of personalism seemed evident for Indian managers. Americans and Australians were found to place the lowest value on individual goals. The data on attitudes toward groups of people and institutions showed that these played a much more significant part in the value system of American managers and a much less significant part in the value system of Indian managers. On values associated with people, the Japanese were surprisingly found to score low on loyalty, trust, and tolerance, which suggested a very low level of humanistic orientation. Both Japanese and Korean managers placed relatively high value on the concept of aggressiveness, just the opposite of Australian and Indian managers. Among ideas about general topics, American managers were found to value change highly while Japanese managers valued caution and rationality. It should be noted with respect to the Japanese data, however, that loyalty was found in another part of the analysis to be significantly correlated with success in that country but not in other countries.

Using deviation scores, England determined that the Japanese were most homogeneous in their value systems. The United States was second in homogeneity, followed in order by Australia, India, and Korea. Factor analysis provided some indications as to the interaction of value concepts. For example, among U.S. and Australian managers power and influence were related in similar patterns but not so with Japan and India. In the former countries the power-influence factors seemed to be related to the general orientation of the individual while in Japan they related to their formal role or dignity of the individual.

8. Cummings and Stevens made a study among business executives of five regions: Central Europe, Greece, Scandinavia, Spain, and United States.[34] A fifty-eight-item questionnaire adapted from the Personality Attitude Schedule of Shure and Meeker was used. The results showed wide variations among executives within regions and much smaller variations between regions, the latter accounting for only about 5 percent of the differences in attitudes.

Four types of attitudes were measured: (1) Conciliation-Belligerence. The scores for Greece and Spain were close together toward the conciliation end of this scale and the U.S. scores significantly toward the belligerance end. Central Europeans and Scandinavians fell between these extremes. (2) Risk-Aversion and Risk-Taking. Here the Central Europeans, Scandinavians, and Greeks were clustered toward the risk-aversion end while the Americans were distinctly toward the risk-taking end. The Spanish were in between. (3) External vs. Internal Control, belief in environmental determination vs. self-determination. The Spanish fell at the external control end of the spectrum here; the Americans at the internal control end with the Greeks close to them; and the Central Europeans and Scandinavians in the middle. (4) Suspiciousness-Trust. The Greek scores showed the greatest suspiciousness and the U.S. data the greatest trust, with the other three regions closely grouped in the middle.

9. Granick analyzed management in Britain, France, the U.S.S.R., and the United States with primary emphasis on the first two.[35] His analysis focused on the effectiveness of managerial adaptation to change in terms of two systems of variables: managerial values and the characteristics of managerial organization. Both determined the enterprise's state of readiness to implement successfully alternative projects. These variables were substantially affected by the values and attitudes of different cultures leading to distinctive national patterns.

Of the several differences identified, the most central was summarized as follows: The British firms were relatively strong at the lower and middle levels of management, but top management seemed incapable of taking and enforcing adaptive decisions. Each company operated as though it consisted of a host of small firms, with coordination lacking and suboptimization rampant. New investment was heavily concentrated in relatively unprofitable product markets because of the unwillingness of top management to depart from what they considered (often incorrectly) to be areas of the company's managerial competence.

In contrast, top management decisions were extremely important in achieving the productivity improvements observed in the French firms. On the other hand, middle management was unaggressive and ineffective; one could observe these managers acting in their own individual interests of professionalism rather than to achieve goals of the company. Four of the six French companies seemed, under normal circumstances, to be quite out of control; middle management did not have the authority or incentive to make decisions, and top management did not receive enough information to make rational decisions.

Intimately related to these characteristics were the managerial personnel patterns in the countries. The British managers were recruited from a wide population base and their top ranks were not among the intellectual elite of the country. The French senior managers were drawn largely from the top graduates of the elite educational institutions. As a consequence they were strong on major corporate decision-making. However, because middle managers were generally excluded from prospects of promotion to the top, they related poorly to overall corporate goals. By contrast, the rather plebeian British managers ran lower level units well but were less effective in top-level decision-making.

A number of other differences were noted. The French were relatively less profit-oriented than the British, being motivated more by a sense of national service in achieving business growth. Long-term planning was relatively undeveloped in both countries as compared to the United States. The author noted that long-range plans were most valuable for those companies that were relatively willing to change their policies, because the gains from eliminating weak activities and starting new ones were better perceived over a long term. Also deterring long-range planning was the greater constraint among both British and French firms in the reduction of employees.

The appointment of foreign nationals to senior positions in foreign affiliates has a special significance in communications which is illustrated by the two possibilities shown in Figure 12–3. In case A the top overseas executive is a local national. It is assumed here that he

**Figure 12–3.** Communications Obstacles and Personnel Assignments

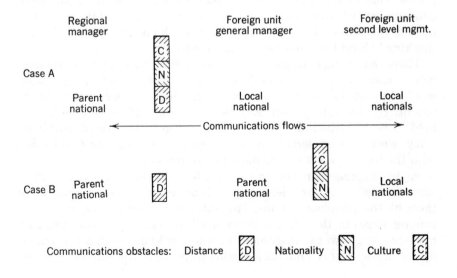

has characteristic cultural and nationality attitudes so that in the break between him and the home office, we have a piling up of obstacles in the combination of culture, nationality, and distance gaps.

In case B we have a parent-country national as a senior man overseas. The communications obstacles are therefore distributed more moderately with the major distance gap between two parent-country nationals and the culture and nationality gaps between a parent-country national and the local nationals below him without the distance impediment.

An intimate picture of these communications problems may be seen in the Racker case, where Mr. Rodriquez, despite long experience with Americans, went through elaborate processes in his communications with his superior Mr. Tarback.[36]

10. A broader exploration of the communications difficulties is provided by results of Hildebrandt's interview survey of 109 German and six American employees in subsidiaries of a variety of U.S. companies in Germany.[37] The group included both German and American general managers as well as line and staff personnel at all levels. Out of the work Hildebrandt derived a composite picture of the aspects of communications that were troublesome, falling under three main headings: channel complexities, linguistics, and culture.

The German managers felt remote from the parent. American members of the executive committee had frequent telephone conversations with the home office but senior Germans, even when proficient in English, felt reluctant to do so because of the cost. German middle managers rarely had direct contacts either in person or by phone. One of them might communicate for years with an American counterpart without ever meeting his respondent. Likewise they missed the values of informal contacts which gave a feel for the thinking behind brief written communications.

There was a high degree of dissatisfaction with formal channels which resulted in considerable bypassing. Subordinates, especially, would bypass the general manager to reach their counterparts in the parent. By the same token, European regional offices were generally held to be an impediment to communication and no significant help. They were viewed largely as coordinators. Direct communication with the parent was used for most decision-making.

As to language barriers, the author found a mixed view. Top management felt the problem was minor while lower management thought the problem serious. Hildebrandt recounted the time-consuming stages in the "linguistic ladder" of getting reports from German-speaking lower management people, working through translation up to headquarters and back again. Important for morale was the fact that German nationals without fluent English had little hope of progressing to the top managerial levels of a subsidiary. They surrounded themselves with bilingual "assistants to" whose bilingual capacity permitted sending reports up and down the linguistic channel. Or, they resigned themselves to retiring in five or ten years, all the time quietly resenting the "young upstarts" who were bilingual.

Hildebrandt described the elaborate rehearsing by Germans weak in English for briefing presentations to visiting parent company executives. A vice president remarked that he was amazed at how well everyone spoke English. This narrow conclusion reflected the separation and seemingly distant touch with realities of the situation.

Assorted cultural differences were mentioned. Some related to the problems of parent people in understanding German ways, for example, their difficulty in grasping the reluctance of German workers to man a night shift. Some related to value systems, the penchant of Americans to move faster in operational changes than Germans, for example. The Germans were also more given to formal report writing compared to the reliance of Americans on informal discussion and brief, "buck-slip" communications. Other differences causing problems were the low mobility of the Germans which deterred shifting them from city to city, their greater concern with formal titles, their formality in personal relations and their tendency to authoritarian management.

The staffing of foreign affiliates is highly dependent upon the type of host nationals seeking positions with MNCs. In earlier years, especially in less developed countries, the MNCs offering good pay and responsible positions were able to attract able local nationals readily. Environmental conditions often aided them as host country economic development was generally too limited and the opportunities in family-dominated local firms too restricted to provide adequate alternatives for ambitious managers. In many countries, the situation is no longer so favorable to the MNCs.

11. The study by Truitt and Blake cited in Chapter 4 illuminated the emerging trend by responses to questions about perceptions of opportunities and interest in working for various types of firms (see p. 146).[38] The results shown in Table 12-2 affirm that in these countries and probably in other relatively advanced LDCs an MNC cannot expect to attract the best available management recruits.

12. Another dimension of this matter was examined in a study of 216 Belgian business students by Vasina seeking information on psychological attitudes relevant to careers in international organizations.[39] Vasina explored three attitudes: (1) interest in working for

Table 12–2.   Views of Opportunities and Conditions in Managerial Positions Elites Attitudes in Chile and Venezuela

| | Chile | | | | Venezuela | | | |
| | Type of Firm | | | | Type of Firm | | | |
| | National | U.S. | Other Foreign | Mixed Ownership | National | U.S. | Other Foreign | Ownership |
|---|---|---|---|---|---|---|---|---|
| What type of company would you recommend your son work for? | 56% | 26% | 5% | 13% | 62% | 21% | 3% | 14% |
| Why? Distribution among four main reasons given: | | | | | | | | |
| More professional opportunities | 35% | 34% | | | 52% | 40% | | |
| Better promotion opportunities | 14 | 12 | | | 27 | 20 | | |
| Support nation | 48 | 0 | | | 18 | 0 | | |
| Better pay | 3 | 54 | | | 3 | 40 | | |
| Opportunities for advancement of local nationals in management: | | | | | | | | |
| Very good | 42% | 8% | | | 42% | 6% | | |
| Good | 35 | 23 | | | 31 | 26 | | |
| Neutral | 15 | 26 | | | 16 | 38 | | |
| Poor | 7 | 28 | | | 10 | 19 | | |
| Very poor | 1 | 14 | | | 1 | 11 | | |

Training efforts for
employees:

| | | | | |
|---|---|---|---|---|
| Very much | 1% | 17% | 22% | 14% |
| Much | 8 | 40 | 25 | 45 |
| Neutral | 26 | 24 | 26 | 25 |
| Little | 32 | 12 | 20 | 11 |
| Very little | 18 | 26 | 7 | 5 |

Source: Nancy S. Truitt and David H. Blake, *Opinion Leaders and Private Investment*. New York: Fund for Multinational Management Education, 1976.

international firms, (2) willingness to work for persons of foreign nationality and culture, and (3) willingness to emigrate for a certain time to other countries. It was found that 23 percent of the students were only interested in working for Belgian firms. Of the balance (77 percent) who were interested in working for international firms, only a little less than half (36 percent) were psychologically fit for such service by criteria 2 and 3.

The survey also gave data on preferences and aversions toward foreign firms. Students' preferences were highest for American (34 percent) and West German (14 percent) firms while the aversions were greatest toward the Japanese (22 percent), Italians (20 percent) and Dutch (17 percent). Overall some 58 percent of the students expressed an aversion to working for a company whose management was from another Common Market country. The majority of the most dynamic students preferred to start their careers with American or West German firms rather than Flemish organizations.

## Focus on the Parent Country National

Consideration of the PCN aspects of staffing focuses particularly on capabilities, behavior, and motivations. Studies that have looked at these characteristics add useful insights to our analysis.

1. Gonzales and Negandhi surveyed 893 U.S. expatriate managers.[40] They could identify no significant distinctions as to family background, education, or other social characteristics between them and U.S. domestic managers. They found that the primary reason given for accepting a foreign assignment was "opportunity for advancement and recognition" for a little over one-third and "desire to travel and live abroad" for another third. Considerable diversity developed in the main advantage given for foreign assignments: higher pay, 17 percent; broader experience and responsibility, 16 percent; learn about people and customs, 15 percent; and more rapid advancement, 14 percent.

The executives were also asked to identify the "factor X" which made for successful work abroad. The main replies were: wife and family adaptable, 20 percent; leadership ability, 19 percent; knowledge of job, 14 percent; knowledge of language of host country, 13 percent; well educated, 13 percent; and respect for laws and people of country, 12 percent. The authors concluded that overseas placement was typically not a preconceived career goal. Chance played a major role in deciding who went overseas, but those who responded exhibited a quality of curiosity and adventure, frequently coupled with strong ambition and impatience with career progress at home.

2. Alpander attempted to determine the differnces in managerial styles of men who had held comparable positions in the United States and abroad in multinational firms.[41] He obtained responses to questionnaires from seventy-five managers, most of them in Europe or Latin America.

The managers' perception of employee attitudes was sought as an important determinant of managerial style. The scaled responses showed that the managers felt the overseas employees were about one-third more resistant to change than those in the United States and somewhat more loyal. Overseas subordinates were believed to be slightly more lazy than Americans, with much stronger differences indicated in the direction of three other attitudes: "Prefer to be led," "Do not want to assume responsibility," and "Have to be closely controlled." A substantial difference was also reported in motivation. Overseas subordinates were felt to be motivated primarily by extrinsic factors (wages, working conditions) while in the United States rewards and job satisfaction were considered primary.

The differences in managerial styles of the U.S. executives were determined according to two basic schemes. First, methods of decision-making were studied with particular reference to the extent of consultation with subordinates. The results showed a pronounced shift toward more authoritarian styles when the men moved abroad. When in the United States, a large majority indicated that most of the time they first presented problems, obtained suggestions, and then made a decision. In their foreign assignment, however, seldom did they consult subordinates. In the majority of the cases, they made their decisions first and then tried to sell their subordinates. Quite a large number did not even bother to sell their decisions.

The second approach identified the degree to which the managers were task- and group-oriented. The men were found to fall in two groups. In the case of Group I the change in managerial style was away from subordinate orientation, support of the social system, warm interpersonal relations, praise as positive source of control, and the tendency to reject the individual as negative source of influence. They drifted instead toward high concern about correction of deviations, organizational identification, increase in controls, tendency to dominate others, and very directive leadership. These executives could be described as having drifted from high to low relationship orientation.

Group II had perceived themselves in the United States as: getting involved with groups and individuals over work, communicating through meetings, having strong coworker orientation and emphasizing teamwork, being interested in finding a source of conflict rather than suppressing it, having a tendency for controlling others by proposing common ideals or settling for a compromise. The same managers identified their managerial style overseas quite differently. The change was toward identifying with the organization and technical system, judging subordinates on the degree of their production, attempting to establish total control over the immediate environment and adapting to paternalistic and domineering attitudes among subordinates. This group of managers were described as having drifted from high task and relationship orientation to high task orientation with low relationship orientation.

Overall the author adhered to the contingency theory of management which, rather than searching for a universal way to manage, assumes that appropriate methods will vary depending upon the situation. Thus the premium in international work was on the ability to shift from a style appropriate at home to one fitting the foreign context. It was determined through the application of several research instruments upon perceived behaviors of the executives that their managerial styles were highly flexible. These managers were successful overseas.

3. Ivancevich and Baker made a study of the satisfactions of a random sample of 127 top and middle managers in foreign assignments for U.S. companies.[42] The framework for the study was Maslow's hierarchy of needs: physiological, security, social, esteem, and self-actualization. For their survey they used the questionnaire designed by Porter, with which he made a 1962 study of a sample of 404 top and middle managers within the United States. The Porter sample provided a basis for comparison of the men in foreign assignments. Porter's questionnaire dropped Maslow's physiological level (food, etc.) as being irrelevant for this level of person and added autonomy as an additional level between esteem and self-actualization. Differences between overseas and domestic managers showed up for each level.

The security needs of top managers overseas were about as well met as those in domestic jobs but the middle managers were substantially less satisfied on this count. The authors speculate that the lower security satisfaction could be accounted for by the fear of being out of the mainstream of company decision-making processes, failing to be considered for promotion and similar reasons.

Under the heading of social needs, the notable difference was the much lower satisfaction of the overseas people in opportunities for friendship. The authors supposed this to result from the social isolation of expatriates from local nationals. The need for esteem of the overseas manager was found to be more adequately met than that of domestic people. The authors noted that the overseas executive's awareness of major contributions made to the host nation by the firm and by himself might provide him with a high degree of gratification.

While it might be assumed that expatriates had more autonomy than did their domestic counterparts, the study showed that the overseas managers felt substantially less satisfaction in their opportunity for independent thought and action. On the other hand, in two other autonomy questions concerning authority and participation in goal setting, the overseas managers felt more satisfaction than those at home.

Overseas and domestic managers were similar in that their needs for self-actualization were the least satisfied of all five categories. Moderate differences appeared between the groups. The overseas people seemed a little more satisfied with opportunities for growth and development, for example, but overall the patterns were similar.

PCNs fall into two general groups when long-run activity patterns are considered: international careerists and those serving abroad for limited periods. The patterns are the result of both company policies and personal preferences. Some companies prefer to have men devote their full careers to international work, feeling that it calls for special capabilities and it is best to focus the efforts of a limited number of managers on it to maximize their effectiveness and that of the organization. Other firms feel that it is better to move a large number of mean through international assignments to integrate the foreign operations more with the domestic activities, to give a broad band of management a good international outlook, and to provide continuing new inputs of parent management skills abroad. The company views are substantially affected by personal preferences of executives. Some of them have a preference for continuing work abroad while others wish either for themselves or for their families' sake to return to the parent country after limited overseas assignments.

Because the limited foreign assignment pattern is widely followed, the experience of managers returning to the parent country is a significant factor in the staffing picture. The image prospective candidates for foreign assignments have of what they may expect when they return is a prime factor in the ability of MNCs to attract men to serve abroad. There has been no systematic research on this subject but a report of a journalist provides substantial information on executive experience.

4. Smith surveyed the problems of U.S. managers returning from foreign assignments to work in the parent organization—"the reentry

crisis of the expatriate executive."[43] Three general areas of anxiety were observed: personal finances, readjustment to the corporate structure, and reacclimation to life in the United States. He found that few, if any, executives ever come out ahead financially in a transfer back to the United States, even with a promotion, and most had to take what amounted to a pay cut. The root of the problem was the benefits companies gave to persuade men to accept foreign assignments. One expert was quoted as estimating that it would take a 50 percent increase in salary in the United States to match the style of living they had abroad. Furthermore, they found that purchasing houses in the United States had become much more expensive when they returned, an average of 10 percent increase in prices per year.

An even more serious shock, because it could have a long-range impact on the executive's career, was the readaptation to corporate life. One of the most attractive aspects of a foreign post for the ambitious executive was the autonomy it allowed. When he returned, no matter how big the promotion, he became the member of an organization again and had to measure his steps carefully. There was also the question of the significance of the foreign assignment. Executives might be encouraged to believe that foreign stints lead to the top. But the reality was uncertain. The author cited a Dun's survey of the fifty largest multinational corporations which showed that only ten of eighty-seven presidents and chairmen had served substantial tours abroad and sixty-nine had no foreign service other than inspection tours. A management consultant was quoted to make the apparent point. "International experience is great. Make sure you get it in the international division at headquarters, right down the corridor from the chairman of the board."[44]

Reentry culture shock for many men lay in status adjustment. Abroad the manager was probably a considerable figure in the business community and perhaps a social lion as well. Back home he was likely to be just another vice president. There were also adjustments in family life. A company psychiatrist is quoted, "When you go abroad, you know that you are a foreigner. You can live in isolation and in many ways that brings a family closer together."[45] Upon return the family had to adjust to pressures of a quite different set of relations and social environment. Likewise the wife who typically had become accustomed to a lifestyle including a staff of servants for cooking and housework had to learn to do most of her own work in suburban American style.

5. A prime requirement of PCN effectiveness abroad is capacity to relate to the host society, to individual local nationals, and to their business system. MNCs typically undertake no more than limited

efforts to prepare managers in this respect prior to departure. Common practices were reported by Ivancevich from a survey of 127 home office executives responsible for training personnel and from 127 expatriates in foreign assignments.[46] A significant deterrent to providing training was the time available. In about 70 percent of cases less than three months elapsed between the time a man was selected for a foreign assignment and the date of departure.

In firms that did provide training, the vast majority concentrated on language study. About half gave attention to the customs in the assignment country. A handful mentioned history, living conditions, political ideology, and law. Geography, exchange rates, government structure, religion, and economics were mentioned by none.

In the brief predeparture period the manager is hard pressed to close out his previous assignment and acquire minimum substantive preparation for the foreign job. Significant training for cultural adaptation is practical in only a few cases and it is further limited by the difficulties of education in this area. The latter are best appreciated by two statements, one describing the skill needed for cultural adaptation and one prescribing an approach to acquiring the skill.

6. Lee proposes the natural self-reference criterion (SRC)—the unconscious reference to one's own cultural values—as the root cause of most international business problems overseas and offers an analytical approach designed to reduce its influence.[47] He quotes Ong's description of the problem: "Our own great American achievement has somehow become a positive psychological handicap. The United States has been a vast and successful working machine for converting into ourselves persons from every nation of the world. We cannot make ourselves over, even imaginatively, into other people. Our thoughtfulness is caught in our assumptions that what we do is never chauvinistic or nationalistic, though what others do may well be."[48]

The SRC habit is seen as one of the most difficult to break. In some circumstances it helps people to succeed in new situations, occasionally even in other cultures. Therefore, its curbing must be specific, not general. The cultural analysis system described by Lee as an effective way to check the SRC influence is a modification of the thinking pattern of the anthropologist, who looks at any item of behavior as functional within the total cultural system of which it is a part. When this thinking pattern is applied to business, it can be seen as a four-step procedure:

Step 1. Define the business problem or goal in terms of the American cultural traits, habits, or norms.

Step 2. Define the business problem or goal in terms of the foreign cultural traits, habits, or norms. Make no value judgments.

Step 3. Isolate the SRC influence in the problem and examine it carefully to see how it complicates the problem.

Step 4. Redefine the problem without the SRC influence and solve for the optimum business goal.

Lee observes that organizations must adapt to a complex environment overseas. Overseas institutions—financial, government, labor, and marketing—are not fitted together in the same way they are in the United States. To illustrate: In one South American country a U.S. company joined with a small group of local capitalists who were destined to be removed from the position of having moderate power in their government to that of having none. Five years after the partnership was formed, the U.S. firm began to suffer delays in licenses to import raw materials and other forms of harassment at the hands of the foreign government.

Lee proposes the following cultural analysis steps in approaching the selection of partnership capital to avoid such a problem.

Step 1. U.S. capital is generally selected on the basis of adequacy and demonstrated integrity.

Step 2. Foreign capital may be selected on the basis of business and government connections, social class, and political comers.

Step 3. The American SRC influence will be to underestimate the role of government in business and industrial operations, and to overestimate the adequacy of warning signs available to U.S. nationals to show up the wrong capital.

Step 4. The method of selecting partners, as it is practiced in the foreign country, should be carefully studied first. Then the partners or stockholders can be chosen as nearly as possible on this basis without jeopardizing the relationship with those institutions that are important to the company's success.

Lee cites as an illustration of a cultural characteristic which appears to present adaptation problems for U.S. nationals overseas the "time-value" difference. For example, a foreign subordinate promises to have a certain job finished by Wednesday. Later it is apparent that this deadline could not have been met and that there probably was no serious intent on his part to try to meet it. The SRC of the U.S. national holds that it is better to tell the boss an agreed-on deadline cannot be met than to have him find out later. But this trait can only be developed in a country where (1) confession is considered good for the soul, (2) the employee has other courses of action open to him if the boss is displeased, (3) the confessor cannot be immediately or easily replaced, and (4) only the eight-hour loyalty is the rule instead of lifetime service with obligations to be on call at all times. The foreigner operates on a more interpersonal system and a part of this system is to avoid disagreements or embarrassment. In his system confession can be very dysfunctional. Moreover, he feels that he has little recourse if he is fired. (His own SRC comes into play here.)

One simple but often resisted solution to the problem is for the person who meters out the assignment to take greater care in seeing to it that it is attainable and well understood, especially the time schedule aspects, even if this means repeating most assignments. This is far more efficient than suffering the continued surprises of important schedules unmet.

7. DeBettignies and Rhinesmith describe their concepts of how to prepare executives for management involving different cultural behavior patterns.[48] Two elements of awareness are required: the manager must become aware of the motivations, values, and goals that condition his own behavior and he must be aware of the new culture in which he will work. The authors contend that managers can operate effectively abroad only when they are: (1) aware of themselves as culturally conditioned individuals, (2) alert to the differences in perception between themselves and others, (3) aware of their own social and emotional needs and attentive to the same needs in others, and (4) willing to work toward meaningful relationships with others through communication and mutual adaptation. They identify four distinctive patterns of human reaction to new and unfamiliar surroundings: "flight," "dependency," "fight," and "adjustment." Their objective is to facilitate adjustment which is regarded as the desirable reaction for the international executive.

Prime attention is given to the learning process which is seen as a three-phase cycle of unfreezing-moving-refreezing. The "unfreezing" process is the most difficult phase requiring that the manager recognize and reconsider the values, standards, and ideals into which he has been frozen by years of conditioning in his society with constant reinforcement from others surrounding him. Once through the unfreezing, the individual can achieve the actual learning in the "moving" phase. He expands his cultural vision, accepts or rejects new experiences and reevaluates his past and present perceptions in order to form new criteria for future decision-making in his work and personal life. In the "refreezing" phase the manager locks in place his new perceptions and ways of behaving to avoid regressing to a previous mode of behavior.

### Staffing Guidelines

Because organization must serve the purposes of strategy, the prevailing staffing patterns described by Franko and other writers in the preceding section are generally sound. We have seen that the communication problems between host country nationals and parent country nationals are great. When HCNs compose all or virtually all of the top management of foreign affiliates, the combination of cultural, nationality, and distance gaps is a tremendous impediment to inputs from the parent organization. Strategies requiring substantial communications from the parent are impossible with such an impediment. The problem is notably great when transmission of resources calls for a heavy flow of skills or when unification strategies require a high degree of coordination of activities between parent and affiliates.

But it is also clear that substantial use of PCNs usually carries a high cost in terms of operational effectiveness of affiliates. There are complications to attracting the best parent personnel to the jobs; they are expensive to maintain abroad; and there are considerable shortcomings in their effectiveness due to cultural and national relationships. These shortcomings in turn result in problems in the internal relationships of the affiliates which reduce their effectiveness. Perhaps more important, along with their adverse effect on promotion prospects they contribute to an unfavorable image of MNCs among management job candidates in host societies. Thus, heavy use of PCNs is a significant obstacle to the MNC in its prime objective of attracting able host country nationals.

A further impediment is the high probability brought out by Zeira's work that this whole area will receive ineffective management attention. The poor communications upward from host country nationals commonly means that those from the parent country do not understand the difficulties within their organizations. And to the extent these difficulties are understood, the PCNs have little incentive to communicate about them to their home organization, both because of reluctance to convey a picture of inadequacies in their own performance and because of perceptions as to degrees of their responsibility for such matters. In addition to these deterrents to communication, the whole matter of internal managerial relationships is likely to have a lower priority than pursuit of strategic objectives and other operational matters, so that it will receive little attention in the crowded channels of communication between parent and affiliates.

This diagnosis leads to the conclusion that staffing is a fundamental weak point of MNC organizations, representing a serious handicap in competitive relations with purely domestic firms. As a practical matter there seems to be an inherent combination of factors leading to loss of effectiveness—substantial use of PCNs to assure communication for primary strategic needs, shortcomings in internal affiliate relations due to inadequacies of PCNs, the best parent nationals are not attracted to the jobs, and consequent shortcomings in HCN performance stemming from the internal situation. The whole situation is inadequately understood and subject to limited corrective action because of the dynamics of MNC objectives and communications relationships.

Realistic prescription of guidelines in these circumstances is not easy. Pragmatic judgment must affirm that MNCs have by and large been successful in their approaches, giving first priority to resource transmission, unification strategy, and operational needs for communication. On the whole the extent of use of parent country nationals has been effective. And since competition results in a trend toward greater efforts to emphasize the special resource and unification capabilities of MNCs, the need to structure the organization to fit these capabilities will continue. It may well be therefore that this situation adds up to one of the fundamental limitations of the scope of MNCs.

Referring back to Figure 12—1, we can sum up the problem by reference to the equation at the bottom. The shortcomings arising from the staffing situation are a major part of the sum of the incremental losses in effectiveness attributed to the communications gaps. The strategy objectives that are a prime factor in causing staffing problems are also the source of the incremental advantages gained by the parent inputs. The crux of the competitive status of the MNC is the balance of the incremental inputs vs. the sum of the related shortcomings. If the inputs are great enough, they can offset the shortcomings and the MNC overall will be able to compete with local national firms. If the inputs are modest and do not offset the deterrents, the MNC will be relatively weak competitively. Thus, quite aside from the direct, marketplace impact of its strategic capabilities, the future of the MNC in foreign markets may be substantially affected by the inherent shortcomings of its mixed staffing characteristics.

To some degree it is realistic to accept the shortcomings fatalistically as part of the nature of MNC operations. But the subject should not be ignored. The adherence to whatever staffing is required at a given time for strategy needs is clearly appropriate. Within the resultant pattern, however, management has substantial scope for improvement of performance. This analysis has suggested major guidelines toward that end.

First, it is clear that there should be incentives and systems to assure that management both at affiliate and parent levels is informed about the performance of the operations.

Second, the mix of elements affecting PCN performance abroad, ranging from selection and training to reentry problems, requires attention, recognizing that where parent nationals can competently handle host nationals, the shortcomings of the system are greatly reduced.

Third, substantial attention to attracting and particularly to developing high quality host country nationals is appropriate. Special attention should be given to develop their capabilities to overcome communications obstacles to strategy implementation. The great need is for host nationals to sufficiently master the parent point of view and the basic capabilities required for skill transmission so that they can serve as efficient communications links in strategy implementation. This would remove the need for PCNs in senior foreign posts and eliminate the range of problems associated with their use.

### NOTES

1. H. Koontz and C. O'Donnell, *Principles of Management: An Analysis of Managerial Functions* (New York: McGraw-Hill, 1972).

2. Mason Haire, Edwin E. Ghiselli, and Lyman W. Porter, *Managerial Thinking* (New York: John Wiley & Sons, 1965), p. 8.

3. For example, see Edward T. Hall, *The Silent Language* (Garden City, N.Y.: Doubleday, 1959) and Edward T. Hall and William F. Whyte, "International Communication," *Human Organization*, Spring 1960, pp. 5–12.

4. For example, see Mason Haire et al., op. cit., and John Fayerweather, *The Executive Overseas* (Syracuse, N.Y.: Syracuse University Press, 1959).

5. Fayerweather, ibid., pp. 145–162.

6. Howard V. Perlmutter, "Social Architectural Problems of the Multinational Firm," *The Quarterly Journal of AIESEC International*, August 1967, pp. 37–38.

7. Gilbert H. Clee and Alfred DiScipio, "Creating a World Enterprise," *Harvard Business Review*, Nov.–Dec., 1959, pp. 77–89.

8. Gilbert H. Clee and Wilbur M. Sachtjen, "Organizing a Worldwide Business," *Harvard Business Review*, Nov.–Dec., 1964, pp. 55–67.

9. Enid Baird Lovell, *The Changing Role of the International Executive* (New York: National Industrial Conference Board, 1966).

10. Ibid., p. 84.

11. John M. Stopford and Louis T. Wells, *Managing the Multinational Enterprise* (New York: Basic Books, 1972).

12. Hans Schollhammer, "Organizational Structures of Multinational Corporations," *Academy of Management Journal*, Sept. 1971, pp. 345–365.

13. Lawrence G. Franko, *European Business Strategies* (Geneva: Business International, 1971).

14. Cedric Suzman, "The Changing Nature of Export Management," *Atlanta Economic Review*, Sept.–Oct. 1975, pp. 15–20.

15. Charles R. Williams, "Regional Management Overseas," *Harvard Business Review*, Jan.–Feb. 1967, pp. 87–91.

16. David A. Heenan and Calvin Reynolds, "RPO's: A Step Toward Global Human Resources Management," *California Management Review*, Fall 1975, pp. 5–9.

17. Roger M. Kenny, "The European Advisory Committee," *The Business Quarterly*, Winter 1975, pp. 86–91.

18. Samuel C. Johnson and Richard M. Thomson, "Active Role for Outside Directors of Foreign Subsidiaries," *Harvard Business Review*, Sept.–Oct. 1974, pp. 13–18.

19. Lawrence G. Franko, "Who Manages Multinational Enterprises?" *Columbia Journal of World Business*, Summer 1973, pp. 30–42.

20. Ibid., p. 37.

21. Jay Galbraith and Anders Edstrom, "International Transfer of Managers," *Columbia Journal of World Business*, Summer 1976, pp. 100–112.

22. Samir M. Youssef, "The Integration of Local Nationals into the Managerial Hierarchy of American Overseas Subsidiaries," *Academy of Management Journal*, Mar. 1973, pp. 24–34.

23. Franko, op. cit., "Who Manages Multinational Enterprises," p. 39.

24. Kenneth Simmonds, "Multinational? Well, Not Quite," *Columbia Journal of World Business*, Fall 1966, pp. 115–122.

25. Christopher Tugendhat, *The Multinationals* (New York: Random House, 1972).

26. Ibid., p. 195.

27. Yoram Zeira, Ehud M. Haavari, and Dafna Izraeli Nundi, "Some Structural and Cultural Factors in Ethnocentric Multinational Corporations and Employee Morale," *Journal of Management Studies*, Feb. 1975, pp. 66–82.

28. Yoram Zeira, "Overlooked Personnel Problems of Multinational Corporations," *Columbia Journal of World Business*, Summer 1975, pp. 96–103.

29. Richard T. Johnson and William S. Ouchi, "Made in Japan (under Japanese Management)" *Harvard Business Review*, Sept.–Oct., 1974, pp. 61–69.

30. M. Y. Yoshino, *Japan's Multinational Enterprises* (Cambridge, Mass.: Harvard University Press, 1971), pp. 161–178.

31. Yasumi Sakamoto, "The Decision-Making Process in Japanese International Joint Ventures," *Management Japan*, Spring 1977, pp. 20–24.

32. Mason Haire, Edwin E. Ghiselli, and Lyman W. Porter, *Managerial Thinking* (New York: John Wiley & Sons, 1966).

33. George W. England, *The Manager and his Values* (Cambridge, Mass.: Ballinger Publishing Company, 1975).

34. L. L. Cummings and O. J. Stevens, "Risk, Fate, Conciliation and Trust," *Academy of Management Journal*, Sept. 1971, pp. 285–304.

35. David Granick, *Managerial Comparison for Four Developed Countries* (Cambridge, Mass.: M.I.T. Press, 1972).

36. John Fayerweather and Ashok Kapoor, *Strategy and Negotiation for the International Corporation* (Cambridge, Mass.: Ballinger Publishing Company 1975), pp. 401–412.

37. H.W. Hilderbrandt, "Communication Barriers Between German Subsidiaries and Parent American Companies," *Michigan Business Review*, July 1973, pp. 6–14.

38. Nancy S. Truitt and David H. Blake, *Opinion Leaders and Private Investment* (New York: Fund for Multinational Management Education, 1976), p. 29.

39. Leopold S. Vasina, "Internationalizing the Firm," *International Studies of Management and Organization*, Winter 1971–72, pp. 351–362.

40. Richard F. Gonzales and Anant R. Negandhi, *The United States Overseas Executive: His Orientations and Career Patterns* (East Lansing: Michigan State University, Graduate School of Business Administration, 1967).

41. Guvenc G. Alpander, "Drift to Authoritarianism: The Changing Managerial Styles of the U.S. Executives Abroad," *Journal of International Business Studies*, Fall 1973, pp. 1–14.

42. John M. Ivancevich and James C. Baker, "Job Satisfaction of American Managers Overseas," *MSU Business Topics*, Summer 1969, pp. 72–79.

43. Lee Smith, "The Hazards of Coming Home," *Dun's Review*, Oct. 1975, pp. 71–73.

44. Ibid., p. 72.

45. Ibid., p. 73.

46. John M. Ivancevich, "Predeparture Training for Overseas," *Training and Development Journal*, Feb. 1969, pp. 36–40.

47. James A. Lee, "Cultural Analysis in Overseas Operations," *Harvard Business Review*, Mar.–Apr. 1966, pp. 106–114.

48. Ibid., p. 107.

49. H.C. deBettignies and S.H. Rhinesmith, "Developing the International Executive," *European Business*, Jan. 1970, pp. 52–57.

✳️ *Chapter 13*

# The Managerial Process

With the organization and staffing patterns in the background as the mechanism of MNC administration, this chapter will examine the processes by which the mechanism functions. Particular attention will be given to three areas: how decisions are made; how skills are transmitted; and how managerial direction is achieved.

## THE ANALYTICAL FRAMEWORK

Analysis of managerial processes is always difficult because of their multifaceted, behavioral character. The analytical approach tends inevitably to focus on one facet at a time which is productive up to a point, but in the achievement of full understanding that approach is inadequate and even misleading. In reality organizations function in response to a complex combination of forces and a total grasp of the managerial process must be able to comprehend both the parts and the totality. The analytical framework presented here is far from perfect by these criteria but it does identify the major parts and gives some sense of the totality.

The main elements of the analytical scheme as shown in Figure 13–1 are the decision-making system, the communication system, and the behavioral dynamics. Visual complexity requires that the diagrams be separated but a realistic sense of the totality requires thinking of them as combined. Cutting through the middle is a line symbolizing the cultural, nationality, and distance gaps with all of their ramifications and implications described in the introduction to Part III.

**Figure 13–1.** Roles, Communications, and Behavioral Dynamics in the MNC Managerial Process

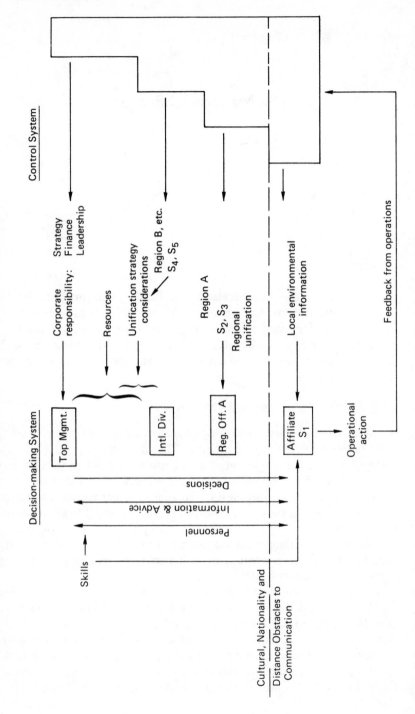

**Figure 13–1.** continued

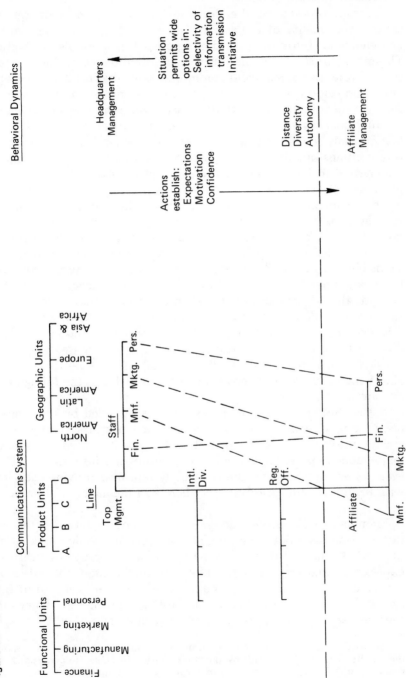

### Decision-making System

The end product of the decision-making system is operational action. The quality of the action it develops is dependent upon two key elements: information and competence in action determination. The main thrust of the analysis is therefore directed at the combination of role assignments and communications that results in the optimum application of these elements. In this part of the analysis only four organizational units are discussed: top corporate management, international division, regional office, and foreign affiliate. The following analysis will deal with the major oversimplications this structure contains but for present purposes the first three units should be understood to be proxies for the assorted variations discussed in the previous chapter.

The main inputs of *information* are on the whole located at certain levels of the organization as shown by the arrows leading to each box at the left in Figure 13−1. Information on overall corporate strategy and finance must come from top management which is responsible for them. Knowledge of resource capabilities may come from varied parts of the parent organization and is available therefore at both the top management and international division levels. Unification considerations such as global product, R&D, and logistic strategies may also be brought in at the top or at the international division level. Where unification is essentially on an area basis, these considerations may enter at the regional office level. Information about the local operating environment is available at the foreign affiliate level.

A substantial volume of information is provided by the management control system.[a] By its nature the control system provides greater information at the operating level than at higher levels, the major constraint being the cost of transmitting information. However, by selective design, the control system may provide each level with feedback data appropriate to its role in the managerial process.

**Elements of Decision-making.**   Competence in action determination encompasses both the intellectual skills of decision-making and the varied qualities that are generally summed up by such terms as experience, maturity, and the like. The intellectual skills are generally greater as one moves up the management scale because of both age and specialization. That is, the more senior men in higher management are presumed to have greater competence, and there are a

---

[a]Control is used here in the common management meaning of ascertaining the results achieved in operations and their relation to plans. It encompasses the functions directed by the controller in corporate management.

variety of specialists in the higher organizational ranks who have superior competence in particular fields, for example, foreign exchange, personnel management, and patent law. But the other qualities contributing to decision-making ability are spread quite widely through organizations. In particular, on many matters people in the lower ranks may have sufficient skill combined with a mature, experienced perspective on management in their areas to make effective decisions.

To the analytical scheme we must now add important elements of *mobility*. Both information and competence in action determination are mobile and they may be transmitted in person or by communication. Personal mobility takes many forms: a specialist in production technology may be sent abroad to apply his expert information to decision-making in establishing a new factory; the chairman of the board may fly to Europe where his knowledge of top corporate goals is applied directly to on-the-spot policy decisions; a foreign affiliate manager may come to the home office bringing his knowledge of local conditions to bear on final budget decisions for his unit for the coming year. Communication options are equally varied. They include reports on foreign operating conditions sent to headquarters, operating manuals put out by the parent organization, advice contained in telephone calls, letters, and other personal contacts from one level to another and, of course, the transmission of actual decisions.

**Locus of Decision-making.**  The mobility characteristics of information and competence in action determination offer a range of options to the MNC in the locus of decision-making. The simplest approach is to assign decision-making on a matter to one spot in the organization and move information and competence to that spot to some degree to improve the quality of the outcome.

Another major option is to split the assignment among two or more spots, each making part of the decision according to the suitability of its situation. A common example of this approach is to have a higher level set broad policies establishing limits of action and then leave specific determination of action within those limits to lower levels.

A third major option is joint decision-making in which two or more parts of the organization engage in an interactive process. The ultimate decision cannot be accurately described as "made" by any one part, others having clearly influenced it greatly. Systems in which action is the result of strongly presented proposals from lower levels, over which higher management exercises final authority fall in this category. Choices among these options must be based upon consideration of the varied criteria bearing on the consequences of the choice of which six are most significant: quality of decisions, timing, cost, efficiency in use of resources, management motivation, and skill transmission.

The immediate concern of management in making any decision must be that its *quality* be high—that the best course of action be chosen. The ideal by this criterion is to draw together all the information that can be useful in making the decision and subject it to the best combination of competence among the management.

*Timing* is a key criterion because the speed with which decisions are made can have a significant impact on their effectiveness. This is notably true in highly competitive marketing situations, but it may also be significant in other areas like finance and labor relations. In general, the time required for decision-making is least if the determinations are made at the spot where action is to be taken. Thus on matters that involve affiliate action the quickest approach is for their managements to make decisions, while major allocations of financial resources are most quickly made in the corporate treasurer's office. The second important determinant of time required for decision-making is the number of people and especially of levels of management involved. A decision in which two or three levels of executives participate will usually take longer than a decision made at only one level.

*Cost* is a limiting criterion in the choice among decision-making options particularly with respect to the mobility characteristics. Transmission of information involves communication expenses and movement of competence is especially costly. Outlays for travel and support of managers dispatched from one level of the organization to another to participate in decision-making are considerable. The cost is further substantially increased when, as is usually the case, the movement of competence also adds to the total management time devoted to the decision-making. For example, when a decision on a marketing plan is made by drawing in a member of the parent staff rather than by the affiliate managers alone, the time of the parent executive must be added to the cost along with his travel expenses.

The *efficiency in use of resources* most commonly involves an extension of the point just made. At a given moment a corporation has available only a finite amount of managerial competence. If a manager is assigned to participate in one decision-making process, not only must the cost of his time be carried by that process but also his time is not available for other possible activities. The question applies regardless of the level of the individual. If a headquarters staff man is sent to one subsidiary, he is not centrally available to help on matters concerning other affiliates. If an affiliate manager is called to headquarters, he is not on the spot to deal with immediate operating problems.

*Motivation* is significant in any pattern of decision-making and particularly relevant in distribution of roles among the major levels of an MNC. The cultural, nationality, and distance gaps create such communications problems that affiliates abroad inevitably must have greater autonomy than domestic counterparts. As a consequence the assurance of positive and usefully directed motivations among the managers at all levels becomes a prime concern. We will deal further with this area in the discussion of behavioral aspects of administration but it has to be noted here because the choice between decision-making options can substantially affect motivations.

*Skill transmission* has a special place in this analysis flagged by the notations on the left side of Figure 13–1. Skills in one sense are already part of the analytical scheme because they are part of competence in action determination. But they are also major components of operating strategy as they are typically prime aspects of resource transmission capability. Thus in considering the movement of that competence, we must consider not only how the movement will affect immediate decision-making but also how it affects skill transmission.

There are many questions that can stem from this duality of goals. Suffice to note one obvious one by way of illustration. Headquarters officers are frequently in a position where they can choose between making a decision on a matter or suggesting to foreign affiliate managers how to approach it and letting them make their own decision. The urgency of the problem, availability of information, and other factors may affect the method employed. But, other things being equal, the decision may often be left to the managers at some sacrifice to the quality of the immediate decision in the interests of long-term achievement of skill transmission.

The range of the options in decision-making locus and the effect of these six criteria present so many permutations that it is impractical to expand further on the analytical scheme. The outline laid out here will suffice as a basis for consideration of the MNC experience to be brought out later in this chapter.

### Control System

The control system is an important adjunct to the decision-making system. However, it also has certain characteristics beyond its simple role in the feedback of information for use in decision-making. One is its impact on skill transmission. The requirements headquarters establishes for operational reporting can have a substantial impact in directing affiliate attention to particular aspects of management, requiring them to perform certain functions regularly and exerting pressure on them in these processes. The control requirements may therefore appreciably shape the types of skills that overseas personnel acquire. These same characteristics will also, of course, tend to steer foreign affiliate decisions in particular directions. For example, if headquarters asks for frequent reports on volume of sales, the affiliates will be moved to push in that direction, while close parent attention to profit margins will result in greater concern for keeping costs in line. Thus the control system is itself an active vehicle for management direction.

The other critical characteristic of control systems is their common bias toward standardization and uniformity. Controllers are statistically oriented. Measurement is their way of life and comparative measurements are a prime objective. In domestic operations comparisons are common and highly effective—productivity of plant A vs. plant B, return on investment of division X vs. division Y. But in international operations measurements are doubtful and many types of comparison are either impossible or dangerous. The major problems lie in the differences in operating conditions among countries, the inaccuracy of some forms of data (notably those related to the environment requiring government or other external information), the character of foreign exchange rates used for translation, and the nature of financial relations among units discussed in Chapter 9 (e.g., transfer prices, royalties, etc.). All of these can grossly distort comparative data among units so that judgments of operating performance based on comparisons of control information may be misleading. Furthermore, the mere fact of establishing standard control systems for all foreign units raises questions because of differences in size, sophistication of management, types of problems encountered, and the like. These observations do not preclude some degree of standardization in control systems nor some forms of comparative analysis. They do emphasize, however, the need to consider carefully the limitations that are wise on both counts.

### Communications System

Communications figured prominently in the discussion of decision-making. However, the direct vertical movements assumed in that discussion grossly oversimplify the realities of the MNC communications needs. The diversity of activities, the spread of operations, the pressures of environment and competition, and the characteristics of individuals combine to foster a quite complex pattern of communications. Even in this discussion we will greatly oversimplify the systems which have evolved in many larger firms but we can identify the main elements affecting the evolution of the systems.

The diagram in the middle of Figure 13—1 provides a framework for this analysis. In Chapter 12, the three dimensions—functional, geographic, and product—noted at the top of the diagram were identified as a fundamental problem of organization design (see p. 487). They reappear now essentially because the problem they pose cannot be satisfactorily solved by direct relationships within the organizational structure and must therefore be largely dealt with by elaborations of the communications system. Depending upon the size and character of the MNC, each of the three dimensions may be present at every level of the organization. As was indicated in Chapter 12, one dimension will normally be designated as having line operational responsibility at each level with others assuming staff roles. The designations will not necessarily be the same at each level. At the lowest level some functional roles, e.g., production and marketing, must assume operational line responsibility with others like personnel in a staff status. However, at higher levels all functional units quite commonly appear in staff positions with product or geographic units carrying the line status.

The organizational scheme shown in Figure 13—1 presents one such situation in rather simplified form but with sufficient body to convey the main point, namely, that there are a great variety of people in varied parts of the organization who have some relation to each other. The characteristics of the relation have to be defined because they are the main determinants of the communications system; they are a combination of operational needs and personal ties.

The operational needs relate essentially to information, skills, and action roles with time and communications obstacles as major variables affecting communication processes. A key factor in the effectiveness of large organizations is specialization; each individual focuses on the acquisition of information and skills in a limited area. In the MNC the potentials for specialization are immense when the permutations of a variety of functions applied to many products in numerous countries are added. A prime challenge for the communications system is to provide the means for relating each specialized unit to the others upon which it is dependent, either because of links in operational tasks or for information and skills which will improve its performance.

The operational needs could be met by communications through the channels indicated by the solid lines in Figure 13—1, which assure that line managers are fully involved in all interactions affecting units under their responsibility. However, time and communications obstacles are major considerations fostering alternatives to this approach for a substantial portion of communications needs. When a production manager in Marseilles encounters a problem with a process developed in a plant in Akron, it makes little sense to require that he send a description of his problem through the French general manager to the regional office in Brussels to the international division in New York and on to Akron with advice to return by the same route. The time consumed would be sufficient to discourage such a communication route. If some oral explanations are involved, the cultural and nationality obstacles will add further to the difficulties. A host of other examples could be cited in which time and communications obstacles of a similar character with greater or less intensity are encountered by following line channels. As a consequence there is substantial operational benefit from establishing direct communications along a myriad of routes of which just a few are suggested by the broken lines in Figure 13–1.

Reinforcing the operational pressures for multiple communications links are personal ties. Let us again consider the production manager in Marseilles and assume he is a young American who was sent abroad to get a new plant started with the expectation that he would return in a couple of years when a Frenchman had been trained to handle the job. There is a French general manager who is competent in marketing, finance, and government relations, and the production manager finds him an agreeable associate. But neither he nor other managers in the affiliate are natural associates by culture, nationality, or professional characteristics. So the production manager finds his chief professional and personal associations in other directions and more than likely these will include in varying ways people in the MNC structure. Among them might be, for example, another American production manager in the firm's Spanish plant, the Englishman who runs the company's plant there, and probably several friends whom he knew in the company's parent operations.

In addition, the young American's contacts will probably be affected by career considerations. His future expectations lie in the parent organization. The Marseilles post was accepted because his superiors felt he was needed and his family was not averse to a brief sojourn in France. But he was concerned in taking the job because he had heard of other men who lost out in the promotion process because their accomplishments abroad were unseen or unappreciated by senior production executives at home. So he is trying to protect his interests by keeping in touch with key production men with whom he had developed good relations. He wants to be sure they remember him and he hopes to impress them with the quality of the work he is doing. It won't do any harm if he can encourage one or two of them to fly over to visit his plant, and if he can get back to the States once or twice before his tour is over, he will surely find a reason to see them. Again this pattern with variations may be found throughout any MNC organization.

The factors just outlined create such great pressures that multiple communications links would come into being informally through natural evolution. And to some degree informal communication is appropriate and no particular concern of management, especially in the personal relationships of individuals. But where the need for communication arises from operational needs, the character of the multiple communications links is of direct concern to management, both to optimize their effectiveness and especially to limit whatever adverse effects they can have.

The emphasis in this discussion has been on the values of direct communication. As long as communication is confined to information, multiple direct links are beneficial and have little if any adverse effects. However, as a practical matter, relationships that affect operations commonly go beyond information. The classic example is the relation between line and staff people, the latter with great frequency assuming an aggressive role in the relationship. The Tice case provides a typical illustration.[1] Hughes, the headquarters staff expert on personnel had no line authority over Finch, the general manager of a Latin American affiliate. But when a salary increase question was referred to him by the office of Birch, the Latin American division manager in headquarters, Hughes was soon found to be communicating directly with Finch in a quite directive tone.

The hazard which is readily identified in this type of case is that the staff man in energetic pursuit of his role will interact with the subordinate levels in ways which disrupt the role of the line organization. If Finch is subject to directives or even strongly worded advice from Hughes and other headquarters staff people, conflicts with the role of Birch are inevitable. The traditional response to this hazard is to push Hughes back into his "proper" staff role of giving advice to Birch and other headquarters people. But that is not a sufficient response to the real character of MNC organizations, even of the Tice size and certainly not in larger firms. Each specialist in the organization, whether he be in a line or staff position, should be expected to energetically advocate the courses of action that his expertise indicates will be best for the firm. This pattern of action is useful to the firm in assuring that each person's competence is put to work and it is natural for the individual who will see a measure of achievement if his recommendations are adopted. It is also to be expected that he will use whatever status he has to reinforce his personal energy in advocacy of his viewpoint. And, since multiple communications links are inevitable, this pattern of behavior will appear in various forms throughout the communications system with consequent continuing hazards for established authority relationships.

The frequency of this sort of situation requires that one look critically at the operating requirements of the communications system. The central requirement must be performance responsibility. The major dimensions of the managerial process, including communication, have to be attuned to assuring that performance responsibility is assumed by individuals and units in the organization with linkages between them which assure that integrated responsibility exists for the enterprise as a whole. In the simple "military" structure that requirement is readily met by the direct vertical progression from top to successively lower levels. Top management assumes overall responsibility. At lower levels, responsibility and comparable authority is subdivided for matters of lesser and more detailed character. Staff people at various levels are clearly limited to advisory roles in relation to line people at their level. But, as the magnitude and complexity of companies have grown, this performance responsibility structure has proved too cumbersome. Instead, two main patterns of evolution have emerged.

The first, which is now well established, is the profit center concept which permits subordinate units to function with a high degree of autonomy within broad policy and planning guidelines set by top management, responsibility being established by operational unity and performance measures, e.g., profit, established for the unit. Although some individual typically has a line supervisory role over each subordinate profit center unit, the assurance of overall performance responsibility for the unit does not depend upon him, but rather on the mechanism of the results achieved by the unit. This key fact loosens up the communications process greatly because it means that the unit as a whole can in principle have any sort of communications relations with other parts of the company without disruption of authority or responsibility roles.

However, the loosening is still limited to the profit center unit as a whole, and technically the only individual who might be said to have fully open communication to the rest of the company would be its senior executive. All others in the unit are still restrained in their relations by their subordinate role in the unit structure and by communication constraints necessary to assure proper authority-responsibility linkages within the unit. Thus the structure typically still follows the general military pattern.

These limitations of the profit center pattern have led to a second stage of evolution which as yet is found only to a moderate extent, the grid or matrix organization. The grid system is not set forth in management doctrine as an alternative to the profit center system, because the latter is typically the broad performance control system even when the grid organization is employed. But in the present context the grid system is a step in the same progression because of its essential assumption with respect to managerial behavior. That assumption is that each manager is accorded a high degree of autonomy and is expected to assume independent responsibility for performance within the range of autonomy given to him. The key implication in terms of our communications analysis is that the manager is then free to establish whatever relations are appropriate for the accomplishment of the performance assigned to him.

Whether the grid concept will be fully and widely adopted is uncertain. In its few present applications the results have been of mixed quality and it is clear that very careful design and conditioning of individuals is essential to make it successful. However, its basic philosophy is highly relevant to the problems of MNCs for which other approaches have proved inadequate because of the needs for multiple communications links. The grid concept encourages the administrative analyst to explore options in which some degree of independent performance responsibility is assigned to each individual. This person then has both the freedom and the requirement to communicate with others anywhere in the organization who can be useful. An established code of constraints is put on the character of the communication to assure that overall performance is not disrupted.

### Behavioral Dynamics

The combination of attributes of the managerial process which affect the individual's response to the organization are, of course, fundamental to the present subject. They are shown at the far right in Figure 13-1. Their special significance to the MNC stems from its worldwide span, the relative autonomy of affiliates, and the great diversity of the members of its organization. In such circumstances the overall influencing of behavior becomes critically dependent upon intangibles—such as organizational norms and loyalty. It is clearly impractical here to delve at any depth into this general subject upon which a massive body of knowledge is available. It is appropriate here to focus on only a few key points of special importance to the MNC situation.

The chief subject of attention must be the managerial staffs of foreign affiliates. Behavioral relations among headquarters personnel are not much different from those among other parts of the senior managerial organization. At the lower level in affiliates, behavior will largely be determined by the local management who are in a position with special characteristics affecting behavior.

The situation of overseas managers is quite different from that of their domestic counterparts. The latter are physically and culturally homogeneous with their superiors and others who can strongly influence their immediate work and future careers. They regularly associate with a number of peers in this homogeneous behavioral environment. They can see relatively well defined career paths within it, sufficient to satisfy the highest aspirations. By contrast, those abroad are physically separated from most of the organization, so they have limited contacts with both superiors and peers. If they are parent nationals, their image of career prospects can be affected substantially by policies on use of expatriates and by the actions of just a few individual superiors. If they are host nationals, the career opportunities in the higher organization are very limited; even in the foreign affiliate there may be significant blocks. The behavior of the host nationals is also notably affected by the differences in culture and nationality between them and superiors and peers, reflected in the way they are treated in their work. To a considerable degree these characteristics are simply facts of life that have to be accepted, handicaps of an international organization with which it learns to live. But to some extent their adverse effects can be minimized and the managerial process can be attuned to compensate for those effects.

**Influences on Behavior.**   Three interrelated influences on behavior can be identified as most significant in this context: expectations, motivation, and confidence. Because of their physical separation and diverse operating conditions, foreign affiliate managers necessarily function more independently than domestic counterparts. Their actions will therefore be governed substantially by *expectations* communicated in other ways than by direct physical contact with supervisors. A variety of mechanisms for conveying expectations are used including policy statements, operating manuals, plans, budgets, control reports, and the like. Employing them to provide an effective pattern of expectations requires careful attention, however, because of two broad problems. First, the rigidity and oversimplification with accompanying gaps and inconsistencies in all such formal mechanisms can be troublesome in the context of operating realities. Such shortcomings in domestic organizations are resolved by oral communication and supervisory flexibility, but these are not readily available to the foreign affiliate management.

Second, there is a tendency toward standardization and uniformity in formal mechanisms which is quite inappropriate for the very diverse character of MNC foreign units. In these circumstances, the challenge for the MNC is to communicate a pattern of expectations which has a broad and universally relevant thrust while being capable of effective application to each situation. These considerations are especially pertinent in large MNCs for which the budget setting process is the major vehicle for communicating expectations. In their study of MNC finance, Robbins and Stobaugh observe:

> The budgetary procedure becomes the structure that guides the financial activities of the subsidiaries without the necessity of constant overview by headquarters. . . . In spite of the apparent willingness on the part of some large firms to make adjustments for "peculiar circumstances" encountered abroad and to judge on the basis of changes from year to year, in fact their managers are trapped by the extensiveness of the international empire. They are forced to return again and again to the use of tangible measures embodied in budgetary guidelines so that subsidiaries might better know what is expected of them and so that headquarters can readily evaluate results.[2]

*Motivation* is to a considerable extent influenced by the expectations of managers. That is, the quantity and quality of their efforts will be determined substantially by what they believe higher management expects of them. But the motivational problem of affiliate managements go well beyond that factor. Central to them are the interrelated elements of morale and opportunity. Vitally affecting these are the career questions noted earlier and, especially for the host country nationals, the manner in which they are handled and the working opportunities they have in the affilaite management.

*Confidence* follows along behind both expectations and motivation as an element which may be either reinforcing or detrimental. Again the structural characteristics of the MNC are critical. When subordinates are separated by distance, culture, and nationality from superiors, the opportunities for misunderstanding, apprehension, and other debilitating influences are greatly increased. The chief counteracting potentials lie in the establishment of confidence. The very factors that create the need also make the establishment of confidence more difficult. So it stands as a critical challenge in the development of effective behavioral dynamics in the MNC organization.

**Influences on Management Action.** Expectations, motivation, and confidence are the prime aspects of behavioral dynamics to which higher MNC management must direct attention in attempting to deal with the special behavioral circumstances of affiliate managers. The other side of those circumstances to which headquarters executives must be attuned is the effect they can have on important aspects of management action, notably selectivity in communication and initiative.

Because of the nature of their situation, the ability of affiliate managers to exercise *selectivity* in communicating information to higher levels is of greater significance than it is for domestic managers. The higher echelons to whom the affiliate managers report are physically separated from the foreign conditions. They are less well informed and less knowing about what to ask for than domestic managers. And then the affiliate managers, because they usually have greater autonomy, are in a position to be more selective in what information they decide to transmit. For routine information on sales, costs, and general environmental reports, these circumstances pose no great problem. However, they can be highly significant in non-routine matters such as competitive problems, new business opportunities, and internal management relations. The general manager of an affiliate can quite easily not communicate such information or do so after considerable delay. The behavioral factors that will influence him in such selective communication decisions are therefore of importance in planning the managerial process.

The question of *initiative* follows a similar line of analysis. The greater autonomy of the affiliate means greater range for its management in making new efforts within its own scope and in generating proposals for top management consideration. The degree of initiative it takes will depend substantially upon the behavioral characteristics of the managers, their imagination and drive. But it is not easy for distant headquarters management to judge the quality of initiative or to manage it. Lack of major creative effort in a given period may be due to either wisdom or lack of initiative. How is a headquarters supervisor to know which? And yet more difficult is the problem of stimulating initiative from headquarters, especially when the need to achieve immediate results appears important for competition. Strong performance pressures from top management may stimulate some managers to greater initiative. Others may simply become more conservative, as they may not want to take the risks involved in new proposals.

These problems would be minor if there were no lack of able managers for foreign affiliates. But the reality for most MNCs, especially for their smaller affiliates in less developed countries, is a limited field due to the difficulty of getting good parent nationals to go abroad and the shortage of good local management personnel. In fact we are dealing here precisely with the heart of the skill transmission process. It is the lack of adequate managerial and entrepreneurial skills in the host country which provides the MNC with much of its opportunity abroad. Thus this particular behavioral aspect of the managerial process is a prime aspect of resource transmission strategy.

## MNC EXPERIENCE

The managerial process in MNCs has received much research attention. There is heavy emphasis in the studies on the centralization-decentralization issue but other aspects have been studied sufficiently to give some sense of practical experience with them as well.

### Locus of Decisions

1. The first work on the locus of decisions was Barlow's survey of twenty-two firms in 1953.[3] He found a range of practices from companies which exercised tight control over subsidiaries to those that gave almost complete operating freedom. He observed, however, that practically all the concerns studied established major policy frameworks within which more or less control was granted to the subsidiaries. The major policies included types of products, product quality, key personnel, accounting and financial methods, and expansion of local operations. But in other matters such as sales plans, negotiations with labor, and local pricing decisions, the policies on delegation were quite diverse. Part of this diversity was due to differences in products or other objective characteristics. But to a considerable degree it stemmed from historical or subjective characteristics and thus did not necessarily represent a well-considered determination as to the most effective balance between centralization versus delegation.

2. More recent work has provided some quantitative measures of the extent of centralization. Wiechmann determined the pattern of headquarters control over the European operations of twenty-seven consumer goods firms shown in Table 13-1.[4] The extent of headquarters direction was determined by ratings for various aspects of operations by both parent and subsidiary executives. The perceptions from both sides were found to be quite similar within each company. Among broad functional areas, finance showed the highest degree of headquarters direction with research and development quite close to it. Manufacturing, marketing, and personnel were close together at

**Table 13–1.  Degree of Headquarters Direction by Business Function and Marketing Group**

| | Degree of Headquarters Direction | | | | | |
| | High | | Moderate | | Low | |
| Function | Companies | Percent | Companies | Percent | Companies | Percent |
|---|---|---|---|---|---|---|
| Finance | 22 | 85% | 3 | 11% | 1 | 4% |
| Manufacturing | 11 | 42 | 7 | 27 | 8 | 31 |
| Research and Development | 18 | 69 | 3 | 12 | 5 | 19 |
| Purchasing | 4 | 15 | 3 | 12 | 19 | 73 |
| Marketing | 12 | 46 | 8 | 31 | 6 | 23 |
| Personnel | 11 | 42 | 6 | 23 | 9 | 35 |
| *Decision Group* | | | | | | |
| Product Policy | 17 | 85% | 3 | 15% | 0 | 0% |
| Pricing | 5 | 25 | 7 | 35 | 8 | 40 |
| Advertising and Promotion | 8 | 40 | 8 | 40 | 4 | 20 |
| Distribution | 7 | 35 | 2 | 10 | 11 | 55 |
| Market Research | 5 | 25 | 3 | 15 | 12 | 60 |

Source: Ulrich E. Wiechmann, *Marketing Management in Multinational Firms.* New York: Praeger, 1976.

a moderate level. Purchasing stood apart as the least centralized function. Within the marketing area, product policy decisions were subject to greatest headquarters control by a wide margin. Advertising and distribution fell in a range of moderate headquarters control, with pricing and market research left substantially in subsidiary control.

The degree of headquarters direction was found to vary chiefly according to product characteristics and to some extent according to characteristics of acquisition and supply. The size of foreign operations and organizational differences (e.g., product line vs. geographic structure) had little apparent influence. Companies in which a limited product line was dominant tended toward greater central direction both because it was more practical and because of the crucial importance of success in the limited line. The direction was typically not so great in non-food lines because of impact of cultural diversity among countries in reception to their products. The existence of a number of subsidiaries that had been independent firms prior to acquisition was a factor favoring greater field autonomy. On the other hand, the development of supply interdependence favored central direction, e.g., a food firm serving all of Europe for a particular product from a single plant.

3. Franko's study of European MNCs provided a somewhat different set of data shown in Table 13−2.[5] The two columns describe the headquarters control exercised over the European and U.S. subsidiaries, the latter clearly being given more scope for independent decisions. The general pattern is similar to Wiechmann's data, finance, for example, being notably centralized in both cases and marketing relatively decentralized. However, Franko's data are more specific as to types of decisions rather than broad functions.

4. Picard surveyed a sample of 56 European MNCs to determine their control over marketing of their U.S. subsidiaries. Most of the firms were British (15), French (14) and German (10) with the balance from seven other countries.[6] The sample was mixed in size of firm and covered a range of consumer and industrial products.

For the operational decisions, the respondents were asked to rate the degree of headquarters control on a scale from 1 representing full affiliate autonomy to 5, complete imposition of decisions by the headquarters. The distribution of responses shown in Table 13−3 was reported for different categories of marketing decisions.

For the most part a large degree of autonomy was given. Parent executives observed that local management had a better feel for competitive pricing needs, U.S. distribution was very difficult for them

**Table 13–2.   Degree of Policy Guidance or Initiation by Headquarters** *(Average score: 1 = no HQ policy guidance, 7 = complete determination by HQ)*

| Policy | European Subsidiaries | U.S. Subsidiaries | Difference |
|---|---|---|---|
| Finished product pricing | 3.5 | 2.7 | .7 |
| Advertising | 3.6 | 2.7 | .7 |
| Brand names | 5.6 | 4.8 | .6 |
| Distribution | 3.4 | 2.3 | .8 |
| Production processes | 5.6 | 4.2 | 1.2 |
| Export pricing | 4.7 | 2.9 | 1.6 |
| Sources of supply for subsidiaries' imports | 3.9 | 3.4 | .4 |
| Sources of supply for U.S. subs-domestic purchases | — | 1.6 | — |
| Product mix | 3.9 | 3.0 | .8 |
| Customer financing and service | 3.4 | 2.6 | .8 |
| Selection of upper-level managers of the subs | 5.6 | 4.7 | .9 |
| Salaries and other remuneration of subs' managers | 5.6 | 4.2 | 1.2 |
| Quantity of subsidiaries' exports | 4.2 | 3.5 | .6 |
| Quantity of subsidiaries' imports | 3.6 | 3.3 | .3 |
| Investment in productive facilities | 6.5 | 5.9 | .6 |
| Financial (i.e. debt vs. equity) structure of subs | 6.0 | 5.6 | .3 |
| Average for all policies | 4.6 | 3.6 | .8 |

*The values shown may not equal the difference between columns 1 and 2 owing to elimination of observations missing for one or the other score.

Note: Number of companies responding: 17 to 19.

Source: Franko, *European Business Strategies in the United States.* Geneva: Business International, 1976.

Table 13-3. Degrees of Headquarters Control of Affiliate Marketing
Decisions in European MNCs

| | Full Affiliate Autonomy | | | | Full Headquarters Control |
|---|---|---|---|---|---|
| | 1 | 2 | 3 | 4 | 5 |
| Pricing | 81% | 11% | 4% | 0% | 4% |
| Distribution | 87 | 2 | 9 | 2 | 0 |
| Advertising and promotion | 74 | 11 | 9 | 2 | 4 |
| New Products | 51 | 8 | 22 | 14 | 6 |
| Product characteristics | 58 | 16 | 8 | 12 | 6 |
| Brand names | 51 | 7 | 19 | 12 | 5 |
| Packaging | 57 | 9 | 18 | 7 | 9 |
| Product line | 47 | 11 | 26 | 12 | 4 |
| Market research | 93 | 0 | 3 | 0 | 3 |

Note: Totals are less than 100% because some firms did not respond in some categories.
Source: Jacques Picard, "How European Companies Control Marketing Decisions Abroad," *Columbia Journal of World Business.* Summer 1977.

to understand, and the U.S. personnel were both closer to the advertising situation and benefited from the perceived leadership of the United States in advertising and promotion. In advertising, however, significant parent influence was pressed by some firms in the interest of conveying a common basic message worldwide. Also some kind of worldwide standardization was desirable since the parent company's experience could be helpful to the subsidiary. Influence on market research was minimal because most firms did not regard decisions on it important.

In product-related decisions the parent role was stronger for several reasons. Often they involved financial investments which were significant to headquarters. Most U.S. affiliates did not have basic research centers so the parents felt more knowledgeable. While diversity among countries was quite tolerable in other marketing matters, global consistency of quality and other product characteristics was important. In many cases also U.S. subsidiaries were dependent upon the parent for components.

While degrees of control over operating decisions varied by category of marketing activity, control of budgetary decisions was generally consistent within firms for all matters. Picard identified firms as falling into six categories in this respect: (1) No budget was presented to the parent, all decisions being made internally (27%); (2) Sales and profit objectives were reported to the parent but it exercised no control (16%); (3) Detailed marketing expenditure plans were presented to headquarters and subject to joint decisions but changes could be made during the year without parent approval (18%); (4) This category was similar to the former except that all but marginal changes during the year required parent clearance (7%); (5) No changes during the year without parent approval were permitted except for shifts of funds from one category to another (12%); and (6) No discretion was allowed to the subsidiary (20%);

The greater degree of parent control on budgetary decisions was explained by the fact that parent executives felt on more familiar ground in budgetary than operating decisions and they perceived a prime responsibility in seeking good return on investment. Picard observed a certain contradiction in results, however, as a close budgetary control could greatly restrict freedom in many operating decisions.

The author noted that other research had shown U.S. firms gave less autonomy than his work indicated for European MNCs. He suggested three main reasons: (1) many European firms were understaffed at the executive level compared to U.S. counterparts, (2) European firms had a longer overseas experience with patterns of delegated authority established in an earlier era when close control was physically less practical, and (3) many U.S. foreign subsidiaries were established after World War II as small units at a time when American marketing was regarded as far superior to that abroad. Another distinction was the greater degree of autonomy European MNCs often gave their subsidiaries in the United States compared to those in Europe. Here the explanations were found in relative size, distance from headquarters and feelings of uncertainty about the U.S. market.

5. Differences between European and U.S. MNCs were explicitly analyzed in Schollhammer's work cited in the previous chapter.[7] Four measures were used to indicate greater degrees of decentralization:

- A greater number of organizational levels between the chief executive and the heads of the foreign units. The U.S. firms all had three to four intervening levels while the Europeans varied from no levels to three.
- Implementation of profit centers. The U.S. firms all had such centers, while only one European firm had a full profit center scheme and three had partial systems.
- Existence of formal task descriptions with specifications of authority. All U.S. firms had such descriptions, compared to only two European firms.

- Ratings of the degree of autonomy given to foreign units as reported by the headquarters and foreign unit managers on a 10-point scale. Differences were small by this measure but the U.S. firms indicated slightly more autonomy.

A related element is the degree of standardized information transmission. Schollhammer determined the number of regular reports sent each month from the field to headquarters. The U.S. firms had from fifteen to twenty reports while the Europeans had from eight to sixteen. For two-thirds of the European firms the largest portion of resports were financial while in the U.S. firms market and sales data were dominant. Combining this finding with the decentralization aspect, the author concluded that all firms showed a high degree of decentralization. However, in the case of the U.S. firms, limits of discretionary authority tended to be more clearly specified and there was a greater emphasis on formal, periodic controls. In the case of European firms, integration and coordination with the overall organization tended to be less clearly structured.

6. Another comparative approach was undertaken by Sim working from the affiliate level.[8] He studied the pattern and degree of decentralization of Malaysian subsidiaries of British, Japanese, and U.S. firms. The study included twenty firms matched according to various key characteristics. The industries covered were consumer products, pharmaceuticals, chemicals, transportation, electronics, electrical goods, and textiles. There were seven British, six Japanese, and seven U.S. subsidiaries.

A four-point decentralization index based on fifteen policy areas was constructed. The author determined the locus of decision-making for each area by depth interviews, observation, and examination of company documents. In addition, local executives' perceptions of the extent of decentralization were obtained by asking them to rate the degree of autonomy for each functional area on a seven-point scale. The executives' perceptions were matched against the decentralization index and a high and significant correlation was found. Performance of the subsidiaries was measured by several indicators including value added per employee, productivity in terms of factor services per unit of value added, sales per employee, growth in sales, labor turnover, absenteeism, and various financial data.

Decentralization was found to be the highest in marketing, personnel and organization, and production and least in finance, ownership, and R&D. In the American subsidiaries, planning and budgeting involved greater head office involvement, and tended to be a "top down" process. For example, targets (sales and profits) and planning format were set by the head office and then used for budgeting by the subsidiary. There was less involvement by the head office in the British subsidiaries, and the process tended to be a "bottom up" one, where the process began at the subsidiary and worked its way up to the head office. In the Japanese firms, targets and budgets were set by the head office, but there was a great deal of interaction between subsidiaries and parent companies.

In the Japanese subsidiaries, planning and decision-making tended to be confined to Japanese executives. On the other hand, American subsidiaries encouraged their employees to participate in planning. British subsidiaries tended to confine their participation and information access to their top management personnel. In terms of control feedback to head office, the largest number of mandatory reports was sent by the American subsidiaries. The use of expatriates in the subsidiaries varied with nationality, with the highest number in Japanese subsidiaries, while the American and British had about the same number of expatriates.

There was a statistically significant difference in the decentralization indices only between the Japanese compared with American and British firms. The former showed a lower degree of decentralization and Sim speculates this may be for two reasons: (1) Japanese firms tended to use operational and managerial control rather than equity ownership to control their subsidiaries. (2) Japanese managers in the subsidiaries tended to be autocratic in their management and did not delegate their authority to the extent that American and British managers did. Sim observed that decentralization was greatest in American subsidiaries, but apparently the difference was not statistically significant.

The results also showed some trend toward greater decentralization in the American and Japanese subsidiaries in recent years and an opposite trend in the British firms. Age was the most significant factor in decentralization; the older subsidiaries were more decentralized. There was also a significant (but weak) relationship between decentralization and import level, and size in terms of total assets. Subsidiaries in the consumer products industries tended to be decentralized, while those in assembly-oriented industries, like electronics and transportation, tended to be less decentralized.

The results showed some evidence that greater decentralization was related to operating success. A significant and positive relationship was found between decentralization and the following performance indicators: sales per employee, value added per employee, factor services per unit of value added, personnel turnover rate, return on sales, and return on total net assets. The relationship between decentralization and growth of sales went in an opposite direction to that hypothesized. This, however, was consistent with the evolution of the units as decentralization and growth both had positive relationships with age of subsidiary. It would seem that the younger and more centralized subsidiary would show greater relative growth of sales due to the smaller base year figure.

### The Decision Process

In studies like those just reviewed, the definition of the locus of decisions is generally the point at which a final determination is made. Although this approach typically gives an accurate sense of the gross distribution of status in decision-making, it oversimplifies the realities of the relative roles of people at different levels and the dynamics of the process by which decision-making is accomplished. Two studies focusing on how decisions were made on new investments provide a more complete picture of this process.

1. The first was Aharoni's analysis of decisions on investment in Israel by thirty-eight U.S. corporations.[9] The basic theme that ran through the whole study was that investments were rarely the result of a single, clear-cut decision. Rather they came about through an accumulation of initiatives, explorations, and commitments which gradually built up momentum so that the final approval, typically by the board of directors, was little more than a formality. He described in detail the various forces affecting this cumulative decision-making process. While economic, profit-oriented considerations had their influence, Aharoni found that in most decisions organizational and human influences were of major importance. For example, earlier decisions and general company policies on such matters as product line or willingness to work in joint—venture arrangements were generally as important as the financial prospects for the specific venture. Likewise, he noted such human considerations as investigators tending to avoid areas of possible friction with other executives, emphasizing that participants in the decision process were a part of the social system.

One of the key characteristics of international investment decisions is the high degree of uncertainty and risk they involve. The author examined carefully the response of management to this problem, noting, for example, skills in use of crude indicators for preliminary screening and the pattern of exploratory searching which companies followed to reduce uncertainty. Another key observation was that the scarce resource in the large firm was not money but management time. The significance of this point was developed in a number of ways in the study—what companies were willing to investigate, the extent of investigation which was feasible, and so forth.

2. In the second study Zwick examined the experience of ten U.S. firms with particular attention to investment decisions in Brazil, India, and the United Kingdom between 1956 and 1964.[10] He observed a problem that was increasingly occupying the attention of MNC managements, namely, the feeling that the gap between top-management investment intentions and lower-level implementation was widening. Given the nature of the appraisal system for overseas investment proposals used by the sample companies, it was not surprising that a control problem should arise.

Standard operating procedures (SOPs) specified what information was to be compiled and how it was to be converted into measures of profitability to facilitate top management's ultimate review. Theoretically the SOPs should assure the chief executives that projections pertaining to such factors as prices, costs, tax rates, and terminal asset values were based on common assumptions.

The chief weakness of the SOPs was their failure to provide guidelines for preliminary screening. They did not indicate what information should be considered during the preliminary evaluations, who should be collecting this information, and where in the organization these critical screenings should be performed.

Proposals originating at lower management levels were subject to several preliminary screenings during the course of which top management might or might not be aware of the projected ventures. These early evaluations occurred outside the framework of the SOPs and were based on both corporate and personal standards. Company personnel discovered that certain types of overseas commitments led to extraordinary management and control problems or excessive supervisory expenses. The purpose of the early screenings was to eliminate by the most cursory of reviews these problematic proposals.

It was more difficult to pinpoint the personal standards that influenced lower-level assessors, but it was reasonable to suggest that before he passed an idea upstairs, the prudent lower-echelon executive would have pondered these questions: If unacceptable proposals result in organizational disenchantment, why submit or support proposals unless it is certain they will be viewed favorably? Will the submission of a proposal further the cause of my career?

If the company evaluation was closely tied to profit-center performance, lower-level personnel tended to focus on the short term. Five years hence these personnel were likely to have new assignments. From their points of view it was undesirable to sacrifice short-term profitability in order to investigate, implement, and carry new ventures.

By the time proposals were prepared for ultimate submission, lower echelons were virtually assured that the opportunities were acceptable in terms of the SOP dictates and the chief executive's current organizational emphasis. The final top-management reviews appeared to be largely a formality. In not a single instance analyzed by the author was a proposal disapproved by the top management during the final assessment. Except for approving certain projects in principle, it would thus appear that top managers played comparatively small roles in both the evaluation and implementation of proposed foreign opportunities. Zwick questioned whether these highly decentralized evaluative procedures yielded conclusions consistent with top-management objectives. They did not guarantee that alleged scarce resources would be optimally allocated among countries and that priorities assigned to investment opportunities in the many countries would correspond to top-management objectives.

### System Patterns

The next set of reports carries us deeper into the system of interactive processes, exploring how major objectives of administration are achieved.

3. In his study of food, soft drink, soap-toiletries, and cosmetic firms cited at the start of this section, Wiechmann set forth two related objectives for headquarters management: how to tie together the business activities of the far-flung subsidiaries and how to transfer skills.[11] The study largely was concerned with how these goals were achieved, primarily through four integrative devices: headquarters direction, acculturation, systems transfer, and personnel transfer. The findings on headquarters direction were reported earlier (see p. 543).

While central direction was taken to be the primary means for achieving integration, exclusive reliance on it was found to be both impractical and counterproductive. Acculturation and systems transfer were therefore subjects of major emphasis, and personnel transfer was of lesser but still appreciable importance. Firms with a low degree of headquarters direction often placed particular emphasis on establishing attitudes and behavior patterns in their subsidiary managers which would lead these men to make decisions that conformed to headquarters intentions. These firms relied on subsidiary managers who were thoroughly committed to corporate objectives and philosophy. Such an approach was noted to be particularly important where strong local initiative was desired. An overuse or abuse of headquarters direction might at times have to be curtailed to maintain the motivation and the organizational loyalty of subsidiary managers. The acculturation process took substantial time during which managers absorbed corporate thinking through varied assignments and interaction in planning and operations work.

In discussing systems transfer, Wiechmann distinguished between "strategy planning," "management control," and "operational control." Strategy planning is high level activity and the other two are directed at specific tasks. Systems transfer focused on management control, notably marketing planning and control which served as prime integrative devices in two-thirds of the companies surveyed. These systems created a way of looking at and analyzing problems; they imposed an internal discipline that might be called "marketing orientation," "good management," or "profit consciousness." Again and again, executives in the mature multinational enterprises said that the factor that really set their firms apart from local competitors was a better and more disciplined system for planning and implementing local marketing efforts. Financial budgeting and control were seen as largely the responsibility of staff people but marketing planning focused on objectives and programs of action so it depended heavily on line personnel over an extended discussion period. If there was one point on which the participating executives agreed almost universally, it was that the give-and-take built into the annual planning and budgeting cycle was at the very heart of multinational marketing.

Related to this subject was the nature of communications. In ranking forms of communication, three-quarters of executives rated personal contact as most important whereas formal reports were generally rated lowest, although the latter generally absorbed the greatest amount of time and effort. Headquarters generally regarded the collection of data in these reports as essential, and the process of collecting it as a control and educational end. However, the field personnel often regarded the work as excessive and of limited value. Wiechmann also noted that the firms generally did not have a highly developed flow of information among subsidiaries and thus were not making effective use of one of the major competitive advantages of being multinational.

In two-thirds of the firms personnel transfers played a minor role. Long-term assignment of marketing personnel abroad was too costly, often produced conflict, and was generally not effective as a means of transferring skills in the view of many executives. On the other hand, short-term visits abroad were generally felt to be quite effective for transfer of skills.

Overall the author found that the current trend was toward greater headquarters direction. Executives expected it to continue because of a natural inclination of top levels to seek power and an urge to keep close watch over critical elements of the business. A major reason was the need to create a uniform product image in a geographical area that was characterized by an increasing tendency for consumers, trade customers, and advertising media to overlap from one country to another. The exception to this trend was in culture-bound products where local autonomy was essential. In mature firms in this class foreign operations were integrated (1) through the transfer of systems, which educated subsidiary managers and standardized the process of decision-making, (2) through the transfer of marketing personnel, and (3) through long periods of acculturation of managers.

4. In the next study Youseff was concerned with control in the sense of the manner in which the MNC parent management exercises influence on affiliate operations.[12] He surveyed 302 multinational corporations to explore the relation of various factors to methods of control. The information was obtained about the controls applied to each company's most recent overseas investment operation.

The study focused on eight control mechanisms. Three were classified as direct controls:

- Nationality, nationality of the top manager of the foreign operation.
- Influence, parent influence over selection and training of top managers.
- Supervision, general supervision by the parent or regional offices.

Five were classed as indirect controls: provision of staff services by the parent company which facilitated checking on its performance (Staff) and standardization among overseas units of four aspects of operations: organization structure, department work flow, product design, and accounting systems. In the survey all of the mechanisms were appraised by a five-point scale except Nationality for which two categories were used: local nationals and others (U.S. and third-country nationals). The survey also identified certain contextual variables: ownership, age of operation, size, length of MNC international involvement, extent of involvement (number of countries in which it had operations), and level of development of host country.

In his first set of analyses the author tested the relation between the various pairs of control mechanisms. He found that the relationships between nationality and most of the other control variables were significant. The percentage of others (U.S. citizens and third-country nationals) tended to increase as more controls were used. However, the relationships were stronger in the case of direct controls (influence and supervision) than with indirect controls. Similarly, correlations between various pairs of control mechanisms were all positive and mostly significant. Except for staff, the correlations among pairs within each group of controls (direct or indirect) were stronger than the correlations among pairs between the two groups. In general, the data tended to support the classification of various control mechanisms as either direct or indirect.

The second set of analyses concerned the relation of the contextual variables to the control mechanisms. The data showed that size and length of involvement had no significant relation to the nature of the mechanisms. Only ownership and age had significant relationships with most of these mechanisms. As ownership increased, various forms of control tended to increase. Also as the operation grew older, the application of direct controls tended to decrease and that of indirect controls tended to increase.

Further analysis of relationships led Youseff to classify the mechanisms into three groups.

• The first groups were mechanisms that involved utilizing the managerial resources and know-how of the parent company including nationality, influence, and staff. The utilization of these mechanisms could be based on the foreign operation's managerial deficiencies and needs. This might explain the fact that the percentage of "others" tended to decrease as the operation grew older and as the country was more developed. Similar tendencies were also evident in the negative and significant correlations between development and staff and between age and influence and age and staff.

• Control mechanisms that involved utilizing the parent company's technological and organizational know-how constituted the second group. These mechanisms included standardizing the operation's structure, work flow, and product design. These activities could be standardized at the beginning stage of a given operation, since the MNC was usually the main source of know-how in these areas. This probably explained why the correlations between these mechanisms and most contextual variables were either statistically insignificant or barely significant.

• The third group were control mechanisms that involved central coordination by the parent company or its regional offices. These mechanisms included direct supervision over the foreign operation by these higher levels. Standardization of accounting practices of various operations also could be included in this category. The application of these control mechanisms could be based on the MNC's desire to maximize the use of its global resources. This might be why supervision and accounting had positive and significant correlations with extent of involvement.

5. Prahalad analyzed the interrelation of strategic decision-making and a matrix structure of organization using a diversified multinational, the Beta corporation and its executive vice president, Dave Austin, as illustrations.[13] Beta had four business aggregates—petrochemicals, pharmaceuticals, consumer products, and mining—and divided its operations into four areas—North America; Europe; Latin America and the Middle East; and Asia, Africa, and Australia. The corporation had functional groups at the second level of organization, for R&D, production, etc. At the top level the matrix structure required approval of major decisions, such as investments, by both business group and area officials, and joint-venture partners also had to be considered. At the second level conflicts took on a different color. For example, the functional groups controlled the deployment of almost all the technical manpower. Another area of conflict was over plant size; functional executives favored larger scale units than area managers.

Thus the number of issues along which coalitions in the matrix might develop and the manner in which they might affect possible investment alternatives were difficult to predict. Somehow, Austin had to link strategic concerns such as "What should our business be?" with the operational realities of managing within a global matrix. Since the complexities of managing multiple businesses worldwide made it practically impossible for Austin to acquire extensive knowledge of all the businesses, he had to rely on lower-level executives for specific judgments. Though ideally the area, function, and business groups represented three equally important components of the matrix, Austin was forced at times to choose one alternative sponsored by a group or a coalition in preference to others. His choice either was determined by his personal evaluation of the alternatives or, more likely, was based on his faith in the judgment of the executive sponsoring the alternative. Irrespective of the reasons for his choice, the fact that he preferred the judgment of one man over another indicated to the organization a certain asymmetry of power.

Much of Prahalad's discussion focused on effects of a shift in relative power from area organizations to a business group which was related to a general shift in strategy toward greater global unification along product lines. Six strategy issues were used to illustrate the analysis.

- Investment decisions.   When a new polypropylene product was introduced in 1970, the area organizations dominated investments. A single plant was built in Europe which the management there felt was adequate. The business group was dissatisfied because in the past they had lost dominant world market positions through inadequate capacity. Thus, when the business group became more influential in 1974 an additional plant was quickly built.
- Control.   The shift to worldwide business group orientation resulted in a movement toward consolidating basic accounting data. Also more operating data were collected in the central organization, considered essential to global planning.
- Joint–ventures.   Joint–venture decisions had previously been made on an ad hoc basis. When business groups assumed dominance with emphasis on worldwide planning, joint–ventures were often found undesirable, notably in investment decisions (capacity and location) and transfer pricing. At the same time, grave doubts were expressed about the desirability of sharing profitability and market-share data worldwide with joint–venture partners.
- Manager mobility and career progression.   When the area groups were ascendant, the emphasis among executives was on development of area-specific skills and affiliations. The worldwide business-group strategy changed the focus to product orientation and movement of personnel among units of product groups.
- Acquisitions.   The change in strategy resulted in acquisitions being directed more toward global plans of the business groups than area conditions.
- Financial strategy.   As the business group assumed the dominant position, the financial policy shifted from having each subsidiary stand on its own feet to greater centralization of financial management.

Prahalad discussed the practical means of implementing strategy-power changes. Top managers moved key individuals around to achieve power shifts. The choice of individuals included consideration of both abilities and orientation. There was also a need to assure a reasonable balance of power. An unintended consequence of having two strong-willed managers, one in the business group and the other in the area organization, would be a debilitating power struggle. On the other hand, if one group became overwhelmingly powerful, the benefits of a matrix structure could be lost, and the organization might tend to assume the characteristics of a product structure. Another mechanism used by top managers to shift relative power was to change the pattern of communication flow in the matrix. For example, when the business group had access to worldwide product data, it could present stronger strategy plans than the area groups that lacked such data. Introduction of a computer model at Beta further simplified the coordination problem. Centralization of data and the use of a standardized format gave an advantage to the planning team and the business group over the area organizations.

## Behavioral Patterns

The final two analyses focus on the behavioral relationships between parent and affiliate organizations.

6. Brooke and Remmers undertook in-depth studies of eighty manufacturing companies and thirty banks.[14] The companies were of nine nationalities located in seven European countries and in the United States. The analysis of organizations focused on roles and communications, with particular attention to the difficulties of serving varied points of view. For example, several contradictory reactions to creation of regional management were reported. Some subsidiary managers saw their jobs as a disciplinary move and others demanded some office nearer their operations, only to react adversely when it was created. Another key problem was what the author called the buffer situation. They found some men in general management posts in foreign countries who were encountering trouble because both the parent and the subsidiaries were essentially organized on product lines. The general managers found it hard to position themselves effectively between home and field men between whom there was a natural product-oriented flow of communication.

The authors coined some new phrases in their conceptualization of key issues in the somewhat fuzzy relationships required in international organizations. They labelled as "recognized informal" the pattern of supplementary relations which the manager had to develop outside the standard line-staff structure, e.g., regular get-togethers of managers of adjoining countries with similar interests. The terms "open" and "close" were used in preference to decentralized and centralized decision-making in an attempt to convey the real philosophy and power structure rather than the mechanics of the decision process. Along with this subject, the authors analyzed the patterns of motivations employed in managing international executives, using the terms "calculative" (essentially financial) and "voluntary" (job interest). They foresaw that strategy demands would require greater closeness but that attracting good men would require more voluntary motivation. Combining these thoughts, they anticipated a trend toward greater personal independence within narrowing limits of decision-making for the foreign managers. Finally, they discussed "repersonalized bureaucracy" as an approach to overcoming communication blocks in product-oriented companies with multiple reporting systems.

7. McKenzie provides a practitioner's analysis of the effect on host country managers of the pattern of headquarters communication with subsidiaries.[15] He observes that complaints that managers in foreign operations are incompetent usually are associated with at least three conditions. First, they are subject to overextensive control systems. Headquarters demands data that are useless for evaluating performance and for communicating its objectives to the local management or motivating it. In one company, headquarters demanded that a production facility abroad report to it daily the number of containers damaged at each point in the production process. The receipt of such detailed data triggers action at headquarters. Detailed suggestions, queries, and instructions flow back to the foreign operation. The inevitable result is that the onus of management shifts to the U.S. headquarters. Such controls take away responsibility in one area and deposit it in another. Ultimately the foreign manager loses (or never develops) the sense of responsibility and proprietary interest that is essential for a chief operating executive. He becomes a man on a string, being pulled this way and that by headquarters demands, attempting to satisfy not the needs of the business but of his advisors.

An example is cited of one company with a manufacturing facility abroad. Production had been paralyzed because it ran out of a basic raw material supplied from the United States and importable without restriction. Through an oversight, the raw material had simply not been ordered, even though the general manager had been specifically queried about his supply by both the president and international vice president. For such an event to occur, a sense of responsibility must be lacking throughout the local organization. Neither the inventory clerk, the worker on the floor, the foreman, nor the plant manager was sufficiently motivated to see that they had enough supplies.

The second symptom develops from the first. The manager really has no grasp of what is going on, even though his reports may be current and correct. Because of the demanded emphasis on individual functional aspects of his business, the manager is often unable to answer vital, but non-routine, questions.

A third common symptom is the irrational fashion in which the manager reacts to either verbal or written isntructions. For example, in one company a headquarters request for a minor accounting change in the handling of one account brought cables from the general manager claiming many hours of extra work when the time actually required was less than one hour per month. Such reactions are symptomatic of a person who is shell-shocked from a bombardment of requests, instructions, and demands from headquarters.

Thus, suspected incompetence leads to excessive controls which in turn verify this incompetence. This dilemma has occurred because of a fundamental misunderstanding of the foreign general manager's role and because of the dual and incongruous position of the headquarters management as both operating expert and judge. The foreign general manager's role is that of the president in the country in which he operates. The U.S. president's board of directors is usually chosen for reasons other than its detailed knowledge of the business. It assumes that the president has this knowledge. His performance is judged on relatively few reports, most of which concern gross input-output comparisons. Within a few broad guidelines, he is usually free to run his business.

This state of affairs is contrasted with the foreign manager's situation. His "board of directors" usually consists of operating management experts who, in total, have more technical know-how in every functional area of the business than he has. But, paradoxically, the chances are that very few, if any, of them have ever experienced the problems of either a chief operating executive or of a board member attempting to assess the performance of its president.

McKenzie observes that this problem is difficult and insidious since the foreign manager actually was responsible for those errors and, if they had not been made, profits would have been greater. The point is that it is not the "board's" place to impose corrective detailed controls any more than it would be for the U.S. president's board to do so. Yet, because of its intricate knowledge of the operation, that is what often happens. Headquarters management, because of its dual role as operating expert and judge, tends to impose extensive controls and restrictions on the new operation in a misguided attempt to reduce the risks and improve performance. And yet the problems facing the foreign manager of a new operation generally cannot be satisfactorily assumed by headquarters any more than the U.S. board of directors can assume the problems of its president. The critical problems require on-the-scene handling, imagination, and freedom to act within broad guidelines. In other words, they require general management handling of the type that the U.S. board would expect from its president.

## GUIDELINES FOR THE MANAGERIAL PROCESS

Guidelines for the managerial process in MNCs must be cast in broad terms because of the unique circumstances of each firm in the complex situation created by communications obstacles, diverse operations, strategy goals, and organizational and staffing characteristics. A few consistent patterns are discernible but beyond them action must in the main be determined by application to each situation of the varied considerations that have been developed in the preceding sections.

For decision-making the clear consensus of both analysis and the several studies of MNC experience supports a broad pattern of assignment according to strategic responsibility and competence. The higher levels of management properly have the primary roles in major decisions on finance, product lines, and other matters in which they are advantageously placed through their central corporate view and capacity for pulling together matters susceptible to unified global strategies. Affiliate managements, on the other hand, are best positioned to make many specific operating decisions in which knowledge of operations and the environment along with the need for speed in decisions are primary considerations. The comparative studies of Schollhammer and Sim suggest only moderate variations in this general pattern among firms of different nations. The more significant variations seem to be among types of firms, confirming that it is broadly the extent of unification vs. fragmentation and other structural variables that determines effective practice.

But more significant is the picture that comes through in many of the studies of the varied patterns of decision-making. Relative roles in the vertical structure were described by Aharoni and Zwick. The assorted horizontal relationships were emphasized in Prahalad's case. The range of means of exerting central influence was brought out by Wiechmann and Youseff. The basic point emerging from all of these studies is that identifying a specific locus of decision-making is a gross oversimplification of the managerial process. In most cases two major phases of the process are at work which result in varied patterns of influence on decisions. First, there is a set of relationships and communications that establishes the environment for the making of specific decisions. These include the acculturation and systems transfer described by Wiechmann, the power relations noted by Prahalad, and the assorted controls analyzed by Yourseff. Second, there are the prevailing pattern of roles, communications and designation of authority and responsibilities of the type described by Aharoni, Prahalad, and Zwick, which result in some degree of participation of two or more levels or units in a large portion of decisions.

It seems quite clear that the effectiveness of the decision-making system will depend very largely on how this complex combination of factors is developed. While it is too complex a combination and too dependent upon the unique characteristics of each firm to permit many general guidelines, two prescriptive observations do seem feasible. First, because of the obstacles to communication, diversity of units, and problems of timing, it is desirable to place maximum reliance in decision-making on preliminary inputs from varied participants rather than on group participation. Second, much the same general approach is favored by the importance of skill transmission as part of MNC strategy giving a prime operational rationale for such elements as Wiechmann's acculturation and systems transfer to supplement their direct value in expediting decision-making.

As to the communications system in an MNC, the consensus of studies in this chapter as well as those of Lovell and Stopford and Wells cited in Chapter 12 affirm that multiple relationships are a necessity to achieve reasonable speed and flexibility of action in such large and complex organizations. McKenzie's practical observations with the Tice case a relevant example are ample indications, however, of the difficulties of making a system of multiple communications function effectively. The ideal is the grid system but in full form it is probably beyond the capabilities of the global strategy requirements, organizational diversity, and multinational staffing of an MNC. For the higher echelons of management, it may be substantially applied but Prahalad's case affirms the difficulty even at that level of making it function smoothly.

However, as a general guideline, it does appear sound to push in the direction of the grid concept, especially in establishing among the organization members the characteristics that make multiple communications work well whether it be in the grid system or in a less sophisticated scheme. Wiechmann's concept of acculturation is a significant contribution in this direction in its thrust toward development of a common approach to management which reduces some of the risks of conflict inherent in multiple communications. The development of a cadre of international executives with close personal relations brought out by the Galbraith-Edstrom study summarized in Chapter 12 is another type of contribution in its facilitation of cross-affiliate communication to aid unification strategies. These add up to an approach that seeks to condition MNC managers and establish an environment in which multiple communications are encouraged but controlled. Codes defining their bounds and character are used to foster useful ends and minimize conflicts, improper pressures, and avoidance of responsibility. These are very broad generalizations, but they do provide a useful direction for effort in what can otherwise become a morass of poorly related roles and communications.

The analysis and MNC experiences with behavioral dynamics provide little basis for general guidelines. McKenzie's analysis and the research of Zeira and his associates reviewed in Chapter 12 reinforce the special problems of expectations, motivations and confidence in handling affiliate personnel. Brooke and Remmers' study proposes some useful insights into relationships in an MNC organization in the concepts of calculative vs. voluntary motivations and development of approaches to providing greater personal independence in decision-making. Their thrust is in the same direction as the application of the grid concept to the communications system, and their points contribute behavioral attributes that are valuable in that mode of operation. Thus the general direction in which the behavioral dynamics of MNC management should move seem to be clearly indicated. But that leaves an admittedly tremendous range of questions of implementation upon which little firm guidance is available. Certainly there is a challenge to sensitively apply the great body of general knowledge in this area to the multicultural, multinational staffs of the global enterprise.

## NOTES

1. John Fayerweather and Ashok Kapoor, *Strategy and Negotiation for the International Corporation* (Cambridge, Mass.: Ballinger Publishing Company, 1976), pp. 413–427.
2. Sidney Robbins and Robert Stobaugh, *Money in the Multinational Enterprise* (New York: Basic Books, 1973), pp. 151–152.
3. E.R. Barlow, *Management of Foreign Subsidiaries* (Boston: Harvard Graduate School of Business Administration, 1953), pp. 84–113.
4. Ulrich E. Wiechmann, *Marketing Management in Multinational Firms* (New York: Praeger, 1976).
5. Lawrence G. Franko, *European Business Strategies in the United States* (Geneva: Business International, 1971).
6. Jacques Picard, "How European Companies Control Marketing Decisions Abroad," *Columbia Journal of World Business*, Summer 1977, pp. 113–121.
7. Hans Schollhammer, "Organizational Structures of Multi-National Corporations," *Academy of Management Journal*, Sept. 1971, pp. 345–365.
8. A.R. Sim, "Decentralized Management of Subsidiaries and Their Performance," *Management International Review*, #2, 1977, pp. 45–52.
9. Yair Aharoni, *The Foreign Investment Decision Process*, (Boston: Harvard Graduate School of Business Administration, 1966).
10. Jack Zwick, "Is Top Management Really on Top?" *Columbia Journal of World Business*, Winter 1966, pp. 87–96.
11. Wiechmann, op. cit.

12, Samir M. Yourseff, "Contextual Factors Influencing Control Strategy of Multinational Corporations," *Academy of Management Journal*, March 1975, pp. 136–221.

13. C.K. Prahalad, "Strategic Choices in Diversified MNCs," *Harvard Business Review*, July-August 1976, pp. 67–78.

14. Michael Z. Brooke and H. Lee Remmers, *The Strategy of Multinational Enterprise*, (Harlow (England): Longman and N.Y.: American Elsevier, 1970).

15. Cameron McKenzie, "Incompetent Foreign Managers?" *Business Horizons*, Spring 1966, pp. 83–90.

# Index

# About the Author

**John Fayerweather** is Professor of Management and International Business at the Graduate School of Business Administration of New York University.

Dr. Fayerweather has played a leading role in the evolution of education for international business for over 30 years. While serving on the faculties of Harvard, Columbia and NYU he authored four previous, textbooks, *Management of International Operations, International Marketing, International Business Management*, and *Strategy and Negotiations for the International Corporation*. He was the first president of the Association for Education in International Business and has worked with several national bodies for advancement of education in the field. His current research concerned with the interaction of nationalism and the strategies of international corporations has resulted in three books, *The Mercantile Bank Affair, International Business-Government Affairs* (ed.) and *Foreign Investment in Canada*, and numerous articles.